DIRECTORY OF TEACHER TRAINING COURSES

Directory of Teacher Training Courses
This first edition published in 2003 by
Trotman and Company Ltd
2 The Green, Richmond, Surrey TW9 1PL

© Trotman and Company Limited 2003

Editorial and Publishing Team

Introductory text Nick Higgins

Additional editorial Anya Wilson

Editorial Mina Patria, Editorial Director; Rachel Lockhart, Commissioning Editor;
Anya Wilson, Editor; Erin Milliken, Editorial Assistant
Production Ken Ruskin Head of Pre-press and Production

Advertising and Sales Jeremy Barton, Advertising and Sponsorship Manager; Mark Tyrell,
Sales Executive
Sales and Marketing Deborah Jones, Head of Sales and Marketing

Managing Director Toby Trotman

Course information is supplied by ECCTIS from the
Course Discover database. Course Discover holds details of over
120,000 courses at more than 1,000 colleges and universities. The service is
managed on behalf of the Department for Education and Skills (DfES).
The courses contained in this book are provided by higher
education institutions in the UK and are recognised and
accredited as award bearing qualifications.

Cover design Pink Frog Ltd
Text design Ursula McLaughlin

British Library Cataloguing in Publication Data
A catalogue record for this book is available from the British Library

ISBN 0 85660 882 3

Typeset by Florence Production Ltd, Stoodleigh, Devon
Printed and bound in Great Britain by
Bell & Bain Ltd

CONTENTS

INTRODUCTION TO THE DIRECTORY

YOUR FIRST STEP TO A TEACHING CAREER

If you are considering a career in teaching, there has never been a better time. Teaching has a great deal to offer: the chance to focus on a subject that inspires you; a clear structure of career development; a competitive salary plus other attractive financial incentives; the opportunity to work with colleagues with similar motivation – not to mention tremendous personal satisfaction from interaction with children and young people and being able to influence their personal development and acquisition of knowledge.

Teaching is about much more than just looking after children – you have to be passionate and dedicated in order to make it a successful and fulfilling career. In the last five years there have been major reforms in education, and teachers' pay and conditions are improving significantly. It is a well-respected and attractive career for anyone talented and hardworking enough to make it their vocation. This book is your first step in acquiring the essential information you need to make your ambition a reality.

In the following chapters we will look in detail at the factors that will influence your future choices and affect your career once you're on your way: from decisions about the level of education you wish to teach at to financing the course you choose to do. Before we look any further though, here are two definitions that will soon become very familiar to you:

- **ITT – Initial Teacher Training.** To become a teacher, you have to complete Initial Teacher Training, which leads to recommendation for Qualified Teacher Status. Details of the different routes you can take for your training will be explored in chapter 3. Institutions where you can undertake your ITT can be found in the Directory.

- **QTS – Qualified Teacher Status. (TQ – Teaching Qualification in Scotland.)** This is the qualification you need to enable you to start your teaching career. After completing your course, as a newly qualified teacher you will then consolidate your skills in an induction year of teaching. At the end of a successful induction year you will achieve Qualified Teacher Status.

This Directory provides details of all ITT and Postgraduate Certificate of Education (PGCE) courses leading to QTS or recommendation for QTS, for both primary and secondary level. This consists of all undergraduate degrees and postgraduate teaching programmes, plus listings of other relevant postgraduate courses for continuing professional development (CPD, see page 26) offered at education institutions throughout the UK.

Course information is supplied by ECCTIS from the Course Discover database. Course Discover holds details of over 120,000 courses at more than 1,000 colleges and universities. The service is managed on behalf of the Department for Education and Skills (DfES). The courses contained in this book are provided by higher education institutions in the UK and are recognised and accredited as award bearing qualifications.

Each entry provides a profile of the institution, its location and facilities, details of the teaching courses offered, contact details of the admissions department and information about how to apply. Undergraduate courses are listed with a description of the course content, followed by PGCE courses and finally other courses for CPD.

After the main body of institutions, there follow two appendices containing respectively information about additional courses that are relevant for CPD or further Teacher Training, and a list of institutions running Further Education PGCE/BEd courses.

The subject index will enable you to identify at a glance which institutions offer the subject areas of your choice at the relevant level. Once you have selected the institutions in the Directory that you are interested in applying to, you should consult that institution's prospectuses and/or websites before making your application.

Before you begin your search for courses in the Directory, it will be useful to have an overview of what you will need to consider before embarking on the road to your career: information about the education system in the UK, types of courses, the application process and funding. The following chapters will serve as an indispensable tool in your future decision-making. Other sources of advice and information for teacher training and applications can be found in Further information, on page 51.

REFORMS IN THE EDUCATION SYSTEM

In the last five years the Department for Education and Skills (DfES) has set in motion a wealth of reforms and investment designed to create a world-class system where the achievements of every child and every school are excellent or improving or both. Teachers are the key resource in the delivery of education, and teacher education and remuneration are rapidly changing to reflect this importance.

Broadly speaking, there are three elements to realising the DfES' ambition for educational reform:

1. investment in infrastructure (technology, school buildings, etc.)
2. changes in the education system (qualifications, curriculum, etc.)
3. modernisation of the teaching profession.

Of these three the latter is perhaps the most important. You can have all the computers, laboratories and sports equipment in the world, but without teachers to engage the imaginations and abilities of young people they are worth little. Similarly, a system of subjects and assessment designed to be more relevant to contemporary society and to keep children in education longer is worthless without the teachers to implement it.

The DfES is using reform to create a new and positive culture of excellence and improvement within teaching, restoring it to the status it deserves as a leading graduate profession.

In modernising teaching the DfES has identified three core objectives:

1. to promote excellent school leadership by rewarding leading professionals properly
2. to recruit, retain and motivate high quality classroom teachers by paying them more
3. to provide better support to all teachers and deploy teaching resources in a more flexible way.

These objectives represent a 'new vision' for teaching, one with good leadership, incentives for excellence, a strong culture of professional development and better support for teachers to focus on teaching rather than the multitude of distractions that have beset the profession in the past.

So, it's all very positive stuff. And while the reforms are still in their infancy and there is still a great deal to do, the early signs are that this approach is working. There are now more teachers employed in the classroom than at any time since 1984, representing an increase of more than 12,000 since 1998, and their pay is now more comparable to other graduate professions. The DfES has pledged to recruit a further 10,000 teachers, 20,000 support staff and 1,000 trained bursars (who will help release school leaders such as headteachers from administrative duties so they can concentrate on the quality of teaching and learning) by 2006. Certainly ambitious, but excellent news for teachers if it is achieved.

THE EDUCATION SYSTEM IN THE UK

This Directory outlines the courses available for your ITT, on completion of which you will be able to enter the classroom to complete your training as a qualified teacher. After at least a year of studying, absorbing information and developing skills, from the time you finish the ITT it will be you imparting knowledge to your pupils. It would be useful therefore for you to have a context in which to place a teaching career. Where would you fit in? What can you expect? This chapter takes you through the structure and content of the education system in the UK – the types of institutions you might work in, the subjects you can teach and the qualifications your pupils will take.

ENGLAND AND WALES

Education in England and Wales is divided into five broad areas:

1   early years

2   primary education

3   secondary education

4   further education

5   higher education.

Primary and secondary levels cover the 11 years' compulsory education that children are required to have between the ages of 5 and 16. Further and higher education are optional and are post-16 and post-18 respectively.

Early years

The government is expanding the number of places available for the under-5s in nurseries, playgroups and in reception classes in schools. It intends to create a free place for every 4-year-old and for the majority of 3-year-olds. It is also setting targets for early years education – such as under-5s being able to count to ten and write their own name by the time they go to school.

Early years education is a new Key Stage – a 'foundation' stage for the more formal curriculum at Key Stage 1 (see below). The early years focus is creating opportunities for childminders and nursery nurses, but primary teachers are also having more contact with under-5s.

Primary and secondary

During compulsory schooling children must receive full-time education suitable for their age, ability, aptitude and special educational needs (SEN). If, for any reason, a child is unable to attend school, their local education authority (LEA) must be satisfied that they are receiving appropriate alternative provision – this can be a private tutor or perhaps their parents.

Primary schools usually teach children up to the age of 11, at which point they will move to a secondary school, but the system does vary from place to place. For example, in some areas 'middle schools' will take children from the age of 9 or 10 and teach them for four years before they move on to secondary education proper.

Most secondary schools are 'comprehensive' in that they do not operate a selection procedure and admit all children of an appropriate age within their catchment area. However, in some parts of England, grammar schools require that pupils pass an entrance exam before they are accepted. As you will see later, the grammar school system is not as prevalent now as it once was.

Within this fairly diverse system of schooling there are four common Key Stages to compulsory education.

- Key Stage 1   5–7-year-olds
- Key Stage 2   7–11-year-olds
- Key Stage 3   11–14-year-olds
- Key Stage 4   14–16-year-olds.

At the end of the first three Key Stages pupils are assessed by National Curriculum tests, while Key Stage 4 assessment takes the form of achievement at GCSE (General Certificate of Secondary Education) level. On completion of Key Stage 4, 16-year-olds have the choice of whether to continue with further education at a school or college or to leave school and seek employment.

Further education

The post-16 sector has several strands – sixth form colleges, tertiary colleges, over 450 further education (FE) colleges and adult education institutes and specialist colleges. Undertaking further education is optional but the government is currently making a great effort to increase the numbers of young people staying on at school after 16.

FE institutions offer a wide range of both academic and vocational courses and qualifications, catering for almost every need. Students wishing to continue studying at a higher level usually make the step up to a higher education institution when they are 18 or 19.

Higher education

Universities and colleges offer higher education (HE) qualifications, including undergraduate and postgraduate degrees, and professional qualifications. In the last decade student numbers studying in UK institutions have risen to nearly two million. This growth rate is projected to continue as the government pursues its lifelong learning and widening participation agenda. The official target is to get half of all young people into HE by 2010.

Examinations and qualifications

In England, Wales and Northern Ireland there are several types of public qualifications. A number of these are new or have changed recently in accordance with 'Curriculum 2000', a set of reforms designed to establish a new National Qualifications Framework.

- GCSE (General Certificate of Secondary Education) – normally taken over two years by 15- and 16-year-olds via a mix of continuous assessment and final examinations. Pupils usually study for GCSEs in up to 10 or 11 subjects. Grades range from A* to G.

- GCE A-level (General Certificate of Education Advanced Level) – normally taken over two years by 17- and 18-year-olds with a greater emphasis on final examinations. Students usually study for A-levels in two to four subjects, with grades running from A to E.

- GCE AS (General Certificate of Education Advanced Subsidiary) – the first half of an A-level but a qualification in its own right. Taking only a year to complete, the AS allows students to study a broader range of subjects. On completion of an AS students can opt to study something else or complete the second half (A2) of the A-level.

- AEA (Advanced Extension Award) – provides the opportunity for the most able students to demonstrate a deeper understanding than required at A-level. Replaced Special Papers and acts as evidence of excellence.

- Vocational A-level (Advanced Vocational Certificate of Education) – formerly the Advanced GNVQ, this is comparable to GCE A-level but applies to more vocational and less academic subjects. Grades range from A to E.

- Vocational AS (Vocational Advanced Subsidiary) – as GCE AS above but with reference to Vocational A-levels.

- GNVQ (General National Vocational Qualification) – this qualification combines general and vocational education with employment. GNVQs are based on the skills required by employers combined with the development and understanding of skills needed in vocational areas such as business, health and engineering. Foundation and Intermediate level GNVQs are equivalent to GCSE study.

- NVQ (National Vocational Qualification) – based on skills, knowledge and competencies required by specific occupations. NVQs are work-based courses assessed by observation within the workplace, oral questioning, practical and written questioning and assignments. Assessed on five levels, NVQ1 to NVQ5.

- HNC and HND (Higher National Certificate/Diploma) – modular courses of vocational study that often form a link between further and higher education. The first year of many degrees can be substituted by an HND.

NORTHERN IRELAND

In Northern Ireland every child between the ages of 4 and 16 receives full-time education – that's 12 years' compulsory schooling. As in England, the majority of pupils switch from primary to 'post-primary' (grammar or secondary) school when they are 11. Grammar schools take pupils up to the age of 19 while secondary schools only go up to 16. To get into a grammar school pupils need to successfully take a 'Transfer Procedure' test.

Compulsory education in Northern Ireland is also divided into four, slightly different, Key Stages, all ending with a set of examinations:

- Key Stage 1   4–8-year-olds
- Key Stage 2   8–11-year-olds
- Key Stage 3   11–14-year-olds
- Key Stage 4   14–16-year-olds.

The qualifications available in Northern Ireland are the same as in England and Wales.

SCOTLAND

The education system in Scotland is quite different to that in the rest of the UK. For a start, the National Curriculum does not apply. LEAs and head-teachers are responsible for the delivery and management of the curriculum, doing so with the support and guidance of Learning and Teaching Scotland, a national public body sponsored by the Scottish Executive Education Department. There are no Key Stages and the nature of qualifications also differs.

In Scotland pupils between the ages of 5 and 16 attend suitable compulsory education just like the rest of the UK. After seven years of primary education they move on to secondary education, usually aged 12. As in the rest of the UK, once they are 16 pupils can choose to pursue further and then higher education, or leave to find a job.

There are no entry restrictions to secondary education in Scotland. Lower secondary education is divided into three stages. The first two years (S1 and S2) provide general education, while the third and fourth years (S3 and S4) are based on specialist and vocational education for all. Standard Grade courses are taken by 14- to 16-year-olds (S3 and S4). These are broadly equivalent to GCSEs and are part of a national programme regulated by the Scottish Qualifications Authority (SQA).

Standard Grade courses take two years to complete, are assessed continually and are available at three levels: Credit, General and Foundation. These are taken according to individual ability.

Further education in Scotland is optional and takes the form of Higher and Advanced Higher courses studied during the fifth and sixth years of secondary education (S5 and S6).

There are five levels to Scottish FE:

- Access

- Intermediate 1

- Intermediate 2

- Higher

- Advanced Higher.

There are 46 FE colleges in Scotland. Their students reflect Scotland's flexible education system, ranging from young people who have just left school to older students, international students, people with or without jobs and people with disabilities and special learning needs. They may be studying industry-designed Scottish Vocational Qualifications (SVQs), Higher National qualifications, General Scottish Vocational Qualifications or the Advanced Higher qualification.

The Scottish Certificate of Education is recognised throughout Britain as the equivalent to GCE A-levels and is usually the entry qualification for university. It is normally taken in secondary schools and assessed by external examination. The Certificate of Sixth Year Studies (CSYS) has now been replaced by the Advanced Higher. The Advanced Higher encourages independent study in preparation for higher education and work. It is assessed by external examination, usually combined with a dissertation or project report.

THE NATIONAL CURRICULUM

In England, Wales and Northern Ireland pupils are required to study a range of subjects at different stages of their schooling according to the National Curriculum. This lays out what should be studied and when, and applies

Table 1.1 The National Curriculum topics and stages

Key Stage	1	2	3	4
Age	5–7	7–11	11–14	14–16
Year groups	1–2	3–6	7–9	10–11
National Curriculum core subjects				
English	*	*	*	*
Mathematics	*	*	*	*
Science	*	*	*	*
National Curriculum non-core foundation subjects				
Art and design	*	*	*	
Citizenship			*	*
Design and technology	*	*	*	*
Geography	*	*	*	
History	*	*	*	
Information and communication technology	*	*	*	*
Modern foreign languages			*	*
Music	*	*	*	
Physical education	*	*	*	*

to pupils of compulsory school age in community and foundation schools, including community special schools and foundation special schools, and voluntary aided and voluntary controlled schools. Table 1.1 illustrates which subjects are studied and when.

The newest of the non-core foundation subjects is citizenship, which became mandatory at Key Stages 3 and 4 in August 2002. Citizenship incorporates the study of different cultures, the political system, economics, spiritualism, the law, human rights and responsibilities, the concept of community, ethnic identities, mutual respect and understanding, self-expression, environment – indeed almost anything about who we are and where we fit into the broader picture.

For each subject the government sets out the knowledge, skills and understanding that pupils of different abilities and maturities are expected to have by the end of each Key Stage. Teachers are responsible for monitoring how pupils are performing against these targets. Standard Assessment Tests (SATs) at the end of Key Stages 1, 2 and 3, and national qualifications are also used as statutory measures of attainment.

As well as the National Curriculum pupils also study religious education through all Key Stages. Sex education also has to be provided, though parents can choose not to have their children attend these lessons. LEAs and school governors determine the content of teaching in these two areas respectively.

There is also some room for schools to customise the curriculum. Many primary schools offer modern foreign languages or personal, social and health education (PSHE)/citizenship on a non-statutory basis.

Secondary schools also teach other non-curriculum subjects such as business studies, classics, law, dance, drama, economics, media and social sciences. This provides pupils with greater choice when it comes to taking GCSEs. At Key Stage 4 certain pupils can also drop up to two National Curriculum subjects (design and technology and modern foreign languages) to follow a programme of work-related learning or to focus on their particular strengths. Those who opt out from part of the National Curriculum must continue to study English, maths, science (unless they are doing work-related learning), IT, PE, sex education and religious education.

Proposed changes to Key Stage 4 Curriculum

Due to come into the pipeline in 2004 are changes in the curriculum for 14- to 16-year-olds. The intention is to introduce greater flexibility and choice; to enable schools to offer programmes that better meet young people's individual needs and strengths, whilst ensuring the core of general learning and experience essential to later learning and employment. The changes relate to, among other things, greater development of information and communications technology (ICT) throughout Curriculum subjects and the nature and scope of a statutory requirement of work-related learning. More information about these proposals can be found on the Qualifications and Curriculum Authority's website, details on page 53.

Special needs provision

Around 20 per cent of school-age children in the UK are estimated to have special educational needs (SEN) at some point in their school career.

A child with SEN can be defined as one who, for a number of reasons, is making significantly slower progress in one or more areas of his or her development than others in the same age group. This could include children who have temporary difficulties with reading or writing or those with an accumulation of physical and mental disabilities. The Royal National Institute for the Blind estimates that 56 per cent of visually impaired children have other disabilities such as physical, hearing, learning or communication difficulties.

Learning difficulties may also be due to a range of physical and medical conditions such as epilepsy, diabetes and cystic fibrosis, emotional and behavioural difficulties or dyslexia, speech difficulties or hyperactivity. However, only 2 per cent of children have special needs to the extent that the long-term, severe and complex nature of the difficulties requires the provision of special schooling or additional resources.

Where are special needs children taught?

Special needs children are taught either in mainstream schools, special schools or special units attached to mainstream schools. The special schools may be LEA maintained or independent, offer boarding or day facilities and be mixed or single sex. Schools may be oriented to a particular disability or aim to teach according to the severity of learning difficulty.

The tendency for children with SEN to be taught in mainstream schools has grown alongside the government's 'inclusive' approach and its accompanying set of targets, legislation and funding. This includes a duty on schools and education authorities to take measures to provide for pupils with disabilities, ranging from improved curriculum materials to better access to buildings.

The promotion of integration also means that special schools will, wherever possible, send pupils to mainstream schools, even if it is only for specific classes. Similarly, mainstream schools may arrange for their pupils to attend special schools. This form of partial integration may give special needs pupils their first experience of an ordinary classroom routine and promote understanding and caring in those who do not have special educational needs.

TYPES OF SCHOOLS

As a teacher you could find yourself working in one of a multitude of different types of school in both the public and private sectors.

Maintained schools

In the state-maintained sector there are three broad categories of school:

1. community

2. foundation

3. voluntary (controlled and aided).

Each of these receives funding from LEAs and is obliged to deliver the National Curriculum, but they do have their own characteristics.

Community schools

The LEA employs the school's staff, owns the school's land and is responsible for deciding which pupils can or cannot be admitted.

Foundation schools

The governing body employs the school's staff and is responsible for admissions arrangements. The school's property is owned by the governing body or a charitable foundation.

Voluntary aided schools

Many voluntary aided schools are church schools. As with foundation schools, the governing body employs the staff and sets admissions arrangements. They are also responsible for meeting some of the capital costs of running the school. The property is normally owned by a charitable foundation.

Voluntary controlled schools

These are almost always church schools, usually Church of England or Roman Catholic. The land and buildings are often owned by a charitable foundation but the LEA employs the staff and has primary responsibility for admissions procedures – hence 'controlled'.

Specialist schools

Any maintained secondary school in England can apply to become a specialist school. Specifically, this arrangement applies to these subject areas:

- technology
- languages
- sports
- arts
- business and enterprise
- engineering
- science
- mathematics and computing.

Specialist schools continue to deliver the National Curriculum but receive extra funding to enable them to build on their particular specialities and strengths. In theory, they add to the richness and diversity of secondary level education. Acting in close partnership with neighbouring schools and the local community, they serve to strengthen relationships between schools and business and raise standards of teaching and learning in their specialist areas. The government has set the target of there being at least 1,500 specialist schools by 2005.

Grammar schools

Grammar schools select pupils according to their academic ability. Since 1995 there have been no new grammar schools, but 'selection' will only end where there is a local demand for it to happen.

Independent schools

Independent schools are schools that receive no direct income from state sources. Their funding comes largely from fees paid by parents. There are many types of independent schools – selective and non-selective, boarding and day, large and small, mixed and single-sex, urban and rural – providing education for children aged from 3 to 18. There are about 2,600 independent schools in the UK, educating more than 600,000 pupils – that's about 7 per cent of all schoolchildren in England. In London this proportion is higher – more like 10 per cent.

The independent sector is well known for having better resourced schools and smaller class sizes than maintained schools and they achieve some of the best examination results. Independent schools also have more flexibility than maintained schools. There is no legal requirement, for example, for them to embrace the National Curriculum, but most do teach its content. They may also be less bound by external financial constraints and some pay above the national salary scales and have more freedom in the allocation of responsibility allowances.

Montessori schools

There are around 800 independent Montessori schools in the UK, following the 'indirect' teaching method defined by Dr Maria Montessori in 1907. It is called an indirect teaching method because the child is given freedom to grow and learn in a natural way but within a carefully planned and structured environment. The Montessori method covers an age range from nursery to 18. Those who wish to teach in Montessori institutions will need to obtain an appropriate Montessori qualification. This will not qualify you to work in UK state schools.

Steiner Waldorf schools

There are 26 Steiner Waldorf schools and 56 early years centres in the UK and Ireland. These are part of an international movement of over 780 schools and 1,500 early years centres named after their originator, the Austrian philosopher educationalist Rudolph Steiner, who founded his first school in 1919. Their educational philosophy stresses the importance of understanding the nature of childhood and the process of growth; this underpins the distinctive Steiner curriculum internationally. Those wishing to teach in Steiner schools should be mature people, be committed to the Steiner philosophy and, ideally, have a degree or recognised teacher training qualification. In addition, applicants will need to take a Steiner accredited course that varies in length from one year full time to up to three years part time.

City Technology Colleges

Although technically independent, CTCs are publicly funded and offer a wide range of vocational qualifications alongside traditional A-levels and their equivalents. They teach the National Curriculum but focus specifically on science, mathematics and technology.

City Academies

Similarly, City Academies are independent schools receiving funding from the government. They are owned and run by sponsors, who provide a significant proportion of the money required to set up the school, with the government covering the remaining costs.

As the name suggests, City Academies are tied in with local community needs, replacing schools in challenging circumstances or where there is an unmet demand for school places. They provide free secondary education to pupils of all abilities, offering a broad and balanced curriculum while specialising in an area such as business, science, technology, languages, arts or sport.

Pupil Referral Units

PRUs are established and maintained by LEAs to provide education for children of compulsory school age who may otherwise not receive suitable education – for example teenage mothers, excluded pupils, school phobics and pupils in the assessment phase of a statement of special educational needs.

Secure Training Centres

STCs were established under the Crime and Disorder Act (1994) and are operated by private providers under contracts managed by the Home Office. There are currently three in operation, holding young people between the ages of 10 and 17 who are provided with formal education for 25 hours a week, 52 weeks of the year. Individuals are assessed on entry to the centre and upon leaving, and have the opportunity to gain mainstream qualifications.

Local Authority Secure Units

These are different to STCs in that local authorities run them with the Youth Justice Board (YJB) purchasing beds. They are generally required to provide education and training 30 hours a week for 38 weeks of the year.

Non-maintained special schools

These are non-profit-making charitable schools, part funded by LEAs according to the placement of special needs pupils.

CURRICULUM 2000 AND THE NATIONAL QUALIFICATIONS FRAMEWORK

One of the core elements of the government's strategy for education is to promote post-16 learning. It believes that the key to increasing numbers in higher education and creating a general culture of 'lifelong learning' is to make staying on at school and pursuing further education a more attractive proposition.

It was with this in mind that, in August 2000, the post-16 curriculum and qualifications framework was subject to some pretty dramatic reforms, known as 'Curriculum 2000'. In fact the changes represented the most radical development in post-16 education in England, Wales and Northern Ireland since the original introduction of GCE A-levels in 1951.

The most significant changes can be summarised as follows:

Pre-Curriculum 2000	*Post-Curriculum 2000*
GCE A-level	Advanced Subsidiary GCE Revised Advanced GCE
Advanced GNVQ	Vocational A-level/ Vocational Advanced Subsidiary
Special Paper	Advanced Extension Award

The underlying purpose of the reforms is to promote higher levels of achievement, to encourage students to undertake broader programmes and to improve flexibility in the post-16 curriculum. By introducing improved vocation-related qualifications and a more precise framework for comparing different kinds of qualifications, Curriculum 2000 has in theory created a more egalitarian, less elitist system of further education.

Curriculum 2000 fits into the broader context of the new National Qualifications Framework. Among other things this has been developed to encourage participation and attainment in education and training; to clarify the relationships between qualifications; and to make it easier for students to take a broad programme and to combine different types of qualifications.

The framework has been designed with the needs of the learner rather than the schools in mind and is intended to be coherent, transparent and inclusive. It contains three broad categories of qualifications:

- General (previously 'academic' – eg GCSE, Advanced GCE, AS GCE)

- Vocationally related (eg Vocational A-level, Vocational AS)

- Occupational (eg National Vocational Qualifications).

These categories are broken down into six levels of attainment, each representing an increasing level of knowledge, understanding, skills and student autonomy in terms of analysis and creative thinking. The framework is summarised in Table 1.2.

Table 1.2 The National Qualifications Framework

	General	Vocation-related	Occupational
Higher level/5			eg NVQ level 5
Higher level/4			eg NVQ level 4
Advanced level/3	eg AS- and A-level	eg Advanced GNVQ, Vocational A-level, Vocational AS	eg NVQ level 3
Intermediate level/2	eg GCSE grades A*–C	eg Intermediate GNVQ	eg NVQ level 2
Foundation level/1	eg GCSE grades D–G	eg Foundation GNVQ	eg NVQ level 1

ROUTES INTO TEACHING

This Directory details all the undergraduate and postgraduate courses that are available in the UK for the study of ITT resulting in Qualified Teacher Status. Before you begin to decide which course to apply for and where, you should be aware of the different routes you can take to gain your QTS. This chapter takes you through these various routes, so that you can decide which one may be right for you.

Anyone wishing to teach in a state-maintained school needs to have QTS. Qualified Teacher Status, regardless of the emphasis of the particular route you choose, theoretically enables you to work in either primary or secondary sectors but, in practice, you will need to take a conversion course if you want to switch between the two.

Teachers in independent schools, further education colleges, sixth form colleges and City Technology Colleges do not formally require QTS but, increasingly, it is becoming difficult to get a job in these institutions without a teaching qualification. Those wishing to teach in the post-16 sector may take a special course designed for it but should be aware that this does not necessarily confer QTS, which will be needed to teach in a state school.

Teachers from Scotland, Northern Ireland and other parts of the European Union may be granted QTS on application to the DfES. Qualified teachers from the European Economic Area countries of Norway, Sweden, Finland, Iceland and Austria are also eligible to apply for recognition.

In addition to obtaining QTS through a course of ITT, newly qualified teachers (NQTs) also need to pass an induction year when they are in employment. While the standards on the induction year are demanding, employers are careful to help their teachers have a successful induction experience.

One of the government's responses to the need for greater numbers of teachers has been to introduce more ways of training and obtaining QTS. The idea is to create a system whereby it is possible for anyone with the potential to become a teacher to do so, regardless of their particular circumstances.

UNDERGRADUATE ROUTE

England, Wales and Northern Ireland

There are more than 50 providers of undergraduate ITT courses in England and Wales. In Northern Ireland there are two providers of undergraduate

Initial Teacher Education (ITE) and further information about providers and entry requirements can be found on the Department of Education for Northern Ireland's website: www.deni.gov.uk. All course details can be found in the Directory. The nature of the courses they provide varies.

Four-year full-time Bachelor of Education (BEd)

This route is primarily for people who wish to train as primary teachers, but there are a few courses geared to those who want to teach in secondary schools, mainly in priority subject areas. Applications should be made via UCAS in the same way as for any other undergraduate degree.

If you take one kind of course and later wish to switch the focus of your teaching career you may be able to take part-time or distance learning conversion courses. However, you will need to gain some solid teaching experience of around two years before contemplating this. Four-year BEd courses include 32 weeks in the classroom and have a distinct emphasis on a specialist subject. A teaching degree is the most popular route into primary teaching.

Three-year full-time BEd

These tend to be six-subject generalist primary teaching degrees with less emphasis on a specialist subject than the four-year BEd, and with less opportunity for extended study at the highest level. As they have to cover much of what the four-year BEd courses offer in a shorter timescale, entry requirements may be more demanding. Three-year BEd courses include 24 weeks in the classroom. Some courses offer a general primary BEd after three years and a subject-specific BA or BSc with QTS after four years.

Three-/four-year full-time BA/BSc with QTS

This qualifies people to teach but has more emphasis on a specialist subject. Most teaching practice tends to take place later in the course but students get some early exposure to schools' work and may withdraw from the education component if they feel they are unsuited to teaching, leaving the course with a BA or BSc and not QTS. Courses include between 24 and 32 weeks in the classroom and are once again applied for via UCAS.

Shortened two-year full-time BEd

More mature applicants who have already completed at least one year on a full-time higher education course or equivalent in an appropriate subject area may be eligible for a two-year BEd. These are offered in priority secondary subjects including maths, modern languages, physics, chemistry, science, music, and design and technology. A small number of courses are also offered in the primary sector.

Some institutions accept work experience instead of higher education as long as the work has involved a high degree of numeracy – accounts and

IT-based jobs are good examples. On a primary course you will spend at least 18 weeks in schools, and on a secondary course at least 24 weeks.

POSTGRADUATE ROUTE

There are over 100 postgraduate courses on offer in England and Wales leading to QTS. The majority of these also carry a university award of the PGCE (Postgraduate Certificate of Education). In Northern Ireland there are five providers of PGCE courses. This is the most popular route into secondary teaching and is increasingly so for primary teaching. The fact that these routes now carry a training bursary/salary will accentuate this trend.

Applications to most postgraduate courses are made through the Graduate Teacher Training Registry (GTTR). The deadline for applications for primary PGCE courses through GTTR is 15 December, although some providers may be prepared to accept late applicants. There is no deadline for application to secondary courses. For more information about post-graduate applications visit the GTTR website: www.gttr.ac.uk

One-year full-time PGCE

This route is for those who have already completed a degree course appro-priate to the subject they wish to teach. There is a requirement that entrants to PGCE courses should have at least 50 per cent of their post-16 educa-tion in National Curriculum subjects. You should therefore choose your first-degree courses with care. Students with a first degree in National Curriculum subjects will be in the strongest position, but other subjects can be interpreted favourably. A combined humanities degree, for example, may still be considered adequate, especially if it is backed up by A-levels in National Curriculum subjects. The one-year PGCE is currently the most popular route into secondary teaching but there are also PGCE places for primary teaching.

Two-year part-time PGCE

There are a limited number of courses, mainly in priority subjects including maths, modern languages, business studies, design and technology, sciences, music and religious education. Many of the prospective students for these courses have family responsibilities or other commitments that prevent them from attending a full-time PGCE course. Courses are run subject to demand and applicants should check with the relevant institution before naming them on the GTTR application form.

Two-year full-time subject conversion PGCE courses

These courses provide extra time to help students build up subject know-ledge in disciplines where there is a shortage of qualified teachers in the secondary age range. They may suit, for example, engineers wanting to teach maths. Applicants must have completed at least one year of higher education study (for instance, through an HND) relevant to the specialist subject.

School Centred Initial Teacher Training

SCITT is a firmly established option for graduates wishing to teach in primary, secondary, sixth form or specialist colleges. SCITT schemes are devised by consortia of schools and usually validated by higher education institutions, enabling them to award a PGCE as well as QTS. The schemes are typically based in groups of local schools but there are also schemes emphasising particular religions, and one national scheme trains teachers in 'outstanding primary schools'.

The certificates they offer count as much as the ones from higher education institutions and their students are just as successful at getting jobs. Indeed many schools and LEAs are partners in SCITT because they want to recruit directly from them.

The majority of schemes are applied to through the GTTR but a small number of schemes choose not to be listed in the *GTTR Handbook* and can be contacted directly. The Teacher Training Agency (TTA) provides the authoritative list of schemes.

The SCITT experience

As the name implies, SCITT schemes offer students a high degree of exposure to schools during their training. While the schemes are all individually approved by the TTA they typically combine a classroom-based approach to training with an entitlement to individual counselling and the support of an appropriate mentor who is also an experienced teacher in the school in which the student is based. The emphasis is on developing competence in classroom management and underpinning this with a progressive introduction to the theory behind the practice of teaching as the students gain confidence in their teaching skills.

Most of the course is spent in a base school but placements are often arranged in other schools to offer a contrasting ethos and extend experience in the specialist subject on secondary courses, or of another Key Stage on primary courses.

Will SCITT throw me in at the deep end?

Absolutely not. Although by the end of your course you will be used to taking your own classes, you will spend much of the early part of the course in structured observing and learning from an experienced teacher. Gradually you will be introduced to teaching through 'team teaching', small-group teaching, part-lesson teaching and then full-lesson teaching under the direct supervision of a mentor. Mentors are specially selected to support you in the subjects you are teaching. They will discuss such things as why lessons have been more or less successful or what particular approaches to teaching a class might be taken.

The transition from observation to contributing through summing up or issuing instructions and eventually to taking your own classes is designed to build confidence. One student described how the process was so gradual that he only realised half-way through a class that, 'Hey, I'm teaching on my own.'

Will there be much reading and study?

Although SCITT courses are highly practical there is still a significant element of study. Courses combine theory with 'on-the-job' training and experience, encouraging students to be analytical, creative and reflective practitioners. All aspects of the course, including self-evaluation, completion of logs while on teaching practice and the completion of essays, are assessed at the rigorous standard expected at postgraduate level. The course involves writing essays covering topics such as how children learn, language and communication in the classroom, issues of gender and race and, for those on secondary courses, the role of your specialist subject in the National Curriculum.

Modular postgraduate provision

A growing number of providers in secondary and primary teacher training are offering modular postgraduate study, which allows trainees to follow more customised courses. The courses are aimed at a wide range of candidates, particularly those in employment seeking to change careers – graduates working as nursery nurses or classroom assistants, or those working in the FE sector who wish to convert, for example.

These courses enable those wishing to study part time or those with family commitments to consider training as a teacher. Candidates will be given an initial assessment of training needs and will have an individual training plan drawn up. For some candidates, such as experienced but unqualified teachers in the independent or FE sector or those who have trained overseas, there may be an opportunity to take the final assessed period of teaching without further training.

FAST TRACK

The Fast Track programme was introduced in August 2000 with the intention of creating the next generation of school leaders sooner rather than later. The idea is to attract the best new graduates, career changers and existing teachers and then provide them with a support structure conducive to accelerated professional development. Given this environment, Fast Track teachers are expected to achieve a leadership position (either as an Advanced Skills Teacher or a member of the leadership group) within the five years that they are on the programme – something that normally takes at least twice that time.

Fast Trackers new to teaching are provided with specially augmented ITT, featuring additional, specialist seminars and tutorials on such subjects as behaviour management. Once qualified they continue to have access to special training events and conferences as well as a Fast Track mentor, Fast Track area coordinator and a host of online resources.

Fast Track teachers agree not to be bound by the same working conditions as other teachers. They are expected to take on responsibilities that contribute to the development of their school and community in addition to their classroom teaching work. This means they must work during evenings, school holidays and the occasional weekend. The good news is that this additional work and responsibility are rewarded by an extra recruitment and retention allowance worth at least £1,914 a year, plus a £5,000 Fast Track training bursary (on top of the £6,000 teacher training bursary). Newly qualified Fast Track teachers also start on point two of the Main Pay Scale, a point higher than most NQTs.

If you think that Fast Track might be the thing for you, you need to apply via the Fast Track website: www.fasttrackteaching.gov.uk. If you are new to teaching then you will have to gain a PGCE from one of the Fast Track ITT providers. Obviously if you already have QTS this won't be necessary. The application and selection process is exhaustive and demanding, but then so is the job!

DISTANCE LEARNING

People who, for reasons of geography or personal circumstance, need to combine home-based study with periods of school experience often choose distance learning. Typically, you may want to combine training with family responsibilities or with a full-time job. Many students on part-time courses may even have jobs in schools as classroom assistants or laboratory technicians. Teachers working in independent schools also use this route to obtain QTS while continuing to teach.

Students taking the route while working or coping with other commitments will find it requires much self-discipline and even more motivation than usual, particularly in the intensive teaching practice periods. However, you will receive support from your personal tutor who will visit you in your school, and from the mentor assigned to you in your chosen school. You will also get a chance to meet other students and exchange experiences on training days that form an essential part of the course.

As with all teacher training courses this route emphasises subject know-ledge, theories of teaching and learning and periods of school-based experience. One of its major advantages, however, is that students can work in schools they nominate themselves. These may be schools that they attended as pupils or schools their own children are attending. The school has to be chosen with care and will only be approved by the training provider if it offers the right range of teaching experience and is willing to provide an experienced teacher to act as a mentor to the student. Teacher training institutions may also be able to advise on schools that have been used in the past and help you when you are approaching schools.

Students combining the course with other responsibilities such as a job will need to ensure that they can arrange to spend blocks of time in schools for their teaching practice. In the first year this involves 180 hours of teaching – the equivalent of six weeks. There is usually a degree of flexibility allowed in the first year in how students timetable their teaching practice, and students have negotiated with schools to offer half-days or three days a week, for example. In the second year the requirement is for 12 weeks in two separate blocks and it is important that students are able to experience this on a full-time basis.

Distance learning provision is being facilitated by the spread of informa-tion technology, with CD-ROMs, e-mail and the Internet being used alongside the more traditional media such as books, videos and audio tapes. Familiarity with this combination of different technologies may be a useful addition to a CV when it comes to applying for jobs.

Distance learning PGCE courses typically last around two years, but the shift towards modular provision means that some students may be able to complete the course more quickly. Approved courses are listed in the **GTTR Guide for Applicants** and on the GTTR website.

EMPLOYMENT-BASED ROUTES

There are two employment-based routes into teaching: the Graduate Teach-ing Programme (GTP) and the Registered Teaching Programme (RTP). These routes are designed to allow schools to employ unqualified teachers on a salaried basis and provide them with an individual training programme leading to QTS.

The GTP and RTP may be particularly suitable for those who have trained overseas, or have relevant teaching experience in further education or inde-pendent schools, for example. Classroom assistants or technicians, or those changing careers, with expertise in priority subjects may also be interested in the programmes. These routes are aimed at mature entrants: you must be aged over 24.

GTPs normally last for one year, though those such as overseas-trained teachers with substantial teaching experience may train in a shorter time; the minimum is three months full time. Applicants must have a degree or equivalent.

The RTP is for those with two years of higher education behind them. The programme will normally last two years. On the RTP, trainees study for a degree at the same time as undertaking their teacher training. QTS is awarded when the trainee has successfully completed both the degree studies and the teacher training. As with the GTP there is provision for shorter programmes in exceptional cases: the minimum is one year full time.

The Teacher Training Agency has a range of literature about these routes into teaching. Visit their website: www.canteach.gov.uk

FURTHER EDUCATION

It is increasingly likely that teachers in FE will be required to have a teaching qualification. However, regardless of future developments, completion of a course will improve your chances of employment. Many teachers in the sector begin their careers on a part-time basis and there are increasing numbers of 'fixed-term' rather than permanent contracts. Information about where you can study courses for teaching in further education and post-compulsory education can be found in the index on page 405.

One-year full-time PGCE (FE)

This route does not carry QTS status and is not designed for those who wish to teach in schools. However, it is a widely recognised route into the FE sector. One-year PGCE (FE) courses are offered on a full-time basis, or part time for those in service. Courses are available in England and Wales and cover a range of subjects, including vocational subjects such as catering and beauty therapy as well as academic subjects. Courses are offered at Bolton Institute, University of Greenwich, Huddersfield University and the University of Wolverhampton. Further information is available from NATFHE (National Association of Teachers in Further and Higher Education, see 'Further information' at the end of this guide).

City & Guilds

These are further and adult education teacher's certificate courses for teaching adults in FE. There are part-time courses at a number of FE colleges that can lead on to the Certificate in Education qualification.

HIGHER EDUCATION

Those seeking posts in higher education will need a very good honours degree together with a higher degree such as a PhD in a relevant field, a proven research record and, most importantly, a list of publications to their name.

Traditionally there has been little emphasis on formal teaching certificates as entry qualifications. Some PGCEs that prepare students for work in the FE sector also include an orientation to higher education but this is by no means the main route into the profession.

Most postgraduate students expect to teach in order to earn their keep during their studies. This provides good experience and a basis for making contacts with other academics. While vacancies are advertised in the national media this kind of networking and the personal recommendations that may flow from it enhance your chances of success.

In response to the changing context of higher education – the growth in student numbers, the drive for wider participation and the creation of more flexible education solutions – the sector is addressing the culture of the academic profession. The main initiative in the area has been the creation of the Institute of Learning and Teaching (ILT). This is a professional institute, open to all academics, with a remit to enhance the status of the teaching profession by validating training courses and developing the use of information technology.

SCOTLAND

There are seven teacher education institutions in Scotland where you can choose to study, offering three routes to a teaching qualification:

- A four-year course leading to the BEd Primary or, for secondary, a four-year course leading to a BEd Technology, Physical Education or Music; apply via UCAS.

- A concurrent degree course, for secondary subjects only; you do not have to make a decision on whether to undertake a teaching qualification until towards the end of the second year. If you decide then that you don't want to teach, you will still qualify with a degree in the subject you have studied. Apply via UCAS.

- A one-year Postgraduate Teacher Certification in Education in Primary or Secondary (a wide range of subjects is available) following a relevant degree; apply via the Graduate Teacher Training Registry.

The University of Strathclyde offers a part-time PGCE leading to the Teaching Qualification (TQ) in primary education. Other institutions are currently developing part-time and distance learning courses.

After examinations the final award of the TQ follows a two-year induction period based on a combination of assessment, external examination and project work. Students must also present their first school and the employing authority with a personal profile recording individual competence and areas of strength.

Teaching in Scotland

By law, all teachers in local authority schools in Scotland must be registered with the General Teaching Council for Scotland (GTCS). The GTCS is responsible for deciding whether a qualification attained outside of Scotland is acceptable (see 'Further information' for contact details).

CONTINUING PROFESSIONAL DEVELOPMENT COURSES

Increasingly, institutions are offering courses that award a higher-level qualification for those who want to develop their professional skills further. Some of the schemes currently on offer include professional bursaries for teachers (see below), and sabbaticals for those teaching in challenging schools. You may also wish to go on a postgraduate course, such as an MA, MSc or MEd.

Some providers run courses for qualified teachers that support priority areas of the curriculum. Providers work in partnership with schools, and courses are increasingly school-focused and flexible in their structure. Priority areas are special educational needs, specialist subject-focused programmes, information and communications technology (ICT) in the curriculum, teaching in the foundation stage and raising achievement/narrowing achievement gaps.

Bursaries for continuing professional development

The government launched the national strategy for continuing professional development (CPD) in March 2001. The strategy offers a wide range of support including sabbaticals and scholarships as well as Professional Bursaries, a scheme launched in April 2002. The Professional Bursaries Scheme entitles qualified teachers to receive a £500 bursary in both their fourth and fifth years of teaching to spend on their own professional development.

Eligible teachers can spend their bursary on any work-related training and development activities they choose, including attending courses, visiting other schools and key sites, work shadowing and arranging guest speakers. To find out more about CPD, visit: www.teachernet.gov.uk/professionaldevelopment/opportunities/bursaries/

RETURNING TO TEACHING

Now that the modernisation of the teaching profession is well under way it is hoped that a number of qualified teachers who had left the job because of the relatively poor conditions will consider returning to the classroom.

GET IN, GET ON!

With two of the UK's leading HE entry guides

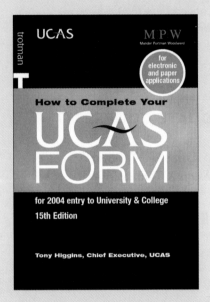

How to Complete Your UCAS Form 2004

Written by Tony Higgins, Chief Executive of UCAS, this is a unique guide that will guide readers through the entire higher education application process. As well as providing insider advice on completing the form, it includes:

- Examples from past applications to help you avoid the common mistakes
- Essential advice on completing the personal statement.

£11.99

The Student Book 2004

Student life isn't just about writing essays or attending lectures – make sure you get the full picture of what life is really like at each UK university and college and decide which institution is the most suitable for you. Includes:

- An A–Z guide on surviving the first year
- Student view sections for each institution, written by recent students.

£16.99

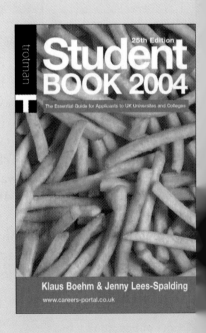

How to Order
Phone: **0870 900 2665**
Online: **www.ordermaster.co.uk**

Naturally teachers who already hold QTS have no need to go through undergraduate or postgraduate initial teacher training before applying for a job. However, they may feel that their skills need brushing up, particularly if they have been away from the profession for some time and they need to work up the confidence to face a class again. For this purpose the Teacher Training Agency (TTA) sponsors a number of returners' courses across the country. They usually last between six and 12 weeks and cover such areas as:

- the National Curriculum

- the National Strategies

- the use of ICT in subject teaching

- assessment of pupils' performance

- classroom and behaviour management.

Participants on these courses receive a training bursary of £150 per week for the duration of the course, up to a maximum of £1,500, and if necessary childcare support.

The TTA also runs the Keeping in Touch (KIT) programme – an information and guidance service for qualified teachers taking a break from the profession. The KIT programme aims to equip potential returners with the knowledge, skills and confidence to make their return as easy and effective as possible.

QUALIFICATIONS

In each entry of the Directory you will see the qualifications required for the teacher training courses on offer, so you will have an idea of what you need to work towards. However, before thinking about the formal academic and vocational qualifications you need to get on to a course you must first consider whether you have the personal qualities that the job demands.

Teaching can be one of the most rewarding and at the same time frustrating experiences. Some children are a delight to work with while others are night-mares, and it may seem as though there's a setback for every breakthrough. But that's what attracts so many people to the profession: the challenge – because it's all the more rewarding to turn a setback into a breakthrough or a little monster into a high achiever than it is to have it easy.

If that doesn't sound like an experience you would like, then perhaps teaching isn't for you. You need to have a passion for working with children – of all kinds and abilities. It's not enough just to like the idea. If you want to be a good teacher, you *really* have to want it. You need to have the commitment and resilience to keep going in the face of adversity and the humility to allow your pupils to shine. You need to be able to communicate with confidence and tackle what could be an unruly mob.

Many of these things are covered in teacher training but you should think about your aptitude for them now – before you start applying. If you are confident that you are cut out for a teaching career then you will probably need some of the following qualifications.

ENTRY REQUIREMENTS FOR TEACHING DEGREES

A minimum of five GCSEs (or the equivalent) at grade C or above, including English language and mathematics. A broad range of GCSE subjects is encouraged for those entering all teaching courses.

Additionally all entrants to ITT primary courses who were born after 1 September 1979 should also have attained GCSE C+, or equivalent, in a single science subject or combined science. At present the science require-ment does not apply to secondary courses.

The GCSE requirements, particularly maths, can be a stumbling block for many applicants but they have been introduced because they are such core education skills. The science GCSE has been brought in for primary courses because teachers in that sector have to teach the broad range of subjects covered by the National Curriculum, which includes science.

Equivalent qualifications are accepted. Typically these include such things as CSE grade 1 or appropriate BTEC National modules. Maths GCSE equivalents for those with BTEC Nationals are numerical methods and finance. English GCSE equivalents include BTEC modules in communication skills and people and organisations. Applicants offering GNVQ Intermediate level qualifications, however, may find that institutions do not accept their maths and English content to be equivalent to GCSE.

For a note on qualifications usually accepted as equivalent to GCSE in mathematics, English and science, contact the Teaching Information Line on 0845 6000 991.

Many colleges offer equivalence tests in English and maths for those without the appropriate qualifications and some are offering similar tests for science. Mature students without the GCSEs but who offer degree or Access courses that have covered core subjects may find that institutions consider them acceptable. A supporting statement from an Access course testifying to the level of maths on the course may even avoid the need for students to take an equivalence test.

Equivalence tests taken at one institution are not transferable to other ITT institutions. The GCSEs are usually needed at the time of application but some institutions will accept students on a provisional basis if they have made arrangements to obtain the GCSEs before the teacher training course begins.

SKILLS TESTS

In addition to the entry requirements students have to pass three national skills tests in numeracy, literacy and ICT before starting their induction period. Most trainees will take the tests shortly before their courses end but undergraduates may choose to take the tests before beginning a PGCE. The tests take around 45 minutes each and focus on the skills that teachers need in their professional role, regardless of their subject. In the numeracy test, for example, mental arithmetic is included as teachers may need to make quick calculations when looking at an OFSTED research report. General arithmetic is included as teachers may, for example, need to compare estimates to the relative progress of classes.

These are two example questions supplied by the TTA from the mental arithmetic part of the numeracy test:

■ In a class of 30 pupils, 85% achieved grade C and above and 5% achieved grades D to G. How many pupils did not achieve a grade?

- A supplier offers schools that spend £500 on equipment a 5% discount. How much is saved on an order of £500?

You can take the tests as many times as you need to pass them. Visit www.canteach.gov.uk to find out more.

A-LEVELS AND TEACHING

You do not necessarily need A-levels to obtain a place on a teacher training course. However, if you are applying with A-levels you must have at least one, and preferably more, in subjects appropriate to the primary or secondary curriculum.

Trainee primary teachers learn to teach all the primary curriculum subjects but may specialise in one or more subjects. Secondary teachers can train to teach National Curriculum subjects and sometimes others that are part of the broader curriculum, for example business studies, economics and sociology. Secondary teachers may teach two or more distinct subjects.

BTEC NATIONAL/GNVQ AND TEACHING

Although 'Vocational' A-levels (AVCEs), formerly GNVQ Advanced level, and BTEC National courses are equivalent to two A-levels, their content may not be relevant to the National Curriculum. In these cases a well-balanced package of qualifications is important for entry into teaching. This should include a good set of GCSEs and you should use the personal statement in your application to draw out the relevance of your vocational course to teaching. Any additional extension units taken should also be included. As noted earlier, GNVQ Intermediate qualifications are not considered to meet the maths and English GCSE requirements.

Admissions tutors pay great attention to the course content applicants are offering. Even students with straight grade As at A-level can encounter problems if the subject matter is inappropriate. Many vocational courses, however, do have a National Curriculum basis in science or art and applicants with merits and distinctions will be able to apply with confidence.

Other courses such as health and social care or leisure and tourism have no National Curriculum subject base and applicants may find it harder to be accepted on to some courses. Applicants on these courses are often accepted on to early years general degrees with QTS and on to some physical education and biology courses. A higher success rate has been achieved where there are close partnerships between schools, FE colleges and local HE institutions. Students embarking on Vocational A-levels should consider taking optional modules that are as relevant as possible to the National Curriculum if they eventually wish to take an ITT course.

Some institutions indicate that a combination of AVCE and a relevant A-level will be required. However, good AVCE students will still be able to find some courses for which institutions are willing to consider them without this added burden.

Contact teacher training admissions tutors for advice, as each institution decides if an applicant's qualifications meet the appropriate criteria.

ACCESS ROUTES TO TEACHING

Some Access courses are recognised as meeting the entry requirements for degree courses with QTS but you should check your acceptability with the institutions offering the teacher training courses that interest you. Courses with maths, English and science components are likely to achieve a more favourable response. Some Access courses provide automatic places on ITT courses for those who pass them.

APPROPRIATE DEGREES FOR PGCE

Candidates for PGCE training, whether for primary, secondary or further education teaching need to hold a first degree, or equivalent qualification appropriate to the curriculum subject they wish to teach. Institutions decide if applicants' qualifications meet these criteria. Those offering overseas degrees will have their degrees checked against the British Council approved list. It is important that you ensure that this check is carried out as soon as possible, and before you submit your application to the Graduate Teacher Training Registry, to avoid disappointment – especially as some overseas degrees are not considered equivalent. Students with qualifications from India and Pakistan, for example, will need to offer an MA or MSc.

APPROPRIATE DEGREES FOR PRIMARY AND SECONDARY TEACHING

Primary teaching

Primary teaching applicants should offer a degree that relates directly to the primary curriculum. Institutions need to 'satisfy themselves that the content of a postgraduate student's first degree provides the necessary foundation for work as a primary school teacher'. Those with degrees in subjects such as sociology, law, philosophy and modern languages may have more difficulty in obtaining a primary teaching place.

However, they can still be considered if they can show that at least 50 per cent of their post-16 education, including A-levels, for example, as well as degrees, has been in subjects related to the National Curriculum. The main concern of admissions tutors is to accept students who will make good primary teachers. However, given the competition for places on primary courses many will feel obliged to favour those whose qualifications are most directly relevant.

You will need to take care to relate your previous post-compulsory education to the curriculum, especially if your degree is not clearly relevant, even to the extent of stressing the percentage of time devoted during your courses to National Curriculum subjects. For example:

BA Caribbean Studies

- 20% devoted to literature – subjects: Black British writers (one module); Shakespeare and race – *The Tempest and Othello*, 3,000-word dissertation;

- 20% devoted to history – subjects: 'Afro-Caribbeans in the Great War', 3000-word dissertation; 'Africans and native Americans' (one module).

Contact university admissions tutors directly for further advice.

Secondary teaching

Secondary teaching applicants, similarly, should have studied their proposed teaching subject to a degree level appropriate to the secondary school curriculum. You will need to demonstrate that your degree course is relevant to the subject you wish to teach.

Those whose degree titles do not obviously relate to the National Curriculum will need to give a breakdown of their degree course content as above. While institutions are at liberty to interpret the content of previous educations most are insisting that at least 50 per cent of an applicant's post-compulsory education must be relevant. The only possible exceptions to this might be religious education, physical education or modern foreign languages for native-speaking foreign national graduates.

The rise of the modular degree has made it more difficult for admissions tutors to assess how relevant certain degree courses are. It is recommended that those with degree courses with titles such as 'combined studies' should be quite explicit in highlighting the relevance of their courses. One admissions tutor on a PGCE English course suggests that applicants write, 'contains literature' against modules such as Caribbean studies or classics, or any others where the literature content may not be obvious.

It is also the case that even those applicants with a directly relevant degree such as maths will still need to be able to discuss the relevance of their degree to the National Curriculum. After all, the content of mathematics degree courses is quite different from the maths a primary school teacher will be teaching.

Postgraduate students do not always need a degree in a National Curriculum subject. Subjects such as politics and law and philosophy, while less acceptable, can have a case made for their relevance. However, it may be more difficult for students with leisure and tourism degrees wishing to teach English or history, for example, to convince admissions tutors that their degrees contain an adequate percentage of National Curriculum material.

Some universities such as Leicester and Nottingham Trent accept psychology degrees and other less explicitly relevant degrees. Such institutions will pay particular attention to candidates' other academic qualifications such as A-levels as well as other qualities applicants may bring. If in doubt, consult the institution's admissions tutor before submitting an application.

HIGHER NATIONAL DIPLOMA (HND) QUALIFICATIONS

Entrants to PGCE courses must have a degree. While an HND is not acceptable there are several routes into teaching for Diplomates – the two-year BEd in shortage secondary subjects available through UCAS and the employment-based Registered Teacher Programme. Alternatively students may transfer on to a relevant three-year degree course and then take a PGCE, or transfer on to a four-year BEd course. HND students applying for a BEd would very probably not be offered any exemptions despite their previous higher education experience and would have to be prepared to take the course from the beginning.

MODERN LANGUAGES

If you want to teach modern foreign languages you must offer a qualification in at least one language at a high level. Many applicants will have studied it to degree level or at least taken it as part of a joint degree.

Interviews will, in part, be conducted in the chosen language and you will need to be fluent for general communication purposes.

Schools have been asked to diversify their language provision, leading to an increase in the demand for French teachers who can also offer Spanish and German. Many applicants now offer a second language, not usually to the same level but possibly to A-level standard, for example.

Strong candidates often speak the language because it is their mother tongue. In a situation where schools are both endeavouring to offer diversity and also having to operate within tight budgets, applicants for jobs who can offer a high proficiency in a mother tongue coupled with another foreign language are much more employable than those only able to offer one language.

ACADEMIC REQUIREMENTS IN SCOTLAND

The minimum entry requirements are set out in *The Memorandum on Entry Requirements to Courses of Teacher Education in Scotland*, available on the Scottish Executive's teaching website: www.teachinginscotland.com They are also outlined on the GTTR website and include the following:

- **For primary**, a degree or equivalent. While there is no one degree that is most appropriate, training institutions will want to ensure that your education provides the foundation for your work as a primary teacher. They will look for evidence that you have studied English and maths, and at least two of the following subjects: science, social studies, expressive arts, religious and moral education, technology, and modern foreign languages. You will also be expected to have had experience of working with children of primary age, preferably in a school environment.

- **For secondary** training your degree must be relevant to the subject you wish to teach. Some secondary subjects have specific requirements. You can get further information from the institution where you wish to study.

Maths and English requirements in Scotland

For primary you will need an SCE Higher Grade pass in English at band C (or equivalent) and an SCE Standard Grade award at grades 1 or 2 in maths (or equivalent).

Those applying with GCSEs should note that the minimum maths requirement is now GCSE at A or B. The minimum English requirement is English language plus English literature at C. The General Teaching Council for Scotland can clarify equivalences.

Information on courses in Scotland not provided through the GTTR is available from the Advisory Service on Entry to Teaching, Cherwood House, 96 Clermiston Road, Edinburgh EH12 6UT, Tel: 0131 314 6000.

APPLICATIONS AND INTERVIEWS

Looking through the Directory will help you choose which teacher training course to apply for. Once that decision has been made, it is then up to you to make sure that your application is successful. Your application has to demonstrate that you have the formal qualifications and personal qualities that it takes to become a good teacher. This is as true for secondary courses where there is a shortfall of applicants as it is of popular primary courses. The standards are high and the process is tough, but this chapter is here to help you maximise your chances of applying successfully.

The fact that some courses are quite small, or some institutions particularly popular may affect the success of your application. Certainly some courses, such as secondary shortage subjects, may be less competitive. However, despite these instances, the focus of admissions tutors remains steady: to select candidates who will not only cope with the demanding courses but also go on to make good teachers.

The government response to the need to attract more teachers has been to create more flexible routes into the profession, not to encourage lower entry standards. The training providers themselves are also keen to maintain demanding entry requirements – only awarding places to capable candidates – because they are judged partly on the number of their students successfully obtaining jobs after completing their courses. So it is extremely unlikely that you will find an easy ride.

Entry procedures for courses demand that admissions tutors interview *all* candidates before they are accepted. This means that your application form for teacher training is particularly important. Interviewers are busy people and they need persuading that it's worth their while devoting time to seeing you. Your application form must therefore make the strongest possible case for your being interviewed.

APPLYING FOR TEACHER TRAINING DEGREE COURSES

If you plan to gain QTS as part of an undergraduate degree course (BA/BSc with QTS or BEd) you must apply through UCAS. This means choosing courses that you like the look of and completing a UCAS form, just as you would for any other subject.

This Directory will provide you with information about all the teacher training courses available in the UK. You should also take care to read the websites and prospectuses published by the individual universities and colleges to make sure that the courses provide what you are looking for and that you can meet the specified entry requirements.

If you are not at a school or college that can provide you with a UCAS form to complete, you can obtain forms from UCAS itself. Many students now apply electronically using the UCAS Electronic Application System (installed at a number of schools, colleges, careers and Connexions services) or via the web.

You may enter up to six choices of courses on your UCAS form. You may apply for fewer than this but, given the competitive nature of the application process, it's better to apply to the maximum number of courses. You don't have to limit your choices to just teacher training courses but it's worth remembering that by sticking with teaching you demonstrate a certain level of commitment to the profession. This is usually a good signal to send to the people considering your application.

The normal deadline for applications via UCAS is 15 January in the year which the course begins. If you submit your form by this date you will definitely be considered for a place on the courses you have applied for. In general though the earlier you apply the better your chance of being called for interview. Late applications are considered at the discretion of individual institutions.

APPLYING FOR PGCE COURSES

The GTTR fields applications for places on most PGCE courses. You will find details about PGCE courses in the UK in this Directory. The GTTR also publishes a free *Guide for Applicants* in September of each year that provides a full list of courses and procedures and the application form.

The GTTR website: www.gttr.ac.uk, also has this information, searchable by your own criteria, as well as an application facility.

Timetable for applications

The creation of flexible, modular routes means that you may be able to start your teacher training course at several different points during the academic year. For courses operating on the standard model the following guidelines apply.

The application forms become available from the GTTR on 1 September. While there is no closing date for secondary applications it is advisable to apply as early as possible as popular courses and subjects can fill up quickly, sometimes by as early as October. Primary and Middle Year courses have an initial closing date of 15 December but places may still be available after this date. In any case it is important that you only apply when you are sure you are going to be able to submit the best application you can and you have been able to research which institutions you want to apply to.

The GTTR does not submit the first batch of applications to colleges until around October of each year and then sends out batches weekly right up until the beginning of courses in the following academic year. However, if you do not have a place by June or July in the year in which you wish to start your training you may need to review your interest in, and suitability for, a career in teaching.

Many students obtain places quite late and the GTTR runs an unplaced student scheme around this time that gives you another chance of obtaining an interview by circulating your details again. You may even apply to institutions direct late in the summer, around August and September, to check if they have any last-minute vacancies, for example through other students withdrawing.

COMPLETING APPLICATION FORMS

Colleges have a legal obligation to interview *all* students before they are accepted on to ITT courses. This means there is less time to interview borderline candidates and makes it all the more important to submit a strong application, whether it is an undergraduate UCAS form or a post-graduate GTTR form. Despite this, admissions tutors continue to be surprised by how many poorly completed application forms they receive. To avoid becoming one of these hopeless cases, you should pay attention to the following general points:

- **Presentation.** Teaching children is all about communicating effectively – a scruffy application form does not inspire confidence that you would be able to do this.

- **Language.** Use standard written English throughout your form. This is the medium used by teachers for communicating in reports, in presenting curriculum policy, in letters to parents, etc.

- **Spelling.** Check your spelling and the correct use of upper and lower case. Application forms with poor spelling and with statements 'SHOUTING' through the use of upper case will be rejected automatically, regardless of their content. Young pupils especially can have problems using upper and lower case properly and teacher training courses simply do not have the time to teach students these basics.

- **Space.** Use all available space. While it is unnecessary to include additional supporting material to reinforce you application, you should make full use of the space allotted on the form to say as much as you can about your suitability.

More specifically, to make sure your application form is a good one you should be aware of the following factors.

Academic background

Teacher training courses generally demand a high academic standard. The Post Graduate Certificate in Education, for example, is precisely that – post-graduate; and those teaching at the primary level need, it is said, an almost Renaissance-like breadth of knowledge to be able to teach the range of subjects demanded by the National Curriculum! Strong academic ability is therefore a key requirement.

Aptitude

Admissions tutors have to make professional judgements very early on about the aptitude of someone for a teaching career. This is why they are obliged to interview everyone they accept on to teacher training courses, but it also makes the application form a crucial first stage in the procedure. You need to use the form to communicate your suitability.

Evidence of work or involvement with young people

ITT course admissions tutors need to be convinced that you know what schools are like. Getting work experience in schools and with children is

an excellent way of developing this knowledge before you start your course and can even be a condition for obtaining a place or gaining an interview.

Current educational issues

You will need to show an understanding of current educational issues. This is particularly important given the extent of recent developments within the sector. You will certainly be asked about such issues in your interview and should also know about the breadth and content of the National Curriculum, relating it to your degree subject where necessary. You need to be clear about what you will be teaching and the age group you will be teaching. Copies of the National Curriculum are available from the DfES and on the DfES website: www.dfes.gov.uk. An understanding of equal opportunities and diversity issues, particularly in urban areas, is also crucial. It would also be a good idea to keep abreast of what's happening in the education press, for example *The Times Education Supplement*.

FURTHER IMPORTANT POINTS ABOUT APPLICATIONS

Health and fitness

All applicants must complete a self-declaration health form. Some may be required to submit to (and pay for!) a formal medical examination. It is unwise to disguise or hide any problems you may have had. Those susceptible to breakdowns, those with drink problems or those who needed to take Valium to get through exams, for example, should consider whether they are in a position to cope with the demands of a teaching career.

'Fitness to teach'

Medical grounds for barring people from teaching only arise where a person is suffering from an illness that implies a risk or potential risk to the safety or welfare of pupils and colleagues. This may be when a person is suffering from mental illness and has displayed psychotic or manic behaviour, or in cases of severe alcohol or drug misuse. DfES Circular 4/99, *Physical and mental fitness to teach of teachers and entrants to initial teacher training* sets out requirements and procedures for fitness to teach. Copies are available from PROLOG on 0845 602 2260.

Criminal convictions

It is a requirement of the Rehabilitation of Offenders Act (1974) that all those seeking entry to the teaching profession disclose any criminal convictions or pending proceedings against them. Before a school employs you, you will be subject to a police check. A criminal conviction will not automatically prevent you from becoming a teacher, but disqualification is automatic for certain serious offences such as rape or unlawful sexual intercourse (after November 1995). Prospective applicants have to give written consent to a police check being made before a school can employ them.

Additionally, the Secretary of State has the power to bar individuals from working with young people on grounds of 'misconduct'. This is not strictly defined, but involves, for example, behaviour that could lead to prosecution for a criminal offence or behaviour that involves an abuse of a teacher.

TEACHER TRAINING AND DISABILITY

DfES regulations stress that training institutions must satisfy themselves that candidates are medically fit for the course and subsequent employment as a teacher. This doesn't discount people with disabilities. Indeed, the Department positively encourages disabled people to apply for the teaching profession:

'Disabled staff can make an important contribution to the overall school curriculum, both as effective employees and in raising the aspirations of disabled pupils and educating non-disabled people about the reality of disability.'

Despite such encouraging statements, applicants with disabilities need to be prepared for a rough ride. Only about 0.1 per cent of teachers are registered as disabled and applicants will need to plan their application carefully to overcome difficulties and pursue their chosen career.

Help others with disabilities into teaching

Skill, the National Bureau for Students with Disabilities, is currently updating its publication *Into Teaching*, which covers opportunities and support for disabled people looking for a teaching career. It is seeking disabled trainees/teachers who would like to write case studies about their experiences in study, training and/or work. Find out how to contribute by visiting the Skill website or go to http://www.teachernet.gov.uk/educationoverview/briefing/Skill/

Getting a job

The same regulations govern employment as cover entry into teacher training, but by this stage you will have the advantage of having demonstrated two of the most important qualities a teacher needs: resilience and dedication. You may also be able to offer the employer's medical examiner letters of recommendation from your course director or from the school where you did your teaching practice.

MAXIMISING YOUR CHANCES

There are a number of ways that you can maximise your chances of a successful application.

Research

You must research the subjects you wish to teach and the context in which you will teach them. In particular you must be familiar with the National Curriculum and issues confronting classroom teachers. The Further information section includes a number of useful starting points for your research.

Other methods of research include: talking to teachers, practitioners and educationalists in your local school or LEA, who are often willing to talk to prospective teachers. Teacher training institutions often have open days or residential sessions over a few days where you can find out more; these might even include some example lessons.

Work experience

Work experience in schools and with children before you start your course is important, not least because leaving your first exposure to school until several months into your course may make it difficult to change if you decide teaching is not right for you. Experience of a modern school and teaching environment will demonstrate to ITT admissions tutors that you are aware of the current situation in schools and are committed to a career in teaching. They will, however, understand that mature applicants with family responsibilities may not be able to spend as much time in a school as younger graduates taking a year off after their degree.

Helping out

It should not be too difficult to find a cooperative school to facilitate your visit, especially if the school is a reasonably large one. Good schools are often keen to encourage interest in the teaching profession. You may offer to help with school trips, remedial reading or even the sports day. The case study at the end of this chapter illustrates how one successful applicant arranged some classroom experience.

You will benefit most from such work experience if you are prepared for it. The class teacher will not have time to look after you during the class and you may well find yourself quickly becoming involved with the pupils. You may think you are 'just a visitor' but pupils will look on you as a resource to help them with their lessons. Be willing to help out and intervene where necessary. Above all, don't pester the teacher, especially during the class.

At the end of your experience you should have found out more about developments in the subject you may want to teach by having spoken to appropriate teachers, and have an idea about the impact of changes in education. Your application form should naturally include details of your personal experience.

Student tutoring

If you are at college or university you might also consider acting as a 'student tutor'. This involves going into local schools to help out – usually in literacy or numeracy classes. You might even be paid for offering this kind of support.

Classroom assistants

Increasing numbers of classroom assistants are being employed to help in schools. You might consider joining them as a way of getting some paid school experience. As an assistant you might help pupils with reading or arithmetic, for example, or on school trips. Many assistants are becoming teachers through joining the Graduate or Registered Teacher Programmes with their schools (see Chapter 3, 'Routes into Teaching').

Teacher training fellowships

These are aimed at motivated and ambitious candidates of African, Caribbean or Asian origin considering a teaching career in England. Fellowships are designed to equip you with the skills required to be successful in the teaching profession, including a period of work-shadowing in a school. Training takes place over weekends and during holidays. It will not interfere with term-time commitments if you are studying. Applicants must be in their final year or have already graduated. For further information contact Windsor Fellowship, The Stables, 138 Kingsland Road, London E2 8DY, Tel: 020 7613 0373.

Mentoring

The National Mentoring Consortium's Teacher Recruitment Project can offer you a six-month mentoring programme. You will be matched with a black or ethnic minority teacher already working in schools and find out what a teaching career is really like. You should be on either a PGCE or in the final year of a degree in a National Curriculum subject. The programme is for those wishing to train to teach in England and is focused mainly on London and south-east England.

For more information contact the programme at the National Mentoring Consortium, Teacher Recruitment Project, University of East London, Room 113, B Block, Longbridge Road, Dagenham, Essex RM8 2AS, Tel: 020 8223 4364.

In England and Wales the Teacher Training Agency will also help individuals find a teacher advocate who can talk to them about a teaching career, find a mentor or even observe a relevant lesson in a school. Contact the Teaching Information Line on 0845 6000 991.

INTERVIEWS

Teaching depends so much on the ability of teachers to communicate well that the interview is an integral part of the admissions procedure. Even students applying from abroad can expect to have to make the journey to attend an interview. You need to be able to convince the interviewer that you will be able to stand in front of a class of pupils and have enough 'presence' to command their attention and respect. If you find it difficult to make eye contact or if your voice is naturally very quiet, you may need to make a conscious effort to change these aspects of yourself.

A number of important topics may feature in the interview:

- commitment to working with pupils of all levels of ability
- evidence of working with children
- a realistic attitude towards children and teaching
- ideas about how to plan a lesson
- knowledge of current issues in education/developments in schools
- realistic but positive view of schools and schooling.

Personal qualities that admissions tutors will be on the look out for are:

- the ability to express yourself clearly and logically in conversation in English
- the capacity to reflect on your own educational experience
- a sense of responsibility and commitment to teaching
- the ability to listen and be sensitive to others
- the potential to relate well with children
- enthusiasm and energy
- a sense of humour
- stamina and robustness
- appearance, maturity and clarity of speech
- competence in learning and an ability to learn quickly.

Typical interview questions include:

- Why do you want to teach?
- What do you know about the National Curriculum?
- How would you deal with an aggressive parent?
- Should pupils have to take exams?

- Maths subject applicant: What makes a good maths teacher?

- How would you motivate an uninterested pupil?

- Secondary applicant: How relevant is your degree to teaching your chosen subject?

- How could your outside interests be used in the classroom?

- English subject applicant: How would you interest a Year 9 pupil in Shakespeare?

Interviews can take different forms. There may be a panel including someone from a local school as well as someone from the ITT institution. You may be interviewed as part of a group of applicants in which you are asked to discuss educational issues. You may also have to take some tests assessing your literacy, numeracy and ICT skills. Sometimes you may be asked to do something practical such as plan and present a lesson or stand at the back of the room and 'project' your voice, or even enter the interview room pretending it is a class of noisy pupils. Be prepared for anything.

6

FUNDING

One of the factors that will affect your student life, whatever you decide to study, is money. The good news is that the DfES has established a number of financial incentives intended to attract new graduates and career changers to the teaching profession. These take the form of training bursaries or other financial sweeteners, created in order to encourage talented people to join the profession who may formerly have discounted teaching as a career in favour of more apparently lucrative graduate professions such as Law. They are explored in detail on page 46.

Studying at undergraduate or postgraduate level is likely to be one of the most stimulating and exciting times of your life. Since 1998 there have been a number of changes that have affected the student experience – the introduction of fees and abolition of grants have meant that rising debts are a seemingly inevitable part of life. The government's White Paper of early 2003, *The Future of Higher Education*, outlined changes to the system of student funding, including the possible introduction of 'top-up' fees, which may come into force from 2006. The benefits of the government's financial incentives will be felt when you have completed your studies and are a qualified teacher, and they will do much to alleviate the debts that you may have built up in along the way. But there are measures you can take to ensure that you don't get buried under an unnecessary mountain of money worries before you qualify.

First, it may be useful to have a look at the financial problems you might encounter and the current funding system that is in place:

- Fees: paid annually by students in England, Wales, Northern Ireland and Scottish students studying outside Scotland

- Loans and grants available

- Cost of living

- Access and Hardship funds and loans.

FEES

In 1998 there began a revolutionary change in the university funding system – fees were introduced, which had previously been paid in full by the government. As a general rule, all UK/EU students have to pay tuition fees unless their parents are earning less than about £20,000 a year. Your local education authority (LEA) if you live in England or Wales, or the

Department of Education (www.deni.gov.uk) if you are in Northern Ireland may assist in paying your fees, provided both you and the course are eligible.

The student portion of fees is means-tested, so how much you need to pay is affected by parental income. The maximum tuition fee contribution is £1,125, but you need to apply to your local government organisation as soon as possible to get the financial support you are entitled to. If you apply too late you could be charged more than £1,125 and you will not have access to the student loan (see below). Scottish students who remain in Scotland to complete their ITT course are in luck, as the Scottish Executive has decided on a different funding package so students do not have to pay fees. Overseas students will be expected to pay for the cost of their education.

European Union nationals studying for a postgraduate qualification that leads to QTS should have their fees paid for them in full. Contact your LEA for more details and to check eligibility. Funding for other postgraduate courses for continued professional development may be more difficult to secure. Contacting the institution to which you are applying is a good way of exploring your options.

Loans and grants

Along with the introduction of fees came the abolition of the maintenance grant, which was compensated for by an increase in the student loan. For information about grants and loans you should contact your LEA if you live in England and Wales, the Department of Education for those of you in Northern Ireland, or the Students Awards Agency (SAAS) if you're in Scotland. For 2003–2004, the maximum loan you can get is £4,000 for students living away from home, £4,930 for students in London living away from home, and £3,165 for students living at home. You are liable to begin making repayments on your loan from the April after you leave your course, once you are earning over the £10,000 threshold salary. See page 47 for information about how the government's financial incentives could affect your loan repayments.

There is financial assistance available in the form of maintenance grants for low-income families. Less well-off students in Wales, Scotland and Northern Ireland may appear to get a better deal than English students, because new systems of non-repayable bursaries and grants, such as the Assembly Learning Grant (ALG) funded by the Welsh Assembly Government, have been introduced in the last two years. For details, contact the relevant authority.

Cost of living

Your student loan is intended to cover the cost of living: lodgings, food, travel, socialising, etc. When you consider that students spend over half their money on accommodation if not living at home, the loan can at first glance seem woefully inadequate. However, it is possible to get by – all you need is the know-how. Refer to books such as *Students' Money Matters* or *Survival on a Shoestring*, both published by Trotman, for essential thrift tips and advice on how to manage your finances.

Access and Hardship funds and loans

These are available through your institution and provide help for students who may need extra financial support for their course and to stay in higher education. They are usually paid as non-repayable grants, although sometimes they can be given as short-term loans. They are particularly useful for students who encounter emergency and unforeseen financial crises. Contact the student support office, the student services office or the students' union of your ITT provider for more information about how and when to apply for a Hardship loan or help from Access funds.

Hardship loans are available for full-time students, and part-time students on teacher training courses, who get into serious financial difficulty during their course. They are available in amounts of £100 up to £500, paid directly into your bank account by the Student Loans Company. From 2004/05 there will be a single source of help available from your college, the Access to Learning Fund. This will replace Hardship Loans and the Access and Hardship Funds, and you will not have to repay this help.

For schemes in Scotland and Northern Ireland, please contact your local education authority.

The DfES produces a booklet called *Financial Support for Higher Education Students*, which outlines the help on offer. You can get a free copy from your LEA or by contacting the DfES's freephone information line: Tel: 0800 731 9133.

The Teaching Information Line (TIL) also offers advice on financial support for students on ITT courses, Tel: 0845 6000 991, Tel: 0845 6000 992 (Welsh speakers).

You can get a copy of the annual publication *Student Support in Scotland – A Guide for Postgraduate Students* from either the SAAS or your chosen Teacher Education Institution (TEI). This publication includes information about student loan arrangements.

Recruitment incentives

These are targeted mainly at people who think 'I'd like to be a teacher but . . .' and can be very generous. Whether you are looking to change career but have responsibilities, or you're a student faced with growing debt, they could well make the difference to you.

Training bursaries

All postgraduate trainee teachers studying in England and Wales who are ordinarily resident in the UK or European Union and are on an eligible course currently receive £6,000 – that's about £150 a week. This is a tax-free sum and does not have to be paid back – it is there purely for you to be able to support yourself during your training.

If you join the Fast Track Teaching programme (details on page 21) and meet the same residential criteria you will also receive a Fast Track bursary of £3,000 – £5,000 at the start of your training year and £2,000 when you start your first Fast Track post.

Secondary Shortage Subject Scheme

Otherwise known as SSSS, this is a response to the chronic teacher shortages in a number of subjects at secondary level education. The SSSS is an additional hardship fund for eligible trainees in these subjects that makes payments based on a needs assessment carried out by individual training providers. The shortage subjects are:

- Design and technology
- Geography
- Information technology
- Mathematics
- Modern foreign languages
- Music
- Religious education
- Science.

If you are under 25 and training to teach one of these subjects at secondary level in England you can receive a maximum of £5,000 through this scheme. Those who are 25 and over could receive up to £7,500. You may also receive a 'golden hello' when you start teaching (see below).

Welsh language incentive

Some students undertaking secondary Initial Teacher Training (ITT) through the medium of Welsh but who need additional assistance to improve their Welsh language skills can receive an extra £1,200. For more information about eligibility contact individual ITT providers.

Welsh placement grant

Undergraduate students living in Wales who are training to become secondary teachers receive an extra grant to support them during their period of school placement. This is £1,000 per year for students on shortage subject courses and £600 on non-shortage subject courses.

'Golden hellos'

Teachers in England and Wales are eligible for an additional £4,000 taxable lump sum upon their second year of teaching one of the following shortage subjects:

- Mathematics
- Science
- English (including drama)
- Modern languages
- Design and technology
- Information and communications technology
- Welsh.

To be eligible for this payment you must have qualified in England or Wales, or hold equivalent qualifications, and must be teaching in England or Wales.

Repayment of student loans

Since September 2002, Newly Qualified Teachers (NQTs) have benefited from the Repayment of Teachers' Loans (RTL) scheme. If you are teaching an eligible priority subject (those listed above) for at least half your teaching time, the government will repay your outstanding Student Loan (from the Student Loans Company) over a period of up to 10 years, as long as you stay in teaching. To be eligible for the Repayment of Teachers' Loans scheme, you must teach within seven months of gaining QTS.

TEACHER SALARIES

Something to look forward to once you qualify and are beyond student hardship, is that teacher salaries are in general improving and are certainly comparable to other professions' starting salaries.

As a NQT, you can expect to start on a scale that ranges from £18,105 to £26,460 (£21,522 to £30,000 in Inner London). If you are a career changer or mature entrant you may, depending on your previous experience, start at a higher level. You will most likely start at point one (M1) on the Main Pay Scale (MPS), which from April 2003 amounts to £18,105 per annum (£21,522 in inner London). By way of comparison, the following are average starting salaries for some other graduate professions:

PR executive	£16,500
advertising sales	£17,000

public services	£17,133
insurance	£17,250
accounting	£17,250

Each year you will move up a point on the MPS until you reach M6 – £26,460. This is known as the 'threshold', when you will be eligible to apply to move on to the Upper Pay Scale (UPS), which has five points running from £28,668 to £33,150 (£34,002 to £39,093 in inner London). These scales are currently reviewed once a year in April.

Advanced Skills Teachers (ASTs) are teachers who have reached standards of excellence in their profession. They are paid on a five-point pay range on the AST pay scale, which extends from £29,757 to £47,469 (£35,700 to £53,412 in inner London). For more information on ASTs, visit www.standards.dfes.gov.uk/ast/. If you take on a leadership role, for example by becoming a headteacher, a deputy or an assistant headteacher, you will be on a five or seven-point pay range drawn from the leadership group pay scale, which ranges over 43 points from £31,416 to £88,155 (£37,359 to £94,098 in inner London). The larger and more challenging the school, the higher up the pay scale a headteacher's salary will be.

In addition to these basic pay scales there are also extra allowances for classroom teachers taking on management responsibilities or for special cases such as those on the Fast Track programme. The starting salary for a teacher on Fast Track is a minimum of £18,984. In subsequent years on the programme, Fast Track teachers receive a recruitment and retention allowance of at least £1,971 for each year they spend working as a Fast Track teacher in addition to the salary and other allowances paid for by the school. Teachers working in London get a regional allowance on top of all that.

With such money being paid and with the government's plans to improve the profession further, there could be no better time to consider a career in teaching.

7

FURTHER INFORMATION

TEACHER TRAINING AGENCY

The TTA is in charge of raising standards in schools by attracting able and committed people to teaching and by improving the quality of teacher training. It can tell you everything you need to know about getting into teaching in England and Wales. It publishes a number of useful booklets, most of which are available to download on its website.

The Teacher Training Agency
Portland House, Stag Place, London SW1E 5TT
Tel: 020 7925 3700
Website: www.canteach.gov.uk

To order copies of TTA publications, call 0845 606 0323 or email

ttapublications@iforcegroup.com

The TTA also runs the teaching information line:

0845 6000 991 (for English speakers)
0845 6000 992 (for Welsh speakers)

DEPARTMENT FOR EDUCATION AND SKILLS

The DfES develops and implements the policy behind education and teaching in England and Wales. It has information about all aspects of education and training.

Website: www.dfes.gov.uk

Teachernet is the DfES's website for teachers and people who work in schools. It provides information about the education system, school management, pay and conditions and professional development, as well as news and useful websites. Website: www.teachernet.gov.uk

TEACHING IN SCOTLAND

Scotland's education system is one of the areas devolved to the Scottish Executive. The Scottish Executive Education Department is responsible for administering policy on pre-school and school education, including the teaching profession.

Scottish Executive Education Department
Victoria Quay
Edinburgh EH6 6QQ

The SEED has a website that can tell you all about teaching and teacher training in Scotland: Website: www.teachinginscotland.com

TEACHING IN NORTHERN IRELAND

Information on courses in Northern Ireland is available from:

The Department of Education
Rathgael House
Balloo Road
Bangor
Co. Down BT19 7PR
Tel: 028 9127 9279
Fax: 028 9127 9100

TEACHER TRAINING

Universities and Colleges Admissions Service (UCAS)
Rosehill
New Barn Lane
Cheltenham
Gloucestershire GL52 3LZ
Tel: 01242 222 444
Website: www.ucas.com

The UCAS website also contains up-to-the-minute details of courses. Alternatively, you can get hold of a copy of the official reference book, *University and College Entrance: The Official Guide* or the smaller, more digestible and free, *UCAS Directory*, available directly from UCAS.

Graduate Teacher Training Register
Rosehill
New Barn Lane
Cheltenham
Gloucestershire GL52 3LZ
Tel: 01242 544 788
Website: www.gttr.ac.uk

Skill – National Bureau for Students with Disabilities
Chapter House
18–20 Crucifix Lane
London SE1 3JW
Tel: 020 7450 0620
Website: www.skill.org.uk

GENERAL TEACHING COUNCILS

These are the professional bodies for the teaching profession in the UK. In order to teach in state education you need to have QTS and be registered with the relevant General Teaching Council.

General Teaching Council for England
344–354 Gray's Inn Road
London WC1X 8BP
Tel: 0870 0010308
Website: www.gtce.org.uk

General Teaching Council for Scotland
Clerwood House
96 Clermiston Road
Edinburgh EH12 6UT
Tel: 0131 314 6000
Website: www.gtcs.org.uk

General Teaching Council for Wales
4th Floor, Southgate House
Wood Street
Cardiff CF10 1EW
Tel: 0292 055 0350
Website: www.gtcw.org.uk

CURRICULA AND QUALIFICATIONS

The National Curriculum Online
Website: www.nc.uk.net

Learning and Teaching Scotland
74 Victoria Crescent Road
Glasgow G12 9JN
Tel: 08700 100 297
Website: www.ltscotland.com

Qualifications and Curriculum Authority
83 Piccadilly
London W1J 8QA
Tel: 020 7509 5555
Website: www.qca.org.uk

Scottish Qualifications Authority
Hanover House
24 Douglas Street
Glasgow G2 7NQ
Tel: 0141 242 2214
Website: www.sqa.org.uk

Northern Ireland:
Council for the Curriculum Examinations and Assessment
29 Clarendon Road
Clarendon Dock
Belfast, BT1 3BG
Tel: 028 9026 1200
Website: http://www.ccea.org.uk/

Qualifications Curriculum and Assessment Authority for Wales
Castle Buildings
Womanby Street
Cardiff CF10 1SX
Tel: 029 2037 5400
Website: www.accac.org.uk

TEACHING ORGANISATIONS

National Union of Teachers
Mabledon Place
London WC1H 9BD
Tel: 020 7388 6191
Website: www.teachers.org.uk

National Association of Teachers in Further and Higher Education
27 Britannia Street
London WC1X 9JP
Tel: 020 7837 3636
Website: www.natfhe.org.uk

SOURCES IN CHAPTERS 1–5

Chapter 1

www.teachernet.gov.uk/teachersloans
www.canteach.gov.uk/teaching/support.htm
www.dfes.gov.uk/studentsupport
www.dfes.gov.uk/leas
Teaching Information Line 0845 6000 991
DfES Student Support Information Line 0800 731 9133

Chapter 2

The education system in the UK

Department for Education and Skills www.dfes.gov.uk
Learning and Teaching Scotland www.ltscotland.com
Learning Wales www.learning.wales.gov.uk

Department of Education Northern Ireland www.deni.gov.uk
Qualifications and Curriculum Authority www.qca.org.uk
Scottish Qualifications Authority www.sqa.org.uk
Qualifications, Curriculum and Assessment Authority for Wales
     www.accac.org.uk
Council for the Curriculum Examinations and Assessment (Northern
     Ireland) www.ccea.org.uk
National Curriculum Online www.nc.uk.net
www.dfes.gov.uk/leas
www.dfes.gov.uk/a-z
www.dfes.gov.uk/sen
www.teachernet.gov.uk
www.canteach.gov.uk
National Association of Special Educational Needs www.nasen.org.uk
www.standards.dfes.gov.uk/specialistschools
Independent Schools Council information service (ISCis)
     www.isis.org.uk
Steiner Waldorf Schools Fellowship www.steinerwaldorf.org.uk
Montessori Foundation www.montessori.org
www.youth-justice-board.gov.uk
Teaching Information Line 0845 6000 991
Guide to Independent Schools by Klaus Boehm and Jenny Lees-
     Spalding, published by Trotman

Chapter 3

www.canteach.gov.uk
www.canteach.gov.uk/teaching/return
www.teachinginscotland.com
www.ucas.com
www.gttr.ac.uk
www.fasttrackteaching.gov.uk
NATFHE www.natfhe.org.uk
General Teaching Council for England www.gtce.org.uk
General Teaching Council for Scotland www.gtcs.org.uk
www.teachernet.gov.uk
www.city-and-guilds.co.uk
Institute for Learning and Teaching in Higher Education
     www.ilt.ac.uk
TTA Keeping in Touch Programme, PO Box 3049, Chelmsford
     CM1 3YT, Tel: 0845 6000 993, helpline@kit-tta.co.uk

Chapter 4

www.canteach.gov.uk
www.teachinginscotland.com
www.ucas.com

www.gttr.ac.uk
www.fasttrackteaching.gov.uk
General Teaching Council for England www.gtce.org.uk
General Teaching Council for Scotland www.gtcs.org.uk
www.teachernet.gov.uk

Chapter 5

www.ucas.com
www.gttr.ac.uk
www.skill.org.uk

INSTITUTIONS

University of Aberdeen

Student Recruitment and Admissions
University Office
Regent Walk
Aberdeen
AB24 3FX
Tel: 01224 272090 / 272091
Fax: 01224 272576
sras@abdn.ac.uk
www.aberdeen.ac.uk

The University was founded by Bishop William Elphinstone in 1495. It is the third oldest university in Scotland and the fifth oldest in the UK and now caters for over 13,000 students. The main campus is King's College in Old Aberdeen, only one mile from the city centre. The Medical School is one mile from the main campus at Foresterhill.

In addition to the recreational facilities the university provides there are five libraries, including one at the Medical School, and extensive computer facilities are available. Halls are available on campus or within a 15-minute walk and accommodation is guaranteed for first-year students.

The Faculty of Education was established in December 2001, following the merger of the University of Aberdeen and Northern College of Education. The faculty offers a range of degree courses and the Post-graduate Certificates in both primary and secondary education. It also offers teachers and other professionals a wide range of undergraduate and postgraduate pro-grammes delivered by distance learning.

HOW TO APPLY

Degree Courses: applications are made through UCAS.
PGCE: applications are made through the GTTR.
Postgraduate: applications are made direct to the institution.

COURSES

BMus (Hons) in Music (Secondary) XW13

4 years full-time

Course offers flexible 2+2 format; 1st 2 years of core study develop students' skills in music; during Years 3 and 4 students choose between an Honours programme in education or music. Students choosing the Honours education route will qualify to teach in secondary schools in Scotland on completion of the course.

Entry requirements: CC to CC: SCE Higher, DD to DD: GCE A- and AS-levels
Contact: Mrs Cathy Reid
01224 283500
c.reid@norcol.ac.uk

BEd (Hons) in Primary Education (3–12 years) X120

4 years full-time

Theory and practice of education and school experience.

School experience: provides students with an understanding of the work of the teacher at each stage of the primary school. Students are placed within the range of primary school provision including a rural school.

Curricular components: 6 areas: environ-mental studies, expressive arts, language arts and mathematics, information tech-nology, religious and moral education.

Assessment by assignments and examina-tions in mathematics.

On the Aberdeen campus Gaelic speaking students are given the opportunity to develop their Gaelic and to be placed in Gaelic medium schools for part of their school experience. Beginners' courses in Gaelic language are offered on both cam-puses.

Roman Catholic students who wish to be eligible to teach in Roman Catholic Schools are required to undertake a distance-learning course offered by St Andrew's College, Glasgow.

This course is offered at the Aberdeen and Dundee campuses.

On completion students are recommended to the General Teaching Council for Scotland for provisional registration. Full registration is awarded on the completion of 2 satisfactory years (or equivalent) of teaching.

Entry requirements: AB to AB: GCE A- and AS-levels, ABB to ABB: SCE Higher
Contact: As above

PGCE in Primary Education (5–11 years) X100

1 year full-time

Entry requirements: Degree from UK University or equivalent, degree must include teaching subject qualifying courses.
Contact: Faculty of Education
Department of Curriculum
Studies
01224 274553
curric@abdn.ac.uk

PGCE in Primary Education (5–11 years, Gaelic medium) X102

1 year full-time
As above

PGCE in Secondary Education (Biology) C1X1

1 year full-time

Entry requirements: Degree from UK University or equivalent, degree must include teaching subject qualifying courses.
Contact: Kerry McKenzie
Registry Assistant
01224 283533
k.mckenzie@norcol.ac.uk

PGCE in Secondary Education (Business Studies) N1X1

1 year full-time

Entry requirements: As above
Contact: Faculty of Education
Department of Curriculum
Studies
01224 274553
curric@abdn.ac.uk

PGCE in Secondary Education (Chemistry) F1X1

1 year full-time
As above

PGCE in Secondary Education (Computing) G5X1

1 year full-time
As above

PGCE in Secondary Education (Drama) W4X1

1 year full-time
As above

PGCE in Secondary Education (English) Q3X1

1 year full-time
As above

PGCE in Secondary Education (Gaelic) Q5X1

1 year full-time
As above

PGCE in Secondary Education (Geography) F8X1

1 year full-time
As above

PGCE in Secondary Education (History) V1X1

1 year full-time
As above

PGCE in Secondary Education (Home Economics) D6X1

1 year full-time
As above

PGCE in Secondary Education (Mathematics) G1X1

1 year full-time
As above

PGCE in Secondary Education (Modern Languages: French) R1X1

1 year full-time
As above

PGCE in Secondary Education (Modern Languages: German) R2X1

1 year full-time
As above

PGCE in Secondary Education (Modern Studies) V9X1

1 year full-time

As above

PGCE in Secondary Education (Physics) F3X1

1 year full-time

As above

PGCE in Secondary Education (Religious Education) V8X1

1 year full-time

As above

PGCE in Secondary Education (Technological Education) J9X1

1 year full-time

As above

Pgcert/PgDip/MEd in Early Education

12 months part-time

Entry requirements: Degree and work experience.

Contact: Joyce Allan
Assistant Registrar
01224 283690
j.allan@norcol.ac.uk

Pgcert/PgDip/MEd in Educational Studies

1 year part-time

Entry requirements: As above

Contact: Janet Clark
Pathway Assistant
01224 283562
j.clark@norcol.ac.uk

PgCert/PgDip/MEd in Information and Communication Technology and Learning

12 months part-time

As above

PgCert/PgDip/MEd in Primary Education

12 months part-time

Entry requirements: Degree and previous experience.

Contact: Joyce Allan
Assistant Registrar
01224 283690
j.allan@norcol.ac.uk

Pgdip in Scottish Qualification for Headship

24 to 36 months part-time

Entry requirements: Degree and at least 5 years' teaching experience.

Contact: Laura Bowie
01224 283653
l.bowie@norcol.ac.uk

Additional Teaching Qualification in Secondary Education

3 to 4 months part-time

Entry requirements: Must be qualified secondary teacher with recent experience, registered with General Teaching Council for Scotland; plus degree with 3 Teaching Subject Qualifying Courses in subject in which student now wishes to train; plus Higher English at grade C.

Contact: Janet Clark
01224 283562
j.clark@abdn.ac.uk

University of Wales, Aberystwyth

Old College
King Street
Aberystwyth
Ceredigion
SY23 2AX
Tel: 01970 623111
Fax: 01970 627410
ug-admissions@aber.ac.uk
www.aber.ac.uk

The University of Wales, Aberystwyth was founded in 1872 and was the first university institution to be established in Wales. It now caters for over 7,000 students, and is situated on the shores of Cardigan Bay.

The Education Department is located in the Old College on the sea-front promenade in the town. The university offers a range of courses from undergraduate degrees to postgraduate teacher training as well as other taught courses. Research opportunities are also available.

There are two other campuses: Penglais (the main one) and Llanbadarn. The Old College has its own specialised library and resources centre and there is also the main Hugh Owen Library for the university and the National Library of Wales on hand as well as extra IT facilities within the academic buildings and halls.

First-year students are guaranteed accommodation and the University has an extensive range of accommodation available for postgraduate students ranging from catered and self-catering rooms on campus and town-based flats, to houses and traditional halls.

HOW TO APPLY

PGCE: applications are made through the GTTR.

Postgraduate: applications are made direct to the institution.

COURSES

**PGCE in Primary Education
(Lower Primary, 3–7) X121**

10 months full-time

Entry requirements: Initial degree in relevant subject, GCSE at grade C or above (or equivalent) in mathematics and English and, for applicants born after 1/9/79, science. Experience of work with children.

Contact: Mrs Eirwen Lewis
            Secretary
            01970 622106
            mel@aber.ac.uk

PGCE in Primary Education (Lower Primary, 3–7, Welsh medium) X123

10 months full-time
As above

PGCE in Primary Education (Upper Primary, 7–11) X171

10 months full-time
As above

**PGCE in Primary Education
(Upper Primary, 7–11, Welsh medium)
X173**

10 months full-time
As above

PGCE in Secondary Education (Biology with Balanced Science) C1X1

10 months full-time

Entry requirements: Initial degree in science with major component biology, and GCSE grade C or above in English language and mathematics; experience of working with children an advantage.

Contact: Mrs Carolyn Gittins
            Secretary
            01970 622105
            cjj@aber.ac.uk

PGCE in Secondary Education (Biology with Balanced Science, Welsh medium) C1XC

10 months full-time
As above

**PGCE in Secondary Education
(Chemistry with Balanced Science) F1X1**

10 months full-time

Entry requirements: Initial degree in science with major component chemistry, and GCSE grade C or above in English language and mathematics; experience of working with children an advantage.

Contact: As above

**PGCE in Secondary Education
(Chemistry with Balanced Science, Welsh medium) F1XC**

10 months full-time
As above

PGCE in Secondary Education (Drama) W4X1

10 months full-time

Entry requirements: Initial degree in drama, and GCSE grade C or above in English language and mathematics; experience of working with children an advantage.

Contact: As above

PGCE in Secondary Education
(Drama, Welsh medium) W4XC

10 months full-time

As above

PGCE in Secondary Education (English)
Q3X1

10 months full-time

Entry requirements: Initial degree in English, and GCSE grade C or above in mathematics; experience of working with children an advantage.

Contact: As above

PGCE in Secondary Education (English, Welsh medium) Q3XC

10 months full-time

As above

PGCE in Secondary Education (French)
R1X1

10 months full-time

Entry requirements: First degree in French and GCSE grade C or above in English language and mathematics; experience of working with children preferred.

Contact: As above

PGCE in Secondary Education (French, Welsh medium) R1XC

10 months full-time

As above

PGCE in Secondary Education
(Geography) F8X1

10 months full-time

Entry requirements: Initial degree required in relevant subject, and GCSE grade C or above in English language and mathematics; experience of working with children preferred.

Contact: As above

PGCE in Secondary Education
(Geography, Welsh medium) F8XC

10 months full-time

As above

PGCE in Secondary Education (German)
R2X1

10 months full-time

Entry requirements: First degree in German, and GCSE grade C or above in English language and mathematics; experience of working with children preferred.

Contact: As above

PGCE in Secondary Education (German, Welsh medium) R2XC

10 months full-time

As above

PGCE in Secondary Education (History)
V1X1

10 months full-time

Entry requirements: Initial degree in history, and GCSE grade C or above in English language and mathematics; experience of working with children an advantage.

Contact: As above

PGCE in Secondary Education (History, Welsh medium) V1XC

10 months full-time

As above

PGCE in Secondary Education (Physics with Balanced Science) F3X1

10 months full-time

Entry requirements: Degree in science, with a major component of physics, and GCSE grade C or above in English language and mathematics; experience of working with children preferred.

Contact: As above

PGCE in Secondary Education (Physics with Balanced Science, Welsh medium) F3XC

10 months full-time

As above

PGCE in Secondary Education (Welsh, Welsh medium) Q5XC

10 months full-time

Entry requirements: Initial degree in Welsh, and GCSE grade C or above in English language and mathematics; experience of working with children preferred.

Contact: As above

Diploma/MEd in Education

Diploma: 3–5 years part-time, MEd: 5 years part-time

Entry requirements: Initial degree/teaching qualification and minimum 2 years' teaching experience required.

Contact: Dr Malcolm Thomas
01970 622103
mlt@aber.ac.uk

Anglia Polytechnic University

Chelmsford Campus
Victoria Road South
Chelmsford
Essex
CM1 1LL
Tel: 01245 493131
Fax: 01245 348740
answers@apu.ac.uk
www.apu.ac.uk

Anglia Polytechnic University's Chelmsford site is based on two campuses within ten minutes' walk of each other, Central Campus and Rivermead Campus. Rivermead is home to the new School of Education as well as extensive student facilities including access to computers, a medical centre and a Learning Resources Centre, which houses the Main Library. The origins of the university go back to 1858 and it was granted university status in 1992.

The School of Education has been offering courses for over 40 years, has developed and expanded and is still introducing new areas of study. The school caters for various levels of teacher education and development including the Initial Teacher Training PGCE at primary and secondary level, a Graduate Teacher Programme and courses for Continuing Professional Development. It also offers Honours degrees, qualifications for Teaching Assistants, teaching qualifications in Post-Compulsory Education and a selection of Master's degrees and research opportunities.

The University offers some on-site accommodation and manages other residences within 1.5 miles of the campus. It can also advise on private accommodation.

HOW TO APPLY

Degree courses: applications are made through UCAS.

PGCE: applications are made through the GTTR for primary and secondary; applications are made direct to the institution for post-compulsory education.

Postgraduate: applications are made direct to the institution.

COURSES

BA (Hons) Primary Education X120

3 years full-time

Course prepares students to teach across the full primary age range (5–11 years); students attend school for 1 day per week during the taught part of the degree, and undertake periods of teaching practice each year; course covers the entire primary curriculum, including use of information and communication technology in each subject; educational issues covered include: different ways in which children develop and learn; professional values; classroom organisation and management; issues of equality; special educational needs; cross-curricular themes such as personal, social and health education and citizenship; in the final year students pursue a specialist study in an area of interest.

Successful completion of this course leads to a recommendation for Qualified Teacher Status (QTS), subject to satisfactory performance in skills tests.

Entry requirements: Tariff: 220 points, BTEC NC/ND, Foundation / access qualification

Contact: Admissions Officer
0845 271 3333
enquiries@apu.ac.uk

PGCE in Post-Compulsory Education

2 years part-time

Entry requirements: Degree or equivalent; applicants should be employed as a teacher or trainer for a minimum of 3 hours per week.

Contact: Gordon Bellamy
g.a.bellamy@apu.ac.uk

PGCE in Primary Education X100

1 year full-time

Entry requirements: Honours degree or equivalent; GCSE grade C or above in English language, mathematics and science (if born on or after 1/9/79); recent experience of working in a primary school.

Contact: Course Administrator, PGCE
(Primary)
01245 493131

PGCE in Secondary Education (Art and Design) W1X1

1 year full-time

Entry requirements: Degree or equivalent in art and design, or with art and design as a substantial component; GCSE grade C or equivalent in English language and mathematics.

Contact: Course Administrator, PGCE
(Secondary)
01245 493131

PGCE in Secondary Education (English) Q3X1

1 year full-time

Entry requirements: Degree or equivalent in English, or with English as a substantial component; GCSE grade C or equivalent in English language and mathematics.

Contact: As above

PGCE in Secondary Education (History with Citizenship) VX1C

1 year full-time

Entry requirements: Degree or equivalent in history, or with history as a substantial component; GCSE grade C or equivalent in English language and mathematics.

Contact: As above

PGCE in Secondary Education (Information and Communication Technology) G5X1

1 year full-time

Entry requirements: Degree or equivalent in information and communication technology (ICT), or with ICT as a substantial component; GCSE grade C or equivalent in English language and mathematics.

Contact: As above

PGCE in Secondary Education (Modern Foreign Languages) R9X1

1 year full-time

Entry requirements: Degree or equivalent in modern foreign languages, or with a modern foreign language as a substantial component; GCSE grade C or equivalent in English language and mathematics.

Contact: As above

PGCE in Secondary Education (Science) F0X1

1 year full-time

Entry requirements: Degree or equivalent in science, or with science as a substantial component; GCSE grade C or equivalent in English language and mathematics.

Contact: As above

MA in Applied Linguistics (Language Teaching and Learning)

1 year full-time, 2 years part-time

This course is offered at the Cambridge campus.

Entry requirements: Honours degree (2.1), or equivalent; 2 years' experience of teaching a language, and/or experienced language learner; in the case of students who are not native English speakers, knowledge of English must be of at least IELTS 6.5 or equivalent.

Contact: Sally Bienias
Postgraduate Course
Administrator
01223 363271 x2010
s.a.bienias@anglia.ac.uk

Pgcert/Pgdip/MA in Education

2–6 years part-time

Entry requirements: Open to professional educators holding degree or equivalent.

Contact: INSET Administrator
    01245 493131 x3509

EdD in Education

3 years part-time

Entry requirements: Master's degree or equivalent in education plus 5 years' experience in the field of education.

Contact: Prof Janet Moyles
    0845 271 3333
    j.moyles@apu.ac.uk

MA in Teaching and Learning, Higher and Further Education

2.5 years part-time

Entry requirements: Applicants should be teachers in post-compulsory and professional education with an Honours degree or equivalent and relevant experience.

Contact: Gordon Bellamy
    01245 493131 x3791
    g.a.bellamy@apu.ac.uk

University of Wales, Bangor

Bangor
Gwynedd
LL57 2DG
Tel: 01248 351151
Fax: 01248 383268
admissions@bangor.ac.uk
www.bangor.co.uk

The University of Wales, Bangor was established in 1884 as one of the original constituent institutions of the University of Wales. It is situated in the Cathedral City of Bangor on the North Wales coast between Snowdon and the sea. It consists of two campuses at Bangor and Wrexham. Bangor has four different sites: Ffriddoedd, College Road, Normal and St. Mary's. All are centrally located for the majority of the departments.

The School of Education formed following the integration of Coleg Normal with the University in 1996 and is situated on the Normal Site. The school offers a wide range of teaching courses leading to honours degrees, certificates and a range of postgraduate qualifications. There are opportunities for research degrees as well as taught courses. Students can take courses in Welsh, English or a bilingual option.

The University offers good computer facilities along with a main library and six other specific libraries including one for education at the Normal Site. The four sites offer over 2,000 places either in catered or self-catered accommodation. First-year students are guaranteed places and there is also some accommodation reserved for postgraduate students.

HOW TO APPLY

Degree courses: applications are made through UCAS.
PGCE: applications are made through the GTTR.
Postgraduate: applications are made direct to the institution.

COURSES

BEd (Hons) in Primary Education (Art and Design) X1W9

3 years full-time

Course comprises a study of the National Curriculum core subjects, education and curricular studies including workshops and seminars in the foundation subjects and religious education, and a major and minor study.

Major study in art, craft and design includes: practical workshops; critical and contextual studies; organisation and management of art in the classroom; teaching experience with children in college and in schools; 24 weeks will be spent in partnership primary schools.

Assessment is by examinations and coursework.

Successful completion leads to a recommendation for Qualified Teacher Status (QTS) on completion of skills tests.

Entry requirements: Tariff: 180 to 220, Irish Leaving Certificates: 270 to 300, BTEC NC/ND, International Baccalaureate
Contact: Mrs Catrin Lewis
      Admissions Secretary
      01248 383012
      eds068@bangor.ac.uk

BEd (Hons) in Primary Education (Design and Technology) X1W2

3 years full-time

Course comprises a study of the National Curriculum core subjects, education and curricular studies including workshops and seminars in the foundation subjects and religious education, and a major and minor study.

The major study in design and technology allows students to become familiar with a wide range of materials, including resistant materials and food and textiles. It also allows them to participate in design activities involving technological concepts. 24 weeks will be spent in partnership primary schools.

Assessment is by examinations and coursework.

Successful completion leads to a recommendation for Qualified Teacher Status (QTS) on completion of skills tests.

Entry requirements: As above
Contact: As above

BEd (Hons) in Primary Education (English) X1Q3

3 years full-time

Course comprises a study of the National Curriculum core subjects, education and curricular studies including workshops and seminars in the foundation subjects and religious education, and a major and minor study.

The major study in English literature will focus mainly on children's literature. 24 weeks will be spent in partnership primary schools.

Assessment is by examinations and coursework.

Successful completion leads to a recommendation for Qualified Teacher Status (QTS) on completion of skills tests.

Entry requirements: As above
Contact: As above

BEd (Hons) in Primary Education (Geography) X1L7

3 years full-time

The course comprises a study of the National Curriculum core subjects, education and curricular studies including workshops and seminars in the foundation subjects and religious education, and a major and minor study.

The major study in geography relates fully to the requirements of the National Curriculum in Wales and England and has a particular focus on learning through field activity. 24 weeks will be spent in partnership primary schools.

Assessment is by examinations and coursework.

Successful completion leads to a recommendation for Qualified Teacher Status (QTS) on completion of skills tests.

Entry requirements: As above
Contact: As above

BEd (Hons) in Primary Education (History) X1V1

3 years full-time

The course comprises a study of the National Curriculum core subjects, education and curricular studies including workshops and seminars in the foundation subjects and religious education, and a major and minor study.

The major study in history aims to provide an understanding of the demands of the National Curriculum history both in terms of content and application in the classroom. The teaching will entail lectures, seminars and workshops and individual research in the classroom. 24 weeks will be spent in partnership primary schools.

Assessment is by examinations and coursework.

Successful completion leads to a recommendation for Qualified Teacher Status (QTS) on completion of skills tests.

Entry requirements: As above
Contact: As above

BEd (Hons) in Primary Education (Mathematics) X1G1

3 years full-time

The course comprises a study of the National Curriculum core subjects, education and curricular studies including workshops and seminars in the foundation subjects and religious education, and a major and minor study.

The major study in mathematics will focus on the development of teaching skills in all areas of the National Curriculum. This will include practical workshops, lectures and seminars and teaching groups of children. 24 weeks will be spent in partnership primary schools.

Assessment is by examinations and coursework.

Successful completion leads to a recommendation for Qualified Teacher Status (QTS) on completion of skills tests.

Entry requirements: As above
Contact: As above

BEd (Hons) in Primary Education (Music) X1W3

3 years full-time

The course comprises a study of the National Curriculum core subjects, education and curricular studies including workshops and seminars in the foundation subjects and religious education, and a major and minor study.

The major study in music will give students the opportunity to perform, compose, analyse and appraise a wide range of music, including examples from Western and non-Western cultures. Studies will be placed within the context of primary education and students will apply their knowledge to the needs of children and the requirements of the National Curriculum. 24 weeks will be spent in partnership primary schools.

Assessment is by examinations and coursework.

Successful completion leads to a recommendation for Qualified Teacher Status (QTS) on completion of skills tests.

Entry requirements: As above
Contact: As above

BEd (Hons) in Primary Education (Physical Education) X1C6

3 years full-time

The course comprises a study of the National Curriculum core subjects, education and curricular studies, including workshops and seminars in the foundation subjects and religious education, and a major and minor study.

The major study in physical education will focus on the teaching of the 6 areas of the subject and on the study and understanding of human movement and development. 24 weeks will be spent in partnership primary schools.

Assessment is by examinations and coursework.

Successful completion leads to a recommendation for Qualified Teacher Status (QTS) on completion of skills tests.

Entry requirements: As above
Contact: As above

BEd (Hons) in Primary Education (Religious Studies) X1V6

3 years full-time

The course comprises a study of the National Curriculum core subjects, education and curricular studies including workshops and seminars in the foundation subjects and religious education, and a major and minor study.

The major study in religious studies provides a general introduction to the sociological, philosophical, ethical, historical, doctrinal, and mythological aspects of religion and a study of the 6 major world religions and methods of incorporating them into the primary curriculum. 24 weeks will be spent in partnership primary schools.

Assessment is by examinations and coursework.

Successful completion leads to a recommendation for Qualified Teacher Status (QTS) on completion of skills tests.

Entry requirements: As above
Contact: As above

BEd (Hons) in Primary Education (Science) X1F0

3 years full-time

The course comprises a study of the National Curriculum core subjects, education and curricular studies including workshops and seminars in the foundation subjects and religious education, and a major and minor study.

The major study in science aims to develop the student's awareness of the nature of scientific enquiry and the implication of supporting children in their learning through science. 24 weeks will be spent in partnership primary schools.

Assessment is by examinations and coursework.

Successful completion leads to a recommendation for Qualified Teacher Status (QTS) on completion of skills tests.

Entry requirements: As above
Contact: As above

BEd (Hons) in Primary Education (Welsh, first or second language) X1Q5

3 years full-time

The course comprises a study of the National Curriculum core subjects, education and curricular studies including workshops and seminars in the foundation subjects and religious education, and a major and minor study. The major study in Welsh aims to enrich awareness of the Welsh language and its literature, both as a source of personal intellectual satisfaction and as a basis for developing the language curriculum in school. 24 weeks will be spent in partnership primary schools.

Assessment is by examinations and coursework.

Successful completion leads to a recommendation for Qualified Teacher Status (QTS) on completion of skills tests.

Entry requirements: As above
Contact: As above

BEd (Hons) in Secondary Education (Design and Technology) X1WF

3 years full-time

Students are provided with a broad foundation in the teaching of technology at Key Stages 3 and 4 and post-16.

Subject study units include: graphics; electronics and mechanisms; construction materials; design; alternative technologies; textiles; robotics and microprocessor control.

Extensive school-based experience: 4-week block placement in each of the 6 semesters.

Assessment by examination and coursework.

Successful completion leads to a recommendation for Qualified Teacher Status (QTS) on completion of skills tests.

Entry requirements: As above
Contact: John Hughes
Course Director
01248 383070
eds087@bangor.ac.uk

PGCE in Primary Education (Lower Primary, 3–8) X121

1 year full-time

Entry requirements: Degree (or equivalent) in subject(s) relevant to primary curriculum, and GCSE minimum grade C (or equivalent) in English language and mathematics, and science if applicant was born after 1/9/79.

Contact: Mrs Catrin Lewis
Admissions Secretary
01248 383012
eds068@bangor.ac.uk

PGCE in Primary Education (Lower Primary, 3–8, Welsh medium) X123

1 year full-time
As above

PGCE in Primary Education (Upper Primary, 7–12) X171

1 year full-time
As above

Primary Education (Upper Primary, 7–12, Welsh medium) X173

1 year full-time
As above

PGCE in Secondary Education (Art and Design) W1X1

1 year full-time

Entry requirements: Degree relevant to National Curriculum subject to be taught, plus GCSE grade C or above (or equivalent qualification) in English language and mathematics.

Contact: Mrs Beryl Hughes
PGCE Secondary Secretary
01248 382933
eds035@bangor.ac.uk

PGCE in Secondary Education (Art and Design, Welsh medium) W1XD

1 year full-time
As above

PGCE in Secondary Education (Biology with Core Science) C1X1

1 year full-time
As above

PGCE in Secondary Education (Biology with Core Science, Welsh medium) C1XD

1 year full-time
As above

PGCE in Secondary Education (Chemistry with Core Science) F1X1

1 year full-time
As above

PGCE in Secondary Education (Chemistry with Core Science, Welsh medium) F1XD

1 year full-time
As above

PGCE in Secondary Education (English) Q3X1

1 year full-time
As above

PGCE in Secondary Education (English, Welsh medium) Q3XD

1 year full-time
As above

PGCE in Secondary Education (French) R1X1

1 year full-time
As above

PGCE in Secondary Education (French, Welsh medium) R1XD

1 year full-time
As above

PGCE in Secondary Education (German) R2X1

1 year full-time
As above

PGCE in Secondary Education (German, Welsh medium) R2XD

1 year full-time
As above

PGCE in Secondary Education (Information Technology) G5X1

1 year full-time
As above

PGCE in Secondary Education
(Information Technology, Welsh
medium) G5XD
1 year full-time
As above

PGCE in Secondary Education
(Mathematics) G1X1
1 year full-time
As above

PGCE in Secondary Education
(Mathematics, Welsh medium) G1XD
1 year full-time
As above

PGCE in Secondary Education (Music)
W3X1
1 year full-time
As above

PGCE in Secondary Education (Music,
Welsh medium) W3XD
1 year full-time
As above

PGCE in Secondary Education (Outdoor
Activities) X1X9
1 year full-time
As above

PGCE in Secondary Education (Outdoor
Activities, Welsh medium) X1XY
1 year full-time
As above

PGCE in Secondary Education (Outdoor
Activities/Art and Design) X9W1
1 year full-time
As above

PGCE in Secondary Education (Outdoor
Activities/Art and Design, Welsh
medium) X9WD
1 year full-time
As above

PGCE in Secondary Education (Outdoor
Activities/Biology with Science) X9C1
1 year full-time
As above

PGCE in Secondary Education (Outdoor
Activities/Biology with Science, Welsh
medium) X9CD
1 year full-time
As above

PGCE in Secondary Education (Outdoor
Activities/Chemistry with Science) X9F1
1 year full-time
As above

PGCE in Secondary Education (Outdoor
Activities/Chemistry with Science, Welsh
medium) X9FD
1 year full-time
As above

PGCE in Secondary Education (Outdoor
Activities/English) X9Q3
1 year full-time
As above

PGCE in Secondary Education (Outdoor
Activities/English, Welsh medium) X9QJ
1 year full-time
As above

PGCE in Secondary Education (Outdoor
Activities/French) X9R1
1 year full-time
As above

PGCE in Secondary Education (Outdoor
Activities/French, Welsh medium) X9RD
1 year full-time
As above

PGCE in Secondary Education (Outdoor
Activities/German) X9R2
1 year full-time
As above

PGCE in Secondary Education (Outdoor
Activities/German, Welsh medium)
X9RG
1 year full-time
As above

PGCE in Secondary Education (Outdoor
Activities/Information Technology)
X9G5
1 year full-time
As above

PGCE in Secondary Education (Outdoor Activities/Information Technology, Welsh medium) X9GN
1 year full-time
As above

PGCE in Secondary Education (Outdoor Activities/Mathematics) X9G1
1 year full-time
As above

PGCE in Secondary Education (Outdoor Activities/Mathematics, Welsh medium) X9GD
1 year full-time
As above

PGCE in Secondary Education (Outdoor Activities/Music) X9W3
1 year full-time
As above

PGCE in Secondary Education (Outdoor Activities/Music, Welsh medium) X9WJ
1 year full-time
As above

PGCE in Secondary Education (Outdoor Activities/Physics with Science) X9F3
1 year full-time
As above

PGCE in Secondary Education (Outdoor Activities/Physics with Science, Welsh medium) X9FJ
1 year full-time
As above

PGCE in Secondary Education (Outdoor Activities/Religious Education) X9V6
1 year full-time
As above

PGCE in Secondary Education (Outdoor Activities/Religious Education, Welsh medium) X9VQ
1 year full-time
As above

PGCE in Secondary Education (Outdoor Activities/Welsh, Welsh medium) X9Q5
1 year full-time
As above

PGCE in Secondary Education (Physical Education) X9C6
1 year full-time
As above

PGCE in Secondary Education (Physical Education, Welsh medium) X9CP
1 year full-time
As above

PGCE in Secondary Education (Physics with Core Science) F3X1
1 year full-time
As above

PGCE in Secondary Education (Physics with Core Science, Welsh medium) F3XD
1 year full-time
As above

PGCE in Secondary Education (Religious Education) V6X1
1 year full-time
As above

PGCE in Secondary Education (Religious Education, Welsh medium) V6XD
1 year full-time
As above

PGCE in Secondary Education (Welsh, Welsh medium) Q5XC
1 year full-time
As above

Diploma/MA/MEd in Education
2–5 years part-time

Entry requirements: Degree or equivalent, or, exceptionally, relevant professional experience.

Contact: Mrs Gwen Hughes
Course Secretary
01248 382932
eds056@bangor.ac.uk

Bath Spa University College

Newton Park
Newton St. Loe
Bath BA2 9BN
Tel: 01225 875875
Fax: 012225 875444
enquiries@bathspa.ac.uk
www.bathspa.ac.uk

The history of the University College goes back to 1898. Bath College of Higher Education was formed in 1975 from the merger of two colleges. The college was granted taught degree-awarding powers in 1992 and in 1999, Privy Council agreement was received to change the name to Bath Spa University College. Bath Spa University College has two campuses in Bath: Newton Park, which is a parkland estate four miles west of Bath leased from the Duchy of Cornwall, and Sion Hill / Somerset Place in Bath. Both campuses provide a range of facilities for the student body of about 4,200.

The School of Education is based at the Newton Park campus. It offers a range of courses from diploma- and undergraduate-level to the PGCE and courses for Continuing Professional Development.

Both campuses have a library that offers access to networked computer services as well as traditional library facilities. Specialist computer facilities are also provided within some subject areas including Education. Social and sporting facilities are also available on site. Accommodation is available on site and there is also privately rented accommodation available.

HOW TO APPLY

PGCE: applications are made through the GTTR.
Postgraduate: applications are made direct to the institution.

COURSES

PGCE in Middle Years (Information and Communications Technology, conversion, 7–14) XGCM

2 years full-time

Entry requirements: Degree in any subject; GCSE English language and mathematics at grade C.
Contact: Ms Clare Furlonger
01225 875514
c.furlonger@bathspa.ac.uk

PGCE in Middle Years (Mathematics, conversion, 7–14) XGCC

2 years full-time

Entry requirements: Degree in any subject; GCSE English language, mathematics and science at grade C.
Contact: Malcolm Hanson
01225 875875

PGCE: Middle Years (Music, 7–14) XWC3

1 year full-time

Entry requirements: Degree in music or with music as a substantial component; alternative music experience considered; GCSE grade C or above in English language, mathematics and science.
Contact: Ms Jo Glover
01225 875523
j.glover@bathspa.ac.uk

PGCE Middle Years/Secondary (Design and Technology, conversion, 7–14/11–18) XWCX

2 years full-time

Entry requirements: Degree; GCSE English language and mathematics at grade C or above.
Contact: Ms Carolyn Goodhew
01225 875517
c.goodhew@bathspa.ac.uk

PGCE in Middle Years/Secondary (English, conversion, 7–14/11–18) XQCH

2 years full-time

Entry requirements: Degree in English or literacy-based subject such as humanities, social sciences and law; GCSE English language, mathematics and science at grade C.
Contact: Susan Hughes
01225 875875

PGCE in Middle Years/Secondary (Science, conversion, 7–14/11–18) XFC0

2 years full-time

Entry requirements: Degree; GCSE English language, mathematics and science at grade C or above.
Contact: Dr David Clark
01225 875448
d.clark@bathspa.ac.uk

PGCE in Primary Education (Advanced Early Years, 3–7) X110

1 year full-time

Entry requirements: Degree; GCSE English language, mathematics and science (for candidates born on or after 1/9/79) at grade C.
Contact: Ms Cathy Hamilton
01225 875875
c.hamilton@bathspa.ac.uk

PGCE in Primary Education (General Primary, 5–11) X100

1 year full-time

Entry requirements: Degree in a subject appropriate to the primary curriculum; GCSE English language, mathematics and science (for candidates born on or after 1/9/79) at grade C.
Contact: Ms Cathy Hamilton
01225 875875
c.hamilton@bathspa.ac.uk

PGCE in Secondary Education (Art and Design) W1X1

1 year full-time

Entry requirements: Degree in art/design or related subject; GCSE English language and mathematics at grade C or above.
Contact: June Bianchi
01225 875651
j.bianchi@bathspa.ac.uk

PGCE in Secondary Education (Design and Technology) W9X1

1 year full-time

Entry requirements: Degree in design and technology or related subject; GCSE English language and mathematics at grade C or above.
Contact: Dr Tim O'Rourke
01225 875464
t.orourke@bathspa.ac.uk

PGCE in Secondary Education (English) Q3X1

1 year full-time

Entry requirements: Degree in English or related subject; GCSE English language and mathematics at grade C or above.
Contact: Mark Browning
01225 875875
m.browning@bathspa.ac.uk

PGCE in Secondary Education (Geography with Information Technology) FX8C

1 year full-time

Entry requirements: Degree with substantial element of geography; GCSE English language and mathematics at grade C or above.
Contact: Mr Fred Martin
01225 875509
f.martin@bathspa.ac.uk

PGCE in Secondary Education (History) V1X1

1 year full-time

Entry requirements: Degree in history or related subject; GCSE English language and mathematics at grade C or above.
Contact: Dr Michael Riley
Secondary History Course Leader
01225 875464
m.riley@bathspa.ac.uk

PGCE in Secondary Education (Information and Communications Technology, conversion) GXM1

2 years full-time

Entry requirements: Degree in any subject; GCSE English language and mathematics at grade C or above.

Contact: Mr Andy Weymouth
01225 875514
a.weymouth@bathspa.ac.uk

PGCE in Secondary Education (Music) W3X1

1 year full-time

Entry requirements: Degree or Graduate Diploma in music; GCSE English language and mathematics at grade C or above.

Contact: Mr Ian Burton
01225 875628
i.burton@bathspa.ac.uk

PGCE in Secondary Education (Religious Education) V6X1

1 year full-time

Entry requirements: Degree in religious studies, theology or related subject; GCSE English language and mathematics at grade C or above.

Contact: Ms Jo Backus
01225 875410
j.backus@bathspa.ac.uk

PGCE in Secondary Education (Science) F0X1

1 year full-time

Entry requirements: Degree in a science subject; GCSE English language and mathematics at grade C or above.

Contact: Bernadette Cass
01225 875875
b.cass@bathspa.ac.uk

PgCert/PgDip/MA/Med in Education/ Professional Studies (Modular Programme for Professional Development)

MA/MEd: 2–6 years part-time

Entry requirements: Qualified Teacher Status or other relevant professional qualification plus substantial recent experience in education, training or other relevant work.

Contact: Dr Steven Coombs
01225 875742
s.coombs@bathspa.ac.uk

University of Bath

Claverton Down
Bath
BA2 7AY
Tel: 01225 388388
Fax: 01225 826366
admissions@bath.ac.uk
www.bath.ac.uk

The University of Bath originated from the Bristol Trade School of 1856 and received its Royal Charter in 1966. It is set in 200-acre grounds and caters for around 8,000 students. As it is a completely purpose-built development all major facilities are located off a single pedestrian parade on the campus. Shops, food courts, bars, laboratories, lecture theatres and the library are grouped around this area, interspersed with accommodation blocks so that all facilities are easily accessible for students. There are extensive computer facilities and the Library and Learning Centre is open 24 hours a day.

The Department of Education offers a range of programmes including undergraduate courses and initial teacher training as well as advanced courses and research degrees. The department houses two leading Centres for Research: the Centre for the Study of Education in an International Context and the Centre for Research in Education and the Environment

HOW TO APPLY

PGCE: applications are made through the GTTR.

Postgraduate: applications are made direct to the institution.

COURSES

PGCE in Middle Years (English, Key Stages 2–3) XQC3

36 weeks full-time

Entry requirements: Degree or equivalent in relevant subject; GCSE grade C or above (or equivalent) in mathematics and English normally required.

Contact: PGCE Course Enquiries
01225 386225/386341
pgce@bath.ac.uk

PGCE in Middle Years (Mathematics, Key Stages 2–3) XGC1

36 weeks full-time
As above

PGCE in Middle Years (Science, Key Stages 2–3) XFCA

36 weeks full-time
As above

PGCE in Secondary Education (English) Q3X1

36 weeks full-time
As above

PGCE in Secondary Education (Geography) F8X1

36 weeks full-time
As above

PGCE in Secondary Education (History) V1X1

36 weeks full-time
As above

PGCE in Secondary Education (Information Technology) G5X1

36 weeks full-time
As above

PGCE in Secondary Education (Mathematics) G1X1

36 weeks full-time
As above

PGCE in Secondary Education (Modern Languages: French/German/Spanish) R9X1

36 weeks full-time
As above

PGCE in Secondary Education (Physical Education) X9C6

36 weeks full-time
As above

PGCE in Secondary Education (Science: Biology) C1X1

36 weeks full-time
As above

PGCE in Secondary Education (Science: Chemistry) F1X1

36 weeks full-time
As above

PGCE in Secondary Education (Science: Earth Science) F6X1

36 weeks full-time
As above

PGCE in Secondary Education (Science: Environmental Science) F9X1

36 weeks full-time
As above

PGCE in Secondary Education (Science: Physics) F3X1

36 weeks full-time
As above

EdD Education

3–5 years full-time or 4–8 year part-time

Entry requirements: Advanced graduate qualification in education or a related field, and appropriate professional experience in the practice of education or a related profession.

Contact: Research Secretary
01225 386545
ed.doc@bath.ac.uk

PgCert/PgDip/MSc Education

1 year full-time

Entry requirements: Degree or relevant experience.

Contact: Gill Brooke-Taylor
Administrator for Postgraduate Research
01225 386545
g.b.brooke-taylor@bath.ac.uk

Advanced Certificate/Advanced Diploma/MA Education (MAEC)

Certificate/Diploma: 1–10 years part-time; MA: 12 months full-time or 2–10 years part-time

Entry requirements: Teaching qualification and/or degree plus 2 years' teaching or other relevant experience.
Contact: Director of Studies
01225 386602/386634
ed.ma@bath.ac.uk

MA English Language Teaching

1 year full-time or 2–10 years part-time

Entry requirements: Degree or equivalent; 2 years' full-time experience in ELT; near native-speaker competence in English.
Contact: Director of Studies for Advanced Courses
Department of Education
01225 386602/386634
ed.ma@bath.ac.uk

Bexley Primary Consortium for Teacher Training

Bexley Education Department
Hill View
Hill View Drive
Dartford
Kent
DA16 3RY
Tel: 020 8240 4000
Fax: 020 8240 4255
patrick.taylor@bexley.gov.uk

The Bexley Primary Consortium for Teacher Training offers graduates a one-year course of Initial Teacher Training. The training is directed by the Head Teachers of successful schools in Bexley. Trainees spend about half of their time in schools, taking increasing responsibility for the work of pupils, groups and whole classes, and the other half in seminars, lectures and courses covering all the professional aspects of teaching.

HOW TO APPLY

Applications are made through the GTTR.

COURSES

PGCE in Primary Education (Foundation and Key Stage 1) X121

1 year full-time

Entry requirements: Degree in relevant subject; GCSE grade C or above in English language and mathematics, and science if born after 1/9/79.
Contact: Patrick Taylor
Course Director
020 8303 7777 x4222
patrick.taylor@bexley.gov.uk

Billericay Educational

PO Box 3477
Billericay
Essex
CM12 0LQ
Tel: 01277 631140
bscitt@rmplc.co.uk
www.billericayscitt.com

The Billericay Educational Consortium was one of two establishments to pioneer the School Centred Initial Teacher Training concept in 1994. The Consortium consists of a group of schools in the Billericay area that have worked together on a range of educational initiatives and projects. The School Centred Initial Teacher Training programme has been developed by some of the schools within the Consortium, creating a 38-week full-time course leading to a PGCE approved by Open University Validation Services.

Trainees spend three days out of most weeks in their base school, where they are involved in the day to day routine of the school. A period of six weeks in the Spring term is spent at a school in the alternative Key Stage and there is a placement in a further Key Stage in the Summer term. The Consortium takes 20 trainees each year.

Each trainee has the use of a laptop whilst on the course, and trainees have access to a quiet study room and library at the Buttsbury Centre. The Consortium can provide details of private rented accommodation in the area.

HOW TO APPLY

Applications are made through the GTTR.

COURSES

PGCE in Primary Education (Lower Primary, 5–8) X121

38 weeks full-time

Entry requirements: Upper 2nd Class degree; experience of working with children.
Contact: Enquiries
01277 631140
bscitt@rmplc.co.uk

PGCE in Primary Education (Upper Primary, 7–11) X171

38 weeks full-time
As above

University of Birmingham

Edgbaston
Birmingham
B15 2TT
Tel: 0121 414 3344
Fax: 0121 414 3971
admissions@bham.ac.uk
www.bham.ac.uk

The University of Birmingham was founded in 1900 and was one of the first redbrick universities. It is mainly based on the campus at Edgbaston in 230 acres of parkland and there is also the nearby Selly Oak campus. The university caters for around 27,000 students.

The School of Education is based on both campuses and is one of the largest schools of its type in Britain. It offers an extensive range of courses that include undergraduate programmes and initial teacher education, as well as post-experience and higher degree courses for those who want to advance their study and continue their professional development.

The Guild of Students, Main Library and sports centre are based on the main campus and there are also student services available on the Selly Oak campus. Students have access to computer clusters based around the university and in individual departments. The university owns a wide range of halls and flats and there are privately owned halls and other accommodation in the local area.

HOW TO APPLY

PGCE: applications are made through the GTTR.

Postgraduate: applications are made direct to the institution.

COURSES

PGCE in Primary Education (Early Years, 3–8) X121 W

1 year full-time

Entry requirements: Relevant Honours degree at a good standard (minimum Lower 2nd class); elements of degree must be in National Curriculum subject; plus GCSE mathematics and English language at grade C or above; or equivalent; applicants born on or after 1/9/79 must have attained at least GCSE grade C, or its equivalent, in science or a science subject; candidates must have minimum 5 days' experience in a mainstream school before starting this course.
Contact: Jean Evanson
0121 415 2357
J.L.Evanson@bham.ac.uk

PGCE in Primary Education (General Primary, 5–11) X100 W

1 year full-time

Entry requirements: As above
Contact: As above

PGCE in Secondary Education (English) Q3X1

1 year full-time

Entry requirements: Degree or equivalent qualification in relevant subject and English language and mathematics at GCSE grade C or above (or equivalent).
Contact: Ms Sue Leach
0121 414 4857/3475
s.d.n.leach@bham.ac.uk

PGCE in Secondary Education (French) R1X1

1 year full-time

Entry requirements: As above
Contact: Dr Carol Gray
0121 414 4806
c.gray@bham.ac.uk

PGCE in Secondary Education (Geography) F8X1

1 year full-time

Entry requirements: As above
Contact: Mr Paul Weeden
0121 414 3467/4810
g.w.butt@bham.ac.uk
p.weeden@bham.ac.uk

PGCE in Secondary Education (German) R2X1

1 year full-time

Entry requirements: As above
Contact: Dr Carol Gray
0121 414 4806
c.gray@bham.ac.uk

PGCE in Secondary Education (History and Citizenship) VX1C

1 year full-time

Entry requirements: Relevant Honours degree; GCSE English and mathematics.
Contact: Alison Gove-Humphries
0121 414 4866

PGCE in Secondary Education (History) V1X1

1 year full-time

Entry requirements: Degree or equivalent qualification in relevant subject and English language and mathematics at GCSE grade C or above (or equivalent).
Contact: Dr Ruth Watts
0121 414 4826
R.E.Watts@bham.ac.uk
I.D.Grosvenor@bham.ac.uk

PGCE in Secondary Education (Mathematics) G1X1

1 year full-time

Entry requirements: As above
Contact: Dr Dave Hewitt
0121 414 4824/4814/4864
d.p.hewitt@bham.ac.uk
p.a.perks@bham.ac.uk
s.a.prestage@bham.ac.uk

PGCE in Secondary Education (Mathematics, conversion) GXC1

2 years full-time

Entry requirements: GCSE grade C (or above) in English language and mathematics, or equivalent, required. Applicants will normally hold A-level (or equivalent) mathematics together with some mathematics as part of their degree. The course is designed for graduates who wish to teach mathematics at secondary school level but who are insufficiently qualified for entry to the 1-year PGCE course.
Contact: Dr Dave Hewitt
0121 414 4824/4814/4864
d.p.hewitt@bham.ac.uk
p.a.perks@bham.ac.uk
s.a.prestage@bham.ac.uk

PGCE in Secondary Education (Physical Education) X9C6

1 year full-time

Entry requirements: Degree or equivalent qualification in relevant subject and English language and mathematics at GCSE grade C or above (or equivalent).

Contact: Ms Heather Shilling
0121 414 4827/4456
h.shilling@bham.ac.uk
J.W.Woodhouse@bham.ac.uk

PGCE in Secondary Education (Religious Education) V6X1

1 year full-time

Entry requirements: As above
Contact: Dr Michael Grimmitt
0121 414 4815
m.h.grimmitt@bham.ac.uk

PGCE in Secondary Education (Science: Biology) C1X1

1 year full-time

Entry requirements: As above
Contact: Dr Roger Lock
0121 414 4825
r.j.lock@bham.ac.uk

PGCE in Secondary Education (Science: Chemistry) F1X1

1 year full-time

Entry requirements: As above
Contact: Dr Allan Soares
Lecturer in Science Education
0121 414 4818
A.B.Soares@bham.ac.uk

PGCE in Secondary Education (Science: Physics) F3X1

1 year full-time

Entry requirements: As above
Contact: Mr Ian Lawrence
0121 414 4833
I.lawrence@bham.ac.uk

PGCE in Secondary Education (Spanish with French) RX41

1 year full-time

Entry requirements: As above
Contact: Ms Carmen D'Arcy
0121 414 4840
c.darcy@bham.ac.uk

Diploma/Advanced Certificate/BPhil/ MEd Continuing Professional Development in Primary Education

MEd: 2–5 years part-time

Entry requirements: Relevant good Honours degree or qualification judged equivalent, successful completion of approved course of professional teacher training and at least 2 years' teaching or other approved experience.
Contact: Chris Swezd
0121 415 2354
C.A.Swezd@bham.ac.uk

EdD Education

36 months full-time or 48 months part-time

Entry requirements: Recognised degree or equivalent and normally at least 2 years' teaching or comparable professional experience.
Contact: Dr Jill Porter
Senior Tutor for Student Research
0121 414 4889
J.M.Porter@bham.ac.uk

Advanced Certificate/PgCert/PgDip/ MEd/BPhil in Information Technology Co-ordination

MEd: 1 year full-time, 2–5 years part-time

Entry requirements: Degree or equivalent and professional experience.
Contact: Ian Selwood
0121 414 4851
I.D.Selwood@bham.ac.uk

Advanced Certificate/PgCert/PgDip/ MEd/BPhil in Information Technology in the Primary/Secondary Classroom

MEd: 2–5 years part-time
As above

EdD Leaders and Leadership in Education

3 years full-time or 4 years part-time

Entry requirements: Good Honours degree or attainment of alternative qualifications and/or evidence of relevant experience.
Contact: Dr Desmond Rutherford
Senior Lecturer
0121 414 4804
r.j.d.rutherford@bham.ac.uk

PgDip/MSc Learning Disability Studies

1 year full-time or 2 years part-time or distance learning

Entry requirements: Good degree in relevant area or professional qualifications plus relevant experience.
Contact: Dr Helen Bradley
Course Tutor
0121 678 2353
h.f.bradley@bham.ac.uk

PgCert/PgDip/MEd/BPhil Management for Learning (Secondary)

2–5 years part-time

Entry requirements: Degree or equivalent and professional experience.
Contact: Dr Desmond Rutherford
Senior Lecturer
0121 414 4804
R.J.D.Rutherford@bham.ac.uk

PgDip/MEd/BPhil Management of Special Education in Developing Countries

1 year full-time or 2–5 years part-time

Entry requirements: For MEd: degree or equivalent plus programme of professional training plus 2 years' relevant professional experience. For Postgraduate Diploma: either degree or equivalent plus 2 years' relevant professional experience or 5 years' relevant professional experience and appropriate educational background. For BPhil: professional qualifications or equivalent of 240 credits obtained after equivalent of 2 years' full-time study and 2 years' relevant professional experience.
Contact: Prof Lynn Davies
Professor of International Education
0121 414 4823
L.Davies@bham.ac.uk
S.Macall@bham.ac.uk

MSc Primary Education, School Improvement, Early Years and Special Education

2 years part-time

Entry requirements: Relevant good Honours degree or qualification judged equivalent, successful completion of approved course of professional teacher training and at least 2 years' teaching or other approved experience, and commitment to school improvement.
Contact: Ann Lance
0121 415 2613
A.C.Lance@bham.ac.uk

Advanced Certificate/PgCert/PgDip/Med/BPhil Special Education (Emotional and Behavioural Difficulties)

1–5 years part-time or 1–5 years distance learning

Entry requirements: For MEd: degree or equivalent plus programme of professional training plus 2 years' relevant professional experience. For Postgraduate Diploma: either degree or equivalent plus 2 years' relevant professional experience or 5 years' relevant professional experience and appropriate educational background. For BPhil: professional qualifications or equivalent of 240 credits obtained after equivalent of 2 years' full-time study and 2 years' relevant professional experience.
Contact: Dr John Visser
0121 414 3603
J.G.Visser@bham.ac.uk

PgCert/PgDip/MEd/BPhil Special Education (Hearing Impairment)

1 year full-time or 2 years part-time or distance learning

Entry requirements: As above
Contact: Dr Steve Powers
0121 414 3471/4876
S.G.Powers@bham.ac.uk

PgCert/PgDip/MEd/BPhil Special Education (Learning Difficulties)

1 year full-time or 2–5 years part-time or 2–5 years distance learning

Entry requirements: As above
Contact: Dr Penny Lacey
Programme Tutor
0121 414 4856/4878/4805
P.J.Lacey@bham.ac.uk

PgCert/PgDip/MEd/BPhil Special Education (Multi-Sensory Impairment)

Distance learning

Entry requirements: As above
Contact: Ms Liz Hodges
0121 414 4873
E.M.Hodges@bham.ac.uk

PgCert/PgDip/MEd/BPhil Special Education (Speech and Language Difficulties)

PgCert: 2–5 years part-time or distance learning; PgDip 2 years distance learning; MEd: 2–5 years part-time or distance learning; BPhil: 2 years distance learning

Entry requirements: As above
Contact: Dr Carol Miller / Dr Deirdre
Martin
Senior Lecturer
0121 414 4853 / 0121 414 4849
C.J.Miller@bham.ac.uk
D.M.Martin@bham.ac.uk

PgDip/BPhil Special Education (Visual Impairment)

Part-time or distance learning

Entry requirements: For PgDip: either degree or equivalent plus 2 years' relevant professional experience or 5 years' relevant professional experience and appropriate educational background; for BPhil: professional qualifications or equivalent of 240 credits obtained after equivalent of 2 years' full-time study and 2 years' relevant professional experience.
Contact: Dr Mike McLinden
0121 414 4837
M.T.McLinden@bham.ac.uk

PgCert/PgDip/MA Teaching English as a Foreign or Second Language

1 year full-time or 2 years sandwich or 15 months mixed mode or distance learning

Entry requirements: Good first degree plus 2 years' teaching experience required, and (for non-native speakers of English) 550 TOEFL score or 6.0 IELTS or Cambridge Certificate of Proficiency.
Contact: Sheila Brady
Secretary, CELS
0121 414 5696
bradysa@bham.ac.uk

Bishop Grosseteste College

Lincoln
LN1 3DY
Tel: 01522 527347
Fax: 01522 530243
registry@bgc.ac.uk
www.bgc.ac.uk

Bishop Grosseteste College is a small institution based on a single-site campus near to the City of Lincoln. There are extensive facilities available for teaching and learning, including the library, theatre and ICT suite and training room in addition to the computer areas in different departments. All facilities are modern and easily accessible. Accommodation is available in halls on campus and there is private accommodation in the local area.

The Education Department offers degree courses, postgraduate programmes including the PGCE at primary and secondary level and also courses for Continuing Professional Development.

HOW TO APPLY

Degree courses: applications are made through UCAS.

PGCE: applications are made through the GTTR.

Postgraduate: applications are made direct to the institution.

COURSES

BA (Hons) in Primary Education X120

3 years full-time

The degree is designed for those who wish to train to teach children specialising in the age range 4–8. Students are trained to teach the range of subjects of the National Curriculum. However, instead of taking just 1 main subject, they study a total of 6:

English, mathematics, science, history, geography, music. 2 of the 6 (English and mathematics) are selected as principal subjects for in-depth study during the 2nd and 3rd years of the course.

The course is very practical in its nature; students learn the craft of teaching, plan, implement and assess all aspects of the primary curriculum, and develop skills in the management of children. This involves spending a great deal of time working with children individually, in small groups, and in classes, which starts during the second week of the course. Course members gain experience of working in a range of urban and rural schools and with children of different ages and needs.

Successful completion of this course leads to a recommendation for Qualified Teacher Status (QTS) after completion of skills tests.

Entry requirements: CC: GCE A- and AS-levels, Foundation / access qualification, Mature entry, SCE Higher.
Contact: Kathleen Taylor
          Course Leader
          01522 527347

PGCE in Primary Education (General Primary, 3–11) X100

1 year full-time or 1 to 3 years part-time

Entry requirements: Honours degree, preferably 2.2 or above; GCSE at grade C or above (or equivalent) in mathematics and English language, plus science for candidates born on or after 1/9/79.
Contact: The College Registry
          01522 527347
          registry@bgc.ac.uk

PGCE in Secondary Education (Art and Design) W1X1

1 year full-time

Entry requirements: Degree in relevant area (preferably 2:2 or above); GCSE mathematics and English at grade C or above (or equivalent).
Contact: The College Registry
          01522 527347
          registry@bgc.ac.uk

PGCE in Secondary Education (English with Drama) QX31

1 year full-time

Entry requirements: Degree in relevant area (preferably 2:2 or above); GCSE mathematics and English at grade C or above (or equivalent).
Contact: The College Registry
          01522 527347
          registry@bgc.ac.uk

PGCE in Secondary Education (Mathematics) G1X1

1 year full-time
As above

PGCE in Secondary Education (Music) W3X1

1 year full-time
As above

PGCE in Secondary Education (Religious Studies) V6X1

1 year full-time
As above

PGCE in Secondary Education (Science) F0X1

1 year full-time
As above

MA in Education

2 years part-time

Entry requirements: 3 years' teaching experience; degree or diploma in education.
Contact: Helen Ashton
          EDS Administrator
          01522 527347
          eds@bgc.ac.uk

Diploma in Professional Studies in Education

2 years part-time

Entry requirements: Initial teaching qualification; accredited prior learning considered.
Contact: Helen Ashton
          EDS Administrator
          01522 527347
          eds@bgc.ac.uk

Certificate in Professional Studies in Education (Classroom Focused Development)

1 year part-time

Entry requirements: Initial teaching qualification; accredited prior learning considered.

Contact: Helen Ashton
EDS Administrator
01522 527347
eds@bgc.ac.uk

Certificate in Professional Studies in Education (Practitioner Research)

1 year part-time
As above

Certificate in Professional Studies in Education (School Focused Development)

1 year part-time
As above

Borough of Poole SCITT

Max Gate Consultancy Ltd
Max Gate
Alington Avenue
Dorchester
Dorset
DT1 2AB
Tel: 01305 262538
Fax: 01305 250978
max.gate@btinternet.com

The Borough of Poole SCITT is a partnership between the Max Gate Consultancy Ltd (the managing agent), local primary schools, the Borough of Poole Local Education Authority and Kingston University. It is accredited by the Teacher Training Agency. The school-centred course is validated for PGCE status by Kingston University.

Upton House, the Borough of Poole's Professional Training Centre, is the Course Centre for the Poole SCITT. It is a large mansion located in a country park on the shores of Poole Harbour. Facilities include a restaurant, library, IT facilities and teaching rooms. In addition to the library, participating schools provide study facilities for trainees. There is also a public library, with study and Internet facilities, in the centre of Poole.

HOW TO APPLY

Applications are made through the GTTR.

COURSES

PGCE in Primary Education (General Primary, 5–11) X100

38 weeks full-time

Entry requirements: Degree in relevant subject; GCSE grade C or above in English language and mathematics, and science if born after 1/9/79.

Contact: Enquiries
01305 262538
max.gate@btinternet.com

Bournemouth and East Dorset SCITT Consortium

Bournemouth and Poole College
The Lansdowne
Bournemouth
BH1 3JJ
Tel: 01202 205460

Bournemouth and East Dorset SCITT Consortium runs a small teacher training programme specialising in Primary Early Years (3–7 age range). It is managed by a group of local schools. Trainees spend 60% of their course based mainly in one school; the course also includes time spent in a nursery setting, a different SCITT school, and two weeks' experience of Key Stage 2.

Trainees are registered as students with Bournemouth and Poole College and with the University of Luton. Students have access to the libraries, resources and computer facilities of both institutions and the resources in local schools. There is also a local Teacher Resource Centre. College Student Services can help to arrange accommodation.

Much of the course is taught at the Bournemouth and Poole College. The PGCE course is validated by the University of Luton.

HOW TO APPLY

Applications are made through the GTTR.

COURSES

PGCE in Primary Education (Lower Primary, 3–7) X121

38 weeks full-time

Entry requirements: Upper 2nd Class degree; GCSE English and mathematics grade C, plus science if born after 1/9/79; knowledge of early years education and Key Stage 1/Foundation curriculum; relevant work experience advantageous.
Contact: Enquiries
01202 205460

Bradford College

Great Horton Road
Bradford
BD7 1AY
Tel: 01274 753004
Fax: 01274 753173
admissions@bilk.ac.uk
www.bilk.ac.uk

The history of Bradford College began in 1832 when the Bradford Mechanics Institute was founded. This grew and developed and in June 23, 1882 the council opened a new Technical School at Great Horton Road. Shortly afterwards, this was renamed Bradford Technical College. It continued to expand and in 1956 it became one of the country's first Colleges of Advanced Technology. A year later this split into the Bradford Institute – which later became The University of Bradford – and the Bradford Technical College. In 1973 the College and the Regional College of Art merged into Bradford College of Art and Technology, then with the merger with the Margaret McMillan College of Education it became Bradford College. In 1982 this became known as the Bradford and Ilkley Community College when it merged with Ilkley College, (which closed in July 1999.) Bradford College has developed to become the second largest of its kind in the country, with a student population of around 36,000.

The Department of Teacher Education is based on the College's McMillan Campus. The department offers degree and Master's courses and also the PGCE at primary and secondary level. There is accommodation near to the campus and a range of sporting and academic facilities are available at the college.

HOW TO APPLY

Degree courses: applications are made through UCAS.
PGCE: applications are made through the GTTR.
Postgraduate: applications are made direct to the institution.

COURSES

BA (Hons) in Primary Education (advanced study of early years) X100

4 years full-time

Specialism is study of early years; educational studies run throughout the course as a means of ensuring professional development and as a challenging discipline in its own right; information and communications technology is embedded in every subject, and students have opportunities to develop their personal skills in information technology.

Successful completion of this course leads to a recommendation for Qualified Teacher Status (QTS), subject to satisfactory performance in skills tests.

Entry requirements: BTEC NC/ND, DipHE, Foundation / access qualification, GCE A- and AS-levels, HND, Mature entry

Contact: Frances Murdoch
        Admissions Tutor
        01274 753004

BA (Hons) in Primary Education (Creative Arts with specialism in Art) X1W1

4 years full-time

All years: educational and professional studies: developing an understanding of children, classrooms, schools and curriculum. Skills in classroom management, pupil assessment, record keeping, developing effective learning environments and catering for individual differences. Courses in art, music, physical education, religious education, history, geography, science, technology, and language will be taken. Thus students are trained to be a class teacher with the ability to foster children's learning in all areas of the curriculum as well as a specialist subject.

Creative Arts (art, drama and music): work on the chosen subject area runs through the course and amounts to half of the total programme.

Placement: each year of the course has block placements (teaching practice) and various forms of school experience.

Successful completion of this course leads to a recommendation for Qualified Teacher Status (QTS), subject to satisfactory performance in skills tests.

Entry requirements: As above
Contact: As above

BA (Hons) in Primary Education (Geography) X1L7

4 years full-time

All years: educational and professional studies: developing an understanding of children, classrooms, schools and curriculum. Skills in classroom management, pupil assessment, record keeping, developing effective learning environments and catering for individual differences. Courses in art, music, physical education, science, technology, and mathematics will be taken. Thus, students are trained to be a class teacher with the ability to foster children's learning in all areas of the curriculum as well as a specialist subject.

Geography: work on the chosen subject area runs through the course and amounts to half of the total programme.

Placement: each year of the course has block placements (teaching practice) and various forms of school experience.

Successful completion of this course leads to a recommendation for Qualified Teacher Status (QTS), subject to satisfactory performance in skills tests.

Entry requirements: As above
Contact: As above

BA (Hons) in Primary Education (History) X1V1

4 years full-time

All years: educational and professional studies: developing an understanding of children, classrooms, schools and curriculum. Skills in classroom management, pupil assessment, record keeping, developing effective learning environments and catering for individual differences. Courses in art, music, physical education, science, technology, mathematics and language will be taken. Thus, students are trained to be a class teacher with the ability to foster children's learning in all areas of the curriculum as well as a specialist subject.

History: work on the chosen subject area runs through the 4 years and amounts to half of the total programme.

Placement: each year of the course has block placements (teaching practice) and various forms of school experience.

Successful completion of this course leads to a recommendation for Qualified Teacher Status (QTS), subject to satisfactory performance in skills tests.

Entry requirements: As above
Contact: As above

BA (Hons) in Primary Education (Language and Literature) X1T9

4 years full-time

All years: educational and professional studies: developing an understanding of children, classrooms, schools and curriculum. Skills in classroom management, pupil assessment, record keeping, developing effective learning environments and catering for individual differences. Courses in art, music, physical education, science, technology, and mathematics will be taken. Thus, students are trained to be a class teacher with the ability to foster children's learning in all areas of the curriculum as well as a specialist subject.

Language and literature: work on the chosen subject area runs through the course and amounts to half of the total programme.

Successful completion of this course leads to a recommendation for Qualified Teacher Status (QTS), subject to satisfactory performance in skills tests.

Placement: each year of the course has block placements (teaching practice) and various forms of school experience.

Entry requirements: BTEC NC/ND, Foundation / access qualification, GCE A- and AS-levels, Mature entry
Contact: As above

BA (Hons) in Primary Education (Mathematics) X1G1

4 years full-time

All years: educational and professional studies: developing an understanding of children, classrooms, schools and curriculum. Skills in classroom management, pupil assessment, record keeping, developing effective learning environments and catering for individual differences. Courses in art, music, physical education, religious education, history, geography, science, technology, and language will be taken. Thus, students are trained to be a class teacher with the ability to foster children's learning in all areas of the curriculum as well as a specialist subject.

Mathematics: work on the chosen subject area runs through the course and amounts to half of the total programme.

Placement: each year of the course has block placements (teaching practice) and various forms of school experience.

Successful completion of this course leads to a recommendation for Qualified Teacher Status (QTS), subject to satisfactory performance in skills tests.

Entry requirements: As above
Contact: As above

BA (Hons) in Primary Education (Religious Studies) X1V6

4 years full-time

All years: educational and professional studies: developing an understanding of children, classrooms, schools and curriculum. Skills in classroom management, pupil assessment, record keeping, developing effective learning environments and catering for individual differences. Courses in art, music, physical education, science, technology, and mathematics will be taken. Thus, students are trained to be a class teacher with the ability to foster children's learning in all areas of the curriculum as well as a specialist subject.

Religious Studies: work on the chosen subject area runs through the course and amounts to half of the total programme.

Placement: each year of the course has block placements (teaching practice) and various forms of school experience.

Successful completion of this course leads to a recommendation for Qualified Teacher Status (QTS), subject to satisfactory performance in skills tests.

Entry requirements: As above
Contact: As above

BA (Hons) in Primary Education (Science) X1F0

4 years full-time

All years: educational and professional studies: developing an understanding of children, classrooms, schools and curriculum. Skills in classroom management, pupil assessment, record keeping, developing effective learning environments and catering for individual differences. Courses in art, music, physical education, technology, mathematics and language will be taken. Thus, students are trained to be a class teacher with the ability to foster children's learning in all areas of the curriculum as well as a specialist subject.

Science: work on the chosen subject area runs through the 4 years and amounts to half of the total programme.

Placement: each year of the course has block placements (teaching practice) and various forms of school experience.

Successful completion of this course leads to a recommendation for Qualified Teacher Status (QTS), subject to satisfactory performance in skills tests.

Entry requirements: As above
Contact: As above

PGCE in Primary Education (Lower Primary, 3–8) X121

Variable or 1 year full-time

Entry requirements: Degree validated by a British university, or a qualification accepted as equivalent by the DfES. The content of the degree needs to be relevant to the primary classroom. Additionally, applicants must hold GCSE (grade C) or O-level passes in English language and mathematics or their equivalent.
Contact: Admissions Officer
01274 753333
admissions@bilk.ac.uk

PGCE in Primary Education (Upper Primary, 7–11) X171

Variable or 1 year full-time

Entry requirements: As above
Contact: As above

PGCE in Key Stages 2–3 Education (Modern Languages) XRC9

1 year full-time

Entry requirements: Degree or equivalent plus GCSE grade C (or equivalent) English and mathematics; proficiency in at least 1 target language and preferably 2 or more.
Contact: As above

PGCE in Key Stages 2–3 Education (Science) XFCA

1 year full-time

Entry requirements: Degree validated by a British university, or a qualification accepted as equivalent by the DfES. The content must include a substantial element of the subject in which the student wishes to specialise. Applicants must hold a GCSE/GCE pass at grade C or above in English language and mathematics or recognised equivalent. Candidates born after 1/9/79 will also need GCSE grade C or above in a science subject or equivalent.
Contact: As above

PGCE in Secondary Education (Information Communication Technology) G5X1

1 year full-time
As above

PGCE in Secondary Education (Mathematics) G1X1

Variable or 1 year full-time

Entry requirements: Degree validated by a British university, or a qualification accepted as equivalent by the DfES. The content must be 50% mathematically based. Applicants must hold a GCSE/GCE pass at grade C or above in English language and mathematics or recognised equivalent. Candidates born after 1/9/79 will also need GCSE grade C or above in a science subject or equivalent.

Contact: As above

PGCE in Secondary Education (Modern Languages) R9X1

1 year full-time

Entry requirements: Degree or equivalent plus GCSE grade C (or equivalent) English and mathematics; proficiency in at least 1 target language and preferably 2 or more.
Contact: As above

PGCE in Secondary Education (Science) F0X1

1 year full-time

Entry requirements: Degree validated by a British university, or a qualification accepted as equivalent by the DfES. The content must include a substantial element of the subject in which the student wishes to specialise. Applicants must hold a GCSE/GCE pass at grade C or above in English language and mathematics or recognised equivalent. Candidates born after 1/9/79 will also need GCSE grade C or above in a science subject or equivalent.
Contact: As above

University of Brighton

Mithras House
Lewes Road
Brighton BN2 4AT
Tel: 01273 600900
Fax: 01273 642825
admissions@brighton.ac.uk
www.brighton.ac.uk

The University of Brighton caters for over 16,000 students in Brighton and Eastbourne. Founded as a School of Art in 1859, it grew to encompass the local technology and teaching colleges and was awarded university status in 1992. It is based on 4 campuses: Moulsecombe, Grand Parade and Falmer in Brighton, and Eastbourne. Both Brighton and Eastbourne overlook the sea, and Eastbourne is bordered by the South Downs.

The School of Education is based in Falmer, a green-field site on the outskirts of Brighton. The Falmer campus has modern halls of residence and good sports facilities, bars and restaurants, and regular bus and train services link it to the city centre. The School offered its first teaching courses in 1909, and merged with the then Brighton Polytechnic in 1976. Current facilities include a new IT suite and library as well as a curriculum centre which contains resources in a range of media for primary and secondary subject areas. In addition to Initial Teacher Training the School also provides educational research and consultancy services and a range of professional development courses for qualified teachers.

HOW TO APPLY

Undergraduate: applications are made through UCAS.

PGCE: applications are made through the GTTR.

Postgraduate: applications are made direct to the institution.

COURSES

BA (Hons) in Business Education (shortened route) X1N2

2 years full-time

This shortened modular degree prepares students to teach business studies in schools and colleges. Students spend approximately 40% of their course in schools, studying alongside a school mentor. In the university students choose from a variety of business modules designed to build on their previous experience and learning. Students are also introduced to the National Curriculum and lesson preparation.

General professional studies modules focus on the education aspects of the degree including classroom management; the Education Reform Act; children with special needs; assessment methods and recent developments in secondary education. In addition to information technology and statistics in Year 1, business studies comprises another 7 modules enabling students to build on their previous learning and experience.

Successful completion of this course leads to a recommendation for Qualified Teacher Status (QTS) after completion of skills tests.

Entry requirements: IELTS: 6.0, HND
Contact: Melanie Norman
Admissions Tutor
01273 643792
m.j.norman@brighton.ac.uk

BA (Hons) in Design and Technology Education X1WF

4 years full-time

Year 1: Design and technology education; information technology; general professional studies; school experience; health and safety; workshop practice; design and designing; structures and mechanism; study skills.

Year 2: Design and technology education; information technology; general professional studies; school experience; design and manufacture; design and graphics; electronics.

Year 3: Design and technology education; information technology; general professional studies; dissertation; discretionaries; mechanisms and systems; structures and materials; computer-aided engineering; microprocessor controls; digital electronics; design and society; food and textiles.

Year 4: Design and technology education; general professional studies; school experience; dissertation; project work.

General professional studies explore issues including teaching and learning methods, assessment issues, the changing school curriculum and special needs. Students become familiar with the latest developments in design and technology teaching.

School experience constitutes more than ¼ of the course, allowing students to work alongside practising teachers.

Successful completion of this course leads to a recommendation for Qualified Teacher Status (QTS) after completion of skills tests.

Entry requirements: Tariff: 240 points, IELTS: 6.0
Contact: Bhavna Prajapat
Admissions Tutor
01273 643432
B.Prajapat@brighton.ac.uk

BA (Hons) in Design and Technology Education (shortened route) X1W2

2 years full-time

Students spend approximately 40% of the course in school, studying alongside a school mentor. At the university students choose from modules designed to build on their previous experience and learning. All students also take education and professional studies components.

Subject teaching studies modules, cover curriculum development in design and technology, such as GNVQ, A- /AS-levels and GCSE, and introduce the National Curriculum, particularly in relation to design and technology and lesson preparation.

General professional studies modules focus on aspects of education, including classroom management, the Education Reform Act, children with special needs, assessment methods and recent developments in secondary education.

Design and technology comprises a range of modules, including areas of design and graphics, product design, structures, mechanisms, electronics and information technology. These equip students with the range of subject skills needed to teach the subject effectively and complement previous experience.

Successful completion of this course leads to a recommendation for Qualified Teacher Status (QTS) after completion of skills tests.

Entry requirements: IELTS: 6.0, HND
Contact: Melanie Norman
01273 643377
m.j.norman@brighton.ac.uk

BA (Hons) in Design and Technology Education (Upper Primary/Lower Secondary) XW12

4 years full-time

Professional modules consider issues related to practical teaching. For the upper primary age range this includes delivery of selected subjects within the National Curriculum so that students develop competence in implementing quality learning and assessing pupil progress. Similarly, for lower secondary, the particular concerns relating to delivery of design and technology are explored.

Additionally, a range of fundamental issues are examined relating to the curriculum as a whole, such as teaching and learning methods, assessment of pupils, and catering for children with special educational needs.

School experience with both age ranges enables students to make an informed choice for their final year specialisation.

Successful completion of this course leads to a recommendation for Qualified Teacher Status (QTS) after completion of skills tests.

Entry requirements: Tariff: 240 points, IELTS: 6.0, BTEC NC/ND
Contact: Bhavna Prajapat
    Admissions Tutor
    01273 643432
    b.prajapat@brighton.ac.uk

BA (Hons) in English Education (Upper Primary/Lower Secondary) XQ13

4 years full-time

Professional modules consider issues related to practical teaching. For the upper primary age range this includes delivery of selected subjects within the National Curriculum so that students develop competence in implementing quality learning and assessing pupil progress. Similarly, for lower secondary, the particular concerns relating to delivery of English are explored.

Additionally, a range of fundamental issues are examined relating to the curriculum as a whole, such as teaching and learning methods, assessment of pupils, and catering for children with special educational needs.

School experience with both age ranges enables students to make an informed choice for their final year specialisation.

Opportunities exist for exchange with student teachers elsewhere in Europe.

Successful completion of this course leads to a recommendation for Qualified Teacher Status (QTS) after completion of skills tests.

Entry requirements: Tariff: 240 points, IELTS: 6.0, BTEC NC/ND
Contact: Roger Neuss
    Admissions Tutor
    01273 643363
    r.neuss@brighton.ac.uk

BA (Hons) in Geography Education (Upper Primary/Lower Secondary) X1L7

4 years full-time

Professional modules consider issues related to practical teaching. For the upper primary age range this includes delivery of selected subjects within the National Curriculum so that students develop competence in implementing quality learning and assessing pupil progress. Similarly, for lower secondary, the particular concerns relating to delivery of geography are explored.

Additionally, a range of fundamental issues are examined relating to the curriculum as a whole, such as teaching and learning methods, assessment of pupils, and catering for children with special educational needs.

School experience with both age ranges enables students to make an informed choice for their final year specialisation.

Opportunities exist for exchange with student teachers elsewhere in Europe.

Successful completion of this course leads to a recommendation for Qualified Teacher Status (QTS) after completion of skills tests.

Entry requirements: Tariff: 240 points, IELTS: 6.0, BTEC NC/ND

Contact: Ian Longman
Admissions Tutor
01273 643426
i.longman@brighton.ac.uk

BA (Hons) in Information Technology Education (shortened) X1G5

2 years full-time

Year 1: Philosophy of information technology in society; general professional studies; personal skills.

Year 2: Subject teaching studies: information technology; practice of teaching; professional development; dissertation.

Entry requirements: HND
Contact: Cathy Wickens
01273 643454
c.a.wickens@brighton.ac.uk

BA (Hons) in Information Technology Education (Upper Primary/Lower Secondary) XG15

4 years full-time

Professional modules consider issues related to practical teaching. For the upper primary age range this includes delivery of selected subjects within the National Curriculum so that students develop competence in implementing quality learning and assessing pupil progress. Similarly, for lower secondary, the particular concerns relating to delivery of English are explored.

Additionally, a range of fundamental issues are examined relating to the curriculum as a whole, such as teaching and learning methods, assessment of pupils, and catering for children with special educational needs.

Opportunities exist for exchange with student teachers elsewhere in Europe.

Successful completion of this course leads to a recommendation for Qualified Teacher Status (QTS) after completion of skills tests.

Entry requirements: Tariff: 240 points, IELTS: 6.0, BTEC NC/ND
Contact: Ian Longman
Admissions Tutor
01273 643426
i.longman@brighton.ac.uk

BA (Hons) in Mathematics Education (shortened route) XG11

2 years full-time

Half of the course is spent in school working with a mentor, the remainder consists of a variety of modules. The mathematics modules are designed to build on previous experience of the subject.

3 modules focusing on various approaches to the teaching and learning of mathematics in the 11–18 range; the details of the National Curriculum, GCSE and A- /AS-levels are all considered, together with the mathematical content of GNVQs; background to teaching modules include classroom management, the Education Reform Act, children with special needs, assessment methods and recent developments in secondary education.

Mathematics modules provide a broad perspective on the elements underlying the school subject – number, algebra, geometry and the history and philosophy of mathematics. Emphasis is placed on the process of mathematical enquiry and the use of information technology.

Successful completion of this course leads to a recommendation for Qualified Teacher Status (QTS) after completion of skills tests.

Entry requirements: IELTS: 6.0, HND
Contact: Melanie Norman
Admissions Tutor
01273 643792
m.j.norman@brighton.ac.uk

BA (Hons) in Mathematics Education (Upper Primary/Lower Secondary) XG1C

4 years full-time

Professional modules consider issues related to practical teaching. For the upper primary age range this includes delivery of selected subjects within the National Curriculum so that students develop competence in implementing quality learning and assessing pupil progress. Similarly, for lower secondary, the particular concerns relating to delivery of mathematics are explored.

Additionally, a range of fundamental issues are examined relating to the curriculum as a whole, such as teaching and learning methods, assessment of pupils, and catering for children with special educational needs.

Opportunities exist for exchange with student teachers elsewhere in Europe.

Successful completion of this course leads to a recommendation for Qualified Teacher Status (QTS) after completion of skills tests.

Entry requirements: Tariff: 240 points; BTEC NC/ND

Contact: Ian Longman
Admissions Tutor
01273 643426
i.longman@brighton.ac.uk

BA (Hons) in Modern Foreign Languages Education (Upper Primary/Lower Secondary) XR19

4 years full-time

Professional modules consider issues related to practical teaching. For the upper primary age range this includes delivery of selected subjects within the National Curriculum so that students develop competence in implementing quality learning and assessing pupil progress. Similarly, for lower secondary, the particular concerns relating to delivery of modern languages are explored.

Additionally, a range of fundamental issues are examined relating to the curriculum as a whole, such as teaching and learning methods, assessment of pupils, and catering for children with special educational needs.

Opportunities exist for exchange with student teachers elsewhere in Europe and in the USA.

Successful completion of this course leads to a recommendation for Qualified Teacher Status (QTS) after completion of skills tests.

Entry requirements: Tariff: 240 points, BTEC NC/ND, International Baccalaureate
Contact: As above

BA (Hons) in Modern Languages Education (shortened route) X1R9

2 years full-time

Students are trained to teach French to 11–18 year olds and a 2nd language, German, Spanish or Italian, to younger pupils. A large part of the 2nd year of the course is spent on placement in a school or college working alongside a school mentor.

Subject teaching modules cover the National Curriculum, GCSE, and A- /AS-level courses. Students are also introduced to professional subject concerns as well as lesson preparation.

General professional studies modules focus on the education aspect, including classroom management, the Education Reform Act, children with special needs, assessment methods and recent developments in secondary education. Students follow modules enabling them to build on their previous experience and learning of French.

Successful completion of this course leads to a recommendation for Qualified Teacher Status (QTS) after completion of skills tests.

Entry requirements: IELTS: 6.0, DipHE, HND
Contact: Melanie Norman
Admissions Tutor
01273 643792
m.j.norman@brighton.ac.uk

BA (Hons) in Physical Education X1C6

4 years full-time

The course provides experience of a range of National Curriculum physical activities, supported by relevant academic and professional studies. Regular opportunities are provided to work with children in schools, in the community and in our own specialist facilities. Of the 48 modules, 13 are allocated to school-based experience.

Physical education modules: In the first 2 semesters, students are introduced to a range of modules including the physiological, psychological and social aspects of physical education; a selection of physical activities; introduction to research methods and approaches to study. In the following semesters (Semesters 3–8) students are able to choose modules which focus on areas such as partnership with the community; exercise and health; leisure and recreation; competitive sport; dance appreciation; special needs; gender and issues in physical education and sport; selected physical activities.

Students are in schools during the 1st semester. Modules focusing on the teacher as a professional are taken throughout the course, preparing for, and following up, school-based semesters 4 and 7 when students become fully integrated into the life and work of 2 schools and their local community.

An exchange programme is available with universities in North America and mainland Europe.

Successful completion of this course leads to a recommendation for Qualified Teacher Status (QTS) after completion of skills tests.

Entry requirements: Tariff: 240 points, International Baccalaureate: 28, IELTS: 6.0, BTEC, NC/ND
Contact: Joan Williams
　　　　　Admissions Tutor
　　　　　01273 643788
　　　　　j.williams@brighton.ac.uk

BA (Hons) in Physical Education (Upper Primary/Lower Secondary) XC16

4 years full-time

Professional modules consider issues related to practical teaching. For the upper primary age range this includes delivery of selected subjects within the National Curriculum so that students develop competence in implementing quality learning and assessing pupil progress. Similarly, for lower secondary, the particular concerns relating to delivery of physical education are explored.

Additionally, a range of fundamental issues are examined relating to the curriculum as a whole, such as teaching and learning methods, assessment of pupils, and catering for children with special educational needs.

Opportunities exist for exchange with student teachers elsewhere in Europe.

Successful completion of this course leads to a recommendation for Qualified Teacher Status (QTS) after completion of skills tests.

Entry requirements: Tariff: 240 points, IELTS: 6.0, BTEC NC/ND
Contact: Ian Longman
　　　　　Admissions Tutor
　　　　　01273 643426
　　　　　i.longman@brighton.ac.uk

BA (Hons) in Primary Education (3–7 years) X100

4 years full-time

Curriculum studies focus on professional concerns relating to the core subjects of English, mathematics and science and an awareness of the breadth of content across all subjects in the primary phase.

Core professional studies examine common issues underpinning the primary school curriculum. In each year the various forms of school experience help students become thoroughly competent and professional.

Specialist subject studies: students choose 1 of the 9 National Curriculum subjects to study in depth.

Successful completion of this course leads to a recommendation for Qualified Teacher Status (QTS) after completion of skills tests.

Entry requirements: Tariff: 240 points, International Baccalaureate: 28, IELTS: 6.0, BTEC NC/ND
Contact: Valerie Snowden
　　　　　Admissions Tutor
　　　　　01273 643425
　　　　　v.snowden@brighton.ac.uk

BA (Hons) in Primary Education (5–11 years) X122

4 years full-time
As above

Entry requirements: as above
Contact: As above

BA (Hons) in Religious Education (Upper Primary/Lower Secondary) XV16

4 years full-time

Professional modules consider issues related to practical teaching. For the upper primary age range this includes delivery of selected subjects within the National Curriculum so that students develop competence in implementing quality learning and assessing pupil progress. Similarly, for lower secondary, the particular concerns relating to delivery of religious studies are explored.

Additionally, a range of fundamental issues are examined relating to the curriculum as a whole, such as teaching and learning methods, assessment of pupils, and catering for children with special educational needs.

Opportunities exist for exchange with student teachers elsewhere in Europe and in the USA.

Successful completion of this course leads to a recommendation for Qualified Teacher Status (QTS) after completion of skills tests.

Entry requirements: As above
Contact: Ian Longman
Admissions Tutor
01273 643426
i.longman@brighton.ac.uk

BA (Hons) in Science Education (shortened route) XF19

2 years full-time

Students complete 2 science teaching studies modules covering curriculum developments and issues in science education. The National Curriculum requirements and entitlements are considered in detail along with other developments, such as GNVQ, A- /AS-levels and GCSE.

Background to teaching modules include: Classroom management; the Education Reform Act; children with special needs; assessment methods and recent developments in secondary education.

Of the science subject modules, all students study 1 on systems, another on science, technology and society and a further module based on information technology in science education. A double module professional dissertation in Year 2 will also have a strong subject focus with direct relevance to teaching the subject at secondary level or post-16 education. In addition, all students have a chance of developing a specialism in the sciences by undertaking 4 modules in their specialist discipline (biology, chemistry or physics) and 3 other modules in the other 2 remaining disciplines.

Nearly 40% of the degree is based in schools where students gain experience of the secondary age and ability range.

Successful completion of this course leads to a recommendation for Qualified Teacher Status (QTS) after completion of skills tests.

Entry requirements: HND
Contact: Melanie Norman
Admissions Tutor
01273 643792
m.j.norman@brighton.ac.uk

BA (Hons) in Science Education (Upper Primary/Lower Secondary) XF10

4 years full-time

Professional modules consider issues related to practical teaching. For the upper primary age range this includes delivery of selected subjects within the National Curriculum so that students develop competence in implementing quality learning and assessing pupil progress. Similarly, for lower secondary, the particular concerns relating to delivery of science are explored.

Additionally, a range of fundamental issues are examined relating to the curriculum as a whole, such as teaching and learning methods, assessment of pupils, and catering for children with special educational needs.

Opportunities exist for exchange with student teachers elsewhere in Europe.

Successful completion of this course leads to a recommendation for Qualified Teacher Status (QTS) after completion of skills tests.

Entry requirements: Tariff: 240 points, IELTS: 6.0, BTEC NC/ND
Contact: Ian Longman
　　Admissions Tutor
　　01273 643426
　　i.longman@brighton.ac.uk

PGCE Post-compulsory Education

1–3 years part-time

Entry requirements: Degree or equivalent plus current involvement in some aspect of post-compulsory education.
Contact: Enquiries
　　01273 643444
　　soeccpd@brighton.ac.uk

PGCE in Primary Education (Lower Primary, 5–8 years) X121

1 year full-time

Entry requirements: Honours degree, normally 2.2 minimum, plus some primary classroom experience; GCSE grade C or equivalent in English language, mathematics and, for those born after 1/9/79, science.
Contact: Linda Nicholls
　　01273 643434
　　l.m.nicholls@brighton.ac.uk

PGCE Primary Education (Upper Primary, 7–11 years) X171

1 year full-time or part-time

Entry requirements: As above
Contact: As above

PGCE in Secondary Education (Art and Design) W1X1

1 year full-time or 16 months part-time

Entry requirements: Degree or equivalent, directly relevant to subject specialism; in addition, GCSE English language and mathematics, minimum grade C, or equivalent; in-house tests available for candidates without qualifications in mathematics and English.
Contact: Jan Hunt
　　01273 643456
　　jan.hunt@brighton.ac.uk

PGCE in Secondary Education (Business Education) N1X1

1 year full-time or 16 months part-time

Entry requirements: As above
Contact: Marian Kenward
　　01273 643374
　　m.a.kenward@brighton.ac.uk

PGCE in Secondary Education (Dance) W4X1

1 year full-time or 16 months part-time

Entry requirements: Entrants should normally have a degree or equivalent qualification which includes a substantial element of practical and theoretical dance; GCSE minimum grade C in English language and mathematics or equivalents also required; all candidates must attend interview before being offered a place.
Contact: Fiona Smith
　　01273 643710
　　fiona.smith@brighton.ac.uk

PGCE in Secondary Education (Design and Technology) W9X1

1 year full-time or 16 months part-time

Entry requirements: Degree or equivalent, directly relevant to subject specialism; in addition, GCSE English language and mathematics, minimum grade C, or equivalent; in-house tests available for candidates without qualifications in mathematics and English.
Contact: Dean Hackett
　　01273 643380
　　d.j.hackett@brighton.ac.uk

PGCE in Secondary Education (Design and Technology, conversion) WXX1

2 years full-time
As above

PGCE in Secondary Education (English) Q3X1

1 year full-time or 16 months part-time

Entry requirements: Degree or equivalent, directly relevant to subject specialism; in addition, GCSE English language and mathematics, minimum grade C, or equivalent; in-house tests available for candidates without qualifications in mathematics and English.

Contact: Joanna Oldham
Admissions Tutor
01273 643394
joanna.oldham@brighton.ac.uk

PGCE in Secondary Education (Geography) F8X1

1 year full-time or 18 months part-time

Entry requirements: As above
Contact: Melanie Norman
01273 643792
m.j.norman@brighton.ac.uk

PGCE in Secondary Education (Information Technology) G5X1

1 year full-time or 16 months part-time

Entry requirements: Applicants should be graduates from relevant field. Suitability of degree will be judged on appropriateness for application to teaching information technology in schools. In addition, GCSEs in English language and mathematics (grade C or above) or equivalents required. In-house tests available for candidates without formal qualifications.
Contact: Cathy Wickens
Admissions Tutor
01273 643454
c.a.wickens@brighton.ac.uk

PGCE in Secondary Education (Information Technology, conversion) GXM1

1 to 3 years part-time

Entry requirements: Degree or equivalent in related area; GCSE English language and mathematics, minimum grade C, or equivalent; in-house tests available for candidates without formal qualifications; potential students are interviewed before being offered a place.
Contact: As above

PGCE in Secondary Education (Mathematics) G1X1

1 year full-time or 16 months part-time

Entry requirements: Degree or equivalent, directly relevant to subject specialism; in addition, GCSE English language and mathematics, minimum grade C, or equivalent; in-house tests available for candidates without qualifications in mathematics and English.

Contact: Carole Plater
01273 643435
c.a.plater@brighton.ac.uk

PGCE in Secondary Education (Mathematics, conversion) GXC1

2 years full-time

Entry requirements: As above
Contact: As above

PGCE in Secondary Education (Modern Foreign Languages) R9X1

1 year full-time or 16 months part-time

Entry requirements: As above
Contact: Christina O'Connell
01273 643911
c.oconnell@brighton.ac.uk

PGCE in Secondary Education (Physical Education) X9C6

1 year full-time or 16 months part-time

Entry requirements: As above
Contact: Andrew Theodoulides
Admissions Tutor
01273 643717
a.theodoulides@brighton.ac.uk

PGCE in Secondary Education (Religious Education) V6X1

1 year full-time or 16 months part-time

Entry requirements: As above
Contact: Roger Homan
01273 643405
r.homan@bton.ac.uk

PGCE in Secondary Education (Science) F0X1

1 year full-time or 16 months part-time

Entry requirements: As above
Contact: Ian Longman
01273 643426
i.longman@brighton.ac.uk

PGCE in Secondary Education (Science, conversion) FXA1

2 years full-time

Entry requirements: Degree or equivalent in related area; GCSE English language and mathematics minimum grade C, or equivalent. In-house tests are available for candidates without formal qualifications. Potential students are interviewed before being offered a place.
Contact: As above

PgCert/PgDip/MA Education

1 year full-time or 2–6 years part-time

Entry requirements: Degree or equivalent or recognised diploma at appropriate standard normally required; course is offered to all those working in education, training and professional development; it is also run in Israel and at the Mauritius Institute of Education.
Contact: Admissions
01273 643444
soeccpd@brighton.ac.uk

EdD Education

4 years part-time

Entry requirements: MA in education or related discipline, and minimum 4 years' professional experience.
Contact: Dave Baker
01273 643433
d.baker@brighton.ac.uk

PgCert Education Management

1–3 years part-time

Entry requirements: Intended for staff within education sector who have managerial responsibility; degree or equivalent would normally be prerequisite.
Contact: Admissions
01273 643444
soeccpd@brighton.ac.uk

PgCert/PgDip/MA English Language Teaching Studies

1 year full-time or 2 years part-time

Entry requirements: Degree or equivalent in relevant area (English, other second language, linguistics, education, psychology); IELTS minimum 6.5; proven interest in language teaching (some experience of language teaching or tutoring, work in a language school or with English language materials).
Contact: Zamy Karimjee
01273 643337
z.karimjee@brighton.ac.uk

PgCert/PgDip/MA Media-Assisted Language Teaching and Learning

1 year full-time or 2 years part-time

Entry requirements: Relevant degree and normally 2 years' language teaching experience; non-native speakers, IELTS grade 7 or equivalent.
Contact: Zamy Karimjee
Admissions
01273 643337
z.karimjee@brighton.ac.uk

PgCert/PgDip/MA Teaching English to Speakers of Other Languages (TESOL)

1 year full-time or 2 years part-time

Entry requirements: Relevant degree or equivalent and normally 2 years' language teaching experience; non-native speakers of English, IELTS 7 or equivalent.
Contact: Zamy Karimjee
01273 643337
z.karimjee@brighton.ac.uk

University of the West of England, Bristol

Frenchay Campus
Coldharbour Lane
Bristol
BS16 1QY
Tel: 0117 965 6261
Fax: 0117 344 3810
admissions@uwe.ac.uk
www.uwe.ac.uk

The University of the West of England, Bristol was established as a university in 1992 but its origins date back to 1595. It now has more than 23,000 students. The University has four Campuses in and around the city of Bristol, with regional centres in Bath and Swindon. Accommodation is available near to each campus and everyone is able to use the facilities on the other campuses at any time. Academic resources include the library and computer services.

The Faculty of Education is located in a new purpose-designed building with specialist facilities and technology. It is the largest centre for teacher education in the West of England and offers undergraduate and postgraduate programmes for Initial Teacher Training and courses for Continuing Professional Development. Students have access to all the university libraries and there is also the Education Resources Centre, which is located in the Learning Resources building.

HOW TO APPLY

Degree courses: applications are made through UCAS.
PGCE: applications are made through the GTTR.
Postgraduate: applications are made direct to the institution.

COURSES

BA (Hons) in Primary Education (Art, early years) WX21

4 years full-time

Students on the initial teacher education (ITE) programme are trained as primary generalist teachers with a subject specialism.

All years: 3 components which feature throughout: subject studies; professional studies; professionally related subject studies.

Students specialise in early years (5–8). They gain experience of teaching the primary school curriculum and an understanding of the general tasks of the primary school teacher. There is frequent school experience including 3 periods of block teaching practice.

Subject specialism: introductory foundation period where students gain experience of a wide range of techniques with emphasis on drawing; As the course progresses students may choose to specialise in 1 or more of the following areas: painting, printmaking, sculpture, ceramics, installation or lens-based media.

Successful completion of this course leads to a recommendation for QTS.

Entry requirements: Tariff: 140 to 180 points, International Baccalaureate: 24, Irish Leaving Certificates: BBC, SCE Higher: BCC, BTEC NC/ND, Portfolio
Contact: Enquiries Officer
Enquiry and Admissions Office
0117 344 3333
admissions@uwe.ac.uk

BSc (Hons) in Primary Education (Biological Science, early years) CX11

4 years full-time

Students on the initial teacher education (ITE) programme are trained as primary generalist teachers with a subject specialism.

All years: 3 components which feature throughout: subject studies; professional studies; professionally related subject studies.

Students specialise in early years (5–8). They gain experience of teaching the primary school curriculum and an understanding of the general tasks of the primary school teacher. There is frequent school experience including 3 periods of block teaching practice.

Subject specialism: Main study areas are: ecosystems; variety of life forms; physiology; genetics and evolution; growth and development. Studies include practical work and field trips.

Successful completion of this course leads to a recommendation for QTS.

Entry requirements: Tariff: 140 to 180 points, International Baccalaureate: 24, Irish Leaving Certificates: BBC, SCE Higher: BCC, BTEC NC/ND
Contact: As above

BA (Hons) in Primary Education (Early Years) X311

4 years full-time

Students on the initial teacher education (ITE) programme are trained as primary generalist teachers with a subject specialism.

All years: 3 components which feature throughout: subject studies; professional studies; professionally related subject studies.

The programme is designed for those who wish to train as specialists in the teaching of children aged 3–8 and is a response to the national shortfall in the number of early years teachers. It focuses on the knowledge and skills necessary to teach early years, with a particular emphasis on child development, and the development of literacy and numeracy, including preparation for teaching those with special educational needs. In addition, students will be prepared to teach across the full primary curriculum for this age range and will spend 32 weeks in schools with periods of school experience during each of the 4 years of the course.

The course should appeal particularly to those who have undertaken employment or voluntary work in early years settings and those who have childcare qualifications. Graduates from this course are expected to take a leading role as literacy or numeracy co-ordinators, as early years co-ordinators or leading the development of special needs provision in primary or nursery schools.

Successful completion of this course leads to a recommendation for QTS.

Entry requirements: Tariff: 140 points, International Baccalaureate: 24, Irish Leaving Certificates: BB-BBC, BTEC NC/ND, European Baccalaureate, Foundation / access qualification
Contact: As above

BA (Hons) in Primary Education (English, early years) QX31

4 years full-time

Students on the initial teacher education (ITE) programme are trained as primary generalist teachers with a subject specialism.

All years: 3 components which feature throughout: subject studies; professional studies; professionally related subject studies.

Students specialise in early years (5–8). They gain experience of teaching the primary school curriculum and an understanding of the general tasks of the primary school teacher. There is frequent school experience and 3 periods of block teaching practice.

Subject specialism includes: genre courses in poetry, drama and fiction from the Renaissance to the 1990s. Particular emphasis on 19th- and 20th-century literature in English, drawing on British, American, Indian and African traditions and European literature in translation. Other modules include practical drama, media and representation and applied literary theory. There are a number of opportunities for personal writing including the presentation of portfolios and more extended pieces of work.

Successful completion of this course leads to a recommendation for QTS.

Entry requirements: Tariff: 140 to 180 points, International Baccalaureate: 24, Irish Leaving Certificates: BBC, SCE Higher: BCC, BTEC NC/ND
Contact: As above

BSc (Hons) in Primary Education (Geography, early years) LX71

4 years full-time

Students on the initial teacher education (ITE) programme are trained as primary generalist teachers with a subject specialism.

All years: 3 components which feature throughout: subject studies; professional studies; professionally related subject studies.

Students specialise in early years (5–8). They gain experience of teaching the primary school curriculum and an understanding of the general tasks of the primary school teacher. There is frequent school experience including 3 periods of block teaching practice.

Subject specialism in human and physical geography includes: the changing geography of the UK; geomorphology and soils; cities in the modern world; interpretation of historic landscapes; global development; climate and ecosystems; fluvial and glacial processes; research methods and dissertation; philosophy and development of geography; 2 field trips (UK and continental Europe).

Successful completion of this course leads to a recommendation for QTS.

Entry requirements: As above
Contact: As above

PGCE in Post-Compulsory Education and Training (PCET) X341

1 year full-time

Entry requirements: Degree or equivalent.
Contact: John Homewood
Award Leader
0117 344 4221
John.Homewood@uwe.ac.uk

PGCE in Primary Education (Early Years, 3–8) X110

1 year full-time

Entry requirements: Degree (2.1 or above) in psychology, sociology, early childhood studies or equivalent, plus relevant work experience.
Contact: Rowan Bullock
Marketing Officer, Faculty of Education
0117 344 4267
education.courses@uwe.ac.uk

PGCE in Primary Education (Later Years, 5–11) X121

1 year full-time

Entry requirements: Degree (2.1 or above) in an area strongly relating to a curriculum subject; good A-levels; GCSE mathematics, science and English; work experience in a primary classroom or with primary-age children.
Contact: As above

PGCE in Secondary Education (Art) W1X1

1 year full-time

Entry requirements: Degree or equivalent in art-related subject, plus GCSE minimum grade C (or equivalent) in English, mathematics and science.
Contact: As above

PGCE in Secondary Education (Business Education) N1X1

1 year full-time

Entry requirements: Degree or equivalent in business-related subject, plus GCSE minimum grade C (or equivalent) in English, mathematics and science; business experience advantageous.
Contact: As above

PGCE in Secondary Education (Design and Technology) W9X1

1 year full-time

Entry requirements: Relevant degree or equivalent, plus GCSE minimum grade C (or equivalent) in English, mathematics and science.
Contact: As above

PGCE in Secondary Education (English) Q3X1

1 year full-time

As above

PGCE in Secondary Education (Geography) F8X1

1 year full-time

As above

PGCE in Secondary Education (History) V1X1

1 year full-time

As above

PGCE in Secondary Education (Mathematics) G1X1

1 year full-time

As above

PGCE in Secondary Education (Modern Foreign Languages) R9X1

1 year full-time

Entry requirements: Relevant degree or equivalent (or graduate native speakers of French or German or Spanish); plus A-level French and GCSE minimum grade C (or equivalent) in English, mathematics and science.

Contact: As above

PGCE in Secondary Education (Science, Biology) C1X1

1 year full-time

Entry requirements: Relevant degree or equivalent, plus GCSE minimum grade C (or equivalent) in English, mathematics and science.

Contact: As above

PgDip in Careers Guidance

1 year full-time

Entry requirements: Degree normally required; other applicants with appropriate skills and expertise may be considered.

Contact: Mary Dempsey
0117 344 4175
Mary.Dempsey@uwe.ac.uk

PgCert/PgDip in Education

1–4 years part-time

Entry requirements: Degree plus teaching qualification and/or experience or Qualified Teacher Status plus substantial experience.

Contact: Jane Tarr
0117 344 4188
Jane.Tarr@uwe.ac.uk

MA in Education

6 years part-time

Entry requirements: Degree and/or substantial experience plus Qualified Teacher Status (or equivalent) plus 3 years' teacher training experience required.

Contact: Carolyn Broomfield
0117 344 4127
Carolyn.Broomfield@uwe.ac.uk

EdD in Education

4 years part-time

Entry requirements: Master's degree or Upper 2nd Class degree or equivalent, plus at least 4 years' experience in relevant professional area.

Contact: Research Manager
0117 344 4226
Eduresearch@uwe.ac.uk

PgCert/PgDip in Further, Adult and Higher Education (FAHE)

2 years part-time

Entry requirements: For current teachers in adult education, higher education, health-related teaching or equivalent.

Contact: John Homewood
0117 344 4221
John.Homewood@uwe.ac.uk

PgCert/PgDip/MA in Guidance (Vocational/Educational)

MA: 2–5 years part-time

Entry requirements: Degree normally required; other applicants with appropriate skills and expertise may be considered.

Contact: Mary Dempsey
0117 344 4176
Mary.Dempsey@uwe.ac.uk

University of Bristol

Senate House
Tyndall Avenue
Bristol
BS8 1TH
Tel: 0117 928 9000
Fax: 0117 925 1424
admissions@bristol.ac.uk
www.bris.ac.uk

The University was founded in 1876 as University College, Bristol and received the Royal charter in 1909. The University is situated in a lively area of the city and although it is not a campus university, the majority of its buildings are only a few minutes' walk from each other.

The School of Education is one of the largest departments in the University of Bristol and is descended from the Bristol Day Training College for Women, which was established in 1892. The school offers a range of graduate programmes including Masters' and doctorate programmes, the PGCE and other courses for Continuing Professional Development.

There are 13 libraries at the university including an Education Library at the School of Education and extensive computer facilities are available. The University guarantees accommodation to postgraduate students new to the University who will be paying fees at the overseas rate. For UK postgraduate students there is accommodation available in the private sector.

HOW TO APPLY

PGCE: applications are made through the GTTR.
Postgraduate: applications are made direct to the institution.

COURSES

PGCE in Secondary Education (Art and Design) W1X1

1 year full-time.

Entry requirements: Good, relevant Honours degree; plus GCSE grade C or above (or equivalent) in English language and mathematics.

Contact: Carole Baker
           PGCE Office, School of
           Education
           0117 928 7002
           Carole.Baker@bristol.ac.uk

PGCE in Secondary Education (Citizenship) L9X1

1 year full-time
As above

PGCE in Secondary Education (English) Q3X1

1 year full-time
As above

PGCE in Secondary Education (Geography) F8X1

1 year full-time
As above

PGCE in Secondary Education (History) V1X1

1 year full-time
As above

PGCE in Secondary Education (Mathematics) G1X1

1 year full-time
As above

PGCE in Secondary Education (Modern Languages) T9X1

1 year full-time
As above

PGCE in Secondary Education (Modern Languages: French with German) RX11

1 year full-time
As above

PGCE in Secondary Education (Modern Languages: French with Italian) RX1C

1 year full-time
As above

PGCE in Secondary Education (Modern Languages: French with Spanish) RXD1

1 year full-time
As above

PGCE in Secondary Education (Modern Languages: French) R1X1

1 year full-time

As above

PGCE in Secondary Education (Modern Languages: German with French) RX21

1 year full-time

As above

PGCE in Secondary Education (Modern Languages: German with Spanish) RXG1

1 year full-time

As above

PGCE in Secondary Education (Modern Languages: Spanish with French) RX41

1 year full-time

As above

PGCE in Secondary Education (Music) W3X1

1 year full-time

As above

PGCE in Secondary Education (Religious Education) V6X1

1 year full-time

As above

PGCE in Secondary Education (Science: Biology) C1X1

1 year full-time

As above

PGCE in Secondary Education (Science: Chemistry) F1X1

1 year full-time

As above

PGCE in Secondary Education (Science: Physics) F3X1

1 year full-time

As above

EdD Education

3 years full-time or 4–5 years part-time

Entry requirements: Aimed at senior educational professionals; good Honours degree or equivalent, advanced qualification in education and minimum 3 years' appropriate professional experience required.

Contact: Dr Tim Bond
Director, EdD Programme
0117 928 7008
jacqui.upcott@bristol.ac.uk

Advanced Diploma/MEd Education

1 year full-time or 2–5 years part-time

Entry requirements: UK Honours degree or equivalent, plus 1 year's relevant professional experience for MEd (except where Psychology of Education taken as a conversion course); ordinary degree/certificate in education plus 1 year's relevant professional experience for Advanced Diploma.

Contact: Mrs Angela Allen
Programme Administrator
0117 928 7048
med-office@bristol.ac.uk

MSc Education, Technology and Society

1 year full-time or up to 5 years part-time

Entry requirements: First degree from a recognised institution with good final grades. 6.5 or above in IELTS for students whose first language is not English. Candidates are also required to have basic computer literacy, which should be broadly equivalent to the standard of the International Driving Licence.

Contact: Keri Facer
Lecturer in Education and Technology
0117 928 7006
Keri.Facer@bristol.ac.uk

MEd Educational Psychology

1 year full-time

Entry requirements: Qualified Teacher Status, minimum 2 years' teaching experience, and Graduate Basis for Registration (GBR) with British Psychological Society; selection includes interview.

Contact: Mrs Norma Meecham
0117 928 7047
norma.meechem@bristol.ac.uk

Bromley Schools' Collegiate

C/o Coopers School
Hawkwood Lane
Chislehurst
Kent BR7 5PS
Tel: 020 8295 3749
Fax: 020 8295 3749
gradteach@coopers.bromley.sch.uk
www.gradteachbromley.co.uk

The Bromley Schools' Collegiate was established in 1993 and offers a School Centred Initial Teacher Training Course for postgraduates who wish to teach in secondary schools. The training throughout the course is based entirely in a consortium of seven successful Bromley secondary schools. Trainees spend some time in each school, but the bulk of the course is spent in two of the schools from September–February and February–July.

HOW TO APPLY

Applications are made direct to the institution.

COURSES

PGCE in Secondary Education (English)
1 year full-time

Entry requirements: Relevant degree; GSCE mathematics and English.
Contact: Enquiries
020 8295 3749
gradteach@coopers.bromley.sch.uk

PGCE in Secondary Education (Geography)
As above

PGCE in Secondary Education (History)
As above

PGCE in Secondary Education (Information Technology)
As above

PGCE in Secondary Education (Mathematics)
As above.

PGCE in Secondary Education (Modern Languages)
As above

PGCE in Secondary Education (Religious Education)
As above

PGCE in Secondary Education (Science)
As above

Brunel University

Hillingdon
London
UB8 3PH
Tel: 01895 274000
Fax: 01895 203096
admissions@brunel.ac.uk
www.brunel.ac.uk/home.html

The development of Brunel University can be traced back to 1928 when Middlesex County Council transferred its Junior Technical School to Acton in west London. Brunel College of Advanced Technology developed from this and expanded to a site at Uxbridge. The college was awarded university status in 1966 and shortly afterwards the Uxbridge campus officially

became part of Brunel University. The Acton site was eventually vacated in 1971. In 1980 the Shoreditch College of Education became part of Brunel University and became the University's second campus. In 1995 the West London Institute of Higher Education was incorporated into the university.

The university is now based at four campuses: Uxbridge, Runnymede, Twickenham and Osterley. Accommodation is available on all of the campuses or in the local area. Academic, sporting and leisure facilities are all available on site.

The Department of Education is based at Twickenham Campus and was formed in 1995 by the merging of Brunel University and the West London Institute of Higher Education. It offers research programmes and courses for academic and professional development as well as Initial Teacher Training at primary and secondary level for both undergraduates and postgraduates.

HOW TO APPLY

Degree courses: applications are made through UCAS.

PGCE: applications are made through the GTTR.

Postgraduate: applications are made direct to the institution.

COURSES

BA (Hons) in Primary Education X120

3 years full-time

Throughout the 3 years, students focus mainly on the core subjects of the National Curriculum (English, mathematics and science) with a strong emphasis on the use of information communications technology to teach these subjects. Students also follow shorter courses of study on the remaining subjects of the primary curriculum (technology, art, geography, history, music, physical education and religious education). Students specialise in either English, mathematics or science in the final year.

All students prepare to teach across the 5–11 age range. The professional studies strand of the award focuses on the wider, cross-curricular issues involved in primary teaching. This strand reinforces the subject specific teaching.

Each year of the award includes extensive school-based work in a variety of contexts. By working in a range of schools students develop their expertise in planning and teaching the primary curriculum as well as participating in all aspects of the teacher's role.

Successful completion of this course leads to a recommendation for Qualified Teacher Status after completion of skills tests.

Entry requirements: Tariff: 220 points, International Baccalaureate: 24, Irish Leav-

ing Certificates: BBBCC, BTEC NC/ND, Foundation / access qualification
Contact: Ms L Thorogood
Admissions Tutor
020 8891 0121 x2028

BSc (Hons) in Secondary Education (Physical Education) X1CP

4 years full-time

Years 1–2: Strong subject base in sport sciences.

Years 3–4: Skills and knowledge required to teach effectively in a secondary school; extensive school-based work; educational studies.

Entry requirements: Tariff: 220 points, International Baccalaureate: 26, Irish Leaving Certificates: BBCCC, BTEC NC/ND, Foundation / access qualification
Contact: Mr P Breckon
Admissions Tutor
020 8891 8362
peter.breckon@brunel.ac.uk

PGCE in Primary Education (General Primary, 5–11) X100

1 year full-time

Entry requirements: Degree or equivalent which is relevant to one of the core subjects of the primary curriculum; GCSE grade C in English language and mathematics.
Contact: John Garvey
Postgraduate Primary Course Leader
020 8891 0121 x2051
school.education@brunel.ac.uk

PGCE in Secondary Education (English) Q3X1

Distance learning or 1 year full-time

Entry requirements: Relevant degree or approved equivalent; GCSE grade C in English language and mathematics.
Contact: Mr Andrew Green
020 8891 0121 x2040
school.education@brunel.ac.uk

PGCE in Secondary Education (Information and Communications Technology) G5X1

1 year full-time

Entry requirements: As above
Contact: Mr Roger Taylor
020 8891 0121 x2040
school.education@brunel.ac.uk

PGCE in Secondary Education (Mathematics) G1X1

Distance learning or 1 year full-time

Entry requirements: Degree with at least 50% of content in mathematics, or approved equivalent; GCSE grade C in English language and mathematics.
Contact: Mr Mark Humble
020 8891 0121 x2040
school.education@brunel.ac.uk

PGCE in Secondary Education (Modern Foreign Languages: French with German) RX11

1 year full-time

Entry requirements: Degree in French and/or German, or degree in which French or German accounts for 50% of content; or native speaker of French or German with a language-related degree; GCSE grade C English language and mathematics, or equivalent.
Contact: Mrs Francoise Allen
Course Leader
020 8891 0121 X2040
school.education@brunel.ac.uk

PGCE in Secondary Education (Modern Foreign Languages: French) R1X1

As above

PGCE in Secondary Education (Modern Foreign Languages: German) R2X1

As above

PGCE in Secondary Education (Physical Education) X9C6

1 year full-time

Entry requirements: Relevant degree or approved equivalent; GCSE grade C in English language and mathematics; practical skills and experience advantageous.

Contact: Mrs Cathy Gower
020 8891 0121 x2040
school.education@brunel.ac.uk

PGCE in Secondary Education (Religious Education) V6X1

1 year full-time

Entry requirements: Relevant degree or approved equivalent; GCSE grade C in English language and mathematics.
Contact: Mrs Lynne Broadbent
020 8891 0121 x2040
school.education@brunel.ac.uk

PGCE in Secondary Education (Science) F0X1

1 year full-time

Entry requirements: As above
Contact: Dr Andrew Cleminson or Mr James Williams
020 8891 0121 x2040
school.education@brunel.ac.uk

PGCE: Secondary Education (Science: Biology) C1X1

Distance learning

Entry requirements: As above
Contact: James Williams
020 8891 0121 x2040
school.education@brunel.ac.uk

PGCE in Secondary Education (Science: Chemistry) F1X1

Distance learning

Entry requirements: As above
Contact: Dr Andrew Cleminson
020 8891 0121 x2040
school.education@brunel.ac.uk

PGCE in Secondary Education (Science: Physics) F3X1

Distance learning

Entry requirements: As above
Contact: Dr Andrew Cleminson
020 8891 0121 x2040
school.education@brunel.ac.uk

EdD in Education

3–4 years full-time, 4–6 years part-time

Entry requirements: Degree or equivalent and relevant initial qualification required, plus, normally, minimum 4 years' relevant professional employment; holders of relevant Master's degree may pursue reduced period of study.

Contact: Dr Keith Wood
        020 8891 8304
        Keith.Wood@brunel.ac.uk

MA in Education

1 year full-time, 2–5 years part-time

Entry requirements: Degree in relevant subject or equivalent, or relevant position in education/training.

Contact: Prof Robert Fisher
        020 8891 0121 x2051
        school.education@brunel.ac.uk

MA in Education (Information Technology)

1 year full-time, 2–5 years part-time

Entry requirements: Degree in relevant subject or equivalent, or relevant position in education/training.

Contact: Roger Taylor
        020 8891 0121 x2051
        school.education@brunel.ac.uk

MA in Education (Primary Education)

1 year full-time, 2–5 years part-time

Entry requirements: As above
Contact: Dr Valsa Koshy
        020 8891 0121 x2051
        school.education@brunel.ac.uk

MA in Education (Educational Management)

1 year full-time, 2–5 years part-time

Entry requirements: As above
Contact: Dr Roy Evans
        020 8891 0121 x2051
        school.education@brunel.ac.uk

MA in Education (Secondary Education)

1 year full-time, 2–5 years part-time

Entry requirements: As above
Contact: Prof Robert Fisher
        020 8891 0121 x2051
        school.education@brunel.ac.uk

MA in Education (Special Educational Needs)

1 year full-time, 2–5 years part-time

Entry requirements: As above
Contact: Dr Roy Evans
        020 8891 0121 x2051
        school.education@brunel.ac.uk

PgCert/PgDip/MA in Guidance and Counselling Skills

1 year full-time, 2–5 years part-time

Entry requirements: As above
Contact: Dr Simon Bradford
        020 8891 0121 x2051
        school.education@brunel.ac.uk

University of Cambridge, Faculty of Education

Homerton Site
Hills Road
Cambridge
CB2 2PH
Tel: 01223 507114
Fax: 01223 507140
mb346@cam.ac.uk
www.educ.ac.uk

The University of Cambridge is one of the oldest universities in the world and one of the largest in the United Kingdom. It currently caters for over 16,500 students. The Faculty of Education was formed from the integration of the former School of Education and Homerton College.

In August 2001 the Faculty of Education became one of the largest groups of educational researchers and teacher educators in the country. Courses offered include the PGCE, undergraduate degree programmes, a range of Continuing Professional Development courses and higher degrees. The Faculty has specialist facilities including a library and information service.

University facilities include a main library, several museums and the botanic gardens.

Most students live in college accommodation but there is also University housing and rented accommodation available.

HOW TO APPLY
PGCE: applications are made through the GTTR.

COURSES

PGCE in Middle Years Education (English, 7–14) XQC3
1 year full-time

Entry requirements: Good Honours degree; GCSE grade C or above in English, mathematics and science; some study of English in degree or A-levels.
Contact: Registry, Homerton College
01223 507114

PGCE in Middle Years Education (Mathematics, 7–14) XGC1
1 year full-time
As above

PGCE in Middle Years Education (Modern Languages, 7–14) XRC9
1 year full-time
As above

PGCE in Middle Years Education (Science, 7–14) XFCA
1 year full-time
As above

PGCE in Primary Education (Early Years, 3–7) X110
1 year full-time

Entry requirements: Good Honours degree in a subject relevant to the primary curriculum required, together with 3 A-levels at grade C or above, and with GCSE grade C or above (or equivalent) in English language and mathematics and science.
Contact: As above

PGCE in Primary Education (General Primary, 5–11) X100
1 year full-time
As above

PGCE in Secondary Education (Art) W1X1
1 year full-time

Entry requirements: Honours degree in art or associated subject required, and GCSE grade C (minimum) or equivalent in English language and mathematics.
Contact: As above

PGCE in Secondary Education (Biology/Science) C1X1
1 year full-time

Entry requirements: Honours degree in biology or associated subject, and GCSE grade C (minimum) or equivalent in English language and mathematics.
Contact: As above

PGCE in Secondary Education (Chemistry/Science) F1X1
1 year full-time

Entry requirements: Honours degree in chemistry or associated subject, and GCSE grade C (minimum) or equivalent in English language and mathematics.
Contact: As above

PGCE in Secondary Education (Classics) Q8X1
1 year full-time

Entry requirements: Honours degree in classics or associated subject required; A-level Latin; GCSE grade C (minimum) or equivalent in English language and mathematics.
Contact: As above

PGCE in Secondary Education (Design and Technology) W9X1
1 year full-time

Entry requirements: Relevant Honours degree; GCSE grade C (minimum) or equivalent in English language and mathematics.
Contact: As above

PGCE in Secondary Education (English and Drama) QX31
1 year full-time

Entry requirements: Degree containing at least 50% English, together with GCSE at grade C or above in mathematics and English language (or equivalents).

Contact: As above

PGCE in Secondary Education (English) Q3X1

1 year full-time

Entry requirements: Honours degree in English/drama or associated subjects required, and GCSE grade C (minimum) or equivalent in mathematics.

Contact: As above

PGCE in Secondary Education (Geography) F8X1

1 year full-time

Entry requirements: Honours degree in geography or in an associated subject which will enable students to cover the full range of secondary work up to GCE A-level standard, and GCSE minimum grade C (or equivalent) in English language and mathematics.

Contact: As above

PGCE in Secondary Education (History) V1X1

1 year full-time

Entry requirements: Honours degree in history or closely associated subject required, and GCSE grade C (minimum) or equivalent in English language and mathematics.

Contact: As above

PGCE in Secondary Education (Mathematics) G1X1

1 year full-time

Entry requirements: Honours degree in mathematics or degree with high mathematical content required, and GCSE grade C (minimum) or equivalent in English language.

Contact: As above

PGCE in Secondary Education (Mathematics, conversion) GXC1

2 years full-time

Entry requirements: Course offers graduates in subjects other than mathematics, who have attained GCE A-level mathematics (or its equivalent) and who have studied some mathematics in their degree course, the opportunity to train to teach mathematics up to A-level standard.

Contact: As above

PGCE in Secondary Education (Modern Languages) R9X1

1 year full-time

Entry requirements: Honours degree required, and GCSE grade C (minimum) or equivalent in English language and mathematics. Applicants should offer 2 languages: either French or German, together with subsidiary language chosen from French, German, Italian, Russian, Spanish.

Contact: As above

PGCE in Secondary Education (Music) W3X1

1 year full-time

Entry requirements: Honours degree in music required, and GCSE minimum grade C (or equivalent) in English language and mathematics.

Contact: As above

PGCE in Secondary Education (Physics/Science) F3X1

1 year full-time

Entry requirements: Honours degree in physics or associated subject, and GCSE grade C (minimum) or equivalent in English language and mathematics.

Contact: As above

PGCE in Secondary Education (Religious Studies) V6X1

1 year full-time

Entry requirements: Honours degree in appropriate subject required, and GCSE minimum grade C (or equivalent) in English language and mathematics.

Contact: As above

Canterbury Christ Church University College

North Holmes Road
Canterbury
Kent CT1 1QU
Tel: 01227 767700
Fax: 01227 470442
admissions@cant.ac.uk
www.cant.ac.uk

Canterbury Christ Church University College is based in the heart of the historic city centre of Canterbury. The College was founded by the Church of England in 1962. The University College is one of the largest Higher Education institutions of its kind with a student population of over 12,000. In addition to the Canterbury Campus a new campus was opened in 2000 at Thanet in East Kent and the third campus, Salomons, is based in West Kent at Tunbridge Wells.

The Faculty of Education offers honours degrees, initial teacher education courses including primary and secondary PGCEs, post-compulsory courses and a wide range of continuing professional development at all levels, including diplomas and higher degrees by taught courses and research.

The College offers catered and non-catered accommodation and a range of academic and leisure facilities are available to students.

HOW TO APPLY

Degree courses: applications are made through UCAS.

PGCE: applications are made through the GTTR (Post-Compulsory Education: applications direct to the institution).

Postgraduate: applications are made direct to the institution.

COURSES

BA (Hons) in Primary Education (Early Years Education) X100

3 years full-time or 4 years full-time

Year 1: Professional studies, core subjects (English, mathematics and ICT) and foundation subjects. All students undertake professional practice experience in schools.

Year 2: Professional studies and core subjects (not including ICT); professional practice placement in student's main Key Stage age group. Students choose 2 subjects from: history; geography; music; art; physical education; ICT; design and technology; religious education; early years; inclusion and special needs; modern foreign languages.

Year 3: Professional studies and professional practice placement in a class within student's main Key Stage age group. All students follow courses in English, mathematics and science; 1 of which is studied at greater depth. Students also choose 1 subject from Year 2 to study at an extended level in Year 3.

Successful completion of this course leads to a recommendation for Qualified Teacher Status (QTS) after completion of the 1st year of teaching.

Entry requirements: Tariff: 160 points, International Baccalaureate: 24, BTEC NC/ND, SCE Higher: CCCC, Irish Leaving Certificates: CCCCC, Foundation / access qualification

Contact: Admissions Office
01227 767700
admissions@cant.ac.uk

BA (Hons) in Primary Education (Lower Primary, 3–8 years) X121

3 years full-time
As above

BA (Hons) in Primary Education (Upper Primary, 5–11 years) X122

3 years full-time
As above

BA (Hons) in Primary Education, Art (Lower Primary) XW11

3 years full-time or 4 years full-time
As above

BA (Hons) in Primary Education, Art (Upper Primary) XWC1

3 years full-time or 4 years full-time
As above

BA (Hons) in Primary Education, English (Lower Primary) XQ13

3 years full-time or 4 years full-time
As above

BA (Hons) in Primary Education, English (Upper Primary) XQC3

3 years full-time or 4 years full-time
As above

BA (Hons) in Primary Education, Geography (Lower Primary) XL17

3 years full-time or 4 years full-time
As above

BA (Hons) in Primary Education, Geography (Upper Primary) XLC7

3 years full-time or 4 years full-time
As above

BA (Hons) in Primary Education, History (Lower Primary) XV11

3 years full-time or 4 years full-time
As above

BA (Hons) in Primary Education, History (Upper Primary) XVC1

3 years full-time or 4 years full-time
As above

BA (Hons) in Primary Education, Mathematics (Lower Primary) XG11

3 years full-time or 4 years full-time
As above

BA (Hons) in Primary Education, Mathematics (Upper Primary) XGC1

3 years full-time or 4 years full-time
As above

BA (Hons) in Primary Education, Music (Lower Primary) XW13

3 years full-time or 4 years full-time
As above

BA (Hons) in Primary Education, Music (Upper Primary) XWC3

3 years full-time or 4 years full-time
As above

BA (Hons) in Primary Education, Physical Education (Lower Primary) X1C6

3 years full-time or 4 years full-time
As above

BA (Hons) in Primary Education, Physical Education (Upper Primary) X1CP

3 years full-time or 4 years full-time
As above

BA (Hons) Primary Education, Religious Studies (Lower Primary) XV16

3 years full-time or 4 years full-time
As above

BA (Hons) in Primary Education, Religious Studies (Upper Primary) XVC6

3 years full-time or 4 years full-time
As above

BA (Hons) in Primary Education, Science (Lower Primary) XC10

3 years full-time or 4 years full-time
As above

BA (Hons) in Primary Education, Science (Upper Primary) XC1A

3 years full-time or 4 years full-time
As above

BA (Hons) in Primary Education, Special Educational Needs XX13

4 years full-time
As above

PGCE in Middle Years (English, Key Stages 2–3) XQC3

1 year full-time

Entry requirements: Degree or equivalent qualification relevant to the subject specialism; GCSE grade C in English and mathematics and, for applicants born on or after 1/9/79, science.

Contact: Postgraduate Admissions Office
         01227 767700
         admissions@cant.ac.uk

PGCE in Middle Years (French, Key Stages 2–3) XRC1

1 year full-time
As above

PGCE in Middle Years (Geography, Key Stages 2–3) XFC8

1 year full-time
As above

PGCE in Middle Years (Mathematics, Key Stages 2–3) XGC1

1 year full-time
As above

PGCE in Middle Years (Music, Key Stages 2–3) XWC3

1 year full-time
As above

PGCE in Middle Years (Religious Studies, Key Stages 2–3) XVC6

1 year full-time
As above

PGCE in Middle Years (Science, Key Stages 2–3) XFCA

1 year full-time
As above

PGCE in Post-Compulsory Education

1 year full-time

Entry requirements: Degree or equivalent with good academic record; competency in communications and numeracy; academic and/or industrial and commercial experience related to chosen curriculum area.
Contact: Postgraduate Admissions Office
    01227 767700
    admissions@cant.ac.uk

PGCE in Primary Education (Lower Primary, 3–7) X121

1 year full-time

Entry requirements: Degree or equivalent; GCSE grade C in English and mathematics and, for applicants born on or after 1/9/79, science.
Contact: Postgraduate Admissions Office
    01227 767700
    admissions@cant.ac.uk

PGCE in Primary Education (Upper Primary, 5–11) X171

1 year full-time
As above

PGCE in Secondary Education (Art and Design) W1X1

1 year full-time

Entry requirements: Degree or equivalent including a substantial element of art, plus English and mathematics at GCSE grade C or above (or equivalent).
Contact: Postgraduate Admissions Office
    01227 767700
    admissions@cant.ac.uk

PGCE in Secondary Education (Art and Design, 14–19) WX1C

1 year full-time

Entry requirements: Degree in art and design area, or unrelated degree with relevant professional experience.
Contact: As above

PGCE in Secondary Education (Citizenship) L9X1

1 year full-time

Entry requirements: Degree or equivalent, plus English and mathematics at GCSE grade C or above (or equivalent).
Contact: As above

PGCE in Secondary Education (Design and Technology) W9X1

1 year full-time

Entry requirements: Degree in design and technology area, or unrelated degree with relevant professional experience.
Contact: As above

PGCE in Secondary Education (English with Drama and Media Studies) Q3X1

1 year full-time

Entry requirements: Degree or equivalent including a substantial element of English literature, plus English language and mathematics at GCSE grade C or above.
Contact: As above

PGCE in Secondary Education (Geography with Fieldwork Planning) F8X1

1 year full-time

Entry requirements: Degree or equivalent including a substantial element of geography, plus English and mathematics at GCSE grade C or above (or equivalent).
Contact: As above

PGCE in Secondary Education (History with Humanities) V1X1

1 year full-time

Entry requirements: Degree in equivalent including a substantial element of history, plus English and mathematics at GCSE grade C or above (or equivalent).
Contact: As above

PGCE in Secondary Education (Information and Communication Technology) G5X1

1 year full-time

Entry requirements: Degree or equivalent qualification relevant to the subject specialism; GCSE in English and mathematics.
Contact: As above

PGCE in Secondary Education (Leisure and Tourism, 14–19) FXVC

1 year full-time

Entry requirements: Degree in leisure and tourism area, or unrelated degree with relevant professional experience.
Contact: As above

PGCE in Secondary Education (Mathematics with Further Mathematics) G1X1

1 year full-time

Entry requirements: Degree or equivalent qualification relevant to the subject specialism; GCSE in English and mathematics (or equivalent).
Contact: As above

PGCE in Secondary Education (Modern Languages: French) R1X1

1 year full-time

Entry requirements: UK candidates: Upper 2nd Class Honours degree in French plus English language and mathematics at GCSE grade C or above (or equivalent); French nationals: Licence de Lettres, Licence de Langues, Licence de Science du Language with mention FLE or equivalent; experience as an assistant(e) in British school is desirable for French students.
Contact: As above

PGCE in Secondary Education (Music with Further Music) W3X1

1 year full-time

Entry requirements: Degree or equivalent qualification relevant to the subject specialism; GCSE in English and mathematics (or equivalent).
Contact: As above

PGCE in Secondary Education (Physical Education) X9C6

1 year full-time
As above

PGCE in Secondary Education (Religious Education with Humanities) V6X1

1 year full-time
As above

PGCE in Secondary Education (Science: Biology with Physics and Chemistry) C1X1

1 year full-time
As above

PGCE in Secondary Education (Science: Chemistry with Physics and Biology) FX11

1 year full-time
As above

PGCE in Secondary Education (Science: Physics with Chemistry and Biology) FX31

1 year full-time
As above

PGCE in Secondary Education French PGCE/Maitrise FLE RXCC

1 year full-time

Entry requirements: Degree or equivalent including a substantial element of French, plus English and mathematics at GCSE grade C or above (or equivalent).
Contact: As above

MA in School Development

Part-time

Entry requirements: Honours degree.
Contact: Suzanne Stokes
    Tel: 01227 767700 x2886
    Email: sjs24@cant.ac.uk

MA in Enabling Learning

Part-time
As above

MA in Subject Leadership

Part-time
As above

MA in Management Studies

Part-time
As above

MA in Philosophy

Part-time
As above

PgDip/MA in Career Education Development and Guidance

MA: 7–15 terms part-time

Entry requirements: Degree with recognised teaching qualification or equivalent professional award; candidates with M-level credits may apply for exemption of up to 50% of the programme.
Contact: Barry Irving
    01892 507504
    b.irving@cant.ac.uk

PgDip/MA (Ed) in Education

MA: 2–6 years part-time

Entry requirements: Honours degree.
Contact: Alun Davies
    01227 782497

PgCert/PgDip/MA in Educational Studies

3 years part-time

Entry reqs: Normally applicants are qualified teachers, although the course may also interest other education professionals, including those from higher education.
Contact: Suzanne Stokes
    Tel: 01227 767700 x2886
    Email: sjs24@cant.ac.uk

PgCert/PgDip/MA in Literacy and Learning

Part-time

Entry reqs: Applicants must be qualified teachers with a first degree and a professional interest in literacy, for example, they may be their school's literacy co-ordinator.
Contact: 01227 767700 x2008

PgDip/MA in Management Studies (Education)

2 years part-time

Entry requirements: Qualified teachers acting in management capacity; or degree or relevant professional qualification and management position in educational context.
Contact: Phil Holden
    01227 782497
    a.c.davies@cant.ac.uk

PgDip/MA in School Development

2 years part-time

Entry requirements: Qualified Teacher Status and, normally, not less than 3 years' experience.
Contact: Angela Barker
    01227 782318
    a.barker@cant.ac.uk

University of Wales Institute, Cardiff

Western Avenue
Cardiff
CF5 2SG
Tel: 029 2041 6070
Fax: 029 2041 6286
uwicinfo@uwic.ac.uk
www.uwic.ac.uk

The University of Wales Institute, Cardiff caters for over 23,000 students. It operates from four main campuses, Colchester Avenue, Cyncoed, Howard Gardens and Llandaff. In addition it has Plas Gwyn, a residential campus with en-suite accommodation, and the small campus at Fairwater, which is used for company conferences and training seminars, as well as providing extra student accommodation.

The School of Education is based at Cyncoed and offers degree courses and PGCEs as well as a range of taught and research postgraduate programmes. The school has its own library and computer facilities and each course within the school has specialist resources.

Students can apply for accommodation in halls of residence and there is also privately rented accommodation available off campus. The Accommodation Office will help to find suitable living arrangements for the students.

HOW TO APPLY

Degree courses: applications are made through UCAS.
PGCE: applications are made through GTTR.
Postgraduate: applications are made direct to the institution.

COURSES

BA (Hons) in Primary Education X120
3 years full-time

Course addresses the full primary age range in the first year (ages 3–11), with later opportunities to specialise in either Early

Years (3–7) or Key Stage 2 (7–11). Further provision in Year 3 is available for specialising in the teaching of under-5s.

School-based work: Over the 3 years, students spend at least 131 days working in local schools. This involves serial days and block practices. Opportunity exists for school practice abroad.

College-based studies: 30 modules are studied with 10 at each of the 3 levels, including subject studies (below) and education studies, which address aspects of child development, teaching competences and wider professional perspectives. There is also provision for Welsh learners and teaching support for study skills, written English language and subject tutorials.

Level 1: All subjects of the primary curriculum are studied, with special emphasis on National Curriculum core subjects.

Levels 2 and 3: Students specialise in 1 teaching subject chosen from the following list: mathematics; religious education; geography; physical education; English; design technology; science; music; art; history; Welsh.

Successful completion of this course leads to a recommendation for Qualified Teacher Status (QTS) after completion of skills tests.

Entry requirements: GCE A- and AS- levels: CC, International Baccalaureate, BTEC NC/ND, SCE Higher: CCCC
Contact: Mrs Margaret Hannay
029 2041 6583
mhannay@uwic.ac.uk

BA (Hons) in Secondary Education (Drama) X1W9
4 years full-time

Subject studied from an academic and practical perspective; elements of theatre history; textual analysis; dramatic genres/playwrights; cultural context of drama; practical exploration of dramatic performance; devising, scripting and development of theatre-in-education programmes enable students to take on role of actor/teachers.

Students are placed in partnership schools in the South Wales area for 4 separate placements. Year 1: serial visits; Year 2: block practice; Year 3: group residency; Year 4: 9-week block practice.

Successful completion of this course leads to a recommendation for Qualified Teacher Status (QTS) after completion of skills tests.

Entry requirements: As above
Contact: Mitch Winfield
029 2041 6535
mwinfield@uwic.ac.uk

BA/BA (Hons) Secondary Education (French) X1R1

2 to 3 years full-time

Course covers subject knowledge, professional understanding and skills.

Level 1: Subject knowledge; information and communications technology; secondary school studies.

Level 2: Subject knowledge; educational and professional studies; secondary partnerships (observation and block teaching placement).

Level 3: Subject knowledge; classroom skills; school placement.

Successful completion of this course leads to a recommendation for Qualified Teacher Status (QTS) after completion of skills tests.

Entry requirements: GCE A- and AS- levels, Age restriction
Contact: Dawn Sadler
Course Director
029 2041 6546
Dsadler@uwic.ac.uk

BA/BA (Hons) in Secondary Education (Music) X1W3

2 years full-time

The course covers subject knowledge, professional understanding and skills.

Successful completion of this course leads to a recommendation for Qualified Teacher Status (QTS) after completion of skills tests.

Entry requirements: As above

Contact: Carol Roese
Course Director
029 2041 6554
croese@uwic.ac.uk

BA/BA (Hons) in Secondary Education (Welsh) X1Q5

2 years full-time
As above

PGCE in Post-Compulsory Education and Training

2 years part-time

Entry requirements: Course is for serving teachers and intending teachers in post-compulsory sector of education and training.
Contact: Mary Carter
Course Director
029 2050 6576
mcarter@uwic.ac.uk

PGCE in Primary Education (3–11) X100

1 year full-time

Entry requirements: Degree from an approved university and GCSE grade C or equivalent in mathematics and English language.
Contact: Mrs Eleri Betts
Course Director
029 2041 6545
uwicinfo@uwic.ac.uk

PGCE in Secondary Education (Art and Design) W1X1

1 year full-time

Entry requirements: Honours degree in art and design; applications also considered from graduates in art history, architecture or related disciplines provided studio work formed a significant component. Additionally, candidates must possess GCSE grade C or above, or the equivalent, in English language and mathematics; students over 25 not holding those qualifications may take an Institute test in either literacy or numeracy.

Contact: Mr P Herrington
Subject Co-ordinator, Art and
Design
029 2041 6518
pherrington@uwic.ac.uk

PGCE in Secondary Education (Design and Technology) W9X1

1 year full-time

Entry requirements: Degree in related discipline required, plus GCSE grade C or above in mathematics and English language, or equivalent.

Contact: Dr Paul Jones
Subject Co-ordinator, Design
and Technology
029 2050 6556
pajones@uwic.ac.uk

PGCE in Secondary Education (English) Q3X1

1 year full-time

Entry requirements: Degree in English or where English has been a substantial component of the course; GCSE grade C (or equivalent) in mathematics and English.

Contact: Lesley James
Subject Co-ordinator, English
029 2041 6526
lcjames@uwic.ac.uk

PGCE in Secondary Education (History) V1X1

1 year full-time

Entry requirements: Degree in history, or where history has been substantial part of course; GCSE grade C (or equivalent) in mathematics and English language.

Contact: Dr Sian Rhiannon Williams
Subject Co-ordinator, History
029 2050 6527
srwilliams@uwic.ac.uk

PGCE in Secondary Education (Mathematics) G1X1

1 year full-time

Entry requirements: Degree in mathematics or where mathematics has been a substantial part of the course; GCSE grade C (or equivalent) in mathematics and English.

Contact: Dr A Cooke
Subject Co-ordinator,
Mathematics
029 2050 6552
arcooke@uwic.ac.uk

PGCE in Secondary Education (Modern Foreign Languages) R9X1

1 year full-time

Entry requirements: Relevant good Honours degree or equivalent, plus GCSE grade C or equivalent in mathematics and English; applications from foreign nationals welcomed.

Contact: Mrs L James
Subject Co-ordinator, Modern
Foreign Languages
029 2050 6546
ljames@uwic.ac.uk

PGCE in Secondary Education (Music) W3X1

1 year full-time

Entry requirements: Relevant good Honours degree plus GCSE grade C or equivalent in mathematics and English.

Contact: Mr P Thomas
Subject Co-ordinator, Music
029 2050 6513
pthomas@uwic.ac.uk

PGCE in Secondary Education (Physical Education) X9C6

1 year full-time

Entry requirements: Degree from approved university in sports-related area of which at least half must be physical education; plus grade C in GCSE mathematics and English or equivalent.

Contact: Ms J S Gadd
Subject Co-ordinator, PE
029 2050 6077
jgadd@uwic.ac.uk

PGCE in Secondary Education (Science) F0X1

1 year full-time

Entry requirements: Degree in science subject plus mathematics and English at GCSE grade C or equivalent.

Contact: Ms Kin Yu
Subject Co-ordinator, Science
029 2050 6567
kyu@uwic.ac.uk

PGCE in Secondary Education (Welsh) Q5X1

1 year full-time

Entry requirements: Degree in Welsh or where Welsh has been a substantial part of course, plus mathematics and English at GCSE grade C or equivalent.

Contact: Mrs H Jones
Subject Co-ordinator, Welsh
029 2050 6528
hcjones@uwic.ac.uk

PgC/PgD/MA in Education

Part-time

Entry requirements: Good Honours degree in an appropriate discipline and Qualified Teacher Status. Applicants without degree qualifications may be considered if they are able to demonstrate an appropriate high level of education involvement. All students will be expected to provide an outline of their potential research focus.

Contact: Mr C Harris
Course Director
029 2041 6780
cjharris@uwic.ac.uk

MA in Education (Art and Design)

1 year full-time, 2–5 years part-time

Entry requirements: Good Honours degree in related discipline and/or appropriate experience.

Contact: Mr P Carter
Subject Leader, Art and Design Education
029 2041 6509
pcarter@uwic.ac.uk

PgC/PgD in Media Education

PgD: 2 years distance learning

Entry requirements: Constitutes part of professional development programme for serving teachers; APL/APEL procedures apply.

Contact: L C James
Course Leader
029 2041 6526
lcjames@uwic.ac.uk

University of Central England in Birmingham

Perry Barr
Birmingham
B42 2SU
Tel: 0121 331 5000
Fax: 0121 356 2875
prospectus@uce.ac.uk
www.uce.ac.uk

Birmingham Polytechnic was designated in 1971 and was initially formed out of five colleges, the Birmingham College of Art, the Birmingham School of Music, the Birmingham College of Commerce, South Birmingham Technical College and North Birmingham Technical College. In 1975 Birmingham City Council introduced a further three colleges into the Polytechnic: the Anstey College of Physical Education, the Bordesley College of Education and the City of Birmingham College of Education. In 1988 Bournville College of Art merged with the Faculty of Art and Design to create the Birmingham Institute of Art and Design and in 1992, university status was awarded. It has since merged with two more colleges, the Birmingham and Solihull College of Nursing and Midwifery and the West Midlands School of Radiography. The University is based on several sites.

The Faculty of Education is based at the Perry Barr campus. Courses cover the entire range of school age-phases from infant to continuing education at every study level from undergraduate to PhD.

Library and computer resources are provided at the university sites and each faculty has computing resources for learning support within its area. Accommodation is available in halls or flats, including some for postgraduate students.

HOW TO APPLY

Degree courses: applications are made through UCAS.

PGCE: applications are made through the GTTR.

Postgraduate: applications are made direct to the institution.

COURSES

BA (Hons) in Primary Education X120

4 years full-time

Choice of 1 option: Art; geography; design and technology; history; English; drama with English; mathematics; music; religious education.

Trains teachers to teach in the 3–11 age range. All students study the core subjects of mathematics, English and science. Special subject studies are designed to train potential subject co-ordinators. Emphasis is given throughout the course to practical experience in schools and all students experience placements in both early years/ National Curriculum Key Stage 1 (3–8 years) and National Curriculum Key Stage 2 (7–11 years).

Successful completion of this course leads to a recommendation for Qualified Teacher Status (QTS) after completion of skills tests.

Entry requirements: Tariff: 160 points, BTEC NC/ND, CCCCC: Irish Leaving Certificates, Foundation / access, qualification, International Baccalaureate, SCE Higher.

Contact: Janet Hill
　　　　Admissions Officer
　　　　0121 33 7300/7315
　　　　janet.hill@uce.ac.uk

PGCE in Post-compulsory Education X341

1 year full-time or 2 years part-time

Entry requirements: Degree from a UK Higher Education institution or a recognised equivalent; grade C GCSE (or its equivalent) in English and mathematics; applicants must also teach for at least 160 hours during course.

Contact: Shulay Crane
　　　　0121 331 7300/7396
　　　　shulay.crane@uce.ac.uk

PGCE in Primary Education (Early Years, 3–8) X110

1 year full-time or 2 years part-time

Entry requirements: Degree from a UK higher education institution in early childhood studies or education: content of entrants' previous education should provide the necessary foundation for work as an early years teacher together with GCSE at grade C or above (or its equivalent) in English and mathematics and, for those born after 1/9/79, similar GCSE qualification in 1 or more science subjects also required; applicants should indicate relevant experience in at least 1 early years setting.

Contact: Kolina Garbutt
　　　　Course Director
　　　　0121 331 7300
　　　　janet.hill@uce.ac.uk

PGCE in Primary Education (General Primary, 5–11) X100

1 year full-time

Entry requirements: Applicants should have a degree or equivalent qualification recognised by the Department for Education and Skills and an education providing the necessary foundation for work as a primary school teacher. GCSE grade C or above (or equivalent) in mathematics and English language required.

Contact: Lynn Fulford
　　　　Course Director
　　　　0121 331 7300/7312
　　　　Janet.Hill@uce.ac.uk

PGCE in Secondary Education (Art and Design) W1X1

1 year full-time

Entry requirements: Applicants should have a degree in an appropriate area of study, relevant background experience/interest and, in addition, GCSE minimum grade C (or equivalent) in English language and mathematics.

Contact: Linda Watts
Admissions Officer
0121 331 5801
webmaster@uce.ac.uk

PGCE in Secondary Education (Drama) W4X1

1 year full-time

Entry requirements: Applicants should normally have a degree or an acceptable equivalent qualification in which drama forms a substantial part. They must also have GCSE at grade C or above (or equivalent) in English language and mathematics (those without these qualifications are offered a special Faculty test). All applicants should be committed to the educational value of drama and have an enthusiasm for working with children.

Contact: Simon Spencer
Course Director
0121 331 7356
Janet.Hill@uce.ac.uk

PGCE in Secondary Education (Music) W3X1

1 year full-time

Entry requirements: Applicants should have a degree or approved graduate diploma in music from a UK University or institution of similar recognised status or have graduated in the arts with a substantial proportion of the degree content having been devoted to studies in music. GCSE grade C or above, or equivalent, required in mathematics and English language.

Contact: As above

PgDip/MA Art and Education

1 year full-time or 2 years part-time

Entry requirements: Normally, appropriate degree or equivalent, teaching qualification and/or previous or concurrent teaching experience required; applications welcomed from those with less conventional educational backgrounds but extensive experience in visual arts/education.

Contact: Monica Keating
Course Director
0121 331 5802/6980
webmaster@uce.ac.uk

PgCert/PgDip/MA Drama in Education

1 year full-time or 2–6 years part-time

Entry requirements: Qualified Teacher Status (via degree or certificate) and teaching experience required.

Contact: Steve Lewis
Course Director
0121 331 7339
kerri.law@uce.ac.uk

PgCert/PgDip/MA Education

PgCert: 1–2 years part-time; PgDip: 3–4 years part-time; MA: 4–6 years part-time

Entry requirements: Degree, UCE Diploma/Certificate, Qualified Teacher Status plus significant experience or other equivalent professional qualification and at least 2 years' work experience.

Contact: Helen Coll
Course Director
0121 331 7339
kerri.law@uce.ac.uk

Central School of Speech and Drama

Embassy Theatre
Eton Avenue
Camden
London NW3 3HY
Tel: 020 7722 8183
Fax: 020 7722 4132
www.cssd.ac.uk

The Central School of Speech and Drama was founded in 1906. The School has two sites in London: the main site at Swiss Cottage and a second site at the Oval site at Kennington Park. Both are within easy access of Central London, so students can take advantage of the easy access to London's social activities.

The School offers undergraduate, postgraduate and teacher training courses. The School Learning and Information Services provide facilities for all course information and communication needs. There is a library and an open-access computer room at the Swiss Cottage site and there is access to all other resources at the Oval site. Although the school does not have accommodation, it can assist with finding residences.

HOW TO APPLY

PGCE: applications are made through the GTTR.

Postgraduate: applications are made direct to the institution.

COURSES

PGCE in Drama (Secondary Education) W4X1

1 year full-time.

Entry requirements: Degree in drama or closely related studies plus GCSE grade C or above (or equivalent) in English language and mathematics; preferably some experience of working with children and young people.
Contact: Pam Shaw
　　　　Course Tutor
　　　　020 7559 3957
　　　　p.shaw@cssd.ac.uk

PGCE in Media Education with English (Secondary Education) P3X1

1 year full-time

Entry requirements: Relevant Honours degree plus GCSE grade C or above (or equivalent) in English language and mathematics; preferably some experience with working with children and young people.
Contact: Symon Quy
　　　　Course Tutor
　　　　020 7559 5964
　　　　s.quy@cssd.ac.uk

PgCert/PgDip/MA in Applied Theatre and Drama Education

1 year full-time, 5 years part-time, 5 years distance learning

Entry requirements: Degree in a relevant subject normally required; programme is designed to serve the needs of teachers, lecturers, arts education professionals, performers and administrators in a range of professional settings in drama, theatre, media and arts education.
Contact: Amanda Stuart-Fisher
　　　　Course Tutor
　　　　020 7559 3960
　　　　a.stuart@cssd.ac.uk

PgCert in Learning and Teaching in Higher Education

2 terms part-time

Entry requirements: Intended for those working in Higher Education, particularly in fields of art and design, performing arts and related humanities; 6–12 months' teaching experience usually required.
Contact: Pam Shaw
　　　　Course Tutor
　　　　020 7722 8183
　　　　p.shaw@cssd.ac.uk

Centre for British Teachers

CfBT Educational Services
Unit 1, The Chambers
East Street
Reading
RG1 4JD
Tel: 0118 902 1649
Fax: 0118 902 1732
pgce@cfbt.org.uk
www.cfbt.com

The Centre for British Teachers was founded in 1965 and is an independent provider of education and training services. Its headquarters are based in Reading but it currently has operations in over 20 countries.

The Centre offers employment-based courses leading to Qualified Teacher Status. There are various training routes available: the PGCE at secondary level validated by the University of Surrey, Roehampton and Graduate Teacher, Registered Teacher or Overseas Trained Teacher programmes.

HOW TO APPLY

All applications are made direct to the institution.

COURSES

PGCE in Secondary Education (Classics)

1 year full-time

Entry requirements: Degree in relevant subject or evidence of equivalent experience; GCSE grade C or above in English language and mathematics, and science if born after 1/9/79.

Contact: Enquiries
0118 902 1649
pgce@cfbt-hq.org.uk

PGCE in Secondary Education (Mathematics)

1 year full-time
As above

PGCE in Secondary Education (Modern Foreign Languages)

1 year full-time
As above

PGCE in Secondary Education (Music)

1 year full-time
As above

PGCE in Secondary Education (Science)

1 year full-time
As above

Chester College

Parkgate Road
Chester
Cheshire
CH1 4BJ
Tel: 01244 375444
Fax: 01244 392820
enquiries@chester.ac.uk
www.chester.ac.uk

Chester College was founded in 1839 and is based on a self-contained campus only a short walk from the city walls. In recent years, the College has developed a new Library and Media Centre, new academic buildings and new sports facilities. The College has expanded its higher education provision through a merger with the Faculty of Higher Education at Warrington Collegiate Institute in 2002.

Accommodation is available on both the main campus and the Warrington campus. Students can also opt to live in halls or College-owned houses a few minutes' walk from Chester campus or in private accommodation nearby.

The School of Education offers Initial Teacher Training courses, programmes for Continuing Professional Development and courses at undergraduate level. Within the school is the Educational Research Unit. It is a regional centre is the focus for research for the school, partner Local Education Authorities, schools and teachers.

HOW TO APPLY

Degree: applications are made through UCAS.
PGCE: applications are made through the GTTR.

Postgraduate: applications are made direct to the institution.

COURSES

BEd (Hons) in Early Years Education (3–7) X100

4 years full-time

The programme has 5 main components: school experience; professional development education; core subjects (mathematics, English and science); information and communications technology (ICT); foundation subjects and religious education; plus specialist subject.

Entry requirements: Tariff: 200 points; BTEC NC/ND, Irish Leaving Certificates: CCCC, SCE Highers: CCCC, Foundation / access qualification.
Contact: Helen Ellis
01244 375444 x3527
h.ellis@chester.ac.uk

PGCE in Primary Education (General Primary, 5–11) X100

1 year full-time

Entry requirements: Good Honours degree (minimum 2:1) which should provide the necessary foundation for work as primary school teacher; GCSE grade C or above (or equivalent) in mathematics, English language and science; candidates must gain experience of working in primary schools before making formal application.
Contact: As above

PGCE in Secondary Education (Art) W1X1

1 year full-time

Entry requirements: Relevant Honours degree (minimum 2:2); GCSE grade C or above, or equivalent in mathematics and English language; 2 weeks' experience in a secondary school.
Contact: As above

PGCE in Secondary Education (Drama) W4X1

1 year full-time
As above

PGCE in Secondary Education (Mathematics) G1X1

Part-time or 1 year full-time
As above

PGCE in Secondary Education (Mathematics, 14–19) G1XC

1 year full-time
As above

PGCE in Secondary Education (Modern Languages: French with German) RX11

1 year full-time
As above

PGCE in Secondary Education (Modern Languages: French with Spanish) RXD1

1 year full-time
As above

PGCE in Secondary Education (Modern Languages: French) R1X1

1 year full-time
As above

PGCE in Secondary Education (Modern Languages: German with French) RX21

1 year full-time
As above

PGCE in Secondary Education (Modern Languages: German with Spanish) RXG1

1 year full-time
As above

PGCE in Secondary Education (Modern Languages: German) R2X1

1 year full-time
As above

PGCE in Secondary Education (Modern Languages: Spanish with French) RX41

1 year full-time
As above

PGCE in Secondary Education (Modern Languages: Spanish with German) RX4C

1 year full-time
As above

PGCE in Secondary Education (Modern Languages: Spanish) R4X1

1 year full-time
As above

PGCE in Secondary Education (Physical Education) X9C6
1 year full-time
As above

PGCE in Secondary Education (Physical Education, 14–19) C6X1
1 year full-time
As above

PGCE in Secondary Education (Religious Education) V6X1
1 year full-time
As above

Certificate in Advanced Study/Diploma in Advanced Study/PgCert/PgDip/MA in Adult Education with Theological Reflection

Certificate: 2 years distance learning, Diploma: 4 years distance learning, MA: 6 years distance learning

Entry requirements: Degree in theology or education (or university experience or qualifications); or accumulated experience of teaching within Christian communities.

Contact: Postgraduate Office
01244 375444 x3510
postgrad@chester.ac.uk

Pgcert/PgDip/MA in Church School Education
2–6 years distance learning

Entry requirements: Degree in theology or education; other candidates considered.

Contact: As above

Certificate in Advanced Study/Diploma in Advanced Study/PgCert/PgDip/MEd in Education

Certificate: 2 years part-time, Diploma: 4 years part-time, MEd: 1 year full-time, 2–6 years part-time

Entry requirements: Open to graduates and non-graduates with professional experience.

Contact: CPD Administrator
01244 375444 x3579

University College Chichester

Bishop Otter Campus
College Lane
Chichester
W. Sussex
PO19 6PE
Tel: 01243 816000
Fax: 01243 816080
admissions@ucc.ac.uk
www.ucc.ac.uk

University College Chichester was founded in 1976 as the West Sussex Institute of Higher Education following the merger of Bishop Otter College Chichester and Bognor Regis College which are now the two campuses of the University College. The title University College Chichester was approved in 1999.

Teacher Education courses at Chichester include programmes for classroom assist-
ants, teaching degrees, the PGCE and Masters and Continuing Professional Development courses for current teachers.

Both campuses provide extensive academic facilities including libraries and computer suites and the Bognor Regis Campus houses the Education Technology Centre and an Education Practice Base. The campus and surrounding local area provide a range of recreational facilities. Accommodation is available in University College residences, rented accommodation and lodgings.

HOW TO APPLY
Degree courses: applications are made through UCAS.

PGCE: applications are made through the GTTR.

Postgraduate: applications are made direct to the institution.

COURSES

BA (Hons) in Mathematics (Key Stage 2/3) G1X1

3 years full-time

Course covers teaching the core subjects of the primary curriculum as well as issues concerning mathematics education; students spend time in school and there are sessions which cover general teaching skills and knowledge; information technology has a high profile throughout the course and students are trained to use computers and education technology for both personal and teaching work.

Successful completion of this course leads to a recommendation for Qualified Teacher Status (QTS) after completion of skills tests.

Entry requirements: Tariff: 160–200
Contact: Admissions
01243 816002

BA (Hons) in Physical Education and Education (Secondary) XC16

4 years full-time

Year 1: Introduction to sport and society; philosophical and research perspectives in physical education; individual and group processes in sport; analysis of human performance-games; principles of movement and skills of observation; introduction to physiology; education: secondary school, teacher and pupil; analysis of human performance-gym/dance.

Year 2: Curriculum skills and knowledge in physical education; psychology of skill acquisition; school experience (9 weeks); analysis of team games; analysis of human performance (outdoor activities); analysis of human performance (track and field, swimming). Elective options: exercise prescription for health and fitness; the social construction of sport; social psychology of coaching and learning.

Year 3: Pedagogical skills in physical education (gym and dance); developmental physiology; analysis of human performance-selected sports; pedagogical skills in physical education; professional issues-research and enquiry in physical education; school experience (9 weeks). Elective options: physiology of training for young people; youth and community sport policy; analysis of coaching practice.

Year 4: Personal study/contextual; enquiry; pedagogical skills in physical education; personal study/professional reflection; school experience (14 weeks).

Successful completion of this course leads to a recommendation for Qualified Teacher Status (QTS) after completion of skills tests.

Entry requirements: BTEC NC/ND, GCE A- and AS- levels: CC, International Baccalaureate, SCE Higher.
Contact: As above

BA (Hons) in Primary Education (Advanced Study of Early Years, ages 3–8) X121

3 years full-time

Successful completion of this course leads to a recommendation for Qualified Teacher Status (QTS) after completion of skills tests.

Entry requirements: Tariff: 240, BTEC NC/ND
Contact: As above

BA (Hons) in Primary Education (English, Key Stage 1/2) Q3X1

3 years full-time
As above

Entry requirements: Tariff: 240
Contact: As above

BA (Hons) in Primary Education (Geography, Key Stage 1/2) L7X1

3 years full-time
As above

BA (Hons) in Primary Education (Information Communications Technology, Key Stage 1/2) G5X1

3 years full-time
As above

BA (Hons) in Primary Education (Mathematics, Key Stage 1/2) G1XC

3 years full-time
As above

PGCE in Primary Education (Advanced Study of Early Years) X110

1 year full-time

Entry requirements: Degree with at least 50% of the modules in a subject taught at primary level. GCSEs in English language, mathematics and science (if born after 1st September, 1979); relevant experience in a state sector UK school preferred.
Contact: As above

PGCE in Primary Education (Information Communications Technology) XG15

1 year full-time

Entry requirements: As above
Contact: Barbara Thompson
01243 816235

MA (Ed) in Education

8 terms part-time

Entry requirements: For classroom teachers.
Contact: Dr Chris Gaine
01243 816000

PgCert/PgDip/MA in Mathematics Education

Part-time

Entry requirements: UK degree or approved equivalent required and either Qualified Teacher Status and minimum 2 years' teaching experience or equivalent professional experience in field of education.
Contact: Admissions
01243 816002

Chiltern Training Group

c/o Challney High School for Boys
Stoneygate Road
Luton
LU4 9TJ
Tel: 01582 493680
Fax: 01582 493680
chilterntraining@yahoo.co.uk

The Chiltern Training Group is a consortium of schools in the South Bedfordshire area. It runs a School Centred Initial Teacher Training course leading to the Postgraduate Certificate in Education awarded by the Univerisity of Luton.

Students are allocated a base school in which they spend the majority of their training.

Support is provided by trained and experienced mentors and each base school has a Professional Tutor who co-ordinates the work of the mentors in their school and oversees the whole experience of the trainees.

HOW TO APPLY

Applications are made through the GTTR.

COURSES

PGCE in Secondary Education (Art) W1X1

1 year full-time

Entry requirements: Degree relevant to subject to be taught, plus GCSE grade C or above (or equivalent) in English language and mathematics.
Contact: Nigel Jones
Chiltern Training Group Art Coordinator
01582 493680
ctg.challney@excite.co.uk

PGCE in Secondary Education (Design and Technology: Food, Resistant Materials and Textiles) W9X1

1 year full-time

Entry requirements: Degree relevant to subject to be taught, plus GCSE grade C or above (or equivalent) in English language and mathematics.
Contact: Mr Steve Davies
Chiltern Training Group Coordinator (Design and Technology)
01582 493680
chilterntraining@yahoo.co.uk

PGCE in Secondary Education (English) Q3X1

1 year full-time

Entry requirements: Degree relevant to subject to be taught, plus GCSE grade C or above (or equivalent) in English language and mathematics.

Contact: Mrs Patrice Evans
Course Co-ordinator (English)
01582 599921
chilterntraining@yahoo.co.uk

PGCE in Secondary Education (Geography) F8X1

1 year full-time

Entry requirements: Degree relevant to subject to be taught, plus GCSE grade C or above (or equivalent) in English language and mathematics.

Contact: Dave Hawkes
Chiltern Training Group Co-ordinator (Geography)
01582 493680
ctg.challney@excite.co.uk

PGCE in Secondary Education (Information Communications Technology) G5X1

1 year full-time

Entry requirements: Degree relevant to subject to be taught, plus GCSE grade C or above (or equivalent) in English language and mathematics.

Contact: Mrs Jackie Rainbow
Chiltern Training Group Co-ordinator (ICT)
01582 599921
chilterntraining@yahoo.co.uk

PGCE in Secondary Education (Mathematics) G1X1

1 year full-time

Entry requirements: Degree relevant to subject to be taught, plus GCSE grade C or above (or equivalent) in English language and mathematics.

Contact: Mr Bob Carson
Chiltern Training Group
Mathematics Co-ordinator

01582 599921
chilterntraining@yahoo.co.uk

PGCE in Secondary Education (Modern Languages) R9X1

1 year full-time

Entry requirements: Degree relevant to subject to be taught, plus GCSE grade C or above (or equivalent) in English language and mathematics.

Contact: Mrs Jacqui Warren
Chiltern Training Group Co-ordinator (MFL)
01582 599921
chilterntraining@yahoo.co.uk

PGCE in Secondary Education (Physical Education) X9C6

1 year full-time

Entry requirements: Degree relevant to subject to be taught, plus GCSE grade C or above (or equivalent) in English language and mathematics.

Contact: Mr John Greetham
Chiltern Training Group Co-ordinator (Physical Education)
01582 599921
chilterntraining@yahoo.co.uk

PGCE in Secondary Education (Religious Education) V6X1

1 year full-time

Entry requirements: Degree relevant to subject to be taught, plus GCSE grade C or above (or equivalent) in English language and mathematics.

Contact: Tina Johns
Chiltern Training Group Co-ordinator (Religious Education)
01582 599921
chilterntraining@yahoo.co.uk

PGCE in Secondary Education (Science, General) FOX1

1 year full-time

Entry requirements: Degree relevant to subject to be taught, plus GCSE grade C or above (or equivalent) in English language and mathematics.

Contact: Brenda Wreaves
Chiltern Training Group
Co-ordinator (Science)

01582 599921
chilterntraining@yahoo.co.uk

Cornwall School Centred Initial Teacher Training

Truro College
College Road
Truro
TR1 3XX
Tel: 01872 267092
Fax: 01872 267059
lindar@trurocollege.ac.uk
www.cornwallscitt.org.uk

Cornwall School Centred Initial Teacher Training is a consortium of 12 local secondary schools and one tertiary college offering opportunities in 11–16 and 11–18 teaching. The course is focused on practical classroom experience within at least two secondary schools, which is further supported by academic study via central training.

HOW TO APPLY

Applications are made direct to the consortium.

COURSES

PGCE in Secondary Education (Design and Technology)

1 year full-time

Entry requirements: Degree in National Curriculum subject; GCSE English and mathematics grade C; relevant school experience or evidence of work with children.

Contact: Linda Robbins
Administrator
01872 267092
lindar@trurocollege.ac.uk

PGCE in Secondary Education (English)

As above

PGCE in Secondary Education (Mathematics)

As above

PGCE in Secondary Education (Modern Languages: French, German, Spanish)

As above

PGCE in Secondary Education (Science)

As above

Crawley College

College Road
Crawley
West Sussex
RH10 1NR
Tel: 01293 442200
Fax: 01293 442399
information@crawley-college.ac.uk
www.crawley-college.ac.uk

Crawley College has four campuses: the main Crawley College site, West Green Centre, Arun House and East Grinstead Learning Centre. All the campuses are within easy reach of local bus and train stations. Learning Resource Centres on each site provide library facilities and computers for internet and private study use.

The college accommodation service can help students find rooms within family homes in the Crawley/Horsham area on either a full-board or self-catering basis. The Students' Association provides social, recreational and cultural facilities. Sports are arranged in conjunction with Crawley Leisure Centre, where students have access to the swimming pool and gym.

The college offers degrees in primary education as well as a part-time Certificate for teachers in the post-compulsory sector.

HOW TO APPLY

Degree courses: applications are made through UCAS.

Certificate: applications are made direct to the institution.

COURSES

BA (Hons) in Primary Teaching (English/Education, Early Years, 3–8 years) X300

4 years full-time

This is a modular degree, in which students consider all aspects of primary education, undertake block teaching practices and are required to specialise in a particular subject study.

Successful completion of this course leads to a recommendation for Qualified Teacher Status (QTS) after completion of the 1st year of teaching.

Entry requirements: BTEC NC/ND, CC: GCE A- and AS-levels, Foundation / access qualification

Contact: Vince Hanley
Head of Department
01293 442277
vbrady@crawley-college.ac.uk

BA (Hons) in Primary Teaching (English/ Education, Key Stage 2, 7–11 years) X500

4 years full-time
As above

Entry requirements: BTEC NC/ND, CC: GCE A- and AS-levels, Foundation / access qualification

Contact: Vince Hanley
Head of Department
01293 442277
vbrady@crawley-college.ac.uk

Cumbria Primary Teacher Training

High Street
Workington
Cumbria
CA14 4ES
Tel: 01900 325060
Fax: 01900 325061
enquiries@cptt.org.uk
www.cptt.org.uk

The Cumbria Primary Teacher Training course is a school-based course set up by a consortium of schools in the Western Lakes and Solway Coast who were anxious to contribute towards Initial Teacher Training but were geographically isolated from existing colleges. The training centre gives access to the Lakes, the coast and Scotland. A wide range of accommodation is available in the area covered by the schools used in course. A list of properties to rent is available from the College's Administration Centre.

The course offers trainees opportunities to become involved in the life of primary schools. Trainees spend nearly twenty weeks in school, allowing them to develop a strong professional bond with teachers and pupils.

HOW TO APPLY

Applications are made direct to the consortium.

COURSES

PGCE in Primary Education

1 year full-time

Entry requirements: Degree; GCSE grade C or above in English, mathematics and science; experience of working with children.

Contact: Enquiries
01900 325060
enquiries@cptt.org.uk

De Montfort University, Bedford

37 Lansdowne Road
Bedford
MK40 2BZ
Tel: 01234 351966
Fax: 01234 793277
admissions@dmu.ac.uk
www.dmu.ac.uk

De Montfort University, Bedford caters for around 3,000 students and is based at two campuses, Lansdowne and Polhill, which are both within walking distance of the town centre. Its history can be traced back to the founding of Bedford Training College for Teachers in 1882 and Bedford Physical Training College in 1903.

The School of Education offers a range of courses including degree courses, initial teacher training via degree or PGCE routes, Graduate Teacher Programmes and also opportunities in Continuing Professional Development through a selection of postgraduate courses.

DMU Bedford's facilities are either campus-based or are within a short distance from either campus. There are extensive academic facilities as well as opportunities for sport and leisure. Accommodation is available in university halls of residence or in privately rented properties.

HOW TO APPLY

Degree courses: applications are made through UCAS.
PGCE: applications are made through the GTTR.
Postgraduate: applications are made direct to the institution.

COURSES

BA (Hons) in Physical Education (Secondary) X1C6 B

4 years full-time

Physical education covers a wide spectrum of activities, including: hockey; netball; soccer; rugby; swimming; athletics; dance; gymnastics; tennis; squash; badminton; basketball; volleyball; sailing; canoeing; yoga; aerobics. The practical work is supported by related theory in physical education. Professional studies and school experience: students develop the basic skills of teaching and gain an understanding of how children grow and learn. School experience supports the university-based work. There are small-scale teaching exercises, extended school placements and structured observation tasks. Professional studies include elements which deal specifically with the teaching of physical education.

Successful completion leads to a recommendation for Qualified Teacher Status (QTS) on completion of skills tests.

Entry requirements: Tariff: 220 to 320 points, BTEC NC/ND, European Baccalaureate, International Baccalaureate, Interview, Mature entry
Contact: Admissions
01234 793279
bed-admissions@dmu.ac.uk

BEd (Hons) in Primary Education X120 B

4 years full-time

Students gain a good understanding of all National Curriculum subjects and have the opportunity to become specialist in 2 subject areas; the course is currently divided into 4 areas: professional studies, school-based experience, curriculum studies, subject studies.

Entry requirements: Tariff: 180 to 240 points, BTEC NC/ND, Irish Leaving Certificates: CCCCC, European Baccalaureate, International Baccalaureate, Mature entry
Contact: As above

PGCE in Middle Years (Key Stages 2/3, 7–14) X180 B

1 year full-time

Entry requirements: 2nd Class Honours degree including 50% of study in a subject relevant to the National Curriculum; GCSE grade C (or equivalent) in English and mathematics, and for candidates born after 1/9/79, science; some experience of working with children.

Contact: Recruitment and Admissions
01234 793279
bed-admissions@dmu.ac.uk

PGCE in Post-Compulsory Education

2 years part-time

Entry requirements: Degree from a UK university (normally 2:2 or above) or equivalent; applicants must be engaged in teaching in post-compulsory (further, higher or adult) education for at least 60 hours per year and have suitable qualifications in the subject taught (at least a National Diploma, NVQ level 3 or equivalent).

Contact: As above

PGCE in Primary Education (Lower Primary, 5–8) X121 B

1 year full-time

Entry requirements: 2nd Class Honours degree including 50% of study in a subject relevant to the National Curriculum; GCSE grade C (or equivalent) in English and mathematics, and for candidates born after 1/9/79, science; some experience of working with children.

Contact: As above

PGCE in Primary Education (Upper Primary, 7–12) X171 B

1 year full-time
As above

PGCE in Secondary Education (Dance) W4X1 B

1 year full-time

Entry requirements: 2nd Class Honours degree in dance, or with a substantial component of dance; GCSE grade C (or equivalent) in English and mathematics, and for candidates born after 1/9/79, science; some experience of working with children.

Contact: As above

PGCE in Secondary Education (English) Q3X1 B

1 year full-time

Entry requirements: 2nd Class Honours degree in which English (or its related components e.g. linguistics, media, drama or language studies) represents at least 50% of the study; GCSE grade C (or equivalent) in English and mathematics, and for candidates born after 1/9/79, science; some experience of working with children.

Contact: As above

PGCE in Secondary Education (Mathematics) G1X1 B

1 year full-time

Entry requirements: 2nd Class Honours degree in mathematics or an area with a substantial application of mathematics such as engineering or business and finance; GCSE grade C (or equivalent) in English and mathematics, and for candidates born after 1/9/79, science; some experience of working with children.

Contact: As above

PGCE in Secondary Education (Physical Education) X9C6 B

1 year full-time

Entry requirements: 2nd Class Honours degree including 50% of study in a subject relevant to the National Curriculum; GCSE grade C (or equivalent) in English and mathematics, and for candidates born after 1/9/79, science; some experience of working with children.

Contact: As above

PGCE in Secondary Education (Science) F0X1 B

1 year full-time

Entry requirements: 2nd Class Honours degree in a science subject or containing a substantial element of science; GCSE grade C (or equivalent) in English and mathematics, and for candidates born after 1/9/79, science; some experience of working with children.

Contact: As above

PgCert/PgDip/MA in Education

2–6 years part-time

Entry requirements: Honours degree or equivalent and Qualified Teacher Status (QTS) or equivalent professional qualification with an educational focus; or CertEd plus Diploma in Educational Studies or substantial teaching experience; all applicants must have a professional background in education.

Contact: As above

PgCert/PgDip/MA in Learning and Teaching

2–5 years part-time

Entry requirements: Degree or equivalent; evidence of relevant teaching work for at least 50 hours in each academic year; holders of CertEd in Further or Higher Education may be admitted.

Contact: As above

De Montfort University, Leicester

The Gateway
Leicester
LE1 9BH
Tel: 0116 255 1551
Fax: 0116 255 0307
enquiry@dmu.ac.uk
www.dmu.ac.uk

The origins of De Montfort University, Leicester go back to 1887 and the University now has a student population of 23,000 students. There are two campuses in Leicester: City Campus is the main site and caters for the majority of the students, and the Charles Frears Campus offers specialist programmes for nursing and midwifery on a site just outside the city centre. The facilities at the City Campus are available to the students on both sites. The University also has several associated colleges.

De Montfort University Leicester offers a PGCE course at secondary level based at Leicester City Campus or a postgraduate programme at post-compulsory level based at Leicester College, one of the associated colleges of the university. Each of the Leicester campuses has its own library supporting the programmes based there and all the libraries offer access to computers. The university has accommodation within close proximity to the campuses or privately rented student housing is available.

HOW TO APPLY

PGCE: applications are made through the GTTR.

Postgraduate: applications are made direct to the institution.

COURSES

PGCE in Secondary Education (Art and Design) W1X1 L

1 year full-time

Entry requirements: Relevant degree and GCSE minimum grade C (or equivalent) in English language and mathematics.
Contact: Colin Brookes
Subject Leader
0116 257 8321
cbrookes@dmu.ac.uk

PGCE in Secondary Education (Design and Technology) W9X1 L

1 year full-time

Entry requirements: 2nd Class Honours degree related to technology, e.g. industrial design, engineering, fashion; GSCE mathematics, English and science at grade C; some experience of working with children.
Contact: Recruitment and Admissions
01234 793279
bed-admissions@dmu.ac.uk

University of Derby

Kedleston Road
Derby
DE22 1GB
Tel: 01332 590500
Fax: 01332 294861
admissions@derby.ac.uk
www.derby.ac.uk

The University of Derby developed from the merger of several local colleges. Derby College of Art and Technology merged with Bishop Lonsdale College to form Derby Lonsdale College of Higher Education in 1977. In 1983, Derby Lonsdale and Matlock Colleges of Higher Education merged to form Derbyshire College of Higher Education and in 1992 the college became a university. It is based at four campuses, Kedleston Road, Mickleover, Brittania Mill and Buxton.

The School of Education and Social Sciences offers a range of courses from degree level and Initial Teacher Training to postgraduate programmes and Continuing Professional Development. There are several Learning Centres on the university sites. The Learning Centre on the Kedleston Road campus provides library and information technology facilities and its resources cover many subjects including education.

The university provides a range of accommodation, most of which is reserved for new students. There is also some reserved exclusively for postgraduates.

HOW TO APPLY

PGCE: applications are made through the GTTR.

Postgraduate: applications are made direct to the institution.

COURSES

PGCE in Primary Education X100

1 year full-time

Entry requirements: Good Honours degree (or equivalent) which contains a substantial element of English, mathematics, science or ICT; other subjects considered if supported by good A-level in 1 of these subjects; GCSE grade C or above (or equivalent) in mathematics and English language and, normally, a science.

Contact: Jon Hewson
PGCE Programme Leader
01332 592128

PGCE in Secondary Education (English) Q3X1

1 year full-time

Entry requirements: Honours degree or equivalent in a related subject; GCSE grade C or above in English and mathematics; applicants from non-traditional routes, mature applicants are also considered.

Contact: Peter Harris
Programme Leader
p.harris@derby.ac.uk

PGCE in Secondary Education (Information and Communication Technology) G5X1

1 year full-time
As above

PGCE in Secondary Education (Mathematics) G1X1

1 year full-time
As above

PgCert/PgDip/MEd/MA/MSc in Continuing Professional Development

1 year full-time, 2–3 years part-time

Entry requirements: Normally, Honours degree or equivalent qualification required, together with professional qualification and 2 years' experience in education; non-graduates with professional qualifications plus classroom experience may qualify for entry; applicants lacking Honours degree or its equivalent may qualify for staged progression to MEd/MA/MSc, registering initially for Certificate stage.

Contact: Doug Briggs
Programme Leader
01332 592132

EdD Education

3–6 years part-time

Entry requirements: Normally, Master's degree, together with relevant professional experience in education.

Contact: Dr John Dolan
Programme Leader
01332 592124

Devon Primary SCITT

Southmead School
Wrafton Road
Braunton
Devon
EX33 2BU
Tel: 01271 812448
Fax: 01271 815783
scitt@southmead.devon.sch.uk
www.dpscitt.ac.uk

The Devon Primary SCITT is a consortium of 11 primary schools in North and South Devon. They provide a workplace-based Initial Teacher Training course where trainees spend the majority of their time working in the classroom alongside skilled teachers. The schools are located in two clusters, Barnstaple-Braunton in the North of the county and Ivybridge-South Hams in the South, which include both large urban and small rural schools. Trainees choose to work in one of the clusters for the whole of the course, but meet together for centrally-based training.

The course covers the full primary age range (5–11 years), and trainees teach in both Key Stages, before specialising in their chosen Key Stage in the final term.

HOW TO APPLY
Applications are made through the GTTR.

COURSES
PGCE in Primary Education (5–11 years) XQ1H

1 year full-time

Entry requirements: Honours degree in subject appropriate to primary curriculum; recent experience of voluntary or paid work in primary school essential.

Contact: Enquiries
01271 812448
scitt@southmead.devon.sch.uk

Devon Secondary Teacher Training Group

Redworth House
Ashburton Road
Totnes
Devon
TQ9 5JZ
Tel: 01803 863067
Fax: 01803 869129
lwright@devon.gov.uk
www.devonscitt.com

The Devon Secondary Teacher Training Group is a consortium of local secondary schools (11–18) and Devon County Council and offers school-based training.

Trainees work alongside experienced heads of department who act as mentors. This is supported by regular training sessions conducted by course tutors and LEA advisers at South Devon Professional Centre, Dartington. The course comprises 28 weeks' school practice with placements in two contrasting schools and 8 weeks' study at the training centre.

HOW TO APPLY
Applications are made through the GTTR.

COURSES
PGCE in Secondary Education (Modern Foreign Languages: French) R1X1

36 weeks full-time

Entry requirements: Degree in (or closely related to) French; GCSE English language and mathematics grade C; trainees are expected to develop proficiency to enable them to teach 2nd foreign language to Key Stage 3 level; experience of working with 11–18 age range desirable.

Contact: Enquiries
01803 863067
lwright@devon.gov.uk

PGCE in Secondary Education (Modern Foreign Languages: German) R2X1

36 weeks full-time

Entry requirements: Degree in (or closely related to) German; GCSE English language and mathematics grade C; trainees are expected to develop proficiency to

enable them to teach 2nd foreign language to Key Stage 3 level; experience of working with 11–18 age range desirable.

Contact: As above

PGCE in Secondary Education (Performing Arts: Drama) W4X1

36 weeks full-time

Entry requirements: Relevant degree; GCSE English language and mathematics grade C; proficiency in performing arts discipline.

Contact: As above

PGCE in Secondary Education (Performing Arts: Music) W3X1

36 weeks full-time

Entry requirements: As above

Contact: As above

Dorset Teacher Training Partnership

Weymouth College
Community Education and Training
  Development
Cranford Avenue
Weymouth
Dorset DT4 7LQ
Tel: 01305 208768
Fax: 01305 208778
judi_osborne@weymouth.ac.uk

The Dorset Teacher Training Partnership comprises approximately 24 local primary schools and Dorset Local Education Authority with Weymouth College acting as managing agent.

Approximately 18 weeks of the course is spent in centre-based study and 20 weeks

in schools. Centre-based study takes place at Weymouth College and ICT Centre Bovington. School-based study and practice takes place in at least two different primary schools. The course offers teaching experience in both rural and urban settings.

HOW TO APPLY

Applications are made through the GTTR.

COURSES

PGCE in Primary Education (General Primary, 5–11) X100

42 weeks full-time

Entry requirements: Degree.

Contact: Judi Osborne
  SCITT Co-ordinator
  01305 208768
  judi_osborne@weymouth.ac.uk

University of Dundee

Perth Road
Dundee
DD1 4HN
Tel: 01382 344000
Fax: 01382 345500

srs@dundee.ac.uk
www.dundee.ac.uk

The University of Dundee was founded in 1881 as University College, Dundee and became part of the University of St Andrews in 1897. It became an independent university in 1967. The university is based on sites at Dundee, Kirkcaldy and Ninewells Hospital and Medical School.

During the growth and development of the institution, the University has merged with Dundee campus of Northern College, absorbed the two local nursing colleges and merged with Duncan of Jordanstone College of Art. These mergers have doubled the University's size and changed the institution dramatically, vastly extending the range of disciplines on offer. The university now has nearly 12,500 students.

The merger with Dundee campus of Northern College in late 2001 created a sixth faculty – the Faculty of Education and Social Work. Available facilities include a library and extensive computer resources with four computer labs in the Computer Education area, two ICT Suites in the library areas and one smaller ICT Suite in the Social Work area. The faculty offers undergraduate courses, postgraduate taught and research programmes including initial teacher training and also courses for Continuing Professional Development.

There are a variety of social, sporting and leisure facilities on campus as well as a wide range of accommodation with some reserved for postgraduate students.

HOW TO APPLY

Degree courses: applications are made through UCAS.

PGCE: applications are made through GTTR.

Postgraduate: applications are made direct to the institution.

COURSES

BEd (Hons) in Primary Education (3–12 years) X120

4 years full-time

Curriculum studies: Environmental studies; expressive arts; language; mathematics; information and communications technology; religious and moral education; personal and social development.

Professional studies: Interprofessional practice; theory and practice of education; placement.

On successful completion of the course, students funded by the SAAS are eligible for the induction year and provisional registration with the GTC for Scotland. Full registration and the entitlement to teach is awarded on successful completion of the induction year.

Entry requirements: Tariff: 220 points, Interview, Mature entry, Work experience

Contact: Lynette McRither
Faculty Assistant – Pre-
Qualifying
01382 464390
l.mcrither@dundee.ac.uk

PGCE in Primary Education X100

1 year full-time

Entry requirements: Degree or equivalent; SCE H-grade passes in English (or a pass offered by any university Arts faculty) and an SCE pass in mathematics at O/S-grade achieved at level 2 or above, or their equivalents.

Contact: Mrs Louise McIntosh
01224 283738
l.mcintosh@norcol.ac.uk

Diploma Advanced Educational Studies

1 year part-time

Entry requirements: Intended for teachers, both in training and in practice, who wish to study theoretical aspects of education in greater depth.

Contact: Fiona Paterson
Education Secretary
01382 344938
f.j.paterson@dundee.ac.uk

PgDip Community Education

1 year full-time

Entry requirements: Degree or equivalent; applicants must have substantial appropriate experience in voluntary or paid work in broad field of community education.

Contact: Alyson Hogg
Dundee Campus
01382 464499
a.hogg@norcol.ac.uk

PgCert/PgDip/MEd Early Education

Distance learning

Entry requirements: For fully registered primary teachers.
Contact: Miss Alda Ritchie
Pathway Administrator
01382 464446
a.ritchie@norcol.ac.uk

MEd Education

1 year full-time or 2–6 years part-time

Entry requirements: Recognised teaching qualification.
Contact: Fiona Patterson
Education Secretary
01382 344938
f.j.paterson@dundee.ac.uk

MSc Educational Psychology

2 years full-time

Entry requirements: Degree in psychology conferring Graduate Basis for Registration (GBR) of the British Psychological Society (BPS) required (applicants to enquire of BPS if in doubt), plus 2 years' full-time (or equivalent) practical experience with children and families, in teaching, or in social work or other welfare agencies.
Contact: Elaine Smith
Course Director
01382 344000
e.f.smith@dundee.ac.uk

Diploma German for Teachers and Others

2 years distance learning

Entry requirements: Higher/A-level German; secondary teaching qualification in another modern foreign language.
Contact: Dr A M K Borthwick
Lecturer in German and French
01382 344535/344899
a.m.k.borthwick@dundee.ac.uk

PgCert/PgDip/MEd Guidance and Pupil Support

Mixed mode

Entry requirements: Must be fully registered teacher.
Contact: Mrs S McIntyre
Course Secretary
01224 283653
s.mcintyre@norcol.ac.uk

Certificate/Diploma/MMEd Medical Education

Certificate: 3 months full-time or 1–4 years distance learning; diploma: 9 months full-time or 1–4 years distance learning; MMEd: 1 year full-time or 1–6 years distance learning.

Entry requirements: For healthcare professionals involved in teaching; healthcare professions qualification.
Contact: Ms Lisa Burton
Courses Administrator
01382 631952
c.m.e.courses@dundee.ac.uk

PgCert/PgDip/MEd Primary Education

3 years part-time

Entry requirements: For fully registered teachers.
Contact: Miss Alda Ritchie
Pathway Administrator
01382 464446
a.ritchie@norcol.ac.uk

PgCert/PgDip/MEd Professional Development in Educational Studies

Distance learning

Entry requirements: For fully registered teachers.
Contact: Mrs J Clark
Pathway Assistant
01224 283562
j.clark@norcol.ac.uk

PgCert Professional Development in Health Education

Distance learning

Entry requirements: As above

Contact: Miss Alda Ritchie
Pathway Administrator
01382 464446
a.ritchie@norcol.ac.uk

PgCert Professional Development in Pastoral Care

1 year distance learning

Entry requirements: As above
Contact: As above

PgCert Professional Development in Primary Science

Distance learning

Entry requirements: As above
Contact: As above

PgCert Professional Development in Rural Education

Distance learning

Entry requirements: For fully registered primary teachers.
Contact: As above

Diploma Spanish for Teachers and Others

2 years distance learning

Entry requirements: Higher/A-level Spanish or equivalent; normally a degree and secondary teaching qualification in another modern foreign language (or appropriate equivalent).
Contact: Mrs L M Hartley
Lecturer in Spanish
01382 344698
L.M.Hartley@dundee.ac.uk

PgCert/PgDip/MEd Special Educational Needs

Mixed mode

Entry requirements: For fully registered teachers/lecturers.
Contact: Ms L Gaffron
Pathway Assistant
01224 283502
l.gaffron@norcol.ac.uk

Certifcate/Diploma/MA Teaching Modern Languages to Adults

Certificate/Diploma: 12 months distance learning; MA: 3 years distance learning

Entry requirements: First degree, native/near native standard in 1 modern language other than English, excellent command of English, language teaching experience.
Contact: Marion Sporing
Programme Director
01382 344894/5488
m.sporing@dundee.ac.uk

University of East Anglia

The Registry
Norwich
Norfolk
NR4 7TJ
Tel: 01603 456161
Fax: 01603 458553
admissions@uea.ac.uk
www.uea.ac.uk

The University of East Anglia was founded in 1963 and received its Royal Charter in 1964. It is based on a 320-acre parkland campus in the outskirts of Norwich two miles from the City centre. It admitted its first 87 students in 1963 and has since expanded to cater for more than 13,000 students today. The university has extensive sporting facilities and there are shops, banks, bars and restaurants on site. Accommodation is mainly based on campus but first-year undergraduate students and new international postgraduate students will be guaranteed a place.

The School of Education and Professional Development was built in 1984. It is based in purpose-built accommodation in an award-winning building at the heart of the campus. It supplies teaching and research facilities for students, including modern information technology networks, a research library, and an archive section in the Main Library. The School offers a wide range of postgraduate taught courses and programmes for practising professionals seeking advanced awards and for students training for teaching.

HOW TO APPLY

PGCE: applications are made through the GTTR.

Postgraduate: applications are made direct to the institution.

COURSES

PGCE in Primary Education with Art (Foundation Years/Key Stage 1) X1WC

1 year full-time

Contact: Dr A Cockburn
   01603 456161
   edu.info@uea.ac.uk

PGCE in Primary Education with Art (Key Stages 1–2) XW11

1 year full-time

Entry requirements: As above
Contact: Dr D W Haylock
   01603 456161
   edu.info@uea.ac.uk

PGCE in Primary Education with Design and Technology (Foundation Years/Key Stage 1) X1WF

1 year full-time

Entry requirements: As above
Contact: Dr A Cockburn
   01603 456161
   edu.info@uea.ac.uk

PGCE in Primary Education with Design and Technology (Key Stages 1–2) XW12

1 year full-time

Entry requirements: As above
Contact: Dr D W Haylock
   01603 456161
   edu.info@uea.ac.uk

PGCE in Primary Education with English (Foundation Years/Key Stage 1) X1QH

1 year full-time

Entry requirements: As above
Contact: Dr A Cockburn
   01603 456161
   edu.info@uea.ac.uk

PGCE in Primary Education with English (Key Stages 1–2) XQ13

1 year full-time

Entry requirements: As above
Contact: Dr D W Haylock
   01603 456161
   edu.info@uea.ac.uk

PGCE in Primary Education with Geography (Foundation Years/Key Stage 1) X1FV

1 year full-time

Entry requirements: As above
Contact: Dr A Cockburn
   01603 456161
   edu.info@uea.ac.uk

Primary Education with Geography (Key Stages 1–2) XF18

1 year full-time

Entry requirements: As above
Contact: Dr D W Haylock
   01603 456161
   edu.info@uea.ac.uk

PGCE in Primary Education with History (Foundation Years/Key Stage 1) X1VC

1 year full-time

Entry requirements: As above
Contact: Dr A Cockburn
   01603 456161
   edu.info@uea.ac.uk

PGCE in Primary Education with History (Key Stages 1–2) XV11

1 year full-time

Entry requirements: As above
Contact: Dr D W Haylock
   01603 456161
   edu.info@uea.ac.uk

PGCE in Primary Education with Information and Communication Technology (Foundation Years/Key Stage 1) X1GM

1 year full-time

Entry requirements: As above
Contact: Dr A Cockburn
   01603 456161
   edu.info@uea.ac.uk

PGCE in Primary Education with Information and Communication Technology (Key Stages 1–2) XG15

1 year full-time

Entry requirements: As above
Contact: Dr D W Haylock
  01603 456161
  edu.info@uea.ac.uk

PGCE in Primary Education with Mathematics (Foundation Years/Key Stage 1) X1GC

1 year full-time

Entry requirements: As above
Contact: Dr A Cockburn
  01603 456161
  edu.info@uea.ac.uk

PGCE in Primary Education with Mathematics (Key Stages 1–2) XG11

1 year full-time

Entry requirements: As above
Contact: Dr D W Haylock
  01603 456161
  edu.info@uea.ac.uk

Primary Education with Music (Foundation Years/Key Stage 1) X1WH

1 year full-time

Entry requirements: As above
Contact: Dr A Cockburn
  01603 456161
  edu.info@uea.ac.uk

Primary Education with Music (Key Stages 1–2) XW13

1 year full-time

Entry requirements: As above
Contact: Dr D W Haylock
  01603 456161
  edu.info@uea.ac.uk

PGCE in Primary Education with Religious Education (Foundation Years/Key Stage 1) X1VP

1 year full-time

Entry requirements: As above
Contact: Dr A Cockburn
  01603 456161
  edu.info@uea.ac.uk

PGCE in Primary Education with Religious Education (Key Stages 1–2) XV16

1 year full-time

Entry requirements: As above
Contact: Dr D W Haylock
  01603 456161
  edu.info@uea.ac.uk

PGCE in Primary Education with Science (Foundation Years/Key Stage 1) X1FA

1 year full-time

Entry requirements: As above
Contact: Dr A Cockburn
  01603 456161
  edu.info@uea.ac.uk

PGCE in Primary Education with Science (Key Stages 1–2) XF10

1 year full-time

Entry requirements: As above
Contact: Dr D W Haylock
  01603 456161
  edu.info@uea.ac.uk

PGCE in Secondary Education (English) Q3X1

1 year full-time

Entry requirements: Honours degree, normally in English, plus A-level at a good standard in chosen subsidiary subject and minimum GCSE grade C, or equivalent, in mathematics.
Contact: Mr T Haydn
  01603 456161
  edu.info@uea.ac.uk

PGCE in Secondary Education (Geography) F8X1

1 year full-time

Entry requirements: Honours degree, normally in geography, plus A-level at a good standard in chosen subsidiary subject and minimum GCSE grade C, or equivalent, in English language and mathematics.
Contact: Mr J Battersby
  01603 456161
  edu.info@uea.ac.uk

PGCE in Secondary Education (History) V1X1

1 year full-time

Entry requirements: Honours degree, normally in history; plus A-level at a good standard in chosen subsidiary subject and minimum GCSE grade C, or equivalent, in English language and mathematics.
Contact: Mr T Haydn
01603 456161
edu.info@uea.ac.uk

PGCE in Secondary Education (Mathematics) G1X1

1 year full-time

Entry requirements: Honours degree, normally in mathematics, plus A-level at a good standard in chosen subsidiary subject and minimum GCSE grade C, or equivalent, in English language.
Contact: Ms S Cramp
01603 456161
edu.info@uea.ac.uk

PGCE in Secondary Education (Modern Languages: French/German) R9X1

1 year full-time

Entry requirements: Honours degree, normally in French/German, plus A-level at a good standard in chosen subsidiary subject and minimum GCSE grade C, or equivalent, in English language and mathematics.
Contact: Dr N Boodhoo
01603 456161
edu.info@uea.ac.uk

PGCE in Secondary Education (Physical Education) X9C6

1 year full-time

Entry requirements: Honours degree in physical education or sports science normally required plus A-level at good standard in chosen subsidiary subject; GCSE grade C or above, or equivalent, in English language and mathematics.
Contact: Ms P Lamb
01603 456161
edu.info@uea.ac.uk

PGCE in Secondary Education (Religious Education) V6X1

1 year full-time

Entry requirements: Honours degree, normally in religious studies, and minimum GCSE grade C, or equivalent, in English language and mathematics.
Contact: Mrs M Agombar
01603 456161
edu.info@uea.ac.uk

PGCE in Secondary Education (Science: Biology) C1X1

1 year full-time

Entry requirements: Honours degree, normally in biology, plus A-level at a good standard in chosen subsidiary subject and minimum GCSE grade C, or equivalent, in English language and mathematics.
Contact: Ms C Still
01603 456161
edu.info@uea.ac.uk

PGCE in Secondary Education (Science: Chemistry) F1X1

1 year full-time

Entry requirements: Honours degree, normally in chemistry, plus A-level at a good standard in chosen subsidiary subject and minimum GCSE grade C, or equivalent, in English language and mathematics.
Contact: Dr R Barton
01603 456161
edu.info@uea.ac.uk

PGCE in Secondary Education (Science: Physics) F3X1

1 year full-time

Entry requirements: Honours degree, normally in physics; plus A-level at a good standard in chosen subsidiary subject and minimum GCSE grade C, or equivalent, in English language and mathematics.
Contact: Dr R Barton
01603 456161
edu.info@uea.ac.uk

EdD Education

4 years part-time

Entry requirements: Aimed at professionals involved in training, professional development and education.

Contact: Sue Page
01603 592625
sue.page@uea.ac.uk

MA Education

1 year full-time

Entry requirements: Applications are invited from qualified teachers and others in allied professions with a significant interest in education; degree is normally required for entry although concessional entry based on other qualifications and/or experience may be considered.

Contact: Mrs E Chapman
International Office
01603 592855
e.chapman@uea.ac.uk

MA Education and Development

12 months full-time

Entry requirements: Good degree or post-graduate diploma plus some professional experience in education, preferably in development situations.

Contact: Steph Simpson
Manager of Postgraduate
Programmes
01603 592807
s.simpson@uea.ac.uk

Advanced Certificate/PgDip/MA Education and Professional Development

2–5 years part-time

Entry requirements: Degree or other appropriate qualification in education, plus teaching experience or experience in educational administration or other appropriate area.

Contact: Mrs Sue Page
01603 456161
sue.page@uea.ac.uk

University of East London

Barking Campus
Longbridge Road
Barking and Dagenham
London
RM8 2AS
Tel: 020 8223 3000
Fax: 020 8507 7799
admiss@uel.ac.uk
www.uel.ac.uk

The University of East London was founded in 1992 but developed from West Ham Technical Institute, which was formed in 1982. There are three campuses, Barking, Docklands and Stratford, all within an easy distance of each other.

The School of Education and Community is based at Barking Campus and offers a broad selection of courses at undergraduate, postgraduate, Master's and PhD level. Primary, secondary and post-compulsory teacher training is available as well as short courses or masters for teachers.

The university has six Learning Resource Centres, a library on each site and access to computers. Sporting and social facilities are also located on all three campuses. Accommodation is available in university residences on campus or in privately rented houses.

HOW TO APPLY

PGCE: applications are made through the GTTR.

Postgraduate: applications are made direct to the institution.

COURSES

PGCE in Primary Education (3–11) X100

1 year full-time

Entry requirements: Degree in discipline relevant to primary curriculum plus GCSE grade C in English language and mathematics, and GCSE grade C in science for applicants born after 1/9/79.

Contact: Frances Brodie
020 8223 2832/2152
brodie@uel.ac.uk

PGCE in Secondary Education (Design and Technology) W9X1

1 year full-time

Entry requirements: Degree in relevant discipline plus GCSE grade C in English language and mathematics, and GCSE grade C in science for applicants born after 1/9/79.

Contact: Kate Tuerena
020 8223 2782
k.tuerena@uel.ac.uk

PGCE in Secondary Education (English) Q3X1

1 year full-time
As above

PGCE in Secondary Education (Mathematics) G1X1

1 year full-time
As above

PGCE in Secondary Education (Modern Foreign Languages: French/Bengali) R9X1

1 year full-time

Entry requirements: As above
Contact: As above

PGCE in Secondary Education (Science) F0X1

1 year full-time

Entry requirements: As above
Contact: As above

Pgcert/Pgdip/MA in Education Practice

PgCert: 2 terms part-time, PgDip: 1 year part-time, MA: 2 years part-time.

Entry requirements: Relevant degree or appropriate experience with Qualified Teacher Status.

Contact: Jennifer Pash
MA EP Administrator
020 8223 2150
j.l.pash@uel.ac.uk

Edge Hill College of Higher Education

St Helens Road
Ormskirk
Lancashire
L39 4QP
Tel: 0800 195 5063
Fax: 01695 579997
enquiries@edgehill.ac.uk
www.edgehill.ac.uk

Edge Hill College of Higher Education is located just outside Ormskirk in Lancashire. It was founded in 1885 as a non-denominational teacher training college, and remains one of the largest providers of teacher education in the UK. There are more than 9,000 degree and diploma students at the college, with a further 6,000 students on professional development and MA/MSc programmes and over 50 MPhil/PhD students. The college benefits from being a short distance from Liverpool, Preston, Southport and Manchester.

Edge Hill has undertaken an extensive programme of redevelopment and expansion in recent years, including new study and sports facilities, and the Learning Innovation Centre which houses modern computing and media facilities. Students have access to Learning Resource Centres and libraries on all the college's sites. Self-catering and catered accommodation in halls of residence and privately rented accommodation is available.

The School of Education provides undergraduate and postgraduate initial teacher education for primary, Key Stages 2–3 and secondary levels. The School also has a wide portfolio of Continuing Professional Development courses and a number of education-related undergraduate degrees.

HOW TO APPLY

Degree courses: applications are made through UCAS.

PGCE: applications are made through the GTTR.

Postgraduate: applications are made direct to the institution.

COURSES

BSc (Hons) in Primary and Secondary Education (Design and Technology, Key Stages 2/3) X1WG

3 years full-time

Specialist subject studies to degree level. In addition, students will study curriculum courses in specialist subject at Key Stage 3. At Key Stage 2 the core curriculum subjects of English, mathematics, science and information technology are covered in addition to the specialist subject. Students will also work in schools, in both primary and secondary, with blocks of teaching in each phase.

Successful completion of this course leads to a recommendation for QTS on completion of skills tests.

Entry requirements: Tariff: 140 points, BTEC NC/ND, Foundation / access qualification

Contact: Enquiries
0800 195 5063
enquiries@edgehill.ac.uk

BA (Hons) in Primary and Secondary Education (English, Key Stages 2/3) X1Q3

3 years full-time
As above

BSc (Hons) in Primary and Secondary Education (Information Technology, Key Stages 2/3) X1G5
3 years full-time
As above

BSc (Hons) in Primary and Secondary Education (Mathematics, Key Stages 2/3) X1GD

3 years full-time
As above

Entry requirements: Tariff: 130 points, BTEC NC/ND, Foundation / access qualification

Contact: As above

BSc (Hons) in Primary and Secondary Education (Science, Key Stages 2/3) X1F0

3 years full-time
As above

Entry requirements: Tariff: 140 points, BTEC NC/ND, Foundation / access qualification

Contact: As above

BA (Hons) in Primary Education (Art) XW11

3 years full-time

Programme comprises the following elements: professional values and practice; primary core curriculum (English, mathematics, science and information and communications technology); primary foundation subjects (geography, history, design and technology, art, physical education, music) and religious education; 3rd year option selected from a range including: special educational needs; the foundation stage; information and communications technology co-ordination; managing a Key Stage; main specialist study or generalist management strand; school-based training.

Successful completion of this course leads to a recommendation for QTS on completion of skills tests.

Entry requirements: Tariff: 160 points, BTEC ND/NC, Foundation / access qualification

Contact: As above

BA (Hons) in Primary Education (English) XQ1H

3 years full-time
As above

BA (Hons) in Primary Education (Generalist) X125

3 years full-time
As above

BA (Hons) in Primary Education (History) XV1C

3 years full-time
As above

BA (Hons) in Primary Education (Mathematics) XG1C

3 years full-time
As above

BA (Hons) in Primary Education (Physical Education) XCC6

3 years full-time
As above

BA (Hons) in Primary Education (Science) XC1C

3 years full-time
As above

BSc (Hons) in Secondary Education (Design and Technology) X1W2

2 years full-time

Teaching Studies: An examination of the nature and function of teaching skills and their link with relevant theory and their practical implementation in the secondary classroom.

Curriculum Studies: The organisation and presentation of design and technology, including assessment and evaluation within the secondary curriculum.

Subject Studies: Students will engage in studio or workshop activities, which will develop and extend their abilities to solve practical problems in a range of materials and technologies.

Successful completion of this course leads to a recommendation for QTS on completion of skills tests.

Entry requirements: Degree, HNC, HND, Professional Qualification
Contact: David Sargeant
01695 584312
sergeand@edgehill.ac.uk

BSc (Hons) in Secondary Education (Design and Technology) X1WF

3 years full-time
As above

Entry requirements: Tariff: 140 points, BTEC NC/ND, Foundation / access qualification
Contact: As above

BSc (Hons) in Secondary Education (Information Technology) X1G4

2 years full-time

Programme comprises the following elements: subject study; subject application; school-based training; professional values and practice. Information technology modules include:

Year 1: Database construction; computer networks; control measuring and modelling; effective information presentation using ICT; planning in ICT.

Year 2: Hypertext and hypermedia systems; intranet design and management; exploring human computer interaction; social, legal, professional and ethical implications of IS/ICT; developing cross-curricular ICT; research in information and communication technology.

Successful completion of this course leads to a recommendation for QTS on completion of skills tests.

Entry requirements: First year of relevant degree course, HNC, HND, Professional Qualification
Contact: Enquiries
0800 195 5063
enquiries@edgehill.ac.uk

BSc (Hons) in Secondary Education (Information Technology) X1GK

3 years full-time

Programme comprises the following elements: subject study; subject application; school-based training; professional values and practice. Information technology modules include:

Year 1: Introduction to computer hardware; foundations of software development; systems analysis; the internet and the world wide web; European Computer Driving Licence.

Year 2: Database construction; computer networks; control measuring and modelling; effective information presentation using ICT; planning in ICT.

Year 3: Hypertext and hypermedia systems; intranet design and management; exploring human computer interaction; social, legal, professional and ethical implications of IS/ICT; developing cross-curricular ICT; research in information and communication technology.

Successful completion of this course leads to a recommendation for QTS on completion of skills tests.

Entry requirements: Tariff:140 points, BTEC NC/ND, Foundation / access qualification

Contact: As above

BSc (Hons) in Secondary Education (Mathematics) X1G1

2 years full-time

Year 1: Advanced calculus; mathematics and computing; statistical inference; mathematical modelling; mathematics curriculum studies 1; teaching studies.

Year 2: 3 modules from: group theory; linear algebra; number theory; numerical analysis; data models and databases; mathematical statistics; mathematical physics; mathematics in sport. Mathematics curriculum studies 2; mathematical education dissertation; teaching studies.

Successful completion of this course leads to a recommendation for QTS on completion of skills tests.

Entry requirements: First year of relevant degree course, HNC, HND, Professional Qualification

Contact: Paul Chambers
        Admissions Unit
        01695 584637
        tunstald@edgehill.ac.uk

BSc (Hons) in Secondary Education (Mathematics) X1GC

3 years full-time

Year 1: Pure mathematics; history of mathematics; probability and statistics; applied mathematics; information systems applications 1 and 2; personal explorations in learning; introduction to contemporary issues in education.

Year 2: Advanced calculus; mathematics and computing; statistical inference; mathematics; modelling; mathematics curriculum studies 1; teaching studies.

Year 3: 3 modules from: group theory; linear algebra; number theory; numerical analysis; data models and databases; mathematical statistics; mathematical physics; mathematics in sport and leisure; mathematics curriculum studies 2; mathematical education dissertation; teaching studies.

Successful completion of this course leads to a recommendation for QTS on completion of skills tests.

Entry requirements: Tariff: 140 points, BTEC NC/ND, Foundation / access qualification

Contact: As above

BSc (Hons) in Secondary Education (Science) X1FA

3 years full-time

Year 1: Science study skills; biodiversity; fundamentals of analysis.

Year 2: Science in schools; cytology, genetics and evolution; the Newtonian worldview.

Year 3: Science in context; the nature of scientific ideas; investigation in science education.

Successful completion of this course leads to a recommendation for QTS on completion of skills tests.

Entry requirements: Tariff: 120 points, BTEC NC/ND, Foundation / access qualification

Contact: Tony Liversidge
        Admissions Unit
        01695 584637
        liversia@edgehill.ac.uk

BSc (Hons) in Secondary Education (Science) X1FB

2 years full-time

Year 1: Science in schools; cytology, genetics and evolution; the Newtonian worldview.

Year 2: Science in context: the nature of scientific ideas; investigation in science education.

Successful completion of this course leads to a recommendation for QTS on completion of skills tests.

Entry requirements: First year of relevant degree course, HNC, HND, Professional Qualification, Work experience
Contact: As above

PGCE in Primary Education (5–11) X100

1 year full-time

Entry requirements: 1st or 2nd Class Honours degree; specialist qualifications in a National Curriculum subject (either C&G, degree studies or grade B at GCE A-level); and GCSE grade B in English language and grade C in mathematics, a science and 2 other National Curriculum subjects.
Contact: Nick Dowrick
        Admissions Unit
        01695 584274

PGCE in Secondary Education (Applied Art and Design) WX1C

1 year full-time

Entry requirements: Honours degree with substantial component of art and design or related area such as textile design, graphic design, architecture, photography; GCSE mathematics and English grade C; appropriate experience welcomed.
Contact: Enquiries
        0800 195 5063
        enquiries@edgehill.ac.uk

PGCE in Secondary Education (Business Education, 14–19) N1X1

1 year full-time or up to 3 years variable

Entry requirements: Degree in business studies or economics or a related discipline, or equivalent; GCSE grade C in mathematics and English language; mature students with additional business experience especially welcome.
Contact: Peter Townley
        Admissions Unit
        01695 584637/584222

PGCE in Secondary Education (Design and Technology) W9X1

1 year full-time or up to 3 years variable

Entry requirements: Good undergraduate degree in related subject area together with GCSE grade C or equivalent in English language and mathematics.
Contact: David Sergeant
        Course Leader
        01695 584458
        sergeand@edgehill.ac.uk

PGCE in Secondary Education (English) QX31

1 year full-time or up to 3 years variable

Entry requirements: Relevant degree, in which English is a substantial component; GCSE in English language and mathematics (grade C or above) or equivalent.
Contact: Carol Evans
        Course Leader
        01695 584341
        evansc@edgehill.ac.uk

PGCE in Secondary Education (French/ French and another Language) R1X1

1 year full-time

Entry requirements: GCSE in English language and mathematics (grade C or above) or equivalent; relevant degree.
Contact: Sue Ainslie
        Course Leader
        01695 584476/584726/584794
        ainslies@edgehill.ac.uk

PGCE in Secondary Education (Geography) F8X1

1 year full-time

Entry requirements: GCSE grade C or above in English language and mathematics (or equivalent), together with good under-graduate degree (or equivalent) in which geography has constituted substantial part.

Contact: Charles Rawding
Course Leader
01695 584207
rawding@edgehill.ac.uk

PGCE in Secondary Education (German/German and another Language) R2X1

1 year full-time

Entry requirements: GCSE in English language and mathematics (grade C or above) or equivalent; relevant degree.

Contact: Sue Ainslie
Course Leader
01695 584476/584726/584794
ainslies@edgehill.ac.uk

PGCE in Secondary Education (History with Citizenship) VX1C

1 year full-time

Entry requirements: Degree in history or in which history features as major part; or joint degree in history and subject relevant to citizenship e.g., religious education, theology, philosophy, peace studies etc; mathematics and English language GCSE grade C or above; some experience in secondary schools.

Contact: Enquiries
0800 195 5063
enquiries@edgehill.ac.uk

PGCE in Secondary Education (History) V1X1

1 year full-time or up to 3 years variable

Entry requirements: GCSE in English language and mathematics (grade C or above) or equivalent; Upper 2nd Class degree with history element relevant to history National Curriculum.

Contact: Ian Phillips
Course Leader
01695 584727
phillipi@edgehill.ac.uk

PGCE in Secondary Education (Information Technology) G5X1

1 year full-time or up to 3 years variable

Entry requirements: GCSE in English language and mathematics (grade C or above) or equivalent, together with relevant Honours degree; recent and relevant practical experience in areas such as network management or consultancy may also be appropriate.

Contact: Tony Hooson
Course Leader
01695 584681
hoosonr@edgehill.ac.uk

PGCE in Secondary Education (Leisure, Travel and Tourism) FXVC

1 year full-time

Entry requirements: 2nd Class Honours degree in area relevant to leisure, travel and tourism, such as geography, leisure and sport, business and leisure; or other degree plus relevant postgraduate experience; GCSE mathematics and English grade C.

Contact: Enquiries
0800 195 5063
enquiries@edgehill.ac.uk

PGCE in Secondary Education (Manufacturing) WX9C

1 year full-time

Entry requirements: Honours degree in manufacturing or related area; GCSE mathematics and English grade C; relevant work experience welcomed.

Contact: Enquiries
0800 195 5063
enquiries@edgehill.ac.uk

PGCE in Secondary Education (Mathematics) G1X1

1 year full-time or up to 3 years variable

Entry requirements: GCSE in English language and mathematics (grade C or above) or equivalent, plus relevant degree or equivalent professional examinations.

Contact: Paul Chambers
Course Leader
01695 584402
chamberp@edgehill.ac.uk

PGCE in Secondary Education (Music) W3X1

1 year full-time

Entry requirements: Good Honours degree.

Contact: Darren Murrall
Course Leader
01695 584221
murralld@edgehill.ac.uk

PGCE in Secondary Education (Physical Education) X9C6

1 year full-time

Entry requirements: Good sports-orientated undergraduate degree, together with GCSE grade C or equivalent in English and mathematics.

Contact: Vicky Harrhy
Course Leader
01695 584386
harrhyv@edgehill.ac.uk

PGCE in Secondary Education (Religious Education with Citizenship) VX6C

1 year full-time

Entry requirements: 2nd Class Honours degree in religious education, theology or related area, or joint Honours degree where 2nd subject is relevant to citizenship; GCSE mathematics and English grade C; relevant work experience welcomed.

Contact: Enquiries
0800 195 5063
enquiries@edgehill.ac.uk

PGCE in Secondary Education (Science) F0X1

1 year full-time

Entry requirements: GCSE in English language and mathematics (grade C or above) or equivalent; relevant degree.

Contact: Tony Liversidge
Course Leader
01695 584640
liversia@edgehill.ac.uk

PGCE in Secondary Education (Spanish/ Spanish and another Language) R4X1

1 year full-time

Entry requirements: GCSE in English language and mathematics (grade C or above) or equivalent; relevant degree.

Contact: Sue Ainslie
Course Leader
01695 584476/584726/584794
ainslies@edgehill.ac.uk

PGCE in Secondary Education (Urdu/ Urdu with another subject) T5X1

1 year full-time
As above

PgDip/MA in Careers Education and Guidance

MA 2–3 years part-time, PgDip 2 years part-time

Entry requirements: Degree, teaching certificate or equivalent.

Contact: Cathryn Jackson
01695 584262

PgCert/PgDip/MA in Early Years Education

MA 2–3 years part-time, PgDip 2 years part-time

Entry requirements: As above
Contact: As above

PgCert/PgDip/MA in Education Management

Part-time

Entry requirements: Applicants should hold management responsibility within their school.

Contact: Cathryn Jackson
01695 584262

PgCert/PgDip/MA in Educational Studies

Part-time

Entry requirements: Degree, teaching certificate, or equivalent.

Contact: As above

PgCert/PgDip/MA in Mentoring

Part-time

Entry requirements: As above
Contact: As above

PgCert/PgDip/MA in Primary Education
Part-time
As above

PgCert/PgDip/MA in Secondary Education
Part-time
As above

PgCert/PgDip/MA in Special Educational Needs
Part-time
As above

University of Edinburgh

Old College
South Bridge
Edinburgh
EH8 9YL
Tel: 0131 650 1000
Fax: 0131 650 2147
communications.office@ed.ac.uk
www.ed.ac.uk

The university is based in the heart of the City of Edinburgh and caters for over 20,000 students. The university has two campuses, Central Campus at George Square and King's Buildings Campus. Academic facilities at the university include the University Library, which holds approximately 3 million printed volumes across its 21 sites which serve the needs of the different faculties and departments. Computer facilities include PC laboratories and PCs in residences.

The Moray House School of Education was created in August 1998 when Moray House Institute of Education merged with the University of Edinburgh. It offers undergraduate study, postgraduate courses in initial education and postgraduate programmes including taught and research degrees.

There is a range of social, sporting and cultural activities on offer at the university in addition to the academic facilities. First year students from outside the city are guaranteed an offer of University accommodation all of which is within walking distance of the University and the city and consists of predominantly modern accommodation blocks with an extensive range of facilities.

HOW TO APPLY

Degree courses: applications are made through UCAS.

PGCE: applications are made through the GTTR.

Postgraduate: applications are made direct to the institution.

COURSES

BEd (Hons) in Design and Technology JX91
4 years full-time

Years 1 and 2: Covers educational studies; product and systems design; students develop knowledge of scientific principles and application to design and technological development; placement.

Years 3 and 4: Placement; technological curriculum and analysis of techniques used in the design process through a practical project and Honours dissertation.

Entry requirements: GCE A- and AS-levels: CC, SCE Highers: BBC
Contact: Undergraduate Office
(Education)
College of Humanities and
Social Science
0131 650 3569
education.faculty@ed.ac.uk

BEd (Hons) in Physical Education XC16
4 years full-time

All years: Education (including school placements); physical education curriculum; physical education perspectives. All students complete dissertation in final year.

Entry requirements: GCE A- and AS-levels: CC, SCE Highers: BBBB
Contact: As above

BEd (Hons) in Primary Education X120
4 years full-time

Years 1 and 2: All students undertake courses of study to prepare them to teach numeracy, language and literacy, environmental studies, expressive arts and religious and moral education, as well as taking the core education courses.

Years 3 and 4: Compulsory courses plus options from: modern languages; Scottish dimensions of the curriculum; science, technology and environment; religious and moral education; home, school and community; information and communication technology; personal, social and health education; pre-school and into school; special educational needs; professional and policy context of teachers' work; thematic teaching; children's fiction.

Entry requirements: GCE A- and AS-levels: CC, SCE Highers: BBB
Contact: As above

PGCE in Primary Education (5–11) X100
1 year full-time

Entry requirements: Degree from a UK university, plus SCE pass in English at Higher Grade (or its equivalent), SCE pass in mathematics at Standard Grade (level 1 or 2) or its equivalent. Selection involves a professional interview.
Contact: Mrs Liz McLaren
Senior Clerical Assistant
0131 651 6610
elizabeth.mclaren@ed.ac.uk

PGCE in Secondary Education (Art and Design) W1X1
1 year full-time

Entry requirements: Either Honours degree in subject to be taught or ordinary degree which contains 3 graduating courses (at levels 1, 2 and 3) in the relevant subject;

candidates are also required to hold SCE Higher English or an equivalent qualification. Selection involves a professional interview.
Contact: Susan Bobby
Senior Clerical Assistant
0131 651 6141
susan.bobby@ed.ac.uk

PGCE in Secondary Education (Biology) C1X1
1 year full-time
As above

PGCE in Secondary Education (Chemistry) F1X1
1 year full-time
As above

PGCE in Secondary Education (Computing) G5X1
1 year full-time
As above

PGCE in Secondary Education (Drama) W4X1
1 year full-time
As above

PGCE in Secondary Education (English) Q3X1
1 year full-time
As above

PGCE in Secondary Education (Geography) F8X1
1 year full-time
As above

PGCE in Secondary Education (History) V1X1
1 year full-time
As above

PGCE in Secondary Education (Mathematics) G1X1
1 year full-time
As above

PGCE in Secondary Education (Modern Languages) R9X1
1 year full-time
As above

PGCE in Secondary Education (Modern Studies) V9X1

1 year full-time

As above

PGCE in Secondary Education (Music) W3X1

1 year full-time

As above

PGCE in Secondary Education (Physics) F3X1

1 year full-time

As above

PGCE in Secondary Education (Religious Education) V6X1

1 year full-time

As above

PGCE in Secondary Education (Technological Education) J9X1

1 year full-time

As above

PgCert in Difficulties in Literacy Development

24 months part-time

Entry requirements: Degree or equivalent professional qualification in a related discipline.

Contact: Dr Gavin Reid
Programme Director
0131 651 6381
Gavin.Reid@ed.ac.uk

PgCert/PgDip/MEd in Advanced Studies in Education

PgCert: 36 months part-time, PgDip: 48 months part-time, MEd: 12 months full-time or 72 months part-time

Entry requirements: Degree or equivalent, a teaching qualification and experience in teaching in a primary or secondary school, in further education, or in some associated sector of education.

Contact: Mr Terry Wrigley
Lecturer
0131 651 6442
Terry.Wrigley@ed.ac.uk

PgCert/PgDip/MEd in Bilingual Learners

PgCert: 3 years part-time, PgDip: 4 years part-time, MEd: 6 years part-time

Entry requirements: Degree or equivalent; candidates should also be qualified teachers with General Teaching Council (GTC) registration.

Contact: Mr John Landon
Senior Lecturer
0131 651 6097
john.landon@ed.ac.uk

PgCert/PgDip/MEd in Early Education

PgCert: 3 years part-time, PgDip: 4 years part-time, MEd: 6 years part-time

Entry requirements: Degree or equivalent, and minimum of 2 years' relevant professional practice.

Contact: Mrs Helen Fraser
Senior Lecturer
0131 651 6597
helen.fraser@ed.ac.uk

PgCert/PgDip/MEd in Inclusive and Special Education

PgCert: 36 months part-time, PgDip: 48 months part-time, MEd: 72 months part-time

Entry requirements: Degree or equivalent; candidates should normally be qualified teachers with General Teachers Council (GTC) registration; designed for teachers of pupils/students with special educational needs, course members may be working in learning support or with learners described as having moderate learning difficulties, physical disabilities or social, emotional and behavioural difficulties.

Contact: Ms Gwynedd Lloyd
Senior Lecturer
0131 651 6445
Gwynedd.Lloyd@ed.ac.uk

PgCert/PgDip/MEd in Information Technology and Education

PgCert: 3 years part-time, PgDip: 4 years part-time, MEd: 6 years part-time

Entry requirements: Degree, 2 years' professional experience, and familiarity with at least 1 information technology application (e.g. word processing) required, and access to desktop computer (Macintosh or Windows) expected.

Contact: Dr Tom Conlon
Senior Lecturer
0131 651 6035
tom.conlon@ed.ac.uk

PgDip/MEd in Deaf Education

PgDip: 4 years part-time, MEd: 6 years part-time

Entry requirements: Degree and registered teacher status required, minimum 2 years' teaching experience, plus experience/strong interest in working with deaf learners.

Contact: Dr Mary Brennan
Senior Lecturer
0131 651 6441/6075
mary.brennan@ed.ac.uk

PgDip/MEd in Specific Learning Difficulties

PgDip: 48 months part-time, MEd: 72 months part-time

Entry requirements: Degree or equivalent; candidates should also normally be qualified teachers with General Teaching Council (GTC) registration; designed for teachers and other professionals who work with pupils who have specific learning difficulties.

Contact: Ms Pamela Deponio
Lecturer
0131 651 6232
PamelaDeponio@ed.ac.uk

PgDip/MEd in Visual Impairment

PgDip: 4 years part-time, MEd: 6 years part-time

Entry requirements: Degree or equivalent; candidates should be qualified teachers with General Teaching Council (GTC) registration.

Contact: Ms Marianna Buultjens
Senior Lecturer
0131 651 6204/6074
marianna.buultjens@ed.ac.uk

Diploma/MSc in Mathematical Education

Diploma: 9 months full-time, MSc: 12 months full-time

Entry requirements: Teaching experience desirable but not essential.

Contact: Dr John Searl
0131 650 5044
j.w.searl@ed.ac.uk

PgCert/PgDip/MSc in Advanced Professional Studies

PgCert: 3 years part-time, PgDip: 4 years part-time, MSc: 1 year full-time or 6 years part-time

Entry requirements: Professional experience in education or related field.

Contact: Mr John Landon
Senior Lecturer
0131 651 6097
john.landon@ed.ac.uk

PgCert/PgDip/MSc in Outdoor Education

PgCert: 3 years part-time, PgDip: 1 years full-time or 4 years part-time, MSc: 1 year full-time or 6 years part-time

Entry requirements: Degree or equivalent experience; primarily for those from professions such as teaching, community education and social work who make use of aspects of outdoor environment as part of their everyday activities.

Contact: Dr Pete Higgins
Senior Lecturer
0131 650 9795
pete.higgins@ed.ac.uk

PgDip/MSc in Education

MSc: 12 months full-time or 24 to 36 months part-time

Entry requirements: Professional experience in education or related field.

Contact: Dr G Donn
0131 651 6310/6305
g.donn@ed.ac.uk

EdD in Education

5 years part-time

Entry requirements: Good undergraduate degree and Master's level award or equivalent professional achievement.

Contact: Prof Mary Simpson
0131 651 6427
mary.simpson@ed.ac.uk

Essex Primary Schools Training Group

Harlow Curriculum Development Centre
Partridge Road
Abbotsweld
Harlow
Essex
CM18 6TE
Tel: 01279 429941
Fax: 01279 411490

The Essex Primary Schools Training Group is made up of a number of local schools and the Essex Local Education Authority. The course has been accredited by the Teacher Training Agency and successful trainees will be awarded qualified teacher status and the Anglia Polytechnic University PGCE.

Trainees will have placements in two schools providing experience of differing age ranges. The administrative base for the course is located in Harlow and the schools are based across Essex.

HOW TO APPLY

Applications are made through the GTTR.

COURSES

PGCE in Primary Education (5–11 years) X100

1 year full-time

Entry requirements: Degree.
Contact: Enquiries
01279 429941

University of Exeter

Northcote House
The Queen's Drive
Exeter
Devon
EX4 4QJ
Tel: 01392 661000
Fax: 01392 263108
admissions@exeter.ac.uk
www.ex.ac.uk

The roots of the University of Exeter can be traced to the establishment of local Schools of Art and Science which merged and expanded to eventually become the University of Exeter in 1955. The institution has since expanded further with the establishment of new schools within the university and the incorporation of external schools and colleges. The university is based at two campuses, Streatham Campus and St. Luke's Campus.

The School of Education and Lifelong Learning is housed at St. Luke's campus where there are specialist facilities such as the large education library, a separate resources library and excellent sporting and recreational facilities. The school runs a wide range of courses from undergraduate degrees to a taught Doctorate course, offering opportunities for research, continuing professional development and initial teacher training.

Accommodation is available on campus in one of the halls of residence or self-catering flats. New students are guaranteed accommodation in their first year of study. There is also private sector accommodation available close to the university.

HOW TO APPLY

Degree courses: applications are made through UCAS.

PGCE: applications are made through the GTTR.

Postgraduate: applications are made direct to the institution.

COURSES

PGCE in Key Stage 2/3 (Design and Technology) XWC9

1 year full-time

Entry requirements: Degree subject(s) must be related to chosen specialist subject; in addition, GCSE grade C or above in English language and mathematics; or equivalent qualifications; For students applying for primary teaching who were born on or after 1 September 1979, GCSE grade C or above (or equivalent) in science(s) will be required (or successful completion of University's special test intended as substitute).

Contact: Initial Teacher Training Office
01392 264837
ed-ipso@exeter.ac.uk

PGCE in Key Stage 2/3 (English) XQC3

1 year full-time

Entry requirements: Degree in relevant area; GCSE grade C or above in English language, mathematics and science.
Contact: As above

PGCE in Key Stage 2/3 (Mathematics) XGC1

1 year full-time

Entry requirements: As above
Contact: As above

PGCE in Key Stage 2/3 (Physical Education) XCC6

1 year full-time

Entry requirements: Degree in related subject plus GCSE grade C or above in English language and mathematics; or equivalent qualifications; for students applying for primary teaching who were born on or after 1 September 1979, GCSE grade C or above in science(s) will be required (or successful completion of university's special test intended as a substitute.

Contact: As above

PGCE in Key Stage 2/3 (Science) XFCA

1 year full-time

Entry requirements: Degree in relevant area; GCSE grade C or above in English language, mathematics and science.
Contact: As above

PGCE in Post-Compulsory Education

1 year full-time or 2 years part-time

Entry requirements: Professional qualification in area to be taught; open to practising lecturers and those with no previous teaching experience.

Contact: Graduate School Office
School of Education and
Lifelong Learning
01392 264815
ed-cpd@exeter.ac.uk

PGCE in Primary Education (Early Years, 3–8) X121

1 year full-time

Entry requirements: Degree in subject(s) related to primary school curriculum; GCSE grade C or above in English language and mathematics or equivalent, plus in science(s) for those born after 1.09.79.

Contact: Initial Teacher Training Office
01392 264837
ed-ipso@exeter.ac.uk

PGCE in Primary Education (Upper Primary, 7–11, English) XQ13

1 year full-time
As above

PGCE in Primary Education (Upper Primary, 7–11, Humanities: Geography and History) XF18

1 year full-time
As above

PGCE in Primary Education (Upper Primary, 7–11, Mathematics) XG11

1 year full-time
As above

PGCE in Primary Education (Upper Primary, 7–11, Music) XW13

1 year full-time
As above

PGCE in Primary Education (Upper Primary, 7–11, Science) XF10

1 year full-time

As above

PGCE in Secondary Education (Art) W1X1

1 year full-time

Entry requirements: Degree in relevant subject area(s); GCSE grade C or above (or equivalent) in English language and mathematics.

Contact: As above

PGCE in Secondary Education (Dance) W4X1

1 year full-time

Entry requirements: Degree in relevant area; GCSE grade C or above in English language, mathematics and science.

Contact: As above

PGCE in Secondary Education (Design and Technology) W9X1

1 year full-time

As above

PGCE in Secondary Education (English with Drama) QX31

1 year full-time

As above

PGCE in Secondary Education (Geography) F8X1

1 year full-time

As above

PGCE in Secondary Education (History with Citizenship) VX1C

1 year full-time

As above

PGCE in Secondary Education (History) V1X1

1 year full-time

As above

PGCE in Secondary Education (Mathematics) G1X1

1 year full-time

As above

PGCE in Secondary Education (Modern Languages: French) R1X1

1 year full-time

As above

PGCE in Secondary Education (Modern Languages: German) R2X1

1 year full-time

As above

PGCE in Secondary Education (Physical Education) X9C6

1 year full-time

As above

PGCE in Secondary Education (Religious Education) V6X1

1 year full-time

As above

PGCE in Secondary Education (Science: Biology) C1X1

1 year full-time

As above

PGCE in Secondary Education (Science: Chemistry) F1X1

1 year full-time

As above

PGCE in Secondary Education (Science: Physics) F3X1

1 year full-time

As above

PgCert/PgDip/MEd Adult Continuing Education

2–5 years part-time

Entry requirements: Teaching qualification or appropriate experience equivalent to at least 2 years' full-time practice.

Contact: Ms Roseanne Benn
01392 262844
R.C.Benn@exeter.ac.uk

PgCert/PgDip/MEd Creative Arts in Education

1 year full-time

Entry requirements: Applicants will normally be qualified teachers, or hold an equivalent professional qualification, or have at least 3 years' experience in their relevant area of professional work; for some programmes applicants must hold good honours degree or equivalent.

Contact: Graduate Studies Office,
Education and Lifelong learning
01392 264838/4815/4728
ed-cpd@exeter.ac.uk

PgCert/PgDip/MEd Education/Educational Studies

2–5 years part-time

Entry requirements: Ability to benefit from these courses constitutes principal criterion for entry. Graduate or professional qualifications are normally sufficient evidence of this. It is often helpful if student has access to schools, colleges or other educational institutions, whether as a teacher, ancillary, school governor, parent or citizen.

Contact: Graduate Studies Office
01392 264 838/815/728
ed-cpd@exeter.ac.uk

MEd Educational Psychology

1 year full-time

Entry requirements: Good Honours degree in psychology (or equivalent recognised by British Psychological Society as conferring graduate basis for registration), postgraduate certificate in education and 2 years' teaching experience.

Contact: As above

EdD Educational Psychology

2–4 years full-time or 4–7 years part-time

Entry requirements: The course is open only to fully qualified educational psychologists with Master's degree and 3 years' professional experience.

Contact: As above

EdD Mathematics Education

2 years full-time or 4 years part-time

Entry requirements: Successful completion of a Master's degree or equivalent in education or related discipline together with at least 3 years' relevant professional experience.

Contact: As above

EdD Professional Studies in Education

2 years full-time or 4 years part-time

Entry requirements: Successful completion of a Master's degree in education or related discipline together with at least 3 years' relevant professional experience.

Contact: As above

PgCert/PgDip/MEd Special Educational Needs

1 year full-time

Entry requirements: Applicants will normally be qualified teachers, or hold an equivalent professional qualification, or have at least 3 years' experience in their relevant area of professional work.

Contact: Graduate Studies Office,
Education and Lifelong Learning
01392 264838
ed-cpd@exeter.ac.uk

EdD Special Educational Needs

2 years full-time or 4 years part-time

Entry requirements: Successful completion of a Master's degree in education or related discipline together with at least 3 years' relevant professional experience.

Contact: As above

MEd/PgDip/PgCert Teaching English as a Foreign Language

1 year full-time

Entry requirements: Applicants will normally be qualified teachers, or hold an equivalent professional qualification, or have at least 3 years' experience in their relevant area of professional work. Aimed at teachers of English as a second or foreign language both from Britain and overseas, education officials, inspectors, those concerned with the organisation of language courses, and teacher trainers.

Contact: As above

EdD Teaching English as a Foreign Language

2 years full-time or 4 years part-time

Entry requirements: Successful completion of a Master's degree in TEFL, TESOL, applied linguistics or related field plus at least 3 years' relevant professional experience.

Contact: Graduate Studies Office
01392 264815/264838/264728
ed-cpd@exeter.ac.uk

Forest Independent Primary Collegiate

Wells Park School and Training Centre
School Lane
Lambourne Road
Chigwell
Essex
IG7 6NN
Tel: 020 8502 6442
Fax: 020 8502 6729
gill@stubbs9996.freeserve.co.uk

The Forest Independent Primary Collegiate (FIPC) is a school-centred teacher training initiative comprising 16 local schools. Their varied geographical backgrounds enable trainees to gain an understanding of schools serving both rural and urban communities. The lead school of the Consortium is Wells Park School and Training Centre, a residential school for children with emotional and behavioural difficulties. The FIPC initiative focuses on training teachers who are not only compe-tent in delivering the curriculum, but who also acquire skills in managing both class and individual behaviour.

Theory is taught at Wells Park and trainees are placed in three of the participating mainstream primary schools during the course of the year, as well as a six-day placement at a special school. Facilities offered at Wells Park include a library, conference and training rooms.

HOW TO APPLY

Applications are made through the GTTR.

COURSES

PGCE in Primary Education (5–11 years) X100

1 year full-time

Entry requirements: Degree.

Contact: Gill Stubbs
Course Administrator
020 8559 6973
gill@stubbs9996.freeserve.co.uk

University of Glasgow

Student Recruitment & Admissions
1 The Square
Glasgow
G12 8QQ
Tel: 0141 339 8855
Fax: 0141 330 3045
stras@gla.ac.uk
www.gla.ac.uk

The University of Glasgow was established in 1451 as the second university to be created in Scotland. The university now has around 19,500 students and most of the departments are located on the Gilmorehill Campus. Glasgow's campus has more listed buildings than any other. The university also has facilities based at the Crichton Campus, which is shared with other institutions, including the University of Paisley.

The Faculty of Education is based at the Gilmorehill Campus and currently consists of four departments. These are the Department of Adult and Continuing Education, the Department of Curriculum Studies, the Department of Educational Studies and the Department of Religious Education. The Department of Educational Studies offers a selection of programmes ranging from initial teacher education, including undergraduate courses and the PGCE, to courses for Continuing Professional Development and post-doctoral research.

The university offers a selection of academic and recreational facilities and students have access to resources and computers within the Faculty of Education. There is accommodation for students in all years of study in residences owned or managed by the University. Accommodation is not guaranteed but there is a register of privately rented property compiled by the Accommodation Office.

HOW TO APPLY

Degree courses: applications are made through UCAS.

PGCE: applications are made through the GTTR.

Postgraduate: applications are made direct to the institution.

COURSES

BEd or BEd (Hons) in Music (Secondary) WX31

4 years full-time

Offered jointly with Royal Scottish Academy of Music and Drama (RSAMD).

Levels 1–4 comprise: Music studies: performing skills; compositional studies; music in its historical/social context.

Educational studies: Professional studies; curriculum studies: music.

School experience: 1st year is spent in primary schools; subsequent years are spent in secondary schools.

On completion students are recommended to the General Teaching Council for Scotland for provisional registration. Full registration is awarded on the completion of 2 satisfactory years (or equivalent) of teaching.

Entry requirements: Audition, GCE A- and AS-levels, Interview, SCE Higher

Contact: Ms Kristen Smith
        0141 330 3461
        ite@educ.gla.ac.uk

BEd (Hons) in Primary Education (3–12 years) X120

4 years full-time

All students are required to follow a course in religious education which leads to award of Catholic Teacher's Certificate in Religious Education.

Course covers: Professional studies: professional understanding and skills needed to teach in primary school.

Curricular studies, main areas of primary curriculum: mathematics; language; religious education; environmental studies; expressive arts; information and communication technology.

School experience: development of understanding, skills and expertise in working in school classroom; affords opportunity to teach at various levels within primary school.

On completion students are recommended to the General Teaching Council for Scotland for provisional registration. Full registration is awarded on the completion of 2 satisfactory years (or equivalent) of teaching.

Entry requirements: Irish Leaving Certificates: BBCC to BBB, SCE Higher: BBCC to BBB, GCE A- and AS-levels: CCC, Foundation / access qualification

Contact: As above

BTheol in Secondary Education (Religious Education) VX61

4 years full-time

The course is designed for those wishing to teach religious education, theology or religious studies in either denominational or non-denominational secondary schools. Students undertake 3 main elements:

Theology and religious studies: Develops the critical and analytical skills required to address the major cultural, theological and spiritual issues of our time.

Professional and education studies: Explores, in the context of Scottish education, how pupils learn and how educators teach most effectively.

School experience: provides the opportunity to try out ideas and develop competence in dealing with people. Additionally, it is designed to develop curriculum planning, assessment, reporting, management and organisation.

Entry requirements: SCE Higher: BBBC, GCE A- and AS-levels: CCD

Contact: As above

BTechEd in Technological Education H111

4 years full-time

Taught jointly by Robert Clark Centre for Technological Education and Department of Educational Studies.

Technology studies levels 1–3 cover: Electronics, materials, mechanics, design, structures, mathematics, practical craft skills, industrial experience.

Level 4: Major project plus options such as product design, sustainable resources and the environments or management studies.

Educational studies levels 1–4: Professional studies; curriculum studies (technology); school experience.

On completion students are recommended to the General Teaching Council for Scotland for provisional registration. Full registration is awarded on the completion of 2 satisfactory years (or equivalent) of teaching.

Entry requirements: SCE Higher: BBCC to BBB, GCE A- and AS-levels: CC, Interview, Mature entry

Contact: Admissions Officer
0141 330 4976
BTechEd@elec.gla.ac.uk

PGCE in Primary Education X100

1 year full-time

Entry requirements: Degree from a UK university or an alternative degree qualification approved by the General Teaching Council for Scotland; plus SCE Higher Grade or equivalent in English and Ordinary or Standard Grade or equivalent in mathematics.

Contact: Mrs Linda Murray
Faculty Office Secretary
0141 330 3461
l.murray@educ.gla.ac.uk

PGCE in Secondary Education (Art and Design) W1X1

1 year full-time

Entry requirements: Degree from a UK university or an alternative degree qualification approved by the General Teaching Council for Scotland; plus SCE Higher Grade or equivalent in English.

Contact: As above

PGCE in Secondary Education (Biology) C1X1

1 year full-time
As above

PGCE in Secondary Education (Business Education) N1X1

1 year full-time
As above

PGCE in Secondary Education (Chemistry) F1X1

1 year full-time
As above

PGCE in Secondary Education (Computing) G5X1

1 year full-time
As above

PGCE in Secondary Education (English) Q3X1

1 year full-time
As above

PGCE in Secondary Education (General Sciences)

1 year full-time
As above

PGCE in Secondary Education (Geography) F8X1

1 year full-time
As above

PGCE in Secondary Education (History) V1X1

1 year full-time

As above

PGCE in Secondary Education (Mathematics) G1X1

1 year full-time

As above

PGCE in Secondary Education (Modern Languages: French) R1X1

1 year full-time

As above

PGCE in Secondary Education (Modern Languages: German with French) R2X1

1 year full-time

As above

PGCE in Secondary Education (Modern Languages: Italian with French) R3X1

1 year full-time

As above

PGCE in Secondary Education (Modern Languages: Spanish with French) R4X1

1 year full-time

As above

PGCE in Secondary Education (Modern Studies) V9X1

1 year full-time

As above

PGCE in Secondary Education (Physics) F3X1

1 year full-time

As above

PGCE in Secondary Education (Religious Studies) V6X1

1 year full-time

As above

PgDip/MSc in Adult and Continuing Education

PgDip: 9 months full-time or 18 months part-time; MSc: 12 months full-time or 24 months part-time

Entry requirements: Degree required (Honours for MSc) and some experience of broad field of adult and continuing educa-

tion; candidates may be admitted either for PgDip or for MSc, with possibility of transfer between them.

Contact: Graduate Secretary
0141 330 4278
graduate@ace.gla.ac.uk

PgCert in Arts in Education

12–24 months part-time

Entry requirements: Appropriate degree or equivalent qualification of comparable level; plus a minimum of 3 years' experience in educational capacity.

Contact: Mr A Laing
Department of Curriculum Studies
0141 330 3402
a.laing@educ.gla.ac.uk

PgCert/PgDip in Early Childhood Education

24 months part-time

Entry requirements: Must be teachers registered with General Teaching Council.

Contact: Ms L Cullen
0141 330 3059
l.cullen@educ.gla.ac.uk

MEd in Education

1 year full-time or 2 years part-time

Entry requirements: First degree and Diploma in education.

Contact: Postgraduate Admissions
0141 330 3202
pgrad@educ.gla.ac.uk

EdD in Education

4–6 years on-line study

Entry requirements: Master's level qualification, or equivalent, in education or a cognate subject area; requests for accreditation of prior learning (APL) and substitution are considered.

Contact: Prof M Peters
Department of Educational Studies
0141 330 3636
m.peters@educ.gla.ac.uk

Pgcert/Pgdip in Educational Management and Leadership

Pgcert: 21 months part-time; Pgdip: 24 months part-time

Entry requirements: Normally, degree or equivalent required and professional training in field of education and/or psychology or related profession e.g. social work, nursery nursing, clinical nursing etc.

Contact: Postgraduate Admissions
0141 330 3202
pgrad@educ.gla.ac.uk

MEd in Psychology

1 calendar year full-time or 2 calendar years part-time

Entry requirements: Degree or equivalent; professional training in field of education or related profession and undergraduate study in psychology equivalent to Level 1 undergraduate psychology.

Contact: As above

Additional Teaching Qualification in Religious Education

Distance learning

Entry requirements: Open to all qualified teachers.

Contact: Mr J Conroy
0141 330 3434
j.conroy@educ.gla.ac.uk

MEd in Religious Education

24 months part-time

Entry requirements: Honours degree in a relevant subject.

Contact: As above

PgDip in School Leadership and Management (Scottish Qualification for Headship)

30 months part-time

Entry requirements: Nomination through local authority or employer.

Contact: Local Authority SQH Co-ordinator

Pgcert/Pgdip in School Management

Pgcert: 24 months part-time; Pgdip: 36 months part-time

Entry requirements: 1st degree or equivalent, GTC registration.

Contact: Postgraduate Admissions
0141 330 3202
pgrad@educ.gla.ac.uk

MSc in Science and Science Education

12 months full-time

Entry requirements: Normally, Honours degree in science subject; educational experience desirable.

Contact: Dr Norman Reid
Director, Centre for Science Education
0141 330 5172
n.reid@mis.gla.ac.uk

Pgcert/Pgdip in Support for Learning

24 months part-time

Entry requirements: Applicants should have full registration with the General Teaching Council of Scotland or equivalent.

Contact: Ms T Boyd
0141 330 3049
t.boyd@educ.gla.ac.uk

PgCert in Teaching for Effective Learning

24 months part-time

Entry requirements: Practising teacher registered with the General Teaching Council.

Contact: Ms V Friel
0141 330 3439
v.friel@educ.gla.ac.uk

Gloucestershire Initial Teacher Education Partnership (SCITT)

St Peter's High School
Stroud Road
Tuffley
Gloucester
GL4 0DE
Tel: 01452 509208
ssykes@st-petershigh.gloucs.sch.uk

The Gloucestershire Initial Teacher Education Partnership is a collaboration between the Gloucestershire Association of Secondary Headteachers, the University of Gloucestershire and local schools. This partnership was established in 1992, and more than 50 secondary schools are now involved. SCITT trainees are based at St Peter's High School in Gloucester.

Trainee teachers spend 25 weeks of the 36-week course in schools. General professional studies training takes place at the University of Gloucestershire.

HOW TO APPLY

Applications are made through the GTTR.

COURSES

PGCE in Secondary Education (Business Studies) N1X1

1 year full-time

Entry requirements: Degree in relevant subject; GCSE mathematics and English grade C.

Contact: Mrs Sheila Sykes
SCITT Co-ordinator
01452 509208
ssykes@st-petershigh.gloucs.sch.uk

PGCE in Secondary Education (Design and Technology) W9X1

1 year full-time
As above

PGCE in Secondary Education (Information Technology) G5X1

1 year full-time
As above

PGCE in Secondary Education (Music) W3X1

1 year full-time
As above

University of Gloucestershire

PO Box 220
The Park Campus
Cheltenham
Gloucestershire
GL50 2QF
Tel: 01242 532700
Fax: 01242 543334
admissions@glos.ac.uk
www.glos.ac.uk

The University of Gloucestershire was established in 2001, having formerly been known as the Cheltenham and Gloucester College of Higher Education. There are four main University campuses, three in Cheltenham, The Park, Pittville and Francis Close Hall, and Oxstalls campus in Gloucester. University accommodation is available in halls on the campuses or in off-campus houses or flats in both Cheltenham and Gloucester.

The School of Education is based at the Francis Close Hall Campus in the centre of Cheltenham. The School offers Initial Teacher Training at undergraduate and postgraduate level, including both primary and secondary PGCEs. Master's degrees and research programmes are also offered.

Library resources and computer facilities are available in Learning Centres at each of the university campuses.

HOW TO APPLY

Degree courses: applications are made through UCAS.

PGCE: applications are made through the GTTR.

Postgraduate: applications are made direct to the institution.

COURSES

BEd (Hons) in Primary Education (Early Primary, 5–8 years) X103

3 years full-time

Course includes: Curriculum and subject studies; teaching methods; experience working in school. Assessment through written assignment, oral presentations and assessment of practical teaching skills. Students also take 2 specialist subjects: 1 from English, mathematics or science and 1 from art, geography, history, information technology, physical education.

Level 1: School experience; learning mathematics and being mathematical; language in use.

Level 2: Block school experience; teaching primary science; teaching primary English.

Level 3: Dissertation; core subject leadership; block school experience.

Successful completion of this course leads to a recommendation for Qualified Teacher Status (QTS) after completion of skills tests.

Entry requirements: Tariff: 160 to 220 points, 26: International Baccalaureate, BTEC NC/ND, Interview, Work experience
Contact: Mr Geoffrey Pryce
Course Leader
01242 532764
gpryce@chelt.ac.uk

BEd (Hons) in Primary Education (Early Primary, 5–8 years, shortened course) X121

2 years full-time

Course includes: Curriculum and subject studies; teaching methods; experience working in school. Assessment through written assignment, oral presentations and assessment of practical teaching skills. Students take 2 specialist subjects: 1 from English, mathematics or science and 1 from art, geography, history, information technology, physical education.

Successful completion of this course leads to a recommendation for Qualified Teacher Status (QTS) after completion of skills tests.

Entry requirements: Age restriction, DipHE, Interview, Work experience
Contact: As above

BEd (Hons) in Primary Education (Key Stage 1 and Nursery, 3–8 years) X101

3 years full-time

Primary teacher training in National Curriculum Key Stage 1 subjects, with specialisation in early childhood development and English.

Level 1: Under 5s specialism; English specialism; school experience.

Level 2: Teaching primary English; teaching foundation subjects; serial school experience.

Level 3: Early years leadership; dissertation subject leadership; block school experience.

Successful completion of this course leads to a recommendation for Qualified Teacher Status (QTS) after completion of skills tests.

Entry requirements: Tariff: 160 to 220 points, 26: International Baccalaureate, BTEC NC/ND, Interview, Work experience
Contact: As above

BEd (Hons) in Primary Education (Key Stage 1 and Nursery, 3–8 years, shortened course) X100

2 years full-time

Primary teacher training in National Curriculum Key Stage 1 subjects, with specialisation in early childhood development and English.

Successful completion of this course leads to a recommendation for Qualified Teacher Status (QTS) after completion of skills tests.

Entry requirements: 26: International Baccalaureate, Age restriction, DipHE, Interview, Work experience
Contact: As above

BEd (Hons) in Primary Education (Later Years, 7–11 years) X102

3 years full-time

Course includes: curriculum and subject studies; teaching methods; experience working in school. Assessment through written assignment, oral presentations and assessment of practical teaching skills. Students take 2 specialist subjects: 1 from English, mathematics or science and 1 from art, geography, history, information technology, physical education.

Level 1: School experience; learning mathematics and being mathematical; language in use.

Level 2: Block school experience; teaching primary science; teaching primary English.

Level 3: Dissertation; core subject leadership; block school experience.

Successful completion of this course leads to a recommendation for Qualified Teacher Status (QTS) after completion of skills tests.

Entry requirements: Tariff: 160 to 220 points, 26: International Baccalaureate, BTEC NC/ND, Interview, Work experience

Contact: As above

BEd (Hons) in Primary Education (Later Years, 7–11 years, shortened course) X122

2 years full-time

Course includes: curriculum and subject studies; teaching methods; experience working in school. Assessment through written assignment, oral presentations and assessment of practical teaching skills. Students take 2 specialist subjects: 1 from English, mathematics or science and 1 from art, geography, history, information technology, physical education.

Successful completion of this course leads to a recommendation for Qualified Teacher Status (QTS) after completion of skills tests.

Entry requirements: Age restriction, BTEC NC/ND, DipHE, International Baccalaureate, Interview

Contact: As above

BEd (Hons) in Primary Education (Physical Education, Key Stage 2, shortened course) X1C6

2 years full-time

Primary teacher training in National Curriculum Key Stage 2 subjects, with specialisation in physical education.

Successful completion of this course leads to a recommendation for Qualified Teacher Status (QTS) after completion of skills tests.

Entry requirements: 12: DipHE, 26: International Baccalaureate, Age restriction, BTEC NC/ND, CCCC: SCE Higher, Interview, Work experience

Contact: As above

PGCE in Primary Education (Lower Primary, 3–7 years) X110

1 year full-time

Entry requirements: GCSE mathematics and English grade C or above (or equivalent), and a degree in a relevant subject for the primary school curriculum; or at least ½ of degree study time spent on an area that relates to the primary curriculum; plus 2 weeks' guided school experience in a primary school and satisfactory school report from head teacher.

Contact: As above

PGCE in Primary Education (Upper Primary, 5–11 years) X100

1 year full-time

Entry requirements: Degree, a significant part of which is in a National Curriculum subject, plus GCSE English language and mathematics; a science subject at GCSE grade C or above is preferred; evidence of successful observation/experience in a primary school or other work with children is strongly recommended; successful applicants are required to complete 2 weeks' of guided school experience in a primary school before commencing the PGCE course.

Contact: As above

PGCE in Secondary Education (Art) W1X1

1 year full-time

Entry requirements: Degree (or equivalent) which includes significant elements related to chosen subject specialism; GCSE mathematics and English grade C or above (or equivalent).

Contact: Alison Scott-Baumann
  Course Leader
  01242 532870
  asbaumann@chelt.ac.uk

PGCE in Secondary Education (Design and Technology) W9X1

1 year full-time

Entry requirements: As above
Contact: Sheila Sykes
  01452 509208

PGCE in Secondary Education (English) Q3X1

1 year full-time

Entry requirements: As above
Contact: Alison Scott-Baumann
  Course Leader
  01242 532870
  asbaumann@chelt.ac.uk

PGCE in Secondary Education (Geography) F8X1

1 year full-time

Entry requirements: As above
Contact: As above

PGCE in Secondary Education (History) V1X1

1 year full-time

Entry requirements: As above
Contact: As above

PGCE in Secondary Education (Information Technology) G5X1

1 year full-time

Entry requirements: As above

Contact: Sheila Sykes
  Course Leader
  01452 509208

PGCE in Secondary Education (Mathematics) G1X1

1 year full-time

Entry requirements: As above
Contact: Alison Scott-Baumann
  Course Leader
  01242 532870
  asbaumann@chelt.ac.uk

PGCE in Secondary Education (Modern Languages) R9X1

1 year full-time

Entry requirements: As above
Contact: As above

PGCE in Secondary Education (Music) W3X1

1 year full-time

Entry requirements: As above
Contact: Sheila Sykes
  01452 509208

PGCE in Secondary Education (Physical Education) X9C6

1 year full-time

Entry requirements: As above
Contact: Alison Scott-Baumann
  Course Leader
  01242 532870
  asbaumann@chelt.ac.uk

PGCE in Secondary Education (Religious Education) V6X1

1 year full-time

Entry requirements: As above
Contact: As above

PGCE in Secondary Education (Science) F0X1

1 year full-time

Entry requirements: As above
Contact: As above

PgCert/PgDip/MEd Educational Leadership

PgCert: 3 months full-time or 24 months part-time; PgDip: 9 months full-time or 36 months part-time; MEd: 12 months full-time or 48 months part-time.

Entry requirements: Qualified Teacher Status plus 2 years' professional experience; or good Honours degree plus 3 years' professional experience/NPHQ award; National Professional Qualification for Headship may be credited towards an award.

Contact: Dr Caroline Mills
Head of Postgraduate Modular Scheme
01242 532928
pms@glos.ac.uk

PgCert Further and Higher Education

1 year part-time

Content covers: teaching and learning; curriculum design and development; professional practice; practice educator.

Entry requirements: For teachers in higher education, and for other professionals involved in education and training.

Contact: As above

PgCert/PgDip/MEd Inclusive Education

PgCert: 3 months full-time or 24 months part-time; PgDip: 9 months full-time or 36 months part-time; MEd: 12 months full-time or 48 months part-time.

Entry requirements: Good degree or equivalent professional qualification or experience, plus qualified teacher status.

Contact: As above

Goldsmiths College, University of London

New Cross
London
SE14 6NW
Tel: 020 7919 7171
Fax: 020 7717 2240
admissions@gold.ac.uk
www.goldsmiths.ac.uk

Goldsmiths College was founded in 1891, and has been part of the University of London since 1904. The College is close to Greenwich and Lewisham, and has excellent public transport links to Central London. There are halls of residence for undergraduate and postgraduate students, and the Accommodation Office provides a private sector accommodation service.

Study resources include the Rutherford Information Services Building (RISB), which brings together the library, computer facilities, language learning and media resources. Goldsmiths offers a variety of clubs and societies, sporting activities and entertainment. Students are also entitled to use the facilities of the University of London Union.

The Department of Educational Studies offers a number of different routes into teaching: an undergraduate degree; a PGCE for primary and secondary teachers; and employment-based routes into teaching (Graduate and Registered Teacher Programme). The department also offers taught Master's and MPhil/PhD programmes.

HOW TO APPLY

Degree courses: applications are made through UCAS.

PGCE: applications are made through the GTTR.

Postgraduate: applications are made direct to the institution.

COURSES

BA (Hons) in Education (Primary, early years) X123

3 years full-time

A specialist subject is chosen from: art; design and technology with computing; English; humanities; mathematics with computing; science, foundation stage.

Year 1: English; mathematics; science; primary curriculum areas including, for example, art, drama, music; teaching studies; professional studies including school experience.

Year 2: English; mathematics; science; 3 subject options chosen from the range available; professional studies including school experience.

Year 3: Specialist subject 1 and 2; teaching studies and education report; professional studies including school experience.

Assessment: Written examinations, coursework and practical assignments.

Successful completion of this course leads to a recommendation for Qualified Teacher Status (QTS) after completion of skills tests.

Entry requirements: SCE Higher: BCCCC, BTEC NC/ND, GCE A- and AS-levels: CC, International Baccalaureate, Irish Leaving Certificates, Work experience
Contact: Dave Boorman
020 7919 7323
d.boorman@gold.ac.uk

BA (Hons) in Education (Primary, junior) X124

3 years full-time
As above

BA (Hons) in Education with Design and Technology (Secondary) X1W2

4 years full-time

All years: Designing and making: students learn to understand and operate responsibly as a designer and technologist in social, cultural, economic, political and environmental contexts employing a range of appropriate skills and practices; teaching and learning: learners and the learning process in the context of formal education, including psychological, cultural, ethical and philosophical perspectives; critical reflection on teaching practices, and how to operate as an effective and professional educator; teaching of design and technology: supporting the development of design and technology capability in 11–18 year-old learners; professional practitioner: integration of skills, values and understandings.

Successful completion of this course leads to a recommendation for Qualified Teacher Status (QTS) after completion of skills tests.

Entry requirements: SCE Higher: BCCCC, BTEC NC/ND, GCE A- and AS-levels: DD, Foundation / access qualification, International Baccalaureate, Irish Leaving Certificates
Contact: Juliet Sprake
Programme Leader
020 7919 7766
admissions@gold.ac.uk

PGCE in Primary Education (Early Years and Key Stage 1, 3–8) X121

1 year full-time

Entry requirements: Degree in a relevant subject and GCSE grade C in English language and mathematics or equivalent; candidates born after 1/9/79 should also have GCSE science at C or above.
Contact: Admissions Office
020 7919 7060
admissions@gold.ac.uk

PGCE in Primary Education (Key Stage 2, 7–11) X171

1 year full-time
As above

PGCE in Secondary Education (Art) W1X1

1 year full-time

Entry requirements: Degree in a relevant subject and GCSE grades A, B or C in English language and mathematics or equivalent qualifications.
Contact: Admissions Office
020 7919 7060
admissions@gold.ac.uk

PGCE in Secondary Education (Biology) C1X1

Part-time or 1 year full-time
As above

PGCE in Secondary Education (Chemistry) F1X1

Part-time or 1 year full-time
As above

PGCE in Secondary Education (Design and Technology) W9X1

Part-time or 1 year full-time

As above

PGCE in Secondary Education (Drama) W4X1

1 year full-time

As above

PGCE in Secondary Education (English) Q3X1

Part-time or 1 year full-time

As above

PGCE in Secondary Education (General Science) F0X1

Part-time or 1 year full-time

As above

PGCE in Secondary Education (Geography) F8X1

1 year full-time

As above

PGCE in Secondary Education (Mathematics) G1X1

1 year full-time

As above

PGCE in Secondary Education (Modern Languages: French) R1X1

1 year full-time

As above

PGCE in Secondary Education (Modern Languages: German) R2X1

1 year full-time

As above

PGCE in Secondary Education (Music) W3X1

1 year full-time

As above

PGCE in Secondary Education (Physics) F3X1

1 year full-time

As above

PGCE in Secondary Education (Social Science and Humanities with Citizenship) L3X1

1 year full-time

As above

MA in Education (Culture, Language and Identity)

1 year full-time, 3 years part-time

Entry requirements: Good Honours degree (at least Upper 2nd class) in relevant subject and appropriate educational experience.

Contact: Dr Carrie Paechter
020 7919 7353
c.paechter@gold.ac.uk

MA in Management of Learning and Teaching

1 year full-time, 2 years part-time

Entry requirements: Degree together with 2 years' teaching experience or equivalent professional qualifications and/or relevant experience.

Contact: Mary-Claire Halvorson
020 7919 7211
m.c.halvorson@gold.ac.uk

Grand Union Training Partnership

Sponne School
Brackley Road
Towcester
Northamptonshire
NN12 6JD
Tel: 01327 350284
Fax: 01327 359061
training@gutp.freeserve.co.uk

The Grand Union Training Partnership is a school-centred initial teacher training consortium centred on four 11–18 comprehensive schools situated in villages and small towns west of Northampton and one 12–18 school in Milton Keynes. Trainees gain practical experience of working in the partnership schools, supervised by a mentor. A general studies programme is provided in co-operation with the University of Leicester, and delivered at the University's centre in Northampton.

HOW TO APPLY

Applications are made through the GTTR.

COURSES

PGCE in Secondary Education (Business Studies with Information Technology) N1X1

1 year full-time

Entry requirements: Degree in relevant subject; GCSE mathematics and English at grade C.

Contact: Enquiries
01327 350284
training@gutp.freeserve.co.uk

PGCE in Secondary Education (English) Q3X1

1 year full-time
As above

PGCE in Secondary Education (French) R1X1

1 year full-time
As above

PGCE in Secondary Education (German) R2X1

1 year full-time
As above

PGCE in Secondary Education (History) V1X1

1 year full-time
As above

PGCE in Secondary Education (Science) F0X1

1 year full-time
As above

University of Greenwich

Maritime Greenwich Campus
Park Row
Greenwich
London
SE10 9LS
Tel: 020 8331 8000 / 0800 005006
Fax: 020 8331 8145
courseinfo@gre.ac.uk
www.gre.ac.uk

The history of the University of Greenwich can be traced back to 1890. Over the years, a range of specialist organisations joined the institution, expanding the diverse selection of subjects available. The name Thames Polytechnic was adopted in 1970 and university status was awarded in 1992. It has Campuses based at Avery Hill, Kingshill, Maritime Greenwich and Medway.

The School of Education and Training is based at the Avery Hill Campus and offers courses in teacher training and degrees in the study of education and related areas. It also runs higher degree programmes and provides Continuing Professional Development for teachers, lecturers and other education professionals and is active in research and consultancy.

The university offers a diverse range of sporting and social facilities and there is accommodation available on and off campus. First-year students are guaranteed a place in university residences.

HOW TO APPLY

Degree courses: applications are made through UCAS.
PGCE: applications are made through the GTTR.

Postgraduate: applications are made direct to the institution.

COURSES

BA/BA (Hons) Primary Teaching Studies (Art) XW11

BA: 3 years full-time; BA (Hons): 4 years full-time

Focus on the development of individual knowledge, understanding and practical skills. Variety of 2-dimensional and 3-dimensional techniques suitable for all levels of primary art education.

Art courses also discuss pedagogical art and design to aid students in their chosen careers, the art curriculum and foundation curriculum.

Successful completion of this course leads to a recommendation for Qualified Teacher Status (QTS) after completion of skills tests.

Entry requirements: International Baccalaureate: 26, SCE Higher: BBB, BTEC NC/ND, GCE A- and AS-levels: CC, Irish Leaving Certificates: CCCCC, Portfolio
Contact: Barbara Huish
0800 005006
courseinfo@greenwich.ac.uk

BA (Hons) Primary Teaching Studies (Design and Technology) XW1F

3 years full-time or 4 years full-time

Introductory course involves textile, food, construction and graphic media while working collaboratively on a chosen scheme. Subsequent courses look at design technology in greater depth and students are given open-ended assignments.

Successful completion of this course leads to a recommendation for Qualified Teacher Status (QTS) after completion of skills tests.

Entry requirements: International Baccalaureate: 26, SCE Higher: BBB, BTEC NC/ND, GCE A- and AS-levels: CC, Irish Leaving Certificates: CCCCC, Foundation / access qualification
Contact: Keith Good
Senior Lecturer
0800 005006
courseinfo@greenwich.ac.uk

BA (Hons) Primary Teaching Studies (Early Years) XX13

3 years full-time or 4 years full-time

Part 1: Focuses on foundation stage of early years (nursery and reception). Provides students with detailed knowledge of the early learning goals and will give them opportunities to develop their own abilities in planning, implementing, assessing and evaluating an appropriate curriculum for this age group.

Part 2: Focuses on Key Stage 1 and relevant National Curriculum. Child development issues, base line assessment and transitions from 1 stage to another are also discussed.

Successful completion of this course leads to a recommendation for Qualified Teacher Status (QTS) after completion of skills tests.

Entry requirements: As above
Contact: Liz Gerrish
Early Years Coordinator
0800 005006
courseinfo@greenwich.ac.uk

BA (Hons) Primary Teaching Studies (English) XQ13

3 years full-time or 4 years full-time

The degree is in 2 parts: Subject study (English) and professional studies, including school placements. Subject study allows students to specialise. Professional studies includes school experience, curriculum studies and general professional development – education studies. Students spend a minimum of 32 weeks in various primary schools.

Curriculum studies develops students all-round abilities to teach the National Curriculum, and in the second half of the programme students focus on a particular pupil age-range. Education studies examines both the principles and the contemporary debates in primary education, including issues in child development and how children learn.

Students also study classroom management and the practical ways of organising pupils' learning. In the final stages, students will have time to extend their subject knowledge, and its application, in terms of learning in the primary school.

Successful completion of this course leads to a recommendation for Qualified Teacher Status (QTS) after completion skills tests.

Entry requirements: International Baccalaureate: 24, SCE Higher: BCCC, BTEC NC/ND, GCE A- and AS-levels: CC, Foundation / access qualification

Contact: Maggie Gravelle
Senior Lecturer
020 8331 9400
m.j.martin@gre.ac.uk

BA (Hons) Primary Teaching Studies (Mathematics) XG11

3 years full-time or 4 years full-time

The course prepares graduates to teach in a primary school, it covers core national curriculum subjects of mathematics, English, science and information and communications technology in depth and includes courses in all the foundation subjects, religious education and education. In addition students study mathematics to higher level. Problem solving and investigation are central to mathematical endeavour and are explicitly included in the mathematics national curriculum. Students are introduced to a range of mathematical problems and encouraged to pose problems from varied starting points. Introduction to a range of mathematical theory about mathematical thinking at adult and child level. Information and communications technology is central to the mathematics courses studied.

Successful completion of this course leads to a recommendation for Qualified Teacher Status (QTS) after completion of skills tests.

Entry requirements: International Baccalaureate: 26, SCE Higher: BBB, BTEC NC/ND, GCE A- and AS-levels: CC, Irish Leaving Certificates: CCCCC
Contact: Geoff Sheath
0800 005006
courseinfo@greenwich.ac.uk

BA (Hons) Primary Teaching Studies (Physical Education) XC16

3 years full-time or 4 years full-time

Successful completion of this course leads to a recommendation for Qualified Teacher Status (QTS) after completion of skills tests.

BA/BA (Hons) Primary Teaching Studies (Science) XF10

BA: 3 years full-time; BA (Hons): 4 years full-time

Science courses are integrated, enabling students to appreciate the relationships between different disciplines. Topics are selected from the National Curriculum and students develop their own knowledge and understanding of these areas. Emphasis is on practical science skills. Science courses also discuss pedagogical matters to prepare students for their chosen careers; additionally students study the core curriculum, foundation curriculum and religious education and undertake school experiences to prepare them to teach in the primary school.

Successful completion of this course leads to a recommendation for Qualified Teacher Status (QTS) after completion of skills tests.

Entry requirements: International Baccalaureate: 24, SCE Higher: BCCC, BTEC NC/ND, GCE A- and AS-levels: CC, Foundation / access qualification
Contact: Jo Mayes
020 8331 9563
j.mayes@greenwich.ac.uk

BA (Hons) Secondary Education (Design and Technology) XWD2

2 years full-time

Students are offered opportunities to: Develop the practical knowledge and theoretical understanding required to successfully work with secondary school children; develop knowledge and understanding of technology within the context of the National Curriculum; undertake personal and teamworking projects based on design and technology; develop their own designing, communicating and making skills.

Successful completion of this course leads to a recommendation for Qualified Teacher Status (QTS) after completion of skills tests.

Entry requirements: GCE A- and AS-levels, HND

Contact: Jim Golden
Principal Lecturer
0800 005006
courseinfo@greenwich.ac.uk

BA (Hons) Secondary Education Studies (Design and Technology)

2 years full-time
As above

Entry requirements: International Baccalaureate: 24, SCE Higher: BCC, BTEC NC/ND, GCE A- and AS-levels: CD, Foundation / access qualification
Contact: Jim Golden
Principal Lecturer
0800 005006
courseinfo@greenwich.ac.uk

PGCE Post-Compulsory Education and Training

1 year full-time or 2 to 6 years part-time

Entry requirements: Candidates are required to be employed full- or part-time in an institution or organisation in the post-compulsory sector, with degree or vocational/professional qualification; accreditation of experience or prior learning (e.g., C&G 730/7307) is offered and can give exemption from study of some units.
Contact: Enquiries
0800 005006
courseinfo@gre.ac.uk

PGCE Primary Education (Lower Primary, 5–8) X121

1 year full-time

Entry requirements: Degree qualification appropriate to the primary school curriculum with GCSE minimum grade C (or equivalent) in English language and mathematics. Applicants who were born on or after 1st September 1979 will also be required to have attained the standard of GCSE grade C in science. The first degree should provide the foundation for work as a teacher in the primary phase.
Contact: Penny Smith
Programme Leader
0800 005006
courseinfo@greenwich.ac.uk

PGCE Primary Education (Upper Primary, 7–11) X171

1 year full-time

Entry requirements: Degree qualification appropriate to 1 of the curriculum areas with GCSE minimum grade C (or equivalent) in English language and mathematics. Applicants who were born on or after 1st September 1979 will also be required to have attained the standard of GCSE grade C in science. The first degree should provide the foundation for work as a teacher in the primary phase.
Contact: Enquiries
0800 005006
courseinfo@gre.ac.uk

PGCE Secondary Education (Art) V1X1

1 year full-time

Entry requirements: Candidates must possess at least GCSE mathematics and English (grades A–C) or equivalent.
Contact: Andy Hudson
Director of Secondary Teacher Education
0800 005006
courseinfo@gre.ac.uk

PGCE Secondary Education (Design and Technology, conversion) WXX1

1 to 3 years mixed mode or 2 years full-time
As above

PGCE Secondary Education (Design and Technology) W9X1

1 year full-time
As above

PGCE Secondary Education (Mathematics) G1X1

1 year full-time

Entry requirements: Degree in mathematics, and GCSE mathematics and English language grade C, or equivalent.
Contact: As above

PGCE Secondary Education (Physical Education) X9C6

1 year full-time

Entry requirements: All candidates must possess at least GCSE mathematics and English (grades A–C) or equivalent.

Contact: As above

PGCE Secondary Education (Science) F0X1

1 year full-time

Entry requirements: Degree in sciences, and GCSE mathematics and English language grade C or equivalent.

Contact: As above

PgDip/MA in Management of Language Learning

MA: 1 year full-time or 2 years part-time

Entry requirements: Degree and some experience in language teaching or training normally required.

Contact: Dr A Benati
020 8331 9048
a.benati@gre.ac.uk

MA in Education

3 to 6 years part-time

Entry requirements: Good Honours degree; applicants should be qualified teachers with 3 years' professional experience.

Contact: Francia Kinchington
020 8331 8058/0800 005 006
f.kinchington@gre.ac.uk

MA in Post-Compulsory Education and Training

1 year full-time

Entry requirements: BEd and 3 years' teaching experience, or Honours degree and teaching qualification plus 3 years' teaching experience, or equivalent. Accreditation of prior learning, including experiential learning can lead to exemption from a number of courses.

Contact: Anne Lahiff
Programme Leader
020 8331 7677/0800 005006
a.t.lahiff@gre.ac.uk

MSc in Education Management

1 year full-time

Entry requirements: Honours degree or equivalent; 2 years' management experience in education or training; accreditation of prior learning, including experiential learning can lead to exemption from a number of courses.

Contact: As above

EdD in Education

Entry requirements: Minimum 3 years' teaching experience normally required, plus either Honours degree, DPSE, relevant postgraduate diploma or DMS, or proof of work at equivalent level.

Contact: Shirley Leathers
CPD Administrative Secretary
S.M.Leathers@gre.ac.uk

University of Hertfordshire

College Lane
Hatfield
Hertfordshire
AL10 9AB
Tel: 01707 284800
Fax: 01707 284870
admissions@herts.ac.uk
www.herts.ac.uk

The University of Hertfordshire is a multi-campus university based close to the City of London. It currently has four campuses on which faculties are based: Bayfordbury, Hatfield, St Albans and Watford, all of which have Learning Resource centres and other student facilities and services. A fifth campus, the De Havilland Campus at Hatfield is opening in September 2003.

The Department of Education is currently based at the Watford Campus but will be moving to the De Havilland Campus. The department runs undergraduate and postgraduate courses leading to recommendation for Qualified Teacher Status and there are also continuing professional development programmes for established teachers. Courses for teaching assistants, early years practitioners and overseas qualified teachers are available and there is an employment-based Graduate Teacher Programme. The university guarantees students a place in university accommodation in the first year of study. There are halls on campus or privately rented accommodation nearby.

HOW TO APPLY

Degree courses: applications are made through UCAS.

PGCE: applications are made through the GTTR.

Postgraduate (and PGCE/CertEd in Post-16 Education): applications are made direct to the institution.

COURSES

BSc (Hons) Mathematics G1XC

4 years full-time

Mathematics components introduce students to virtually all of the topics found in modern A-level syllabuses and give students the knowledge and skills to cope with future developments in teaching; the final year project has strong links with teaching.

Entry requirements: Tariff: 180, International Baccalaureate: 26, BTEC NC/ND
Contact: University Admissions Office
01707 284800
admissions@herts.ac.uk

BEd/BEd (Hons) Primary Education (for students with overseas qualifications) X101

BEd: 2 years full-time; BEd (Hons): 2 years full-time or 3 years mixed mode

2 main areas: professional training and 1 subject study. Choices of subject study include language and communications, mathematics and religious studies. Professional training is school focused and includes all areas of the National Curriculum, cross-curricular themes, the study of educational issues. Students will either specialise in the 3–7 years or the 8–11 years age range.

Successful completion of this course leads to a recommendation for Qualified Teacher Status (QTS) after completion of skills tests.

Entry requirements: International qualifications, Interview
Contact: As above

BEd (Hons) Primary Education with Art XW11

3 years full-time

Combines a programme of academic study with professional training; specialist subjects; professional training is focused in schools and on all areas of the National Curriculum, cross-curricular issues, attainment targets and assessment procedures, as well as on a range of educational issues; there are at least 32 weeks of school-based work throughout the 3 years of study.

Specialism in education: General Professional Studies courses cover such areas as: assessment, recording and reporting; children's learning and teaching in the primary school; early years education (3–8 years); equal opportunities; the European dimension in education; special educational needs.

The art course involves theoretical and practical work in: painting; printmaking; photography; ceramics; sculpture; creative dress; embroidery; textile printing; dyeing and weaving; study visits.

Successful completion of this course leads to a recommendation for Qualified Teacher Status (QTS) after completion of skills tests.

Entry requirements: Tariff: 180–220, Irish Leaving Certificates: 370, BTEC NC/ND, Foundation / access qualification, International Baccalaureate, Interview, SCE Higher
Contact: As above

BEd (Hons) Primary Education with English Literature and Language XQ13

3 years full-time

Combines a programme of academic study with professional training.

Specialist subjects

Professional training: Focused in schools and on all areas of the National Curriculum, cross-curricular issues, attainment targets and assessment procedures, as well as on a range of educational issues. There are at least 32 weeks of school-based work throughout the 3 years of study.

Specialism in education: General Professional Studies course covers such areas as: assessment, recording and reporting; children's learning and teaching in the primary school; early years education (3–8 years); equal opportunities; the European dimension in education; special educational needs.The English course considers literature within the context of other media: film, theatre, television and encourages students to develop their understanding of the 3 principal literary genres: prose, poetry and drama through the study of Renaissance literature and early novels. Later the emphasis is placed on the modern period. 2 options: the tragic vision or American literature.

Successful completion of this course leads to a recommendation for Qualified Teacher Status (QTS) after completion of skills tests.

Entry requirements: As above
Contact: As above

BEd (Hons) Primary Education with Mathematics XG11

3 years full-time

Combines a programme of academic study with professional training; specialist subjects; professional training: focused in schools and on all areas of the National Curriculum, cross-curricular issues, attainment targets and assessment procedures, as well as on a range of educational issues. There are at least 32 weeks of school-based work throughout the 3 years of study.

Specialism in education: General Professional Studies course covers such areas as: assessment; recording and reporting;

children's learning and teaching in the primary school; early years education (3–8 years); equal opportunities; European dimension in education; special educational needs.

Successful completion of this course leads to a recommendation for Qualified Teacher Status (QTS) after completion of skills tests.

Entry requirements: As above
Contact: As above

BEd (Hons) Primary Education with Science XF1A

3 years full-time

Combines a programme of academic study with professional training; specialist subjects; students specialise in their chosen subject; professional training: focused in schools and on all areas of the National Curriculum, cross-curricular issues, attainment targets and assessment procedures, as well as on a range of educational issues; there are at least 32 weeks of school-based work throughout the 3 years of study. Specialism in education: General Professional Studies course covers such areas as: assessment, recording and reporting; children's learning and teaching in the primary school; early years education (3–8 years); equal opportunities; European dimension in education; special educational needs.The science course has been designed to meet the requirements of the National Curriculum.

Successful completion of this course leads to a recommendation for Qualified Teacher Status (QTS) after completion of skills tests.

Entry requirements: As above
Contact: As above

PGCE Post-16 Education and Training

2 years part-time

Entry requirements: Candidates required to be employed in a teaching or training role for minimum of 6 hours a week throughout the programme.
Contact: CPD Admissions Office
01707 285766
V.Chick@herts.ac.uk

PGCE Primary Education (Foundation-Key Stage 1) X121

1 year full-time

Entry requirements: GCSE grade C or above (or equivalent) in English Language, mathematics and science, together with an appropriate good Honours degree awarded by a British University, or an award recognised as equivalent by the Department for Education and Employment; 2 weeks' continuous work experience in a state primary school.

Contact: University Admissions Office
01707 284800
Admissions@herts.ac.uk

PGCE in Primary Education (Foundation-Key Stage 1) X125

2 years part-time
As above

PGCE Primary Education (Key Stages 1–2) X171

1 year full-time
As above

Entry requirements: GCSE grade C or above (or equivalent) in English Language, mathematics and science, together with an appropriate good Honours degree awarded by a British University, or an award recognised as equivalent by the Department for Education and Employment; 2 weeks' continuous work experience in a state primary school.

Contact: As above

PGCE Secondary Education (Art) W1X1

1 year full-time or 2 years part-time

Entry requirements: An appropriate degree, plus GCSE grade C or above (or equivalent) in mathematics and English language. Mature applicants and students from ethnic minorities are especially welcome.

Contact: As above

PGCE Secondary Education (English) Q3X1

1 year full-time or 2 years part-time
As above

PGCE Secondary Education (French with German) RX11

1 year full-time or 2 years part-time
As above

PGCE Secondary Education (French with Spanish) RXD1

1 year full-time or 2 years part-time
As above

PGCE Secondary Education (French) R1X1

1 year full-time or 2 years part-time
As above

PGCE Secondary Education (Geography) F8X1

1 year full-time or 2 years part-time
As above

PGCE Secondary Education (German with French) RX21

1 year full-time or 2 years part-time
As above

PGCE Secondary Education (Mathematics) G1X1

1 year full-time or 2 years part-time
As above

PGCE Secondary Education (Science) F0X1

1 year full-time or 2 years part-time
As above

PgCert/PgDip/MA/MEd in Education

Part-time

Entry requirements: Degree with QTS or equivalent for post-16 sector and relevant experience.

Contact: INSET Unit
01707 285766
V.Chick@herts.ac.uk

PgDip in Education of Deaf Children

2 year part-time

Entry requirements: Qualified Teacher Status.

Contact: As above

High Force Education

Darlington and Dales Teacher Training
Green Lane
Barnard Castle
County Durham
DL12 8LG
Tel: 01833 630487
Fax: 01833 690316
kturnbull100@durhamlea.org.uk
www.highforceeducation.org.uk

High Force Education offers School Centred Initial Teacher Training in 11 schools in the Darlington to Teesside area. The course structure includes time in the Central Study and Support Area (CSSA) based in Barnard Castle Church of England Primary School as well as in-school teaching practice. Trainees follow the taught part of the course on Monday and Tuesday in the CSSA and then have time in the classrooms of a range of schools during Wednesday, Thursday and Friday. The CSSA is equipped with computer facilities and a library.

HOW TO APPLY
Applications are made through the GTTR.

COURSES
PGCE in Primary Education (5–11 years) X100
1 year full-time

Entry requirements: Degree in relevant subject; GCSE grade C or above in English language and mathematics, and science if born after 1/9/79.
Contact: Enquiries
01833 630487
k.turnbull100@durhamlea.
org.uk

University of Huddersfield

Queensgate
Huddersfield
Kirklees
HD1 3DH
Tel: 01484 422288
Fax: 01484 516151
admissions@hud.ac.uk
www.hud.ac.uk

The University of Huddersfield was granted university status in 1992 and was formerly Huddersfield Polytechnic. The main campus is located adjacent to the town-centre. Amongst the academic buildings are the award-winning conversions of historic mill buildings.

Teacher training and education at Huddersfield has developed since the mid-20th century. Firstly the Technical Teacher Training College was founded in 1947 and was principally concerned with establishing full-time programmes of basic training. In 1963 the name was changed to College of Education (Technical) and in 1974 the separate institution merged with Huddersfield Polytechnic and a Faculty of Education was formed which facilitated the development of degree programmes. By 1992 when the polytechnic became a university the faculty had an established research expertise. Now named The School of Education and Professional Development, it provides a range of programmes at undergraduate and postgraduate level including PGCE courses. It is based in the newly refurbished Lockside building on Firth Street

The university has library and computer resources available as well as a range of student service and facilities on campus. There is a selection of student accommodation available in privately owned halls of residence and shared houses and priority is given to first-year students.

HOW TO APPLY
Degree courses: applications are made through UCAS.

PGCE: applications are made through the GTTR.

Postgraduate and part-time/in-service courses: applications are made direct to the institution.

COURSES

BEd/BEd (Hons) in Secondary Education (Business Studies) XN11

BEd: 2 years full-time, BEd (Hons): 3 years mixed mode

All years: Study of subject specialism supported by 2 school placements; and general professional studies: knowledge and skills to create effective learning environments in schools; understanding of the broad issues which affect teaching and learning; how teachers produce effective learning; how to develop the skills pupils need to gain access to the curriculum; also covers: special educational needs; pastoral care; problems experienced with pupils such as bullying, truancy, race and gender issues; economic and industrial understanding; enterprise; careers; environmental issues; citizenship and health.

BEd (Hons) is awarded after further year of part-time study associated with 1st teaching post.

Successful completion of this course leads to a recommendation for Qualified Teacher Status (QTS) after completion of skills tests.

Entry requirements: HNC, HND
Contact: Prof David Newbold
01484 478275

BEd/BEd (Hons) in Secondary Education (Design and Technology) XW12

BEd: 2 years full-time, BEd (Hons): 3 years mixed mode
As above

BEd/BEd (Hons) in Secondary Education (Information and Communication Technology) XG15

BEd: 2 years full-time, BEd (Hons): 3 years mixed mode
As above

Entry requirements: As above
Contact: Roger Crawford
Senior Lecturer
01484 478264
r.a.crawford@hud.ac.uk

BEd/BEd (Hons) in Secondary Education (Mathematics) XG11

BEd: 2 years full-time, BEd (Hons): 3 years mixed mode
As above

BEd/BEd (Hons) in Secondary Education (Music) XW13

BEd: 2 years full-time, BEd (Hons): 3 years mixed mode
As above

BEd/BEd (Hons) in Secondary Education (Science) XF10

BEd: 2 years full-time, BEd (Hons): 3 years mixed mode

The course is continuous and progressive through the 2 years. All specialist subjects are supported by general professional studies and include placements in 2 secondary schools. General professional studies are designed to give the student the knowledge and skills to create effective learning environments in schools and an understanding of the broad issues which affect teaching and learning. It emphasises how teachers produce effective learning and also how to develop the skills pupils need to gain access to the curriculum. More general aspects of school life are also studied: special educational needs; pastoral care; problems experienced with pupils such as bullying, truancy, race and gender issues; economic and industrial understanding; enterprise; careers; environmental issues; citizenship and health.

At the end of the 2 years successful students receive the award of BEd; after a further year of part-time study associated with the 1st teaching post students are able to gain the award of BEd (Hons).

Successful completion of this course leads to a recommendation for Qualified Teacher Status (QTS) after completion of skills tests.

Entry requirements: As above
Contact: Mr David Thompson
01484 478213

BEd/BEd (Hons) in Upper Primary/Lower Secondary Education (Design and Technology, 7–14) X1WF
BEd: 2 years full-time, BEd (Hons): 3 years mixed mode
As above

PGCE in Middle Years (Design and Technology, Key Stages 2–3) XWCX
38 weeks full-time

Entry requirements: Relevant degree, and GCSE English language, science and mathematics at grade C or above (or equivalent).
Contact: Anne Gibson
01484 478240/4
f.a.gibson@hud.ac.uk

PGCE in Post-Compulsory Education and Training (in-service)
2 years part-time evening only

Entry requirements: Degree in subject to be taught with at least 2 years' post-qualification experience in this area; applicants must be employed to teach for at least 150 hours during course.
Contact: Roy Fisher
Admissions Tutor
01484 478269
r.fisher@hud.ac.uk

PGCE in Post-Compulsory Education and Training (pre-service)
1 year full-time

Entry requirements: Degree or equivalent qualification; at least 3 years' relevant work experience in area to be taught.
Contact: Mel Ashmore
Admissions Tutor
01484 478216/69
sepd@hud.ac.uk

PGCE in Secondary Education (Business Studies with Citizenship) NX1C
1 year full-time

Entry requirements: 2:2 degree or above in relevant subject area; mathematics and English GCSE.

Contact: Neil Denby
01484 478112

PGCE in Secondary Education (Business Studies) N1X1
1 year full-time

Entry requirements: Qualifications and expertise in an appropriate subject area; mathematics and English language at GCSE grade C (or equivalent).
Contact: Bob Butroyd
01484 478220
r.butroyd@hud.ac.uk

PGCE in Secondary Education (Business Studies, conversion) NXC1
2 years full-time

Entry requirements: Appropriate qualifications and expertise (and some industrial experience) plus mathematics and English language at GCSE grade C or above (or equivalent).
Contact: As above

PGCE in Secondary Education (Design and Technology) W9X1
1 year full-time

Entry requirements: Qualifications (degree) and expertise in an appropriate subject area (and some industrial experience) plus mathematics and English language at GCSE grade C or above (or equivalent).
Contact: Mr A Turner
Senior Lecturer
01484 478244
a.turner@hud.ac.uk

PGCE in Secondary Education (Design and Technology, conversion) WXX1
2 years full-time
As above

PGCE in Secondary Education (History) V1X1
1 year full-time

Entry requirements: 2:2 degree or above in relevant subject area; mathematics and English GCSE.
Contact: Claire Smith
01484 478102

PGCE in Secondary Education (Information Technology) G5X1

1 year full-time

Entry requirements: Degree (minimum Lower 2nd Class) in an information technology related discipline, or substantial practical experience in information technology; GCSE English and mathematics at grade C or above (or equivalent).
Contact: Roger Crawford
01484 478264
r.a.crawford@hud.ac.uk

PGCE in Secondary Education (Information Technology, conversion) GXM1

2 years full-time

Entry requirements: Applicants must have at least a Lower 2nd Class degree containing substantial component of information technology or substantial practical experience.
Contact: As above

PGCE in Secondary Education (Mathematics) G1X1

1 year full-time

Entry requirements: Minimum Lower 2nd Class degree in a mathematical discipline, or substantial practical experience; GCSE English and mathematics at grade C or above (or equivalents).
Contact: As above

PGCE in Secondary Education (Mathematics, conversion) GXC1

2 years full-time

Entry requirements: As above
Contact: As above

PGCE in Secondary Education (Music) W3X1

1 year full-time

Entry requirements: Good Honours degree and Grade 8 on main instrument, plus mathematics and English language at GCSE grade C level or above (or equivalent) required; piano skills and A-level music advisable.

Contact: Lesley-Anne Pearson
Course Leader
01484 478263
l.pearson@hud.ac.uk

PGCE in Secondary Education (Music, conversion) WXH1

2 years full-time

Entry requirements: Appropriate degree and appropriate main instrument/music skills, plus mathematics and English language at GCSE grade C level or above (or equivalent).
Contact: As above

PGCE in Secondary Education (Science, conversion) FXA1

2 years full-time

Entry requirements: Minimum Lower 2nd Class Honours science degree and GCSE English language and mathematics at grade C or above (or equivalent). Plus A-level passes in 2 of the following: physics, chemistry, biology or equivalent GNVQ standard.
Contact: Mr D Thompson
01484 478213
d.thompson@hud.ac.uk

PGCE in Secondary Education (Science: Biology) C1X1

1 year full-time

Entry requirements: Relevant degree (minimum Lower 2nd Class), and GCSE English language and mathematics at grade C or above (or equivalent), together with GCE A-level passes or GNVQ (or equivalent) in at least 2 science subjects at grade C or above.
Contact: As above

PGCE in Secondary Education (Science: Chemistry) F1X1

1 year full-time
As above

PGCE in Secondary Education (Science: Physics) F3X1

1 year full-time
As above

EdD in Education

3.5–7 years part-time

Entry requirements: Relevant Master's degree or equivalent.

Contact: Dr Paul Oliver
Programme Leader
01484 478212
p.oliver@hud.ac.uk

MA in Education (Human Resource Development)

12 months full-time

Entry requirements: Degree in professional area (such as BEd); or first degree plus recognised professional qualification (such as PGCE or CertEd); or diploma in professional studies in education: all entrants will normally have 2 years' full-time experience in an appropriate professional area.

Contact: Dr D B Brady
Pathway Leader
01484 478252
d.b.brady@hud.ac.uk

PgCert/PgDip/MA in Professional Development

PgCert/PgDip: 1 year part-time, MA: 3 years part-time

Entry requirements: Honours degree preferred; non-standard applicants can be admitted after interview with tutors and reference from employer.

Contact: Mrs H Swift
Head of Continuing Professional Development
01484 478203
h.d.swift@hud.ac.uk

University of Hull

Admissions Office
Cottingham road
Hull
Kingston-upon-Hull
HU6 7RX
Tel: 01482 466100
Fax: 01482 442290
admissions@hull.ac.uk
www.hull.ac.uk

The University of Hull was founded in 1927 and is based in the suburbs of the City of Hull. It later merged with Scarborough Campus and some academic buildings are based there in addition to the Hull Campus.

The University offers a range of undergraduate and postgraduate programmes including PGCE courses and taught and research opportunities. Courses are run from the Scarborough School of Education, Centre for Educational Studies and also through the Educational Development Team.

Both campuses have shops and restaurants and a variety of social and leisure facilities. There are libraries on both sites and also computer facilities in clusters around the campuses and in some residences. A range of accommodation is available for undergraduates and postgraduates. PGCE students will be assisted in finding private accommodation.

HOW TO APPLY

Degree courses: applications are made through UCAS.

PGCE: applications are made through the GTTR.

Postgraduate: applications are made direct to the institution.

COURSES

BSc (Hons) in Professional Studies in Primary Education with Biological Studies XC11 S

3 years full-time

Modular programme that provides the knowledge and skills necessary for a generalist primary school teacher and for a potential curriculum leader. A range of modules develop the ability to plan, teach and assess effectively across the primary curriculum. Students specialise in biological studies. At least 34 weeks will be spent in school, focusing on either the 3–8 or 7–11 age range.

Successful completion of this course leads to a recommendation for Qualified Teacher Status (QTS) after completion of skills tests.

Entry requirements: Tariff: 200 points, BTEC NC/ND, Foundation / access qualification

Contact: Ruth James
Admissions Tutor
01723 362392
r.james@hull.ac.uk

BA (Hons) in Professional Studies in Primary Education with English XQ13 S

3 years full-time

Students spend a significant amount of time (over 24 weeks) on school placement.

English subject specialism offers modules on 'literary' aspects of English with a strong focus on language studies, literary theory and cultural studies. The literature modules examine poetry and forms of literature, classic realism, modernism and postmodernism, and children's literature. Social aspects of language are examined through the relationships between language and society, language and gender, and language and power.

Teaching Studies modules cover theoretical aspects of education as well as informing the development of classroom-based skills such as planning, assessing children's work and teaching techniques. During the first 2 years students study the primary core subjects of English, mathematics and science.

Entry requirements: As above
Contact: David Cox
01723 357240
d.cox@hull.ac.uk

BA (Hons) in Professional Studies in Primary Education with Information and Communications Technology XGC1 S

BA (Hons): 3 years full-time

Level 1: Foundation, ideas and skills; information and communications technology (ICT) system fundamentals; human computer interaction; programming and authoring systems.

Level 2: Generic applications and effects; database systems and information management; ICT futures.

Level 3: ICT and schools; ICT in practise; ICT co-ordination in schools.

Successful completion of this course leads to a recommendation for Qualified Teacher Status (QTS) after completion of skills tests.

Entry requirements: Tariff: 200 points, BTEC NC/ND, Foundation / access qualification
Contact: Peter Williams
Course Co-ordinator
01723 357219
P.Williams@hull.ac.uk

BA (Hons) in Professional Studies in Primary Education with Mathematics XG11 S

3 years full-time

Modular programme which provides the knowledge and skills necessary for a generalist primary school teacher and for a potential curriculum leader. A range of modules develop the ability to plan, teach and assess effectively across the primary curriculum. Students specialise in mathematics. At least 34 weeks will be spent in school, focusing on either the 3–8 or 7–11 age range.

Successful completion of this course leads to a recommendation for Qualified Teacher Status (QTS) after completion of skills tests.

Entry requirements: Tariff: 180 points, Foundation / access qualification
Contact: Bill Holmes
Admissions Tutor
01723 357308
B.Holmes@hull.ac.uk

PGCE in Primary Education (Early Years) X121 S

1 year full-time

Entry requirements: Good Honours degree, plus GCSE grade C or above in English, mathematics and science.

Contact: PGCE Admissions Secretary
01723 362392
education@hull.ac.uk

PGCE in Primary Education (General Primary, 5–11) X100

1 year full-time

Entry requirements: Degree in subject(s) relevant to the primary school curriculum required; in addition, GCSE minimum grade C (or equivalent) in English language and mathematics (and, for those born on or after 1/9/79, science).

Contact: PGCE Admissions Secretary
01482 465406
education@hull.ac.uk

PGCE in Secondary Education (Balanced Science: Biology) C1X1

1 year full-time

Entry requirements: Degree relevant to subject applicant wishes to teach, and GCSE minimum grade C (or equivalent) in English language and mathematics.

Contact: As above

PGCE in Secondary Education (Balanced Science: Chemistry) F1X1

1 year full-time
As above

PGCE in Secondary Education (Balanced Science: Physics) F3X1

1 year full-time
As above

PGCE in Secondary Education (Business Studies) N1X1

1 year full-time
As above

PGCE in Secondary Education (English) Q3X1

1 year full-time
As above

PGCE in Secondary Education (French) R1X1

1 year full-time
As above

PGCE in Secondary Education (Geography) F8X1

1 year full-time
As above

PGCE in Secondary Education (German) R2X1

1 year full-time
As above

PGCE in Secondary Education (History) V1X1

1 year full-time
As above

PGCE in Secondary Education (History with Citizenship) VX1C

1 year full-time
As above

PGCE in Secondary Education (Mathematics) G1X1

1 year full-time
As above

PGCE in Secondary Education (Mathematics, conversion) GXC1

2 years full-time
As above

PGCE in Secondary Education (Religious Education) V6X1

1 year full-time
As above

PGCE in Secondary Education (Religious Education with Citizenship) VX6C

1 year full-time
As above

PGCE in Secondary Education (Spanish) R4X1

1 year full-time
As above

Advanced Certificate/Advanced Diploma/MEd in Early Years Education

Part-time

Entry requirements: Applicants should be qualified teachers with experience of working in an early years setting.

Contact: Postgraduate Admissions Secretary
01482 466898
education@hull.ac.uk

EdD in Education

3 years full-time, 5 years part-time

Entry requirements: Master's degree, together with appropriate professional experience.

Contact: As above

MEd in Education

12 months full-time, 9 years part-time

Entry requirements: Degree and PGCE or CertEd and 3–4 years' experience required.

Contact: As above

MEd in Information Communication Technology for Teaching English to Speakers of Other Languages

Part-time

Entry requirements: Applicants will usually be graduates who hold a teaching qualification in the teaching of English to speakers of other languages plus a minimum of 3 years' teaching experience in that field.

Contact: As above

MEd in Inclusive Education

9 years part-time

Entry requirements: Applicants should be qualified teachers, either at primary or secondary level.

Contact: As above

Institute of Education, University of London

20 Bedford Way
London
WC1H 0AL
Tel: 020 7612 6000
Fax: 020 7612 6126
info@ioe.ac.uk
www.ioe.ac.uk

The Institute of Education is a graduate college of the University of London. It was founded in 1902 to deliver high quality teacher training. The Institute has expanded its activities over the years, and now offers courses leading to higher degrees in all areas of education and related aspects of the social sciences and professional practice. It is also a centre for educational research and a forum for debate on educational issues.

The Institute is located in Bloomsbury in central London, close to bus, rail and underground links. It is part of the campus of the University of London and close to other colleges. Most students study in the Institute's main building, which houses the Institute library. In addition to the Institute's own facilities, students have access to the cafeteria, bar, theatre workshop, swimming pool, gymnasium and badminton and squash courts in the University of London Union.

The Institute offers Initial Teacher Training in primary, secondary and post-compulsory education, and a range of Master's and doctoral programmes in education and related fields.

HOW TO APPLY

PGCE: applications are made through the GTTR.

Postgraduate: applications are made direct to the institution.

COURSES

PGCE in Adult Literacy and English for Speakers of Other Languages

1 year part-time

Entry requirements: Stage 2 initial teacher qualification; applicants should be currently employed as teacher of adult literacy or ESOL teaching for at least 6 hours per week; should be able to show evidence that they have: a minimum of 60 hours' experience of teaching adult literacy as independent teacher; excellent personal language and literacy skills.

Contact: Registry
Initial Teacher Education
020 7612 6123
pgce.enquiries@ioe.ac.uk

PGCE in Post-Compulsory Education X341

1 year full-time or 4 to 6 terms part-time

Entry requirements: Degree from UK universities, or other qualification accepted as equivalent by the Institute; competence in both English language and mathematics; qualification should be in an area of strong relevance to the post-compulsory curriculum.

Contact: Registry
Initial Teacher Education
020 7612 6123
pgce.enquiries@ioe.ac.uk

PGCE in Primary Education (Foundation and Key Stage 1 or Key Stage 1 and 2) X100

1 year full-time or 5 terms part-time

Entry requirements: Degree (preferably 2.2 or above), or equivalent or graduate qualification which is acceptable to the Institute; GCSE (grade C minimum) in English language and mathematics, or approved equivalent examinations; applicants born on or after 1/9/79 must also have GCSE science; recent experience of state primary schools and of work with young children is essential.

Contact: Registry
Initial Teacher Education
020 7612 6123
pgce.enquiries@ioe.ac.uk

PGCE in Secondary Education (Art and Design) W1X1

1 year full-time or 4 terms part-time

Entry requirements: Degree, equivalent or graduate qualification accepted by the Institute as appropriate in any field of art

and design, including history of art and design and allied disciplines; GCSE minimum grade C or approved equivalent in both English language and mathematics; evidence of recent practical work.

Contact: Registry
Initial Teacher Education
020 7612 6123
pgce.enquiries@ioe.ac.uk

PGCE in Secondary Education (Business and Economics) NX11

1 year full-time

Entry requirements: Degree or equivalent, or graduate qualification accepted by the Institute, in business studies, economics or closely related subjects; GCSE minimum grade C or approved equivalent in English language and mathematics; applicants should ideally have some business or commercial experience.

Contact: Registry
Initial Teacher Education
020 7612 6123
pgce.enquiries@ioe.ac.uk

PGCE in Secondary Education (Citizenship) L9X1

1 year full-time

Entry requirements: Honours degree, equivalent, or graduate qualification accepted by the Institute in social science, philosophy, political studies, history, humanities or related subjects; GCSE at grade C or above in English language and mathematics, or approved equivalent; recent experience of working with young people, especially in an inner-city setting, advantageous.

Contact: Registry
Initial Teacher Education
020 7612 6123
pgce.enquiries@ioe.ac.uk

PGCE in Secondary Education (English with Drama) QX31

1 year full-time

Entry requirements: Degree, equivalent or graduate qualification accepted by the

Institute in English or drama with substantial elements of language and literature; GCSE grade C or above in English language and mathematics or approved equivalent; applicants should also have some practical experience in drama work.

Contact: Registry
        Initial Teacher Education
        020 7612 6123
        pgce.enquiries@ioe.ac.uk

PGCE in Secondary Education (English) Q3X1

1 year full-time

Entry requirements: Degree, equivalent or graduate qualification accepted by the Institute in English literature, English language and linguistics, or a combination of these; GCSE grade C or above in English language and mathematics, or approved equivalent.

Contact: Registry
        Initial Teacher Education
        020 7612 6123
        pgce.enquiries@ioe.ac.uk

PGCE in Secondary Education (Geography) F8X1

1 year full-time

Entry requirements: Degree, equivalent or graduate qualification accepted by the Institute in geography, environmental science or related subjects (including planning, geology and development education); GCSE at grade C or above in English language and mathematics, or approved equivalent qualifications.

Contact: Registry
        Initial Teacher Education
        020 7612 6123
        pgce.enquiries@ioe.ac.uk

PGCE in Secondary Education (History) V1X1

1 year full-time

Entry requirements: Degree, equivalent, or graduate qualification accepted by the Institute; GCSE at grade C or above in English language and mathematics; degree should be in history or a joint degree with a substantial history component; applicants should also have recent experience of work with young people.

Contact: Registry
        Initial Teacher Education
        020 7612 6123
        pgce.enquiries@ioe.ac.uk

PGCE in Secondary Education (Information and Communications Technology) G5X1

1 year full-time

Entry requirements: Degree, equivalent or graduate qualification accepted by the Institute; GCSE at grade C or above in English language and mathematics or equivalent qualifications; degree in ICT, or study of ICT as a postgraduate qualification or as part of first degree; candidates with substantial experience as an ICT specialist considered.

Contact: Registry
        Initial Teacher Education
        020 7612 6123
        pgce.enquiries@ioe.ac.uk

PGCE in Secondary Education (Mathematics) G1X1

1 year full-time

Entry requirements: Degree, equivalent or graduate qualification accepted by the Institute in mathematics or with mathematics as a substantial component; GCSE at grade C or above in English language and mathematics, or equivalent qualifications.

Contact: Registry
        Initial Teacher Education
        020 7612 6123
        pgce.enquiries@ioe.ac.uk

PGCE in Secondary Education (Modern Foreign Languages: French) R1X1; PGCE in Secondary Education (Modern Foreign Languages: German with French) RX21; PGCE in Secondary Education (Modern Foreign Languages: French with German) RX11; PGCE in Secondary Education (Modern Foreign Languages: French with

Spanish) RXD1; PGCE in Secondary Education (Modern Foreign Languages: Spanish with French) RX41

1 year full-time

Entry requirements: Honours degree, equivalent or graduate qualification accepted by the Institute; GCSE at grade C or above in English language and mathematics or approved equivalent; candidates should have spent the equivalent of 1 academic year in the country where their foreign language is spoken, or if their degree is in 2 languages, 6 consecutive months in each of the countries concerned.

Contact: Registry
Initial Teacher Education
020 7612 6123
pgce.enquiries@ioe.ac.uk

PGCE in Secondary Education (Music) W3X1

1 year full-time or 4 terms part-time

Entry requirements: Music degree, equivalent or graduate qualification accepted by the Institute; degree or equivalent in a subject other than music also considered if student can provide evidence of musical competence at an acceptable level; GCSE at grade C or above in English language and mathematics, or equivalent qualification.

Contact: Registry
Initial Teacher Education
020 7612 6123
pgce.enquiries@ioe.ac.uk

PGCE in Secondary Education (Religious Education) V6X1

1 year full-time

Entry requirements: Degree, equivalent or graduate qualification accepted by the Institute in theology, religious studies, social science or a closely related discipline; GCSE at grade C or above in English language and mathematics or equivalent qualifications.

Contact: Registry
Initial Teacher Education
020 7612 6123
pgce.enquiries@ioe.ac.uk

PGCE in Secondary Education (Science: Biology) C1X1; PGCE in Secondary Education (Science: Chemistry) F1X1; PGCE in Secondary Education (Science: General) F0X1; PGCE in Secondary Education (Science: Physics) F3X1

1 year full-time

Entry requirements: Degree, equivalent or graduate qualification accepted by the Institute in biological, physical, geological, combined or applied sciences, engineering, or related subjects; GCSE at grade C or above in English language and mathematics or equivalent qualification.

Contact: Registry
Initial Teacher Education
020 7612 6123
pgce.enquiries@ioe.ac.uk

PGCE in Secondary Education (Social Science with Humanities) L3X1

1 year full-time

Entry requirements: Degree, equivalent or graduate qualification accepted by the Institute in the social sciences or humanities; GCSE at grade C or above in English language and mathematics or equivalent qualifications; candidates should be able to demonstrate the willingness and subject knowledge to teach history or religious education at Key Stage 3 (ages 11 to 14).

Contact: Registry
Initial Teacher Education
020 7612 6123
pgce.enquiries@ioe.ac.uk

MA in Adult Basic Skills Education

2–4 years part-time

Entry requirements: Good Honours degree or equivalent plus at least a year's experience of teaching adult basic skills.

Contact: Registry
Further Professional Development
020 7612 6100/6101
fpd.enquiries@ioe.ac.uk

MA in Art and Design in Education

2–4 years part-time

Entry requirements: Good Honours degree in a relevant subject and a minimum of 2 years' relevant experience.

Contact: Registry
Further Professional
Development
020 7612 6100/6101
fpd.enquiries@ioe.ac.uk

MA in Citizenship Education

1 year full-time, 2–4 years part-time

Entry requirements: Honours degree in approved subject.

Contact: Registry
Further Professional
Development
020 7612 6100/6101
fpd.enquiries@ioe.ac.uk

MA in Comparative Education

1 year full-time, 2–4 years part-time

Entry requirements: Good Honours degree in a relevant subject and 2 years' teaching experience or PGCE.

Contact: Registry
Further Professional
Development
020 7612 6100/6101
fpd.enquiries@ioe.ac.uk

MA in Curriculum Studies

1 year full-time, 2–4 years part-time

Entry requirements: Approved teaching qualification or 2 years' relevant experience plus good Honours degree.

Contact: Registry
Further Professional
Development
020 7612 6100/6101
fpd.enquiries@ioe.ac.uk

EdD in Education

4 years part-time

Entry requirements: At least 4 years' full-time experience in relevant professional area and, normally, Master's degree; applicants will be asked to provide details of

grades obtained in Master's degree, and copy of, or substantial extract from, Master's dissertation

Contact: Registry
Research Degrees
020 7612 6103/6670
doc.enquiries@ioe.ac.uk

MA in Education (Early Years)

1 year full-time, 2–4 years part-time

Entry requirements: Good Honours degree or equivalent in a relevant subject plus 2 years' relevant experience.

Contact: Registry
Further Professional
Development
020 7612 6100/6101
fpd.enquiries@ioe.ac.uk

EdD in Education (International)

4 years part-time

Entry requirements: At least 4 years' full-time experience in relevant professional area and, normally, Master's degree; applicants will be asked to provide details of grades obtained in Master's degree, and copy of, or substantial extract from, Master's dissertation

Contact: Registry
Research Degrees
020 7612 6103/6670
doc.enquiries@ioe.ac.uk

MA in Education (Psychology)

1 year full-time, 2–4 years part-time

Entry requirements: Good Honours degree plus teaching qualification or relevant experience.

Contact: Registry
Further Professional
Development
020 7612 6100/6101
fpd.enquiries@ioe.ac.uk

Advanced Diploma in Education and Psychology for Special Needs

1 year full-time, 2–5 years part-time

Entry requirements: Qualifications beyond A-level and experience of schools or adult education.

Contact: Registry
Further Professional
Development
020 7612 6100/6101
fpd.enquiries@ioe.ac.uk

Advanced Diploma in Education and Psychology for Special Needs (Children with Disabilities of Sight)

1 year full-time, 2–5 years part-time

Entry requirements: Qualified Teacher Status plus relevant SEN experience.

Contact: Registry
Further Professional
Development
020 7612 6100/6101
fpd.enquiries@ioe.ac.uk

MA in Educational Management and Administration

1 year full-time, 2–4 years part-time

Entry requirements: Good Honours degree (or equivalent) and 2 years' management experience.

Contact: Registry
Further Professional
Development
020 7612 6100/6101
fpd.enquiries@ioe.ac.uk

MA in Effective Learning

1 year full-time, 2–4 years part-time

Entry requirements: Good Honours degree and normally at least 2 years' teaching experience.

Contact: Registry
Further Professional
Development
020 7612 6100/6101
fpd.enquiries@ioe.ac.uk

MA in Evaluation and Assessment

1 year full-time, 2–4 years part-time

Entry requirements: Good Honours degree and approved teaching qualification; applications considered on an individual basis.

Contact: Registry
Further Professional
Development

020 7612 6100/6101
fpd.enquiries@ioe.ac.uk

MA in Geography in Education

1 year full-time, 2 years distance learning, 2–4 years part-time

Entry requirements: Good Honours degree in geography or a related subject plus teaching qualification or 2 years' teaching experience required for standard programme; QTS is not a formal requirement for the distance learning programme.

Contact: Registry
Further Professional
Development
020 7612 6100/6101
fpd.enquiries@ioe.ac.uk

MA in History in Education

1 year full-time, 2–4 years part-time

Entry requirements: BEd with Honours in an appropriate area of study or approved degree or equivalent with Honours in history.

Contact: Registry
Further Professional
Development
020 7612 6100/6101
fpd.enquiries@ioe.ac.uk

MA in Inclusive Education

2 years part-time

Entry requirements: Honours degree or 2 years' relevant professional experience and qualifying essay or portfolio.

Contact: Registry
Further Professional
Development
020 7612 6100/6101
fpd.enquiries@ioe.ac.uk

MA in Information and Communications Technology in Education

1 year full-time, 2–4 years part-time

Entry requirements: Good Honours degree plus evidence of ICT knowledge and experience (for example, degree, diploma course, or practical experience of using ICT in teaching) and evidence of educational

knowledge and experience (education degree, PGCE or teaching experience).
Contact: Registry
Further Professional
Development
020 7612 6100/6101
fpd.enquiries@ioe.ac.uk

MA in Lifelong Learning

1 year full-time, 2–4 years part-time

Entry requirements: Good Honours degree or 2 years' professional experience and qualifying essay or portfolio.
Contact: Registry
Further Professional
Development
020 7612 6100/6101
fpd.enquiries@ioe.ac.uk

MA in Literacy Learning and the Development of Early Literacy (academic route)

1 year full-time, 2–4 years part-time

Entry requirements: Good Honours degree in a relevant subject or equivalent, plus 2 years' relevant experience.
Contact: Registry
Further Professional
Development
020 7612 6100/6101
fpd.enquiries@ioe.ac.uk

MA in Literacy Learning and the Development of Early Literacy (professional route)

2 years mixed mode

Entry requirements: Honours degree in a relevant subject or equivalent, plus 2 years' relevant experience; applicants should normally be based in the UK and be seconded by their local education authority.
Contact: Registry
Further Professional
Development
020 7612 6100/6101
fpd.enquiries@ioe.ac.uk

MA Mathematics Education

1 year full-time, 2–4 years part-time

Entry requirements: Good Honours degree in mathematics or in education with relevant experience.
Contact: Registry
Further Professional
Development
020 7612 6100/6101
fpd.enquiries@ioe.ac.uk

Advanced Diploma/Certificate in Minority Ethnic Achievement

Diploma: 2–4 years part-time, Certificate: 1–4 years part-time

Entry requirements: Qualified Teacher Status; non-graduates or those without QTS may be able to enter through the submission of 1 or more qualifying essays.
Contact: Registry
Further Professional
Development
020 7612 6100/6101
fpd.enquiries@ioe.ac.uk

MA in Music Education

1 year full-time, 2–4 years part-time

Entry requirements: Good Honours degree plus teaching qualification or minimum 2 years' teaching experience; alternative qualifications and experience considered.
Contact: Registry
Further Professional
Development
020 7612 6100/6101
fpd.enquiries@ioe.ac.uk

MA in Policy Studies in Education

1 year full-time, 2–4 years part-time

Entry requirements: Good Honours degree in sociology, economics or related area, plus relevant professional experience or teaching qualification.
Contact: Registry
Further Professional
Development
020 7612 6100/6101
fpd.enquiries@ioe.ac.uk

MA in Primary Education

1 year full-time, 2–4 years part-time

Entry requirements: Good Honours degree and primary school teaching experience, either in the UK or abroad.

Contact: Registry
Further Professional
Development
020 7612 6100/6101
fpd.enquiries@ioe.ac.uk

MA in Religious Education

1 year full-time, 2–4 years part-time

Entry requirements: Good Honours degree plus some experience of working in field of religious education in the state, independent or supplementary sector (e.g. Sunday schools).

Contact: Registry
Further Professional
Development
020 7612 6100/6101
fpd.enquiries@ioe.ac.uk

MA in School Effectiveness and School Improvement

1 year full-time, 2–4 years part-time

Entry requirements: Good Honours degree plus 2 years' experience of employment in schools.

Contact: Registry
Further Professional
Development
020 7612 6100/6101
fpd.enquiries@ioe.ac.uk

MA in Science Education

1 year full-time, 2–4 years part-time

Entry requirements: Good Honours degree and experience in teaching science or working in a science-related field of education.

Contact: Registry
Further Professional
Development
020 7612 6100/6101
fpd.enquiries@ioe.ac.uk

MA/MSc in Special Education (Inclusion and Disability Studies/Psychological Perspectives)

1 year full-time, 2–4 years part-time

Entry requirements: Good Honours degree plus minimum 2 years' post-qualification experience working with children, young people or adults with special educational needs (SEN).

Contact: Registry
Further Professional
Development
020 7612 6100/6101
fpd.enquiries@ioe.ac.uk

MA in Teaching

2–3 years mixed mode

Entry requirements: Good Honours degree plus evidence of good PGCE (and successful induction year if applicable) and strong references.

Contact: Registry
Further Professional
Development
020 7612 6100/6101
fpd.enquiries@ioe.ac.uk

MA in Teaching English to Speakers of Other Languages

1 year full-time, 2 years part-time, 2 years distance learning

Entry requirements: Good Honours degree in relevant field; teaching qualification and 2 years' relevant teaching experience.

Contact: Registry
Further Professional
Development
020 7612 6100/6101
fpd.enquiries@ioe.ac.uk

MA in Values in Education (Philosophical Perspectives)

1 year full-time, 2–4 years part-time

Entry requirements: Good Honours degree including some study of philosophy or a related subjects, plus experience of some form of educational work.

Contact: Registry
Further Professional
Development
020 7612 6100/6101
fpd.enquiries@ioe.ac.uk

Isle of Man College

Homefield Road
Douglas
Isle of Man
IM2 6RB
Tel: 01624 648200
Fax: 01624 648201
enquiries@iomcollege.ac.im
www.iomcollege.ac.im

The Isle of Man College is spread over two sites. The main college building overlooks Douglas Bay, and a new higher education campus is under development on an adjacent site. The college does not have its own accommodation, but staff can assist students in finding accommodation in the local area.

Learning resources include a modern library, a range of lecture and seminar rooms and computer resource centres. Leisure facilities include a common room, refectory, cafe, restaurant, concert hall, sauna, solarium, hair salon and beauty therapy suite. The Students' Union provides a range of social activities.

The College offers teacher training in further, adult and higher education at PGCE or Certificate level, as well as a primary PGCE.

HOW TO APPLY

Applications are made direct to the institution.

COURSES

PGCE in Further, Adult and Higher Education

2 years part-time

Entry requirements: Degree
Contact: Mrs A Gundry
01624 648221

PGCE in Primary Education

2 years part-time
Contact: Mrs Jan Quayle
Secretary, Adult Leisure and Recreation
01624 648204
janice.quayle@college.doe.gov.im

Jewish Primary Schools Consortium

Bet Meir
44a Albert Road
Hendon
London
NW4 2SJ
Tel: 020 8457 9713
Fax: 020 8457 9707
jpsc@aje.org.uk

The Jewish Primary Schools Consortium is made up of 12 schools. The School Centred Initial Teacher Training course is offered by the Jewish Teacher Training Partnership, which is part of the Agency for Jewish Education, in collaboration with consortium schools and partner universities. Successful trainees will be qualified to teach in any school either inside or outside the Jewish network.

HOW TO APPLY

Applications are made through the GTTR.

COURSES

PGCE in Primary Education (3–11 years)
X104

1 year full-time

Entry requirements: Degree in relevant subject; GCSE mathematics and English grade C.
Contact: Enquiries
020 8457 9713
jpsc@aje.org.uk

Keele University

Keele
Staffordshire
ST5 5BG
Tel: 01782 621111
Fax: 01782 632343
aaa30@keele.ac.uk
www.keele.ac.uk

The University was founded in 1949 as the University College of North Staffordshire, and became Keele University in 1962. It is situated on an estate of 650 acres, with extensive woods, lakes and parkland, the central feature of which is 19th-century Keele Hall.

Keele is a campus university and has the highest proportion (around 70%), of full-time students in campus residence of any university in the country. On-campus accommodation includes halls of residence and self-catering flats. The student residences are within easy walking distance of campus restaurants, the Students' Union and teaching buildings. The library, computer laboratories and leisure centre are all situated on campus. The Students' Union organises entertainment including club nights, comedy and live bands, and supports a wide range of clubs and societies.

The Education Department at Keele is a major provider of secondary Initial Teacher Training. The department also offers degree-level study in education, postgraduate and Continuing Professional Development courses.

HOW TO APPLY

Degree courses: applications are made through UCAS.

PGCE: applications are made through the GTTR.

Postgraduate: applications are made direct to the institution.

COURSES

PGCE in Secondary Education (English) Q3X1

1 year full-time

Entry requirements: Degree with at least 50% of the content in English and GCSE minimum grade C (or equivalent) in English is required but special tests are available in mathematics.

Contact: Mr D Miller
01782 583124
eda30@educ.keele.ac.uk

PGCE in Secondary Education (French) R1X1

1 year full-time

Entry requirements: Degree with at least 50% of the content in French and GCSE minimum grade C (or equivalent) in mathematics and English is required although special tests are available.

Contact: Mr D Miller
01782 583124
eda30@educ.keele.ac.uk

PGCE in Secondary Education (Geography) F8X1

1 year full-time

Entry requirements: Degree with at least 50% of content in geography and GCSE minimum grade C (or equivalent) in English language and mathematics is required although special tests are available.

Contact: Mr D Miller
01782 583124
eda30@educ.keele.ac.uk

PGCE in Secondary Education (German with French) RX21

1 year full-time

Entry requirements: Degree with at least 50% of the content in German and an A-level French (or equivalent) and GCSE minimum grade C (or equivalent) in English language and mathematics is required although special tests are available.

Contact: Mr D Miller
01782 583124
eda30@educ.keele.ac.uk

PGCE in Secondary Education (History) V1X1

1 year full-time

Entry requirements: Degree with at least 50% of the content in history and GCSE minimum grade C (or equivalent) in English and mathematics is required although special tests are available.
Contact: Mr D Miller
01782 583124
eda30@educ.keele.ac.uk

PGCE in Secondary Education (Information Technology, conversion) GXM1

2 years full-time

Entry requirements: Any degree and GCSE minimum grade C (or equivalent) in English language and mathematics; interest or work-related experience in information technology.
Contact: Mr D Miller
01782 583124
eda30@educ.keele.ac.uk

PGCE in Secondary Education (Information Technology/Computer Science) GX1C

1 year full-time

Entry requirements: Degree with at least 50% of the content in information communication technology and GCSE minimum grade C (or equivalent) in English and mathematics; special tests available.
Contact: Mr D Miller
01782 583124
eda30@educ.keele.ac.uk

PGCE in Secondary Education (Mathematics) G1X1

1 year full-time

Entry requirements: Degree with at least 50% of the content in mathematics and GCSE minimum grade C (or equivalent) in mathematics and English; special tests are available in English.
Contact: Mr D Miller
01782 583124
eda30@educ.keele.ac.uk

PGCE in Secondary Education (Mathematics, conversion) GXC1

2 years full-time

Entry requirements: Any degree, A-level or equivalent in mathematics, plus some mathematical component in the degree; GCSE minimum grade C (or equivalent) in English language and mathematics.
Contact: Mr D Miller
01782 583124
eda30@educ.keele.ac.uk

PGCE in Secondary Education (Science, conversion) FXA1

2 years full-time

Entry requirements: A degree in an area of science with insufficient science to enable students to follow the 1 year PGCE; GCSE minimum grade C (or equivalent) in English language and mathematics.
Contact: Mr D Miller
01782 583124
eda30@educ.keele.ac.uk

PGCE in Secondary Education (Science: Biology) C1X1

1 year full-time

Entry requirements: Degree with at least 50% of the content in biology together with at least an A-level grade C (or equivalent) in another science. GCSE minimum grade C (or equivalent) in English and mathematics; special tests available.
Contact: Mr D Miller
01782 583124
eda30@educ.keele.ac.uk

PGCE in Secondary Education (Science: Chemistry) F1X1

1 year full-time

Entry requirements: Degree with at least 50% of the content in chemistry and at least an A-level grade C (or equivalent) in another science. GCSE minimum grade C (or equivalent) in English and mathematics; special tests available.
Contact: Mr D Miller
01782 583124
eda30@educ.keele.ac.uk

PGCE in Secondary Education (Science: Geology) F6X1

1 year full-time

Entry requirements: Degree with at least 50% of the content in geology and an A-level grade of at least grade C (or equivalent) in another science and GCSE minimum grade C (or equivalent) in English and mathematics; special tests available.
Contact: Mr D Miller
01782 583124
eda30@educ.keele.ac.uk

PGCE in Secondary Education (Science: Physics) F3X1

1 year full-time

Entry requirements: Degree with at least 50% of the content in physics together with at least an A-level grade C (or equivalent) in another science and GCSE minimum grade C (or equivalent) in English and mathematics; special tests available.
Contact: Mr D Miller
01782 583124
eda30@educ.keele.ac.uk

PGCE in Secondary Education (Social Science: Sociology/Psychology/Politics) L3X1

1 year full-time

Entry requirements: Degree with at least 50% of the content in a social science and GCSE minimum grade C (or equivalent) in English and mathematics is required although special tests are available. An A-level or equivalent in a National Curriculum Subject also required.
Contact: Mr D Miller
01782 583124
eda30@educ.keele.ac.uk

PGCE in Secondary Education (Spanish with French) RX41

1 year full-time

Entry requirements: Degree with at least 50% of the content in Spanish and an A-level (or equivalent) in French, GCSE minimum grade C (or equivalent) in mathematics and English; special tests are available.
Contact: Mr D Miller
01782 583124
eda30@educ.keele.ac.uk

EdD in Education

4 years part-time

Entry requirements: Master's degree, e.g. MSc/MA/MBA/MEd in field of education, education management, or sociology of education.
Contact: Prof M David
01782 583576
m.david@educ.keele.ac.uk

PgCert/PgDip/MBA in Education

MBA: 2 years distance learning, PgDip 18 months, PgCert 10 months

Entry requirements: Normally, good Honours degree; non-graduates with appropriate professional experience considered for admission to PgDip; designed for those in full-time employment in Local Education Authorities but open to others with relevant experience and commitment.
Contact: Dorothy Tyson
Course Secretary
01782 583126
eda04@keele.ac.uk

MA in Effective Education and Management

24 months distance learning

Entry requirements: Normally good Honours degree; non-graduates with appropriate professional experience considered for admission to diploma course; intended for those in full-time education employment but open to others with relevant experience and commitment.
Contact: Dorothy Tyson
Course Secretary
01782 583126
eda04@keele.ac.uk

Kent and Medway Training

c/o Leigh City Technology College
Green Street
Green Road
Dartford
Kent
DA1 1QE
Tel: 01322 271212
Fax: 01322 271232
jwi@leighctc.kent.sch.uk

Kent and Medway Training Group runs a School Centred Initial Teacher Training course within a consortium of 14 secondary schools in the Kent and Medway area. Successful completion of the course leads to Qualified Teacher Status and a Postgraduate Certificate in Education validated by the Open University Validation Service.

Training is mainly based in two schools and students also have the opportunity to gain experience in a primary school. During each placement students are supported by a subject specialist who has been trained to act as a Mentor, as well as a Senior Member of staff who oversees the placement.

HOW TO APPLY

Applications are made through the GTTR.

COURSES

PGCE in Secondary Education (Business Studies) N1X1
1 year full-time

Entry requirements: Degree in relevant subject; GCSE English language and mathematics grade C.
Contact: Brenda Smith
Course Administrator
01322 271212
bsm@leighctc.kent.sch.uk

PGCE in Secondary Education (Design and Technology) W9X1
1 year full-time
As above

PGCE in Secondary Education (English) Q3X1
1 year full-time
As above

PGCE in Secondary Education (Mathematics) G1X1
1 year full-time
As above

PGCE in Secondary Education (Modern Foreign Languages) R9X1
1 year full-time
As above

Languages offered: French, German, Italian, Spanish, Japanese.

PGCE in Secondary Education (Science) F0X1
1 year full-time
As above

King Alfred's Winchester

Sparkford Road
Winchester
SO22 4NR
Tel: 01962 841515
Fax: 01962 842280
admissions@wkac.ac.uk
www.wkac.ac.uk

King Alfred's was founded by the Church of England in 1840 to train schoolmasters for church elementary schools. It is now one of the country's largest providers of primary Initial Teacher Training. The College has approximately 5,500 students. It is situated a ten-minute walk from Winchester city centre, and is 15 minutes by rail from Southampton.

Accommodation is available in four catered halls of residence on campus, or in self-catering rooms at West Downs student village, a few hundred metres from the main campus. Private rented accommodation is available in Winchester. The

College's library includes a substantial extension opened in 2000. There are networked PCs for students' use in the library and in IT centres on campus. The Students' Union provides leisure and recreation activities, and students can participate in a range of sports clubs and other societies.

In addition to Initial Teacher Training courses, King Alfred's offers Master's degrees and research opportunities in educational studies.

HOW TO APPLY

Degree courses: applications are made through UCAS.

PGCE: applications are made through the GTTR.

Postgraduate: applications are made direct to the institution.

COURSES

BA (Hons) in Primary Education (Early Years) X1X3

4 years full-time

All years: 4 major elements: Curriculum studies; professional studies; subject studies; school experience.

Successful completion of this course leads to a recommendation for Qualified Teacher Status (QTS) after completion of skills tests.

Entry requirements: Tariff: 220 points, International Baccalaureate: 24, Foundation / access qualification: 60%, Irish Leaving Certificates: BBCCC, BTEC NC/ND, Work experience

Contact: Liz Mullarkey
Admissions Assistant
01962 827273
e.mullarkey@wkac.ac.uk

BA (Hons) in Primary Education with Art (Lower Primary) XW11

4 years full-time

There are 4 major elements in all years of the course.

Professional Education Studies: Gives students the general professional training to be a class teacher in a primary school.

School Experience: Students work in schools in all years for block periods of between 5 and 10 weeks and on occasional days throughout the course.

Special Subject: Art is studied in depth. Includes: visual imagery; constructing visual forms; collation and selection of visual information; analysis of selected aspects of the visual language; exploration of 2- and 3-dimensional forms; multimedia applications.

Applied Studies: Students learn how to teach specialist subject.

Successful completion of this course leads to a recommendation for Qualified Teacher Status (QTS) after completion of skills tests.

Entry requirements: As above
Contact: As above

BA (Hons) in Primary Education with Art (Upper Primary) XWC1

4 years full-time
As above

BA (Hons) in Primary Education with Drama with English (Lower Primary) XW14

4 years full-time

There are 4 major elements in all years of the course.

Professional Education Studies: Gives students the general professional training to be a class teacher in a primary school.

School Experience: Students will work in schools in all years for block periods of between 5 and 10 weeks and on occasional days throughout the course.

Special Subject: Drama is studied in depth. Includes: analysis of the language of performance; study of classic dramatic texts and plays written by black and Asian playwrights; exploration of the role of drama and theatre as tools for social and cultural intervention; group project.

Applied Studies: Students learn how to teach specialist subject.

Successful completion of this course leads to a recommendation for Qualified Teacher Status (QTS) after completion of skills tests.

Entry requirements: As above
Contact: As above

BA (Hons) in Primary Education with Drama with English (Upper Primary) XWC4

4 years full-time
As above

BA (Hons) in Primary Education with English (Lower Primary) XQ13

4 years full-time

There are 4 major elements in all years of the course.

Professional Education Studies: Gives students the general professional training to be a class teacher in a primary school.

School Experience: Students work in schools in all years for block periods of between 5 and 10 weeks and on occasional days throughout the course.

Special Subject: English. Includes: poetry 1530–1998; text and context; Medieval literature; Milton and the century of revolution; the 18th century; British romantic poetry and culture; 19th-century fictions and culture; Shakespeare and the early modern drama; modernism and post-modernism; language in society; children's literature; autobiography; narrative; creative writing.

Applied Studies: Students learn how to teach specialist subject.

Successful completion of this course leads to a recommendation for Qualified Teacher Status (QTS) after completion of skills tests.

Entry requirements: As above
Contact: As above

BA (Hons) in Primary Education with English (Upper Primary) XQC3

4 years full-time
As above

BA (Hons) in Primary Education with Geography (Lower Primary) XF18

4 years full-time

There are 4 major elements in all years of the course.

Professional Education Studies: Gives students the general professional training to be a class teacher in a primary school.

School Experience: Students work in schools in all years for block periods of between 5 and 10 weeks and on occasional days throughout the course.

Special Subject: Geography is studied in depth.

Applied Studies: Students learn how to teach specialist subject.

Successful completion of this course leads to a recommendation for Qualified Teacher Status (QTS) after completion of skills tests.

Entry requirements: As above
Contact: As above

BA (Hons) in Primary Education with Geography (Upper Primary) XFC8

4 years full-time
As above

BA (Hons) in Primary Education with History (Lower Primary) XV11

4 years full-time

There are 4 major elements in all years of the course.

Professional Education Studies: Gives students the general professional training to be a class teacher in a primary school.

School Experience: Students work in schools in all years for block periods of between 5 and 10 weeks and on occasional days throughout the course.

Special Subject: History is studied in depth.

Applied Studies: Students learn how to teach specialist subject.

Successful completion of this course leads to a recommendation for Qualified Teacher Status (QTS) after completion of skills tests.

Entry requirements: As above
Contact: As above

BA (Hons) in Primary Education with History (Upper Primary) XVC1

4 years full-time
As above

BA (Hons) in Primary Education with Mathematics (Lower Primary) XG11

4 years full-time

All years, 4 major elements: Curriculum studies; professional studies; subject studies; school experience.

Successful completion of this course leads to a recommendation for Qualified Teacher Status (QTS) after completion of skills tests.

Entry requirements: As above
Contact: As above

BA (Hons) in Primary Education with Mathematics (Upper Primary) XGC1

4 years full-time
As above

BA (Hons) in Primary Education with Physical Education (Lower Primary) XC16

4 years full-time

There are 4 major elements in all years of the course.

Professional Education Studies: Gives students the general professional training to be a class teacher in a primary school.

School Experience: Students work in schools in all years for block periods of between 5 and 10 weeks and on occasional days throughout the course.

Special Subject: Human movement studies are studied in depth. Includes: the development of physical education and sport; the contemporary sporting agenda; the way in which children acquire and learn motor skills; the relationship between physical growth, maturity and motor development; the way in which physical education and sport impacts on healthy lifestyles; the impact on the child when motor skill learning breaks down; tensions between the developing sporting culture and educational values; issues relating to access, opportunity and ownership in sport and physical education; group project.

Applied Studies: Students learn how to teach specialist subject.

Successful completion of this course leads to a recommendation for Qualified Teacher Status (QTS) after completion of skills tests.

Entry requirements: As above
Contact: As above

BA (Hons) in Primary Education with Physical Education (Upper Primary) XCC6

4 years full-time
As above

BA (Hons) in Primary Education with Religious Studies (Lower Primary) XV16

4 years full-time

There are 4 major elements in all years of the course.

Professional Education Studies: Gives students the general professional training to be a class teacher in a primary school.

School Experience: Students work in schools in all years for block periods of between 5 and 10 weeks and on occasional days throughout the course.

Special Subject: Religious studies are studied in depth. Includes: different approaches to the study of religions; great religious traditions of the world; contemporary approaches to the Bible; primal religions; science and religion; women and religion; liberation theologies; Christian mysticism; the Gospels; philosophy of religions; ethics; nature and religion; new religious movements; mythology; Buddhism; religion in Britain since 1945; Judaism after the Holocaust; contemporary Christian theology; Zen Buddhism.

Applied Studies: Students learn how to teach specialist subject.

Successful completion of this course leads to a recommendation for Qualified Teacher Status (QTS) after completion of skills tests.

Entry requirements: As above

Contact: As above

BA (Hons) in Primary Education with Religious Studies (Upper Primary) XVC6

4 years full-time

As above

BA (Hons) in Primary Education with Science (Lower Primary) XC11

4 years full-time

There are 4 major elements in all years of the course.

Professional Education Studies: Gives students the general professional training to be a class teacher in a primary school.

School Experience: Students work in schools in all years for block periods of between 5 and 10 weeks and on occasional days throughout the course.

Special Subject: Social biology is studied in depth.

Applied Studies: Students learn how to teach specialist subject.

Successful completion of this course leads to a recommendation for Qualified Teacher Status (QTS) after completion of skills tests.

Entry requirements: As above

Contact: As above

BA (Hons) in Primary Education with Science (Upper Primary) XCC1

4 years full-time

As above

BA (Hons) in Special Educational Needs X360

4 years full-time

Successful completion of this course leads to a recommendation for Qualified Teacher Status (QTS) after completion of skills tests.

Entry requirements: As above

Contact: As above

PGCE in Primary Education (5–8) X121

1 year full-time

Entry requirements: Degree from any approved university, with either a significant element in a subject relevant to the National Curriculum, or a broader degree supported by other qualifications and/or experience; GCSE grade C or above, or equivalent qualifications, in mathematics and English language and, for applicants born on or after 1/9/79, a science subject.

Contact: Niak Whittall
Postgraduate Admissions
01962 827235
N.Whittall@wkac.ac.uk

PGCE in Primary Education (7–11) X171

1 year full-time

As above

Certificate/Diploma in Advanced Educational Studies (Professional Enquiry)

Diploma: up to 5 years part-time

Entry requirements: Degree or Qualified Teacher Status or equivalent.

Contact: Karen Sayers
Programme Administrator
01962 827375
k.sayers@wkac.ac.uk

Certificate/Diploma in Advanced Educational Studies (Special Educational Needs)

Diploma: up to 5 years part-time

Entry requirements: As above

Contact: As above

MA(Ed) in Education (Professional Enquiry)

Up to 7 years part-time

Entry requirements: Degree and Qualified Teacher Status or equivalent.

Contact: As above

MA in Educational Studies (Theory and Practice)

2–7 years part-time

Entry requirements: Relevant Honours degree.

Contact: Janice De Sousa
Course Director
01962 827432
j.desousa@wkac.ac.uk

King's College London, University of London

Strand
Westminster
London
WC2R 2LS
Tel: 020 7836 5454
Fax: 020 7836 1799
ceu@kcl.ac.uk
www.kcl.ac.uk

King's College London was established by King George IV in 1829 and became one of the founding colleges of the University of London. In 1908, King's College School and King's College Hospital School became independent colleges. King's was reconstituted by Royal Charter as a constituent college of the University of London in 1980, and was united with the School of Medicine and Dentistry in 1983. The College expanded through mergers with Queen Elizabeth College and Chelsea College, the Institute of Psychiatry, and the United Medical and Dental Schools of Guy's and St Thomas' Hospitals. It is now a multi-faculty institution with over 17,000 students.

The main King's College site is the Strand campus on the banks of the River Thames. The Department of Education and Professional Studies is based at the Waterloo campus. King's College first entered the field of education in 1890, offering courses in initial teacher education. The department now provides a range of taught and research-oriented courses at undergraduate, PGCE, Master's and doctoral levels.

The College's information resources include libraries, archives, computing services and multimedia/audio-visual services. The Information Services Centre at the Waterloo campus holds the education collection, among others. Computing facilities are available across the campuses in rooms and clusters. Applicants may apply to the College's catered or self-catering residences and to the University of London's intercollegiate residences. Advice and information about private sector accommodation is available.

HOW TO APPLY

PGCE: applications are made through the GTTR.

Postgraduate: applications are made direct to the institution.

COURSES

PGCE in Secondary Education (Classics) Q8X1

1 year full-time

Entry requirements: Latin to at least AS-level standard, relevant degree, GCSE grade C or above (or equivalent) in English language and mathematics.

Contact: Ms Lois Thorley
020 7848 3170
lois.thorley@kcl.ac.uk

PGCE in Secondary Education (English) Q3X1

1 year full-time

Entry requirements: Degree closely related to subject of PGCE and GCSE grade C or above (or equivalent) in mathematics and English language.
Contact: As above

PGCE in Secondary Education (French with German) RX11

1 year full-time

Entry requirements: Degree closely related to subject of PGCE and GCSE grade C or above (or equivalent) in mathematics and English language. Applicants should offer 2 languages, with qualifications equivalent to at least AS-level in the subsidiary language.
Contact: As above

PGCE in Secondary Education (French with Spanish) RXD1

1 year full-time

Entry requirements: As above
Contact: As above

PGCE in Secondary Education (German with French) RX21

1 year full-time

Entry requirements: As above
Contact: As above

PGCE in Secondary Education (Spanish with French) RX41

1 year full-time

Entry requirements: As above
Contact: As above

PGCE in Secondary Education (Information and Communications Technology) G5X1

1 year full-time

Entry requirements: Degree (or equivalent) in any subject with at least 2nd class Honours, and substantial IT experience/expertise; additionally, GCSE grade C or above (or equivalent) in English language and mathematics.
Contact: As above

PGCE in Secondary Education (Mathematics) G1X1

1 year full-time

Entry requirements: Degree closely related to subject of PGCE and GCSE grade C or above (or equivalent) in mathematics and English language.
Contact: As above

PGCE in Secondary Education (Religious Education) V6X1

1 year full-time

Entry requirements: Degree closely related to subject of PGCE and GCSE grade C or above (or equivalent) in mathematics and English language.
Contact: As above

PGCE in Secondary Education (Science: Biology) C1X1

1 year full-time

Entry requirements: Degree closely related to subject of PGCE and GCSE grade C or above (or equivalent) in mathematics and English language.
Contact: As above

PGCE in Secondary Education (Science: Chemistry) F1X1

1 year full-time

Entry requirements: Degree closely related to subject of PGCE and GCSE grade C or above (or equivalent) in mathematics and English language.
Contact: As above

PGCE in Secondary Education (Science: Physics) F3X1

1 year full-time

Entry requirements: Degree closely related to subject of PGCE and GCSE grade C or above (or equivalent) in mathematics and English language.
Contact: As above

MA in Applied Language Studies in Education

1 year full-time, 2–4 years part-time

Entry requirements: Minimum 2:2 degree, plus PGCE or equivalent; normally have a minimum of 2 years' teaching experience related to the focus of the chosen degree.
Contact: As above

MA in Classics Education

1 year full-time, 2–4 years part-time
As above

MA in Computers in Education

1 year full-time, 2–4 years part-time
As above

MA in Education and Professional Studies

1 year full-time, 2–4 years part-time

Entry requirements: Minimum 2:2 degree, plus PGCE or equivalent; normally minimum of 2 years' teaching experience related to focus of the chosen degree when applying for specialist subject programme.
Contact: Dr Meg Maguire
    020 7848 3150
    meg.maguire@kcl.ac.uk

MA in Education Management

1 year full-time, 2–4 years part-time

Entry requirements: Minimum 2:2 degree, plus PGCE or equivalent; normally have a minimum of 2 years' teaching experience related to the focus of the chosen degree.
Contact: Ms Lois Thorley
020 7848 3170
lois.thorley@kcl.ac.uk

MA in Language, Ethnicity and Education
1 year full-time, 2–4 years part-time
As above

MA in Mathematics Education
1 year full-time, 2–4 years part-time
As above

MA in Modern Foreign Languages Education
1 year full-time, 2–4 years part-time
As above

MA in Religious Education
1 year full-time, 2–4 years part-time
Entry requirements: Minimum 2:2 degree; applicants must satisfy the school that they are sufficiently well prepared to undertake both the educational and religious components of the programme; English language requirements for applicants whose first language is not English: IELTS 7.0, TOEFL 600 (written at level 6 and spoken 60).
Contact: Dr Andrew Wright
020 7848 3148
andrew.wright@kcl.ac.uk

MA in Science Education
1 year full-time, 2–4 years part-time
Entry requirements: Minimum 2:2 degree, plus PGCE or equivalent; normally have a minimum of 2 years' teaching experience related to the focus of the chosen degree.
Contact: Ms Lois Thorley
020 7848 3170
lois.thorley@kcl.ac.uk

MA in Urban Education
1 year full-time, 2–4 years part-time
Entry requirements: Minimum 2:2 degree, plus PGCE or equivalent; normally have a minimum of 2 years' teaching experience related to the focus of the chosen degree.
Contact: Ms Lois Thorley
020 7848 3170
lois.thorley@kcl.ac.uk

EdD in Education
4 years part-time
Entry requirements: Normally, Master's degree or its overseas equivalent and minimum 4 years' professional experience required; applicants whose first language is not English need IELTS 7.0, TOEFL 600 (paper based), 250 (computer based)
Contact: Prof Deryn Watson
020 7848 3106
deryn.watson@kcl.ac.uk

Kingston University

Cooper House
40–46 Surbiton Road
Kingston upon Thames
London
KT1 2HX
Tel: 020 8547 2000
Fax: 020 8547 7857
admissions-info@kingston.ac.uk
www.kingston.ac.uk

Kingston University is located just 25 minutes from central London in Kingston upon Thames and has a student population of about 17,000. It is based on five sites: Dorich House, Kingston Hill, Knights Park, Penrhyn Road and Roehampton Vale.

The University has Learning Resource Centres at Knights Park, Penrhyn Road and Kingston Hill. There is also a library at Roehampton Vale. University halls are available within close proximity to the campuses for first-year students and there is a selection of university-managed and private accommodation in the nearby area.

The Faculty of Education is based at Kingston Hill and educational resources are located in the Learning Resources Centre on site. The faculty offers undergraduate degrees, the PGCE at primary and secondary level and also programmes for Continuing Professional Development and research degrees.

HOW TO APPLY

Degree courses: applications are made through UCAS.

PGCE: applications are made through the GTTR.

Postgraduate: applications are made direct to the institution.

COURSES

BA (Hons) in Primary Education (Art and Drama, 5–11 years) XW11

3 years full-time

The following themes are studied in all years of the course: subject specialism; school experience (24 weeks is spent in school across the 3 years; students are placed in a different school each year); core subject National Curriculum areas (English, mathematics, information and communications technology and science); broader curriculum subjects (art, history and geography, performing arts, physical education and religious education); pedagogic and professional issues.

Successful completion of this course leads to a recommendation for Qualified Teacher Status (QTS) after completion of skills tests.

Entry requirements: Tariff: 180 points, including 80 in specialist subject at A2 or 160 in a 12-unit AVCE

Contact: School Admissions Officer
020 8547 8145
educationoffice@kingston.ac.uk

BA (Hons) in Primary Education (English, 5–11 years) XQD3

3 years full-time
As above

BA (Hons) in Primary Education (Geography, 5–11 years) XF18

3 years full-time

As above

BA (Hons) in Primary Education (History, 5–11) XVD1

3 years full-time
As above

BA (Hons) in Primary Education (Science, 5–11 years) XC11

3 years full-time
As above

PGCE in Primary Education (General Primary, 3–11) X100

1 year full-time

Entry requirements: Degree; GCSE grade C or above in mathematics and English, and for candidates born on or after 1/9/79, science.

Contact: Maureen Stevens
Admissions Officer
020 8547 8145/2000 x5071
m.stevens@kingston.ac.uk

PGCE in Secondary Education (Business Studies) N1X1

1 year full-time

Entry requirements: Degree with at least 50% of studies in subject relevant to the specialism; additionally GCSE minimum grade C in English and mathematics (plus science if born after 1/9/79).

Contact: As above

PGCE in Secondary Education (History) V1X1

1 year full-time

Entry requirements: As above
Contact: As above

PGCE in Secondary Education (Modern Languages: French) R1X1

1 year full-time

Entry requirements: As above
Contact: As above

PGCE in Secondary Education (Modern Languages: German) R2X1

1 year full-time
As above

PGCE in Secondary Education (Modern Languages: Spanish) R4X1
1 year full-time
As above

PGCE in Secondary Education (Music) W3X1
1 year full-time
As above

PGCE in Secondary Education (Science: Biology) C1X1
1 year full-time
As above

PGCE in Secondary Education (Science: Chemistry) F1X1
1 year full-time
As above

PGCE in Secondary Education (Science: Physics) F3X1
1 year full-time
As above

MA in Education
2 years part-time
Entry requirements: Applicants will normally have a degree, or equivalent, and at least 2 years' professional experience in education or a related area; applicants without a degree will be considered on the basis of their qualifications and relevant professional experience.
Contact: Sylvia Mullett
Course Co-ordinator
020 8547 8073
s.mullett@kingston.ac.uk

Pgcert/PgDip in Professional Studies in Education
PgDip: 1 year part-time
Entry requirements: Qualified Teacher Status and teaching experience; other candidates from field of education and training also considered.
Contact: As above

Leeds Metropolitan University

Calverley Street
Leeds
LS1 3HE
Tel: 0113 283 2600
Fax: 0113 283 3114
course-enquiries@lmu.ac.uk
www.lmu.ac.uk

The origins of Leeds Metropolitan University can be traced back to 1824 when the Leeds Mechanics Institute was founded. In 1868 this became the Leeds Institute of Science, Art and Literature and later Leeds College of Technology. Two more colleges were founded in the 1840s, Leeds College of Art and Leeds College of Commerce and in 1874 the Yorkshire Training School of Cookery was founded. In the early 1950s the Leeds local education authority decided to relocate the four colleges on a central site, the present City Campus. Leeds Polytechnic was formed in 1970 and enlarged in 1976 with the addition of the James Graham College and the City of

Leeds and Carnegie College. The Polytechnic became an independent Higher Education Corporation on 1 April 1989 and in September 1992 Leeds Polytechnic gained university status and changed its name to Leeds Metropolitan University. It has since merged with Harrogate College.

The School of Education and Professional Development offers various routes in Initial Teacher Training. There are a selection of degree courses, PGCE courses and also a range of postgraduate programmes. The university provides extensive academic resources in Learning Centres in which there are library, IT and media facilities. There are also facilities on the campus for sports and leisure. University-owned or privately rented accommodation is available.

HOW TO APPLY
Degree courses: applications are made through UCAS.
PGCE: applications are made through the GTTR.

Postgraduate: applications are made direct to the institution.

COURSES

BA (Hons) in Early Childhood Education (2-year route) X111

2 years full-time

All years: English; mathematics; science; professional studies; information technology; school experience. Provides opportunity to study foundation subjects of the National Curriculum and religious education in the context of curriculum for children in the 3–8 age range.

Entry requirements: DipHE
Contact: Course Enquiries
0113 283 3113
course-enquiries@lmu.ac.uk

BA (Hons) in Early Childhood Education (4-year route) X110

4 years full-time

All years: English; mathematics; science; professional studies; information technology; school experience. Provides opportunity to study foundation subjects of the National Curriculum and religious education in the context of curriculum for children in the 3–8 age range.

Specialist subject modules: practical and theoretical aspects of early childhood education.

Entry requirements: Tariff: 180 to 220 points, International Baccalaureate: 28, BTEC NC/ND
Contact: As above

BA (Hons) in Primary Education X120

4 years full-time

Course covers teaching at Key Stage 1 and 2. All years: core and specialist subjects: design technology; English; history; mathematics; physical education; professional studies; ICT. Foundation in all other subjects of National Curriculum is provided during 1st 3 years. Placements within partner schools continue throughout the course.

Entry requirements: As above
Contact: As above

BA (Hons) in Secondary Physical Education XC16

4 years full-time

10 modules delivered jointly by the University and its partner schools. Modules include: professional and educational studies; main subject studies; teaching practice; school placement 1 (single module): develops basic classroom skills; school placement 2 (double module).

Successful completion of this course leads to a recommendation for Qualified Teacher Status (QTS) after completion of skills tests.

Entry requirements: Tariff: 220 points, International Baccalaureate: 28, BTEC NC/ND
Contact: As above

PGCE in Primary Education X121

1 year full-time

Entry requirements: 2nd Class Honours degree, together with GCSE grade C in English, mathematics, and a science or equivalent; evidence is also required of previous study of childhood (e.g. psychology, sociology) at degree or A-level standard.
Contact: As above

PGCE in Primary Education (5–11) X171

1 year full-time, part-time

Entry requirements: 2nd Class Honours degree, together with GCSE grade C in English, mathematics, and a science or equivalent; evidence is also required of previous study of childhood (e.g. psychology, sociology) at degree or A-level standard.
Contact: As above

PGCE in Secondary Education (Physical Education) X9C6

1 year full-time

Entry requirements: Lower 2nd class Honours degree relevant to the teaching of physical education, as well as strong practical experience in a number of the National Curriculum areas; GCSEs grade C (or equivalent) in English language and mathematics required.

Contact: As above

EdD in Education

4 years full-time

Entry requirements: Honours degree or equivalent required; applicants should normally have minimum 3 years' practical professional experience in provision of learning.

Contact: As above

MPhil/PhD in Education and Professional Development

MPhil: 2 years full-time, PhD: 3 years full-time; part-time

Entry requirements: Honours degree or equivalent in a relevant subject; non-standard applications considered on their individual merits.

Contact: As above

MBA in Education Leadership

2 years part-time

Entry requirements: Designed for school heads, LEA inspectors, or senior managers in post-16 compulsory education and training.

Contact: As above

PgCert/PgDip/MA in Educational Leadership

MA: 3 years part-time, PgDip: 2 years part-time, PgCert: 1 year part-time

Entry requirements: Degree or teaching certificate required, or relevant work experience; considerable scope for accreditation of work-based activities.

Contact: As above

MA in Physical Education

2–3 years part-time

Entry requirements: Degree in a relevant subject; each application considered individually.

Contact: As above

PgCert/PgDip/MA in Professional Education

Part-time

Entry requirements: Degree or equivalent plus 3 years' experience within education or training field required; non-graduates considered on basis of their current role and personal level of professional development.

Contact: As above

MA in Professional Education and Development

Full-time or part-time

Entry requirements: Degree or equivalent; or PgCert or PgDip; or prior uncertificated learning and/or sub-degree qualifications to graduate level.

Contact: As above

PgCert/PgDip in Professional Studies in Education

1 year part-time

Entry requirements: Qualified Teacher Status (QTS); scope for accreditation of work-based activities; credit can be given for prior or concurrent certificated or experiential learning.

Contact: As above

MA in Teaching Studies

Full-time or part-time

Entry requirements: Degree or equivalent; or PgCert or PgDip; or prior uncertificated learning and/or sub-degree qualifications to graduate level.

Contact: As above

The following course is available at Leeds Metropolitan University, Harrogate College Faculty:

PGCE in Education (post-16 sector, in-service)

2 years part-time

Entry requirements: Degree or equivalent required and employment in a teaching or training capacity for a minimum of 150 hours for the duration of the course; candidates who can demonstrate prior learning and/or experience are eligible for exemption from certain course elements.

Contact: Sue Knight

01423 878211

University of Leeds

Woodhouse Lane
Leeds
LS2 9JT
Tel: 0113 243 1751
Fax: 0113 244 3923
prospectus@leeds.ac.uk
www.leeds.ac.uk

The University of Leeds is one of the largest universities in the UK with over 29,000 students. The university was formally established in 1904 but its history can be traced back to the nineteenth century with the founding of the Leeds School of Medicine in 1831 and then the Yorkshire College of Science in 1874.

The School of Education is one of the largest in the country. Apart from courses in initial teacher training the school offers programmes for educators including a range of taught Master's courses specialising in different aspects of education and research degrees. A selection of courses at undergraduate level are also available.

The University's Leeds campus is situated in the heart of Leeds providing a range of cultural, sporting and social opportunities. Academic resources are available in the School of Education Library and there are additional resources available in the Main Library and computer facilities on campus. University residences and sports and leisure facilities are also based on the campus.

HOW TO APPLY

PGCE: applications are made through the GTTR.

Postgraduate: applications are made direct to the institution.

COURSES

PGCE in Primary Education (5–11 with emphasis 5–8/7–11) X171

1 year full-time

Entry requirements: UK Honours degree or equivalent, plus GCSE grade C or above (or equivalent) in English language and math-

ematics, and in science: candidates should also be able to demonstrate a commitment to teaching as a career, i.e. experience in primary schools or work with primary age children.

Contact: M A Bryant
Admissions Officer, ITT Office,
School of Education
0113 233 4523/4524
m.a.bryant@education.leeds.ac.uk

PGCE in Secondary Education (Art and Design) W1X1

1 year full-time

Entry requirements: All applicants are expected to be well qualified with a relevant degree and some experience of teaching and/or working with young people: the content of the degree must be at least 60% art related and applicants with a degree in art history must be able to provide evidence of their practical art making skills: all applicants will have to present a portfolio of their work at interview: some familiarity with educational issues and the National Curriculum will also be expected: applicants will also need GCSE grade C or above (or equivalent) in English and mathematics.

Contact: As above

PGCE in Secondary Education (Design and Technology: Textiles) W9X1

1 year full-time

Entry requirements: Degree/graduate diploma in textile arts, textile science, technology, multidisciplinary design, fashion/dress and allied areas; plus GCSE grade C or above (or equivalent) in English and mathematics.

Contact: As above

PGCE in Secondary Education (Drama) W4X1

1 year full-time

Entry requirements: Applicants should have, or expect to obtain, a degree in Theatre or Performing Arts or a joint degree in drama with another subject: graduates in related subject areas may be considered: all applicants are expected to be well qualified and to have had some experience of teaching or working with young people or adults and to be conversant with the nature of the teaching profession, the drama curriculum in schools and its place in the English National Curriculum: graduates also need GCSE grade C or above (or equivalent) in English and mathematics.

Contact: As above

PGCE in Secondary Education (English) Q3X1

1 year full-time

Entry requirements: Degree in English or a joint degree in English and another subject; graduates in other subjects will be considered if English has formed a major part of their undergraduate studies or if they have taught English; plus GCSE grade C or above (or equivalent) in English and mathematics.

Contact: As above

PGCE in Secondary Education (French) R1X1

1 year full-time

Entry requirements: Degree in French with substantial residence in a country where French is the main language; native speakers of French may be admitted with degrees in cognate subject areas; plus GCSE grade C or above (or equivalent) in English and mathematics.

Contact: As above

PGCE in Secondary Education (Geography) F8X1

1 year full-time

Entry requirements: Single subject Honours degree in geography or broadly-based or joint honours degree in which geography is a strong element; plus GCSE grade C or above (or equivalent) in English and mathematics.

Contact: As above

PGCE in Secondary Education (German) R2X1

1 year full-time

Entry requirements: Degree in German with substantial residence in a country where German is the main language; native speakers of German may be admitted with degrees in cognate subject areas; plus GCSE grade C or above (or equivalent) in English and mathematics.

Contact: As above

PGCE in Secondary Education (History) V1X1

1 year full-time

Entry requirements: Degree in history or joint degree in history with another subject; graduates in related areas (e.g. art history, archaeology) will also be considered; plus GCSE grade C or above (or equivalent) in English and mathematics.

Contact: As above

PGCE in Secondary Education (Information Technology) G5X1

1 year full-time

Entry requirements: Candidates are expected to have a degree in computer studies, information technology, business information systems or a related subject. Graduates with good honours degrees in other disciplines having considerable emphasis on information technology and mature candidates whose work since graduating has developed competence in information technology to a high level will be considered. As important as knowledge of information technology are candidates' commitment to teaching and enthusiasm for the subject.

Contact: As above

PGCE in Secondary Education (Mathematics) G1X1

1 year full-time

Entry requirements: Applicants should have a degree in mathematics or a joint degree in mathematics with another subject, plus GCSE grade C or above (or

equivalent) in English and mathematics. Graduates in other subject combinations will be considered only if mathematics has formed a substantial part of their whole degree, either directly taught as mathematics or applied within specific areas of the degree e.g. thermodynamics. A guide to "substantial" is at least 50% of the degree should be identifiable as mathematics or mathematically based.
Contact: As above

PGCE in Secondary Education (Music) W3X1

1 year full-time

Entry requirements: Applicants should have a degree or degree equivalent qualification in music or music and another subject, a wide range of musical experience and skills and enthusiasm to teach; plus GCSE grade C or above (or equivalent) in English and mathematics.
Contact: As above

PGCE in Secondary Education (Religious Education) V6X1

1 year full-time

Entry requirements: Degree in theology, religious studies or a joint degree in theology/religious studies and a related subject e.g. philosophy, sociology; plus GCSE grade C or above (or equivalent) in English and mathematics.
Contact: As above

PGCE in Secondary Education (Science: Biology) C1X1

1 year full-time

Entry requirements: UK Honours degree, joint degree or an equivalent qualification in a biological subject plus normally A-level in physics or chemistry or an equivalent qualification.
Contact: As above

PGCE in Secondary Education (Science: Chemistry) F1X1

1 year full-time

Entry requirements: UK Honours degree or equivalent in chemistry or a closely related field, plus normally A-level biology or physics (or equivalent) plus GCSE grade C or above (or equivalent) in English and mathematics.
Contact: As above

PGCE in Secondary Education (Science: Physics) F3X1

1 year full-time

Entry requirements: UK Honours degree or equivalent in physics or a related subject plus normally A-level biology or chemistry (or equivalent) and GCSE grade C or above (or equivalent) in English and mathematics. Most engineering degrees are acceptable.
Contact: As above

PGCE in Secondary Education (Social Science) L3X1

1 year full-time

Entry requirements: UK Honours degree or equivalent in a social science (economics or business studies preferred), plus GCSE grade C or above (or equivalent) in English and mathematics.
Contact: As above

PGCE in Secondary Education (Spanish) R4X1

1 year full-time

Entry requirements: Degree in Spanish with substantial residence in a country where Spanish is the main language; native speakers of Spanish may be admitted with degrees in cognate subject areas; plus GCSE grade C or above (or equivalent) in English and mathematics.
Contact: As above

PgDip/MEd in Deaf Education

MEd: 24 months distance learning

Entry requirements: Degree and/or appropriate professional qualification, and at least 2 years' experience in teaching the deaf or other relevant professional work.
Contact: Higher Degrees and Diplomas
Office, School of Education
0113 233 4690/4528
med@education.leeds.ac.uk

PgDip/MEd in Education

12 months full-time, 24 months part-time
As above

EdD in Education

3 years full-time, 5 years part-time

Entry requirements: Applicants normally hold 1st degree and/or appropriate professional qualification, together with Master's degree; students who gained their Master's degree within 5 years prior to EdD application may apply for accreditation of up to 60 credits (3 modules) of EdD degree.

Contact: Dr Sally Beveridge
Postgraduate Research Tutor
0113 343 4537
research@education.leeds.ac.uk

Certificate in Education

12 months part-time

Entry requirements: Candidates must be experienced teachers who hold Qualified Teacher Status.

Contact: Higher Degrees and Diplomas
Office, School of Education
0113 233 4690/4528
diploma@education.leeds.ac.uk

Advanced Diploma in Education of Children with Severe Learning Difficulties

2 years part-time

Entry requirements: Teaching qualification.
Contact: As above

Advanced Diploma in Education of Deaf Children

2 years part-time

Entry requirements: Teaching qualification and Council for the Advancement of Communication with Deaf People (CACDP) level 1.

Contact: Pam Knight
Course Tutor
0113 233 4582
diploma@education.leeds.ac.uk

Certificate in Emotional and Behavioural Difficulties

12 months part-time

Entry requirements: Candidates must be experienced teachers.

Contact: Higher Degrees and Diplomas
Office, School of Education
0113 233 4690/4528
diploma@education.leeds.ac.uk

PgDip/MEd in Information Technology, Multimedia and Education

12 months full-time, 24 months part-time, distance learning

Entry requirements: Degree and/or appropriate professional qualification, and at least 2 years' experience in teaching or other relevant professional work.

Contact: Higher Degrees and Diplomas
Office, School of Education
0113 233 4690/4528
med@education.leeds.ac.uk

PgDip/MEd in International Educational Management

12 months full-time, 24 months part-time
As above

Certificate in Learning Difficulties

12 months part-time

Entry requirements: Candidates must be experienced teachers who hold Qualified Teacher Status.

Contact: Higher Degrees and Diplomas
Office
0113 233 4567/4528

PgDip/MEd in Lifelong Learning

1 year full-time, 2 years part-time

Entry requirements: Degree and 2 years' professional experience in a field of lifelong learning.

Contact: Higher Degrees and Diplomas
Office, School of Education
0113 233 4690/4528
med@education.leeds.ac.uk

EdD in Lifelong Learning

3–4 years full-time, 5–7 years part-time

Entry requirements: Degree; most students have already completed a Master's degree and have substantial experience in education as teachers/administrators etc.

Contact: Janet Barton
Secretary, Lifelong Learning
Institute
0113 233 3147
j.c.barton@leeds.ac.uk

Certificate in Music Technology for Schools

12 months part-time

Entry requirements: Candidates must be experienced teachers who hold Qualified Teacher Status.
Contact: Higher Degrees and Diplomas
Office, School of Education
0113 233 4690/4528
diploma@education.leeds.ac.uk

PgDip/MEd in Primary Education

12 months full-time, 24 months part-time

Entry requirements: Degree and/or appropriate professional qualification and at least 2 years' experience in field of primary education.
Contact: Higher Degrees and Diplomas
Office, School of Education
0113 233 4690/4528
med@education.leeds.ac.uk

Certificate in Primary Subject Leadership (English)

12 months part-time

Entry requirements: Candidates must normally be experienced teachers who hold Qualified Teacher Status.
Contact: Higher Degrees and Diplomas
Office, School of Education
0113 233 4690/4528
diploma@education.leeds.ac.uk

PgDip/MEd in Religious Education

12 months full-time, 24 months part-time

Entry requirements: Degree and/or appropriate professional qualification, and at least 2 years' experience in teaching or other relevant professional work.
Contact: Higher Degrees and Diplomas
Office, School of Education
0113 233 4690/4528
med@education.leeds.ac.uk

PgDip/MEd in School Management and Leadership

24 months part-time
As above

PgDip/MEd in Science Education

12 months full-time, 24 months part-time
As above

PgDip/MEd in Secondary Curriculum Leadership (English Language and Literature)

12 months full-time, 24 months part-time
As above

PgDip/MEd in Secondary Curriculum Leadership (General)

24 months part-time
As above

PgDip/MEd in Secondary Curriculum Leadership (Geography)

12 months full-time, 24 months part-time
As above

PgDip/MEd in Secondary Curriculum Leadership (Mathematics)

12 months full-time, 24 months part-time
As above

PgDip/MEd in Secondary Curriculum Leadership (Modern Languages)

12 months full-time, 24 months part-time
As above

PgDip/MEd in Secondary Curriculum Leadership (Music)

12 months full-time, 24 months part-time
As above

PgDip/MEd in Secondary Curriculum Leadership (Science)

12 months full-time, 24 months part-time
As above

PgDip/MEd in Special Educational Needs

12 months full-time, 24 months part-time
As above

PgDip/MEd in Teaching English to Speakers of Other Languages

12 months full-time, 24 months part-time
As above

PgDip/MEd in Teaching English to Speakers of Other Languages

24 months distance learning

As above

PgDip/MEd in Teaching English to Speakers of Other Languages (Young Learners)

12 months full-time, 24 months part-time

As above

Certificate in Use of Basic Counselling Skills in Education

12 months part-time

Entry requirements: Candidates must normally be experienced teachers who hold Qualified Teacher Status.

Contact: Higher Degrees and Diplomas Office, School of Education
0113 233 4690/4528
diploma@education.leeds.ac.uk

University of Leicester

University Road
Leicester
LE1 7RH
Tel: 0116 252 2522
Fax: 0116 252 2200
admissions@le.ac.uk
www.le.ac.uk

The University of Leicester is based on a campus overlooking Leicester City centre, which is about one mile away. It is one of the older universities in the country. Founded in 1921 with nine students it was granted its Royal Charter in 1957. The University's buildings represent over a century of architectural styles. The first building, the Fielding Johnson with its Georgian style, dates from 1837 and the Engineering Building which was designed by architects Gowan and Stirling in 1963 and is now a Grade 2 listed building.

The School of Education was formed in 1962 when the Department of Education and the Institute of Education were merged. It provides programmes of Initial Teacher Training and Continuing Professional Development for all phases of schooling and offers taught courses, distance learning or research programmes for qualified teachers or lecturers. The Education Library is based in the school and there are two computer suites available. The Main Library is on the central campus and also offers additional computer facilities.

The university provides catered and self-catered accommodation and first-year undergraduates are guaranteed a place in university owned residences. There is some accommodation reserved for postgraduates but it is not guaranteed. Private accommodation is an alternative.

HOW TO APPLY

PGCE: applications are made through the GTTR.

Postgraduate: applications are made direct to the institution.

COURSES

PGCE in Primary Education (Lower Primary, 3–7) X110

1 year full-time

Entry requirements: British university degree or equivalent; plus GCSE grade C (or equivalent) in mathematics and English language; plus for those born on or after 1 September 1979 GCSE grade C (or equivalent) in a science subject; plus GCE A-level (or equivalent), and/or experience in degree course, and/or other relevant professional qualifications or experience in chosen subject specialism.

Contact: Ms B D'sa
Primary PGCE Office
0116 252 3677
pgce.primary@le.ac.uk

PGCE in Primary Education (Upper Primary, 5–11) X171

1 year full-time

As above

PGCE in Secondary Education (Biology) C1X1

1 year full-time

Entry requirements: As above
Contact: Ms M Middleton
Secondary PGCE Office
0116 252 3689
pgce.secondary@le.ac.uk

PGCE in Secondary Education (Chemistry) F1X1

1 year full-time
As above

PGCE in Secondary Education (Citizenship) L9X1

1 year full-time
As above

PGCE in Secondary Education (Co-ordinated Science) F0X1

1 year full-time
As above

PGCE in Secondary Education (English and Media)   QX31

1 year full-time
As above

PGCE in Secondary Education (English) Q3X1

1 year full-time
As above

PGCE in Secondary Education (French with German) RX11

1 year full-time
As above

PGCE in Secondary Education (French with Italian) RX1C

1 year full-time
As above

PGCE in Secondary Education (French) R1X1

1 year full-time
As above

PGCE in Secondary Education (Geography) F8X1

1 year full-time
As above

PGCE in Secondary Education (History) V1X1

1 year full-time
As above

PGCE in Secondary Education (Mathematics) G1X1

1 year full-time
As above

PGCE in Secondary Education (Physics) F3X1

1 year full-time
As above

PGCE in Secondary Education (Social Science) L3X1

1 year full-time
As above

MA in Applied Linguistics and the Teaching of English to Speakers of Other Languages

1 year full-time, 2–5 years part-time, 30 months distance learning

Entry requirements: 2nd Class Honours degree or equivalent normally required plus at least 3 years' experience of teaching English to speakers of other languages.
Contact: Julie Thomson
0116 252 3675/5782
jt22@le.ac.uk/hw8@le.ac.uk

EdD in Education

2–3 years full-time, 3–5 years part-time

Entry requirements: Relevant Master's degree or equivalent and minimum 3 years' professional experience required.
Contact: Mrs R Holmes
Course Administrator
0116 252 3691
rsh6@le.ac.uk

MSc in Educational Leadership

3–5 years part-time

Entry requirements: Degree in relevant discipline; teaching qualification and 2 years' teaching experience.

Contact: Mrs Carolyn Marriott
Senior Administrator
01604 630180
cjm17@le.ac.uk

Advanced Certificate in Educational Management

1 year part-time

Entry requirements: Applicants should be qualified teachers or graduates with a minimum of 3 years' appropriate professional experience.

Contact: As above

MA in Leadership for Learning

3–5 years part-time

Entry requirements: Degree in relevant discipline; teaching qualification and 2 years' teaching experience.

Contact: As above

PgDip/MA in Primary Education

2–5 years distance learning

Entry requirements: Qualified teachers with, normally, at least 2nd Class Honours degree or its equivalent and 3 years' teaching experience.

Contact: Clare Harley
Course Clerk
0116 252 3669

PgCert/PgDip/MA in Professional Studies in Education

1 year full-time, 2–5 years part-time

Entry requirements: Good Honours degree/ advanced diploma in education, preferably with 2/3 years' teaching experience.

Contact: Fiona Belton
0116 252 3669
fvmbl@le.ac.uk

Lindisfarne Initial Teacher Training

University of Northumbria
School of Health, Community and
    Education Studies
Coach Lane Campus
Coach Lane
Newcastle upon Tyne
NE7 7XA
Tel: 0191 215 6463

The School Centred Initial Teacher Training (SCITT) programme is run by a consortium of Northumberland schools with the University of Northumbria acting as managing agent. The participating schools are located in the region of Amble and Alnwick in Northumberland. The course offers training experience at Key Stages 1 and 2, in early years and in middle schools.

HOW TO APPLY

Applications are made through the GTTR.

COURSES

PGCE in Primary Education (Lower Primary, 3–8) X121

38 weeks full-time

Entry requirements: Honours degree; GCSE mathematics, English language and science grade C.

Contact: Judith Speed
Admissions Administrator
0191 215 6653
judithmaria.speed@unn.ac.uk

PGCE in Primary Education (Upper Primary, 7–11) X171

38 weeks full-time
As above

Liverpool Hope

Hope Park
Liverpool
L16 9JD
Tel: 0151 291 3000
Fax: 0151 291 3100
admissions@hope.ac.uk
www.hope.ac.uk

Liverpool Hope's history stretches back over 150 years, when the Church of England Diocese of Chester and the Roman Catholic Sisters of Notre Dame established separate teacher education colleges for women in Warrington (St Katharine's) and Liverpool city centre (Notre Dame). A second Catholic teacher education college, Christ's College, opened in 1965. In 1980 these three colleges joined in an ecumenical federation under the title of Liverpool Institute of Higher Education (LIHE). In 1995 a unified ecumenical College was established under the name Liverpool Hope. Hope now offers a wide range of programmes to its 9,000 students.

The College has locations across the city of Liverpool. The main campus is Hope Park, a landscaped campus situated four miles from the city centre. Campus facilities include a library, two chapels, and a new all-weather pitch, nursery and sports hall. Accommodation is available in student residences at Hope Park and Everton campuses and at Aigburth Park. Privately rented accommodation is available in Liverpool.

Liverpool Hope is one of the largest teacher training providers in the UK. Initial Teacher Training is offered at degree or PGCE level. Full-time, part-time and flexible modular study is available, and the flexible PGCE is also offered at Hope's site in Ripon. Liverpool Hope is a member of the Merseyside and Cheshire Consortium offering an employment-based Graduate Teaching Programme. There are also courses for primary-trained teachers returning to the classroom or secondary-trained teachers wishing to move into primary teaching.

HOW TO APPLY

Degree courses: applications are made through UCAS.

PGCE: applications are made through the GTTR.

Postgraduate: applications are made direct to the institution.

COURSES

BA (Hons) in Advanced Study of Early Years (3–8) X121
4 years full-time

Professional Studies: Level 1: child development and the curriculum; introduction to the core subjects of the National Curriculum (English; mathematics and science); religious education; preparation for school-based experience; the role of the teacher; foundation studies; includes work in schools in Semester 2. Level 2: Further study of teaching and assessment; classroom organisation; discipline; remaining foundation subjects of the National Curriculum are introduced (art; history; geography; music; physical education and technology); includes work in schools in Semester 3; conclusion of the National Curriculum; religious education studies; research of an education issue of the student's choice; reflective practitioner course (critical reading; research skills; self-presentation; organisation and interpersonal skills); professional teacher module (preparation for the legal, contractual and pastoral aspects of role as teacher); includes work in schools in Semesters 6 and 8.

Advanced Study of Early Years: Students take modules from those available in the BA/BSc (Hons) Combined Studies degree.

Successful completion of this course leads to a recommendation for Qualified Teacher Status (QTS) after completion of skills tests.

Entry requirements: GCE A- and AS-levels: CC

Contact: Admissions
0151 291 3295
admission@hope.ac.uk

BA (Hons) in Art (Middle School and Key Stage 2) X1WC

4 years full-time

Professional Studies: Level 1: child development and the curriculum; introduction to the core subjects of the National Curriculum (English; mathematics and science); religious education; preparation for school-based experience; the role of the teacher; foundation studies; includes work in schools in Semester 2. Level 2: Further study of teaching and assessment; classroom organisation; discipline; remaining foundation subjects of the National Curriculum are introduced (art; history; geography; music; physical education and technology); includes work in schools in Semester 3; conclusion of the National Curriculum and religious education studies; research of an education issue of the student's choice; reflective practitioner course (critical reading; research skills; self-presentation; organisation and interpersonal skills); professional teacher module (preparation for the legal, contractual and pastoral aspects of role as teacher); includes work in schools in Semesters 6 and 8.

Art: Modules from the study and practice of painting, printmaking and sculpture; in Semesters 1 to 3, students take 1 art module in each semester; 3 modules are taken in each of Semesters 4 and 5.

Successful completion of this course leads to a recommendation for Qualified Teacher Status (QTS) after completion of skills tests.

Entry requirements: BTEC NC/ND, GCE A- and AS-levels: CC, International Baccalaureate, SCE Higher

Contact: As above

BA (Hons) in Art (Nursery and Key Stage 1) X1W1

4 years full-time
As above

BA (Hons) in English (Key Stage 1) X1Q3

4 years full-time

Professional Studies: Level 1: child development and the curriculum; introduction to the core subjects of the National Curriculum (English; mathematics and science); religious education; preparation for school-based experience; the role of the teacher; foundation studies; includes work in schools in Semester 2. Level 2: Further study of teaching and assessment; classroom organisation; discipline; remaining foundation subjects of the National Curriculum are introduced (art; history; geography; music; physical education and technology); includes work in schools in Semester 3; conclusion of the National Curriculum; religious education studies; research of an education issue of the student's choice; reflective practitioner course (critical reading; research skills; self-presentation; organisation and interpersonal skills); professional teacher module (preparation for the legal, contractual and pastoral aspects of role as teacher); includes work in schools in Semesters 6 and 8.

English: Level 1: foundation course: literary studies; narrative; poetry; drama. Level 2: Core modules: readers and reading/s; children's literature; Shakespeare; language; option modules: 1 19th-century module and 1 other option; 1 20th-century module.

Successful completion of this course leads to a recommendation for Qualified Teacher Status (QTS) after completion of skills tests.

Entry requirements: BTEC NC/ND, GCE A- and AS-levels: CC, International Baccalaureate, SCE Higher

Contact: As above

BA (Hons) in English (Key Stage 2) X1QH

4 years full-time
As above

BA (Hons) in English Language (Key Stage 1) X1Q9

4 years full-time

Professional Studies: Level 1: child development and the curriculum; introduction to the core subjects of the National Curriculum (English; mathematics and science); religious education; preparation for school-based experience; the role of the teacher; foundation studies; includes work in schools in Semester 2. Level 2: Further study of teaching and assessment; classroom organisation; discipline; remaining foundation subjects of the National Curriculum are introduced (art; history; geography; music; physical education and technology); includes work in schools in Semester 3; conclusion of the National Curriculum; religious education studies; research of an education issue of the student's choice; reflective practitioner course (critical reading; research skills; self-presentation; organisation and interpersonal skills); professional teacher module (preparation for the legal, contractual and pastoral aspects of role as teacher); includes work in schools in Semesters 6 and 8.

English Language: Level 1: 1 module in each semester; general introduction to linguistics and important aspects of the subject such as discourse. Levels 2–3: modules in linguistics; history of English language; varieties of English; theories of discourse.

Entry requirements: BTEC NC/ND, GCE A- and AS-levels: CC, International Baccalaureate, SCE Higher
Contact: As above

BA (Hons) in English Language (Key Stage 2) X1QX

4 years full-time
As above

BA (Hons) in Geography (Key Stage 1) X1F8

4 years full-time

Professional Studies: Level 1: child development and the curriculum; introduction to the core subjects of the National Curriculum (English; mathematics and science); religious education; preparation for school-based experience; the role of the teacher; foundation studies; includes work

in schools in Semester 2. Level 2: Further study of teaching and assessment; classroom organisation; discipline; remaining foundation subjects of the National Curriculum are introduced (art; history; geography; music; physical education and technology); includes work in schools in Semester 3; conclusion of the National Curriculum and religious education studies; research of an education issue of the student's choice; reflective practitioner course (critical reading; research skills; self-presentation; organisation and interpersonal skills); professional teacher module (preparation for the legal, contractual and pastoral aspects of role as teacher); includes work in schools in Semesters 6 and 8.

Geography: Students take modules from those available in the BA/BSc (Hons) Combined Studies degree.

Successful completion of this course leads to a recommendation for Qualified Teacher Status (QTS) after completion of skills tests.

Entry requirements: BTEC NC/ND, GCE A- and AS-levels: CC, International Baccalaureate, SCE Higher
Contact: As above

BA (Hons) in Geography (Key Stage 2) X1FV

4 years full-time
As above

BA (Hons) in History (Key Stage 1) X1V1

4 years full-time

Professional Studies: Level 1: child development and the curriculum; introduction to the core subjects of the National Curriculum (English; mathematics and science); religious education; preparation for school-based experience; the role of the teacher; foundation studies; includes work in schools in Semester 2. Level 2: Further study of teaching and assessment; classroom organisation; discipline; remaining foundation subjects of the National Curriculum are introduced (art; history; geography; music; physical education and technology); includes work in schools in Semester 3; conclusion of the National Curriculum and religious education studies; research of an education issue of the student's choice; reflective practitioner course (critical reading; research skills; self-presentation; organisation and interpersonal skills); professional teacher module (preparation for the legal, contractual and pastoral aspects of role as teacher); includes work in schools in Semesters 6 and 8.

History: Students take modules from those available in the BA/BSc (Hons) Combined Studies degree.

Successful completion of this course leads to a recommendation for Qualified Teacher Status (QTS) after completion of skills tests.

Entry requirements: BTEC NC/ND, GCE A- and AS-levels: CC, International Baccalaureate, SCE Higher

Contact: As above

BA (Hons) in History (Key Stage 2) X1VC

4 years full-time
As above

BA (Hons) in Information Technology (Key Stage 1) X1G5

4 years full-time

Professional Studies: Level 1: child development and the curriculum; introduction to the core subjects of the National Curriculum (English; mathematics and science); religious education; preparation for school-based experience; the role of the teacher; foundation studies; includes work in schools in Semester 2. Level 2: Further study of teaching and assessment; classroom organisation; discipline; remaining foundation subjects of the National Curriculum are introduced (art; history; geography; music; physical education and technology); includes work in schools in Semester 3; conclusion of the National Curriculum and religious education studies; research of an education issue of the student's choice; reflective practitioner

course (critical reading; research skills; self-presentation; organisation and interpersonal skills); professional teacher module (preparation for the legal, contractual and pastoral aspects of role as teacher); includes work in schools in Semesters 6 and 8.

Information Technology: Students take modules from those available in the BA/BSc (Hons) Combined Studies degree.

Successful completion of this course leads to a recommendation for Qualified Teacher Status (QTS) after completion of skills tests.

Entry requirements: BTEC NC/ND, GCE A- and AS-levels: CC, International Baccalaureate, SCE Higher

Contact: As above

BA (Hons) in Information Technology (Key Stage 2) X1G4

4 years full-time
As above

BA (Hons) in Mathematics (Key Stage 1) X1G1

4 years full-time

Professional Studies: Level 1: child development and the curriculum; introduction to the core subjects of the National Curriculum (English; mathematics and science); religious education; preparation for school-based experience; the role of the teacher; foundation studies; includes work in schools in Semester 2. Level 2: Further study of teaching and assessment; classroom organisation; discipline; remaining foundation subjects of the National Curriculum are introduced (art; history; geography; music; physical education and technology); includes work in schools in Semester 3; conclusion of the National Curriculum and religious education studies; research of an education issue of the student's choice; reflective practitioner course (critical reading; research skills; self-presentation; organisation and interpersonal skills); professional teacher module (preparation for the legal, contractual and pastoral aspects of role as teacher); includes work in schools in Semesters 6 and 8.

Mathematics: Students take modules from those available in the BA/BSc (Hons) Combined Studies degree.

Successful completion of this course leads to a recommendation for Qualified Teacher Status (QTS) after completion of skills tests.

Entry requirements: BTEC NC/ND, GCE A- and AS-levels: CC, International Baccalaureate, SCE Higher
Contact: As above

BA (Hons) in Mathematics (Key Stage 2) X1GC
4 years full-time
As above

BA (Hons) in Music (Key Stage 1) X1W3
4 years full-time

Professional Studies: Level 1: child development and the curriculum; introduction to the core subjects of the National Curriculum (English; mathematics and science); religious education; preparation for school-based experience; the role of the teacher; foundation studies; includes work in schools in Semester 2. Level 2: Further study of teaching and assessment; classroom organisation; discipline; remaining foundation subjects of the National Curriculum are introduced (art; history; geography; music; physical education and technology); includes work in schools in Semester 3; conclusion of the National Curriculum and religious education studies; research of an education issue of the student's choice; reflective practitioner course (critical reading; research skills; self-presentation; organisation and interpersonal skills); professional teacher module (preparation for the legal, contractual and pastoral aspects of role as teacher); includes work in schools in Semesters 6 and 8.

Music: Students take modules from those available in the BA/BSc (Hons) Combined Studies degree.

Successful completion of this course leads to a recommendation for Qualified Teacher Status (QTS) after completion of skills tests.

Entry requirements: BTEC NC/ND, GCE A- and AS-levels: CC, International Baccalaureate, SCE Higher
Contact: As above

BA (Hons) in Music (Key Stage 2) X1WH
4 years full-time
As above

BA (Hons) in Special Needs (Key Stage 1) X161

Successful completion of this course leads to a recommendation for Qualified Teacher Status (QTS) after completion of skills tests.
Contact: As above

BA (Hons) in Special Needs (Key Stage 2) X163
As above

BA (Hons) in Sport Studies (Key Stage 1) X1C6
4 years full-time

Professional Studies: Level 1: child development and the curriculum; introduction to the core subjects of the National Curriculum (English; mathematics and science); religious education; preparation for school-based experience; the role of the teacher; foundation studies; includes work in schools in Semester 2. Level 2: Further study of teaching and assessment; classroom organisation; discipline; remaining foundation subjects of the National Curriculum are introduced (art; history; geography; music; physical education and technology); includes work in schools in Semester 3; conclusion of the National Curriculum and religious education studies; research of an education issue of the student's choice; reflective practitioner course (critical reading; research skills; self-presentation; organisation and interpersonal skills); professional teacher module (preparation for the legal, contractual and pastoral aspects of role as teacher); includes work in schools in Semesters 6 and 8.

Sport, Recreation and Physical Education: Students take modules from those available in the BA/BSc (Hons) Combined Studies degree.

Successful completion of this course leads to a recommendation for Qualified Teacher Status (QTS) after completion of skills tests.

Entry requirements: BTEC NC/ND, GCE A- and AS-levels: CC, International Baccalaureate, SCE Higher

Contact: As above

BA (Hons) in Sport Studies (Key Stage 2) X1CP

4 years full-time

As above

BA (Hons) in Theology and Religious Studies (Key Stage 1) X1V6

4 years full-time

Professional Studies: Level 1: child development and the curriculum; introduction to the core subjects of the National Curriculum (English; mathematics and science); religious education; preparation for school-based experience; the role of the teacher; foundation studies; includes work in schools in Semester 2. Level 2: Further study of teaching and assessment; classroom organisation; discipline; remaining foundation subjects of the National Curriculum are introduced (art; history; geography; music; physical education and technology); includes work in schools in Semester 3; conclusion of the National Curriculum and religious education studies; research of an education issue of the student's choice; reflective practitioner course (critical reading; research skills; self-presentation; organisation and interpersonal skills); professional teacher module (preparation for the legal, contractual and pastoral aspects of role as teacher); includes work in schools in Semesters 6 and 8.

Theology and Religious Education: Compulsory module: the Jewish and Christian tradition; 3 modules from: movies, morality and religion; philosophy and its influence on religion; New Testament studies; Muslims in Britain; Judaism and contemporary Jewish experience; Christian ethics;

Hinduism; 2 modules from: Jews and Judaism, contemporary Jewish experience; unity and diversity within Islam; Hinduism, historic expressions; ecumenical ethics; early Christian belief and practice; theology in the early 20th century; extended essay on an approved topic under tutorial supervision.

Successful completion of this course leads to a recommendation for Qualified Teacher Status (QTS) after completion of skills tests.

Entry requirements: BTEC NC/ND, GCE A- and AS-levels: CC, International Baccalaureate, SCE Higher

Contact: As above

BA (Hons) in Theology and Religious Studies (Key Stage 2) X1VP

4 years full-time

As above

PGCE in Primary Education (Lower Primary) X121

1 year full-time

Entry requirements: At least a 2.2 degree, the components of which should be relevant to the primary curriculum; GCSE grade C or above (or equivalent) in English language and mathematics and, if born on or after 1/9/79, science.

Contact: Sheila Hayes
        Admissions Secretary
        0151 291 3258
        Hayess@hope.ac.uk

PGCE in Primary Education (Lower Primary) X125

2 years part-time

As above

PGCE in Primary Education (Upper Primary) X171

1 year full-time

As above

PGCE in Primary Education (Upper Primary) X175

2 years part-time

As above

PGCE in Secondary Education (English with Drama) QX31

1 year full-time

Entry requirements: Relevant degree; GCSE grade C or above (or equivalent) in English language and mathematics.
Contact: As above

PGCE in Secondary Education (English) Q3X1

1 year full-time, 1–2 years part-time
As above

PGCE in Secondary Education (Geography) F8X1

1 year full-time, 1–2 years part-time
As above

Secondary Education (History with Citizenship) VX1C

1 year full-time
As above

PGCE in Secondary Education (History) V1X1

1 year full-time
As above

PGCE in Secondary Education (Information Technology) G5X1

1 year full-time, 1–2 years part-time
As above

PGCE in Secondary Education (Mathematics) G1X1

1 year full-time, 1–2 years part-time
As above

PGCE in Secondary Education (Modern Languages: French) R1X1

1 year full-time, 1–2 years part-time
As above

PGCE in Secondary Education (Modern Languages: German) R2X1

1 year full-time, 1–2 years part-time
As above

PGCE in Secondary Education (Modern Languages: Spanish) R4X1

1 year full-time, 1–2 years part-time
As above

PGCE in Secondary Education (Music) W3X1

1 year full-time
As above

PGCE in Secondary Education (Physical Education) X9C6

1 year full-time
As above

PGCE in Secondary Education (Religious Education) V6X1

1 year full-time, 1–2 years part-time
As above

PgCert/PgDip/MA/MSc in Education Studies

Up to 5 years, full-time or part-time

Entry requirements: Good Honours degree, Qualified Teacher Status, and experience in a teaching situation at time of entry.
Contact: Kathryn Curr
Postgraduate Administrator
0151 291 3445
currk@hope.ac.uk

Liverpool John Moores University

Roscoe Court
4 Rodney Street
Liverpool
Merseyside L1 2TZ
Tel: 0151 231 2121

Fax: 0151 231 5632
recruitment@livjm.ac.uk
www.livjm.ac.uk

The University has developed since 1823 when a small mechanics library was established. The institution grew and expanded by merging and amalgamating with different colleges and eventually became the

Liverpool Polytechnic. In 1992, the Polytechnic became Liverpool John Moores University and now has over 25,000 students.

The School of Education offers a two-, three- or four-year degree programme with Qualified Teacher Status for undergraduates and for postgraduate students there is the opportunity to study the one-year PGCE in either primary or secondary teaching. A range of other postgraduate programmes is available. All education courses are based at the IM Marsh campus, in the Liverpool suburb of Aigburth. The campus has extensive facilities including a Learning Resource Centre, sports hall, fitness room, swimming pool and Student Union Bar. University owned or private accommodation is available.

HOW TO APPLY

Degree courses: applications are made through UCAS.

PGCE: applications are made through the GTTR.

Postgraduate: applications are made direct to the institution.

COURSES

BA (Hons) in Primary and Secondary Education (Design and Technology) XJ19

3 years full-time

Prepares students for work in junior schools (Key Stage 2), in secondary schools (Key Stage 3), middle schools or within clusters of primary and secondary schools. The course in partnership with schools, provides students with a sound knowledge of their chosen subject area. It provides experiences which allow for the progressive development of a broad range of professional competencies and an understanding of the whole school and its curriculum and the society in which it operates.

Successful completion of this course leads to a recommendation for Qualified Teacher Status (QTS) after completion of skills tests.

Entry requirements: Tariff: 110 to 160 points, Irish Leaving Certificates: BBB, BTEC NC/ND, Foundation / access qualification

Contact: Enquiry Management Team
0151 231 5090
recruitment@livjm.ac.uk

BA (Hons) in Primary and Secondary Education (Mathematics) XG11

3 years full-time

Year 1: 30 credits are made up of subject study including: science, mathematics; English; foundation studies; a primary education module; subject application. Many of the modules include work in the classroom and students will have 2 block experiences in a junior school classroom. Year 2: 30 credits made up of subject study including: science; mathematics; English; a secondary education module; subject application. Many of these modules include work in the classroom and students have 2 block experiences in a lower secondary classroom. Year 3: 30 credits made up of: subject study including; science; mathematics; English; contemporary education module; classroom enquiry; subject application. Many of the modules include work in the classroom and students have a 5-week block final experience in either primary or secondary following a 10-day in-school preparation period.

Successful completion of this course leads to a recommendation for Qualified Teacher Status (QTS) after completion of skills tests.

Entry requirements: As above
Contact: As above

BA (Hons) in Primary and Secondary Education (Physical Education) XCIP

3 years full-time

Prepares students for work in junior schools (Key Stage 2), in secondary schools (Key Stage 3), middle schools or within clusters of primary and secondary schools. The course in partnership with schools, provides students with a sound knowledge of their chosen subject area. It provides experiences which allow for the progressive development of a broad range of professional competencies and an understanding of the whole school and its curriculum and the society in which it operates.

Successful completion of this course leads to a recommendation for Qualified Teacher Status (QTS) after completion of skills tests.

Entry requirements: As above
Contact: As above

BSc (Hons) in Primary and Secondary Education (Science) XF10

3 years full-time

Year 1: 30 credits are made up of subject study including: science, mathematics; English; foundation studies; a primary education module; subject application. Many of the modules include work in the classroom and students have 2 block experiences in a junior school classroom. Year 2: 30 credits made up of subject study including: science; mathematics; English; a secondary education module; subject application. Many of these modules include work in the classroom and students have 2 block experiences in a lower secondary classroom. Year 3: 30 level 3 credits made up of: subject study including; science; mathematics; English; contemporary education module; classroom enquiry; subject application. Many of the modules include work in the classroom and students have a 5-week block final experience in either primary or secondary following a 10-day in-school preparation period.

Successful completion of this course leads to a recommendation for Qualified Teacher Status (QTS) after completion of skills tests.

Entry requirements: As above
Contact: As above

BA (Hons) in Primary Education (Mathematics, English, Science) X120

4 years full-time

All yrs: A modular course in partnership with schools, including core curriculum studies (English, mathematics and science); foundation studies (history, geography, music, art, technology, information technology, religious education and physical education); an integrative education and professional studies strand; in the final year of the course specialist options include mathematics, English or science.

Successful completion of this course leads to a recommendation for Qualified Teacher Status (QTS) after completion of skills tests.

Entry requirements: Tariff: 180 to 220 points, BTEC NC/ND, Irish Leaving Certificates: CCCC, Foundation / access qualification, International Baccalaureate
Contact: As above

BEd/BEd (Hons): Secondary Education (Information Technology) X1G5

2 years full-time

This programme concentrates on broadening personal skills and awareness in information technology whilst preparing for a career in teaching. The programme is intended to enable students to develop their understanding of how information technology plays a central part in supporting the development of the learning of young people.

Successful completion of this course leads to a recommendation for Qualified Teacher Status (QTS) after completion of skills tests.

Entry requirements: Age restriction: 21 or over, First year of relevant degree course, HND
Contact: As above

BA (Hons) in Secondary Education (Physical Education) XC1Q

4 years full-time

A modular course in which students from all routes undertake education modules (some as options in later years of the course): learning and teaching, information technology and study skills, interpersonal relations: class management and control, differentiation in school and society, assessment and evaluation, personal and social education, curriculum: design, innovation and research, European dimensions, teaching and professional ethics, equal opportunities, schools/industry links, teacher socialisation, schooling and deviance. Subject study includes sport development and culture, practical sports studies, responses to exercise, health and performance-related fitness, aesthetic development, sport and life-style, and a placement in sport, industry or the community. Modules from the dance route can be selected in the 3rd or 4th years. A 2nd subject is taken from art and design, English or science. Subject application is studied in every year of the course, and school experience in a range of schools is undertaken each year.

Successful completion of this course leads to a recommendation for Qualified Teacher Status (QTS) after completion of skills tests.

Entry requirements: Tariff: 240 points, BTEC NC/ND, Irish Leaving Certificates: CCC, Foundation / access qualification
Contact: As above

PGCE in Primary Education (Early Years, 3–8) X121

1 year full-time

Entry requirements: Degree in relevant subject plus GSCE grade C or equivalent in English language, mathematics and science.
Contact: As above

PGCE in Secondary Education (Art and Design) W1X1

1 year full-time

Entry requirements: Degree or degree equivalent in the specialist subject and GCSE grade C or above, or equivalent, in English language and mathematics.
Contact: As above

PGCE in Secondary Education (Design and Technology) W9X1

1 year full-time

Entry requirements: Degree or degree equivalent in the specialist subject or a related area involving materials, design, engineering, food or textiles; plus GCSE

grade C or above, or equivalent, in English language and mathematics.
Contact: As above

PGCE in Secondary Education (Food/Textile Technology) D6X1

As above

PGCE in Secondary Education (Information Technology, conversion) GXM1

2 years full-time

Entry requirements: Degree in any subject plus GCSE grade C or equivalent in English language and mathematics.
Contact: As above

PGCE in Secondary Education (Modern Languages: French) R1X1

1 year full-time

Entry requirements: Degree or degree equivalent in the specialist subject(s) and GCSE grade C or above, or equivalent, in mathematics and English language.
Contact: As above

PGCE in Secondary Education (Modern Languages: German) R2X1

As above

PGCE in Secondary Education (Modern Languages: Spanish) R4X1

As above

PGCE in Secondary Education (Physical Education) X9C6

1 year full-time

Entry requirements: Degree or degree equivalent in the specialist subject or a related area, and GCSE grade C or above or equivalent in English language and mathematics.
Contact: As above

PGCE in Secondary Education (Science: Biology) C1X1

1 year full-time

Entry requirements: Degree or degree equivalent in science and GCSE grade C or above, or equivalent, in English language and mathematics.
Contact: As above

PGCE in Secondary Education (Science: Chemistry) F1X1

1 year full-time

As above

PGCE in Secondary Education (Science: Physics) F3X1

1 year full-time

As above

MA in Education Studies/Education Management

Part-time

Entry requirements: Designed for experienced teachers, lecturers and those working in related professions; degree or equivalent required including qualification in education; special admission arrangements available for non-graduate (CertEd) teachers.

Contact: As above

MA in Special Educational Needs

Part-time evening

As above

London Diocesan Board for Schools

36 Causton Street
Westminster
London
SW1P 4AU
Urban Learning Foundation
56 East India Dock Road
Poplar
London
E14 6JE
Tel: 020 7987 0033
Fax: 020 7536 0107

The London Diocesan Board for Schools works with Church of England schools across London. It offers school-centred initial teacher training for the early years (3–8) in partnership with the Urban Learning Foundation and a consortium of 20 schools in east and north-east London. The training programme is focused on teaching in the inner city, and includes experience in nurseries as well as schools. More than half the course takes place in schools, where training is provided by serving teachers. Taught sessions are based at the Urban Learning Foundation. Students will be part of a group of around 30 trainees.

HOW TO APPLY

Applications are made through the GTTR.

COURSES

PGCE in Primary Education (Early Years, 3–8) X110

1 year full-time

Entry requirements: Degree; GCSE mathematics, English language and science grade C.

Contact: Leanne Price
Course Administrator
020 7536 7012
leanne.price@ulf.org.uk

London Metropolitan University

166–220 Holloway Road
London N7 8DB
Tel: 020 7713 4200
Fax: 020 7753 3272
admissions@londonmet.ac.uk
www.londonmet.ac.uk

London Metropolitan University was formed on 1st August 2002 following the merger of the University of North London and London Guildhall University. The University has two campuses, London City Campus and London North Campus. It now caters for around 28,000 students.

The Department of Education offers degree courses, the PGCE at primary and secondary level, programmes for Continuing Professional Development and also research opportunities.

There are a range of sporting and leisure facilities available at the university and recent developments have taken place to provide a new Learning Centre and extensive access to computer facilities. University accommodation is available close to either campus and there is also privately rented housing available.

HOW TO APPLY
Degree courses: applications are made through UCAS.
PGCE: applications are made through the GTTR.
Postgraduate: applications are made direct to the institution.

COURSES
BA (Hons) in Education, Mathematics (Secondary Education) XG11
2 years full-time

Designed to prepare mature students for mathematics teaching in inner-city secondary schools.

Year 1 (subject study): Problem-solving; algebraic structures; geometry and number theory; communication mathematics; analysis; probability and statistics; math-

ematics modelling; evaluation teaching and learning.

Year 2: (professional): Range of issues including planning; teaching; class management; assessment. 2 school block practices of 6 and 11 weeks and 3 school-based projects.

Successful completion of this course leads to a recommendation for Qualified Teacher Status (QTS) after completion of skills tests.
Entry requirements: Tariff: 120, HND
Contact: Admissions Office
020 7133 4200
Admissions@londonmet.ac.uk

BA (Hons) in Education, Music (Secondary Education) XW19
Successful completion of this course leads to a recommendation for Qualified Teacher Status (QTS) after completion of skills tests.
Entry requirements: Tariff: 120
Contact: As above

PGCE in Primary Education (3–8 Early Years Route) X124
38 weeks full-time
Entry requirements: Relevant degree and some experience of working with primary aged or young children in urban, multicultural, multilingual contexts; GCSE grade C or equivalent in mathematics, English language and science; candidates who are bilingual or multilingual in community languages particularly welcome.
Contact: Postgraduate Admissions
020 7753 3333
admissions@unl.ac.uk

PGCE in Primary Education (5–11 Upper Primary Route) X174
38 weeks full-time
As above

PGCE in Secondary Education (Citizenship) L9X1
36 weeks full-time
Entry requirements: Relevant degree, and GCSE grade C or above (or equivalent) in English and mathematics.

Contact: As above

PGCE in Secondary Education (English with Media/Drama) QX31

36 weeks full-time

Entry requirements: Degree or degree-level knowledge in subject to be taught, plus GCSE grade C or equivalent in English language and mathematics.
Contact: As above

PGCE in Secondary Education (Mathematics) G1X1

1 year full-time

Entry requirements: Degree in mathematics; GCSE grade C or equivalent in English language.
Contact: As above

PGCE in Secondary Education (Mathematics, conversion) GXC1

2 years full-time

Entry requirements: Degree in another subject and mathematics qualification/experience beyond A-level; GCSE grade C or equivalent in English language.
Contact: As above

PGCE in Secondary Education (Modern Languages) R9X1

36 weeks full-time

Entry requirements: Degree or degree-level knowledge in subject to be taught, plus GCSE grade C or equivalent English language and mathematics; native speakers can have a degree in another subject.
Contact: As above

PGCE in Secondary Education (Music) W3X1

1 year full-time

Entry requirements: Degree in music or a related subject; GCSE grade C or equivalent in English language and mathematics.
Contact: As above

PGCE in Secondary Education (Music, conversion) WXH1

2 years full-time

Entry requirements: Degree in subject other than music and a music qualification beyond A-level; GCSE grade C or equivalent in English language and mathematics.
Contact: As above

PGCE in Secondary Education (Physical Education) X9C6

1 year full-time

Entry requirements: Degree or half-degree in sports science or related subject area, plus GCSE grade C or equivalent in English language and mathematics.
Contact: As above

MA in Early Childhood Education

2–3 years part-time

Entry requirements: Degree or qualification in teaching or social work; alternative qualifications or experience will be considered.
Contact: As above

PgCert/PgDip/MA in Education

1 year full-time, 2 years part-time

Entry requirements: Appropriate Honours degree, or equivalent.
Contact: As above

MA in Jewish Education

3 years part-time

Entry requirements: Degree or equivalent.
Contact: As above

PgCert/PgDip/MA in Managing School Improvement

MA: 2 years part-time

Entry requirements: Qualified Teacher Status and a minimum of 1 year's experience as a teacher.
Contact: As above

Loughborough University

Loughborough
Leicestershire
LE11 3TU
Tel: 01509 263171
Fax: 01509 223905
admissions@lboro.ac.uk
www.lboro.ac.uk

Loughborough University has around 12,000 students and is based on a 216-acre campus just outside Loughborough. It was granted university status in 1966. Sports, leisure and academic facilities are all located on campus as well as one of the biggest Student Unions in the country.

There is a main library at Loughborough and computer facilities are available 24 hours a day. Catered or self-catered accommodation is available for over 5,000 students on or near the main site or there is the option of renting privately. Some of the private accommodation is University-managed.

The Teacher Education Unit provides Initial Teacher Training for postgraduates only, in a selection of subjects.

HOW TO APPLY

PGCE: applications are made through the GTTR.

COURSES

PGCE in Secondary Education (Design and Technology) W9X1
1 year full-time

Entry requirements: Applicants should hold a degree or approved equivalent, and should be prepared to demonstrate the relevance of their degree to the curriculum subject they wish to teach; in addition, applicants should have attained minimum GCSE grade C (or equivalent standard) in English language and mathematics.

Contact: Mrs Fiona McLaughlin
    Programme Administrator
    01509 222762
    f.mclaughlin@lboro.ac.uk

PGCE in Secondary Education (Physical Education) X9C6
1 year full-time
As above

Applicants for physical education as the main subject to be taught are normally required to offer a subsidiary teaching subject from: geography, English, history, mathematics, science.

PGCE in Secondary Education (Science, Biology) C1X1
1 year full-time
As above

PGCE in Secondary Education (Science, Chemistry) F1X1
1 year full-time
As above

PGCE in Secondary Education (Science, Physics) F3X1
1 year full-time
As above

Manchester Metropolitan University

All Saints Building
All Saints
Manchester
M15 6BH
Tel: 0161 247 2000
Fax: 0161 247 6390
enquiries@mmu.ac.uk
www.mmu.ac.uk

The Manchester Metropolitan University caters for over 30,000 students and is based at seven campuses: five in the Manchester area, All Saints and Aytoun, City Centre, Didsbury, Elizabeth Gaskell and Hollings and Manchester and North West, and two at Alsager and Crewe in Cheshire.

The Institute of Education is one of the largest teacher training establishments in the country and offers courses in Initial Teacher Training and programmes for Continuing Professional Development. It also runs Graduate and Registered Teacher programmes. The Institute is based on two campuses, Didsbury and Alsager and Crewe but the course of study for any individual will be undertaken at one campus only.

There are seven site libraries including one containing education resources at the Didsbury campus. There is also access to computer, sporting and leisure facilities. University or privately rented accommodation is available.

HOW TO APPLY

Degree courses: applications are made through UCAS.
PGCE: applications are made through GTTR.

Postgraduate: applications are made direct to the institution.

COURSES

BA (Hons) in Primary Education X120 A
4 years full-time

Students choose 1 main subject and an alternative main subject from: Art and design; design and technology; drama; early years; English; geography; history; literacy and numeracy; mathematics; music; religious studies; science. Students will cover the whole of the primary curriculum, take 1 specialist subject and study how to plan, teach and assess within the whole curriculum.

The course is organised into 3 phases, with assessment and progression points at the end of Years 1, 3 and 4. There is an opportunity to specialise in either the early or later years stages of primary education in Year 3 onwards.

Successful completion of this course leads to a recommendation for Qualified Teacher Status (QTS) after completion of skills tests.

Entry requirements: Tariff: 240 points, BTEC NC/ND, SCE Higher: CCCC, Irish Leaving Certificates: CCCCCCC, Foundation / access qualification, International Baccalaureate
Contact: Primary Office
0161 247 2028/2026
d.davies@mmu.ac.uk

BA (Hons) in Primary Education X120 D
4 years full-time
As above

BA (Hons) in Secondary Education (Business and Information Communications Technology) XNC1 A
3 years full-time

Year 1: Subject studies units in business and ICT education, education studies.

Years 2 and 3: Subject studies (business and ICT); application studies; professional studies; school placement.

Successful completion of this course leads to a recommendation for Qualified Teacher Status (QTS) after completion of skills tests.

Entry requirements: GCE A- and AS-levels

Contact: R Forrester
Subject Leader, Business
Education
0161 247 5112
r.forrester@mmu.ac.uk

**BA (Hons) in Secondary Education
(Business and Information
Communications Technology) XNC1 D**

3 years full-time
As above

**BA (Hons) in Secondary Education
(Business and Information
Communications Technology, shortened)
XN11 A**

2 years full-time or 3 to 4 years part-time

Students undertake a range of business and information technology education units and take related work in educational and application studies. 24 weeks' practical school experience is also undertaken, with appropriate professional courses. The course prepares mature students for a career in secondary or further education.

Successful completion of this course leads to a recommendation for Qualified Teacher Status (QTS) after completion of skills tests.

Entry requirements: DipHE, HNC, HND
Contact: Faculty Admissions Office
0161 247 2991

**BA (Hons) in Secondary Education
(Business and Information
Communications Technology, shortened)
XN11 D**

2 years full-time or 3 to 4 years part-time
As above

**BA (Hons) in Secondary Education
(Design and Technology) XWC2 A**

3 years full-time

After a strong emphasis on subject studies in year 1, students additionally study professional studies and undertake 24 weeks of school placement in Years 2 and 3.

Successful completion of this course leads to a recommendation for Qualified Teacher Status (QTS) after completion of skills tests.

Entry requirements: Tariff: 160 points, BTEC NC/ND, Foundation / access qualification, Interview, Mature entry, NVQ, Portfolio
Contact: Jim Morley
Subject Co-ordinator
0161 247 5387
j.w.morley@mmu.ac.uk

**BA (Hons) in Secondary Education
(Design and Technology) XWC2 D**

3 years full-time
As above

**BA (Hons) in Secondary Education
(Design and Technology, shortened)
XW12 A**

2 years full-time or 3 to 4 years part-time

Students take a range of design and technology courses and take related work in educational and application studies. 24 weeks' practical school experience is also undertaken, with appropriate professional courses. The course prepares mature students for a career in secondary or further education.

Successful completion of this course leads to a recommendation for Qualified Teacher Status (QTS) after completion of skills tests.

Entry requirements: DipHE, HNC, HND
Contact: Faculty Admissions Office
0161 247 2991

**BA (Hons) in Secondary Education
(Design and Technology, shortened)
XW12 D**

2 years full-time or 3 to 4 years part-time
As above

**BA (Hons) in Secondary Education
(Mathematics) XG11 A**

3 years full-time

Emphasis is placed on developing mathematical competencies which support the teaching of the National Curriculum. The mathematical content and methods of teaching on the course use the same frameworks that inform teaching in the classroom.

The course clarifies these frameworks in units of study which collectively are called mathematics in the professional context. This contains work on information technology and methods of presenting mathematics to pupils: it stresses the place of language in the classroom and develops the professional competencies expected of the new teacher.

There is a substantial school-based element. Students are placed in schools to practise their professional competencies in both serial attachments and block experiences.

Successful completion of this course leads to a recommendation for Qualified Teacher Status (QTS) after completion of skills tests.

Entry requirements: Tariff: 160 points, BTEC NC/ND, International Baccalaureate, SCE Higher

Contact: Mr G Frank-Keyes
           Admissions Tutor
           0161 247 2354/2007
           d.chesters@mmu.ac.uk

BA (Hons) in Secondary Education (Mathematics) XG11 D

3 years full-time
As above

BA (Hons) in Secondary Education (Mathematics, subject conversion) XGC1 A

2 years full-time

The course includes the equivalent of 1 year's study of mathematics together with: a study of that subject in its professional context; an element which contains the methodology and skills of teaching the chosen subject; a practical school-based element which has both serial attachments and block school experiences. This element involves 120 days over the 2 years. The school-based work will be supported and supervised by teachers.

This course prepares teachers for the National Curriculum 11–16 and, in addition, to contribute to post-16 and A-level subject teaching. It is characterised by its concentration of practical skills and a thorough professional preparation underpinned by appropriate theoretical frameworks. Students are invited to join with tutors in negotiating course experiences to meet individual backgrounds and needs.

Successful completion of this course leads to a recommendation for Qualified Teacher Status (QTS) after completion of skills tests.

Entry requirements: BTEC NC/ND, HND, International Baccalaureate, SCE Higher

Contact: As above

BA (Hons) in Secondary Education (Mathematics, subject conversion) XGC1 D

2 years full-time
As above

BA (Hons) in Secondary Education (Mathematics, with foundation year) XG1D

4 years full-time including foundation year

Foundation year: Application of number, Levels 2–3; foundation information technology; skills for lifelong learning.

Emphasis is placed on developing mathematical competencies which support the teaching of the National Curriculum. The mathematical content and methods of teaching on the course use the same frameworks that inform teaching in the classroom.

The course clarifies these frameworks in units of study which collectively are called mathematics in the professional context. This contains work on information technology and methods of presenting mathematics to pupils: It stresses the place of language in the classroom and develops the professional competencies expected of the new teacher.

There is a substantial school-based element. Students are placed in schools to practise their professional competencies in both serial attachments and block experiences.

Successful completion of this course leads to a recommendation for Qualified Teacher Status (QTS) after completion of skills tests.

Entry requirements: Tariff: 40 to 100 points, IELTS: 5.5, BTEC NC/ND, SCE Higher: CC, Irish Leaving Certificates: CCC, Work experience
Contact: Dr Nicola Hughes
University Foundation Scheme Leader
0161 247 1168
foundationyear@mmu.ac.uk

BA (Hons) in Secondary Education (Physical Education) XC16 A
3 years full-time or 5 years part-time

Successful completion of this course leads to a recommendation for Qualified Teacher Status (QTS) after completion of skills tests.

Entry requirements: Tariff: 240 points, BTEC NC/ND, SCE Higher: CCCCC, Interview, Mature entry, Work experience
Contact: Sue Jones
Secondary PE Co-ordinator
0161 247 5462
s.r.jones@mmu.ac.uk

BA (Hons) in Secondary Education (Physical Education) XC16 D
3 years full-time or 5 years part-time
As above

PGCE in Middle Years Education (7–14) X180 M
2 years full-time

Entry requirements: Honours degree (preferably 2nd Class or above) relevant to main subject; plus GCSE English, mathematics and science at grade C, or equivalent.
Contact: Primary Education Office
0161 247 2026
primaryed.cse@mmu.ac.uk

PGCE in Primary Education (3–7) X110 C
1 year full-time

Entry requirements: Degree or equivalent and GCSE grade C or above (or equivalent) in English language and mathematics and science.

Contact: Mrs Brenda Keogh
Faculty Admissions Office
0161 247 2991
admissions.ca@mmu.ac.uk

PGCE in Primary Education (3–7) X110 M
1 year full-time

Entry requirements: As above
Contact: Primary Education Office
0161 247 2006/7
primaryed.cse@mmu.ac.uk

PGCE in Primary Education (5–11) X100 C
1 year full-time

Entry requirements: As above
Contact: Mrs Brenda Keogh
Faculty Admissions Office
0161 247 2991
admissions.ca@mmu.ac.uk

PGCE in Primary Education (5–11) X100 M
1 year full-time

Entry requirements: As above
Contact: Primary Education Office
0161 247 2006/7
primaryed.cse@mmu.ac.uk

PGCE in Secondary Education (Art and Design) W1X1 M
1 year full-time

Entry requirements: Degree (1st or 2nd Class Honours), or equivalent, in an appropriate subject and GCSE grade C or above, or equivalent, in English language and mathematics.
Contact: Dolores Chesters
Secondary Education Office
0161 247 2007/2006
d.chesters@mmu.ac.uk

PGCE in Secondary Education (Business and Information Technology Education) N1X1 C
1 year full-time

Entry requirements: Degree or equivalent in a relevant subject (economics graduates are eligible); GCSE grade C or above (or equivalent) in English language and mathematics.

Contact: Sandra Speed
0161 247 5055
s.speed@mmu.ac.uk

PGCE in Secondary Education (Design and Technology: Resistant Materials) W9X1C

1 to 3 years part-time

Entry requirements: Recognised degree or equivalent qualification; GCSE grade C or above (or equivalent) in English language and mathematics.

Contact: Sandra Speed
0161 247 5005
s.speed@mmu.ac.uk

PGCE in Secondary Education (Design and Technology: Resistant Materials, conversion) WXX1 C

2 years full-time
As above

PGCE in Secondary Education (Design and Technology: Food Technology with Textiles) W2X1 M

1 year full-time

Entry requirements: Degree (1st or 2nd Class Honours), or equivalent, in an appropriate subject, and GCSE grade C, or equivalent, in English language and mathematics.

Contact: Dolores Chesters
Secondary Education Office
0161 247 2007/2006
d.chesters@mmu.ac.uk

PGCE in Secondary Education (Drama) W4X1 M

1 year full-time

Entry requirements: Single or combined degree in drama (1st or Upper 2nd Class); experience of working with young people in educational settings; GCSE grade C or equivalent in English language and mathematics.

Contact: As above

PGCE in Secondary Education (English with Special Educational Needs) QX31 M

1 year full-time

Entry requirements: Degree (1st or 2nd Class Honours), or equivalent, in an appropriate subject, and GCSE grade C, or equivalent, in English language and mathematics.

Contact: Dolores Chesters
Secondary Education Office
0161 247 2007/2006
d.chesters@mmu.ac.uk

PGCE in Secondary Education (English) Q3X1 C

1 year full-time

Entry requirements: Recognised degree or equivalent qualification; GCSE grade C or above (or equivalent) in English language and mathematics.

Contact: Sandra Speed
Faculty Admissions Office
0161 247 5055
s.speed@mmu.ac.uk

PGCE in Secondary Education (English) Q3X1 M

1 year full-time

Entry requirements: Degree (1st or 2nd Class Honours), or equivalent, in an appropriate subject, and GCSE grade C, or equivalent, in English language and mathematics.

Contact: Dolores Chesters
Secondary Education Office
0161 247 2007/2006
d.chesters@mmu.ac.uk

PGCE in Secondary Education (Geography) F8X1 C

1 year full-time

Entry requirements: Recognised degree or equivalent qualification; GCSE grade C or above (or equivalent) in English language and mathematics.

Contact: Sandra Speed
Faculty Admissions Office
0161 247 5055
s.speed@mmu.ac.uk

PGCE in Secondary Education (Geography) F8X1 M

1 year full-time

Entry requirements: Degree (1st or 2nd Class Honours), or equivalent, in an appropriate subject, and GCSE grade C, or equivalent, in English language and mathematics.

Contact: Dolores Chesters
Secondary Education Office
0161 247 2007/2006
d.chesters@mmu.ac.uk

PGCE in Secondary Education (History) V1X1 M

1 year full-time
As above

PGCE in Secondary Education (Mathematics) G1X1 M

1 year full-time
As above

PGCE in Secondary Education (Mathematics, conversion) GXC1 M

2 years full-time

Entry requirements: Degree (1st or 2nd Class Honours), or equivalent, containing 1 year's study of mathematics plus A-level (or equivalent) in mathematics and GCSE grade C, or equivalent, in English.

Contact: As above

PGCE in Secondary Education (Modern Foreign Languages: French) R1X1 M

1 year full-time

Entry requirements: Degree (1st or 2nd Class Honours), or equivalent, in an appropriate subject, and GCSE grade C, or equivalent, in English language and mathematics; native speakers of French welcome.

Contact: As above

PGCE in Secondary Education (Modern Foreign Languages: German) R2X1 M

1 year full-time

Entry requirements: Degree (1st or 2nd Class Honours), or equivalent, in an appropriate subject, and GCSE grade C, or equivalent, in English language and mathematics; native speakers of German welcome.

Contact: As above

PGCE in Secondary Education (Modern Foreign Languages: Spanish) R4X1 M

1 year full-time

Entry requirements: Degree (1st or 2nd Class Honours), or equivalent, in an appropriate subject, and GCSE grade C, or equivalent, in English language and mathematics; native speakers of Spanish welcome.

Contact: As above

PGCE in Secondary Education (Music with Specialist Strings Teaching) WX31 M

2 years full-time

Entry requirements: Degree (1st or 2nd Class Honours), or equivalent, in an appropriate subject, and GCSE grade C, or equivalent, in English language and mathematics.

Contact: As above

PGCE in Secondary Education (Music) W3X1 M

1 year full-time
As above

PGCE in Secondary Education (Religious Education) V6X1 M

1 year full-time
As above

PGCE in Secondary Education (Science: Biology) C1X1 C

1 to 3 years part-time

Entry requirements: Recognised degree or equivalent qualification; GCSE grade C or above (or equivalent) in English language and mathematics.

Contact: Sandra Speed
Faculty Admissions Office
0161 247 5055
s.speed@mmu.ac.uk

PGCE in Secondary Education (Science: Biology) C1X1 M

1 year full-time

As above

Entry requirements: Degree (1st or 2nd Class Honours), or equivalent, in an appropriate subject, and GCSE grade C, or equivalent, in English language and mathematics.

Contact: Dolores Chesters
　　　　Secondary Education Office
　　　　0161 247 2007/2006
　　　　d.chesters@mmu.ac.uk

PGCE in Secondary Education (Science: Chemistry) F1X1 C

1 to 3 years part-time

Entry requirements: Recognised degree or equivalent qualification; GCSE grade C or above (or equivalent) in English language and mathematics.

Contact: Sandra Speed
　　　　Faculty Admissions Office
　　　　0161 247 5055
　　　　s.speed@mmu.ac.uk

PGCE in Secondary Education (Science: Chemistry) F1X1 M

1 year full-time

Entry requirements: Degree (1st or 2nd Class Honours), or equivalent, in an appropriate subject, and GCSE grade C, or equivalent, in English language and mathematics.

Contact: Dolores Chesters
　　　　Secondary Education Office
　　　　0161 247 2007/2006
　　　　d.chesters@mmu.ac.uk

PGCE in Secondary Education (Science: Physics) F3X1 C

1 to 3 years part-time

Entry requirements: Recognised degree or equivalent qualification; GCSE grade C or above (or equivalent) in English language and mathematics.

Contact: Sandra Speed
　　　　Faculty Admissions Office

0161 247 5055
s.speed@mmu.ac.uk

PGCE in Secondary Education (Science: Physics) F3X1 M

1 year full-time

Entry requirements: Degree (1st or 2nd Class Honours), or equivalent, in an appropriate subject, and GCSE grade C, or equivalent, in English language and mathematics.

Contact: Dolores Chesters
　　　　Secondary Education Office
　　　　0161 247 2007/2006
　　　　d.chesters@mmu.ac.uk

PGCE in Secondary Education (Social Sciences and Citizenship) LX31 M

1 year full-time

As above

Postgraduate and Continuing Professional Development Courses – Didsbury

PgDip/MA/MEd/MSc in Education

3–5 years part-time

Entry requirements: Degree, teaching qualification and minimum 3 years' experience in teaching or allied occupation normally required.

Contact: Ms B Jackson
　　　　Continuing Professional
　　　　Development
　　　　0161 247 2012
　　　　education.cse@mmu.ac.uk

EdD in Educational Practitioner Studies

2 years part-time evening, part-time weekend

Entry requirements: Master's degree required, other qualifications considered; aimed at practitioners in range of professional settings including: teaching; nursing; management of training; and educational support and evaluation.

Contact: Prof Tony Brown
　　　　Course Leader
　　　　0161 247 2243
　　　　a.m.brown@mmu.ac.uk

MA/MEd in Special Educational Needs

1 year full-time, 3–5 years part-time

Entry requirements: Applicants should be qualified professionals in education with some experience and/or diploma in special educational needs.

Contact: M Johnson
Senior Lecturer
0161 247 2011/2
m.johnson@mmu.ac.uk

Diploma in Professional Studies in Special Educational Needs

2 years part-time

Entry requirements: Qualified Teacher Status and minimum 2 years' teaching experience normally required, exceptionally, holders of alternative professional qualifications admitted.

Contact: Ms B Jackson
Continuing Professional
Development
0161 247 2012
education.cse@mmu.ac.uk

PgDip/MA in Teaching

MA: 3 years part-time

Entry requirements: Honours degree, teaching qualification and 3 years' teaching experience normally required.

Contact: Dr John Powell
Course Lecturer
0161 247 2011/2012/2376
cpddidsbury@mmu.ac.uk

PgDip in Teaching Pupils with Specific Learning Difficulties

1 year part-time

Entry requirements: Qualified Teacher Status (QTS); teachers must be able to carry out practical teaching sessions with pupils with specific learning difficulties or be holders of Diploma in Teaching in SpLD.

Contact: Dr J Robertson
Course Leader
0161 247 205
cpddidsbury@mmy.ac.uk

Postgraduate and Continuing Professional Development Courses – Crewe

EdD in Education

4–6 years part-time

Entry requirements: Normally, Master's degree or equivalent required, and minimum 4 years' experience of working in a professional educational role.

Contact: Prof Tony Brown
Programme Leader
0161 247 2243
a.m.brown@mmu.ac.uk

PgCert/PgDip/MSc in Education Leadership and Management

MSc: 3 years part-time

Entry requirements: Good Honours degree or similar, management experience is also required.

Contact: CPD Office, Institute of
Education
0161 247 5582

Certificate in Professional Studies in Individual/Special Educational Needs

Part-time or mixed mode

Entry requirements: Qualified Teacher Status, or other relevant professional qualification.

Contact: Kath Hughes
CPD Administrator
0161 247 5057
k.m.hughes@mmu.ac.uk

Certificate in Professional Studies in Mentoring

1 year part-time

Entry requirements: Qualified Teacher Status.

Contact: As above

MA in Post-Compulsory Education and Training

2–3 years part-time

Entry requirements: Good degree or equivalent qualification, exceptional entry may be possible, and accreditation of prior learning (APL).

Contact: CPD Office, Institute of Education
0161 247 5582

Certificate/Diploma in Professional Studies in Primary Art Education

Entry requirements: Qualified Teacher Status and professional experience.

Contact: As above

Certificate in Professional Studies in Education

2–6 years part-time

Entry requirements: CATS Points: 180; Work experience

Contact: Dr Paul Goggin
Professional Development Programme Co-ordinator
0161 247 5082
p.f.goggin@mmu.ac.uk

Certificate in Professional Studies in Education (stage 1)

2 terms part-time

Entry requirements: Qualified Teacher Status.

PgCert/PgDip/MA in Professional Studies in Education

2–3 years part-time

Entry requirements: Honours degree, although other combinations of qualifications and experience may be acceptable equivalents. Professional experience is also a requirement, but can be acquired during the course.

Contact: CPD Office, Institute of Education
0161 247 5582

Diploma in Teaching in Specific Learning Difficulties

1–3 years part-time

Entry requirements: Qualified Teacher Status.

Contact: As above

University of Manchester

Oxford Road
Manchester
M13 9PL
Tel: 0161 275 2000
Fax: 0161 275 2106
ug-admissions@man.ac.uk
www.man.ac.uk

The University of Manchester originated from Owens College, which was established in 1851 in Richard Cobden's house on Quay Street, Manchester. The College moved to the first buildings on the present site on Oxford Road in 1873. The College was granted a Royal Charter in April 1880 as the Victoria University, a federal institution which established colleges in Leeds and Liverpool which were granted their independence in 1903 becoming the Universities of Leeds and Liverpool respectively, creating the Victoria University of Manchester. The University now has more than 18,000 students.

The University has extensive computer services and the library is one of the three largest in the country. There are many sporting and social facilities and both catered and non-catered halls are available within a few miles of the campus with new undergraduate students guaranteed a place. Several halls are reserved exclusively for postgraduate students.

The Faculty of Education runs undergraduate degrees and postgraduate options including PGCE courses and both taught and research programmes. The faculty has its own resource centre and computer unit.

HOW TO APPLY

PGCE: applications are made through the GTTR.

Postgraduate: applications are made direct to the institution.

COURSES

PGCE in Primary Education (5–11) X501

1 year full-time

Entry requirements: Degree or approved equivalent in subject relevant to primary national curriculum, and GCSE grade C or equivalent in English language and mathematics; entrants born on or after 1/9/79 also need GCSE grade C in a science subject or subjects.

Contact: Mrs P Warburton
Course Secretary
0161 275 3456
janet.grimshaw@man.ac.uk

PGCE in Secondary Education (Biology) C1X1

1 year full-time or 1 to 3 years part-time

Entry requirements: Relevant degree required and GCSE grade C or equivalent in English language and mathematics.
Contact: As above

PGCE in Secondary Education (Business Studies) N1X1

1 year full-time
As above

PGCE in Secondary Education (Chemistry) F1X1

1 year full-time or 1 to 3 years part-time
As above

PGCE in Secondary Education (Design and Technology) W9X1

1 year full-time
As above

PGCE in Secondary Education (Economics and Business Studies) L1X1

1 year full-time
As above

PGCE in Secondary Education (English) Q3X1

1 year full-time or 1 to 3 years part-time
As above

PGCE in Secondary Education (Information Technology) G5X1

1 year full-time
As above

PGCE in Secondary Education (Mathematics) G1X1

1 year full-time or 1 to 3 years part-time
As above

PGCE in Secondary Education (Modern Languages: French) R1X1

1 year full-time
As above

PGCE in Secondary Education (Modern Languages: German) R2X1

1 year full-time
As above

PGCE in Secondary Education (Modern Languages: Spanish) R4X71

1 year full-time
As above

PGCE in Secondary Education (Physics) F3X7

1 year full-time or 1 to 3 years part-time
As above

PGCE in Secondary Education (Science) F0X1

1 to 3 years part-time
As above

MEd in Communications, Education and Technology

1 year full-time, 2–5 years part-time

Entry requirements: Degree, teaching qualification or other approved qualification required.
Contact: Dr S Ralph
Course Director
0161 275 3398
sue.ralph@man.ac.uk

EdD in Education

3 years full-time, 4–6 years part-time

Entry requirements: Applicants should be working as senior professionals in a context that involves education and should already have obtained a Master's degree in education or an equivalent qualification in a related discipline.

Contact: Prof M West
Dean, Faculty of Education
0161 275 3463/3617
janet.grimshaw@man.ac.uk

Advanced Diploma in Education of Hearing Impaired Children

1 year full-time

Entry requirements: Candidates must hold Qualified Teacher Status.

Contact: Wendy McCracken
Programme Director
0161 275 3366
wendy.mccracken@man.ac.uk

Diploma/MEd in Educational Leadership and School Improvement

Diploma: 9 months full-time, MEd: 1 year full-time, 2–5 years part-time

Entry requirements: First degree or graduate-equivalent qualification.

Contact: Dr Marie Brown
Course Director
0161 275 3432
marie.brown@man.ac.uk

MEd in Educational Technology and English Language Teaching

Distance learning

Entry requirements: Degree from an approved university, initial qualification in teaching and 3 years' relevant teaching experience, e-mail facility and access to world wide web.

Contact: Mr G Motteram
Senior Lecturer in Education
0161 275 3431
gary.motteram@man.ac.uk

MEd in Educational Technology and TESOL

1 year full-time, 2–5 years part-time

Entry requirements: Degree or other approved qualification.

Contact: As above

MEd in English Language Teaching

Distance learning

Entry requirements: Degree from an approved university, or Qualified Teacher Status and advanced post-qualification award, or equivalent qualifications and experience.

Contact: Richard Fay
Programme Director
0161 275 3467
richard.fay@man.ac.uk

MEd in Further Professional Studies in Hearing Impairment

5 years distance learning

Entry requirements: Candidates must be qualified and experienced teachers of the deaf.

Contact: Mr R Baker
Programme Director
0161 275 3387
richard.baker@man.ac.uk

MEd in Hearing Impairment International

1 year full-time

Entry requirements: Candidates must hold teaching diploma or an initial degree.

Contact: Wendy McCracken
Programme Director
0161 275 3366
wendy.mccracken@man.ac.uk

MEd in Information and Communication Technology

1 year full-time, 2 years part-time

Entry requirements: Degree; exceptional entry possible for experienced teachers.

Contact: Ivy Brember
Director of Computing Services,
Faculty of Education
0161 275 3471
I.Brember@man.ac.uk

PgCert in Social Development and Citizenship Education

1 year full-time

Entry requirements: Honours degree or equivalent required; course intended for primary and secondary school teachers in British schools.

Contact: George Skinner
Programme Director
0161 275 3506
george.skinner@man.ac.uk

Diploma of Advanced Study in Special and Inclusive Education

9 months full-time

Entry requirements: Degree from an approved university, or Qualified Teacher Status and advanced post-qualification award, or equivalent qualifications and experience.

Contact: Dr Pauline Davis
Course Director
0161 275 3343
pauline.s.davis@man.ac.uk

Diploma of Advanced Study/MEd in Special and Inclusive Education

MEd: 1 year full-time, 2–5 years part-time
As above

MEd in Teaching of English to Speakers of Other Languages

1 year full-time, 2–5 years part-time

Entry requirements: First degree, initial teaching qualification minimum; 3 years' relevant full-time teaching experience; IELTS 7.0 required for non-native speakers.

Contact: John Burgess
Lecturer in Education (TESOL)
0161 275 3453/3467/3476
Michael.Beaumont@man.ac.uk

Marches Consortium (SCITT)

Grange Court
Pinsley Road
Leominster
Herefordshire
HR6 8ZG
Tel: 01568 615510
Fax: 01568 516340
scitt@marchesconsortium.org
www.marchesconsortium.org

The Marches Consortium is a large partnership of primary and secondary schools, sixth form colleges, universities, training providers and community groups. The partner schools and colleges are located in Herefordshire, Worcestershire, Shropshire, the West Midlands and Wales.

Trainees spend a minimum of 20 weeks in school, in two different placements. They attend an average of one training session per week run by subject specialists.

HOW TO APPLY

Applications are made through the GTTR.

COURSES

PGCE in Middle Years Education (Citizenship, 7–14 years) XLC9

36 weeks full-time

Entry requirements: Degree; GCSE mathematics, English language at grade C, and science if born after 1/9/79.

Contact: Enquiries
01568 615510
scitt@marchesconsortium.org

PGCE in Middle Years Education (Design and Technology, 7–14 years) XWC9

36 weeks full-time
As above

PGCE in Middle Years Education (Geography, 7–14 years) XFC8

36 weeks full-time
As above

PGCE in Middle Years Education (History, 7–14 years) XVC1

36 weeks full-time
As above

PGCE in Middle Years Education (Information Technology, 7–14 years) XGC5

36 weeks full-time
As above

PGCE in Middle Years Education (Mathematics, 7–14 years) XGC1

36 weeks full-time
As above

PGCE in Middle Years Education
(Modern Foreign Languages, 7–14 years)
XRC9
36 weeks full-time
As above

PGCE in Middle Years Education
(Music, 7–14 years) XWC3
36 weeks full-time
As above

PGCE in Middle Years Education
(Physical Education, 7–14 years) XCC6
36 weeks full-time
As above

PGCE in Middle Years Education
(Religious Education, 7–14 years) XVC6
36 weeks full-time
As above

PGCE in Middle Years Education
(Science, 7–14 years) XFCA
36 weeks full-time
As above

PGCE in Secondary Education
(Citizenship) L9X1
37 weeks full-time
As above

PGCE in Secondary Education (Design
and Technology) W9X1
37 weeks full-time
As above

PGCE in Secondary Education
(Geography) F8X1
37 weeks full-time
As above

PGCE in Secondary Education (History)
V1X1
37 weeks full-time
As above

PGCE in Secondary Education
(Information Technology) G5X1
37 weeks full-time
As above

PGCE in Secondary Education
(Mathematics) G1X1
37 weeks full-time
As above

PGCE in Secondary Education (Modern
Foreign Languages) R9X1
37 weeks full-time
As above

PGCE in Secondary Education (Music)
W3X1
37 weeks full-time
As above

PGCE in Secondary Education (Physical
Education) X9C6
37 weeks full-time
As above

PGCE in Secondary Education (Religious
Education) V6X1
37 weeks full-time
As above

PGCE in Secondary Education (Science)
F0X1
37 weeks full-time
As above

Maryvale Institute

Maryvale House
Old Oscott Hill
Kingstanding
Birmingham
B44 9AG
Tel: 0121 360 8118
Fax: 0121 366 6786
maryvale.institute@dial.pipex.com
www.maryvale.ac.uk

Maryvale Institute specialises in part-time
and distance learning courses in theology,
religious education and catechesis. The site
of Maryvale has been in Catholic occupation since the Middle Ages. From 1794 to
1838 it was the home of Oscott College,
the first Seminary to open in England
after the Reformation. The college moved
to larger purpose-built premises and received the name 'Maryvale' in 1846. From

1851–1980 the Sisters of Mercy ran an orphanage and established a school for poor children. The present Catholic college developed out of the Adult Centre for catechetics opened in 1980. The Institute has a library and bookshop.

The Institute offers a distance-learning PGCE and the Catholic Certificate in Religious Studies, which is a requirement for teachers in Catholic schools. Postgraduate courses are available in pastoral and educational subjects.

HOW TO APPLY

Applications are made directly to the institution.

COURSES

PGCE in Secondary Education (Religious Education)

18 months part-time

Entry requirements: Degree in theology, religious studies or cognate areas or recognised equivalent, plus grade C standard in GCSE English language and mathematics.
Contact: Mrs Maureen Shiel
Postgraduate Programme
Secretary
0121 325 2408
cdcs.maryvale@dial.pipex.com

PgCert/PgDip/MA in Chaplaincy in Catholic Schools

MA: 30 months distance learning

Entry requirements: Honours degree or equivalent professional qualifications (e.g. Teacher's Certificate) normally required; eligibility restricted to existing and potential chaplains and their lay collaborators.
Contact: As above

PgCert/PgDip/MA in Leadership and Vision for Catholic Schools

MA: 30 months distance learning

Entry requirements: Applicants should be aspiring head teachers or head teachers in first 2 years of office; if entrant is an aspiring head teacher they must be undertaking or have completed a National Professional Qualifications for Head Teachers (NPQH) course.
Contact: As above

PgCert/PgDip/MA in Religious Education Curriculum Leadership in Catholic Schools

MA: 30 months distance learning

Entry requirements: Honours degree or equivalent professional qualifications (e.g. Teacher's Certificate) normally required; eligibility restricted to existing and potential co-ordinators/subject leaders of religious education in primary and secondary schools.
Contact: As above

Middlesex University

White Hart Lane
Enfield
London
N17 8HR
Tel: 020 8411 5898
Fax: 020 8411 5649
admissions@mdx.ac.uk
www.mdx.ac.uk

Middlesex was granted university status in 1992. It was formed in 1973 as a polytechnic with the merger of Enfield College of Technology, Hendon College of Technology and Hornsey College of Art but the history of its development goes back to the nineteenth century.

Middlesex University is the sixth largest in the UK and has several campuses across north London: Cat Hill, Enfield, Hendon, Tottenham, Trent Park and Archway and Hospitals. The facilities are based in buildings ranging from modern centres to buildings that have existed for centuries including a mansion house and country park estate and purpose-built sites. The sport and leisure facilities at each campus are available to all students. Halls of residence or privately rented accommodation are located on campus or within close proximity.

The School of Life Long Learning and Education is based at the Trent Park and Tottenham sites. The school offers courses for the primary and secondary phases of education and also a range of postgraduate programmes for existing teachers.

HOW TO APPLY

Degree courses: applications are made through UCAS.

PGCE: applications are made through the GTTR.

Postgraduate: applications are made direct to the institution.

COURSES

BA (Hons) Primary Education X120 P

3 years full-time

Course trains students to teach at Key Stages 1 and 2; comprises a specialist subject and 6 additional subjects: English, mathematics, science, art, design and technology, information technology and history; students choose to focus on either Key Stage 1 (5–7) or Key Stage 2 (8–11) in the 3rd year.

Entry requirements: GCE A- and AS-levels, BTEC NC/ND, Foundation / access qualification

Contact: Admissions Enquiries
020 8411 5898
admissions@mdx.ac.uk

PGCE in Primary Education X100

1 year full-time

Entry requirements: Degree or equivalent qualification; GCSE minimum grade C in mathematics, English language and science; 50% of first degree should be in a National Curriculum subject or a combination of National Curriculum subjects.

Contact: Christine Khwaja
Curriculum Leader
020 8411 5166
c.khwaja@mdx.ac.uk

PGCE in Secondary Education (Art and Design) W1X1

1 year full-time

Entry requirements: Degree in art history, art and design, architecture, or expressive arts or visual studies, providing studio work formed significant part of the degree; portfolio required; GCSE grade C or above (or equivalent) in English language and mathematics.

Contact: Peter Shipley
Curriculum Leader
020 8411 5609
p.shipley@mdx.ac.uk

PGCE in Secondary Education (Business Studies) N1X1

1 year full-time

Entry requirements: Relevant degree; English language and mathematics GCSE grade C (or equivalent).

Contact: As above

PGCE in Secondary Education (Design and Technology) W9X1

1 year full-time

Entry requirements: Degree or equivalent qualification; GCSE minimum grade C (or equivalent) in mathematics and English; applicants will have a practical capability with some experience in art or a design discipline or an aspect of technology.

Contact: As above

PGCE in Secondary Education (Design and Technology, conversion) WXX1

2 years full-time

Entry requirements: As above
Contact: As above

PGCE in Secondary Education (Drama) W4X1

1 year full-time

Entry requirements: Degree or equivalent in drama; GCSE minimum grade C (or equivalent) in English language and mathematics.

Contact: As above

PGCE in Secondary Education (English) Q3X1

1 year full-time

As above

Entry requirements: Degree in English, or combined or related subject degrees with a high proportion of English; English and mathematics equivalent to GCSE grade C.
Contact: As above

PGCE in Secondary Education (Geography) F8X1

1 year full-time

Entry requirements: Relevant degree; English language and mathematics GCSE grade C (or equivalent).
Contact: As above

PGCE in Secondary Education (Information Technology) G5X1

1 year full-time

Entry requirements: Relevant degree plus GCSE minimum grade C (or equivalent) in English language and mathematics.
Contact: As above

PGCE in Secondary Education (Mathematics) G1X1

1 year full-time

Entry requirements: Relevant degree; English language and mathematics GCSE grade C (or equivalent).
Contact: As above

PGCE in Secondary Education (Modern Languages) R9X1

1 year full-time

Entry requirements: Relevant modern languages Honours degree (Upper 2nd Class); plus GCSE minimum grade C (or equivalent) in English language and mathematics.
Contact: As above

PGCE in Secondary Education (Music) W3X1

1 year full-time

Entry requirements: Degree or equivalent in music; GCSE minimum grade C (or equivalent) in English language and mathematics.
Contact: As above

PGCE in Secondary Education (Physical Education) X9C6

1 year full-time

Entry requirements: Relevant degree; English language and mathematics GCSE grade C (or equivalent).
Contact: As above

PGCE in Secondary Education (Science) F0X1

1 year full-time

Entry requirements: Relevant degree; English language and mathematics GCSE grade C (or equivalent).
Contact: As above

PgCert/PgDip in Leadership and Management Teaching and Learning Social Inclusion

PgCert: 1 year part-time

Entry requirements: Normally for graduates with QTS but candidates without these qualifications would be considered.
Contact: Vicky MacLeod
Curriculum Leader
020 8411 6160
v.macleod@mdx.ac.uk

MA in Lifelong Learning

5 semesters part-time

Entry requirements: Degree.
Contact: Deborah Jack
020 8411 6251/6369
d.jack@mdx.ac.uk

PgDip/MA in Special Educational Needs

2–3 years part-time, distance learning

Entry requirements: Qualified Teacher Status and experience in teaching normally required; applicants need access to a classroom or groups of pupils.
Contact: Diane Montgomery
020 8411 5658
j.lewis@mdx.ac.uk

PgDip/MA in Specific Learning Difficulties

2–3 years part-time, distance learning

Entry requirements: As above
Contact: As above

Mid-Essex SCITT Consortium

Chelmer Valley High School
Court Road
Broomfield
Essex
CM1 7ER
Tel: 01245 443480
Fax: 01245 441568
midess_scitt@btconnect.com
www.middessexscitt.org

The Mid-Essex Consortium offers school-centred initial teacher training in nine local secondary schools. Training is available in seven subjects, leading to a PGCE awarded by the University of Greenwich.

HOW TO APPLY

Applications are made through the GTTR.

COURSES

PGCE in Secondary Education (Art and Design) W1X1

36 weeks full-time

Entry requirements: Degree in relevant subject; GCSE grade C or above in English language and mathematics, and science if born after 1/9/79; recent relevant experience in secondary school an advantage.

Contact: Enquiries

01245 443480
midess_scitt@btconnect.com

PGCE in Secondary Education (English) Q3X1

36 weeks full-time
As above

PGCE in Secondary Education (Geography) F8X1

36 weeks full-time
As above

PGCE in Secondary Education (Information Technology) G5X1

36 weeks full-time
As above

PGCE in Secondary Education (Mathematics) G1X1

36 weeks full-time
As above

PGCE in Secondary Education (Modern Languages) R9X1

36 weeks full-time
As above

PGCE in Secondary Education (Science) F0X1

36 weeks full-time
As above

National SCITT in Outstanding Primary Schools

School of Education
University of Nottingham
Jubilee Campus
Nottingham
NG8 1BB
Tel: 0115 951 4543
Fax: 0115 951 4499
Beverly.tribbick@nottingham.ac.uk
www.nottingham.ac.uk/education/courses/
initial-teacher-training

The National SCITT in Outstanding Primary Schools is a consortium of over 40 primary schools recognised by OFSTED as nationally outstanding. The PGCE is validated by the University of Nottingham.

HOW TO APPLY

Applications are made through the GTTR.

COURSES

PGCE in Primary Education (5–11 years) X100

38 weeks full-time

Entry requirements: Upper 2nd Class Honours degree or equivalent, of which component is in subject within National Curriculum; GCSE grade C or above in English language and mathematics.

Contact: Beverly Tribbick
Enquiries Secretary
0115 951 4517
beverly.tribbick@nottingham.ac.uk

North East Essex Coastal Confederation Initial Teacher Training

Clacton County High School
Walton road
Clacton on Sea
Colchester
Essex
CO15 6DZ
Tel: 01255 431949
Fax: 01255 421377
teach@coastalscitt.co.uk
www.coastalscitt.co.uk

The North East Essex Coastal Confederation Initial Teacher Training offers a full time PGCE at secondary level in the subjects of English, maths, science, history and information technology. Clacton County High School is the lead school of the confederation and there is a designated base located on site. There are five other schools within the confederation at present.

Students are enrolled in Suffolk College and have access to all the student support and resource facilities based there. The PGCE is validated by the University of East Anglia.

HOW TO APPLY

Applications are made through the GTTR.

COURSES

PGCE in Secondary Education (English)
Q3X1
38 weeks full-time

Entry requirements: Degree in relevant area; GCSE grade C or above in English language and mathematics, and science if born after 1/Sep/79.

Contact: Enquiries
01255 431949
teach@coastalscitt.co.uk

PGCE in Secondary Education (History)
V1X1
38 weeks full-time
As above

PGCE in Secondary Education (Information Technology) G5X1
38 weeks full-time
As above

PGCE in Secondary Education (Mathematics) G1X1
38 weeks full-time
As above

PGCE in Secondary Education (Science)
F0X1
38 weeks full-time
As above

University of Newcastle Upon Tyne

6 Kensington Terrace
Newcastle Upon Tyne
NE1 7RU
Tel: 0191 222 6000
Fax: 0191 222 6139
admissions-enquiries@ncl.ac.uk
www.ncl.ac.uk

The University developed from the School of Medicine, which was established in 1834, and Armstrong College, which was founded in 1871 for the teaching of physical sciences. These colleges formed one division of the federal University of Durham. In 1937 the Newcastle Colleges merged to form King's College and, when the federal University was dissolved in 1963, King's College became the University of Newcastle upon Tyne. The campus is based on the northern side of the city centre.

The University has a range of sporting and social facilities as well as an award-winning library and there are extensive computer services available. The School of Education, Communication and Language Sciences offers both undergraduate and postgraduate degrees, initial teacher training and a wide range of research opportunities. Aside from the main academic facilities students have access to the Education Resource Centre.

Catered halls and university flats are available to both undergraduates and postgraduates. Most accommodation is within easy walking distance of the university or has good links to the campus.

HOW TO APPLY

PGCE: applications are made through the GTTR.

Postgraduate: applications are made direct to the institution.

COURSES

PGCE in Key Stage 2/3 (General Science, 7–14) XFCA

1 year full-time

Entry requirements: Relevant degree and GCSE grade C or above (or equivalent) in mathematics, English language and a science subject.

Contact: Admissions Office
0191 222 5594
admissions-enquiries@ncl.ac.uk

PGCE in Key Stage 2/3 (Mathematics, 7–14) XGC1

1 year full-time
As above

PGCE in Key Stage 2/3 (Modern Languages: French, 7–14) XRC1

1 year full-time
As above

PGCE in Primary Education (Advanced Early Years, 3–5) X110

1 year full-time

Entry requirements: Degree, of which 50% should have been in an area or areas directly relevant to the primary school curriculum; GCSE or O-level passes (grades A–C) in English language, mathematics and a science subject.
Contact: As above

PGCE in Primary Education (Lower Primary, 3–8) X121

1 year full-time
As above

PGCE in Primary Education (Upper Primary, 7–11) X171

1 year full-time
As above

PGCE in Primary Education (Upper Primary, Advanced French Specialism, 7–11) XR11

1 year full-time
As above

PGCE in Secondary Education (Biology, Core Science) C1X1

1 year full-time

Entry requirements: Degree in subject to be taught or closely related subjects; GCSE or O-level passes (grades A–C) in English language and mathematics.
Contact: As above

PGCE in Secondary Education (Chemistry, Core Science) F1X1

1 year full-time
As above

PGCE in Secondary Education (English, includes Drama) QX31

1 year full-time
As above

PGCE in Secondary Education (French with German) RX11

1 year full-time
As above

PGCE in Secondary Education (French with Spanish) RXD1

1 year full-time
As above

PGCE in Secondary Education (French) R1X1

1 year full-time
As above

PGCE in Secondary Education (Geography) F8X1

1 year full-time
As above

PGCE in Secondary Education (German with French) RX21

1 year full-time
As above

PGCE in Secondary Education (German with Spanish) RX2C
1 year full-time
As above

PGCE in Secondary Education (German) R2X1
1 year full-time
As above

PGCE in Secondary Education (History) V1X1
1 year full-time
As above

PGCE in Secondary Education (Mathematics) G1X1
1 year full-time
As above

PGCE in Secondary Education (Physics, Core Science) F3X1
1 year full-time
As above

PGCE in Secondary Education (Religious Education) V6X1
1 year full-time
As above

PGCE in Secondary Education (Spanish with French) RX41
1 year full-time
As above

PGCE in Secondary Education (Spanish with German) RX4C
1 year full-time
As above

BPhil in Education
1 year full-time
Entry requirements: Initial teaching qualification plus teaching experience and DAES/Advanced Diploma in education or equivalent depending upon point of entry.
Contact: As above

MEd in Education
24–36 months part-time
Entry requirements: Degree, teaching qualification and teaching experience.
Contact: As above

MEd in Education
1 year full-time
As above

EdD in Education
2 years full-time, 4 years part-time
Entry requirements: Degree (or equivalent) and teaching qualification (or equivalent).
Contact: As above

MEd in Education (Educational Management) delivered in Abu Dhabi
24 months part-time
Entry requirements: Degree or equivalent, with professional qualification and significant professional experience; appropriate level of English (IELTS 6.5, TOEFL 575 or equivalent).
Contact: As above

MEd in Education (Special Educational Needs) delivered in Hong Kong
24 months part-time
Entry requirements: Degree, professional qualification and professional experience with appropriate level of English (IELTS 6.5, TOEFL 575 or equivalent).
Contact: As above

MEd in Education (TESOL) delivered in the United Arab Emirates
24 months part-time
Entry requirements: Degree and work experience required.
Contact: As above

Advanced Diploma/BPhil in Educational Studies (Early Years Practitioners)
BPhil: 12 months full-time, Advanced Diploma: 24 months full-time
Entry requirements: Appropriate professional qualification with appropriate professional experience.
Contact: As above

MEd in Guidance and Counselling (Special Educational Needs)
24 months part-time
Entry requirements: Degree and work experience required.
Contact: As above

Newman College of Higher Education

Genners Lane
Bartley Green
Birmingham
B32 3NT
Tel: 0121 476 1181
Fax: 0121 476 1196
registry@newman.ac.uk
www.newman.ac.uk

Newman College was founded in 1968 and was originally designed for teacher training. The college is situated to the south west of Birmingham next to the green belt area and has modern purpose-built buildings. The campus offers a range of academic and recreational facilities and accommodation is available in halls or in private housing in the local area.

The college runs initial teacher training courses at degree level and also the PGCE at primary and secondary level. Alternatively there are employment-based routes through Graduate and Registered Teacher Programmes. Taught higher degree and research programmes are also offered and a course for qualified teachers going back into teaching is available.

HOW TO APPLY

Degree courses: applications are made through UCAS.
PGCE: applications are made through the GTTR.
Postgraduate: applications are made direct to the institution.

COURSES

English (Key Stages 2/3) XQ1H
BA (Hons): 4 years full-time
BEd (Hons): 3 years full-time

Year 1: English language and English literature (including drama and theatre); Key Stage 1 and 2 core subjects: English; mathematics; science; ICT; education studies (Key Stages 1 and 2); religious education; school experience: placement in a primary school.

Year 2: English language and English literature (including drama and theatre); Key Stage 1 and 2 core subjects: English; mathematics; science; ICT; education studies (Key Stages 2 and 3); English at Key Stage 3; school placement teaching at Key Stage 3.

Year 3: English language and English literature; Key Stage 1 and 2 core subjects: English; mathematics; science; ICT; education studies (Key Stages 1 and 2); religious education; school experience: placement teaching at Key Stage 3.

Year 4: BA (Hons): English language and English literature; advanced subject applications: specialist areas of English teaching at Key Stage 2 and Key Stage 3; school placement teaching at Key Stage 2 and Key Stage 3.

Successful completion of this course leads to a recommendation for Qualified Teacher Status (QTS) on completion of skills tests.

Entry requirements: Tariff: 160 points, International Baccalaureate: 24, AVCEs, BTEC NC/ND, SCE Higher: CCC, Irish Leaving Certificates: CCCDD, Foundation / access qualification
Contact: Jenny Daniels
        Head of English
        0121 476 1181 x2253
        j.c.daniels@newman.ac.uk

Information and Communications Technology (Key stages 2/3) XG15

BEd (Hons): 3 years full-time
BSc (Hons): 4 years full-time

Year 1: Teaching ICT at Key Stage 2; fundamentals of information technology; measuring, sensing and control.

Year 2: Global communications and networks; computer programming; teaching ICT at Key Stage 3.

Year 3: Multimedia authoring; information technology in education; advanced database applications

Year 4: BSc (Hons): Teaching and learning strategies; special study.

Successful completion of this course leads to a recommendation for Qualified Teacher Status (QTS) on completion of skills tests.

Entry requirements: As above
Contact: Linda Harrries
Head of ICT
0121 476 1181 x2333
l.harries@newman.ac.uk

Primary Education (5–11 years) X101

BA (Hons): 4 years full-time
BEd (Hons): 3 years full-time

The BEd Honours degree leads to a teaching qualification after 3 years' study. Students choose 1 major subject from: art; English; history; information and communications technology; theology. There is an extensive programme of school experience in each year, courses in the National Curriculum core and foundation subjects, plus educational studies. The course covers both upper and lower primary age ranges.

Year 4: BA (Hons): Students have an opportunity to develop skills and subject knowledge to become subject specialists; leads to recommendation for Qualified Teacher Status (QTS) on completion of skills tests.

Throughout the course emphasis is given to topics such as class management, child development, cross-curricular issues and the use of educational technology.

Entry requirements: Tariff: 160 points, BTEC NC/ND, Irish Leaving Certificates, Work experience
Contact: Chris Wilkinson
Admissions Registrar
0121 476 1181 x2205
registry@newman.ac.uk

Primary Education (5–11 years) X103

BEd (Hons): 3 years full-time
BSc (Hons): 4 years full-time

Students choose 1 major subject from: biology; geography; mathematics; physical education and sports studies; there is an extensive programme of school experience in each year, courses in the National Curriculum core and foundation subjects, plus

educational studies; the course covers both upper and lower primary age ranges.

Year 4: BSc (Hons): Students have the opportunity to develop skills and subject knowledge to become subject specialists; leads to a recommendation for Qualified Teacher Status (QTS) after completion of skills tests.

Throughout the course emphasis is given to topics such as class management, child development, cross-curricular issues and the use of educational technology.

Entry requirements: Tariff: 160 points, BTEC NC/ND, Irish Leaving Certificates: CCCDD, Work experience
Contact: As above

Science (Key Stages 2/3) XF10

BEd (Hons): 3 years full-time
BSc (Hons): 4 years full-time

This course gives students a thorough understanding of teaching science at Key Stage 2/3. In addition students will learn about the National Curriculum including mathematics and English.

Entry requirements: Tariff: 160 points, International Baccalaureate: 24, BTEC NC/ND, SCE Higher: CCC, Irish Leaving Certificates: CCCDD, Foundation / access qualification
Contact: Dr Des Bowden
Head of Science
0121 476 1181 x2294
d.j.bowden@newman.ac.uk

Secondary English (11–16 years) XQ13

BA (Hons): 4 years full-time
BEd (Hons): 3 years full-time

Year 1: Introduction to literary studies; introduction to language studies; expressive English 1; people in school.

Year 2: Language of spoken and written texts; expressive English 2; pre-20th century literature; teaching and learning in secondary schools.

Year 3: Language and genre; 20th-century literature; critical approaches; educational studies.

Year 4: BA (Hons): Language options; literature options; special study (language or literature). Typical options include: language and learning; contemporary women writers; American literacy and film studies; children's literature; drama and poetry 1576–1700.

School placements in secondary school or college during each year of the course.

Successful completion of this course leads to a recommendation for Qualified Teacher Status (QTS) on completion of skills tests.

Entry requirements: As above
Contact: Dr Jenny Daniels
Head of English
0121 476 1181 x2253
j.c.daniels@newman.ac.uk

BA (Hons) in Secondary English (11–18 years) X1Q3

4 years full-time

Year 1: An introduction to literacy and language studies; expressive English 1 (creative writing; drama and theatre production); people in schools.

Year 2: Language of spoken and written texts; expressive English 2 (creative writing; drama and theatre production); pre-20th century literature; teaching and learning in secondary schools.

Year 3: Language and genre; 20th-century literature; critical approaches; education studies.

Year 4: Language and literature options; special study (language or literature).

The course will give students the skills to teach A-level English literature and language. Students develop classroom skills and undertake teaching placements in a secondary school or college.

Successful completion of this course leads to a recommendation for Qualified Teacher Status (QTS) on completion of skills tests.

Entry requirements: As above
Contact: As above

BA (Hons) in Secondary English (14–19 years) XQC3

4 years full-time

Year 1: Introduction to literary studies; introduction to language studies; expressive English 1; people in school.

Year 2: Language of spoken and written texts; expressive English 2; pre-20th-century literature; etching and learning in secondary schools.

Year 3: Language and genre; 20th-century literature; critical approaches; education studies.

Year 4: Language options; literature options; special study (language or literature). Typical options include: language and learning; contemporary women writers; American literary and film studies; children's literature; drama and poetry 1576–1700.

Students develop classroom skills and undertake teaching placement in a secondary school or college during each year of the course.

Successful completion of this course leads to a recommendation for Qualified Teacher Status (QTS) on completion of skills tests.

Entry requirements: As above
Contact: As above

PGCE in Middle Years Education (Information and Communications Technology, Key Stage 2/3) XGC5

1 year full-time

Entry requirements: Good degree in an appropriate subject; those wishing to teach at secondary level should have high information technology content in their degree plus experience in school setting, e.g. as volunteer.

Contact: Course Contact
0121 476 1181 x2333
l.harries@newman.ac.uk

PGCE in Primary Education X100

1 year full-time

Entry requirements: Nationally recognised graduate qualification; applicants must have GCSE grade A–C in English language, mathematics and, if born after 1/9/79, science; good Honours graduates preferred
Contact: Mr S Walker
Programme Leader
0121 476 1181 x2245
s.a.walker@newman.ac.uk

PGCE in Primary Education with French XR11
36 weeks full-time
Entry requirements: Good degree preferably in national curriculum subject; fluent French language skills (written and oral) up to A-level standard English and mathematics at GCSE grade C or above (or equivalent) and science GCSE at grade C or above for applicants born after 1/9/79.
Contact: As above

PGCE in Secondary Education (Citizenship) L9X1
1 year full-time
Entry requirements: Recognised degree in a subject relevant to the citizenship curriculum; plus GCSE grade C or above in English and mathematics.
Contact: As above

PGCE in Secondary Education (English) Q3X1
1 year full-time
Entry requirements: Degree in relevant area; GCSE mathematics and English grade C or above; relevant work experience welcomed.
Contact: As above

PGCE in Secondary Education (Physical Education) X9C6
1 year full-time
Entry requirements: Degree in which sports studies or related subject forms a significant element; Gcses in mathematics and English at grade C or above; experience of working with young people welcomed.
Contact: Dr Yahya Al-Nakeeb
0121 476 1181 x2268
y.al-nakeeb@newman.ac.uk

PGCE in Secondary Education (Religious Education) V6X1
1 year full-time
Entry requirements: Recognised degree in which theology or religious studies forms significant part, and GCSE grade C or above in English language and mathematics; or equivalent qualifications.
Contact: Mr Paul Walsh
Programme Leader
0121 476 1181 x2233
p.walsh@newman.ac.uk

PgCert/PgDip/MA/MEd in Education
Part-time
Entry requirements: Relevant good Honours degree normally required and teaching qualification or similar professional experience.
Contact: Mrs H Dunphy
Programme Leader
0121 476 1181 x2249
h.m.dunphy@newman.ac.uk

University of Wales College, Newport

Caerleon Campus
PO Box 101
Newport
NP18 3YG
Tel: 01633 432432
Fax: 01633 432850

uic@newport.ac.uk
www.newport.ac.uk

The University of Wales College, Newport is based around two main campuses, Allt-Yr-Yn in Newport and the Caerleon Campus. A third, Fairoak, is situated in the centre of the town and is the centre for the art and design foundation course.

The School of Education is situated on Caerleon Campus. It benefits from specialist facilities and there are library and computer services on hand. Courses on offer include degree courses and PGCEs as well as a range of postgraduate programmes.

First-year students are guaranteed places in halls of residence which are found at the Caerleon Campus with all the university facilities close to hand. There is also the option of privately rented accommodation, which the Student Accommodation Office can advise on.

HOW TO APPLY

Degree courses: applications are made through UCAS.

PGCE: applications are made through the GTTR.

Postgraduate: applications are made direct to the institution.

COURSES

BSc (Ed) in Design and Technology X1W2

2 years full-time

The main course elements in both years are:

Subject studies: Covers study of design and technology.

Teaching studies: This includes subject application, educational studies and 24 weeks' practical teaching. The University has established partnerships with secondary schools including Welsh Medium schools so as to provide integrated studies with teaching experience during the course.

During the first year of the course, safety and first aid courses are provided and there is an opportunity to develop study and IT skills. Laptop computers are available for short-term loan.

Successful completion of this course leads to a recommendation for Qualified Teacher Status (QTS) after completion of skills tests.

Entry requirements: Mature entry

Contact: University Information Centre
01633 432432
uic@newport.ac.uk

BSc (Ed) in Mathematics with Information and Communications Technology X1GC

2 years full-time

This is a shortened degree programme designed specifically to utilise the experience and expertise of mature students with appropriate qualifications who wish to enter the teaching profession.

The main course elements in both years are: teaching studies; subject studies.

Subject studies covers the study of mathematics and information technology. Students will gain a specialist knowledge and understanding of topics arising from the Programmes of Study in the National Curriculum to enable them to develop teaching skills which will enhance the teaching and learning of mathematics and information technology in the secondary school. There will be an emphasis upon practical and investigative work and 'hands on' experience. The teaching and learning methods used are designed to build up confidence, competence and independence as learners.

Teaching studies includes subject application, educational studies and 24 weeks of practical teaching.

Assessment: assessment is based on course work, including projects, written examinations and practical teaching competence.

Successful completion of this course leads to a recommendation for Qualified Teacher Status (QTS) after completion of skills tests.

Entry requirements: As above

Contact: As above

BSc (Ed) in Mathematics with Science X1G1

2 years full-time

This is a shortened degree programme designed specifically to utilise the experience and expertise of mature students with appropriate qualifications who wish to enter the teaching profession.

The main course elements in both years are: teaching studies; subject studies.

Subject studies covers the study of mathematics and science. Students will gain a specialist knowledge and understanding of topics arising from the Programmes of Study in the National Curriculum to enable them to develop teaching skills which will enhance the teaching and learning of mathematics and science in the secondary school. There will be an emphasis upon practical and investigative work and 'hands on' experience. The teaching and learning methods used are designed to build up confidence, competence and independence as learners.

Teaching studies includes subject application, educational studies and 24 weeks of practical teaching.

Assessment: assessment is based on course work, including projects, written examinations and practical teaching competence.

Successful completion of this course leads to a recommendation for Qualified Teacher Status (QTS) after completion of skills tests.

Entry requirements: As above
Contact: As above

BA (Hons) in Primary Education X120

3 years full-time

Consists of 3 components: curriculum studies; teaching studies including school focused component; subject studies.

Curriculum Studies: To cover all areas of the National Curriculum: mathematics core studies; English core studies; science core studies; art; geography; history; music; physical education; religious education; technology; Welsh or Welsh history and culture.

Teaching Studies: Workshops: practical sessions where skills and techniques are practiced. Serial visits to schools linked to workshops and supported by school and Tutors. Block school experience (Year 1: 6 weeks, Year 2: 5 weeks, Year 3: 11/12 weeks).

Subject Studies: During the second year of the course, students will be required to select 3 subjects to study in greater depth; 1 from each category below:

1 from: music; physical education; religious education; Welsh. 1 from: mathematics; science; geography. 1 from: technology; English; art; history.

In the 3rd year, 2 of these 3 subjects will be studied, 1 as a major and the other as a minor.

Successful completion of this course leads to a recommendation for Qualified Teacher Status (QTS) after completion of skills tests.

Entry requirements:

Tariff: 160 to 200, BTEC NC/ND, Irish Leaving Certificates: CCCCC, International Baccalaureate, SCE Higher
Contact: As above

PGCE in Post-Compulsory Education and Training X341

1 year full-time or 2 years part-time

Entry requirements: Applicants should be graduates and (part-time option) be employed as teachers/trainers in the post-compulsory sector of education part-time (or for full-time option) or be intending to teach in post-16 full-time.
Contact: As above

PGCE in Primary Education (5–11/12) X100

1 year full-time

Entry requirements: Degree or approved equivalent; GCSE grade C or above (or equivalent) in English language and mathematics is also required. Applicants born after 1/9/79 must also have GCSE science at grade C or above.
Contact: As above

PGCE in Secondary Education (Design and Technology) W9X1

1 year full-time

Entry requirements: Degree or equivalent in a subject relevant to design and technology, and English language and mathematics at GCSE grade C or above or equivalent.

Contact: As above

PGCE in Secondary Education (Information and Communication Technology) G5X1

1 year full-time

Entry requirements: Degree or equivalent in a subject relevant to information and communications technology, and English language and mathematics at GCSE grade C or above or equivalent.

Contact: As above

PgCert/PgDip/MA in Art Education

1 year full-time, 2–5 years part-time

Entry requirements: Normally, good Honours degree or other suitable academic/professional qualifications (if over 25), as well as relevant experience.

Contact: As above

PgCert/PgDip/MA in Creative Arts in Education

1 year full-time, 2–5 years part-time
As above

PgCert/PgDip/MA in Curriculum Studies

1 year full-time, 2–5 years part-time
As above

PgCert/PgDip/MA in Early Years Education

1 year full-time, 2–5 years part-time
As above

PgCert/PgDip/MA in Education

1 year full-time, 2–5 years part-time
As above

PgCert/PgDip/MA in Education Management

1 year full-time, 2–5 years part-time
As above

PgCert/PgDip/MA in Education Practice

2–5 years part-time evening

Entry requirements: Must be qualified teacher working towards national standards

identified in framework of professional standards and qualifications; degree or, if over 25, relevant experience, required.

Contact: As above

PgCert/PgDip/MA in Environmental Education

1 year full-time, 2–5 years part-time

Entry requirements: Normally, good Honours degree or other suitable academic/professional qualifications (if over 25), as well as relevant experience.

Contact: As above

MA in Post-Compulsory Education and Training

2–5 years part-time evening

Entry requirements: Normally, good Honours degree or equivalent academic/professional qualifications, and (if over 25) relevant experience; credit may be claimed for 1 or more modules as a result of previous study, or achievement and learning in work and/or community.

Contact: As above

PgCert/PgDip/MA in Religious Education

1 year full-time, 2–5 years part-time

Entry requirements: Normally, good Honours degree or other suitable academic/professional qualifications (if over 25) as well as relevant experience.

Contact: As above

PgCert/PgDip/MA in Special Educational Needs

1 year full-time, 2–5 years part-time

Entry requirements: Normally, good Honours degree or equivalent academic/professional qualifications (if over 25), and relevant experience.

Contact: As above

PgCert/PgDip/MA in Special Educational Needs (Dyspraxia)

1 year full-time, 2–5 years part-time
As above

PgCert/PgDip/MA in Special Educational Needs (Emotional and Behaviour Difficulties)

1 year full-time, 2–5 years part-time

As above

PgCert/PgDip/MA in Special Educational Needs (Hearing Impairment)

1 year full-time, 2–5 years part-time

As above

PgCert/PgDip/MA in Special Educational Needs (Severe Learning Difficulties)

1 year full-time, 2–5 years part-time

As above

PgCert/PgDip/MA in Special Educational Needs (Special Educational Needs in Ordinary Schools)

1 year full-time, 2–5 years part-time

As above

PgCert/PgDip/MA in Special Educational Needs (Specific Learning Difficulties)

1 year full-time, 2–5 years part-time

As above

PgCert/PgDip/MA in Special Educational Needs (Speech and Language Difficulties)

1 year full-time, 2–5 years part-time

As above

PgCert/PgDip/MA in Special Educational Needs (Visual Impairment)

1 year full-time, 2–5 years part-time

As above

North Bedfordshire Consortium

Samuel Whitbread Community College
Shefford Road
Clifton
Bedford
Bedfordshire
SG17 5QS
Tel: 01462 817445
Fax: 01462 815577
marionkirton@northbedscitt.org.uk
www.northbedscitt.org.uk

The North Bedfordshire SCITT Consortium was established in 1996 and offers the PGCE (validated by De Montfort University, Leicester) leading to Qualified Teacher Status. Students can specialise in one of a selection of subjects.

Students train in two schools, the base school, in which the majority of time will be spent, and a complementary school. Training will cover the middle and upper phases of school. Lectures are held both in school and at De Montfort University in Bedford. Trainees will have access to a mentor in each of the base and complementary schools.

HOW TO APPLY

Applications are made through the GTTR.

COURSES

PGCE in Secondary Education (Art) W1X1

36 weeks full-time

Entry requirements: Relevant degree; GCSE English and mathematics grade C.

Contact: Marion Kirton
Administrator
01462 817445
marionkirton@northbedsscitt.org.uk

PGCE in Secondary Education (English) Q3X1

36 weeks full-time

As above

PGCE in Secondary Education (Geography) F8X1

36 weeks full-time

As above

PGCE in Secondary Education (History) V1X1

36 weeks full-time

As above

PGCE in Secondary Education (Physical Education) X9C6
36 weeks full-time
As above

PGCE in Secondary Education (Science) F0X1
36 weeks full-time
As above

North East Partnership

University of Northumbria
School of Health, Community and Education Studies
Coach Lane Campus
Coach Lane
Newcastle upon Tyne
NE7 7XA
Tel: 0191 215 6462
Fax: 0191 215 6404
hs.admissions@unn.ac.uk

The North East Partnership is a consortium of secondary schools in the north east of England, which provides school-centred initial teacher training with Northumbria University acting as managing agent. Professional practice is undertaken and assessed in two different schools in the consortium.

HOW TO APPLY

Applications are made through the GTTR.

COURSES

PGCE in Secondary Education (Physical Education) X9C6
1 year full-time

Entry requirements: Degree in a subject which will allow the student to teach physical education at secondary level; mature candidates with career profiles to graduate equivalent are also considered for entry; GCSE grade C or above or equivalent in English language and mathematics.
Contact: Sue Lyle
        Programme Leader
        0191 215 6462
        sue.lyle@unn.ac.uk

North East Wales Institute of Higher Education

Plas Coch
Mold Road
Wrexham
LL11 2AW
Tel: 01978 290666
Fax: 01978 290008
www.newi.ac.uk

The origins of the North East Wales Institute of Higher Education can be traced back to 1887 when the school of Science and Art, later renamed the Denbighshire Technical College, was established in Wrexham. As demand grew for post-compulsory education, the three main colleges of the County of Clwyd, Denbighshire Technical College, Cartrefle Teacher Training College and Kelsterton College, were merged. The merger created the North East

Wales Institute of Higher Education, one of the largest colleges of its kind in Britain. In 1993 it became an associated college of the University of Wales.

The Department of Education offers a range of courses including primary education with qualified teaching status, early childhood studies and education studies at degree level and the PGCE for post-compulsory education. It also operates two research centres: the Centre for Applied Educational Research and the Professional Development Centre.

The university is based on two campuses, Regent Street where art and design courses are based and Plas Coch. The campuses are within five minutes' walk of each other and close to the centre of Wrexham. All students have access to the library and computer resources on campus and the recreational facilities on site and in the local area. There is university owned accommodation on or off campus and there is private accommodation available.

HOW TO APPLY

Degree courses: applications are made through UCAS.

PGCE: applications are made direct to the institution.

Postgraduate courses: applications are made direct to the institution.

COURSES

BA (Hons) in Education (Primary) X103

3 years full-time

Years 1–2: 3 core subjects of English, mathematics and science, as well as a 4th subject chosen from art, geography, history, physical education or Welsh.

Year 3: Specialism in 1 of these subjects or to study the Early Years modules to specialise in teaching pupils aged 3–5 years.

School experience: Students also undertake school experience with a chance of working in several primary schools with the full primary range, from 3–12 years.

Education and Professional Studies: This section of the course considers classroom management issues and the theory underlying the practice in primary schools. Areas covered include: the school as a social and learning organisation; the context of education; assessment and evaluation; the foundation subjects of the National Curriculum. The course becomes age-specific in the professional aspects studied in the 3rd year, when students opt to teach either 3–8 year old or 7–12 year old children.

Successful completion of this course leads to a recommendation for Qualified Teacher Status (QTS) after completion of skills tests.

Entry requirements: BTEC NC/ND, DD: GCE A- and AS-levels, International Baccalaureate, SCE Higher
Contact: Jan Bagguley
01978 293084
j.bagguley@newi.ac.uk

PGCE in Education and Training (Post-Compulsory)

2 years part-time

Entry requirements: For uncertified teachers in FE, Adult, Community Education, Nurse Education, or other training establishments.
Contact: As above

Certificate in Training of Teachers of Pupils with Specific Learning Difficulties

Part-time

Entry requirements: Teaching qualification required.
Contact: As above

Diploma in Education of Children with Special Educational Needs

1 year full-time or 2 years part-time

Entry requirements: Applicants should be qualified teachers.
Contact: Ms M Bowen
01978 293361
m.bowen@newi.ac.uk

Diploma in Education of Children with Special Educational Needs (Severe Learning Difficulties)

1 year full-time or 2 years part-time

Entry requirements: Applicants should be qualified teachers with at least 2 years' teaching experience.
Contact: As above

PgCert in Special Educational Needs in Ordinary Schools

1 year part-time

Entry requirements: Applicants should be qualified teachers with at least 2 years' teaching experience.
Contact: As above

MA in Education

5 years part-time evening

Entry requirements: Degree or professional experience.
Contact: Jan Bagguley
01978 293084
j.bagguley@newi.ac.uk

Northampton Teacher Training Partnership

Northampton School for Boys
Billing Road
Northampton
NN1 5RT
Tel: 01604 258662
Fax: 01604 258659
nttp@nsb.northants.sch.uk
www.nsb.northants.sch.uk/nttp

The Northampton Teacher Training Partnership consists of nine schools, the main one being Northampton School for Boys. The others consist of a girls' school and seven mixed schools and all the participants are middle or secondary schools.

The partnership offers training in the subjects of Maths, Design and Technology, English and Science. The course consists of Professional Studies led by Leicester University, subject-related studies led by mentors, Northampton Inspection and Advisory Service and bought-in providers, and practical teaching experience.

HOW TO APPLY

Applications are made direct to the institution.

COURSES

PGCE in Secondary Education (Design and Technology)
1 year full-time

Entry requirements: Relevant degree; GCSE grade C or above in English language and mathematics.
Contact: Administrator
        01604 258662
        nttp@nsb.northants.sch.uk

PGCE in Secondary Education (English)
1 year full-time
As above

PGCE in Secondary Education (Mathematics)
1 year full-time
As above

PGCE in Secondary Education (Science)
1 year full-time
As above

University College Northampton

Park Campus
Boughton Green Road
Northampton
NN2 7AL
Tel: 01604 735500
Fax: 01604 720636
admissions@northampton.ac.uk
www.northampton.ac.uk

University College Northampton is based at two campuses, Park Campus and Avenue Campus two miles apart from each other. Park Campus is the main site set in 80 acres on the northern edge of Northampton. Recent developments have included purpose-built accommodation, new recreational facilities and newly extended Library and Information Technology Centre. Avenue Campus also has on-site facilities and a bus service runs between the two campuses. Around 9,000 students are currently at the university. Aside from the residences provided by the university, there is accommodation available in the private sector.

The School of Education offers a broad range of taught undergraduate and postgraduate courses and opportunities to study for research degrees. Courses for Initial Teacher Education include the PGCE at primary level. There are also programmes for Continuing Professional Development.

HOW TO APPLY

Degree courses: applications are made through UCAS.
PGCE: applications are made through GTTR.

Postgraduate: applications are made direct to the institution.

COURSES

BA (Hons) in Early Years Education X101

3 years full-time

All years: Foundations of literacy and numeracy; science; information and communications technology; religious education; two foundation subjects from: art; geography; history; physical education.

Successful completion of this course leads to a recommendation for Qualified Teacher Status (QTS) after completion of skills tests.

Entry requirements: GCE A- and AS-levels, Interview

Contact: School of Education
01604 735500 x2018

BA (Hons) in Primary Education (5–11 years) X120

3 years full-time

All years: Specialisation in 1 or more subjects of the National Curriculum with particular attention to training in the teaching of English, mathematics and science; school-based work with experienced teachers, including early experience of whole class and group responsibility; study in all areas of the National Curriculum and religious education, at specialist or other levels; development of generic teaching skills, including those required for planning and managing the curriculum, managing classes and the behaviour of individuals, matching teaching to the differential learning needs of children and the assessment of children's learning; research and reflection on educational issues and practices as the basis for curriculum development, personal professional status, and to underpin continuing professional development.

Successful completion of this course leads to a recommendation for Qualified Teacher Status (QTS) after completion of skills tests.

Entry requirements: GCE A- and AS-levels

Contact: Academic Registrar
01604 735500

PGCE in Primary Education (3–8) X121

1 year full-time

Entry requirements: A degree or a recognised equivalent and GCSE grade C or equivalent in both English language and mathematics.

Contact: Faculty Registry
01604 735500 x2099

PGCE in Primary Education (7–11) X171

1 year full-time

As above

Northumbria DT Partnership (SCITT)

University of Northumbria
School of Health, Community and
   Education Studies
Coach Lane Campus
Coach Lane
Newcastle upon Tyne
NE7 7XA
Tel: 0191 215 6469

Northumbria DT Partnership provides a school-centred secondary PGCE course validated by the University of Northumbria. The partnership specialises in training teachers in specialised areas within the subject of Design and Technology: Food and Textiles, Textiles and Graphics or Food and Health and Social Care. The partnership is made up of a consortium of fifteen schools. Students are based in two of the schools during the course with some additional experience in primary schools.

Students have access to all university facilities including libraries and electronic resources. Tutors and mentors are provided in the schools where most of the lectures take place.

HOW TO APPLY

Applications are made through the GTTR.

PGCE in Secondary Education (Design and Technology) W9X1

36 weeks full-time

Entry requirements: Relevant degree; GCSE English and mathematics at grade C; candidates also require portfolio (essential for textiles and graphics applicants) or dissertation/project (all applicants, but essential for food, and health and social care streams.

Contact: Margaret Chapman
Programme Leader
0191 215 6418
margaret.chapman@unn.ac.uk

Northumbria University, Newcastle Campuses

Ellison Building
Ellison Place
Newcastle upon Tyne
Tyne and Wear
NE1 8ST
Tel: 0191 232 6002
Fax: 0191 227 4017
rg.admissions@northumbria.ac.uk
www.northumbria.ac.uk

Northumbria University is based at four campuses. The largest, City Campus and Coach Lane Campus, are in the city of Newcastle upon Tyne. Longhirst Campus is located ten miles north of Newcastle in Northumberland, and the Carlisle Campus is situated in the heart of the city of Carlisle in Cumbria. Northumbria University was first established as a polytechnic in 1969 and awarded university status in September 1992. The student population is now almost 22,000.

Courses are run from the School of Health, Community and Education Studies which is based at the Coach Lane Campus. The school offers undergraduate courses and range of postgraduate programmes including the primary PGCE, the option of School Centred Initial Teacher Training PGCE at primary and secondary level and also options for further study for professionals.

Students have access to all the campus facilities and the Newcastle campuses are close to the main shopping and entertainment centres. Each campus is equipped with a library, computer resources and has some accommodation. There is also privately rented accommodation in the local areas.

HOW TO APPLY

Degree courses: applications are made through UCAS.

PGCE: applications are made through the GTTR.

Postgraduate: applications are made direct to the institution.

COURSES

BA (Hons) in Primary Education X120

3 years full-time

Advanced study of early years; the early years curriculum; thinking, learning and creativity; core subjects; information and communications technology in education; school placements.

Successful completion of this course leads to a recommendation for Qualified Teacher Status (QTS) after completion of the 1st year of teaching.

Entry requirements: International Baccalaureate: 24, Tariff: 280 points, European Baccalaureate: 60%, Irish Leaving Certificates: BCCC, BTEC NC/ND, Foundation / access qualification, Work experience

Contact: Admissions Team
0191 215 6333
hs.admissions@northumbria.ac.uk

PGCE in Further Education and Training

1 to 2 years part-time

Entry requirements: Applicants should have access to group of learners, hold a degree from a UK university and be capable of fulfilling the academic study.

Contact: As above

PGCE in Primary Education (Early Years, 3–8) X121

1 year full-time

Entry requirements: Degree from a UK University or recognised equivalent qualification; plus GCSE grade C or above (or equivalent) in mathematics and English language and a science subject; applicants must have had some experience of British schools and/or primary aged children before they attend for interview.

Contact: As above

PGCE in Primary Education (Later Years, 7–11) X171

1 year full-time

As above

PGCE in Secondary Education (Visual Arts) W1X1

1 year full-time

Entry requirements: Degree or equivalent qualification containing a significant art element of appropriate level and scope; competence in information and communications technology also expected.

Contact: As above

Nottingham Trent University

Burton Street
Nottingham
NG1 4BU
Tel: 0115 941 8418
marketing@ntu.ac.uk
www.ntu.ac.uk

Nottingham Trent University is the fourth largest in the United Kingdom with a student population of over 23,000. The university has three sites: City campus is based in the heart of Nottingham, Clifton campus is about four miles from the City centre and Brackenhurst campus is based about 12 miles from Nottingham. The university has recently invested in developing its facilities and now offers extensive computing facilities in IT resource rooms and PC clusters across all sites, library resources and virtual e-library. Students also have access to a range of sporting and social activities. Accommodation is available in halls or university managed residences and the university also has an accreditation scheme for local private sector accommodation.

The Faculty of Education is organised into two academic departments: the Department of Primary Education and the Department of Secondary and Tertiary Education. The faculty offers Initial

Teacher training courses, degree and postgraduate programmes and research opportunities. Continuing Professional Development programmes are also available for established teachers.

HOW TO APPLY

Degree courses: applications are made through UCAS.

PGCE: applications are made through the GTTR.

Postgraduate: applications are made direct to the institution.

COURSES

Primary Education X101

BA: 4 years full-time, BA (Hons): 4 years full-time

Years 1–2: Students learn to teach all subjects of the national curriculum effectively with a broad curriculum focus.

Years 3–4: Gradual shift towards the development of curriculum areas of particular strength. These areas may be selected from the core curriculum (English, mathematics, science) or from the areas of design and technology, geography, history, physical education and art. Primary strand students select either lower primary 5–8 or upper primary 7–11 as an age phase emphasis. This decision is made at the start of year 3.

Successful completion of this course leads to a recommendation for Qualified Teacher Status (QTS) after completion of skills tests.

Entry requirements: GCE A- and AS-levels: BBC-BCC, AVCE, BTEC NC/ND, Irish Leaving Certificates, Mature entry, SCE Higher,
Contact: Admissions Office
0115 848 6711
edu.admin@ntu.ac.uk

Primary Education (Early Years) X100

BA: 4 years full-time, BA (Hons): 4 years full-time

Early Years (3–8 years): Students study some modules specific to the early years range and some modules that give the 3–11 age range perspective. This is to enable students to work effectively within the broader primary phase of education. As students move through the course the focus on early years is emphasised.

Successful completion of this course leads to a recommendation for Qualified Teacher Status (QTS) after completion of skills tests.

Entry requirements: AVCEs: BB, GCE A- and AS-levels: BCC to BBC, BTEC NC/ND, Irish Leaving Certificates, Mature entry, SCE Higher
Contact: As above

PGCE in Further Education and Training
1 year full-time or 2 years part-time

Entry requirements: Applicants should have appropriate qualifications or experience in the field of their teaching.
Contact: Gill Goodchild
Course Leader
0115 848 3718
gillian.goodchild@ntu.ac.uk

PGCE in Primary Education X100
1 year full-time

Entry requirements: Degree and GCSE/O-level or equivalent in English, mathematics and science; in addition, candidates are encouraged to demonstrate an interest in and awareness of current primary practice.

Contact: Kathryn Whitt
0115 848 6719
edu.admin@ntu.ac.uk

PGCE in Secondary Education (Business Education) N1X1
1 year full-time

Entry requirements: Suitable degree (or degree equivalent) and GCSE minimum grade C (or equivalent) in mathematics and English language.
Contact: As above

PGCE in Secondary Education (Design and Technology) W9X1
1 year full-time
As above

PGCE in Secondary Education (English) Q3X1
1 year full-time
As above

PGCE in Secondary Education (Information Communications Technology) G5X1
1 year full-time
As above

PGCE in Secondary Education (Mathematics) G1X1
1 year full-time
As above

PGCE in Secondary Education (Science: Biology) C1X1
1 year full-time
As above

PGCE in Secondary Education (Science: Chemistry) F1X1
1 year full-time
As above

PGCE in Secondary Education (Science: Physics) F3X1
1 year full-time
As above

Pgcert/Pgdip/MA in Education

Entry requirements: Normally an Honours degree, but graduate-equivalent knowledge, abilities and skills can also serve as an entry point, professionally relevant experience is also required

Contact: Sue Brewill
Course Administrator
0115 848 6789
sue.brewill@ntu.ac.uk

University of Nottingham

University Park
Nottingham
NG7 2RD
Tel: 0115 951 5151
Fax: 0115 951 3666
undergraduate-enquiries@nottingham.ac.uk
www.nottingham.ac.uk

The University of Nottingham is a multi-campus university, with three UK campuses. A fourth campus opened in Malaysia in 2000. The UK campuses are Jubilee Park, Sutton Bonington and University Park. Over 23,000 students currently attend the university.

The School of Education is located on Jubilee Park and students benefit from state-of-the-art technology and modern facilities, including on-site accommodation, restaurants, library and computing centre. Further facilities including the main library are available at University Park only one mile away. The Faculty of Education is one of the largest in the country and is a recognised centre for research in education with staff of international repute. The school provides opportunities at degree level for practising teachers and continuing professional development for teachers, educators and other professionals. Initial Teacher Training is offered as a full time or part time course at secondary level and as School Centred Initial Teacher Training at primary level.

The university offers well-equipped, modern accommodation for postgraduate students conveniently close to the campuses so that all necessary facilities are nearby.

HOW TO APPLY

PGCE: applications are made through the GTTR.

Postgraduate: applications are made direct to the institution.

COURSES

PGCE in Secondary Education (English) Q3X1

1 year full-time or up to 3 years part-time

Entry requirements: UK degree or its equivalent, plus GCSE grade A, B or C in English language and mathematics or their equivalent; in addition to the qualifications listed above, a candidate's suitability for teaching will be assessed by interview, by considering reports from referees and by evaluating previous related experience.

Contact: Secretary, Faculty of Education
0115 951 4472
june.lemon@nottingham.ac.uk

PGCE in Secondary Education (French with German) RX11

1 year full-time or up to 3 years part-time

Entry requirements: UK degree (or its equivalent) in the relevant languages, plus GCSE grade A, B or C in English language and mathematics or their equivalents; in addition to the qualifications listed above, a candidate's suitability for teaching will be assessed by interview, by considering reports from referees and by evaluating previous related experience.

Contact: As above

PGCE in Secondary Education (French with Japanese) RX1D

1 year full-time or up to 3 years part-time

Entry requirements: Relevant UK degree or its equivalent, plus GCSE grade A, B or C in English language and mathematics or their equivalents. In addition to the qualifications listed above, a candidate's suitability for teaching will be assessed by interview, by considering reports from referees and by evaluating previous related experience.
Contact: As above

PGCE in Secondary Education (French with Russian) RXC1

1 year full-time or up to 3 years part-time

Entry requirements: As above
Contact: As above

PGCE in Secondary Education (French with Spanish) RXD1

1 year full-time or up to 3 years part-time

Entry requirements: As above
Contact: As above

PGCE in Secondary Education (French) R1X1

1 year full-time or up to 3 years part-time

Entry requirements: As above
Contact: As above

PGCE in Secondary Education (Geography through medium of French or German) FX81

1 year full-time

Entry requirements: Relevant UK degree or its equivalent, plus GCSE grade A, B or C in English language and mathematics or their equivalent; in addition, a candidate's suitability for teaching will be assessed by interview, by considering reports from referees and by evaluating previous related experience; candidates should have at least A-level (or equivalent) capability in the relevant foreign language.
Contact: As above

PGCE in Secondary Education (Geography) F8X1

1 year full-time

Entry requirements: Relevant UK degree or its equivalent, plus GCSE grade A, B or C in English language and mathematics or their equivalent; in addition to the qualifications listed above, a candidate's suitability for teaching will be assessed by interview, by considering reports from referees and by evaluating previous related experience.
Contact: As above

PGCE in Secondary Education (German with French) RX21

1 year full-time or up to 3 years part-time

Entry requirements: As above
Contact: As above

PGCE in Secondary Education (German with Russian) RXFD

1 year full-time or up to 3 years part-time

Entry requirements: As above
Contact: As above

PGCE in Secondary Education (History through medium of French or German) VX11

1 year full-time

Entry requirements: Relevant UK degree or its equivalent, plus GCSE grade A, B or C in English language and mathematics or their equivalent; in addition, a candidate's suitability for teaching will be assessed by interview, by considering reports from referees and by evaluating previous related experience; candidates should have at least A-level (or equivalent) capability in the relevant foreign language.
Contact: As above

PGCE in Secondary Education (History) V1X1

1 year full-time

Entry requirements: Relevant UK degree or its equivalent, plus GCSE grade A, B or C in English language and mathematics or their equivalent' in addition to the qualifications listed above, a candidate's suitability for teaching will be assessed by interview, by considering reports from referees and by evaluating previous related experience.

Contact: As above

PGCE in Secondary Education (Japanese) T4X1

1 year full-time or up to 3 years part-time
As above

Secondary Education (Mathematics) G1X1

1 year full-time
As above

PGCE in Secondary Education (Russian with French) RX71

1 year full-time or up to 3 years part-time
As above

PGCE in Secondary Education (Russian with German) RX7C

1 year full-time or up to 3 years part-time
As above

PGCE in Secondary Education (Science: Biology) C1X1

1 year full-time or up to 3 years part-time
As above

PGCE in Secondary Education (Science: Biology, through medium of French or German) CX11

1 year full-time

Entry requirements: UK relevant science degree or its equivalent, plus GCSE grade A, B or C in English language and mathematics or their equivalent; in addition, a candidate's suitability for teaching will be assessed by interview, by considering reports from referees and by evaluating previous related experience; candidates should have at least A-level (or equivalent) capability in the relevant foreign language.

Contact: As above

PGCE in Secondary Education (Science: Chemistry) F1X1

1 year full-time or up to 3 years part-time

Entry requirements: Relevant UK degree or its equivalent, plus GCSE grade A, B or C in English language and mathematics or their equivalent; in addition to the qualifications listed above, a candidate's suitability for teaching will be assessed by interview, by considering reports from referees and by evaluating previous related experience.

Contact: As above

PGCE in Secondary Education (Science: Chemistry, through medium of French or German) FX11

1 year full-time

Entry requirements: UK relevant science degree or its equivalent, plus GCSE grade A, B or C in English language and mathematics or their equivalent; in addition, a candidate's suitability for teaching will be assessed by interview, by considering reports from referees and by evaluating previous related experience; candidates should have at least A-level (or equivalent) capability in the relevant foreign language.

Contact: As above

PGCE in Secondary Education (Science: Physics) F3X1

1 year full-time or up to 3 years part-time

Entry requirements: Relevant UK degree or its equivalent, plus GCSE grade A, B or C in English language and mathematics or their equivalent; in addition to the qualifications listed above, a candidate's suitability for teaching will be assessed by interview, by considering reports from referees and by evaluating previous related experience.

Contact: As above

PGCE in Secondary Education (Science: Physics, through medium of French or German) FX31

1 year full-time

Entry requirements: Relevant UK science degree, or its equivalent, plus GCSE grade A, B or C in English language and mathematics or their equivalent; in addition, a

candidate's suitability for teaching will be assessed by interview, by considering reports from referees and by evaluating previous related experience; candidates should have at least A-level (or equivalent) capability in the relevant foreign language.
Contact: As above

PGCE in Secondary Education (Spanish with French) RX41

1 year full-time or up to 3 years part-time

Entry requirements: Relevant UK degree or its equivalent, plus GCSE grade A, B or C in English language and mathematics or their equivalent; in addition to the qualifications listed above, a candidate's suitability for teaching will be assessed by interview, by considering reports from referees and by evaluating previous related experience.
Contact: As above

Diploma/MA in Behavioural and Emotional Development

2 years part-time

Entry requirements: Degree and 2 years' relevant professional experience.

PgCert in Continuing Education (Post-Compulsory Education)

1 year full-time, 2 years part-time

Entry requirements: Normally, degree or equivalent.
Contact: Stephen Drodge
Course Director
0115 951 3042
stephen.drodge@nottingham.ac.uk

Diploma/MA in Continuing Professional Development and School Improvement

MA: 1 year full-time, 2 years part-time; Diploma: 2 years part-time

Entry requirements: Degree and teaching qualification.
Contact: Dr Mark Hadfield
0115 951 4417
mark.hadfield@nottingham.ac.uk

Diploma/MA in Educational Leadership

2–4 years part-time

Entry requirements: Degree or equivalent plus at least 2 years' experience in relevant field.
Contact: Linda Ellison
Enquiries Secretary
0115 951 4543/4444
linda.ellison@nottingham.ac.uk

EdD in Educational Leadership

4 years part-time

Entry requirements: Master's degree and relevant professional experience.
Contact: Professor Christopher Day
School of Education
0115 951 4473
christopher.day@nottingham.ac.uk

Diploma/MA in Educational Management

2–4 years part-time

Entry requirements: Degree or equivalent plus at least 2 years' experience in relevant field.
Contact: Linda Ellison
Enquiries Secretary
0115 951 4543/4444
linda.ellison@nottingham.ac.uk

Diploma/MA in English Language Teacher Development

1 year full-time

Entry requirements: Degree at a good standard, 2 years of relevant teaching experience, and (if non-native speaker of English) IELTS score of 6.5.
Contact: Jean Brewster
Enquiries Secretary
0115 951 4543/4451
jean.brewster@nottingham.ac.uk

Diploma/MA in English Language Teaching

1 year full-time, 2 years part-time

Entry requirements: Degree at a good standard, 2 years of relevant teaching experience, and (if non-native speaker of English) IELTS score of 6.5.

Contact: Dr Barbara Sinclair
0115 951 4513
barbara.sinclair@nottingham.ac.uk

Diploma/MA in Learning and Teaching

2 years part-time

Entry requirements: Degree and relevant teaching experience.
Contact: Dr Eric Parkins
School of Education
0115 951 4425
eric.parkins@nottingham.ac.uk

EdD in Lifelong Education

2 years full-time, 4 years part-time

Entry requirements: Master's degree from approved university and minimum of 2 years' appropriate professional experience.
Contact: Prof W J Morgan
Course Director
0115 951 3717
John.Morgan@nottingham.ac.uk

Diploma/MA in Lifelong Education

1 year full-time, 2–4 years part-time

Entry requirements: Graduate qualification or equivalent experience; in addition, for non-native speakers, English language requirement of 6.0 IELTS score or 550 TOEFL score.
Contact: Dr Mark Dale
Course Director
0115 951 3708
Mark.Dale@nottingham.ac.uk

EdD in Literacy

2 years full-time, 4 years part-time

Entry requirements: Must be teacher with Master's degree and current involvement in the education, training and development of teachers.
Contact: Enquiries Secretary
0115 951 4543
education-enquiries@nottingham.ac.uk

EdD in School Improvement and Continuing Professional Development

2 years full-time, 4 years part-time

Entry requirements: Applicants usually senior professionals with at least 5 years' experience and Master's degree; applicants whose native language is not English must have average 7.0 on IELTS.
Contact: As above

Diploma/MA in Special Needs

1 year full-time, 2 years part-time

Entry requirements: Normally, degree plus training and experience in teaching or training.
Contact: Dr Eric Parkins
0115 951 4543/4425
eric.parkins@nottingham.ac.uk

EdD in Teacher Education

2 years full-time, 4 years part-time

Entry requirements: Must be teacher with Master's degree and current involvement in the education, training and development of teachers.
Contact: Dr Do Coyle
Enquiries Secretary
0115 951 4543/4429
do.coyle@nottingham.ac.uk

MA in Teaching

2–4 years part-time

Entry requirements: Qualified Teacher Status.
Contact: Dr Peter Gates
0115 951 4432
peter.gates@nottingham.ac.uk

Diploma/MA in Teaching Content through a Foreign Language

2–4 years part-time

Entry requirements: Degree or equivalent, plus relevant experience in the field of teaching content subjects through a foreign language.
Contact: Dr Philip Hood
0115 951 4426
philip.hood@nottingham.ac.uk

Open University

Walton Hall
Milton Keynes
MK7 6AA
Tel: 01908 274066
Fax: 01908 653744
www.open.ac.uk/courses

The Open University admitted its first students in 1971 and is Britain's largest university with over 200,000 people studying its courses. Students can study from home or work with the help of locally based tutors and regional study centres.

The Faculty of Education and Language Studies offers training for teacher assistants, a range of undergraduate courses, an initial teacher training programme and postgraduate courses for professional development.

HOW TO APPLY

All applications should be made direct to the institution.

COURSES

PGCE in Secondary Education (Design and Technology) (EXT880)

36 months mixed mode

Entry requirements: Degree of which at least half and preferably two-thirds (at least 180 credit points) should comprise studies relevant to the subject you intend to teach; GCSE grade A–C, or equivalent, in English language and mathematics.

Contact: Course Information and Advice Centre
01908 653231
general-enquiries@open.ac.uk

PGCE in Secondary Education (Geography) (EXG880)

36 months mixed mode
As above

PGCE in Secondary Education (Mathematics) (EXM880)

36 months mixed mode
As above

PGCE in Secondary Education (Modern Foreign Languages: French) (EXF880)

36 months mixed mode
As above

PGCE in Secondary Education (Modern Foreign Languages: German) (EXD880)

36 months mixed mode
As above

PGCE in Secondary Education (Modern Foreign Languages: Spanish) (EXB880)

36 months mixed mode
As above

PGCE in Secondary Education (Music) (EXN880)

36 months mixed mode
As above

PGCE in Secondary Education (Science) (EXS880)

36 months mixed mode
As above

Credits from The Open University in Developing Inclusive Curricula: Equality and Diversity in Education (E829)

9 months distance learning

Entry requirements: Normally first degree (or equivalent); or at least 2 courses that lead to the Open University's Advanced Diploma in Education (or an equivalent qualification); or the Open University's Certificate in Continuing Professional Development; or QTS and at least 3 years' teaching experience. Applicants are expected to have some experience in education or an allied field.

Contact: As above

Credits from the Open University in Developing Practice in Primary Education (E842)

9 months distance learning

Entry requirements: Normally first degree (or equivalent); or an Open University Advanced Diploma in Education (or an equivalent qualification); or at least 2 courses that lead to the Open University's Certificate in Continuing Professional

Development; or QTS and at least 3 years' teaching experience.

Contact: As above

Credits from the Open University in Difficulties in Literacy Development (E801)

12 months distance learning

Entry requirements: First degree (or the equivalent), OU Advanced Diploma in education (or equivalent professional qualification), OU Certificate of Continuing Professional Development or QTS with at least 3 years' teaching experience. Candidates must be experienced teachers or other professionals working in an educational setting. Current employment at an educational institution or access to an institution is also required.

Contact: As above

Credits from the Open University in Early Professional Development for Teachers (E853)

12 months distance learning

Entry requirements: Applicants should be recently qualified teachers seeking professional development and career enhancement.

Contact: As above

Credits from the Open University in Educational Management in Action (E828)

9 months distance learning

Entry requirements: Normally, first degree (or the equivalent); or an Open University Advanced Diploma in Education (or an equivalent qualification); or at least 2 courses that lead to the Open University's Certificate in Continuing Professional Development; or QTS and at least 3 years' teaching experience. Students are expected to have some experience in education or an allied field.

Contact: As above

Credits from the Open University in Educational Research in Action (E835)

9 months distance learning

Entry requirements: First degree (or the equivalent), OU Advanced Diploma in education (or equivalent professional qualification), OU Certificate of Continuing Professional Development or QTS with at least 3 years' teaching experience. Candidates must be experienced teachers or other professionals working in an educational setting. Current employment at an educational institution or access to an institution is also required.

Contact: As above

Credits from the Open University in Guidance and Counselling in Learning (E839)

9 months distance learning

Entry requirements: Normally first degree (or the equivalent); or an Open University Advanced Diploma in Education (or an equivalent qualification); or at least 2 courses that lead to the Open University's Certificate in Continuing Professional Development; or QTS and at least 3 years' teaching experience. Applicants are expected to have some experience in education or an allied field, but need not be practising teachers.

Contact: As above

Credits from the Open University in Leading and Managing for Effective Education (E849)

9 months distance learning

Entry requirements: Normally, first degree (or the equivalent); or an Open University Advanced Diploma in Education (or an equivalent qualification); or at least 2 courses that lead to the Open University's Certificate in Continuing Professional Development; or QTS and at least 3 years' teaching experience.

Contact: As above

Credits from the Open University in Leading Professional Development in Education (E843)

9 months distance learning

Entry requirements: Normally first degree (or the equivalent); or an Open University Advanced Diploma in Education (or an equivalent qualification); or at least 2 courses that lead to the Open University's Certificate in Continuing Professional Development; or QTS and at least 3 years' teaching experience. Applicants are expected to have some experience in education or an allied field, but need not be practising teachers.
Contact: As above

Credits from the Open University in Learning, Curriculum and Assessment (E836)
9 months distance learning
As above

Credits from the Open University in Learning, Curriculum and Assessment (EZX836)
9 months on-line study
As above

Credits from the Open University in Supporting Lifelong Learning (E845)
9 months distance learning
As above

Credits from the Open University/PgCert in Professional Development for Special Educational Needs Co-ordinators (E831/C30)
12 months distance learning
Entry requirements: Normally first degree (or the equivalent); or an Open University Advanced Diploma in Education (or an equivalent qualification); or at least 2 courses that lead to the Open University's Certificate in Continuing Professional Development; or qualified teacher status and at least 3 years' teaching experience. Applicants must also be experienced teachers working in school.
Contact: As above

Credits from the Open University/ Certificate in Professional Development with Information and Communication Technology (E851/C19)
5 months distance learning

Entry requirements: Applicants must have a teaching qualification and access to a school and must have successfully completed E850 Teaching and Learning with Information and Communication Technology.
Contact: As above

PgCert: Professional Studies in Education (C27)
Distance learning
Entry requirements: Applicants should normally hold degree (in any area) or equivalent; or OU Advanced Diploma in Education or Certificate in Continuing Professional Development; or QTS and at least 3 years' teaching experience. Applicants without these qualifications, but with substantial relevant professional experience, may also be admitted. Students will usually need to be able to work with learners, but not necessarily in a formal teaching situation.
Contact: As above

PgDip in Professional Studies in Education (D52)
Distance learning
As above

Advanced Diploma in Special Needs in Education (D06)
Distance learning
Entry requirements: First degree (or the equivalent), OU Advanced Diploma in education (or equivalent professional qualification), OU Certificate of Continuing Professional Development or QTS with at least 3 years' teaching experience. Candidates must be experienced teachers working in a school.
Contact: As above

Supporting Lifelong Learning (E845) MA/MEd in Education (F01)
Distance learning
Entry requirements: Applicants must have either degree (in any subject area) or equivalent; or successful completion of OU Advanced Diploma in Education; or a minimum of 2 courses which lead to OU Certificate in Continuing Professional

Development; or QTS and at least 3 years' teaching experience. Applicants without these qualifications, but with substantial relevant professional experience, may also be admitted.

Students will usually need to be able to work with learners, but not necessarily in a formal teaching situation.

Contact: As above

EdD in Education (F08)

Distance Learning

Entry requirements: OU Master's degree in education or alternative qualification (not necessarily in education) that meets the following criteria: study must have been formally taught and assessed at a level equivalent to that of a Master's degree (postgraduate diplomas are not eligible); the minimum period of study must have been the equivalent of at least a full-time academic year.

Contact: As above

Oxford Brookes University

Gipsy Lane
Headington
Oxford
OX3 0BP
Tel: 01865 484848
Fax: 01865 483616
query@brookes.ac.uk
www.brookes.ac.uk

The history of Oxford Brookes University dates back to 1865 when the Oxford School of Art was founded. It gradually developed and expanded to become Oxford Polytechnic in 1970 and finally became a University in 1992.

The Westminster Institute of Education was founded in April 2000 through the merger of Westminster College and the School of Education at Oxford Brookes University. Initial teacher training courses include the PGCE at primary, secondary and post-compulsory levels and also degree courses at primary level. There is also a range of postgraduate taught and research degrees.

Students have access to extensive library and computer services as well as the sporting and social facilities on campus. Accommodation is available in halls for undergraduate and postgraduate students or there is privately rented accommodation in the nearby area.

HOW TO APPLY

Degree courses: applications are made through UCAS.

PGCE: applications are made through the GTTR.

Postgraduate: applications are made direct to the institution.

COURSES

BA (Hons) in Primary Education (work-based) X110

3 years full-time

Successful completion of this course leads to a recommendation for Qualified Teacher Status (QTS) after completion of skills tests.

Entry requirements: Candidates should be over 24 years of age upon qualification and be working part-time in a mainstream primary school, or have access to mainstream pupils for part of the week. Minimum of 2 years' experience working with children and hold GCSE or equivalent in mathematics and English language at grade C or above, with evidence of study at A-level standard. Candidates also require NNEB, LSA or STA.

Contact: Trudy McAuley
01865 488297.

BA (Hons) in Primary Initial Teacher Training X101

3 years full-time or 6 years part-time day

Year 1: Primary schooling; the range of primary curriculum subjects; primary age range of 5 to 11; school experience.

Years 2 and 3: English specialism; focus on ages 5 to 8 or 7 to 11; learning, teaching and the curriculum; school experience, block and serial placements.

Successful completion of this course leads to a recommendation for Qualified Teacher Status (QTS) after completion of skills tests.

Entry requirements: International Baccalaureate: 25, Irish Leaving Certificates: CCCCC, GCE A- and AS-levels: DDD to CC

Contact: Dr R Bainbridge
01865 485885
rmbainbridge@brookes.ac.uk

PGCE in Post-Compulsory Education X341

1 year full-time or 2 years part-time

Entry requirements: Degree and English and mathematics at GCSE grade A*–C or equivalent. Students without English and mathematics requirement will be expected to achieve NVQ key skills in communication and application of numbers before graduation.

Contact: Elizabeth Browne
Course Secretary
01865 488292
pgcecpd_ioed@brookes.ac.uk

PGCE in Primary Education X100

38 weeks full-time

Entry requirements: Applicants must hold an appropriate degree of the United Kingdom, or an equivalent qualification recognised by the Department for Education and Skills, and GCSE at grade C or above (or equivalent qualification) in English language and mathematics, plus science. Additionally, applicants will be asked for evidence of work with groups of children, including minimum 2 weeks' observation in a state primary school. Applicants will also have to meet medical criteria.

Contact: Rosemary Caunt
Programme Administrator
01865 488390
pgceprim_ioed@brookes.ac.uk

PGCE in Primary Education (Early Years) X121

38 weeks full-time

As above

PGCE in Secondary Education (Art and Design) W1X1

1 year full-time

Entry requirements: Applicants should be graduates and should have completed an appropriately substantial amount of study in the subjects(s) in which they intend to specialise. In addition, applicants must have achieved at least a grade C pass at GCSE, or the equivalent, in mathematics and English. The government requires all trainees to pass tests in numeracy, literacy and information and communications technology, and opportunities to sit these tests will be offered during the course.

Contact: Secondary PGCE Administrator
01865 488549
pgcesec_ioed@brookes.ac.uk

PGCE in Secondary Education (English) Q3X1

1 year full-time

As above

PGCE/Maitrise in Secondary Education (French) RXCC

1 year full-time

As above

PGCE in Secondary Education (Geography) F8X1

37 weeks full-time

As above

PGCE in Secondary Education (Mathematics) G1X1

37 weeks full-time

As above

PGCE in Secondary Education (Modern Foreign Languages) R9X1

37 weeks full-time

As above

PGCE in Secondary Education (Music)
W3X1
37 weeks full-time
As above

PGCE in Secondary Education (Religious
Education) V6X1
1 year full-time
As above

PGCE in Secondary Education (Science)
F0X1
37 weeks full-time
As above

PgCert in Educational Studies (Special
Educational Needs)
1 year part-time

Entry requirements: Qualified teacher
status, degree (or equivalent qualification)
and minimum 2 years' teaching experience.
Contact: Caroline Roaf
         Course Leader
         01865 488284
cpd_ioed@brookes.ac.uk

Pgdip in Educational Studies (Hearing
Impairment)
2 years part-time

Entry requirements: Teaching qualification
required and minimum 1 year's teaching
experience; aimed at candidates wishing to
train as teachers of deaf students.

Contact: Georgina Glenny
         Course Secretary
         01865 488299
         cpd-ioed@brookes.ac.uk

MA in Education
1 years full-time, 2 years open learning,
2 to 5 years part-time

Entry requirements: Applicants should be
qualified teachers/lecturers with minimum
3 years' teaching experience; they should
normally have undertaken study at undergraduate level or equivalent, but may also
be accepted on the basis of substantial professional experience and standing.
Contact: Ashley Tagg
         Course Administrator
         01865 488284
         cpd_ioed@brookes.ac.uk

EdD in Education
3 years full-time or 4 years part-time

Entry requirements: Honours degree or
Master's degree in education or a related
discipline; and at least 5 years' professional
experience.
Contact: Janet Warren
         01865 488563
         jwarren@brookes.ac.uk

University of Oxford

University Offices
Wellington Square
Oxford
OX1 2JD
Tel: 01865 270059
Fax: 01865 270708
graduate.admissions@admin.ox.ac.uk
www.ox.ac.uk

Oxford is the oldest University in the
English-speaking world. It has over 16,500
students and there are 39 colleges and six
permanent private halls.

The Department of Educational Studies
was established in 1892 and is presently situated at Norham Gardens bordering on the
university parks. The department offers
teacher training, Continuing Professional
Development through the Diploma
courses, Master's and Doctoral programmes and research opportunities. The
department library specialises in the field of
education and areas of related interest.
Resources are also available in the other
university libraries. The education holdings
at Oxford Brookes University and at the
Institute of Education in London are also
recommended.

The Department of Educational Studies has extensive ICT facilities with two rooms for teaching purposes and for use by individual PGCE students. Additional computers and ICT equipment are located in the Library Resources area.

Accommodation is provided in the colleges or associated university-owned buildings. There is also private accommodation near to university colleges and facilities.

HOW TO APPLY

PGCE: applications are made through the GTTR.

Postgraduate: applications are made direct to the institution.

COURSES

PGCE in Secondary Education (Biology) C1X1

1 year full-time

Entry requirements: Relevant degree and GCSE grade C or above, or equivalent, in English language and mathematics.
Contact: Mrs Olga Clarke
            PGCE Course Secretary
            01865 274020
            olga.clarke@edstud.ox.ac.uk

PGCE in Secondary Education (Chemistry) F1X1

1 year full-time
As above

PGCE in Secondary Education (English) Q3X1

1 year full-time
As above

PGCE in Secondary Education (Geography) F8X1

1 year full-time
As above

PGCE in Secondary Education (History) V1X1

1 year full-time
As above

PGCE in Secondary Education (Mathematics) G1X1

1 year full-time
As above

PGCE in Secondary Education (Modern Languages: French with German) RX11

1 year full-time
As above

PGCE in Secondary Education (Modern Languages: French with Italian) RX1C

1 year full-time
As above

PGCE in Secondary Education (Modern Languages: French with Spanish) RXD1

1 year full-time
As above

PGCE in Secondary Education (Modern Languages: French) R1X1

1 year full-time
As above

PGCE in Secondary Education (Modern Languages: German with French) RX21

1 year full-time
As above

PGCE in Secondary Education (Modern Languages: Italian with French) RX31

1 year full-time
As above

PGCE in Secondary Education (Physics) F3X1

1 year full-time
As above

PgDip in Educational Studies

2 years part-time

Entry requirements: Candidates should be practising teachers within reach of Oxford, with 3 years' educational experience.
Contact: Secretary for Higher Degrees
            01865 274018
            rosalind.gerring@edstud.ox.
            ac.uk

MSc in Educational Studies (Comparative and International Studies in Education)
1 year full-time
Entry requirements: Good Honours degree.
Contact: As above

MSc in Educational Studies (Professional Development in Education)
2 years part-time
Entry requirements: Good Honours degree.
Contact: As above

University of Paisley

Paisley Campus
High Street
Paisley
Renfrewshire
PA1 2BE
Tel: 0141 848 3000
Fax: 0141 887 0812
uni-direct@paisley.ac.uk
www.paisley.ac.uk

The University of Paisley was founded in 1897 to offer vocational courses. It began offering degree courses in the early 1900s and was awarded university status in 1992. There are currently over 10,000 students at the university.

The university has three campuses, Paisley Campus, Ayr Campus and Dumfries Campus. The Faculty of Education and Media studies is located at Ayr Campus. The faculty offers a range of undergraduate and postgraduate teacher education programmes and students have access to specialist teaching resources.

Ayr Campus has a library, extensive computer facilities, accommodation, Students' Union and sports facilities based on site. Apart from the university owned halls and flats which are available and there is also private accommodation available near to the campuses.

HOW TO APPLY

Degree courses: applications are made through UCAS.

PGCE: applications are made direct to the institution.

COURSES

BEd/BEd (Hons) in Primary Education
X120 A
4 years full-time
Year 1: 5 main curricular areas: environmental studies; expressive arts; language; mathematics; religious education plus professional studies. School experience in middle primary at end of the year.

Year 2: Curricular and professional studies plus 1 advanced level option. Courses focus on upper primary level, preparing students for solo school experience in primary 6 or 7.

Year 3: Studies relate to the pre-school and lower primary groups. Curricular and professional studies plus a second advanced level option. 2 periods of school experience in the 3–8 age group. A core course module in special educational needs.

Year 4: Major applied educational study and dissertation; 1 other advanced level option. 1 period of school experience at end of Semester 1.

On completion students are recommended to the General Teaching Council for Scotland for provisional registration. Full registration is awarded on the completion of 2 satisfactory years (or equivalent) of teaching.

Entry requirements: GCE A- and AS-levels: CCD to BB, AVCEs, SCE Higher: BBBB, BTEC NC/ND, European Baccalaureate, International Baccalaureate, Irish Leaving Certificates
Contact: Tom Hamilton
Admissions Officer
01292 886223

PGCE in Primary Education

9 months full-time

Entry requirements: Degree or equivalent qualification; in addition, candidates should hold H-grade English and O/S-grade or GCSE grade C (or above) passes in mathematics, or equivalent.

Contact: Robert Stefani
Programme Leader
01292 886285/886309

PGCE in Secondary Education (Biology with Science)

9 months full-time

Entry requirements: Degree or equivalent qualification required; within the degree, candidates must hold 3 graduating passes (equivalent to 2 years' full-time study) in a subject which they wish to teach; SCE H-grade English or its equivalent is also required.

Contact: Ian Smith
Programme Leader
01292 886272

PGCE in Secondary Education (Business Education)

9 months full-time

As above

PGCE in Secondary Education (Computing)

9 months full-time

As above

Secondary Education (English)

9 months full-time

As above

Secondary Education (Mathematics)

9 months full-time

As above

Secondary Education (Modern Languages)

9 months full-time

As above

Secondary Education (Religious Education)

9 months full-time

As above

PgCert/PgDip/MEd in Education

PgCert: 1–2 years part-time, PgDip: 3–4 years part-time, MEd: 4–6 years part-time

Entry requirements: Applicants should normally be teachers or other professionals working in the field of education, with a degree or equivalent qualification and at least 2 years' experience in an educational context.

Contact: Kay Livingston
01292 886319/886309
kay.livingstone@paisley.ac.uk

University of Plymouth

Drake Circus
Plymouth
PL4 8AA
Tel: 01752 600600
Fax: 01752 232141
admissions@plymouth.ac.uk
www.plymouth.ac.uk

The University of Plymouth has an educational history dating back to 1862. It now caters for over 27,000 students and its faculties are based at four campuses: Exeter, Exmouth, Plymouth and Seale-Hayne.

Within the Faculty of Arts and Education based at the Exeter and Exmouth campuses is the School of Education. In addition to the university facilities, student teachers have access to specialised materials and resources such as the School Practice collection in the library. The school itself has a range of specialist subject facilities. There are undergraduate and postgraduate courses, research opportunities in Teacher Education and both primary and secondary initial teacher training courses are available.

The university has a wide range of IT facilities and services throughout the university, some within the faculties. A range of social and sporting facilities are available to students and there is conveniently located university managed and privately rented accommodation. The Student Accommodation Services can help with living arrangements.

HOW TO APPLY

Degree courses: applications are made through UCAS.

PGCE: applications made through the GTTR.

Postgraduate: applications are made direct to the institution.

COURSES

BEd (Hons) in Art and Design and General Primary (5–11 years) X1WX

4 years full-time

Students follow 1 main subject option: Art and design. In addition, all students follow a range of professional courses related to the age phase of 3–8 years and undertake a variety of practical teaching and research experiences in schools. A programme of education studies introduces students to the general principles of education.

Opportunities exist for some subject courses and school experience to be undertaken overseas.

Successful completion of this course leads to a recommendation for Qualified Teacher Status (QTS) after completion of skills tests.

Entry requirements: GCE A- and AS-levels: E, BTEC NC/ND, International Baccalaureate, SCE Higher

Contact: Miss D Wright
Programme Director
01395 255367
d1wright@plymouth.ac.uk

BEd (Hons) in Early Childhood Studies (3–8 years) X121

4 years full-time

Students follow 1 main subject option: early childhood studies. In addition, all students follow a range of professional courses related to the age phase of 3–8 years and undertake a variety of practical teaching and research experiences in schools. A programme of education studies introduces students to the general principles of education.

Opportunities exist for some subject courses and school experience to be undertaken overseas.

Successful completion of this course leads to a recommendation for Qualified Teacher Status (QTS) after completion of skills tests.

Entry requirements: GCE A- and AS-levels, BTEC NC/ND, International Baccalaureate, SCE Higher

Contact: As above

BEd (Hons) in English in Education and General Primary (5–11 years)

4 years full-time

Students follow 1 main subject option: English. In addition, all students follow a range of professional courses related to the age phase of 3–8 years and undertake a variety of practical teaching and research experiences in schools. A programme of education studies introduces students to the general principles of education.

Opportunities exist for some subject courses and school experience to be undertaken overseas.

Successful completion of this course leads to a recommendation for Qualified Teacher Status (QTS) after completion of skills tests.

Entry requirements: As above
Contact: As above

BEd (Hons) in History and General Primary (5–11 years)

4 years full-time

Students follow 1 main subject option, history. In addition, all students follow a range of professional courses related to the age phase of 3–8 years and undertake a variety of practical teaching and research experiences in schools. A programme of education studies introduces students to the general principles of education.

Opportunities exist for some subject courses and school experience to be undertaken overseas.

Successful completion of this course leads to a recommendation for Qualified Teacher Status (QTS) after completion of skills tests.

Entry requirements: As above
Contact: As above

BEd (Hons) in Information Communication Technology and General Primary (5–11 years) X1G5

4 years full-time

Students follow 1 main subject option, information communication technology (ICT). In addition, all students follow a range of professional courses related to the age phase of 3–8 years and undertake a variety of practical teaching and research experiences in schools. A programme of education studies introduces students to the general principles of education.

Opportunities exist for some subject courses and school experience to be undertaken overseas.

Successful completion of this course leads to a recommendation for Qualified Teacher Status (QTS) after completion of skills tests.

Entry requirements: As above
Contact: As above

BEd (Hons) in Mathematics and General Primary (5–11 years) X1G1

4 years full-time

Students follow 1 main subject option, mathematics. In addition, all students follow a range of professional courses related to the age phase of 3–8 years and undertake a variety of practical teaching and research experiences in schools. A programme of education studies introduces students to the general principles of education.

Opportunities exist for some subject courses and school experience to be undertaken overseas.

Successful completion of this course leads to a recommendation for Qualified Teacher Status (QTS) after completion of skills tests.

Entry requirements: GCE A- and AS-levels, BTEC NC/ND, International Baccalaureate, SCE Higher
Contact: As above

BEd (Hons) in Music and General Primary (5–11 years) X1W3

4 years full-time

Students follow 1 main subject option, music. In addition, all students follow a range of professional courses related to the age phase of 3–8 years and undertake a variety of practical teaching and research experiences in schools. A programme of education studies introduces students to the general principles of education.

Opportunities exist for some subject courses and school experience to be undertaken overseas.

Successful completion of this course leads to a recommendation for Qualified Teacher Status (QTS) after completion of skills tests.

Entry requirements: As above
Contact: As above

BEd (Hons) in Physical Education and General Primary (5–11 years)

4 years full-time

Students follow 1 main subject option, physical education. In addition, all students follow a range of professional courses related to the age phase of 3–8 years and undertake a variety of practical teaching and research experiences in schools. A programme of education studies introduces students to the general principles of education.

Opportunities exist for some subject courses and school experience to be undertaken overseas.

Successful completion of this course leads to a recommendation for Qualified Teacher Status (QTS) after completion of skills tests.

Entry requirements: As above
Contact: As above

BEd (Hons) in Science and General Primary (5–11 years) X1F9

4 years full-time

Students follow 1 main subject option, science. In addition, all students follow a range of professional courses related to the age phase of 3–8 years and undertake a variety of practical teaching and research experiences in schools. A programme of education studies introduces students to the general principles of education.

Opportunities exist for some subject courses and school experience to be undertaken overseas.

Successful completion of this course leads to a recommendation for Qualified Teacher Status (QTS) after completion of skills tests.

Entry requirements: As above
Contact: As above

PGCE in Primary Education (5–11) X100

1 year full-time

Entry requirements: Degree or equivalent; plus GCSE grade C (or equivalent qualification) in English language, mathematics and at least one science.
Contact: Admissions Office
01395 255309
rse-admissions@plymouth.ac.uk

PGCE in Secondary Education (Art and Design) W1X1

1 year full-time

Entry requirements: Degree or equivalent. Portfolio of work which represents a broad involvement in the subject.
Contact: Admissions Office / Howard Jones, Pathway Co-ordinator
01395 255309 /
rse-admissions@plymouth.ac.uk /
hfjones@plymouth.ac.uk

PGCE in Secondary Education (Drama) W4X1

1 year full-time

Entry requirements: Degree in drama, theatre and performance or related areas, with significant experience of practical theatre and a wide interest in popular culture including television and film; GCSE or equivalent at grade C or above in mathematics and English language required; alternative tests available for otherwise qualified candidates.
Contact: Admissions Office
01395 255309
rse-admissions@plymouth.ac.uk

PGCE in Secondary Education (English) Q3X1

1 year full-time

Entry requirements: Degree or equivalent approved by DfES, with relevance to English; plus GCSE grade C or above (or equivalent) in mathematics and English language.
Contact: Admissions Office / Phil Norman, Pathway Co-ordinator
01395 255309
rse-admissions@plymouth.ac.uk /
prnorman@plymouth.ac.uk

PGCE in Secondary Education (Geography) F8X1

1 year full-time

Entry requirements: Degree, or equivalent.
Contact: Admissions Office / David Cragg, Pathway Co-ordinator
01395 255309
rse-admissions@plymouth.ac.uk /
dcragg@plymouth.ac.uk

PGCE in Secondary Education (Mathematics) G1X1

1 year full-time

Entry requirements: A degree or equivalent, plus GCSE at grade C or above, or equivalent pass, in mathematics and English language. Alternative tests are available for otherwise qualified candidates.

Contact: Admissions Office / Alan
McClean, Pathway Co-ordinator
01395 255309
rse-admissions@plymouth.ac.uk /
amclean@plymouth.ac.uk

**PGCE in Secondary Education (Music)
W3X1**

1 year full-time

Entry requirements: Degree or equivalent
plus GCSE at grade C or above, or equivalent pass in mathematics and English
language. Alternative tests available for
otherwise qualified candidates.

Contact: Admissions Office /
Will Mcburnie, Pathway Co-
ordinator
01395 255309
rse-admissions@plymouth.ac.uk /
wmcburnie@plymouth.ac.uk

**Pgdip/MA in Education (integrated
Master's programme)**

2–5 years part-time

Entry requirements: Degree or equivalent
and/or appropriate experience.

Contact: School of Graduate Studies
01395 255478
gsaeadmissions@plymouth.ac.uk

Portsmouth Primary SCITT

Dame Judith Professional Centre
Sundridge Close
Portsmouth
PO6 3JL
Tel: 02392 373432
portsmouth_scitt@hotmail.com

Portsmouth Primary SCITT was set up in
September 2000. Each school in the consortium serves a very different catchment
area. In practice, this means that Portsmouth SCITT is able to offer a range of
training experiences to prospective candidates.

Trainees spend a total of twenty weeks in
the classroom. Each term is made up of half
a term of lectures in primary subjects, based
mainly at the Professional Centre, followed
by half a term of teacher training at Key
Stage 1 and 2. Trainees undertake a total

of three teaching practices covering the
primary age range of 5–11 years. Two practices take place in one school and the third
practice in another with a contrasting
catchment area to the first school.

HOW TO APPLY

Applications are made through the GTTR.

**PGCE in Primary Education (English,
5–11) XQ1H**

1 year full-time

Entry requirements: Degree in relevant
subject; GCSE grade C or above in English
language and mathematics, and science if
born after 1/Sep/79.

Contact: As above

**PGCE in Primary Education
(Mathematics, 5–11) XG1C**

1 year full-time
As above

University of Portsmouth

University House
Winston Churchill Avenue
Portsmouth
PO1 2UP
Tel: 023 9284 8484
Fax: 023 0284 3082
admissions@port.ac.uk
www.port.ac.uk

The University of Portsmouth caters for
over 18,000 students and is based on three
campuses. The main one is Guildhall
Campus and is situated in the heart of the
city centre. The others, Milton and Lang-
stone, are a few kilometres to the East of
Guildhall but are easily accessible with a
free bus service and a cycle route.

The School of Education and Continuing Studies is situated in the St Georges Building on the Guildhall Campus. The school offers a selection of taught and research postgraduate courses in addition to the Initial Teacher Training secondary programme. There are computer facilities within the building and throughout the university and resources are available in the university libraries.

The university has halls of residence and student lodgings available and there is also privately rented accommodation in the surrounding area.

HOW TO APPLY

PGCE: applications made through the GTTR.

Postgraduate: applications are made direct to the institution.

COURSES

PGCE in Secondary Education (Business Studies) N1X1

1 year full-time

Entry requirements: Relevant degree or equivalent; GCSE (grades A–C) mathematics and English language.

Contact: Maureen Lines
Senior Course Administrator
023 9284 5213
maureen.lines@port.ac.uk

PGCE in Secondary Education (English) Q3X1

1 year full-time
As above

PGCE in Secondary Education (Mathematics) G1X1

1 year full-time
As above

PGCE in Secondary Education (Modern Languages: French with German) RX11

1 year full-time
As above

PGCE in Secondary Education (Modern Languages: French with Spanish) RXD1

1 year full-time
As above

PGCE in Secondary Education (Modern Languages: French) R1X1

1 year full-time
As above

PGCE in Secondary Education (Science) F0X1

1 year full-time
As above

MA in Education (Advanced Professional Practice)

2 years part-time

Entry requirements: Honours degree relevant to teaching role, or teaching qualification, or employment in teaching/training role required; accreditation of prior learning/prior experiential learning possible.

Contact: Dr Angela Race
Course Leader
023 9284 5203
angela.race@port.ac.uk

MSc in Education and Training Management

1 year full-time, 2 years part-time

Entry requirements: Degree or other academic qualifications which are recognised as equivalent to a degree.

Contact: Pat Stallard
Course Leader
023 9284 5224/5206
pat.stallard@port.ac.uk

Primary Catholic Partnership

C/o Holy Family Catholic Primary School
Mansel Road West
Southampton
SO16 9LP
Tel: 023 8077 9753
Fax: 023 8077 9809
jshaw.pcp@bigfoot.com
www.pcp-scitt.org.uk

The Primary Catholic Partnership provides School Centred Initial Teacher Training at primary level based on the Catholic philosophy of education. Part of the course includes four modules of the Catholic Certificate of Religious Studies. On completion of the course trainees are awarded Qualified Teacher Status and the PGCE which is awarded by St Mary's College, Strawberry Hill, a college of the University of Surrey.

The training base is in an independent building on the site of the lead school, Holy Family Catholic Primary School in Southampton. Trainees have access to Southampton University Hartley and New College libraries and computer facilities in the lead school, training base and the university. New College library houses the Primary Curriculum Resource Centre. There are twenty schools involved in the partnership within a thirty mile radius of Southampton including six on the Isle of Wight. Students will need to find privately owned accommodation in the area.

HOW TO APPLY

Applications are made through the GTTR.

COURSES

PGCE in Primary Education (5–11 years) X100

1 year full-time

Entry requirements: Relevant degree; GCSE grade C or above in English language and mathematics.

Contact: Tracey Cooney
Administrator
023 8077 9753
tcooney.pcp@bigfoot.com

Queen's University of Belfast

University Road
Belfast
County Antrim
BT7 1NN
Tel: 028 9024 5133
Fax: 028 9024 7895
admissions@qub.ac.uk
www.qub.ac.uk

Queen Victoria founded the Queen's University of Belfast in 1845. The academic buildings and facilities are based on campus not far from Belfast City Centre with the Ulster Museum and Botanic Gardens also located on site. The university is closely linked with St. Mary's and Stranmillis colleges and also Omagh College and Armagh College of Further and Higher Education.

The Faculty of Legal, Social and Educational Sciences is the largest faculty in the University and was established in 1997 when the faculties of Law, Social Sciences and Education merged. It offers a range of programmes at the university and also at St Mary's and Stranmillis. The Graduate School of Education is the main provider of secondary school teachers in Northern Ireland and degree programmes at primary and secondary level are run at the associated colleges of St. Mary's and Stranmillis. Postgraduate taught masters or research degrees are available.

The university caters for 23,000 students and there are a variety of social and sporting facilities available. There is accommodation available in university or privately owned residences and all students have access to the library and computer resources.

HOW TO APPLY

Applications are made direct to the institution.

COURSES

PGCE in Secondary Education (Biology)

1 year full-time

Entry requirements: Degree or equivalent; plus GCSE grade C or above (or equivalent) in English language and mathematics.
Contact: Assistant Director
028 9033 5941
c.shannon@qub.ac.uk

PGCE in Secondary Education (Chemistry)

1 year full-time
As above

PGCE in Secondary Education (Economics)

1 year full-time
As above

PGCE in Secondary Education (English)

1 year full-time
As above

PGCE in Secondary Education (Information Technology)

1 year full-time
As above

PGCE in Secondary Education (Languages)

1 year full-time
As above

PGCE in Secondary Education (Mathematics)

1 year full-time
As above

PGCE in Secondary Education (Physics)

1 year full-time
As above

PGCE in Secondary Education (Politics)

1 year full-time
As above

PGCE in Secondary Education (Religious Education)

1 year full-time
As above

PGCE in Secondary Education (Science)

1 year full-time
As above

EdD in Education

3 years full-time, 4 years part-time

Entry requirements: Recognised degree with appropriate higher level qualification plus 5 years' full-time professional experience in field of management in education.
Contact: Administrator, Graduate School
of Education
028 9033 5941
cpu.edu@qub.ac.uk

Advanced Certificate/DASE/MEd/MSc in Education

Up to 5 years part-time

Entry requirements: Candidates should normally be qualified teachers holding Honours degree or equivalent qualification and having at least 2 years' teaching experience, or hold degree or equivalent qualification with significant experience of working in an education or training context plus at least 5 years' teaching experience.
Contact: As above

Certificate/Diploma in Professional Development (Education)

Part-time

Entry requirements: For qualified teachers or graduates with significant experience of working in an education or training context.
Contact: As above

MA in English Language Teaching

12 months full-time

Entry requirements: Degree; at least 6.5 in the International English Language Testing Service (IELTS) test.
Contact: Dr A Ridgway
028 9027 3807
tefl@qub.ac.uk

MSSc in Lifelong Learning

3 years part-time

Entry requirements: Honours degree or equivalent plus relevant professional qualification in education or training; or degree or equivalent qualification with significant experience of working in education or training context.

Contact: Rob Mark
028 9033 5163
r.d.mark@qub.ac.uk

University of Reading

Whiteknights House
PO Box 217
Reading
RG6 6AH
Tel: 0118 987 5123
Fax: 0118 378 8924
schools.liaison@rdg.ac.uk
www.rdg.ac.uk

Founded in 1860 and awarded the Royal Charter in 1926, the University of Reading is based mainly at Whiteknights Campus in 300 acres of landscaped grounds. It has two other campuses, Bulmershe Campus and London Road, which are situated a short distance away from Whiteknights. The university caters for over 13,000 students.

The Institute of Education is one of the largest departments of its kind in the university sector and is located on the Bulmershe Campus. They offer a wide selection of courses at both undergraduate and postgraduate level and also Master's degrees. There are other courses of Continuing Professional Development.

Aside from the Main Library at Whiteknights there is the Music Library and also the Bulmershe Library which specialises in education and community. There is a substantial network of PCs with over 400 available to students and most departments have their own specialist computer labs. There is also a 24-hour computer lab in the centre of the campus. A wide range of accommodation is available in halls and students housing for undergraduates and postgraduates and there is also the option of renting privately.

HOW TO APPLY

Degree courses: applications are made through UCAS.

PGCE: applications made through the GTTR.

Postgraduate: applications are made direct to the institution.

COURSES

BA (Ed) (Hons) in Art Specialism X1W1
4 years full-time

Professional studies: Term 1: Introduction to university study and to schools. Role of the classroom teacher; aspects of the social, emotional and intellectual development of children and the context of the school; 3 core subjects of the National Curriculum are introduced; school experience; practical teaching.

Terms 2 onwards: Professional framework: 2 courses: early years (age range 3–7 years); later primary years (age range 7–12 years). Students choose 1 by the end of the first year. Throughout the rest of the degree students develop their understanding of children's learning; of a range of approaches to teaching; of curriculum planning, evaluation and assessment; of classroom organisation and management; of the legal requirements of the profession and the wider life of the school community. Curriculum studies will ensure that students have the knowledge, understanding and skill to teach all areas of the primary curriculum, while school experience will be a feature throughout.

Art specialism: Part 1: Aims to provide an introduction to a wide range of ideas, materials and processes. Many of these will relate directly to work in schools; others will extend skills and provide personal insight into the underlying processes of art making. Towards the end, projects become more open-ended, giving scope for personal initiative. Also, study of range of topics drawn from the history of art and design. Part 2: Students will work independently, discussing work in individual tutorials and small group seminars; will also examine some of the underlying processes of teaching and learning in art, and prepare for practice in schools.

Successful completion of this course leads to a recommendation for Qualified Teacher Status (QTS) after completion of skills tests.

Entry requirements: Tariff: 180, International Baccalaureate: 28, BTEC NC/ND
Contact: Admissions Office
0118 378 8815
fasug@rdg.ac.uk

BA (Ed) (Hons) in English Specialism X1Q3

4 years full-time

Professional studies: Term 1: Introduction to university study and to schools. Role of the classroom teacher; aspects of the social, emotional and intellectual development of children and the context of the school; 3 core subjects of the National Curriculum are introduced; school experience; practical teaching.

Terms 2 onwards: Professional framework: 2 courses: early years (age range 3–7 years); later primary years (age range 7–12 years). Students choose 1 by the end of the first year. Throughout the rest of the degree students develop their understanding of children's learning; of a range of approaches to teaching; of curriculum planning, evaluation and assessment; of classroom organisation and management; of the legal requirements of the profession and the wider life of the school community. Curriculum studies will ensure that students have the knowledge, understanding and skill to teach all areas of the primary curriculum, while school experience will be a feature throughout.

English specialism: Terms 2–4: units include: childhood and autobiography; craft of writing; realisation of text: language and communication; women writing, women reading; heritage and multicultural literature; Shakespeare and the modern world. Terms 10–12: a special study linked to a core unit on children's literature; 2 options from: modern drama; modern British poetry; popular culture; television narrative.

Successful completion of this course leads to a recommendation for Qualified Teacher Status (QTS) after completion of skills tests.

Entry requirements: As above
Contact: As above

BA (Ed) (Hons) in Music Specialism X1W3

4 years full-time

Professional studies: Term 1: Introduction to university study and to schools. Role of the classroom teacher; aspects of the social, emotional and intellectual development of children and the context of the school; 3 core subjects of the National Curriculum are introduced; school experience; practical teaching.

Terms 2 onwards: Professional framework: 2 courses: early years (age range 3–7 years); later primary years (age range 7–12 years). Students choose 1 by the end of the first year. Throughout the rest of the degree students develop their understanding of children's learning; of a range of approaches to teaching; of curriculum planning, evaluation and assessment; of classroom organisation and management; of the legal requirements of the profession and the wider life of the school community. Curriculum studies will ensure that students have the knowledge, understanding and skill to teach all areas of the primary curriculum, while school experience will be a feature throughout.

Music specialism: The course has been designed with a strong practical emphasis. Terms 2–4: main instrumental (or vocal) study; creative work, including composition and arrangement; musical and classroom skills; music style and context;

microtechnology in music; music in education.

Terms 10–12: preparation of a special study; plus 3 music electives from: performance; composition; listening in the curriculum; music and theatre; music technology.

Successful completion of this course leads to a recommendation for Qualified Teacher Status (QTS) after completion of skills tests.

Entry requirements: As above
Contact: As above

PGCE in Primary Education (Early Years, 3–8) X121

1 year full-time

Entry requirements: Degree in an appropriate subject with GCSE minimum grade C or equivalent in mathematics, English language and science. Faculty mathematics test also offered. Candidates should be able to show at interview that they have a wide range of life experiences, including work in school with young children, and should be able to speak about those experiences in an enthusiastic and articulate manner.

Contact: Mrs C Adamson
Course Secretary
0118 931 8870

PGCE in Primary Education (Upper Primary, 7–12/13) X171

1 year full-time
As above

PGCE in Secondary Education (Art and Design) W1X1

1 year full-time

Entry requirements: Degree related to subject, English and mathematics GCSE minimum grade C or equivalent.
Contact: Mrs M Mitchell
Course Secretary
0118 931 8870
essmitma@reading.ac.uk

PGCE in Secondary Education (Drama) W4X1

1 year full-time
As above

PGCE in Secondary Education (English) Q3X1

1 year full-time
As above

PGCE in Secondary Education (Geography) F8X1

1 year full-time
As above

PGCE in Secondary Education (History) V1X1

1 year full-time
As above

PGCE in Secondary Education (Mathematics) G1X1

1 year full-time
As above

PGCE in Secondary Education (Modern Foreign Languages: French, conversion route) RXD1

2 years full-time

Entry requirements: Course will cater for those with a degree in a subject which normally offers little opportunity for teacher training (e.g. philosophy, politics, sociology) and who wish to become teachers of French; will also cater for graduates in a less taught language such as Spanish, Russian, Urdu.
Contact: As above

PGCE in Secondary Education (Modern Foreign Languages: French) R1X1

1 year full-time

Entry requirements: Degree related to subject, English and mathematics GCSE minimum grade C or equivalent.
Contact: As above

PGCE in Secondary Education (Modern Foreign Languages: German) R2X1

1 year full-time
As above

PGCE in Secondary Education (Music) W3X1

1 year full-time
As above

PGCE in Secondary Education (Physical Education) X9C6
1 year full-time
As above

PGCE in Secondary Education (Science: Biology) C1X1
1 year full-time
As above

PGCE in Secondary Education (Science: Chemistry) F1X1
1 year full-time
As above

PGCE in Secondary Education (Science: Physics) F3X1
1 year full-time
As above

Pgdip/MA in English and Language in Education
MA: 1 year full-time, 3–8 years part-time; PgDip 2–4 years part-time

Entry requirements: For graduate teachers, advisers, or lecturers, normally with minimum 2 years' teaching experience; candidates with other qualifications considered.
Contact: Mr A C Goodwyn
Course Leader
0118 931 8837
p.m.parry@reading.ac.uk

Pgdip/MA in Inclusive Education
MA: 1 year full-time, 3–8 years part-time; PgDip: 2–4 years part-time

Entry requirements: Graduate teachers with minimum 2 years' experience who hold positions of responsibility/management positions within a primary, secondary or special school; teachers who have successfully completed further professional studies courses within Faculty may be eligible for admission with advanced standing.
Contact: Mrs Rosemary Jones
Course Secretary
0118 931 8857
r.k.jones@reading.ac.uk

Pgdip/MA in Information Technology in Education
1 year full-time, 2–3 years part-time

Entry requirements: For graduate teachers with at least 2 years' teaching experience; other applicants considered; some experience of information technology expected.
Contact: Dr P Carmichael
Course Leader
0118 931 8869
p.carmichael@rdg.ac.uk

Pgdip/MSc in Managing School Improvement
MSc: 3–8 years part-time, PgDip: 2 years part-time

Entry requirements: Graduate teachers with minimum 2 years' experience who hold positions of responsibility/management positions within a primary, secondary or special school.
Contact: Prof Brian Fidler
Course Leader
0118 931 8632/8857
f.b.fidler@reading.ac.uk

Pgdip/MA in Music Education
MA: 1 year full-time, 3–5 years part-time; PgDip: 2–4 years part-time

Entry requirements: For graduate teachers, advisers, lecturers with minimum 2 years' experience.
Contact: G Cox
Course Leader
0118 931 8837
p.m.parry@reading.ac.uk

Pgdip/MA in Music Teaching in Professional Practice
MA: 1–3 years part-time

Entry requirements: Applicants should be teaching individual pupils or small groups, will normally have received a professional training, and should hold relevant music/instrumental qualifications.
Contact: Ms D Brewis
0118 931 8843
d.brewis@reading.ac.uk

MA in Organisation, Planning and Management in Education

1 year full-time, 2 years part-time

Entry requirements: For graduate qualified teachers with minimum 2 years' teaching experience, or those with other relevant professional qualifications and experience (for example, administration of education, curriculum development), from UK and overseas.

Contact: Dr K J Brehony
Course Leader

0118 931 8860
m.king@reading.ac.uk

PgDip/MA in Primary Education

MA: 3–8 years part-time, Pgdip: 2–4 years part-time

Entry requirements: Experience of teaching in the primary sector.

Contact: N Rassool
Course Leader
0118 931 8857
n.rassool@reading.ac.uk

Redcar and Cleveland College

Corporation Road
Redcar
TS10 1EZ
Tel: 01642 473132
Fax: 01642 490856
cinfo@cleveland.ac.uk
www.cleveland.ac.uk

Redcar and Cleveland College is based on the North East coast 50 miles south of Newcastle and 20 miles north of Whitby. It was formed in 1994 when Cleveland College of Further Education merged with Sir William Turners Sixth Form College. The combined institution was initially called Cleveland Tertiary College, but changed its name to Redcar and Cleveland College in 1997.

The college has three campuses: the main campus and Connections campus in Red-

car, and the Loftus campus. All the campuses are easily accessible by car and bus, and the main campus is also accessible by train.

HOW TO APPLY

Applications are made direct to the institution.

COURSES

PGCE in Further Education

1 to 2 years part-time

Entry requirements: Current teaching/training work of at least 150 hours and appropriate subject qualifications; candidates with a basic teaching qualification follow 1-year programme.

Contact: Sheila Rooth
01642 473132

Royal Academy of Dance

36 Battersea Square
Wandsworth
London
SW11 3RA
Tel: 020 7326 8000
Fax: 020 7924 3129
info@rad.org.uk
www.rad.org.uk

The Royal Academy of Dance is the largest examining and teacher education organisation for classical ballet in the world. It was formed in 1920 by a small group of dance professionals as the Association of Teachers of Operatic Dancing in Great Britain. In 1935 the Association was granted a Royal Charter and became the Royal Academy of Dance. There are currently 1,200 students in full-time or part-time teacher training with the Academy.

The Academy's resources include a library containing more than 5,000 titles covering all aspects of ballet and dance. Books on education and psychology form a growing part of the library's collection. Facilities are also available for viewing videos and listening to CDs or audiocassettes. Students at the Academy have access to a physiotherapy treatment room, gymnasium, performance space, music studio, and computer room.

HOW TO APPLY

Applications are made direct to the institution.

COURSES

PGCDT in Dance Teaching (14–19 years)

1 year full-time

Entry requirements: Appropriate UK undergraduate degree; equivalent qualification in dance studies or related subject with substantial dance component accepted; GCSE grade C in English and mathematics.

Contact: Sian Emmett
Programme Officer
020 7326 8034
semmett@rad.org.uk

Royal Northern College of Music

124 Oxford Road
Manchester
Greater Manchester
M13 9RD
Tel: 0161 907 5200
Fax: 0161 273 7611
info@rncm.ac.uk
www.rncm.ac.uk

The roots of the college go back to the late 19th century when Sir Charles Hallé, the founder of the Hallé Orchestra, established the Royal Manchester College of Music. Royal Manchester College amalgamated with the Northern School of Music in 1973 to form the present-day Royal Northern College of Music.

There is a range of academic and leisure facilities at the college including the library, IT facilities and Student Union. Some accommodation is available in student halls near to the main college building. The college offers a PGCE course with Specialist Strings Teaching held in collaboration with Manchester Metropolitan University.

HOW TO APPLY

Applications are made through the GTTR.

COURSES

PGCE in Secondary Education in Music (specialist strings teaching)

1 year full-time

Entry requirements: For graduates in music of universities and conservatoires, who wish to specialise in instrumental teaching; in addition to degree or equivalent qualification, GCSE minimum grade C in English and mathematics, or equivalent achievement, is required.

Contact: Penny Stirling
Director of the Junior Strings Project
0161 273 6283

Royal Scottish Academy of Music and Drama

100 Renfrew Street
Glasgow
G2 3DB
Tel: 0141 332 4101
Fax: 0141 332 8901

registry@rsamd.ac.uk
www.rsamd.ac.uk

The Royal Scottish Academy of Music and Drama originated from the Anderson Institute which was established in 1846. It gradually expanded and developed incorporating the School of Music and later the

College of Drama and was renamed in 1968. The academy received degree awarding powers in 1994.

The Bachelor of Education course is offered by the Royal Scottish Academy of Music and Drama in Collaboration with the Faculty of Education, University of Glasgow.

HOW TO APPLY

Applications are made direct to the institution.

COURSES

BEd/BEd (Hons) in Music

BEd: 3 years full-time, BEd (Hons): 4 years full-time

The course is offered in collaboration with the Faculty of Education, University of Glasgow.

Music studies, professional training and school experience are offered concurrently throughout 4 years.

All students on this course initially pursue 3 performance studies which must include keyboard and singing (the third normally being an orchestral instrument).

Principal performance studies from: piano; harpsichord; organ; voice; violin; viola; violoncello; double bass; guitar; harp; flute; oboe; clarinet; saxophone; bassoon; horn; trumpet; trombone; tuba; cornet; euphonium; timpani; percussion.

Techniques of teaching are incorporated in instrumental study.

Examples of additional studies are: practical musicianship; arranging and orchestration; compositional studies; instrumental modules; electronic and recording techniques.

On completion students are recommended to the General Teaching Council for Scotland for provisional registration. Full registration is awarded on the completion of 2 satisfactory years (or equivalent) of teaching.

Entry requirements: Audition, DD to AA: GCE A- and AS-levels, Interview, SCE Higher

Contact: Dr Peter Inness
Associate Director of Music
0141 332 4101
p.inness@rsamd.ac.uk

PgDip in Music (Teaching)

1 year full-time or 2 to 5 years part-time

Entry requirements: Normally applicants must have either music degrees or diplomas or be graduates in another discipline and hold an external performance or teaching Diploma; at least 2 years' appropriate teaching experience is also required.

Contact: Ms Pamela Flanagan
Head of Educational Music
0141 332 4101
P.Flanagan@rsamd.ac.uk

Sheffield Hallam University

City Campus
Howard Street
Sheffield
S1 1WB
Tel: 0114 225 5555
Fax: 01114 225 4023
undergraduate-admissions@shu.ac.uk
www.shu.ac.uk

The origins of Sheffield Hallam University go back to 1843 when Sheffield School of Design was founded. In 1969 it became one of the colleges that merged with the city's College of Technology to form Sheffield Polytechnic. In 1976 the Polytechnic was renamed Sheffield City Polytechnic when it absorbed the city's two teacher training colleges and in 1992, the City Polytechnic was awarded university status and became

Sheffield Hallam University. Today, with more than 24,000 students, the University is the country's sixth largest. The University has three campuses; City Campus located in the heart of the city centre and Collegiate Crescent Campus and Psalter Lane Campus which are located in the south-west of the city.

The School of Education is based on the Collegiate Crescent Campus. The Collegiate Learning Centre holds extensive collections of educational reference material in addition to specialist subject and teaching resources. The school offers undergraduate and taught and research postgraduate programmes of study as well as teacher training courses and opportunities for Continuing Professional Development.

The university has three learning centres one of which is based at the Collegiate campus. University owned and managed accommodation is available or there is the option of renting privately.

HOW TO APPLY

Degree courses: applications are made through UCAS.

PGCE: applications are made through the GTTR.

Postgraduate: applications are made direct to the institution.

COURSES

BA/BA (Hons) Early Years Education (Advanced Early Years, 3–7) X121

3 years full-time

All years: Core subjects of English, mathematics and science together with information and communications technology; plus a subject specialism.

Successful completion of this course leads to a recommendation for Qualified Teacher Status (QTS) after completion of skills tests.

Entry requirements: Tariff: 220, Foundation / access qualification, Professional Qualification
Contact: Di Chilvers
Course Leader
0114 225 2306
education@shu.ac.uk

BA/BA (Hons) Early Years Education (Design and Technology, 3–7) XJ19

3 years full-time
As above

Entry requirements: Tariff: 220, BTEC NC/ND, Foundation / access qualification
Contact: Margaret Noble
Subject Leader
0114 225 2306
education@shu.ac.uk

BA/BA (Hons) Early Years Education (English, 3–7) XQ13

3 years full-time
As above

Entry requirements: Tariff: 240, BTEC NC/ND, Foundation / access qualification
Contact: Jim McDonagh
Subject Leader
0114 225 2306
education@shu.ac.uk

BA/BA (Hons) Early Years Education (Geography, 3–7) XF18

3 years full-time
As above

Entry requirements: Tariff: 220, BTEC NC/ND, Foundation / access qualification
Contact: David Owen
Subject Leader
0114 225 2306
education@shu.ac.uk

BA/BA (Hons) Early Years Education (Information and Communications Technology, 3–7) XG15

3 years full-time
As above
Contact: Richard Pountry
Subject Leader
0114 225 2306
education@shu.ac.uk

BA/BA (Hons) Early Years Education (Mathematics, 3–7) XG1D

3 years full-time
As above

Contact: Ian Dall
    Subject Leader
    0114 225 2306
    education@shu.ac.uk

BA/BA (Hons) Early Years Education (Science, 3–7) XF10

3 years full-time

As above

Entry requirements: Tariff: 220, Foundation / access qualification

Contact: Tricia Young
    Subject Leader
    0114 225 2306
    education@shu.ac.uk

BA/BA (Hons) Primary Education (Design and Technology, 5–11) XJC9

3 years full-time

All years: Subject knowledge: National Curriculum preparation, courses in English; mathematics; science; Education and professional studies: links theory to practice; blocks of time in primary schools in each year; personal and study skills: use of information technology in learning and teaching; cross-curricular theme; consideration of gender; multicultural issues; special educational needs; research project on primary education; equal opportunities.

Successful completion of this course leads to a recommendation for Qualified Teacher Status (QTS) after completion of skills tests.

Entry requirements: Tariff: 220, BTEC NC/ND, Foundation / access qualification: 12 credits

Contact: Margaret Noble
    Subject Leader
    0114 225 2306
    education@shu.ac.uk

BA/BA (Hons) Primary Education (English, 5–11) XQC3

3 years full-time

As above

Entry requirements: Tariff: 240, BTEC NC/ND, Foundation / access qualification: 12 credits

Contact: Jim McDonagh
    Subject Leader
    0114 225 2306
    education@shu.ac.uk

BA/BA (Hons) Primary Education (Geography, 5–11) XFC8

3 years full-time

As above

Entry requirements: Tariff: 220, BTEC NC/ND, Foundation / access qualification: 12 credits

Contact: David Owen
    Subject Leader
    0114 225 2306
    education@shu.ac.uk

BA/BA (Hons) Primary Education (Information and Communications Technology, 5–11) XGC5

3 years full-time

As above

Contact: Richard Pountney
    Subject Leader
    0114 225 2306
    education@shu.ac.uk

BA/BA (Hons) Primary Education (Mathematics, 5–11) XGC1

3 years full-time

As above

Contact: Ian Dall
    Subject Leader
    0114 225 2306
    education@shu.ac.uk

BA/BA (Hons) Primary Education (Science, 5–11) XF1B

3 years full-time

As above

Entry requirements: Tariff: 220, Foundation / access qualification: 12 credits

Contact: Tricia Young
    Subject Leader
    0114 225 2306
    education@shu.ac.uk

BSc/BSc (Hons) Secondary Education (Design and Technology) XW12

3 years full-time

All years: Range of design and technology units; education; applied design and technology; classroom and teaching skills; school placements.

Successful completion of this course leads to a recommendation for Qualified Teacher Status (QTS) after completion of skills tests.

Entry requirements: Tariff: 160, BTEC NC/ND
Contact: John Lee
0114 225 2306
education@shu.ac.uk

BSc/BSc (Hons) Secondary Education (Design and Technology) XWC2

2 years full-time
As above

Entry requirements: Tariff: 160, BTEC NC/ND, C&G, First year of relevant degree course, HND, NVQ
Contact: Peter Grover
Subject Leader
0114 225 2306
education@shu.ac.uk

BSc/BSc (Hons) Secondary Education (Mathematics) XG11

3 years full-time

Mathematics; education; applied mathematics; teaching skills.

Successful completion of this course leads to a recommendation for Qualified Teacher Status (QTS) after completion of skills tests.

Entry requirements: Tariff: 140, Foundation / access qualification
Contact: Sue Elliott
Senior Lecturer
0114 225 2306
education@shu.ac.uk

BSc/BSc (Hons) Secondary Education (Mathematics) XG1C

2 years full-time
1 year of mathematics, followed by 1 year (school-based) of applied mathematics; education; classroom and teaching skills.

Successful completion of this course leads to a recommendation for Qualified Teacher Status (QTS) after completion of skills tests.

Entry requirements: CATS points: 120, HND
Contact: Mr John Routledge
Subject Leader
0114 225 2306
education@shu.ac.uk

BSc/BSc (Hons) Secondary Education (Science) X1F0

2 years full-time

Year 1: Science subjects (chemistry, physics, biology).

Year 2: School-based professional year with education; applied science; education and teaching skills.

Successful completion of this course leads to a recommendation for Qualified Teacher Status (QTS) after completion of skills tests.

Entry requirements: Tariff: 160, Credits from The Open University, HND, HNC, International Baccalaureate, SCE Higher
Contact: Mr Ken Mannion
Subject Leader
0114 225 2603
education@shu.ac.uk

BSc/BSc (Hons) Secondary Education (Science) XFC0

3 years full-time

Units in science (biology, chemistry, physics); education; subject application; teaching skills.

Successful completion of this course leads to a recommendation for Qualified Teacher Status (QTS) after completion of skills tests.

Entry requirements: Tariff: 160, Irish Leaving Certificates: BBBB, Credits from The Open University, International Baccalaureate, Mature entry, SCE Higher
Contact: Mr Terry Hudson
Subject Leader
0114 225 2306
education@shu.ac.uk

PGCE Early Years Education (3–7) X121

1 year full-time

Entry requirements: Degree awarded by a British university or equivalent; GCSE grade C or above (or equivalent qualifications) in English language, mathematics and science. Previous education should provide the necessary foundation for work as a teacher in the subject(s) that are to be taught.

Contact: Customer Services
0114 225 2306
education@shu.ac.uk

PGCE Post-Compulsory Education and Training X341

1 or 2 years part-time

Entry requirements: Degree or equivalent, part-time course is an in-service programme for those already teaching 100 hours or more in each of the 2 years of the programme; interview.

Contact: Pat Smith
Course Leader
0114 225 2306
education@shu.ac.uk

PGCE Primary Education (5–11) X100

Variable or 1 year full-time or 18 months part-time

Entry requirements: Degree in relevant subject, generally 1st or 2nd Class; GCSE grade C (or equivalent) in English language and mathematics.

Contact: Graham Peacock
Course Leader, Part Time PGCE
0114 225 2306
education@shu.ac.uk

PGCE Secondary Education (Business Education) N1X1

Variable or 1 year full-time

Entry requirements: UK university degree in a subject relevant to business education, and GCSE grade C or above (or equivalent) in mathematics and English language.

Contact: Mr Herb Gray
Admissions Tutor
0114 225 2295/2306
education@shu.ac.uk

PGCE Secondary Education (Design and Technology) W9X1

Variable or 1 year full-time

Entry requirements: UK university degree; substantial experience relevant to the area of technology in the National Curriculum in the subject they intend to teach; GCSE at grade C or above (or equivalent) in mathematics and English language.

Contact: Peter Grover
Admissions Tutor
0114 225 2306
education@shu.ac.uk

PGCE Secondary Education (Design and Technology, conversion) WXX1

2 years full-time

Entry requirements: Degree awarded by a British university, or recognised equivalent, and GCSE grade C or above (or equivalent) in English language and mathematics. This 2-year PGCE course is aimed at graduates whose previous qualifications and experience are related to design and technology but who lack elements needed for entry to (standard) 1-year PGCE course.

Contact: As above

PGCE Secondary Education (English) Q3X1

Variable or 1 year full-time

Entry requirements: UK university degree or equivalent in the subject they intend to teach; GCSE grade C or above (or equivalent) in mathematics and in English language.

Contact: Paul Dickinson
Senior Lecturer, English Centre
0114 225 2306
education@shu.ac.uk

PGCE Secondary Education (Information and Communications Technology) G5X1

Variable or 1 year full-time

Entry requirements: Relevant degree and GCSE mathematics and English language at grade C or above, or equivalent qualifications.

Contact: John Chatterton
Senior Lecturer, Education and Foundation Studies Centre
0114 225 2306
education@shu.ac.uk

PGCE Secondary Education (Mathematics) G1X1

Variable or 1 year full-time

Entry requirements: UK university degree or equivalent in mathematics or equally appropriate subject, together with GCSE at grade C or above or equivalent in mathematics and English language.

Contact: Jim Smith
Admissions Tutor
0114 225 2306
education@shu.ac.uk

PGCE Secondary Education (Mathematics, conversion) GXC1

2 years full-time

Entry requirements: The course is designed for graduates in subjects other than mathematics. Applicants must have passes at GCSE grade C or above (or equivalent) in English and mathematics. Prospective candidates will be expected to have continued their study of mathematics to A-level. They must have the equivalent of 1 year of mathematical study at degree level.

Contact: Hilary Povey
Admissions Tutor, Assistant Director
0114 225 2306
education@shu.ac.uk

PGCE Secondary Education (Modern Foreign Languages) R9X1

Variable or 1 year full-time

Entry requirements: UK university degree or equivalent in the language(s) they intend to teach (choice from: French, German, Spanish) and GCSE at grade C or above (or equivalent) in mathematics and English language.

Contact: Mr Chris Willan
Admissions Tutor, Senior Lecturer, Education and Foundation Studies Centre
0114 225 2306
education@shu.ac.uk

PGCE Secondary Education (Modern Foreign Languages, conversion) RXX1

2 years full-time

Entry requirements: UK University degree or equivalent required, and GCSE grade C or above in English language and mathematics. Applicants will be expected to have an A-level pass in their main language (French or German or Spanish) and be able to produce evidence of continued study of that language to a high level, either for their degree or as a substantial part of their degree work. Applicants with alternative proof of linguistic competence (e.g., those who have lived abroad or foreign nationals) may be considered. No previous experience is expected in the 2nd language.

Contact: As above

PGCE Secondary Education (Religious Education) V6X1

Variable or 1 year full-time

Entry requirements: Degree or equivalent, plus GCSE (or equivalent) at grade C or above in mathematics and English language; the degree should be appropriate to religious education.

Contact: Liz Dwyer
Admissions Tutor
0114 225 2306
education@shu.ac.uk

PGCE Secondary Education (Science: Biology, Chemistry, Physics) F0X1

Variable or 1 year full-time

Entry requirements: UK university degree (or equivalent) in science and GCSE at grade C or above (or equivalent) in mathematics and English language.

Contact: John Wardle
Senior Lecturer
0114 225 2306
education@shu.ac.uk

PGCE Secondary Education (Science: Biology, Chemistry, Physics, conversion) FXA1

2 years full-time

Entry requirements: GCSE passes at grade C or above (or equivalent) mathematics and English.

Contact: As above

PgCert/PgDip/MA in Early Childhood Studies

1 year full-time, 1–6 years part-time

Entry requirements: Degree or Certificate in education; some relevant professional experience.

Contact: Ross Garrick
0114 225 2306
education@shu.ac.uk

PgCert/PgDip/MA in Education

1 year full-time, 3–6 years part-time

Entry requirements: Degree or Certificate in education and some relevant professional experience.

Contact: Reg Tooth
Programme Co-ordinator
0114 225 2278/2306
education@shu.ac.uk

EdD in Education (Professional Leadership)

Part-time

Entry requirements: Applicants normally have a Master's degree and are experienced professionals who work in an education or training context.

Contact: Customer Services
0114 225 2306
education@shu.ac.uk

PgCert/PgDip/MA in Education of Children and Young People with Autism

PgCert: 15 months part-time, PgDip 2 years part-time

Entry requirements: Applicants are normally qualified teachers with an interest in the field of autism or graduates in a related field.

Contact: Nick Hodge
Senior Lecturer in Education,
Foundation Study Centre
0114 225 5645/2306
education@shu.ac.uk

PgCert/PgDip/MA in Further and Higher Education

1 year full-time, 3–6 years part-time

Entry requirements: Normally, degree or certificate in education required, and some relevant professional experience.

Contact: Jacquie Daniels
Senior Lecturer in CPD Centre,
FHE Area Co-ordinator
0114 225 2306
education@shu.ac.uk

PgCert/PgDip/MSc in Information Communication Technology in Education

1 year full-time, 1–6 years part-time

Entry requirements: Degree or certificate in education; some relevant professional experience.

Contact: John Chatterton
0114 225 2306
education@shu.ac.uk

PgCert/PgDip/MA in Language and Literacy

1 year full-time, 3–6 years part-time

Entry requirements: Degree plus relevant experience normally required; non-graduates will also be considered, on basis of qualifications and experience.

Contact: Guy Merchant
Area Co-ordinator, Senior
Lecturer, English Centre
0114 225 2306
education@shu.ac.uk

PgCert/PgDip/MSc in Leadership and Management in Education

1 year full-time, 3–6 years part-time

Entry requirements: Degree plus relevant management experience normally required; non-graduates will also be considered, on basis of qualifications and experience.

Contact: Kath Aspinwall
Subject Leader
0114 225 2306
education@shu.ac.uk

PgCert in Managing Study Support

1 year full-time, 1–6 years part-time

Entry requirements: Degree or Certificate in education; some relevant professional experience.

Contact: Customer services
School of Education
0114 225 2306
education@shu.ac.uk

PgCert/PgDip/MSc in Mathematics Education

1 year full-time, 3–6 years part-time

Entry requirements: Degree or Certificate in education, and some relevant professional experience.

Contact: Tansy Hardy
Area Co-ordinator
0114 225 2306
education@shu.ac.uk

PgCert/PgDip/MSc in Multimedia Education and Consulting

1 year full-time, 3 years part-time

Entry requirements: Normally a degree or equivalent in education, computer science or closely related field or degree in any subject area together with relevant experience in teaching, training, digital media production or consultancy; access to on-line facilities; internet skills, web searching skills and independent study skills.

Contact: Brian Hudson
0114 225 2306
education@shu.ac.uk

PgCert/PgDip/MA in Professional Development and Training

1 year full-time, 3–6 years part-time

Entry requirements: Degree plus relevant experience normally required; non-graduates will also be considered, on basis of qualifications and experience.

Contact: John Williams
Senior Lecturer, CPD Centre
0114 225 2306
education@shu.ac.uk

PgCert in Quality and Management in Education

1 year full-time, 1–6 years part-time

Entry requirements: Degree or certificate in education; some relevant personal experience.

Contact: Sean Cavan
0114 225 2306
education@shu.ac.uk

PgCert/PgDip/MSc in Science Education

1 year full-time, 3–6 years part-time

Entry requirements: Degree or Certificate in education, and some relevant professional experience.

Contact: Mick Nott
0114 225 2306
education@shu.ac.uk

PgCert/PgDip/MA in Special Educational Needs

2.5 years part-time

Entry requirements: Normally, a degree, professional experience of working with any age, phase of education, or special educational needs children and/or young people .

Contact: John Stirton
SEN Area Co-ordinator
0114 225 2306
education@shu.ac.uk

PgCert in Subject Leadership

1 year full-time, 1–6 years part-time

Entry requirements: Degree or certificate in education; some relevant professional experience.

Contact: Guy Merchant
0114 225 2306
education@shu.ac.uk

PgCert/PgDip/MA in Teaching English to Speakers of Other Languages (TESOL)

PgCert: 48 weeks distance learning. PgDip: 2–3 years distance learning or part-time. MA: 2–3 years distance learning or part-time

Entry requirements: Vary according to level

Contact: Customer Services
0114 225 2240
tesol@shu.ac.uk

University of Sheffield

Western Bank
Sheffield
S10 2TN
Tel: 0114 222 2000
Fax: 0114 222 1415
ug-admissions@shef.ac.uk
www.shef.ac.uk

Based on the Western Bank Campus half a mile from the city centre the University of Sheffield developed from three local institutions: the Sheffield School of Medicine, Firth College and the Sheffield Technical School. It was granted university status in 1905 and there are now around 16,500 full-time students at the university, and a further 4,000 students studying part-time.

The School of Education is based in the department of Social Sciences and offers a diverse selection of courses from higher degrees to taught and research postgraduate programmes. The initial teacher education programme offers a secondary PGCE course but not a primary one.

There is a main library as well as several specialised libraries on campus. There are also extensive computer facilities available based in staffed IT centres around the campus and computer rooms. There are halls of residence and self-catering accommodation available with some reserved specifically for postgraduates and mature students.

HOW TO APPLY

PGCE: applications made through the GTTR.

Postgraduate: applications are made direct to the institution.

COURSES

PGCE in Secondary Education (English) Q3X1

1 year full-time

Entry requirements: Degree or equivalent in English or with a strong element of English. GCSE grade C or equivalent in English language and mathematics.
Contact: Ann Whorton
0114 222 8081
ite@sheffield.ac.uk

PGCE in Secondary Education (French with German) RX11

1 year full-time

Entry requirements: Degree or equivalent in French or German or with a strong element of French/German. GCSE grade C or equivalent in English language and mathematics.
Contact: As above

PGCE in Secondary Education (French with Russian) RXC1

1 year full-time

Entry requirements: Degree or equivalent in French/Russian or with a strong element of French/Russian. GCSE grade C or equivalent in English language and mathematics.
Contact: As above

PGCE in Secondary Education (French with Spanish) RXD1

1 year full-time

Entry requirements: Degree or equivalent in French/Spanish or with a strong element of French/Spanish. GCSE grade C or equivalent in English language and mathematics.
Contact: As above

PGCE in Secondary Education (French) R1X1

1 year full-time

Entry requirements: Degree or equivalent in French or with a strong element of French. GCSE grade C or equivalent in English language and mathematics.
Contact: As above

PGCE in Secondary Education (Geography) F8X1

1 year full-time

Entry requirements: Degree or equivalent in Geography or with a strong element of Geography. GCSE grade C or equivalent in English language and mathematics.
Contact: As above

PGCE in Secondary Education (German with French) RX21

1 year full-time

Entry requirements: Degree or equivalent in German/French or with a strong element of German/French. GCSE grade C or equivalent in English language and mathematics.
Contact: As above

PGCE in Secondary Education (German with Russian) RXFD

1 year full-time

Entry requirements: Degree or equivalent in German/Russian or with a strong element of German/Russian. GCSE grade C or equivalent in English language and mathematics.
Contact: As above

PGCE in Secondary Education (German with Spanish) RX2C

1 year full-time

Entry requirements: Degree or equivalent in German/Spanish or with a strong element of German/Spanish. GCSE grade C or equivalent in English language and mathematics.
Contact: As above

PGCE in Secondary Education (German) R2X1

1 year full-time

Entry requirements: Degree or equivalent in German or with a strong element of German; GCSE grade C or equivalent in English language and mathematics.
Contact: As above

PGCE in Secondary Education (History) V1X1

1 year full-time

Entry requirements: Degree or equivalent in History or with a strong element of History. GCSE grade C or equivalent in English language and mathematics.
Contact: As above

PGCE in Secondary Education (Mathematics) G1X1

1 year full-time

Entry requirements: Degree or equivalent in mathematics or with a strong element of mathematics. GCSE grade C or equivalent in English language and mathematics.
Contact: As above

PGCE in Secondary Education (Science) F0X1

1 year full-time

Entry requirements: Degree or equivalent in a teaching subject or with a strong element of a teaching subject. GCSE grade C or equivalent in English language and mathematics.
Contact: As above

PGCE in Secondary Education (Spanish with French) RX41

1 year full-time
As above

Entry requirements: Degree or equivalent in Spanish/French or with a strong element of Spanish/French. GCSE grade C or equivalent in English language and mathematics.
Contact: As above

PGCE in Secondary Education (Spanish with German) RX4C

1 year full-time
As above

MA in E-Learning

24–48 months distance learning

Entry requirements: Degree or equivalent professional experience.
Contact: Carole Worboys
CPD Courses Administrator
0114 222 8127
cpd@sheffield.ac.uk

MA in Early Childhood Education

2–4 years distance learning

Entry requirements: Degree and teaching qualification or Advanced Diploma in Educational Studies plus 4 years' teaching experience.
Contact: As above

MA in Education (Policy and Practice)

12 months full-time

Entry requirements: Degree and teaching qualification or BEd and 2 years' teaching or other relevant experience; advanced diploma in educational studies and at least 4 years' teaching or other relevant experience. Candidates with other relevant training and experience are welcome to apply.
Contact: As above

MEd Educational Management

2–4 years part-time

Entry requirements: Upper 2nd class degree or advanced qualification in education.
Contact: As above

MEd in English Language Teaching

2–4 years distance learning

Entry requirements: Degree and teaching qualification or Advanced Diploma in Educational Studies plus 4 years' teaching experience.
Contact: As above

MEd in Inclusive Education

2–4 years distance learning

Entry requirements: Degree and teaching qualification, or BEd and 2 years' teaching experience, or Advanced Diploma in Educational Studies plus 4 years' teaching experience.
Contact: As above

MEd in Literacy

24–72 months part-time

Entry requirements: Graduate, qualified teacher with at least 2 years' service, plus English language qualification of at least IELTS 6.0 or TOEFL 550.
Contact: As above

MEd in E-learning

2 years distance learning

Entry requirements: Degree or equivalent professional qualification. Students need a PC or MAC computer, a printer, access to the Internet and an email address.
Contact: As above

EdD in Education

Part-time

Entry requirements: Students come from a wide range of backgrounds including: nursery, primary and secondary schools, further and higher education institutions, social and welfare work, healthcare education and clinical practitioners, trades and business training organisations. The majority are in middle and senior managerial level positions.
Contact: Sheila Melbourne
Course Secretary
0114 222 8096
s.melbourne@sheffield.ac.uk

Shire Foundation

Luton Learning Resource Centre
Strangers Way
Luton
LU4 9ND
Tel: 01582 538228
Fax: 01582 538206
mcfarlaneg@luton.gov.uk

The Shire Foundation offers school-centred training in a consortium of Luton schools. Trainees are based in one of the schools but have teaching practices in other schools during training. The course is accredited by the Teacher Training Agency and on successful completion of the course students will be awarded Qualified Teacher Status and the Post Graduate Certificate in Education through the University of Luton.

Trainees are allocated a base school and trainees have the opportunity to visit other schools and LEA resource centres. Teaching practice takes place in at least two of the consortium or associate schools. Trainees are registered at the University of Luton and lectures, tutorials and workshops take place there or at the LLRC in Luton. Accommodation can be arranged through the university.

The Shire base is effectively sited at the local teachers' centre for Luton and therefore offers excellent resources support to trainees. Students have access to study facilities at the Shire central bases and the LEA's ICT facility suite.

HOW TO APPLY

Applications are made through the GTTR.

COURSES

PGCE Primary Education (General Primary, 3–11 years) X100
1 year full-time

Entry requirements: Relevant degree; GCSE grade C or above in English language and mathematics.

Contact: Jane Morrissey
Administrator
01582 538228
morriseyj@luton.gov.uk

Somerset Teacher Education Programme

Education Development Service
The Holway Centre
Keats Road
Taunton
Somerset
TA1 2JB
Tel: 01823 349306
Fax: 01823 349301
SCITT@somerset.gov.uk

The Somerset Teacher Education Programme is a school-based course leading to Qualified Teacher Status with the PGCE awarded by the University College Worcester. It consists of 25 local primary schools working in partnership with University College Worcester and Somerset LEA.

Trainees spend over 60% of the 38-week course in schools. Each trainee will have a school-based tutor from the first teaching practice school, and a course tutor chosen from the advisers and lecturers involved in delivering the theoretical aspects of the course. The individual schools provide the majority of facilities and resources needed and library access, study facilities and IT facilities are provided through the Education Development Service in Taunton, the main training centre for Somerset LEA.

HOW TO APPLY

Applications are made through the GTTR.

COURSES

PGCE Primary Education (5–11 years) X100
38 weeks full-time

Entry requirements: Relevant degree; GCSE grade C or above in English language and mathematics, and science if born after 1/Sep/79.

Contact: Tony Whiteley
Course Manager
01823 349306
SCITT@somerset.gov.uk

South Bank University

103 Borough Road
Southwark
London
SE1 0AA
Tel: 020 7928 8989
Fax: 020 7815 8273
enrol@sbu.ac.uk
www.sbu.ac.uk

South Bank University caters for over 17,000 students and is based on three campuses in the London area and one in Essex. Southwark is the main campus and the Perry Library and Learning Resources Centre are located there. Wandsworth Campus is the location of the Faculty of the Built Environment and is three miles away from the main campus. The Essex campus is based on two hospital sites in Essex and East London. Both the Wandsworth and Essex campuses have their own libraries and facilities. University residences are available within a ten-minute walk of the main campus or there is the option of privately rented accommodation.

The Division of Education offers the PGCE at primary level, Graduate and Registered Teacher Programmes and a route to Qualified Teacher Status for overseas trained teachers.

HOW TO APPLY

PGCE: applications are made through the GTTR.

Postgraduate: applications are made direct to the institution.

COURSES

PGCE Primary Education (Early Years, 3–7, Foundation and Key Stage 1) X110

1 year full-time

Entry requirements: Good Honours degree in subject relevant to the primary curriculum including GCSE grade C or above (or equivalent) in English language and mathematics; candidates born after 1/9/79 also need GCSE grade C or above in science subject or subjects.

Contact: Admissions Office
020 7815 7815

PGCE Primary Education (General Primary, 5–11) X100

1 year full-time, 2 years variable, part-time
As above

South London Teacher Training

C/o Haberdashers' Aske's Hatcham College
Pepys Road
New Cross
Lewisham
London
SE14 5SF
Tel: 020 7652 9500
Fax: 020 7252 9531
sltt@hahc.org.uk
www.hahc.org.uk/SLTT/SLTT.htm

South London Teacher Training offers School Centred Initial Teacher Training for graduates. Successful trainees are awarded Qualified Teacher Status and the Postgraduate Certificate of Education validated by the Open University. Training is offered for the 11–19 age group in three subjects; English, Sciences (Biology, Chemistry, Physics or Combined Science) or Modern Foreign Languages (French, German or Spanish with a subsidiary in Italian or Russian).

Haberdashers' Aske's Hatcham College is used as the base for trainees and provides study facilities and a common room. There are ten other schools in the consortium all within a five mile range of the college. Teaching practice takes place in two of the schools but trainees are given the opportunity to experience each of the other schools.

HOW TO APPLY

Applications are made direct to the institution.

COURSES

PGCE Secondary Education (English)

37 weeks full-time

Entry requirements: Degree in relevant subject; GCSE grade C or above in English language and mathematics, and science if born after 1/9/79; recent experience with children in primary school.

Contact: Enquiries
020 7652 9500
sltt@hahc.org.uk

PGCE Secondary Education (Modern Foreign Languages)
37 weeks full-time
As above

PGCE Secondary Education (Science)
37 weeks full-time

Entry requirements: As above
Contact: Enquiries
020 7652 9500
sc-clarke@hahc.org.uk

South West Teacher Training

West Exe Technology College
Hatherleigh Road
Exeter
Devon
EX2 9JU
Tel: 01392 686165
Fax: 01392 686165
swtt@westexetc.devon.sch.uk
www.swtt.net

The South West School Centred Initial Teacher Training programme was initiated in 1993. It specialises in training teachers in Design and Technology, Information Technology, French, German and Science for the age range 11–19.

HOW TO APPLY

Applications are made through the GTTR.

COURSES

PGCE Secondary Education (Design and Technology) W9X1
40 weeks full-time

Entry requirements: Degree in engineering, science (especially physics), design (especially industrial or commercial design) or technology; GCSE grade C or above in English language and mathematics, and science if born after 1/9/79.
Contact: Enquiries
01392 686165
swtt@westexetc.devon.sch.uk

PGCE Secondary Education (Information and Communication Technology) G5X1
40 weeks full-time

Entry requirements: Relevant degree; GCSE grade C or above in English language and mathematics, and science if born after 1/9/79.
Contact: As above

PGCE Secondary Education (Modern Languages: French) R1X1
40 weeks full-time

Entry requirements: Degree in French; GCSE grade C or above in English language and mathematics, and science if born after 1/9/79.
Contact: As above

PGCE Secondary Education (Modern Languages: German) R2X1
40 weeks full-time

Entry requirements: Degree in German; GCSE grade C or above in English language and mathematics, and science if born after 1/9/79.
Contact: As above

PGCE Secondary Education (Science) F0X1
40 weeks full-time

Entry requirements: Degree in relevant science-related area; GCSE grade C or above in English language and mathematics, and science if born after 1/9/79.
Contact: As above

University of Southampton

Highfield
Southampton
SO17 1BJ
Tel: 023 8059 5000
Fax: 023 8059 3037
educate@soton.ac.uk
www.soton.ac.uk

The University of Southampton is a multi-campus university with teaching and research facilities spread over campuses in Southampton and Winchester. These are Avenue Campus, Boldrewood, Highfield Campus, New College, Southampton Oceanography Centre, Winchester School of Art and Southampton General Hospital. It was granted University status in 1952 and now has around 19,000 students.

The School of Education is based in the Faculty of Social Sciences on the Highfield Campus. In addition to the PGCE in primary and secondary education, the School offers undergraduate programmes for teachers and trainers in the post-compulsory sector. Advanced programmes including Master's and research degrees span a broad range.

The university has extensive library services and is well equipped with computer facilities. There is a wide range of accommodation available for undergraduates and postgraduates and first-year students are guaranteed a place. The majority of the halls of residence are within a ten-minute walk of Highfield. There is also private accommodation in Portswood, which is also near to Highfield.

HOW TO APPLY

PGCE: applications made through the GTTR.

Postgraduate: applications are made direct to the institution.

COURSES

PGCE in Primary Education (General Primary) X100

1 year full-time

Entry requirements: Degree required and GCSE grade C or above (or equivalent) in English language, mathematics and science.

Contact: Claire Mooney
ITE Office, Research and
Graduate School of Education
023 8059 2413
pgceite@soton.ac.uk

PGCE in Secondary Education (Biology and Science) C1X1

1 year full-time

Entry requirements: Degree in a subject appropriate to the subjects to be taught, and GCSE grade C or above (or equivalent) in mathematics and English language.

Contact: Mr Patrick Fullick
ITE Office, Research and
Graduate School of Education
023 8059 2413
pgceite@soton.ac.uk

PGCE in Secondary Education (Chemistry and Science) F1X1

1 year full-time
As above

PGCE in Secondary Education (English) Q3X1

1 year full-time

Entry requirements: As above

Contact: Ms Kate Domaille
ITE Office, Research and
Graduate School of Education
023 8059 2413
pgceite@soton.ac.uk

PGCE in Secondary Education (Geography) F8X1

1 year full-time

Entry requirements: As above

Contact: Prof Nick Foskett
ITE Office, Research and
Graduate School of Education
023 8059 2413
pgceite@soton.ac.uk

PGCE in Secondary Education (History) V1X1

1 year full-time

Entry requirements: As above

Contact: Mr Richard Harris
ITE Office, Research and
Graduate School of Education
023 8059 2413
pgceite@soton.ac.uk

PGCE in Secondary Education (Information Technology) G5X1

1 year full-time

Entry requirements: As above

Contact: Mr John Woollard
ITE Office, Research and
Graduate School of Education
023 8059 2413
pgceite@soton.ac.uk

PGCE in Secondary Education (Mathematics) G1X1

1 year full-time

Entry requirements: As above

Contact: Mr Keith Jones
ITE Office, Research and
Graduate School of Education
023 8059 2413
pgceite@soton.ac.uk

PGCE in Secondary Education (Modern Languages: French) R1X1

1 year full-time

Entry requirements: As above

Contact: Mr Mike Smith
ITE Office, Research and
Graduate School of Education
023 8059 2413
pgceite@soton.ac.uk

PGCE in Secondary Education (Modern Languages: German) R2X1

1 year full-time

Entry requirements: A degree in a subject appropriate to the subjects to be taught, and GCSE grade C or above (or equivalent) in mathematics and English language, and A-level German or equivalent.

Contact: As above

PGCE in Secondary Education (Modern Languages: Spanish) R4X1

1 year full-time

Entry requirements: A degree in a subject appropriate to the subjects to be taught, and GCSE grade C or above (or equivalent) in mathematics and English language, and A-level Spanish or equivalent

Contact: As above

PGCE in Secondary Education (Music) W3X1

1 year full-time

Entry requirements: A degree in a subject appropriate to the subjects to be taught, and GCSE grade C or above (or equivalent) in mathematics and English language.

Contact: Rebecca Berkley
ITE Office, Research and
Graduate School of Education
023 8059 2413
pgceite@soton.ac.uk

PGCE in Secondary Education (Physical Education) X9C6

1 year full-time

Entry requirements: As above

Contact: Dr Gary Kinchin
ITE Office, Research and
Graduate School of Education
023 8059 2413
pgceite@soton.ac.uk

PGCE in Secondary Education (Physics and Science) F3X1

1 year full-time

Entry requirements: As above

Contact: Mr Patrick Fullick
ITE Office, Research and
Graduate School of Education
023 8059 2413
pgceite@soton.ac.uk

PGCE in Secondary Education (Religious Education) V6X1

1 year full-time

Entry requirements: Good degree in religious studies or theology; degrees in other subjects may be acceptable with evidence of the study of religion or religions.

Contact: Ms Sam Jordan
023 8059 2413
pgceite@soton.ac.uk

MA in Applied Linguistics for Language Teaching

1 year full-time

Entry requirements: Good degree and 2 years' language teaching or related experience.

Contact: Prof Ros Michell
Masters Admissions Secretary
023 8059 3476
rgseaco@soton.ac.uk

MSc (Ed) Biology Education

1 year full-time, 2 years part-time

Entry requirements: Recognised professional qualification and minimum 2 years' post-qualifying experience required.

Contact: Dr Mary Ratcliffe
Masters Admissions Secretary
023 8059 3476
rgseaco@soton.ac.uk

MSc in Computer-Based Learning and Training

1 year full-time, 2 years part-time

Entry requirements: Good Honours degree required and adequate professional experience.

Contact: John Woollard
Masters Admissions Secretary
023 8059 3476
rgseaco@soton.ac.uk

EdD in Education

3 years full-time, 4 years part-time

Entry requirements: Normally, Master's degree plus appropriate professional experience.

Contact: Michael Erben
Masters Admissions Secretary
023 8059 3476
rgseaco@soton.ac.uk

MA in English Language Teaching

1 year full-time, 2 years part-time

Entry requirements: Degree or equivalent plus minimum 2 years' relevant professional experience.

Contact: Prof Ros Michell
Masters Admissions Secretary
023 8059 3476
rgseaco@soton.ac.uk

MSc (Ed) in Environmental Sciences Education

1 year full-time, 2 years part-time

Entry requirements: Good Honours degree, recognised professional qualification and minimum 5 years' post-qualifying experience.

Contact: Prof Nick Foskett
Masters Admissions Secretary
023 8059 2763
rgseaco@soton.ac.uk

MSc (Ed) in Geography Education

1 year full-time

Entry requirements: Recognised professional qualification and minimum 5 years' post-qualifying experience.

Contact: As above

MA (Ed) in Geography Education/Environmental Education

1 year full-time, 2 years part-time

Entry requirements: Degree or equivalent required, plus minimum 2 years' relevant professional experience.

Contact: As above

MA (Ed) in Institutional and Professional Development

1 year full-time, 2 years part-time

Entry requirements: As above

Contact: Dr Gill Clarke
Master's Admissions Secretary
023 8059 3476
rgseaco@soton.ac.uk

MA (Ed) in Management and Professional Studies Education

1 year full-time, 2 years part-time

Entry requirements: Good Honours degree, recognised professional qualification and minimum 3 years' post-qualification experience.

Contact: Dr Terry Martin
Master's Admissions Secretary
023 8059 3476
rgseaco@soton.ac.uk

MA (Ed) in Mathematics Education

1 year full-time, 2 years part-time

Entry requirements: Degree or equivalent required and practical experience in education or related professional field.

Contact: Dr Keith Jones
Master's Admissions Secretary
023 8059 3476
rgseaco@soton.ac.uk

MA (Ed) in Physical Education

1 year full-time, 2 years part-time

Entry requirements: Good Honours degree, recognised professional qualification and minimum 3 years' post-qualifying experience.

Contact: Dr Gill Clarke
Master's Admissions Secretary
023 8059 3476
rgseaco@soton.ac.uk

MSc (Ed) Physics/Chemistry Education

1 year full-time, 2 years part-time

Entry requirements: Recognised professional qualification and minimum 5 years' post-qualifying experience.

Contact: Dr Mary Ratcliffe
Master's Admissions Secretary
023 8059 3476
rgseaco@soton.ac.uk

MA (Ed) in Science and Technology Education

1 year full-time, 2 years part-time

Entry requirements: Good Honours degree, recognised professional qualification and minimum 3 years' post-qualifying experience.

Contact: As above

MSc in Specific Learning Difficulties (Dyslexia)

1 year full-time, 2 years part-time

Entry requirements: Applicants will normally have a background in teaching or relevant, related experience in an educational setting such as speech and language therapy or educational psychology.

Contact: Geraldine Price
023 8059 3476
rgseaco@soton.ac.uk

College of St Mark and St John

Derriford Road
Plymouth
PL6 8BH
Tel: 01752 636700
Fax: 01752 636819
admissions@marjon.ac.uk
www.marjon.ac.uk

The College of St Mark and St John is situated a short distance from Plymouth. It is a Church of England voluntary college, and its constituent colleges, St John's, Battersea and St Mark's, Chelsea, date back to the 1840s. The College of St Mark and St John moved from London to Plymouth in 1973. Since 1991, it has been affiliated to the University of Exeter, which accredits it to run undergraduate and postgraduate programmes.

The College has an academic community of approximately 5,000 people. It is based on a single campus, which has academic areas, accommodation for more than 500 students, sports facilities, library, computing facilities, bars, dining areas and shops all on one site. The campus gives access to the Cornwall and Devon coast and Dartmoor National Park, as well as to the city of Plymouth.

In addition to primary and secondary Initial Teacher Training, the Faculty of Education, Sport and Technology offers courses in continuing professional development for teachers. The International Education Centre provides in-service development and postgraduate courses for English language teachers and trainers.

HOW TO APPLY

Degree courses: applications are made through UCAS.

PGCE: applications are made through the GTTR.

Postgraduate: applications are made direct to the institution.

COURSES

BEd (Hons) in Primary Education X120

4 years full-time

General primary course; students focus on either Foundation Stage and Key Stage 1, working with children aged 3–8 or Key Stage 1 and Key Stage 2, working with children aged 5–11.

Successful completion of this course leads to a recommendation for Qualified Teacher Status (QTS) on completion of skills tests.

Entry requirements: Tariff: 120 points, BTEC NC/ND, SCE Higher: CCCC, International Baccalaureate, Irish Leaving Certificates

Contact: Mr Tony Brown
01752 636700 x3132

BEd (Hons) in Primary Education (Art and Design) X1WG

2 years full-time

Entry requirements: Overseas students only. International teaching qualification with 3 years' teaching experience.

Contact: Admissions Office
01752 636827
admissions@marjon.ac.uk

BEd (Hons) in Secondary Education (Design and Technology) X1W2

4 years full-time

Professional Education: Understanding how teachers teach, how schools operate, how children learn and equally important, why some do not learn. Wide range of practical and intellectual activities including observing practice in schools and talking to teachers in their own classrooms and at Marjon. Lectures; seminars; films; conferences; collaborative group projects. Students undertake the bulk of their college-based professional work in their well-equipped specialist subject areas.

School Experience: Students begin with day visits and gradually take more responsibility for the pupil's learning. Each year of the course gives regular experience of working in schools and contains blocks of full-time teaching practice. In the final year a full term is spent working in schools.

Subject Specialism: Courses in design and technology in each year of the course.

Successful completion of this course leads to a recommendation for Qualified Teacher Status (QTS) on completion of skills tests.

Entry requirements: Tariff: 80 points, BTEC NC/ND, International Baccalaureate, Irish Leaving Certificates

Contact: As above

BEd (Hons) in Secondary Education (Design and Technology) X1WF

2 years full-time

Entry requirements: Overseas students only. International teaching qualification with 3 years' teaching experience.

Contact: As above

BEd in Secondary Education (Design and Technology) XW12

2 years full-time

4 areas covered in both years of the course are: subject studies: product design; engineering; silversmithing; jewellery; welding fabrication; casting; ceramics; photography; graphics; polymer technology; electronics; computer numerical control; computer-aided design. Professional studies: preparation of materials, planning lessons, studying ways in which teachers and pupils communicate, learning how teachers work together, and how to monitor teaching; educational studies; school experience.

Successful completion of this course leads to a recommendation for Qualified Teacher Status (QTS) on completion of skills tests.

Entry requirements: Age restriction: 21 or over, AVCEs, BTEC NC/ND, DipHE, GCE A- and AS-levels, International Baccalaureate, Irish Leaving Certificates, Work experience
Contact: As above

BEd in Secondary Education (Mathematics with Information Technology) XG11

2 years full-time

4 areas covered in both years of the course are: subject studies: shape and number; statistical analytical methods; techniques of mathematical modelling; analysis; options. Professional studies: preparation of materials; lesson planning; studying ways in which teachers and pupils communicate; learning how teachers work together and how to monitor your teaching. Educational studies; school experience.

Successful completion of this course leads to a recommendation for Qualified Teacher Status (QTS) on completion of skills tests.

Entry requirements: Age restriction: 21 or over, AVCEs, BTEC NC/ND, Credits from The Open University, DipHE, GCE A- and AS-levels, International Baccalaureate, Irish Leaving Certificates, Work experience
Contact: Roger Fentem
01752 636700 x4347

BEd (Hons) in Secondary Education (Mathematics with Physical Education) XGC1

4 years full-time

Professional Education: Understanding how teachers teach, how schools operate, how children learn and equally important, why some do not learn. Wide range of practical and intellectual activities including observing practice in schools and talking to teachers in their own classrooms and at Marjon. Lectures; seminars; films; conferences; collaborative group projects.

Students undertake the bulk of their college-based professional work in their well-equipped specialist subject areas.

School Experience: Students begin with day visits and gradually take more responsibility for the pupil's learning. Each year of the course gives regular experience of working in schools and contains blocks of full-time teaching practice. In the final year a full term is spent working in schools.

Subject Specialism: Courses in design and technology in each year of the course.

Successful completion of this course leads to a recommendation for Qualified Teacher Status (QTS) on completion of skills tests.

Entry requirements: Tariff: 80 points, BTEC NC/ND, SCE Higher: CCCC, International Baccalaureate, Irish Leaving Certificates
Contact: Admissions Office
01752 636827
admissions@marjon.ac.uk

BEd (Hons) in Secondary Education (Mathematics) X1GC

4 years full-time

Professional Education: Understanding how teachers teach, how schools operate, how children learn and equally important, why some do not learn. Wide range of practical and intellectual activities including observing practice in schools and talking to teachers in their own classrooms and at Marjon. Lectures; seminars; films; conferences; collaborative group projects. Students undertake the bulk of their college-based professional work in their well-equipped specialist subject areas.

School Experience: You will begin with day visits and gradually take more responsibility for the pupil's learning. Each year of the course gives regular experience of working in schools and contains blocks of full-time teaching practice. In the final year you spend a full term working in schools.

Subject Specialism: Courses in mathematics in each year of the course.

Successful completion of this course leads to a recommendation for Qualified Teacher Status (QTS) on completion of skills tests.

Entry requirements: Tariff: 80 points, BTEC NC/ND, SCE Higher: CCCC, International Baccalaureate, Irish Leaving Certificates
Contact: As above

BEd (Hons) in Secondary Education (Mathematics) X1GD

2 years full-time

Entry requirements: Overseas students only. International teaching qualification with 3 years' teaching experience.
Contact: As above

BEd (Hons) in Secondary Education (Physical Education) X1XH

4 years full-time

Professional Education: Understanding how teachers teach, how schools operate, how children learn and, equally important, why some do not learn. Wide range of practical and intellectual activities including observing practice in schools and talking to teachers in their own classrooms and at Marjon. Lectures; seminars; films; conferences; collaborative group projects. Students undertake the bulk of their college-based professional work in their well-equipped specialist subject areas.

School Experience: Students begin with day visits and gradually take more responsibility for the pupils' learning. Each year of the course gives regular experience of working in schools and contains blocks of full-time teaching practice. In the final year a full term is spent working in schools.

Subject Specialism: Physical education is studied throughout the 4 years of the course. In years 1 and 2 a supportive subject is followed chosen from: educational information technology; English; geography; history; mathematics; religious studies; science. Successful completion of this course leads to a recommendation for Qualified Teacher Status (QTS) on completion of skills tests.

Entry requirements: Tariff: 120 points, BTEC NC/ND, SCE Higher: CCCC, International Baccalaureate, Irish Leaving Certificates
Contact: Jim Christophers
01752 636700 x3133

BEd (Hons) in Secondary Education (Science) X1FA

2 years full-time

Entry requirements: Overseas students only. International teaching qualification with 3 years' teaching experience.
Contact: Admissions Office
01752 636827
admissions@marjon.ac.uk

PGCE in Primary Education (Lower Primary, 5–8) X121

1 year full-time

Entry requirements: Honours degree of which the chosen curriculum specialism should form a substantial part; GCSE in mathematics and English grade C or above, and science for those born after 1/9/79.
Contact: As above

PGCE in Primary Education (Upper Primary, 7–11) X171

1 year full-time

Entry requirements: As above
Contact: Mr P Foster
01752 636700 x2051

PGCE in Secondary Education (Art) W1X1

1 year full-time

Entry requirements: Approved degree or recognised equivalent (not HNC/HND) in relevant subject; GCSE grade C or above, or equivalent, in mathematics and English language.
Contact: Admissions Office
01752 636827
admissions@marjon.ac.uk

PGCE in Secondary Education (Design and Technology) W9X1

1 year full-time

Entry requirements: As above

Contact: Mr S Gold
Route Leader
01752 636700 x5530

PGCE in Secondary Education (English) Q3X1

1 year full-time

Entry requirements: As above
Contact: Ms M Brown
Route Leader
01752 636700 x6506

PGCE in Secondary Education (Geography with Information Technology) FX8C

1 year full-time
As above

PGCE in Secondary Education (Information Technology) G5X1

1 year full-time

Entry requirements: As above
Contact: Jon Coupland
Route Leader
01752 636700 x4337

PGCE in Secondary Education (Mathematics) G1X1

1 year full-time

Entry requirements: As above
Contact: Mr R Fentem
Route Leader
01752 636700 x4347

PGCE in Secondary Education (Modern Foreign Languages) R9X1

1 year full-time

Entry requirements: As above
Contact: Mr B Lien
Route Leader
01752 636700 x3017

PGCE in Secondary Education (Physical Education) X9C6

1 year full-time

Entry requirements: As above
Contact: Mrs J Arthur
Route Leader
01752 636700 x8703

PGCE in Secondary Education (Religious Education) V6X1

1 year full-time

Entry requirements: As above
Contact: Ms C Bowness
Route Leader
01752 636700 x2016

PGCE in Secondary Education (Science with Biology, Chemistry or Physics) F0X1

1 year full-time

Entry requirements: As above
Contact: Dr B Allmark
PGCE Secondary Course Leader
01752 636700 x5601

PgCert/PgDip/MEd in English Language Teaching in Higher Education

MEd: 1 year full-time, part-time

Entry requirements: Degree, plus 2 years' minimum professional (teaching) experience; IELTS 6.5 for non-native speakers.
Contact: Dr Tony Wright
Course Leader
01752 636821
inted@marjon.ac.uk

PgCert/PgDip/MEd in Professional Development (International)

Part-time

Entry requirements: Degree, plus 2 years' minimum professional (teaching) experience; IELTS 6.5 for non-native English speakers.
Contact: Dr Tony Wright
Course Leader
01752 636821
inted@marjon.ac.uk

MA in Theology (Church School Education/Religious Education)

3 years part-time, 3 years distance learning

Entry requirements: Good Honours degree or equivalent.
Contact: Admissions Office
01752 636827
admissions@marjon.ac.uk

Pgcert/PgDip/MEd in Trainer Development (English Language Teaching)

1 year full-time, part-time

Entry requirements: Degree, plus 2 years' minimum professional (teaching) experi-

ence; IELTS 6.5 for non-native English speakers.

Contact: Dr Tony Wright
Course Leader
01752 636821
inted@marjon.ac.uk

St Martin's College

Bowerham Road
Lancaster
Lancashire
LA1 3JD
Tel: 01524 384384
Fax: 01524 384385
admissions@ucsm.ac.uk
www.ucsm.ac.uk

St Martin's College was founded in 1963 by the Church of England as a College of Education to train teachers. The college now caters for over 10,000 students and has three main campuses in Lancaster, Ambleside, Carlisle and also has sites in Barrow, Whitehaven, Chislehurst and Tower Hamlets. The development of the college has seen a merger with Lakeland College of Nursing and Ambleside's Charlotte Mason College in the 1990s. Shortly afterwards in 1998, the Carlisle campus was opened. The college has expanded and developed and the students have access to a library, audio-visual resource centre, sports facilities and teaching rooms.

The college offers both undergraduate teacher training programmes leading to Qualified Teacher Status and the PGCE at primary and secondary level. There is also a range of in-service and Continuing Professional development courses. Some of the courses are run at more than one university site and all the degree qualifications are awarded by Lancaster University. There are halls of residence on or near each of the main campuses or there is the option of privately rented property.

HOW TO APPLY

Undergraduate courses: applications are made through UCAS.

PGCE: applications are made through the GTTR.

Postgraduate courses: applications are made direct to the institution.

BA (Hons) Advanced Study of Early Years Education (3–11 years) X104 T

3 years full-time

Offered in conjunction with the Urban Learning Foundation, London.

Successful completion of this course leads to a recommendation for Qualified Teacher Status (QTS) after completion of skills tests.

Entry requirements: Tariff: 160
Contact: Admissions
01524 384384
admissions@ucsm.ac.uk

BA (Hons) Advanced Study of Early Years Education (3–8 years) X101 C

3 years full-time

General primary teaching course with special option in the teaching of early years (ages 3–8).

Entry requirements: As above
Contact: Fran Dale
01228 616202

BSc (Hons) Advanced Study of Early Years Education (3–8 years) X121 A

3 years full-time
As above

Entry requirements: As above
Contact: Margaret Hartley
01539 430211

BA (Hons) Drama Education (5–11 years) X1WL A

3 years full-time

General primary teaching course with specialist study in drama; specialist modules: drama and text for the curriculum; the roots of drama; working in role; study of drama application ; drama and the humanities; drama and values: the subject co-ordinator's role; special study (double module).

Successful completion of this course leads to a recommendation for Qualified Teacher Status (QTS) after completion of skills tests.

Entry requirements: As above
Contact: Admissions
01524 384384
admissions@ucsm.ac.uk

BA (Hons) Education and Art and Design (Primary Education) XW31

4 years full-time

Year 1: Professional studies; English; mathematics; science and IT; teaching studies plus 1 day per week in school; 4-week teaching placement; courses in main subject.

Year 2: Professional studies; National Curriculum subjects; personal and social education; teaching studies plus 1 day per week in school for 10 weeks; cross-curricular approaches; 5-week teaching placement; 2 modules from main subject.

Year 3: Professional studies; English; mathematics; science; teaching studies plus 1 day per week in school for 8 weeks; special educational needs; 8-week teaching placement; 2 modules from main subject.

Year 4: Professional studies; elective; Curriculum co-ordination and 1 day per week in school; 3 week teaching in school; at least 4 modules from main subject.

Main subject Part 1: Courses in art and design exploring both practical studies in the studios with related art theory.

Part 2: Turning points in 20th-century art and design; independent art history topic; analytical and expressive figure drawing; nomination practical studies; history and theory of art and design; digital image creation and manipulation.

Successful completion of this course leads to a recommendation for Qualified Teacher Status (QTS) after completion of skills tests.

Entry requirements: Tariff: 160; International Baccalaureate: 28, SCE Higher: BBCC, BTEC NC/ND
Contact: As above

BSc (Hons) Education and Biological Studies (Primary Education) XC31

4 years full-time

Year 1: Professional studies; English; mathematics; science and IT; teaching studies plus 1 day per week in school; 4-week teaching placement; course in main subject.

Year 2: Professional studies; National Curriculum subjects; personal and social education; teaching studies plus 1 day per week in school for 10 weeks; cross curricular approaches; 5-week teaching placement; 2 modules in main subject.

Year 3: Professional studies; English; mathematics; science; teaching studies plus 1 day per week in school for 8 weeks; special educational needs; 8-week teaching placement; 2 modules in main subject.

Year 4: Professional studies; elective; Curriculum co-ordination and 1 day per week in school; 3 weeks teaching in school; at least 4 modules in main subject.

Main subject Part 1: Study skills; freshwater ecology; human exercise physiology; biochemistry; biophysics.

Part 2: Cell biology; microbiology; human biology; animal behaviour; the functioning plant; woodland ecology; molecular form and function; evolutionary genetics; energy and molecular biology; science and society; research methods; individual practical dissertation.

Successful completion of this course leads to a recommendation for Qualified Teacher Status (QTS) after completion of skills tests.

Entry requirements: As above
Contact: As above

BA (Hons) Education and Drama (Primary Education) XW34

4 years full-time

Year 1: Professional studies; English; mathematics; science and information technology; teaching studies plus 1 day per week in school; 4-week teaching placement; courses in main subject.

Year 2: Professional studies; National Curriculum subjects; personal and social education; teaching studies plus 1 day per week in school for 10 weeks; cross-curricular approaches; 5-week teaching placement; 2 modules from main subject.

Year 3: Professional studies; English; mathematics; science; teaching studies plus 1 day per week in school for 8 weeks; special educational needs; 8-week teaching placement; 2 modules from main subject.

Year 4: Professional studies; elective; Curriculum co-ordination and 1 day per week in school; 3-week teaching in school; at least 4 modules from main subject.

Drama specialist modules: Drama and the social situation; drama and text for the curriculum; drama as communication; the roots of drama; drama and the humanities; working in role; study of drama application; drama and the community; drama and values; drama subject specialist teaching and leadership in the primary school.

Successful completion of this course leads to a recommendation for Qualified Teacher Status (QTS) after completion of skills tests.

Entry requirements: Tariff: 160, International Baccalaureate: 28, SCE Higher: BCCC, BTEC NC/ND

Contact: As above

BA (Hons) Education and Early Childhood Education (including 3–5 years) X110

3 years full-time

Entry requirements: Tariff: 160, Irish Leaving Certificates: BBBCC, SCE Higher: BBBC, BTEC NC/ND, SCE Advanced Higher: CC, Interview, Work experience

Contact: As above

BA (Hons) Education and English (Primary Education) XQ33

4 years full-time

Year 1: Professional studies; English; mathematics; science and information technology; teaching studies plus 1 day per week in school; 4-week teaching placement; courses in main subject.

Year 2: Professional studies; National Curriculum subjects; personal and social education; teaching studies plus 1 day per week in school for 10 weeks; cross-curricular approaches; 5-week teaching placement; 2 modules from main subject.

Year 3: Professional studies; English; mathematics; science; teaching studies plus 1 day per week in school for 8 weeks; special educational needs; 8-week teaching placement; 2 modules from main subject.

Year 4: Professional studies; elective; Curriculum co-ordination and 1 day per week in school; 3-week teaching in school; at least 4 modules from main subject.

Main subject Part 1: Approaches to literature: modern texts in relation to a variety of critical approaches developing independent critical skills and working on contemporary poets, plays and novels.

Part 2: Working with texts; narrative; modules on the English language; further modules including those on aspects of the subject relevant to teachers. Specialist pathways are available in: language; children's literature; creative writing; historic literature.

Successful completion of this course leads to a recommendation for Qualified Teacher Status (QTS) after completion of skills tests.

Entry requirements: Tariff: 160, International Baccalaureate: 28, SCE Higher: BBBC, BTEC NC/ND

Contact: As above

BA (Hons) Education and Geography (Primary Education) XL37

4 years full-time

Year 1: Professional studies; English; mathematics; science and information technology; teaching studies plus 1 day per week in school; 4-week teaching placement; courses in main subject.

Year 2: Professional studies; National Curriculum subjects; personal and social education; teaching studies plus 1 day per week in school for 10 weeks; cross-curricular approaches; 5-week teaching placement; 2 modules from main subject.

Year 3: Professional studies; English; mathematics; science; teaching studies plus 1 day per week in school for 8 weeks; special educational needs; 8-week teaching placement; 2 modules from main subject.

Year 4: Professional studies; elective; Curriculum co-ordination and 1 day per week in school; 3-week teaching in school; at least 4 modules from main subject.

Main subject Part 1: Geographical enquiry; human and physical geographical systems.

Part 2: Information management in geography; geographical thought and practice (including foreign field class). Physical modules: atmospheric processes; geomorphological processes; biogeographical systems; environmental hazards; quaternary geomorphology; Karst geomorphology; coastal processes; environmental conservation. Core modules: human and physical systems; geographical enquiry; information management in geography; geographic thought and process. Human modules: rural management; economic geography; historical geography; landscape studies; international geopolitics; leisure and recreation; urban issues; landscape of industry; tourism; culture and religion; retailing geography; Western Europe; Sub-Sahara Africa; urban management.

Successful completion of this course leads to a recommendation for Qualified Teacher Status (QTS) after completion of skills tests.

Entry requirements: Tariff: 160, International Baccalaureate: 28, SCE Higher: BCCC, BTEC NC/ND

Contact: As above

BA (Hons) Education and History (Primary Education) XV31

4 years full-time

Year 1: Professional studies; English; mathematics; science and IT; teaching studies plus 1 day per week in school; 4-week teaching placement; courses in main subject.

Year 2: Professional studies; National Curriculum subjects; personal and social education; teaching studies plus 1 day per week in school for 10 weeks; cross-curricular approaches; 5-week teaching placement; 2 modules from main subject.

Year 3: Professional studies; English; mathematics; science; teaching studies plus 1 day per week in school for 8 weeks; special educational needs; 8-week teaching placement; 2 modules from main subject.

Year 4: Professional studies; elective; curriculum co-ordination and 1 day per week in school; 3-week teaching in school; at least 4 modules from main subject.

Main subject Part 1: 2 or 4 from: aspects of modern European history 1860–1918; Nazism and communism; history in action (an introduction to the historian's craft); history in the community; modern British Imperialism.

Part 2: 8 from: Roman Britain; Saxon and Viking England; the Early Tudors; the reign of Elizabeth; British society in the Industrial Revolution; Victorian society; British politics and society 1918–1940; British politics and society 1940–74; the USA 1900–45; the USA 1945–92.

Successful completion of this course leads to a recommendation for Qualified Teacher Status (QTS) after completion of skills tests.

Entry requirements: As above

Contact: As above

BSc (Hons) Education and Information and Communications Technology (Primary Education) XG35

4 years full-time

Successful completion of this course leads to a recommendation for Qualified Teacher Status (QTS) after completion of skills tests.

Entry requirements: As above
Contact: As above

BSc (Hons) Education and Mathematics (Primary Education) XG31

4 years full-time

Year 1: Professional studies; English; mathematics; science and IT; teaching studies plus 1 day per week in school; 4-week teaching placement; courses in main subject.

Year 2: Professional studies; National Curriculum subjects; personal and social education; teaching studies plus 1 day per week in school for 10 weeks; cross-curricular approaches; 5-week teaching placement; 2 modules from main subject.

Year 3: Professional studies; English; mathematics; science; teaching studies plus 1 day per week in school for 8 weeks; special educational needs; 8-week teaching placement; 2 modules from main subject.

Year 4: Professional studies; elective; Curriculum co-ordination and 1 day per week in school; 3-week teaching in school; at least 4 modules from main subject.

Main subject Part 1: Foundations of mathematics: the language and structure of mathematics; applications of mathematics and statistics: modelling real life by mathematics and problem-solving methods and use of computer software in mathematical investigations; mathematics and art: mathematics and visual imagery; logic: useful thinking skills.

Part 2: 10 or more modules chosen from: real analysis; linear geometry; further applications of mathematics and statistics; group theory; different geometrics; complex analysis and geometry; history and philosophy of mathematics; numerical analysis; independent study in mathematics; mathematics models in finance; graph theory; number theory; advanced applications of

mathematics and statistics; modelling mechanical systems; Galois theory; operations research.

Successful completion of this course leads to a recommendation for Qualified Teacher Status (QTS) after completion of skills tests.

Entry requirements: As above
Contact: As above

BA (Hons) Education and Music (Primary Education) XW33

4 years full-time

Year 1: Professional studies; English; mathematics; science and IT; teaching studies plus 1 day per week in school; 4-week teaching placement; courses in main subject.

Year 2: Professional studies; National Curriculum subjects; personal and social education; teaching studies plus 1 day per week in school for 10 weeks; cross-curricular approaches; 5-week teaching placement; 2 modules from main subject.

Year 3: Professional studies; English; mathematics; science; teaching studies plus 1 day per week in school for 8 weeks; special educational needs; 8-week teaching placement; 2 modules from main subject.

Year 4: Professional studies; elective; Curriculum co-ordination and 1 day per week in school; 3-week teaching in school; at least 4 modules from main subject.

Main subject Part 1: Main instrument/vocal study and supporting practical musicianship; composition and instrumentation; performance practice seminars; foundation and contextual studies in music.

Part 2: Performance with supporting studies; style and repertoire, contextual studies; 20th-century studies; composition and arranging; primary school music; 2nd subject.

Successful completion of this course leads to a recommendation for Qualified Teacher Status (QTS) after completion of skills tests.

Entry requirements: As above
Contact: As above

BSc (Hons) Education and Physical Education (Primary Education) XX31

4 years full-time

Part 1: Modules provide an introduction to and foundation for the academic study of physical education; students analyse: the physiology of exercise, skill acquisition, contemporary issues in sport.

Part 2: Students study a variety of areas in a context that relates to National Curriculum physical education including: health-related exercise; sports coaching; games; dance; gymnastics; athletics; swimming; outdoor experience; outdoor leadership.

Successful completion of this course leads to a recommendation for Qualified Teacher Status (QTS) after completion of skills tests.

Entry requirements: As above
Contact: As above

BA (Hons) Education and Religious Studies (Primary Education) XV36

4 years full-time

Year 1: Professional studies; English; mathematics; science and IT; teaching studies plus 1 day per week in school; 4-week teaching placement; courses in main subject.

Year 2: Professional studies; National Curriculum subjects; personal and social education; teaching studies plus 1 day per week in school for 10 weeks; cross-curricular approaches; 5-week teaching placement; 2 modules from main subject.

Year 3: Professional studies; English; mathematics; science; teaching studies plus 1 day per week in school for 8 weeks; special educational needs; 8-week teaching placement; 2 modules from main subject.

Year 4: Professional studies; elective; curriculum co-ordination and 1 day per week in school; 3-week teaching in school; at least 4 modules from main subject.

Main subject Part 1: Introduction to religious studies; an investigation of 2 faiths:

Christianity and Hinduism. 2 or 4 further elements chosen from: what is religion?; critical approaches to the study of religion; Christian theology; Sikhism.

Part 2: Subjects studied include: Jesus in the Synoptic tradition; applied religion and secular ethics 1 and 2; explorations in religion 1 and 2; Islam: belief and values; mission, conversion and dialogue; modern Christian theology; Judaism; Hindu and Buddhist ethics; independent dissertation; second subject.

Successful completion of this course leads to a recommendation for Qualified Teacher Status (QTS) after completion of skills tests.

Entry requirements: As above
Contact: As above

BA (Hons) Education and Special Educational Needs (Primary Education) X360

4 years full-time

Successful completion of this course leads to a recommendation for Qualified Teacher Status (QTS) after completion of skills tests.

Entry requirements: Tariff 160.
Contact: As above

BA (Hons) English and Education (Secondary Education) X1Q3

3 years full-time

The main focus of the course is teaching your specialist subject to the 11–16 age range; students also gain some experience in either Key Stage 2 (7–11) or sixth form (16–18).

Successful completion of this course leads to a recommendation for Qualified Teacher Status (QTS) after completion of skills tests.

Entry requirements: Tariff: 160
Contact: As above

BA (Hons) English and Literacy Education (5–11 years) X1Q2 A

3 years full-time

General primary teaching course for ages 5–11. Includes special study of English and literacy option.

Successful completion of this course leads to a recommendation for Qualified Teacher Status (QTS) after completion of skills tests.

Entry requirements: As above
Contact: Margaret Hartley
         01539 430211

BA (Hons) English and Literacy Education (5–11 years) X1QJ C

3 years full-time

General primary teaching course with special option in the study of literacy.

Successful completion of this course leads to a recommendation for Qualified Teacher Status (QTS) after completion of skills tests.

Entry requirements: As above
Contact: Fran Dale
         01228 616202

BA (Hons) English and Literacy Education (Primary Education) X1X3 T

3 years full-time
As above
Contact: As above

BSc (Hons) Geographical and Environmental Education (5–11 years) X1F8 A

3 years full-time

General primary teaching course with special option in the teaching of geography and environmental education.

Successful completion of this course leads to a recommendation for Qualified Teacher Status (QTS) after completion of skills tests.

Entry requirements: Tariff: 160
Contact: Margaret Hartley
         01539 430211

BA (Hons) Geography and Education (Secondary Education) XLC7

3 years full-time

The main focus of the course is teaching your specialist subject to the 11–16 age range; students also gain some experience in either Key Stage 2 (7–11) or sixth form (16–18).

Successful completion of this course leads to a recommendation for Qualified Teacher Status (QTS) after completion of skills tests.

Entry requirements: As above
Contact: Admissions
         01524 384384
         admissions@ucsm.ac.uk

BA (Hons) Geography Education (Secondary Education) XLCT C

3 years full-time
As above
Contact: As above

BA (Hons) History and Education (Secondary Education) XV1C

3 years full-time
As above
Contact: As above

BA (Hons) History and Education (Secondary Education) XVD1 C

3 years full-time
As above
Contact: As above

BA (Hons) History Education (5–11 years) XVDD C

4 years full-time

Combines primary teaching with degree studies in history. Opportunity to opt out of QTS route after Year 2. Teaching studies emphasis in Years 3 and 4.

Successful completion of this course leads to a recommendation for Qualified Teacher Status (QTS) after completion of skills tests.

Entry requirements: As above
Contact: Fran Dale
         01228 616202

BA (Hons) Information and Communications Technology Education (5–11 years) XG15 A

3 years full-time

Successful completion of this course leads to a recommendation for Qualified Teacher Status (QTS) after completion of skills tests.

Entry requirements: As above
Contact: As above

BSc (Hons) Information and Communications Technology Education (5–11 years) XG1M C

4 years full-time

Combines general primary teaching with degree studies in information technology. Teaching emphasis in Years 3 and 4 with the chance to opt out of QTS route after Year 2.

Successful completion of this course leads to a recommendation for Qualified Teacher Status (QTS) after completion of skills tests.

Entry requirements: As above
Contact: Fran Dale
01228 616202

BA (Hons) Information Technology and Education (Secondary Education) XG1N C

3 years full-time

The main focus of the course is teaching your specialist subject to the 11–16 age range; students also gain some experience in either Key Stage 2 (7–11) or sixth form (16–18).

Successful completion of this course leads to a recommendation for Qualified Teacher Status (QTS) after completion of skills tests.

Entry requirements: As above
Contact: As above

BSc (Hons) Mathematics and Education (Secondary Education) XG1D

3 years full-time

Years 1 and 2: Secondary school mathematics: shape and space, algebra, number, calculus, probability and statistics; educational and professional studies: approaches to teaching and learning mathematics and becoming familiar with texts, schemes of work etc; school experience including regular attachment to a secondary school and block school experience.

Successful completion of this course leads to a recommendation for Qualified Teacher Status (QTS) after completion of skills tests.

Entry requirements: DipHE, HNC, HND
Contact: Admissions
01524 384384
admissions@ucsm.ac.uk

BA (Hons) Music Education (5–11 years) X1WJ C

3 years full-time

Successful completion of this course leads to a recommendation for Qualified Teacher Status (QTS) after completion of skills tests.

Entry requirements: Tariff: 160
Contact: Admissions
01524 384384
admissions@ucsm.ac.uk

BSc (Hons) Numeracy and Mathematics Education (5–11 years) X1G0 C

3 years full-time

General primary teaching course with special option in the teaching of numeracy and mathematics.

Successful completion of this course leads to a recommendation for Qualified Teacher Status (QTS) after completion of skills tests.

Entry requirements: As above
Contact: Fran Dale
01228 616202

BSc (Hons) Numeracy and Mathematics Education (5–11 years) X1GY A

3 years full-time

General primary teaching course with special option in the teaching of numeracy and mathematics.

Successful completion of this course leads to a recommendation for Qualified Teacher Status (QTS) after completion of skills tests.

Entry requirements: As above
Contact: Margaret Hartley
01539 430211

BA (Hons) Numeracy and Mathematics Education (Primary) X1G9 T

3 years full-time
As above

BSc (Hons) Physical Education (5–11 years) X1C6 A

3 years full-time

General primary teaching course with a special option in the teaching of physical education.

Successful completion of this course leads to a recommendation for Qualified Teacher Status (QTS) after completion of skills tests.

Entry requirements: As above
Contact: Margaret Hartley
    01539 430211

BA (Hons) Physical Education and Education (Secondary Education) XC16

3 years full-time

The main focus of the course is teaching your specialist subject to the 11–16 age range; students also gain some experience in either Key Stage 2 (7–11) or sixth form (16–18).

Successful completion of this course leads to a recommendation for Qualified Teacher Status (QTS) after completion of skills tests.

Entry requirements: As above
Contact: Admissions
    01524 384384
    admissions@ucsm.ac.uk

BA (Hons) Religious Education and Education (Secondary Education) XV1Q

3 years full-time
As above

BA (Hons) Religious Studies and Education (Secondary Education) XVCQ C

3 years full-time
As above

BSc (Hons) Religious Studies Education (5–11 years) XV1P C

4 years full-time

Combines primary teaching with degree studies in religious studies. Teaching emphasis in Years 3 and 4 with the chance to opt out of QTS route after Year 2.

Successful completion of this course leads to a recommendation for Qualified Teacher Status (QTS) after completion of skills tests.

Entry requirements: As above

Contact: Fran Dale
    01228 616202

BSc (Hons) Science and Education (Secondary Education) X1Y0

3 years full-time

The main focus of the course is teaching your specialist subject to the 11–16 age range; students also gain some experience in either Key Stage 2 (7–11) or sixth form (16–18).

Successful completion of this course leads to a recommendation for Qualified Teacher Status (QTS) after completion of skills tests.

Entry requirements: As above
Contact: Admissions
    01524 384384
    admissions@ucsm.ac.uk

BSc (Hons) Science Education (5–11 years) XF10 A

3 years full-time

General primary teaching course with a special option in the teaching of science.

Successful completion of this course leads to a recommendation for Qualified Teacher Status (QTS) after completion of skills tests.

Entry requirements: As above
Contact: Margaret Hartley
    01539 430211

PGCE Primary Education (5–11, Key Stage 1 or 2) X100

1 year full-time

Entry requirements: Students taking this course should have degree relevant to the school curriculum and understanding of pupils in this age range; passes in English language and mathematics at GCSE grade C or equivalent are required, or recognised equivalent qualifications; candidates born after 1/9/79 must have grade C GCSE in science subject or subjects. Candidates should have 5–6 GCSEs (grade C or above) in National Curriculum subjects and at least an A-level, and ideally a significant part of their degree, in a National Curriculum subject.

Contact: Frances Higgin
Postgraduate Admissions Officer
f.higgin@ucsm.ac.uk

PGCE Primary Education (5–11, Key Stage 1 or 2) X103
Flexible
Entry requirements: As above
Contact: As above

PGCE Secondary Education (Art) W1XC
1 year full-time
Entry requirements: All candidates should have an art-based degree containing a large element of practical/studio based work. Passes in English language and mathematics at GCSE or equivalent are required, or recognised equivalent qualifications.
Contact: As above

PGCE Secondary Education (Biology with Combined Science) C1X1
1 year full-time
Entry requirements: All applicants should have graduated in an appropriate subject. Passes in English language and mathematics at GCSE or equivalent are required, or recognised equivalent qualifications. Mature entrants are encouraged.
Contact: As above

PGCE Secondary Education (Chemistry with Combined Science) F1X1
1 year full-time
Entry requirements: All candidates should have graduated in an appropriate subject. Passes in English language and mathematics at GCSE or equivalent are required, or recognised equivalent qualifications.
Contact: As above

PGCE Secondary Education (Citizenship with History) LX91 C
1 year full-time
Entry requirements: Applicants should have an appropriate degree and either A-level history or history as a component of their degree; GCSE English language and mathematics at grade C required.
Contact: As above

PGCE Secondary Education (English including Drama and Media Studies) QX31
1 year full-time
Entry requirements: Applicants should have graduated in an appropriate subject. Passes in English language and mathematics at GCSE or equivalent are required, or recognised equivalent qualifications.
Contact: As above

PGCE Secondary Education (French with German) RX11
1 year full-time
As above

PGCE Secondary Education (French with Italian) RX1C
1 year full-time
As above

PGCE Secondary Education (French with Spanish) RXD1
1 year full-time
As above

PGCE Secondary Education (French) R1X1
1 year full-time
As above

Maitrise/PGCE Secondary Education (French) RXCC K
1 year full-time
Entry requirements: As above
Contact: Lola Davies
Administrator
01524 384500

PGCE Secondary Education (Geography) F8X1
1 year full-time
Entry requirements: All candidates should have graduated in an appropriate subject, normally including geography. Passes in English language and mathematics at GCSE or equivalent are required, or recognised equivalent qualifications.
Contact: Frances Higgin
Postgraduate Admissions Officer
01524 384500
f.higgin@ucsm.ac.uk

PGCE Secondary Education (Geography, conversion) FXV1 L

2 years full-time

Entry requirements: Graduates in any discipline considered, as course includes subject conversion; GCSE pass (C or above) in English and mathematics, A-level in geography or equivalent; some post A-level study in geography also required; mature students with non-standard qualifications encouraged.

Contact: As above

PGCE Secondary Education (German with French) RX21

1 year full-time

Entry requirements: All candidates should have graduated in an appropriate subject. Passes in English language and mathematics at GCSE or equivalent are required, or recognised equivalent qualifications.

Contact: As above

PGCE Secondary Education (German with Italian) RX2D

1 year full-time
As above

PGCE Secondary Education (German with Spanish) RXG1

1 year full-time
As above

PGCE Secondary Education (German) R2X1

1 year full-time
As above

PGCE Secondary Education (German, with Hauptschulqualifikation Austria HSQA) RXFD K

1 year full-time

Entry requirements: Degree in appropriate subject; GCSE English language and mathematics at grade C or above, or equivalent, required.

Contact: Lola Davies
Administrator
01524 384500

PGCE Secondary Education (History) V1X1

1 year full-time

Entry requirements: All candidates should have graduated in an appropriate subject. Passes in English language and mathematics at GCSE or equivalent are required, or recognised equivalent qualifications.

Contact: Frances Higgin
Postgraduate Admissions Officer
01524 384500
f.higgin@ucsm.ac.uk

PGCE Secondary Education (Information and Communication Technology) G5X1 L

1 year full-time or variable

Entry requirements: All candidates should have graduated in a related subject; passes in English language and mathematics at GCSE (grade C or above) or equivalent are required or recognised equivalent qualifications.

Contact: As above

PGCE Secondary Education (Information Technology, conversion) GXM1 L

2 years full-time

Entry requirements: Graduates in any discipline considered, as course includes subject conversion; GCSE pass (C or above) in English and Maths, A-level in information technology or equivalent; experience of work in information technology field considered, some post A-level study also required; mature students with non-standard qualifications encouraged.

Contact: As above

PGCE Secondary Education (Mathematics) G1X1 L

1 year full-time or variable

Entry requirements: All candidates should have graduated in an appropriate subject, normally including mathematics. Passes in English language and mathematics at GCSE or equivalent are required, or recognised equivalent qualifications. Mature students are encouraged.

Contact: As above

PGCE Secondary Education (Mathematics, conversion) GXC1 L

24 months full-time

Entry requirements: Graduates in any discipline considered, as course includes subject conversion. GCSE pass in English and A-level mathematics, or other equivalent qualifications. Some post A-level study in mathematics also required. Mature students with non-standard qualifications encouraged.

Contact: As above

PGCE Secondary Education (Physics with Combined Science) F3X1 L

1 year full-time

Entry requirements: All candidates should have graduated in an appropriate subject. Passes in English language and mathematics at GCSE or equivalent are required, or recognised equivalent qualifications.

Contact: As above

PGCE Secondary Education (Religious Education with Personal, Social and Moral Education) VX61 L

1 year full-time

Entry requirements: All candidates should have graduated in an appropriate subject, normally including some religious education. Passes in English language and mathematics at GCSE or equivalent are required, or recognised equivalent qualifications.

Contact: As above

PGCE Secondary Education (Science) F0X1 L

Variable

As above

PGCE Secondary Education (Science, conversion) FXA1 L

2 years full-time

Entry requirements: Graduates in any discipline considered, as course includes subject conversion; GCSE pass (C or above) in English and Maths, A-level in a science or equivalent; some post A-level study in science also required; mature students with non-standard qualification encouraged.

Contact: As above

PGCE Secondary Education (Spanish with French) RX41

1 year full-time

Entry requirements: All candidates should have graduated in an appropriate subject. Passes in English language and mathematics at GCSE or equivalent are required, or recognised equivalent qualifications.

Contact: As above

PGCE Secondary Education (Spanish with German) RX4C

1 year full-time

As above

PgCert/PgDip/MA in Education

1–5 years part-time

Entry requirements: Good Honours degree and minimum 1 year's professional experience; teachers without a good Honours degree can be considered for entry via AP(E)L.

Contact: Linda Sharpe
01524 384604
l.sharpe@ucsm.ac.uk

PgCert/PgDip/MA in Education (Developing of Teacher Expertise)

Part-time

As above

PgCert/PgDip/MA in Education (English Education)

2–5 years part-time

As above

PgCert/PgDip/MA in Education (Leadership and Management)

Part-time

As above

PgCert/PgDip/MA in Education (Science and Mathematics Education)

2–5 years part-time

As above

PgCert/PgDip/MA in Education (Special Educational Needs)

Part-time

As above

Certificate of Advanced Studies in Mentorship

Part-time

Entry requirements: Qualified Teacher Status and experience.

Contact: Jo Taylor
01524 384467

Certificate of Attendance in Primary Updating and Retraining

Part-time

As above

St Mary's University College, Belfast

191 Falls Road
Belfast
BT12 6FE
Tel: 028 9032 7678
Fax: 028 9033 3719
admissions@stmarys-belfast.ac.uk
www.stmarys-belfast.ac.uk

St Mary's University College is an independent Catholic institution linked academically to the Queen's University of Belfast, which validates its degrees, and the Department of Education for Northern Ireland. The origins of the college can be traced back to 1900 when the Dominican Sisters opened St Mary's Training College, on the present Falls Road site, with an enrolment of 100 women students.

For nearly 50 years after that, the college was concerned with the education of women students and their preparation for teaching in primary schools. In 1949 a men's department was established at Trench House and in 1961 it was constituted St Joseph's Training College. The two colleges were amalgamated in 1970, and St Mary's University College came formally into existence in September 1985.

The College is primarily involved in the training and ongoing professional development of teachers for the Catholic schools sector, but is also involved in the professional development of all teachers in all types of schools. It operates at undergraduate and post-graduate levels and offers a range of courses and awards of an educational and related nature. The College currently has 590 students. The College's facilities include a library and resources centre, sports hall and IT rooms.

HOW TO APPLY

Degree courses: applications are made through UCAS.

PGCE: applications are made direct to the institution.

Postgraduate: applications are made direct to the institution.

COURSES

BEd (Hons) in Education (Primary) with Art and Design XW11

4 years full-time

Students take modules in 4 areas: education studies; curriculum studies; school-based teaching experience; subject studies. Subjects are chosen from: art and design; English; geography; history; Irish; mathematics; music; physical education; religious studies; science.

Entry requirements: Tariff: 260, Irish Leaving Certificates, Foundation / access qualification

Contact: Mr Paddy Bradley
Academic Registrar
028 9032 7678
p.bradley@stmarys-belfast.ac.uk

BEd (Hons) in Education (Primary) with English XQ13

4 years full-time

As above

Entry requirements: Tariff: 280, Irish Leaving Certificates, Foundation / access qualification

Contact: As above

BEd (Hons) in Education (Primary) with Geography XL17

4 years full-time

As above

Entry requirements: Tariff: 280, Irish Leaving Certificates

Contact: As above

BEd (Hons) in Education (Primary) with History XV11

4 years full-time

As above

Entry requirements: Tariff: 260, Irish Leaving Certificates

Contact: As above

BEd (Hons) in Education (Primary) with Irish XQ15

4 years full-time

As above

BEd (Hons) in Education (Primary) with Mathematics XG11

4 years full-time

As above

Entry requirements: Tariff: 240, Irish Leaving Certificates

Contact: As above

BEd (Hons) in Education (Primary) with Music XW13

4 years full-time

As above

Entry requirements: Tariff: 240, Irish Leaving Certificates, Foundation / access qualification

Contact: As above

BEd (Hons) in Education (Primary) with Physical Education XX13

4 years full-time

As above

Entry requirements: Tariff: 280, Irish Leaving Certificates

Contact: As above

BEd (Hons) in Education (Primary) with Religious Studies XV16

4 years full-time

As above

BEd (Hons) in Education (Primary) with Science XF10

4 years full-time

As above

Entry requirements: Tariff: 260, Irish Leaving Certificates, Foundation / access qualification

Contact: As above

BEd (Hons) in Education (Secondary) with Business Studies XN11

4 years full-time

Students take a main subject from: Business studies; religious studies; technology and design; plus a subsidiary subject from: English; geography; history; information and communications technology. Technology and design students are required to take information and communications technology as their subsidiary. In addition students take educational studies and undertake school-based teaching experience.

Entry requirements: Tariff: 240, BTEC NC/ND, Irish Leaving Certificates

Contact: As above

BEd (Hons) in Education (Secondary) with Religious Studies XVC6

4 years full-time

As above

Entry requirements: Tariff: 240, Irish Leaving Certificates

Contact: As above

BEd (Hons) in Education (Secondary) with Technology and Design XW12

4 years full-time

Contact: As above

PGCE in Primary Education (5–11, Irish Medium)

1 year full-time

Entry requirements: Degree from a recognised university, or diploma or other qualification approved as equivalent; plus GCSE grade C or above (or equivalent) in English language and mathematics. In addition, knowledge of Irish (both written and

oral) at a high level required. Candidates must normally be at least 20 years of age. **Contact:** Dr Gabrielle Nig Uidhir
Irish Medium Development Officer
01232 327678

MEd/MSc in Education

3–5 years part-time

Entry requirements: Honours degree or equivalent plus at least 2 years' professional experience in an education or training context; or degree or equivalent qualification with at least 5 years' professional experience in an education or training context.

Contact: A Rice
In-Service Co-ordinator
028 9032 7678
a.rice@stmarys-belfast.ac.uk

St Mary's College

Strawberry Hill
Waldegrave Road
Richmond upon Thames
London
TW1 4SX
Tel: 020 8240 4000
Fax: 020 8240 4255
www.smuc.ac.uk

Founded in 1850 St Mary's College is a college of the University of Surrey. A wide range of courses is available leading to degrees awarded by the university. The students union at the college offers a range of activities and there are also sports facilities available on the campus. Accommodation is available in halls or in self-catering residences at Twickenham.

The School of Education offers education courses at degree level, the PGCE at primary and secondary level and other postgraduate courses for Continuing Professional Development.

HOW TO APPLY

Degree courses: applications are made through UCAS.

PGCE: applications are made through the GTTR.

Postgraduate: applications are made direct to the institution.

COURSES

BA (Hons) Primary Education with an Advanced Subject X320

4 years full-time

Courses address professional values and practice; planning, expectation and targets; teaching strategies; monitoring and assessment; classroom management and inclusion.

Importance is given to the core subjects of English, Mathematics, Science and Information Communications Technology (ICT). Emphasis is also given to Religious Education and trainees have the opportunity to study for the Catholic Certificate in Religious Studies (CCRS). Courses are provided in all foundation subjects of the National Curriculum. Trainees begin their studies across a broad range of subjects and subsequently make choices and study these selected subjects in greater depth. School experience is an integral part of each year of study.

Successful completion of this course leads to a recommendation for Qualified Teacher Status (QTS) after completion of skills tests.

Entry requirements: Tariff: 140 to 160, BTEC NC/ND, Irish Leaving Certificates, International Baccalaureate.

Contact: Eileen Olnick
020 8240 4162
olnicke@smuc.ac.uk

BA (Hons) Primary Teaching Studies X120

3 years full-time

Successful completion of this course leads to a recommendation for Qualified Teacher Status (QTS) after completion of skills tests.

Entry requirements: AVCEs, BTEC NC/ND, Irish Leaving Certificates: CCCC, SCE Higher: CCCC, GCE A- and AS-levels: CD to CC

Contact: As above

BA (Hons) Secondary Education (Physical Education) X140

4 years full-time

There are 3 main strands which develop throughout the programme: subject knowledge; the subject in context; and school/professional experience.

Year 1: Subject knowledge: introductory blocks in sport science and physical education encompass the theoretical and practical concepts of sport science and physical education including physiological aspects of performance, socio-cultural aspects of sport and physical education, and psychological aspects of movement control and acquiring skills. Subject in context: includes practical work and 2 theoretical themes of school and community and special populations. Professional/school experience: 2 school-based modules, 1 focusing on the primary school and 1 on the secondary school. Additional professional qualifications on games and gymnastics are taken as well as an introductory course in information technology.

Year 2: Options in sport science: research methods; physiological responses to exercise; sport and exercise psychology; applied mechanics of sport; fundamentals of physical activity; fitness and health; introduction to coaching; individual sports, games and artistic activities. Options in physical education covering National Curriculum areas: pedagogy; school-based courses on the physical education teacher and the pupil in physical education.

Year 3: Subject knowledge: application of theoretical principles developed in previous years, within a specific physical education context. Subject in context: further practical work with specialisation in either 'school and community' or 'special populations'. Professional/school experience: subject pedagogy and the physical education curriculum. 12 weeks are entirely devoted to subject pedagogy and 2 blocks of school-based experience in partnership schools. A further information technology course focuses on presentational skills.

Year 4: Choice of 1 of the 2 areas in the subject in context module; principles of school-based research prior to dissertation in semester two. Professional/school experience: subject pedagogy plus a block of continuous school-based experience.

Successful completion of this course leads to a recommendation for Qualified Teacher Status (QTS) after completion of skills tests.

Entry requirements: Tariff: 180, Irish Leaving Certificates: BBCC, BTEC NC/ND, International Baccalaureate, SCE Higher

Contact: Mrs Moira Packer
Programme Director
020 8240 4179
packerm@smuc.ac.uk

PGCE Primary Education (Primary, 5–11) X100

1 year full-time

Entry requirements: 2nd Class degree from a UK university of the CNAA or recognised equivalent qualification that has clear relevance to the National Curriculum for pupils; applicants are expected to have organised and undertaken work experience with primary aged children; minimum grade C in GCSE English, mathematics and science.

Contact: Mr John Rankmore / Ms Mona Farrugia
Director of Primary ITT /
Postgraduate Admissions Officer
020 8240 4139 / 020 8240 4027
farrugim@smuc.ac.uk

PGCE Primary Education (Primary, 5–11) X103

Part-time
As above

PGCE Secondary Education (Classics) Q8X1

1 year full-time

Entry requirements: Degree from a UK university or equivalent which has a significant proportion of content relevant to classics; students must have Latin to beyond A-level, preferably with some Greek and at least a grade C in GCSE (or equivalent) mathematics and English language; candidates should have recently visited and assisted/observed in a mainstream United Kingdom secondary school, preferably 11–18.

Contact: Ms Mona Farrugia / Robert Vertes
Postgraduate Admissions Officer / Secondary PGCE Admissions Tutor
020 8240 4027 /
020 8240 4154
farrugim@smuc.ac.uk /
bobv@smuc.ac.uk

PGCE Secondary Education (Geography) F8X1

1 year full-time

Entry requirements: Degree (normally 2:1 or above) from a UK university or equivalent which has a significant proportion of content relevant to geography, a balance of human and physical geography preferred; at least a grade C in GCSE (or equivalent) mathematics and English language; candidates should have recently visited and assisted/observed in a mainstream United Kingdom secondary school, preferably 11–18.

Contact: As above

PGCE Secondary Education (Mathematics) G1X1

1 year full-time

Entry requirements: Degree from a UK university or equivalent which has a significant proportion of content relevant to mathematics; allied subjects such as economics, physics, engineering disciplines, psychology, computing considered providing applicant has A-Level and significant undergraduate study of mathematics/mathematical topics; at least grade C in GCSE (or equivalent) mathematics and English language; candidates should have recently visited and assisted/observed in a mainstream United Kingdom secondary school, preferably 11–18.

Contact: As above

PGCE Secondary Education (Modern Foreign Languages) R9X1

1 year full-time

Entry requirements: Degree from a UK university or equivalent which has a significant proportion of content relevant to the subject you wish to teach; a significant proportion of the degree must be in French or another modern foreign language; applicants offering a language other than French must have some knowledge of French; at least grade C in GCSE (or equivalent) mathematics and English language; candidates should have recently visited and assisted/observed in a mainstream United Kingdom secondary school, preferably 11–18.

Contact: As above

PGCE Secondary Education (Religious Education) V6X1

1 year full-time

Entry requirements: Degree from a UK university or equivalent which has a significant proportion of content relevant to religious education; background in both theology and religious studies and awareness of the need to be able to teach about 6 major world faiths; at least grade C in GCSE (or equivalent) mathematics and English language; candidates should have recently visited and assisted/observed in a mainstream United Kingdom secondary school, preferably 11–18.

Contact: As above

PGCE Secondary Education (Science) F0X1

1 year full-time

Entry requirements: Degree of a UK university of the CNAA or a recognised equivalent qualification that has a significant proportion of content relevant to science; sufficient undergraduate study to teach all 3 sciences (biology, chemistry and physics) to Key Stage 3, 2 sciences to Key Stage 4 and at least 1 to A-Level; at least grade C in GCSE (or equivalent) mathematics and English language; candidates should have recently visited and assisted/observed in a mainstream UK secondary school, preferably 11–18.

Contact: As above

Diploma/MA in Education for School Improvement (CPD)

Part-time

Entry requirements: Open to qualified teachers at all levels
Contact: Dr Rosie Penny
Programme Director
020 8240 4197
pennyr@smuc.ac.uk

Staffordshire University

College Road
Stoke on Trent
ST4 2DE
Tel: 01782 294000
Fax: 01782 295704
public@staffs.ac.uk
www.staffs.ac.uk

Staffordshire University caters for approximately 15,000 full-time and 2,500 part-time students. It is situated on three campuses: Stoke, Stafford and Lichfield. The Stoke campus is based in the heart of the City of Stoke-on-Trent. Stafford campus is 18 miles from the Stoke campus and a short bus ride from Stafford town centre. There is a regular University minibus service between the two main campuses. The Lichfield campus is 11 miles by road from Stafford and is situated in the centre of Lichfield in a new purpose-built building. The university has halls of residence at the Stoke and Stafford Campuses and there is also private accommodation available which is registered at the university.

The University developed from the Staffordshire Polytechnic in September 1992 which had been created from the merger of the Staffordshire College of Technology in Stafford, the Stoke-on-Trent College of Art, and the North Staffordshire College of Technology based in Stoke. It now caters for 17,000 students and there are a variety

of sport and recreational facilities available, a large Student's Union and extensive library and computing facilities. The university offers teacher training via the PGCE route in specialised subjects.

HOW TO APPLY

PGCE: applications are made through the GTTR.

COURSES

PGCE Secondary Education (Business Studies and Information Technology) NX11

1 year full-time

Entry requirements: At least a 2:2 Honours degree or equivalent in economics, business or management, plus GCSE mathematics and English at grade C or above (or equivalent), mature students with a non-business degree but with appropriate work experience may also be considered.
Contact: Helen Howie
PGCE Administrator
01782 294085
cebe@staffs.ac.uk

PGCE Secondary Education (Economics and Business Education) L1X1

1 year full-time

Entry requirements: At least a 2:2 Honours degree or equivalent in economics, business or management, plus GCSE mathematics and English at grade C or above (or equivalent), mature students with a non-business or economics degree but with appropriate work experience may also be considered.

Contact: Peter Davies
Course Tutor
01782 294085
p.i.davies@staffs.ac.uk

University of Stirling

Stirling
FK9 4LA
Tel: 01786 473171
Fax: 01786 466800
admissions@stir.ac.uk
www.stir.ac.uk

The University of Stirling was opened in 1967 on a brand new campus built on the estate of the 18th-century Airthrey Castle. It has two additional campuses: the Highland Campus situated in the grounds of Raigmore Hospital in Inverness and the Western Isles Campus located in Stornoway.

The Institute of Education was created in 1998 and is located on the main campus. It is the location of two major research centres in the areas of Lifelong Learning (with Glasgow Caledonian University), and Language in Society. The Institute offers Teacher Education within a concurrent programme leading to degree qualifications with a Diploma in Education, and a Teacher Qualification in Further Education, which may be taken at either undergraduate or postgraduate level. There are other undergraduate degrees, a range of Master's programme, including two completely web-based degrees, and opportunities for Doctoral studies or research degrees.

The library at the university is centrally located and students have access to computers with a variety of IT resources. All first-year students are guaranteed accommodation and there is also some especially reserved for postgraduates.

HOW TO APPLY

Degree courses: applications are made through UCAS.

Postgraduate: applications are made direct to the institution.

COURSES

BSc/BSc (Hons) in Secondary Education (Biology) CX11

BSc: 3 years full-time, BSc (Hons): 4 years full-time

Includes 21 weeks of school and teaching experience.

Years 1 and 2: Biology core units in: cell biology; physiology; ecology; introductory genetics; education units in: human relationships in the classroom; the curriculum; society and schools; 3 weeks' school experience.

Year 3: Advanced biology courses in animal and plant diversity; structure and functional biology; experimental biology; principles and analysis; microbiology; plant ecophysiology; education units in: teaching strategies; curriculum studies; 6 vacation weeks; 1 day per week school experience during semester.

Year 4: Honours biology courses including research project; education dissertation.

Year 4.5: Teaching practice.

On completion students are recommended to the General Teaching Council for Scotland for provisional registration. Full registration is awarded on the completion of 2 satisfactory years (or equivalent) of teaching.

Entry requirements: GCE A- and AS-levels: BCD, International Baccalaureate: 26, SCE Higher: BBCC, BTEC NC/ND
Contact: As above

BA/BA (Hons) in Secondary Education (Business Studies) NX11

BA: 3 years full-time, BA (Hons): 4 years full-time

Includes 21 weeks of school and teaching experience.

Semesters 1 and 2: Human relationships in the classroom: teachers and pupils attitudes, teachers' perception of pupils, teaching styles, language in classrooms, classroom groups; curriculum, society and schools including the 5–14 Curriculum in Scotland, and the National Curriculum in England and Wales; business studies.

Semester 4: Subject studies (business studies); teaching and learning; lesson planning; teaching small groups of children with video-feedback.

Semester 5: Subject studies (business studies); planning, teaching and evaluating units of work; practical work.

Semester 6: Subject studies (business studies); Education of pupils with learning difficulties; subject teaching in schools; research methods in education (Honours only).

Semester 7 (Ordinary degree): Curriculum studies and instructional techniques; classroom management; final teaching practice.

Semesters 7 and 8 (Honours degree): Dissertation in education (majoring in education only) or subject studies (business studies) only.

Semester 9 (Honours only): Curriculum studies and instructional techniques; classroom management; final teaching practice.

On completion students are recommended to the General Teaching Council for Scotland for provisional registration. Full registration is awarded on the completion of 2 satisfactory years (or equivalent) of teaching.

Entry requirements: GCE A- and AS-levels: BBC, SCE Higher: BBBB, International Baccalaureate: 30, BTEC NC/ND
Contact: As above

BA/BA (Hons) in Secondary Education (Business Studies/Computing Science) NX21

BA: 3 years full-time, BA (Hons): 4 years full-time

On completion students are recommended to the General Teaching Council for Scotland for provisional registration. Full registration is awarded on the completion of 2 satisfactory years (or equivalent) of teaching.

Entry requirements: As above
Contact: As above

BSc/BSc (Hons) in Secondary Education (Computing Science) GX41

BSc: 3 years full-time, BSc (Hons): 4 years full-time

Includes 21 weeks of school and teaching experience.

Semesters 1 and 2: Human relationships in the classroom: teachers and pupils attitudes, teachers' perception of pupils, teaching styles, language in classrooms, classroom groups; curriculum, society and schools including the 5–14 Curriculum in Scotland, and the National Curriculum in England and Wales; subject studies (Computing Science).

Semester 4: Subject studies (Computing science); teaching and learning; lesson planning; teaching small groups of children with video-feedback.

Semester 5: Subject studies (Computing science); planning, teaching and evaluating units of work; practical work.

Semester 6: Subject studies (Computing science); Education of pupils with learning difficulties; subject teaching in schools; research methods in education (Honours only).

Semester 7 (Ordinary degree): Curriculum studies and instructional techniques; classroom management; final teaching practice.

Semesters 7 and 8 (Honours degree): Dissertation in education (majoring in education only) or subject studies (Computing science) only.

Semester 9 (Honours only): Curriculum studies and instructional techniques; classroom management; final teaching practice.

On completion students are recommended to the General Teaching Council for Scotland for provisional registration. Full registration is awarded on the completion of 2 satisfactory years (or equivalent) of teaching.

Entry requirements: GCE A- and AS-levels: CCD, International Baccalaureate: 26, SCE Higher: BBCC, BTEC NC/ND
Contact: As above

BSc/BSc (Hons) in Secondary Education (Computing Science/Mathematics) GX91
BSc: 3 years full-time, BSc (Hons): 4 years full-time

On completion students are recommended to the General Teaching Council for Scotland for provisional registration. Full registration is awarded on the completion of 2 satisfactory years (or equivalent) of teaching.

Entry requirements: As above
Contact: As above

BA/ BA (Hons) in Secondary Education (English Studies) QX31
BA: 3 years full-time, BA (Hons): 4 years full-time

Includes 21 weeks of school and teaching experience.

Semesters 1 and 2: Human relationships in the classroom: teachers and pupils attitudes, teachers' perception of pupils, teaching styles, language in classrooms, classroom groups; curriculum, society and schools including the 5–14 Curriculum in Scotland, and the National Curriculum in England and Wales; subject studies (English studies).

Semester 4: Subject studies (English studies); teaching and learning; lesson planning; teaching small groups of children with video-feedback.

Semester 5: Subject studies (English studies); planning, teaching and evaluating units of work; practical work.

Semester 6: Subject studies (English studies); Education of pupils with learning difficulties; subject teaching in schools; research methods in education (Honours only).

Semester 7 (Ordinary degree): Curriculum studies and instructional techniques; classroom management; final teaching practice.

Semesters 7 and 8 (Honours degree): Dissertation in education (majoring in education only) or subject studies (English studies) only.

Semester 9 (Honours only): Curriculum studies and instructional techniques; classroom management; final teaching practice.

On completion students are recommended to the General Teaching Council for Scotland for provisional registration. Full registration is awarded on the completion of 2 satisfactory years (or equivalent) of teaching.

Entry requirements: GCE A- and AS-levels: BBC, International Baccalaureate: 30, SCE Higher: BBBB, HNC, HND
Contact: As above

BA/BA (Hons) in Secondary Education (English Studies/Film and Media Studies) QXH1
BA: 3 years full-time, BA (Hons): 4 years full-time

On completion students are recommended to the General Teaching Council for Scotland for provisional registration. Full registration is awarded on the completion of 2 satisfactory years (or equivalent) of teaching.

Entry requirements: GCE A- and AS-levels: BBC, International Baccalaureate: 32, SCE Higher: ABBB
Contact: As above

BA/BA (Hons) in Secondary Education (English Studies/Post-colonial Literature) QX21
BA: 3 years full-time, BA (Hons): 4 years full-time

Includes 21 weeks of school and teaching experience.

Semesters 1 and 2: Human relationships in the classroom: teachers and pupils attitudes, teachers' perception of pupils, teaching styles, language in classrooms, classroom groups; curriculum, society and schools including the 5–14 Curriculum in Scotland, and the National Curriculum in England and Wales.

Semester 4: Subject studies (English studies and post-colonial literature); teaching and learning; lesson planning; teaching small groups of children with video-feedback.

Semester 5: Subject studies (English studies and post-colonial literature); planning, teaching and evaluating units of work; practical work.

Semester 6: Subject studies (English studies and post-colonial literature); education of pupils with learning difficulties; subject teaching in schools; research methods in education (Honours only).

Semester 7 (Ordinary degree): Curriculum studies and instructional techniques; classroom management; final teaching practice.

Semesters 7 and 8 (Honours degree): Dissertation in education (majoring in education only) or subject studies (English studies and post-colonial literature) only.

Semester 9 (Honours only): Curriculum studies and instructional techniques; classroom management; final teaching practice.

On completion students are recommended to the General Teaching Council for Scotland for provisional registration. Full registration is awarded on the completion of 2 satisfactory years (or equivalent) of teaching.

Entry requirements: GCE A- and AS-levels: BBC, International Baccalaureate: 30, SCE Higher: BBBB, BTEC NC/ND
Contact: As above

BA/BA (Hons) in Secondary Education (English/History) QXHC

BA: 3 years full-time, BA (Hons): 4 years full-time

On completion students are recommended to the General Teaching Council for Scotland for provisional registration. Full registration is awarded on the completion of 2 satisfactory years (or equivalent) of teaching.

Entry requirements: As above
Contact: As above

BA/BA (Hons) in Secondary Education (English/Religious Studies) QXJ1

BA: 3 years full-time, BA (Hons): 4 years full-time
As above

Entry requirements: GCE A- and AS-levels: BBC, International Baccalaureate: 30, SCE Higher: BBBB, HNC, HND
Contact: As above

BSc/BSc (Hons) in Secondary Education (Environmental Science, Geography) FX81

BSc: 3 years full-time, BSc (Hons): 4 years full-time
As above

Entry requirements: GCE A- and AS-levels: CCD, International Baccalaureate: 26, SCE Higher: BBCC, BTEC NC/ND
Contact: As above

BA/BA (Hons) in Secondary Education (French) RX11

BA: 4 years full-time with time abroad, BA (Hons): 5 years full-time with time abroad

Includes 21 weeks of school and teaching experience.

Semesters 1 and 2: Human relationships in the classroom: teachers and pupils attitudes, teachers' perception of pupils, teaching styles, language in classrooms, classroom groups; curriculum, society and schools including the 5–14 Curriculum in Scotland, and the National Curriculum in England and Wales; subject studies (French).

Semester 4: Subject studies (French); teaching and learning; lesson planning; teaching small groups of children with video-feedback.

Semester 5: Subject studies (French); planning, teaching and evaluating units of work; practical work.

Semester 6: Subject studies (French); Education of pupils with learning difficulties; subject teaching in schools; research methods in education (Honours only).

Semester 7 (Ordinary degree): Curriculum studies and instructional techniques; classroom management; final teaching practice.

Semesters 7 and 8 (Honours degree): Dissertation in education (majoring in education only) or subject studies (French) only.

Semester 9 (Honours only): Curriculum studies and instructional techniques; classroom management; final teaching practice.

Residence abroad: Students normally spend an additional year abroad in a French-speaking country.

On completion students are recommended to the General Teaching Council for Scotland for provisional registration. Full registration is awarded on the completion of 2 satisfactory years (or equivalent) of teaching.

Entry requirements: GCE A- and AS-levels: CCC, International Baccalaureate: 28, SCE Higher: BBCC, BTEC NC/ND
Contact: As above

BA/BA (Hons) in Secondary Education (French/German) RXC1

BA: 3 years full-time, BA (Hons): 4 years full-time

On completion students are recommended to the General Teaching Council for Scotland for provisional registration. Full registration is awarded on the completion of 2 satisfactory years (or equivalent) of teaching.

Entry requirements: As above
Contact: As above

BA/BA (Hons) in Secondary Education (French/Spanish) RXD1

BA: 3 years full-time, BA (Hons): 4 years full-time

As above

Entry requirements: GCE A- and AS-levels: CCC, International Baccalaureate: 28, SCE Higher: BBCC, HNC, HND
Contact: As above

BA/BA (Hons) in Secondary Education (German) RX21

BA: 4 years full-time, BA (Hons): 5 years full-time with time abroad

Includes 21 weeks of school and teaching experience.

Semesters 1 and 2: Human relationships in the classroom: teachers and pupils attitudes, teachers' perception of pupils, teaching styles, language in classrooms, classroom groups; curriculum, society and schools including the 5–14 Curriculum in Scotland, and the National Curriculum in England and Wales; subject studies (German).

Semester 4: Subject studies (German); teaching and learning; lesson planning; teaching small groups of children with video-feedback.

Semester 5: Subject studies (German); planning, teaching and evaluating units of work; practical work.

Semester 6: Subject studies (German); Education of pupils with learning difficulties; subject teaching in schools; research methods in education (Honours only).

Semester 7 (Ordinary degree): Curriculum studies and instructional techniques; classroom management; final teaching practice.

Semesters 7 and 8 (Honours degree): Dissertation in education (majoring in education only) or subject studies (German) only.

Semester 9 (Honours only): Curriculum studies and instructional techniques; classroom management; final teaching practice.

Residence abroad: Students normally spend an additional year abroad in a German-speaking country.

Students may join the introductory German or advanced German course depending on entry qualifications.

On completion students are recommended to the General Teaching Council for Scotland for provisional registration. Full registration is awarded on the completion of 2 satisfactory years (or equivalent) of teaching.

Entry requirements: GCE A- and AS-levels: CCC, International Baccalaureate: 28, SCE Higher: BBCC, BTEC NC/ND
Contact: As above

BA/BA (Hons) in Secondary Education (German/Spanish) RXF1

BA: 3 years full-time, BA (Hons): 4 years full-time

On completion students are recommended to the General Teaching Council for Scotland for provisional registration. Full registration is awarded on the completion of 2 satisfactory years (or equivalent) of teaching.

Entry requirements: GCE A- and AS-levels: CCC, International Baccalaureate: 28, SCE Higher: BBCC, HNC, HND

Contact: As above

PGCE in Secondary Education (History) VX11

BA: 3 years full-time, BA (Hons): 4 years full-time

Entry requirements: GCE A- and AS-levels: CCC, International Baccalaureate: 28, SCE Higher: BBBC, BTEC NC/ND,

Contact: As above

BA/BA (Hons) in Secondary Education (History/Politics) LX21

BA: 3 years full-time, BA (Hons): 4 years full-time

On completion students are recommended to the General Teaching Council for Scotland for provisional registration. Full registration is awarded on the completion

of 2 satisfactory years (or equivalent) of teaching.

Entry requirements: GCE A- and AS-levels: BCC, International Baccalaureate: 30, SCE Higher: BBBC
Contact: As above

BA/BA (Hons) in Secondary Education (History/Religious Studies)

BA: 3 years full-time, BA (Hons): 4 years full-time
As above

Entry requirements: GCE A- and AS-levels: BCC, International Baccalaureate: 28, SCE Higher: BBBC, BTEC NC/ND
Contact: As above

BSc/BSc (Hons) in Secondary Education (Mathematics and its Applications) GXC1

BSc: 3 years full-time, BSc (Hons): 4 years full-time

Includes 21 weeks of school and teaching experience.

Semesters 1 and 2: Human relationships in the classroom: teachers and pupils attitudes; teachers' perception of pupils; teaching styles; language in classrooms; classroom groups; curriculum; society and schools including the 5–14 Curriculum in Scotland and the National Curriculum in England and Wales; subject studies (mathematics and its applications).

Semester 4: Subject studies (mathematics and its applications); teaching and learning; lesson planning; teaching small groups of children with video-feedback.

Semester 5: Subject studies (mathematics and its applications); planning, teaching and evaluating units of work; practical work.

Semester 6: Subject studies (mathematics and its applications); education of pupils with learning difficulties; subject teaching in schools; research methods in education (Honours only).

Semester 7 (Ordinary degree): Curriculum studies and instructional techniques; classroom management; final teaching practice. Semesters 7 and 8 (Honours degree): Dissertation in education (majoring in education only) or subject studies (mathematics and its applications) only.

Semester 9 (Honours only): Curriculum studies and instructional techniques; classroom management; final teaching practice.

On completion students are recommended to the General Teaching Council for Scotland for provisional registration. Full registration is awarded on the completion of 2 satisfactory years (or equivalent) of teaching.

Entry requirements: GCE A- and AS-levels: CCD, International Baccalaureate: 26, SCE Higher: BBCC, HNC, HND
Contact: As above

BSc/BSc (Hons) in Secondary Education (Mathematics) GX11

BSc: 3 years full-time, BSc (Hons): 4 years full-time

Includes 21 weeks of school and teaching experience.

Semesters 1 and 2: Human relationships in the classroom: teachers and pupils attitudes; teachers' perception of pupils; teaching styles; language in classrooms; classroom groups; curriculum; society and schools including the 5–14 Curriculum in Scotland and the National Curriculum in England and Wales; subject studies (mathematics and its applications).

Semester 4: Subject studies (mathematics and its applications); teaching and learning; lesson planning; teaching small groups of children with video-feedback.

Semester 5: Subject studies (mathematics and its applications); planning, teaching and evaluating units of work; practical work.

Semester 6: Subject studies (mathematics and its applications); education of pupils with learning difficulties; subject teaching in schools; research methods in education (Honours only).

Semester 7 (Ordinary degree): Curriculum studies and instructional techniques; classroom management; final teaching practice.

Semesters 7 and 8 (Honours degree): Dissertation in education (majoring in education only) or subject studies (mathematics and its applications) only.

Semester 9 (Honours only): Curriculum studies and instructional techniques; classroom management; final teaching practice.

On completion students are recommended to the General Teaching Council for Scotland for provisional registration. Full registration is awarded on the completion of 2 satisfactory years (or equivalent) of teaching.

Entry requirements: As above
Contact: As above

BA/BA (Hons) in Secondary Education (Religious Studies) VX61

BA: 3 years full-time, BA (Hons): 4 years full-time

Includes 21 weeks of school and teaching experience.

Semesters 1 and 2: Human relationships in the classroom: teachers and pupils attitudes, teachers' perception of pupils, teaching styles, language in classrooms, classroom groups; curriculum, society and schools including the 5–14 Curriculum in Scotland, and the National Curriculum in England and Wales; subject studies (religious studies).

Semester 4: Subject studies (religious studies); teaching and learning; lesson planning; teaching small groups of children with video-feedback.

Semester 5: Subject studies (religious studies); planning, teaching and evaluating units of work; practical work.

Semester 6: Subject studies (religious studies); education of pupils with learning difficulties; subject teaching in schools; research methods in education (Honours only).

Semester 7 (Ordinary degree): Curriculum studies and instructional techniques; classroom management; final teaching practice.

Semesters 7 and 8 (Honours degree): Dissertation in education (majoring in education only) or subject studies (religious studies) only.

Semester 9 (Honours only): Curriculum studies and instructional techniques; classroom management; final teaching practice.

On completion students are recommended to the General Teaching Council for Scotland for provisional registration. Full registration is awarded on the completion of 2 satisfactory years (or equivalent) of teaching.

Entry requirements: GCE A- and AS-levels: CCC, International Baccalaureate: 26, SCE Higher: BBCC BTEC NC/ND
Contact: As above

BA/BA (Hons) in Secondary Education (Spanish) RX41

BA: 4 years full-time with time abroad, BA (Hons): 5 years full-time with time abroad

Includes 21 weeks of school and teaching experience.

Semesters 1 and 2: Human relationships in the classroom: teachers and pupils attitudes; teachers' perception of pupils; teaching styles; language in classrooms; classroom groups; curriculum, society and schools including the 5–14 Curriculum in Scotland, and the National Curriculum in England and Wales; subject studies (Spanish).

Semester 4: Subject studies (Spanish); teaching and learning; lesson planning; teaching small groups of children with video-feedback.

Semester 5: Subject studies (Spanish); planning, teaching and evaluating units of work; practical work.

Semester 6: Subject studies (Spanish); Education of pupils with learning difficulties; subject teaching in schools; research methods in education (Honours only).

Semester 7 (Ordinary degree): Curriculum studies and instructional techniques; classroom management; final teaching practice.

Semesters 7 and 8 (Honours degree): Dissertation in education (majoring in education only) or subject studies (Spanish) only.

Semester 9 (Honours only): Curriculum studies and instructional techniques; classroom management; final teaching practice.

Residence abroad: Students normally spend an additional year abroad in a Spanish-speaking country.

Students may join the introductory Spanish or advanced Spanish course depending on entry qualifications.

On completion students are recommended to the General Teaching Council for Scotland for provisional registration. Full registration is awarded on the completion of 2 satisfactory years (or equivalent) of teaching.

Entry requirements: GCE A- and AS-levels: CCC, International Baccalaureate: 31, SCE Higher: BBBC, BTEC NC/ND
Contact: As above

MPhil/EdD in Education

MPhil: 3–4 years part-time, EdD: 4–6 years part-time

Entry requirements: Degree and/or MA/MEd and minimum 3 years' relevant professional experience; 2 satisfactory references; outline of the area of research.
Contact: Prof Richard Edwards
Programme Director
01786 466264
rge1@stir.ac.uk

PgCert/PgDip/MSc in Lifelong Learning

PgCert: 1–2 years on-line study, PgDip 2–4 years on-line study, MSc 2.5–5 years on-line study

Entry requirements: Recognised degree normally required; exceptionally, access could be gained to programme on basis of qualification deemed equivalent to a first degree or on basis of relevant prior experiential learning.

Contact: Dr Roy Canning
01786 467613
Roy.Canning@stir.ac.uk

Pgcert/Pgdip/MEd in Management for Tertiary Education

MEd: 36 months part-time

Entry requirements: Degree and either an appropriate professional qualification or at least 2 years' relevant experience. Non-graduates with appropriate professional qualifications or experience may exceptionally be admitted to the PgCert or PgDip. Candidates also require access to a suitable work setting.

Contact: As above

Pgcert/Pgdip/MEd in Professional Enquiry in Education

MEd: 36 months part-time

Entry requirements: Applicants must be nominated by their employer and have access to suitable setting in order to undertake work-based action learning. Applicants aiming to address the Chartered Teacher Standard must be either registered or eligible to register with the General Teaching Council for Scotland and have a minimum of 5 years' teaching experience.

Contact: MEd Secretary
01786 467606
educ-pg@stir.ac.uk

Pgdip in School Leadership and Management (SQH)

2 years part-time

Entry requirements: For senior managers in schools who are sponsored by their employers and are Scottish Teaching Council registered teachers. Participants must have access to management development opportunities in a school as much of the course is delivered as work-based learning.

Contact: Dr Jenny Reeves
Director of CPD
01786 466276
cjr1@stir.ac.uk

Pgcert/Pgdip in Teaching (Further Education)

PgCert: 2 semesters full-time, 6 semesters part-time, PgDip: 3 semester full-time, 8 semesters part-time

Entry requirements: Degree or equivalent qualification.

Contact: Dr Brenda Morgan-Klein
Course Director
01786 467603
education.tqfe@stir.ac.uk

Pgcert/Pgdip/MSc in Teaching English to Speakers of Other Languages

MSc: 11 months full-time, 23 months part-time

Entry requirements: Degree in any discipline accepted, non-native speakers of English must have reached minimum IELTS 6.5 or TOEFL 600.

Contact: Mrs Stephanie Tytler
Associate Director CELT
01786 467934
hwm1@stir.ac.uk

Pgcert/Pgdip/MEd in Technology-Enhanced Learning

MEd: 36 months on-line study

Entry requirements: Degree and either an appropriate professional qualification or at least 2 years' relevant experience. Non-graduates with appropriate professional qualifications or experience may exceptionally be admitted to the PgCert or PgDip.

Contact: Dr Roy Canning
01786 467613
roy.canning@stir.ac.uk

Stranmillis University College

Stranmillis Road
Belfast
County Antrim
BT9 5DY
Tel: 028 9038 1271
Fax: 028 9066 4423
registry@stran-ni.ac.uk
www.stran-ni.ac.uk

Stranmillis University College was founded in 1922 and is situated on a campus set in 46 acres of woodland. It has expanded and improved to include modern halls of residence, Information Technology Centre, Learning Resource Unit and purpose built Library. There is also a wide range of sports and leisure facilities available to students. Stranmillis has a student population of around 700 and all qualifications are validated and awarded by Queen's University of Belfast which is located a short distance from the college.

The college offers initial teacher training at primary and secondary level through a degree route, the PGCE in educational psychology and early years and also postgraduate programmes including opportunities for Continuing Professional Development.

HOW TO APPLY

Undergraduate courses: applications are made through UCAS.
PGCE: applications are made direct to the institution.

COURSES

BEd (Hons) Primary Education (Art and Design, 3–13 years) XW11
4 years full-time
School-based work including teaching practice.

Curriculum Studies: Students gain knowledge of the subjects of the Northern Ireland curriculum at a level which will support effective classroom teaching at both Key Stages 1 and 2.

Art and design modules include: Foundation studies; visual and interpretative studies; studies in 2- and 3-dimensional design in the areas of ceramics, drawing and painting and textiles; dissertation; option.

Successful completion of this course leads to a recommendation for Qualified Teacher Status (QTS) after completion of skills tests.

Entry requirements: AVCEs: BBC, GCE A- and AS-levels: BBC, Interview
Contact: Miss Mae Watson
Director of Academic and Information Services
028 9038 1271
registry@stran.ac.uk

BEd (Hons) Primary Education (Dramatic Art and English, 3–13 years) XW14
4 years full-time
Course includes: Education Studies: Study of the whole process of schooling and the social contexts within which it takes place. Courses cover pupils and their education, foundation of the curriculum, teachers in schools and an option.

Professional Studies: School-based work including teaching practice.

Curriculum Studies: Students gain knowledge of the subjects of the Northern Ireland curriculum at a level which will support effective classroom teaching at both Key Stages 1 and 2.

Dramatic art with English modules include: Foundation studies in drama and English; theatre studies; Anglo-Irish literature; theatre and critical studies; dissertation.

Successful completion of this course leads to a recommendation for Qualified Teacher Status (QTS) after completion of skills tests.

Entry requirements: AVCEs: BBC, GCE A- and AS-levels: BBC, Foundation / access qualification, Interview
Contact: As above

BEd (Hons) Primary Education (English, 3–13 years) XQ13

4 years full-time

Course includes: Education Studies: Study of the whole process of schooling and the social contexts within which it takes place. Courses cover pupils and their education, foundation of the curriculum, teachers in schools and an option.

Professional Studies: School-based work including teaching practice.

Curriculum Studies: Students gain knowledge of the subjects of the Northern Ireland curriculum at a level which will support effective classroom teaching at both Key Stages 1 and 2.

English modules include: Genre study; thematic study (man and nature; comedy); Anglo-Irish literature; curriculum option and literary theory; 20th-century literature and option study; dissertation.

Successful completion of this course leads to a recommendation for Qualified Teacher Status (QTS) after completion of skills tests.

Entry requirements: GCE A- and AS-levels: BBB, Foundation / access qualification, Interview

Contact: As above

BEd (Hons) Primary Education (Geography, 3–13 years) XL17

4 years full-time

Course includes: Education Studies: Study of the whole process of schooling and the social contexts within which it takes place. Courses cover pupils and their education, foundation of the curriculum, teachers in schools and an option.

Professional Studies: School-based work including teaching practice.

Curriculum Studies: Students gain knowledge of the subjects of the Northern Ireland curriculum at a level which will support effective classroom teaching at both Key Stages 1 and 2.

Geography modules include: Geographical education; development studies: local and

global; principles of physical geography; principles of human geography; Europe and its neighbours; physical option chosen from geomorphology or biogeography; human option chosen from social or historical geography; dissertation.

Successful completion of this course leads to a recommendation for Qualified Teacher Status (QTS) after completion of skills tests.

Entry requirements: As above
Contact: As above

BEd (Hons) Primary Education (History, 3–13 years) XV11

4 years full-time

Course includes: Education Studies: Study of the whole process of schooling and the social contexts within which it takes place. Courses cover pupils and their education, foundation of the curriculum, teachers in schools and an option.

Professional Studies: School-based work including teaching practice.

Curriculum Studies: Students gain knowledge of the subjects of the Northern Ireland curriculum at a level which will support effective classroom teaching at both Key Stages 1 and 2.

History modules include: History of Ireland and her neighbours from the fifth to the thirteenth century; European history 1870–1963; Irish history 1850–1922; British history 1865–1939; Ulster politics, partition and the establishment of Northern Ireland c1900–1950; dissertation.

Successful completion of this course leads to a recommendation for Qualified Teacher Status (QTS) after completion of skills tests.

Entry requirements: As above
Contact: As above

BEd (Hons) Primary Education (Information Technology, 3–13 years) XG15

4 years full-time

Course includes: Education Studies: Study of the whole process of schooling and the social contexts within which it takes place.

Courses cover pupils and their education, foundation of the curriculum, teachers in schools and an option.

Professional Studies: School-based work including teaching practice.

Curriculum Studies: Students gain knowledge of the subjects of the Northern Ireland curriculum at a level which will support effective classroom teaching at both Key Stages 1 and 2.

Information Technology modules include: Structured programming; computer hardware; microprocessor architecture; modular programming; multi-media systems; database technology; dissertation.

Successful completion of this course leads to a recommendation for Qualified Teacher Status (QTS) after completion of skills tests.

Entry requirements: AVCEs: BCC, GCE A- and AS-levels: BCC, Foundation / access qualification, Interview
Contact: As above

BEd (Hons) Primary Education (Mathematics, 3–13 years) XG11

4 years full-time

Course includes: Education Studies: Study of the whole process of schooling and the social contexts within which it takes place. Courses cover pupils and their education, foundation of the curriculum, teachers in schools and an option.

Professional Studies: School-based work including teaching practice.

Curriculum Studies: Students gain knowledge of the subjects of the Northern Ireland curriculum at a level which will support effective classroom teaching at both Key Stages 1 and 2.

Mathematics modules include: Calculus, mechanics and discrete mathematics; linear algebra, analysis and data handling; operational research; finite mathematics; 2 modules form: topics in applied mathematics; computer algebra; dissertation.

Successful completion of this course leads to a recommendation for Qualified Teacher Status (QTS) after completion of skills tests.

Entry requirements: GCE A- and AS-levels: BBB, Interview
Contact: As above

BEd (Hons) Primary Education (Music, 3–13 years) XW13

4 years full-time

Course includes: Education Studies: Study of the whole process of schooling and the social contexts within which it takes place. Courses cover pupils and their education, foundation of the curriculum, teachers in schools and an option.

Professional Studies: School-based work including teaching practice.

Curriculum Studies: Students gain knowledge of the subjects of the Northern Ireland curriculum at a level which will support effective classroom teaching at both Key Stage 1 and 2.

Music modules include: Western music 1660–1830; performance and listening skills; baroque and classical composition; music in the primary curriculum; Western music 1830–present; 19th and early 20th-century composition; special historical topics; applied compositional and analytical studies 1500–1900; performance skills; keyboard skills; assessment of music at Key Stages 1 and 2; the role of the co-ordinator; 20th-century techniques and styles; dissertation; orchestration, arranging and editing; instrumental techniques; conducting skills.

Successful completion of this course leads to a recommendation for Qualified Teacher Status (QTS) after completion of skills tests.

Entry requirements: Audition, GCE A- and AS-levels: BCC, Foundation / access qualification, Interview
Contact: As above

BEd (Hons) Primary Education (Physical Education, 3–13 years) XX13

4 years full-time

Course includes: Education Studies: Study of the whole process of schooling and the social contexts within which it takes place. Courses cover pupils and their education, foundation of the curriculum, teachers in schools and an option.

Professional Studies: School-based work including teaching practice.

Curriculum Studies: Students gain knowledge of the subjects of the Northern Ireland curriculum at a level which will support effective classroom teaching at both Key Stages 1 and 2.

Physical education modules include: Childhood studies in physical education; movement studies in physical education; investigations in physical education; issues in physical education.

Successful completion of this course leads to a recommendation for Qualified Teacher Status (QTS) after completion of skills tests.

Entry requirements: AVCEs: BBC, GCE A- and AS-levels: BBC, Foundation / access qualification, Interview
Contact: As above

BEd (Hons) Primary Education (Religious Studies, 3–13 years)

4 years full-time

Course includes: Education Studies: Study of the whole process of schooling and the social contexts within which it takes place. Courses cover pupils and their education, foundation of the curriculum, teachers in schools and an option.

Professional Studies: School-based work including teaching practice.

Curriculum Studies: Students gain knowledge of the subjects of the Northern Ireland curriculum at a level which will support effective classroom teaching at both Key Stages 1 and 2.

Religious Studies modules include: Biblical studies; education into religion; the history and faith of the early church; the reforma-tion and varieties of Christian experience; Christian morality; religion and ideologies; theology and education; dissertation.

Successful completion of this course leads to a recommendation for Qualified Teacher Status (QTS) after completion of skills tests.

Entry requirements: GCE A- and AS-levels: BBB, Foundation / access qualification, Interview
Contact: As above

BEd (Hons) Primary Education (Science, 3–13 years) XF10

4 years full-time

Course includes: Education Studies: Study of the whole process of schooling and the social contexts within which it takes place. Courses cover pupils and their education, foundation of the curriculum, teachers in schools and an option.

Professional Studies: School-based work including teaching practice.

Curriculum Studies: Students gain knowledge of the subjects of the Northern Ireland curriculum at a level which will support effective classroom teaching at both Key Stages 1 and 2.

Science modules include: Structure and function; interactions; energy; the natural history of Ireland; the biology of the individual; cell biology; population biology; dissertation.

Successful completion of this course leads to a recommendation for Qualified Teacher Status (QTS) after completion of skills tests.

Entry requirements: AVCEs: BBB, GCE A- and AS-levels: BBB, Foundation / access qualification, Interview
Contact: As above

BEd (Hons) Secondary Education (Business Studies, 11–18 years) XN11

4 years full-time

Course includes: Education Studies: study of the whole process of schooling and the social contexts within which it takes place. Courses cover pupils and their education, foundation of the curriculum, teachers in schools and an option.

Professional Studies: Teaching practice and acquisition of classroom skills; school-based work, including teaching practice.

Business studies modules include: Business environment; business accounting; marketing; human resource management; information technology skills for business; management studies; management and cost accounting; financial management; European/international studies; business policy; operations management/management information systems; dissertation.

Successful completion of this course leads to a recommendation for Qualified Teacher Status (QTS) after completion of skills tests.

Entry requirements: AVCEs: BCC, GCE A- and AS-levels: BCC, Interview
Contact: As above

BEd (Hons) Secondary Education (Religious Studies, 11–18 years) XVC6

4 years full-time

Course includes: Education Studies: study of the whole process of schooling and the social contexts within which it takes place. Courses cover pupils and their education, foundation of the curriculum, teachers in schools and an option.

Professional Studies: Teaching practice and acquisition of classroom skills. School-based work, including teaching practice.

Religious studies modules include: Biblical studies; education into religion; the history and faith of the early church; the reformation and varieties of Christian experience; Christian morality; religion and ideologies; theology and education; dissertation.

Successful completion of this course leads to a recommendation for Qualified Teacher Status (QTS) after completion of skills tests.

Entry requirements: GCE A- and AS-levels: BCC, Foundation / access qualification, Interview
Contact: As above

BEd (Hons) Secondary Education (Technology and Design, 11–18 years) XW12

4 years full-time

Course includes: Education Studies: study of the whole process of schooling and the social contexts within which it takes place. Courses cover pupils and their education, foundation of the curriculum, teachers in schools and an option.

Professional Studies: Teaching practice and acquisition of classroom skills. School-based work, including teaching practice.

Technology and design modules include: Product design and manufacture; systems design; computer based systems; dissertation.

Successful completion of this course leads to a recommendation for Qualified Teacher Status (QTS) after completion of skills tests.

Entry requirements: AVCEs: CCC, GCE A- and AS-levels: CCC, Interview
Contact: As above

PGCE Early Years

36 weeks full-time

Entry requirements: Upper 2nd Class Honours degree, preferably in early years; degrees in curriculum areas, education, psychology are also acceptable; substantial experience working with children in a structured early years environment is essential.
Contact: As above

PGCE Education (Educational Psychology)

36 weeks full-time

Entry requirements: Minimum requirements are GCSE at least at grade C in English, science and mathematics and an Upper 2nd Class Honours degree in psychology. Applicants who wish to proceed to the MSc in Developmental and Educational Psychology of Queen's University of Belfast should make simultaneous application to Queen's for a place and entry to Stranmillis is conditional on acceptance; all students are required to teach for 2 years prior to progressing to educational psychology training courses.
Contact: As above

University of Strathclyde

McCance Building
16 Richmond Street
Glasgow
G1 1XQ
Tel: 0141 552 440
Fax: 0141 552 0775
scls@mis.strath.ac.uk
www.strath.ac.uk

The University was founded in 1796 as Anderson's Institution and became the University of Strathclyde in 1964. It is located in the city of Glasgow and currently has over 20,000 students. It is based on two campuses: John Anderson Campus in the city centre and Jordanhill Campus in the West End of Glasgow.

The Faculty of Education is based on the Jordanhill Campus and aside from the extensive computer facilities that are available at the university, students have access to the largest education research library in Scotland. The faculty offers opportunities for postgraduate study and research and a wide range of courses for further professional development for qualified teachers and other professionals as well as degree and PGCE courses.

Strathclyde has a campus village in the heart of the city with accommodation for undergraduates and postgraduates. Over 1,440 students live there and a further 500 live in other university accommodation within close walking distance. The Jordanhill Campus has its own halls of residence on site and there is further accommodation available through private rental.

HOW TO APPLY

Degree courses: applications are made through UCAS.

PGCE: applications are made through the GTTR.

Postgraduate: applications are made direct to the institution.

COURSES

BSc/BSc (Hons) in Biological Sciences with Teaching Qualification (Secondary)
C1X1

BSc: 3 years full-time, BSc (Hons): 4 years full-time

Year 1: Classes in bioscience, chemistry and education; bioscience topics include: cellular structure and function; inheritance; molecular biology and biotechnology; microbial and plant bioscience; animal bioscience; statistics for bioscience; introductory classes on education studies and science education are supported with school experience.

Year 2: Bioscience is studied in greater depth; courses include: nutrition and metabolism; cell biology; molecular biology and genetics; introductory microbiology and human physiology; a course is also taken in organic chemistry associated with biological processes; practical bioscience laboratory course develops further competence in the operation of biological apparatus, plus computer and communication skills associated with the biological sciences; education classes focus on effective learning and teaching, with a science education course which leads to periods of school experience.

Year 3: Advanced study in: plant biology and ecology; biochemistry in health and disease; molecular and cellular biology; microbiology; practical course which gives hands-on experience of modern biotechnology; continuing studies in education and biological education.

Year 4: Bioscience component focuses on biomedical science (with particular reference to human biology) and environmental biotechnology; there are also classes on: role of science in society; science communication; laboratory safety; biological education; an individual project occupies 25% of the year.

Year 5: Semester 1: school management; cross-curricular issues in biology teaching;

project in education; extended block of school experience.

On completion students are recommended to the General Teaching Council for Scotland for provisional registration. Full registration is awarded on the completion of 2 satisfactory years (or equivalent) of teaching.

Entry requirements: GCE A- and AS-levels: BBC, SCE Higher: BBC

Contact: Mr Charles Shaw / Mr Nicky Souter
Contact for Bioscience / Contact for Education
0141 548 2467 / 0141 950 3560
c.shaw@strath.ac.uk /
n.t.souter@strath.ac.uk

BSc (Hons) in Chemistry with Teaching Qualification (Secondary) FX11

4 years full-time

In each year, in addition to the core elements of the Chemistry MSci, there are 3 credits provided by the Faculty of Education, 1 of which is in practical school experience. The final written examinations are taken in the summer of Year 4, followed by a 3-month period the next autumn devoted entirely to education studies, a project in education and further school experience.

Entry requirements: GCE A- and AS-levels: BCC, SCE Higher: BBBB to AAB

Contact: Dr Debbie Willison / Paul Chambers
Academic Co-ordinator /
Contact for Education
0141 548 3281 / 0141 950 3410
d.willison@strath.ac.uk /
paul.chambers@strath.ac.uk

BSc/BSc (Hons) in Mathematics with Teaching Qualification (Secondary) G1X1

BSc: 3 years full-time, BSc (Hons): 4 years full-time

Years 1–3: Classes in mathematics and education, together with school experience.

Year 4: Almost entirely on mathematics-based classes; final semester is devoted to topics in education and school experience.

On completion students are recommended to the General Teaching Council for Scotland for provisional registration. Full registration is awarded on the completion of 2 satisfactory years (or equivalent) of teaching.

Entry requirements: GCE A- and AS-levels: BCC, SCE Higher: BBBB to ABBC

Contact: Dr Chris Coles / Paul Chambers
Contact for Mathematics /
Contact for Education
0141 548 3718 / 0141 950 3410
c.w.coles@strath.ac.uk /
p.chambers@strath.ac.uk

BSc (Hons) in Physics with Teaching Qualification (Secondary) F3X1

4 years full-time

This course integrates physics with teaching methods and practice. Covers the syllabus of the Honours physics degree plus the curriculum and classroom experience required for General Teaching Council recognition. All Years: Education classes; teaching experience; physics. Final semester: extended teaching practice.

Entry requirements: GCE A- and AS-levels: CC, SCE Higher: BBCC to BBB

Contact: Dr Ronal Brown / Paul Chambers
Contact for Physics / Contact for Education
0141 548 3378 / 0141 950 3410
ronal.brown@strath.ac.uk /
p.chambers@strath.ac.uk

BEd (Hons) in Primary Education X120

4 years full-time

Core programmes: Professional studies; environment; expressive arts; language; mathematics; religious and moral education; educational computing; independent study; major project; school experience and preparation for teaching.

Students also take 4 Faculty modules: Information and communication technology; social justice in professional roles; enquiry and research skills; personal development in a professional context.

Elective/option modules: Variety of curricular and cross-curricular options which build on the core programmes or consider issues crossing the various areas of the curriculum of Scottish primary schools, e.g. special needs in education; opportunity to develop an interest in areas, such as modern languages in the primary school, educational computing, Gaelic-medium education.

School placement in each year of the course, amounting to 25% of the total course.

On completion students are recommended to the General Teaching Council for Scotland for provisional registration.

Entry requirements: GCE A- and AS-levels: CCD to BB, SCE Higher: BBBC to BBBB
Contact: Ms J Moffat
        0141 950 3343
        j.j.moffat@strath.ac.uk

PGCE in Primary Education X100

36 weeks full-time

Entry requirements: Degree from UK university or CNAA, plus Higher English and Standard Grade mathematics at 2 or better; evidence of having worked with young people or general public, an understanding of modern primary education and an ability to relate to people will be taken into consideration.
Contact: Lynda Keith
        0141 950 3212
        l.keith@strath.ac.uk

PGCE in Secondary Education (Art and Design) W1X1

1 year full-time

Entry requirements: Degree from higher education institution in UK or degree of equivalent standard from institution outside UK; degree should normally contain passes in minimum of 3 years' progressive study in subjects student wants to teach; applicants must also have Higher English at C or above, or equivalent qualification.
Contact: Nicky Souter
        Course Director
        0141 950 3560
        PGCES@strath.ac.uk

PGCE in Secondary Education (Biology with Science) C1X1

1 year full-time
As above

PGCE in Secondary Education (Business Education) N1X1

1 year full-time
As above

PGCE in Secondary Education (Chemistry with Science) F1X1

1 year full-time
As above

PGCE in Secondary Education (Classics) Q8X1

1 year full-time
As above

PGCE in Secondary Education (Community Languages with another subject) Q9X1

1 year full-time
As above

PGCE in Secondary Education (Computing)   G5X1

1 year full-time
As above

PGCE in Secondary Education (Drama) W4X1

1 year full-time
As above

PGCE in Secondary Education (Economics with another subject) L1X1

1 year full-time
As above

PGCE in Secondary Education (English)
Q3X1
1 year full-time
As above

PGCE in Secondary Education (Gaelic)
Q5X1
1 year full-time
As above

PGCE in Secondary Education
(Geography)   F8X1
1 year full-time
As above

PGCE in Secondary Education (Greek)
Q7X1
1 year full-time
As above

PGCE in Secondary Education (History)
V1X1
1 year full-time
As above

PGCE in Secondary Education (Home
Economics) D6X1
1 year full-time
As above

PGCE in Secondary Education (Latin)
Q6X1
1 year full-time
As above

PGCE in Secondary Education
(Mathematics) G1X1
1 year full-time
As above

PGCE in Secondary Education (Modern
Languages: French) R1X1
1 year full-time
As above

PGCE in Secondary Education (Modern
Languages: German) R2X1
1 year full-time
As above

PGCE in Secondary Education (Modern
Languages: Italian) R3X1
1 year full-time
As above

PGCE in Secondary Education (Modern
Languages: Spanish) R4X1
1 year full-time
As above

PGCE in Secondary Education (Modern
Studies) V9X1
1 year full-time
As above

PGCE in Secondary Education (Modern
Studies) V9X1
1 year full-time
As above

PGCE in Secondary Education (Music)
W3X1
1 year full-time
As above

PGCE in Secondary Education (Physical
Education) X9C6
1 year full-time
As above

PGCE in Secondary Education (Physics
with Science) F3X1
1 year full-time
As above

PGCE in Secondary Education (Religious
Education) V6X1
1 year full-time
As above

PGCE in Secondary Education
(Technology Education) J9X1
1 year full-time
As above

PgCert in Careers Education
Part-time evening

Entry requirements: Relevant qualification,
e.g. degree or equivalent, and normally, but
not invariably, teaching qualification with
minimum of 2 years' teaching experience.
Contact: Sheila Semple
Course Director
0141 950 3326
sheila.m.semple@strath.ac.uk

PgCert/PgDip/MSc in Guidance

Part-time

Entry requirements: Fully-registered secondary teachers with at least 3 years' teaching experience, although applications from staff in other sectors of education, e.g. primary and FE, will be considered.
Contact: Mike Hough
  Course Director
  0141 950 3622
  m.t.hough@strath.ac.uk

PgCert/PgDip in Language and Teaching

Part-time

Entry requirements: Degree or equivalent qualification and recognised teaching qualification in primary, secondary or further education, or diploma from college of education; in each case, applicants should have 2 years' relevant post-qualification experience and full GTC registration.
Contact: Margaret Ritchie/ Sandra
  Dunbar
  0141 950 3234
  margaret.ritchie@strath.ac.uk

PgCert/PgDip/MSc in Management in Education

Full-time or part-time

Entry requirements: Designed to meet needs of teachers and related professionals who aspire to or currently hold management posts in educational establishments.
Contact: Mr D Fenton
  0141 950 3211
  d.n.fenton@strath.ac.uk

Pgcert in Mathematics Recovery

2 years part-time

Entry requirements: Degree or equivalent; students must have access to appropriate situations to complete the assessment requirements; those working in management or higher education will need a primary school willing to act as their base school.
Contact: Dr Penny Mann
  0141 950 3746
  penelope.mann@strath.ac.uk

Pgcert/PgDip in Modern Languages in the Primary School

Part-time

Entry requirements: The course is aimed at teachers in primary schools, who are registered with the General Teaching Council, who have a degree and have completed the Modern Languages Primary School National Training Programme, and who are currently engaged in teaching modern languages in a primary context.
Contact: John de Cecco
  0141 950 3230
  J.DeCecco@strath.ac.uk

Pgcert in Post-School Education

9 months full-time, 2 years part-time

Entry requirements: Normally, 240 SCOTCATS points at levels 1 and 2; opportunities exist for the Accreditation of Prior Learning.
Contact: Liz McFarlan
  0141 950 3154
  e.mcfarlan@strath.ac.uk

Pgcert in Post-School Educational Management

Part-time

Entry requirements: Degree or equivalent professional qualification plus 2 years' experience in a post-school setting.
Contact: Anne Nicolson
  0141 950 3613
  a.e.nicolson@strath.ac.uk

Additional Teaching Qualification in Primary Education

18 weeks full-time

Entry requirements: Applicants should be qualified secondary teachers with full registration with General Teaching Council for Scotland and, normally, minimum 5 years' post-qualifying teaching experience; knowledge and experience of the primary sector is desirable.
Contact: Ms M McNaughton
  0141 950 3567
  m.j.mcnaughton@strath.ac.uk

PgCert in Primary Mathematics

Part-time

Entry requirements: Recognised teaching qualification in primary education plus 2 years' teaching experience.

Contact: Mr D Clarke
0141 950 3402
david.clarke@strath.ac.uk

PgCert in Primary Science

Part-time

Entry requirements: As above
Contact: Dr Rae Condie
Course Director
0141 950 3400
rae.condie@strath.ac.uk

PgDip in School Leadership and Management

2.5 years part-time

Entry requirements: 5 years' or more teaching experience and registered with the GTC: candidates will be selected by their employers by merit or having shown potential to develop competencies required for effective school leadership and management.

Contact: Michelle Oates
0141 950 3217
michelle.oates@strath.ac.uk

PgCert/PgDip in Science Education 5–14

Part-time evening

Entry requirements: Primary or secondary teaching qualification plus 2 years' relevant post-qualification professional experience.
Contact: Dr Isobel Robertson
Course Director
0141 950 3415
i.j.robertson@strath.ac.uk

Additional Teaching Qualification in Secondary Education

18 weeks full-time

Entry requirements: Applicants should be qualified secondary teachers with full registration with General Teaching Council for Scotland and, normally, minimum 5 years' post-qualifying teaching experience.
Contact: Anne Welsh
Course Director
0141 950 3207
a.h.welsh@strath.ac.uk

PgCert/PgDip/MSc in Support for Learning

Part-time

Entry requirements: Degree or equivalent plus recognised teaching qualification in primary, secondary or further education; 2 years' post-qualification experience; full GTC registration.
Contact: Kathleen Clark
Course Director
0141 950 3335
K.a.clark@strath.ac.uk

Suffolk and Norfolk Primary SCITT

South Suffolk Professional Development Centre
Paul's Road
Ipswich
Suffolk
IP2 0AN
Tel: 01473 583533
Fax: 01473 583519

The Suffolk and Norfolk Primary SCITT partnership is made up of 60 primary schools, the Suffolk College of Further and Higher Education and Suffolk and Norfolk LEA. Trainees are allocated a base school in which they will spend the majority of their school-based training. During the course trainees will spend time in at least one other SCITT partnership school and also have centre-based work.

Students have access to a training room with computer facilities and the SCITT bases are newly refurbished and also include computer facilities. All trainees will receive support from school-based mentors.

HOW TO APPLY

Applications are made direct to the institution.

COURSES

PGCE Primary Education (3–11 years)
38 weeks full-time

Entry requirements: Degree in relevant subject; GCSE grade C or above in English language and mathematics, and science if born after 1/9/79.
Contact: Enquiries
01473 583533

Suffolk College

Ipswich
Suffolk
IP4 1HY
Tel: 01473 255885
Fax: 01473 2300054
info@suffolk.ac.uk
www.suffolk.ac.uk

Suffolk College has been an accredited college of the University of East Anglia since 1992. It is based on a site close to Ipswich town centre, which offers library, computing, sports and leisure facilities for all students. Accommodation is available in lodgings or privately rented houses and flats near to the university.

All education courses are run from the Department of Social Studies. The college offers teacher training at primary, secondary and post-compulsory level. Primary and secondary PGCEs are offered in conjunction with local SCITT providers.

HOW TO APPLY

All applications are made direct to the institution.

COURSES

PGCE Post-Compulsory Education and Training
11 months full-time or 2 years part-time

Entry requirements: Degree required; students are also required to have access to 200 hours of teaching experience for duration of programme.
Contact: Sharon Wardman-Browne
Course Leader
01473 296645

PGCE Secondary Education (Design and Technology)
1 year full-time

Entry requirements: Relevant degree and minimum grade C in GCSE English language and mathematics or equivalent.
Contact: Rob Knee
Programme Co-ordinator
01502 405989

PGCE Secondary Education (Modern Foreign Languages)
1 year full-time
As above

University of Sunderland

Langham Tower
Ryhope Road
Sunderland
Tyne & Wear
SR2 7EE
Tel: 0191 515 2000
Fax: 0191 515 3805
student-helpline@sunderland.ac.uk
www.sunderland.ac.uk

The University of Sunderland is situated in the heart of the city and caters for around 11,000 students. The School of Education and Lifelong Learning is currently based in several buildings in and around the centre of the city of Sunderland but also makes extensive use of other University facilities. It will shortly be moving to two buildings, the Forster Building on the City Centre Campus at Chester Road and the David Goldman Centre on the Tom Cowie

Campus at St Peter's.

As well as PGCE courses the school provides an extensive range of professional and academic programmes of study in education at degree level, Continuing Professional Development programmes. There are several libraries providing specialised support for a range of subjects and all sites have computer facilities. Resources for education can be found in the Murray Library. The university has a wide range of modern accommodation and first-year students are guaranteed a place. There is also some purpose-built accommodation available for postgraduates.

HOW TO APPLY

Degree courses: applications are made through UCAS.

PGCE: applications are made through the GTTR.

Postgraduate (and PGCE Further Education): applications are made direct to the institution.

COURSES

BA (Hons) in Business Education (11–18 years) XN11

2 years full-time

Course develops a solid knowledge of business and its related areas; covers skills needed to apply subject knowledge in the classroom; 130 days spent in schools and colleges, as well as lectures, seminars, open learning, and project and group work.

Modules of study available include: Microeconomics; business and information studies; marketing and financial applications; designing and producing for a market; applied business statistics; business policy and strategy; finance and economics; management accounting; business economics; assessment in business and economic education; business evaluation and enhancement; European business and enterprise; education/industry links; industrial relations.

All students undertake the secondary professional practice programme.

Completion leads to recommendation for Qualified Teacher Status (QTS) after completion of skills tests.

Entry requirements: HND, International Baccalaureate: 24

Contact: Student Helpline
0191 515 3000
student-
helpline@sunderland.ac.uk

BA(Hons)/BSc (Hons) in Design and Technology Education XW12

3 years full-time

Course equips students to teach within the fields of design and technology meeting the needs of the National Curriculum in secondary schools. Course focuses on fundamental activities of designing and making, developing conceptual, creative and practical skills. Students spend over 130 days in schools and colleges, and also undergo a work placement in an industrial or commercial organisation.

Subjects include: Design and technology; graphical communication; visual design; electronic systems; product design; information technology; material technology and testing; microcomputing; design analysis; assessment in theory and practice; personal and social education; problem behaviour in children; comparative education; current issues in technology education; educational enquiry.

Teaching combines project and group work, lectures, seminars, work placement, and open learning. Assessment is by presentations, essays and examinations.

Successful completion of this course leads to a recommendation for Qualified Teacher

Entry requirements: Tariff: 160, International Baccalaureate: 24, BTEC NC/ND

Contact: Lynn Shrubb
Recruitment Officer
0191 515 3000
student-helpline@sunderland.
ac.uk

BA (Hons) in Education (Information Technology, Key Stages 2–3) XG1M

3 years full-time

Successful completion of this course leads to a recommendation for Qualified Teacher Status (QTS) after completion of skills tests.

Entry requirements: GCE A- and AS-levels: CC, International Baccalaureate: 24, BTEC NC/ND, SCE Higher: CCCCC
Contact: Student Helpline
0191 515 3000
student-helpline@sunderland.
ac.uk

BA/BA (Hons) in English Education (11–18 years) XQ13

3 years full-time

Degree develops knowledge of literature, language, drama and media studies, and provides the skills to teach these subjects to National Curriculum requirements in the 11–18 age range. Students spend 130 days in schools and colleges to provide the professional skills and experience required for teaching.

Level 1: Introduction to education; exploring issues through drama; literature in the secondary school; studying and writing about literature 1 and 2; text and performance 1; and language in childhood. Plus 1 option in language or literature.

Level 2: History; theory; criticism; critical approaches; teaching and learning; describing English. 1 option from drama and 1 from range of literature.

Level 3: Compulsory professional year programme in schools and colleges. Contemporary poetry; Shakespeare and young people; poetry in the secondary school. Teaching is through lectures, seminars, projects and group work. A variety of assessment methods are operated.

Successful completion of this course leads to a recommendation for Qualified Teacher Status (QTS) after completion of skills tests.

Entry requirements: GCE A- and AS-levels: CC, BTEC NC/ND, Foundation / access qualification, SCE Higher
Contact: As above

BA (Hons) in Geography Education (11–18 years) XL17

3 years full-time

Students spend 130 days in schools and colleges to gain the professional skills and experience required for teaching.

Level 1: Physical geography; human geography; cartography and fieldwork; introduction to education. 3 options from: tourism; geology; geomorphology; social environment; environmental issues; resources and sedimentation.

Level 2: European field course; integrated geography; Caribbean development; Third World development; teaching and learning. 2 options from: European studies; introduction to geographical information systems; tourism and travel; applied geomorphology; energy resources; energy production; geographical information systems applications; global environmental issues; ecotourism.

Level 3: Secondary professional programme. 2 options from: personal and social education; contemporary issues in education; classroom studies; assessment in practice; exceptional children and the nature of special education.

Teaching is via professional placements, lectures, seminars, and resource-based learning. Assessment includes examinations and continuous assessment.

Completion leads to recommendation for Qualified Teacher Status (QTS) after completion of skills tests.

Entry requirements: GCE A- and AS- levels: CC, International Baccalaureate, 24, BTEC NC/ND
Contact: As above

BA (Hons) in Information Technology Education (11–18 years) XG15

2 years full-time

Year 1: Information technology across the curriculum; extended microcomputing skills; desktop publishing; computer-based design tools; microcomputer control; multimedia; data modelling; research and applications project; information technology and society; microcomputer programming; option.

Year 2: Professional year: lesson planning and evaluation; classroom management; motivation; behaviour management; educating for differentiation; contemporary issues relating to the National Curriculum. Practical blocks of teaching practice.

Assessment of the programme will be through assignments related to the various modules of study.

Successful completion of this course leads to a recommendation for Qualified Teacher Status (QTS) after completion of skills tests.

Entry requirements: GCE A- and AS-levels, HND, BTEC NC/ND
Contact: As above

BA (Hons) in Information Technology Education (11–18 years) XGC5

3 years full-time

Successful completion of this course leads to a recommendation for Qualified Teacher Status (QTS) after completion of skills tests.

Entry requirements: GCE A- and AS-levels: CC, International Baccalaureate: 24, SCE Higher: CCCCC
Contact: As above

BSc (Hons) in Mathematics Education (11–18 years) XG11

2 years full-time

Students spend a minimum of 120 days in schools or colleges. Teaching combines lectures, seminars, open learning, practical project and group work. Assessment is done mainly through continuous coursework evaluation.

Modules of study include: Structure and pattern 1 and 2; using and applying; information technology in mathematics 1 and 2; foundations of mathematical modelling; statistics in action; mechanics in action; the nature of mathematics; the development of mathematics; development of geometric thinking.

All students follow the secondary professional year programme.

Successful completion of this course leads to a recommendation for Qualified Teacher Status (QTS) after completion of skills tests.

Entry requirements: First year of relevant degree course, GCE A- and AS-levels, HNC, HND
Contact: Mr John Below
Senior Lecturer in Mathematics
0191 515 2371
john.below@sunderland.ac.uk

BA (Hons) in Music Education (11–18 years) XW13

2 years full-time

Year 1: Music technology and its applications; composing in context; music for everyday life; practical work in music education; music for performance; creative uses of music technology.

Year 2: All students follow the secondary professional year programme.

Successful completion of this course leads to a recommendation for Qualified Teacher Status (QTS) after completion of skills tests.

Entry requirements: Audition, GCE A- and AS-levels, BTEC NC/ND, First year of relevant degree course,

HND, Interview
Contact: Mr P Kay
Senior Lecturer in Music Education
0191 515 3891
peter.kay@sunderland.ac.uk

BA (Hons) in Primary Education (7–11 years) X122

4 years full-time or 4 years full-time with time abroad

This primary education programme prepares students to teach in primary schools in the junior age range (7–11 years). Students develop the competence needed in the classroom, and an awareness of the primary curriculum and how to teach it. Development of in-depth knowledge of National Curriculum subjects is combined with modules in teaching and learning skills. This focuses on children's differences including children with special needs and 'gifted' children.

Assessment is by continuous evaluation in the form of essays, reports, individual and group seminar presentations, and work placement performance.

At level 1, students study English; mathematics; and science, and options from history; music; geography; technology; art; physical education and religious education.

Successful completion of this course leads to a recommendation for Qualified Teacher Status (QTS) after completion of skills tests.

Entry requirements: GCE A- and AS-levels: BC to BB, AVCEs, BTEC NC/ND
Contact: Student Helpline
0191 515 3000
student-helpline@sunderland.ac.uk

BA (Hons) in Primary Education (Early Years, 3–8) X121

4 years full-time

Course includes: Specialist focus in either the 3–8 years age range; broad range of subjects; 2 specialisms acquiring an in-depth knowledge at an academic and school level in 1 core and 1 foundation National Curriculum subject.

Successful completion of this course leads to a recommendation for Qualified Teacher Status (QTS) after completion of skills tests.

Entry requirements: Tariff: 180

Contact: Lyn Shrubb
Recruitment Officer
0191 515 3000
student-helpline@sunderland.ac.uk

BSc (Hons) in Science Education (11–18 years) XF10

2 years full-time

Year 1: Modules of study (including options in physics, biology or chemistry routes): exploration of science; scientific investigation; energy forces and materials; electricity, magnetism and electronics; waves, atoms and molecules; environmental biology; metabolic processes; molecular biology; essential principles of chemistry; physics of the universe; introduction to earth sciences; the exploration of science; information technology for science; mathematics for science.

Year 2: All students follow the secondary professional year programme.

Successful completion of this course leads to a recommendation for Qualified Teacher Status (QTS) after completion of skills tests.

Entry requirements: GCE A- and AS-levels, HND
Contact: Student Helpline
0191 515 3000
student-helpline@sunderland.ac.uk

PGCE in Further Education X180

2 years part-time

Entry requirements: Aimed at teachers, lecturers and trainers in the post-16 sector. Applicants should have relevant experience.
Contact: As above

PGCE in Key Stage 2/3 Education (7–14) X180

1 year full-time

Entry requirements: Degree in a science-, mathematics- or ICT-related subject.

Contact: Student Helpline
0191 515 3000
student-helpline@sunderland.
ac.uk

PGCE in Primary Education (4–11) X100

2 years full-time

Entry requirements: Relevant degree or other recognised and approved equivalent qualification, plus GCSE grade C or above (or equivalent) in English language and mathematics and science.

Contact: Ms Christine Taylor
0191 515 2395
christine.taylor@sunderland.
ac.uk

PGCE in Secondary Education (Business Education) N1X1

1 year full-time

Entry requirements: Relevant degree or other recognised and approved equivalent qualification. In addition, GCSE grade C or above (or equivalent) in English language and mathematics. University entrance test available for mature applicants who do not hold these GCSEs.

Contact: Larry Hunter
0191 515 2395
helen.chambers@sunderland.
ac.uk

PGCE in Secondary Education (Business Education, 2 years) NXC1

2 years full-time

Entry requirements: GCSE grade C or above in mathematics and English language (or equivalent); good Honours degree in a relevant subject area; prior teaching/training experience.

Contact: As above

PGCE in Secondary Education (Design and Technology) W9X1

1 year full-time

Entry requirements: Relevant degree or other recognised and approved equivalent qualification. In addition, GCSE grade C or above (or equivalent) in English language and mathematics. University entrance test

available for mature applicants who do not hold these GCSEs.

Contact: Ms Sue Cooke
0191 515 2395
helen.chambers@sunderland.
ac.uk

PGCE in Secondary Education (Design and Technology, 2 years) WXX1

2 years full-time

Entry requirements: GCSE grade C or above in mathematics and English language (or equivalent); good Honours degree in a relevant subject area; prior teaching/training experience.

Contact: As above

PGCE in Secondary Education (English) Q3X1

1 year full-time

Entry requirements: Relevant degree or other recognised and approved equivalent qualification. In addition, GCSE grade C or above (or equivalent) in English language and mathematics. University entrance test available for mature applicants who do not hold these GCSEs.

Contact: Ms Kath McColl
0191 515 2395
helen.chambers@sunderland.
ac.uk

PGCE in Secondary Education (Geography) F8X1

1 year full-time

Entry requirements: As above
Contact: Mr Steve Watts
0191 515 2395
helen.chambers@sunderland.
ac.uk

PGCE in Secondary Education (Information Technology) G5X1

1 year full-time

Entry requirements: As above
Contact: Christopher Jones
0191 515 2395
helen.chambers@sunderland.
ac.uk

PGCE in Secondary Education (Information Technology, 2 years) GXM1

2 years full-time

Entry requirements: GCSE grade C or above in mathematics and English language (or equivalent); good Honours degree in a relevant subject area; prior teaching/training experience.

Contact: As above

PGCE in Secondary Education (Mathematics) G1X1

1 year full-time

Entry requirements: Relevant degree or equivalent; GCSE grade C or above in English language and mathematics.

Contact: Christine Farnsworth
0191 515 2395
christine.farnsworth
@sunderland.ac.uk

PGCE in Secondary Education (Mathematics, 2 years) GXC1

2 years full-time

Entry requirements: Degree in mathematics or subject with high mathematical content.

Contact: Mr John Below
Senior Lecturer in Mathematics
Education
0191 515 2371
john.below@sunderland.ac.uk

PGCE in Secondary Education (Modern Foreign Languages) R9X1

1 year full-time

Entry requirements: A relevant degree or other recognised and approved equivalent qualification. In addition, GCSE grade C or above (or equivalent) in English language and mathematics. University entrance test available for mature applicants who do not hold these GCSEs.

Contact: Mr Bob Wass
0191 515 2442
bob.wass@sunderland.ac.uk

PGCE in Secondary Education (Music) W3X1

1 year full-time

Entry requirements: As above

Contact: Mr Peter Kay
Senior Lecturer in Music
Education
0191 515 3891/2395
peter.kay@sunderland.ac.uk

PGCE in Secondary Education (Music, 2 years) WXH1

2 years full-time

Entry requirements: Appropriate degree or recognised qualification in music-related area plus GCSE English language and mathematics at grade C.

Contact: As above

PGCE in Secondary Education (Science) F0X1

1 year full-time

Entry requirements: Relevant degree or other recognised and approved equivalent qualification. In addition, GCSE grade C or above (or equivalent) in English language and mathematics. University entrance test available for mature applicants who do not hold these GCSEs.

Contact: Alex Docherty
0191 515 2395
helen.chambers@sunderland.
ac.uk

PGCE in Secondary Education (Science, conversion) FXA1

2 years full-time

Entry requirements: GCSE grade C or above in mathematics and English language (or equivalent); good Honours degree in a relevant subject area; prior teaching/training experience.

Contact: As above

MA in Education (Children's Literature)

1 year full-time, 3 years part-time

Entry requirements: Honours degree or equivalent.

Contact: Sylvia Briggs
0191 515 2395
sylvia.briggs@sunderland.ac.uk

MA in Education (Design and Technology)

1 year full-time, 3 years part-time

As above

PgCert/PgDip/MA Education (Music)

1 year full-time, 2 years part-time

Entry requirements: Appropriate degree and relevant experience; applications from non-graduates may be considered.

Contact: Student Helpline
0191 515 3000
student-
helpline@sunderland.ac.uk

PgCert/PgDip/MA in Education (Post-16)

1 year full-time, 2 years part-time

Entry requirements: As above
Contact: Caroline Walker Gleaves
0191 515 2395
sylvia.briggs@sunderland.ac.uk

PgCert/PgDip/MA in Education (Special Educational Needs)

1 year full-time, 2 years part-time

Entry requirements: As above

Contact: Prof Joe Elliot
0191 515 2395
joe.elliot@sunderland.ac.uk

PgCert/PgDip/MA in Education (Teaching and Learning with Information and Communication Technology)

1 year full-time, 2 years part-time

Entry requirements: As above
Contact: Dr John Grey
0191 515 2395
sylvia.briggs@sunderland.ac.uk

PgCert/PgDip/MA in Teaching English to Speakers of Other Languages

Mixed mode

Entry requirements: Normally degree or equivalent teaching qualification and English teaching experience (normally 3 years).

Contact: Dr Felicity Breet
Principal Lecturer
0191 515 2200
felicity.breet@sunderland.ac.uk

University of Surrey, Roehampton

Roehampton
Whitelands College
West Hill
Wandsworth
London
SW15 3SN
Tel: 020 8392 3232
Fax: 020 8392 3470
enquiries@roehampton.ac.uk
www.roehampton.ac.uk

The University of Surrey, Roehampton is located six miles from the heart of London and set in beautiful parkland. The university has a collegiate structure created by the federation of four teacher training colleges in 1975 when it became known as the Roehampton Institute. These were White-lands College, Southlands College, Digby Stuart College and Froebel College. On the

federation with the University of Surrey in 2000 it changed its name to the University of Surrey, Roehampton and now has over 7,000 students.

Based at Froebel College the School of Education Studies and School of Initial Teacher Education offers undergraduate degree and PGCE courses as well as providing opportunities for Continuing Professional Development through taught and research postgraduate programmes. Students have access to a range of facilities and services and the Learning Resources Centre houses an extensive library as well as computing and media facilities.

Accommodation is available both on and off campus. Whitelands College has accommodation specifically aimed at mature or postgraduate students.

HOW TO APPLY

Degree courses: applications are made through UCAS.

PGCE: applications are made through the GTTR.

Postgraduate: applications are made direct to the institution.

COURSES

BA (Hons) in Primary Education (Art and Design, 3–8 years) X1W2

3 years full-time

Core curriculum studies: English, mathematics, science, and information communication technology, give students an appropriate level of knowledge and understanding in the core areas of the National Curriculum as well as addressing how to teach these subjects at the Primary level and shows how ICT supports learning across the curriculum; each course is related to the work with children undertaken in the weekly school placement.

Foundation subjects: Art and design, design and technology, geography, history, music, physical education and religious studies courses introduce the student to the breadth of primary curriculum and examine the interrelationship of these areas of knowledge and their relationship to the core curriculum subjects and ICT.

Subject specialism: Develops the knowledge, skills and understanding of the student; teaching and learning courses provide a unifying link across the programme relating to the understanding of children's learning and cross-curricular issues to classroom practice.

School experience: Placement is in a different school each year with a total of 120 days in school throughout the entire programme; 1 day a week is typically spent in a primary school, teaching and observing; period of Block School Experience ranging from 4 to 9 weeks; progress is supported and monitored through a partnership between the school and university and is recorded in the professional development profile.

Successful completion of this course leads to a recommendation for Qualified Teacher Status (QTS) after completion of skills tests.

Entry requirements: GCE A- and AS-levels: CDD, International Baccalaureate: 26, BTEC NC/ND, Mature entry

Contact: Enquiries Office
020 8392 3232
enquiries@roehampton.ac.uk

BA (Hons) in Primary Education (Art and Design, 7–11 years) X1WF

3 years full-time
As above

BA (Hons) in Primary Education (Design and Technology, 3–8 years) X1J9

3 years full-time
As above

BA (Hons) in Primary Education (Design and Technology, 7–11 years) X1JX

3 years full-time
As above

BA (Hons) in Primary Education (Early Childhood Studies, 3–8 years) X1X3

3 years full-time
As above

Entry requirements: GCE A- and AS-levels: CDD, International Baccalaureate: 26, BTEC NC/ND, Credits from The Open University, Mature entry, SCE Higher

Contact: As above

BA (Hons) in Primary Education (English, 3–8 years) X1QJ

3 years full-time
As above

Entry requirements: As above
Contact: As above

BA (Hons) in Primary Education (English, 7–11 years) X1Q3

3 years full-time
As above

Entry requirements: GCE A- and AS-levels: CDD, International Baccalaureate: 26, BTEC NC/ND, Mature entry, SCE Higher
Contact: As above

BA (Hons) in Primary Education
(Geography, 3–8 years) X1L7

3 years full-time
As above

BA (Hons) in Primary Education
(Geography, 7–11 years) X1LR

3 years full-time
As above

BA (Hons) in Primary Education
(History, 3–8 years) X1V1

3 years full-time
As above

BA (Hons) in Primary Education
(History, 7–11 years) X1VC

3 years full-time
As above

BA (Hons) in Primary Education (Music,
3–8 years) X1W3

3 years full-time
As above

BA (Hons) Primary Education (Music,
7–11 years) X1WH

3 years full-time
As above

BA (Hons) in Primary Education
(Physical Education, 3–8 years) X1C6

3 years full-time
As above

BA (Hons) in Primary Education
(Physical Education, 7–11 years) X1XH

3 years full-time
As above

BA (Hons) in Primary Education
(Religious Education, 3–8 years) X1VQ

3 years full-time
As above

BA (Hons) in Primary Education
(Religious Education, 7–11 years) X1VP

3 years full-time
As above

BA (Hons) in Primary Education
(Sciences, 3–8 years) X1F0

3 years full-time
As above

BA (Hons) in Primary Education
(Sciences, 7–11 years) X1FA

3 years full-time
As above

PGCE in Early Years (3–6 years) X110

1 year full-time

Entry requirements: Degree awarded in the
UK or by an approved university outside
the UK, or an acceptable equivalent; GCSE
grade C or above in mathematics and
English language, or equivalent; candidates
born after 1/9/79 must also have GCSE
grade C or above in science.

Contact: As above

PGCE in Early Years and Lower Primary
(Art and Design) X1WC

1 year full-time
As above

PGCE in Early Years and Lower Primary
(Design and Technology) X1WF

1 year full-time
As above

PGCE in Early Years and Lower Primary
(English) X1QH

1 year full-time
As above

PGCE in Early Years and Lower Primary
(Geography) X1FV

1 year full-time
As above

PGCE in Early Years and Lower Primary
(History) X1VC

1 year full-time
As above

PGCE in Early Years and Lower Primary
(Information Communication
Technology) X1GM

1 year full-time
As above

PGCE in Early Years and Lower Primary
(Mathematics) X1GC

1 year full-time
As above

PGCE in Early Years and Lower Primary (Music) X1WH

1 year full-time

As above

PGCE in Early Years and Lower Primary (Physical Education) X1CP

1 year full-time

As above

PGCE in Early Years and Lower Primary (Religious Education) X1VP

1 year full-time

As above

PGCE in Early Years and Lower Primary (Science) X1FA

1 year full-time

As above

PGCE in Secondary Education (Art and Design) W1X1

1 year full-time

Entry requirements: Degree awarded in the UK or by an approved university outside the UK; or an acceptable graduate-equivalent qualification. In addition, applicants must hold GCSE (minimum grade C) mathematics and English language (or their recognised equivalents) and those born on or after 1/9/79 must have attained the standard required to achieve GCSE grade C in science(s).

Contact: As above

PGCE in Secondary Education (Biology) C1X1

1 year full-time

As above

PGCE in Secondary Education (Business Studies) N1X1

1 year full-time

Entry requirements: Degree awarded in the UK or by an approved university outside the UK; or an acceptable graduate-equivalent qualification. In addition, applicants must hold GCSE (minimum grade C) mathematics and English language (or their recognised equivalents) and those born on or after 1/9/79 must have attained the stan-

dard required to achieve GCSE grade C in science(s).

The course is particularly suitable for those candidates who have industrial or commercial experience and such graduates are especially welcome to apply.

Contact: As above

PGCE in Secondary Education (Chemistry) F1X1

1 year full-time

Entry requirements: Degree awarded in the UK or by an approved university outside the UK; or an acceptable graduate-equivalent qualification. In addition, applicants must hold GCSE (minimum grade C) mathematics and English language (or their recognised equivalents) and those born on or after 1/9/79 must have attained the standard required to achieve GCSE grade C in science(s).

Contact: As above

PGCE in Secondary Education (Design and Technology) W9X1

1 year full-time

Entry requirements: Degree awarded in the UK or by an approved university outside the UK; or an acceptable graduate-equivalent qualification. In addition, applicants must hold GCSE (minimum grade C) mathematics and English language (or their recognised equivalents) and those born on or after 1 September 1979 must have attained the standard required to achieve GCSE grade C in science(s).

Applications are invited from graduates whose degree has included a substantial element of technology, for example: food technology, engineering, design and textiles.

Contact: As above

PGCE in Secondary Education (English) Q3X1

1 year full-time

Entry requirements: Degree awarded in the UK or by an approved university outside the UK; or an acceptable graduate-equivalent qualification. In addition, applicants must hold GCSE (minimum grade C) mathematics and English language (or their recognised equivalents) and those born on or after 1/9/79 must have attained the standard required to achieve GCSE grade C in science(s).

The course in English is suitable for mature students with work experience and such graduates are encouraged to apply.

Contact: As above

PGCE in Secondary Education (History) V1X1

1 year full-time

Entry requirements: Applicants must hold: a degree awarded in the UK or by an approved university outside the UK; or an acceptable graduate-equivalent qualification. In addition, applicants must hold GCSE minimum grade C (or recognised equivalent) in mathematics and English language.

Contact: As above

PGCE in Secondary Education (Mathematics) G1X1

1 year full-time

Entry requirements: Degree awarded in the UK or by an approved university outside the UK; or an acceptable graduate-equivalent qualification. In addition, applicants must hold GCSE (minimum grade C) mathematics and English language (or their recognised equivalents) and those born on or after 1/9/79 must have attained the standard required to achieve GCSE grade C in science(s).

PGCE Secondary Mathematics is open to candidates who have a single subject degree or a joint degree in which mathematics formed a substantial part. Applications are also invited from students with a degree in other disciplines with a strong mathematical content, such as engineering and management science.

Contact: As above

PGCE in Secondary Education (Modern Languages) R9X1

1 year full-time

Entry requirements: Applicants must hold: a degree relevant to the language(s) to be taught, awarded in the UK or by an approved university outside the UK; or an acceptable graduate-equivalent qualification. In addition, applicants must hold GCSE (minimum grade C) or recognised equivalent in mathematics and English language.

Contact: As above

PGCE in Secondary Education (Music) W3X1

1 year full-time

Entry requirements: Degree awarded by British or approved overseas university, or equivalent qualification in appropriate subject (such as successful completion of 3-year graduate-equivalent diploma, e.g. GRSM, GTCL, GLCM, GNSM, GBSM, FRCO; or an approved diploma (of a music college) in performance; or FTCL Diploma); plus GCSE (grade C or above) in mathematics and English language, or the equivalent.

Contact: As above

PGCE in Secondary Education (Physics) F3X1

1 year full-time

Entry requirements: Degree awarded in the UK or by an approved university outside the UK; or an acceptable graduate-equivalent qualification. In addition, applicants must hold GCSE (minimum grade C) mathematics and English language (or their recognised equivalents) and those born on or after 1/9/79 must have attained the standard required to achieve GCSE grade C in science(s).

Contact: As above

PGCE in Secondary Education (Religious Education) V6X1

1 year full-time

Entry requirements: Applicants must hold an approved degree awarded in the UK or by an approved university outside the UK, or an equivalent qualification. In addition, candidates must hold GCSE minimum grade C (or equivalent) in English language and mathematics; approved degree subjects include religious studies or affiliated subjects such as philosophy, sociology, English, anthropology and some aspects of classical studies.
Contact: As above

PGCE in Secondary Education (Science) F0X1

1 year full-time

Entry requirements: Applicants must hold a degree awarded in the UK or by an approved University outside the UK, or an equivalent qualification. In addition, candidates must hold GCSE English language (grade C or above) or equivalent. The graduate subject is normally expected to be in the area, or an acceptable allied area, to which entry is sought. Candidates who have successfully completed an approved degree in science welcomed. Mature students with work experience and such graduates are invited to apply.
Contact: As above

PGCE in Upper Primary (Art and Design) XW11

1 year full-time

Entry requirements: Degree awarded in the UK or by an approved university outside the UK, or an acceptable equivalent; GCSE grade C or above in mathematics and English language, or equivalent; candidates born after 1/9/79 must also have GCSE grade C or above in science.
Contact: As above

PGCE in Upper Primary (Design and Technology) XW12

1 year full-time
As above

PGCE in Upper Primary (English) XQ13

1 year full-time
As above

PGCE in Upper Primary (Geography) XF18

1 year full-time
As above

PGCE in Upper Primary (History) XV11

1 year full-time
As above

PGCE in Upper Primary (Information Communication Technology) XG15

1 year full-time
As above

PGCE in Upper Primary (Mathematics) XG11

1 year full-time
As above

PGCE in Upper Primary (Music) XW13

1 year full-time
As above

PGCE in Upper Primary (Music) XWC3

1 year full-time, part-time
As above

PGCE in Upper Primary (Physical Education) XC16

1 year full-time
As above

PGCE in Upper Primary (Religious Education) XV16

1 year full-time
As above

PGCE in Upper Primary (Science) XF10

1 year full-time
As above

PgDip/MA in Art, Craft and Design Education

18 months full-time, 2–4 years part-time

Entry requirements: Degree with art, craft or design education component required, or degree with qualification leading to QTS, or CertEd plus evidence of DfES-recognised professional experience; applicants lacking formal qualifications in art, craft and design may be required to complete a qualifying assignment and/or present a portfolio of documentary evidence of intellectual and professional development resulting from prior experiential learning.

Contact: As above

Certificate of Professional Development in Children with Literacy Problems

1 year full-time/part-time

Entry requirements: Applicants should be qualified teachers with experience at middle management level, considering the move to senior management and whole-school responsibility

Contact: As above

PgDip/MA in Early Childhood Studies

1 year full-time, 2–4 years part-time evening

Entry requirements: Degree in education (or with education as significant component), early childhood studies, social work or health studies, social policy or degree in another discipline and significant interest in childhood studies, or comparable professional award plus relevant experiential learning; applicants not meeting standard entry requirements may be required to undertake qualifying assignment and/or present portfolio of documentary evidence of intellectual and professional development resulting from prior experiential learning.

Contact: As above

PgDip/MA in Education

1 year full-time, 2–4 years part-time

Entry requirements: Degree in education, or degree plus PGCE or Certificate with qualified teacher status, or comparable professional award with relevant experience; graduates in non-cognate disciplines considered; non-standard applicants may be required to qualify for entry by assignment and/or portfolio documenting intellectual and professional development resulting from prior experiential learning.

Contact: As above

EdD in Education

Part-time

Entry requirements: Course is aimed at education professionals who have completed Master's level study.

Contact: As above

Certificate of Professional Development in Gifted Education

Part-time

Entry requirements: Applicants should be early years, primary and secondary teachers who work with, or have an interest in working with, gifted and talented children.

Contact: As above

Certificate of Professional Development in Preparation for Senior Management (Primary)

6 months part-time

Entry requirements:
As above

Certificate of Professional Development in Preparation for Senior Management (Secondary)

10 months part-time weekends and evenings

Entry requirements: Applicants should be qualified teachers with experience at middle management level, considering the move to senior management and whole-school responsibility

Contact: As above

Certificate in Return to Teaching (Primary)

6 months part-time

Entry requirements: Applicants will be qualified teachers seeking return to employment, or qualified secondary teachers who wish to learn more about primary education.

Contact: As above

Certificate in Return to Teaching (Secondary)

6 months part-time

Entry requirements: Applicants will be qualified teachers seeking return to employment.

Contact: As above

University of Surrey

Guildford
Surrey
GU2 7XH
Tel: 01483 300800
Fax: 01483 300803
admissions@surrey.ac.uk
www.surrey.ac.uk

The University of Surrey is built on a hillside leading up to Guildford Cathedral. It is based on a compact campus with all social, academic and sports facilities within walking distance of most of the accommodation. The library is located at the heart of the campus and there are computer facilities available in PC rooms as well as in most of the individual schools,

The Department of Educational studies specialises exclusively in post-school learning and carries out research and consultancy on the education and training of adults. The department offers an extensive programme of postgraduate courses. The Master's courses enable experienced professionals, in education, training and management, to upgrade their skills and knowledge, and the Doctoral programme enables individuals to study adult learning. Based in the School of Arts the department has purpose-built facilities, including dedicated space for postgraduate students.

The Accommodation Services can advise on finding places to live. There is accommodation available in halls on and off campus and there is also privately rented accommodation in the area.

HOW TO APPLY

Degree courses: applications are made through UCAS.
Postgraduate: applications are made direct to the institution.

COURSES

BSc (Hons) in Chemistry with Science Education F107
4 years full-time

Years 1–3: Study of chemistry and complementary education modules: the nature of science; science in the school curriculum; information technology in school science; learning science.

Year 4: 1-year initial teaching training course at University of Surrey Roehampton leading to PGCE and recommendation for Qualified Teacher Status (QTS).

Entry requirements: GCE A- and AS-levels: BCC

Contact: Dr Brendan Howlin
Admissions Tutor
01483 686834
b.howlin@surrey.ac.uk

PgCert/PgDip/MSc in Applied Professional Studies in Education and Training
PgCert: 12 months distance learning, PgDip: 24 months distance learning, MSc: 12 months full-time or 30 to 36 months distance learning

Entry requirements: Recognised degree or equivalent professional qualification; relevant professional experience.

Contact: Dr David Hay
Director of Studies
01483 683158
d.hay@surrey.ac.uk

PgCert/PgDip/MSc in Applied Professional Studies in Educational Technology
PgCert: 12 months distance learning, PgDip: 24 months distance learning, MSc: 12 months full-time or 36 months distance learning
As above

PgCert/PgDip/MSc in Applied Professional Studies in Lifelong Learning
PgCert: 12 months full-time or 12 months distance learning, PgDip: 12 months full-time or 24 months distance learning, MSc: 12 months full-time or 36 months distance learning
As above

PgDip/Msc in Research Methods (Education/Social and Educational Studies)

Msc: 1 year full-time or 2 years part-time

Entry requirements: At least 2 years' professional experience, plus a degree from the University of Surrey, another approved university or awarding body, or an appropriate and approved professional or other qualification.

Contact: Dr Thomas Black
Director of Studies
01483 689197
t.black@surrey.ac.uk

PgDip/Msc in Teaching and Learning

PgDip: 2 years part-time, MSc: 2 years part-time

Entry requirements: Degree or equivalent, and/or relevant professional qualification; must be employed in a teaching or training capacity; those without a first degree may be considered for exceptional entry.

Contact: Dr Jocelyn Robson
Director of Studies
01483 683170/689188
T-and-L@surrey.ac.uk

EdD in Education

3 years full-time or 4 to 5 years part-time

Entry requirements: Honours degree and at least 4 years' relevant professional experience.

Contact: Mrs Adrienne Wilson
Administrative Assistant
01483 689639
a.m.wilson@surrey.ac.uk

University of Sussex

Sussex House
Falmer
Brighton
BN1 9RH
Tel: 01273 606755
Fax: 0273 678335
ug.admissions@sussex.ac.uk
www.sussex.ac.uk

The University of Sussex was founded in the 1960s and received its Royal Charter in August 1961. The university is located in a designated Area of Outstanding Natural Beauty on the edge of the Sussex Downs. The University campus is large and self-contained with lecture theatres, seminar rooms, libraries, laboratories, accommodation, restaurants, bars, shops and sports facilities all within easy walking distance. The seaside town of Brighton is a few minutes away.

The Institute of Education offers initial teacher education including the PGCE and a Graduate Teacher Programme, postgraduate taught programmes and doctoral programmes. The University library and computer services cater for the academic needs of the students.

Accommodation is situated on campus and most is allocated to new undergraduates. The University guarantees housing for all new full-time research students in their first year of study and for non-EU students taking Master's degrees. Graduate housing is available both on campus in the Brighthelm residences and off campus in Kings Road on the seafront. There are also other residences in Brighton and Hove.

HOW TO APPLY

PGCE: applications are made through the GTTR.

Postgraduate: applications are made direct to the institution.

COURSES

PGCE in Middle Years (Mathematics, 7–14) XGC1

1 year full-time

Entry requirements: Approved degree, or other qualification (e.g. of a professional body) recognised as being equivalent to a first degree; GCSE English language and mathematics grade C, or equivalent.
Contact: PGCE Admissions
01273 678405
usie.oite@sussex.ac.uk

PGCE in Middle Years (Modern Languages, 7–14) XRC9

1 year full-time
As above

PGCE in Middle Years (Science, 7–14) XFCA

1 year full-time
As above

PGCE in Secondary Education (Citizenship with History) LX91

1 year full-time

Entry requirements: Degree and GCSE grade C English language and mathematics.
Contact: PGCE Admissions
01273 678405

PGCE in Secondary Education (English) Q3X1

1 year full-time

Entry requirements: Graduate of an approved institution of higher education or equivalent qualification (e.g. of a profes-sional body) and GCSE minimum grade C in English language and mathematics, or equivalents; degree (or equivalent) should be in specialist subject; school experience desirable.
Contact: Dr Penny Searls
Course Director
01273 678405
m.p.searls@sussex.ac.uk

PGCE in Secondary Education (Geography) F8X1

1 year full-time
As above

PGCE in Secondary Education (History) V1X1

1 year full-time
As above

PGCE in Secondary Education (Mathematics) G1X1

1 year full-time
As above

PGCE in Secondary Education (Modern Languages) R9X1

1 year full-time
As above

PGCE in Secondary Education (Music) W3X1

1 year full-time, 2 years part-time
As above

PGCE in Secondary Education (Science) F0X1

1 year full-time
As above

Entry requirements: As above
Contact: Dr V Griffiths
Course Director
01273 678405
m.p.searls@sussex.ac.uk

EdD in Education

4 years part-time

Entry requirements: Good Honours degree and preferably a Master's degree; relevant professional qualifications and experience may be acceptable in exceptional cases.
Contact: Dr Harry Torrance
01273 678260
margmr@sussex.ac.uk

MA in Education (School Improvement and Professional Development)

2 year part-time

Entry requirements: Upper 2nd Class Honours degree, plus PGCE, and in-service teacher status.
Contact: Postgraduate Admissions
01273 678412
pg.admissions@sussex.ac.uk

Pgdip/MA in Education Studies

Pgdip: 2 years full-time, 4 years part-time; MA: 3 years full-time, 5 years part-time

Entry requirements: Intended for teachers and administrators able to work independently on particular topic or topics they wish to study in depth.

Contact: Postgraduate Admissions
01273 678412
pg.admissions@sussex.ac.uk

MA in International Education

1 year full-time, 18 months distance learning, 2 years sandwich

Entry requirements: Degree plus minimum 2 years' relevant work experience, usually overseas, plus satisfactory standard of English.

Contact: Margaret Ralph
01273 678260
margmr@sussex.ac.uk

MA in Special Educational Needs

2 years part-time

Entry requirements: Applicants should be practising teachers.

Contact: Institute of Education
01273 678568
usie.gso@sussex.ac.uk

Swansea Institute of Higher Education

Mount Pleasant
Swansea
SA1 6ED
Tel: 01792 481000
Fax: 01792 481085
enquiry@sihe.ac.uk
www.sihe.ac.uk

The Swansea Institute of Higher Education is an Associated College of the University of Wales. It achieved the status of an independent Higher Education Corporation in 1992. It developed from its predecessors, the Colleges of Technology, Art and Teacher Training which had been established in the area prior to 1900. The Institute is based on three campuses: Mount Pleasant near to the City Centre, Alexandra Road, the former Swansea College of Art, also close to the City Centre and Townhill which is located high above the city with views of Swansea Bay.

The School of Education is based on Townhill Campus. It offers undergraduate and postgraduate programmes including the PGCE at secondary level. Qualified Teacher Status at primary level can be obtained through the degree programme. Students have access to the Library and computing services on the campuses as well as the sporting and leisure facilities. Accommodation is available on all three campuses or in the private sector.

HOW TO APPLY

Degree courses: applications are made through UCAS.

PGCE: applications are made through the GTTR.

Postgraduate: applications are made direct to the institution.

COURSES

BA (Hons) Primary Education X120

3 years full-time or 4 years full-time

The course is designed to meet directly the demands of the National Curriculum and all recent developments in the primary school. It includes substantial periods of time in schools and classrooms.

It provides a broad spectrum of subject knowledge to enable students to teach across the whole curriculum. In the 4-year course students also have the opportunity to select subjects of their choice for further study.

Professional development is centred on education and professional studies in which the emphasis is placed entirely on teachers, children, and learning in the primary school. The core areas of the National

Curriculum, English, mathematics and science, form 3 substantial components for all students.

Throughout the course there are periods of attachment to local primary schools. These are carefully designed to allow students to begin teaching securely and to increase the range of their skills and understandings to the point where, by the end of the course, they can stand on their own feet as competent, lively and versatile practitioners, ready to begin their careers in the modern education service.

Successful completion of this course leads to Qualified Teacher Status (QTS) on completion of skills tests.

Entry requirements: BTEC NC/ND, GCE A- and AS-levels: CC, International Baccalaureate, SCE Higher

Contact: Mrs Helen Davies
Admissions Tutor/Programme Director
01792 481000

PGCE Secondary Education (Art and Design) W1X1

1 year full-time

Entry requirements: Degree in art or related subject; GCSE or equivalent mathematics and English at grade C or above.

Contact: Shan Samuel-Thomas
PGCE Art Programme Director
01792 481024 x2024
shansamuel-thomas@sihe.ac.uk

PGCE Secondary Education (Business Studies) N1X1

1 year full-time

Entry requirements: Honours degree in Business studies, or with a high proportion of Business studies together with relevant experience, or an ordinary degree in Business studies combined with relevant experience, plus GCSE passes (grade C or above) in English and Mathematics or equivalents, plus all applicants must meet the secretary of states requirements for the physical and mental fitness to teach.

Contact: Mr Simon Evans
PGCE Programme Director
01792 481176/24
simon.evans@sihe.ac.uk

Diploma in Professional Development in Education

5 years part-time

Entry requirements: Applicants should be serving primary or secondary teachers.

Contact: Ken Jones
Head of School of Education
01792 481254
Ken.jones@sihe.ac.uk

MA (Ed)/PgDip in Education

MA (Ed): 5 years part-time

Entry requirements: Applicants should be serving primary or secondary school teachers, especially those holding (or aspiring to) posts of senior responsibility and possessing good Honours degree.

Contact: Dr Sue Lyle
Programme Director
01792 481254
sue.lyle@sihe.ac.uk

University of Wales, Swansea

Singleton Park
Swansea
SA2 8PP
Tel: 01792 205678
Fax: 01792 295874
admissions@swan.ac.uk
www.swan.ac.uk

Founded in 1920, the University of Wales, Swansea is one of the original colleges of the University of Wales (created in 1893). The main campus in Singleton Park is 1½ miles from Swansea city centre and overlooks Swansea Bay and the Bristol Channel. Hendrefoelan Campus is about 1¾ miles north west of Singleton. It now has over 10,000 students.

The Department of Education is situated on Hendrefoelan campus. It offers courses including Early Childhood Studies, primary and secondary PGCEs and other postgraduate programmes. It has a major role in running courses of Continuing Professional Development for practising teachers and is the main provider of courses on Special Needs in education throughout Wales and the south-west region of England. A specialist Education Library is situated at Hendrefoelan as well as extensive ICT facilities.

There are three halls on campus known as the Singleton Halls. All the campus facilities are available for these halls. Most self-catering accommodation is situated at Hendrefoelan and is served by a regular Unibus service. On site are a bar, shop, fast-food takeaway, launderette, doctor's surgery and tennis courts. There are some University Managed Houses in the Uplands and Brynmill areas of the city and also number of houses and flats in the city.

HOW TO APPLY

PGCE: applications are made through the GTTR.

Postgraduate: applications are made direct to the institution.

COURSES

PGCE in Primary Education (Lower Primary, 3/5–8) X121
1 year full-time

Entry requirements: Degree and GCSE grade C or above in English language, mathematics and science; A-level (minimum grade C) in National Curriculum subject required if first degree is non-National Curriculum.
Contact: Mrs Gill Harper-Jones
         Primary Admissions Tutor
         01792 518682
         g.c.harper-jones@swansea.ac.uk

PGCE in Primary Education (Upper Primary, 7–11) X171
1 year full-time
As above

PGCE in Secondary Education (Design and Technology) W9X1
1 year full-time

Entry requirements: Relevant degree, and GCSE grade C or above in English language and mathematics.
Contact: Mr Dave Hendley
         PGCE Secondary Admissions
         and Course Tutor
         01792 518682
         d.r.hendley@swansea.ac.uk

PGCE in Secondary Education (English) Q3X1
1 year full-time
As above

Entry requirements: As above
Contact: Ms Betty Morris
         PGCE Course Tutor
         01792 518682
         b.morris@swansea.ac.uk

PGCE in Secondary Education (French with German) RX11
1 year full-time
As above

Entry requirements: As above

Contact: Mr Nigel Norman
PGCE Course Tutor
01792 518682
n.a.norman@swansea.ac.uk

PGCE in Secondary Education (French with Spanish) RXD1

1 year full-time
As above

PGCE in Secondary Education (French) R1X1

1 year full-time
As above

PGCE in Secondary Education (Geography) F8X1

1 year full-time
As above

Entry requirements: As above
Contact: Mr Duncan Hawley
PGCE Course Tutor
01792 518682
d.j.hawley@swansea.ac.uk

PGCE in Secondary Education (German with French) RXG1

1 year full-time
As above

Entry requirements: As above
Contact: Mr Nigel Norman
PGCE Course Tutor
01792 518682
n.a.norman@swansea.ac.uk

PGCE in Secondary Education (History) V1X1

1 year full-time
As above

Entry requirements: As above
Contact: Mr Alan Kelly
PGCE Course Tutor
01792 518682
A.G.B.Kelly@swansea.ac.uk

PGCE in Secondary Education (Information Technology) G5X1

1 year full-time

Entry requirements: Relevant degree, study beyond GCSE in second subject (mathematics, physics or design and technology)

and GCSE grade C or above in English language and mathematics; or equivalent.
Contact: Dr Steven Kennewell
PGCE Course Tutor
01792 518682
s.e.kennewell@swansea.ac.uk

PGCE in Secondary Education (Mathematics with Information Technology, 11–16) GX11

1 year full-time

Entry requirements: Degree with reasonable mathematical content plus experience with information technology, and GCSE grade C or above in English language and mathematics.
Contact: Dr Howard Tanner
PGCE Course Tutor
01792 518682
h.f.tanner@swansea.ac.uk

PGCE in Secondary Education (Mathematics) G1X1

1 year full-time

Entry requirements: Relevant degree, and GCSE grade C or above in English language and mathematics; or equivalent; although degree in mathematics is preferred, students with degrees in engineering, physics, economics, statistics and psychology are often acceptable.
Contact: Dr Howard Tanner
PGCE Course Tutor
01792 518682
h.f.tanner@swansea.ac.uk

PGCE in Secondary Education (Science 11–16) F0XC

1 year full-time

Entry requirements: Relevant degree and GCSE grade C or above in English language and mathematics.
Contact: Dr Chris Turner
PGCE Course Tutor
01792 518649
c.k.turner@swansea.ac.uk

PGCE in Secondary Education (Science: Biology) C1X1

1 year full-time

Entry requirements: As above
Contact: Ms Pam Bashford
    PGCE Course Tutor
    01792 518629
    P.J.Bashford@swansea.ac.uk

PGCE in Secondary Education (Science: Chemistry) F1X1

1 year full-time

Entry requirements: As above
Contact: Dr John Parkinson
    PGCE Course Tutor
    01792 518682
    j.parkinson@swansea.ac.uk

PGCE in Secondary Education (Science: Physics) F3X1

1 year full-time

Entry requirements: As above
Contact: Mr Chris Turner
    PGCE Course Tutor
    01792 518682
    c.k.turner@swansea.ac.uk

PGCE in Secondary Education (Welsh) Q5X1

1 year full-time

Entry requirements: As above
Contact: Mr Tim Samuel
    PGCE Course Tutor
    01792 518682
    T.Samuel@swansea.ac.uk

MA (Ed) in Education

1 year full-time, 2–5 years part-time

Entry requirements: Degree or relevant experience; non-graduates with at least 2 years' professional experience in education considered.
Contact: Dr Steve Kennewell
    Director of Graduate Studies
    01792 518639
    s.e.kennwell@swansea.ac.uk

University of Teesside

Middlesborough
TS1 3BA
Tel: 01642 218121
Fax: 01642 384201
reg@tees.ac.uk
www.tees.ac.uk

In 1992 Teesside Polytechnic was approved to become the University of Teesside. Student numbers have risen from around 8,000 to over 17,000 and extensive investment has taken place to create a 21st century campus. The University of Teesside is situated on a large compact site in the centre of Middlesbrough so all the learning and teaching facilities, support services, student accommodation and the Students' Union are within easy walking distance. It has a Learning Resource Centre, combining traditional library services with high-tech computing and multimedia resources.

The Education Department is located in the School of Arts and Media. It offers PGCE courses, postgraduate taught courses and research opportunities as well as programmes to aid continuing professional development for qualified and practising teachers.

University Managed Residences situated on the campus or University Managed Housing rooms in the private sector are both available to accommodate students. Places on campus are reserved exclusively to first year students.

HOW TO APPLY

PGCE: applications are made through the GTTR.

Postgraduate: applications are made direct to the institution.

COURSES

PGCE in Initial Teacher Training (English) XQC3

1 year full-time

Entry requirements: Degree or equivalent qualification with English as a major component; some prior experience of work with children normally required.

Contact: Admissions Enquiries
01642 384019

PGCE in Initial Teacher Training (Science) XFCA

1 year full-time

Entry requirements: Degree or equivalent qualification with a science as a major component and, normally, prior experience of work with children.

Contact: As above

PgDip in Curriculum Leadership

1 year part-time evening

Entry requirements: Open to qualified and practising teachers who have successfully completed a relevant postgraduate certificate.

Contact: As above

MA in Education

1 year part-time evening

Entry requirements: Completion of PgCert and PgDip; exemptions possible based on prior learning.

Contact: As above

PgCert in Foundation Stage

1 year part-time evening

Entry requirements: For practising teachers in primary education including support teachers, classroom teachers, subject specialists and members of senior management.

Contact: As above

PDD in In-Service Education

2 terms part-time evening

Entry requirements: For practising teachers.

Contact: As above

PgCert in Key Stage 2/3 Transition

1 year part-time evening
As above

PgCert in Literacy at Key Stage 3

1 year part-time evening

Entry requirements: Applicants should be teachers of English at Key Stage 3.

Contact: As above

PgCert in Meeting and Managing Special Educational Needs in Mainstream Schools

1 year part-time evening

Entry requirements: Applicants should be qualified teachers and should either be carrying out the role of Special Educational Needs Co-ordinator or should be preparing to do so.

Contact: As above

PgCert in Primary ICT

1 year part-time evening

Entry requirements: For practising teachers.

Contact: As above

PgCert in Primary Literacy

1 year part-time evening
As above

PgCert in Primary Numeracy

1 year part-time evening
As above

PgCert in Teaching Pupils with Specific Learning Difficulties (Dyslexia) within the School Context

1 year part-time evening
As above

Thames Primary Consortium

78 Willingale Way
Southend
SS1 3SX
Tel: 01702 586744
teaching@blueyonder.co.uk

The consortium offers school-based training leading to Qualified Teacher Status and the PGCE which is awarded by the University of Luton. Students are assigned to a home school for a large part of the course but will also experience other schools during the course.

There are 22 schools within the consortium situated on the north bank of the river Thames. The schools are infant, junior or primary and are located in the Laindon and Basildon areas toward the west and the Benfleet, Hadleigh and Southend areas towards the east.

HOW TO APPLY

Applications are made through the GTTR.

COURSES

PGCE Primary Education (Lower Primary, 5–8) X121
1 year full-time

Entry requirements: Degree in relevant area; GCSE grade C or above in English language and mathematics, and science if born after 1/9/79.
Contact: Enquiries
01702 586744
teaching@blueyonder.co.uk

PGCE Primary Education (Upper Primary, 7–11) X171
1 year full-time
As above

Titan Partnership Ltd

St. Georges Post 16 Centre
Great Hampton Row
Birmingham
B19 3JG
Tel: 0121 212 4567
Fax: 0121 233 3383
teachertraining@titan.org.uk
www.titan.org.uk

The Titan Partnership Ltd is an educational charity made up of fifty nurseries, primary and secondary schools, a college, business groups and training providers and is based in the Handsworth, Aston and Nechells area of Birmingham. It focuses on the special needs of the inner city and how to promote the potential of the children to employers.

The partnership runs School Centred Initial Teacher Training (SCITT) and also Graduate Teacher Programmes at secondary level. The Titan Secondary SCITT consists of six secondary schools and leads to Qualified Teacher Status with the PGCE accredited by the Open University. A range of facilities and some accommodation is available for students at the training schools. Students also have access to teacher resource bases.

HOW TO APPLY

Applications are made through the GTTR.

COURSES

PGCE Secondary Education (English) Q3X1
36 weeks full-time

Entry requirements: Degree in relevant area; GCSE grade C or above in English language and mathematics, and science if born after 1/9/79.
Contact: Enquiries
0121 212 4567
teachertraining@titan.org.uk

PGCE Secondary Education (Information Technology) G5X1
36 weeks full-time
As above

PGCE Secondary Education
(Mathematics) G1X1
36 weeks full-time
As above

PGCE Secondary Education (Modern
Languages: French and Urdu) R9X1
36 weeks full-time
As above

PGCE Secondary Education (Physical
Education) X9C6
36 weeks full-time
As above

PGCE Secondary Education (Religious
Education) V6X1
36 weeks full-time
As above

PGCE Secondary Education (Science)
F0X1
36 weeks full-time
As above

PGCE Secondary Education (Technology)
J9X1
36 weeks full-time
As above

Trinity and All Saints College

Brownberrie Lane
Horsforth
Leeds
LS18 5HD
Tel: 0113 283 7100
Fax: 0113 283 7321
admissions@tasc.ac.uk
www.tasc.ac.uk

Trinity and All Saints College is an accredited college of the University of Leeds, with the university awarding the degrees and diplomas for all the courses. It opened in 1966 as two colleges on a single site and has been offering degrees of the University of Leeds since 1974. In 1980 the colleges formally merged into a single institution. and in 1991 it was designated a full College of the University.

The College is situated six miles north west of Leeds on a campus in 40 acres of landscaped grounds. There are nine halls of residence and a wide range of facilities. Additional shops, pubs and restaurants can be found in nearby Horsforth. Academic facilities include a library, twelve computer laboratories and a new Learning Centre.

The Faculty of Education offers an undergraduate degree with Qualified Teacher Status for prospective primary teachers or a secondary PGCE with the option to specialise in a selection of subjects.

HOW TO APPLY

Degree courses: applications are made through UCAS.
PGCE: applications are made through the GTTR.

COURSES

BA (Hons) Primary Education with English (5–8 years specialism) X1Q3
4 years full-time

Year 1: Narrative and poetry; knowledge about language.

Year 2: Medieval language and literature; communication skills workshop.

Entry requirements: SCE Higher: BCCCC, BTEC NC/ND, AVCEs: CC, Irish Leaving Certificates: CCCC, GCE A- and AS-levels: CCD, Mature entry
Contact: Ms Jean Walton
        Director of Primary Education
        0113 283 7140
        j_walton@tasc.ac.uk

BA (Hons) Primary Education with English (7–11 years specialism) X1QH
4 years full-time
As above

BA (Hons) Primary Education with History (5–8 years specialism) X1V1
4 years full-time

Year 1: Patterns and periodisation; the historian's craft.

Year 2: Problems in history; research and discover.

Year 3: Special subject study.

Entry requirements: BTEC NC/ND, AVCEs: CC, Irish Leaving Certificates: CCCC, SCE Higher: CCCCC, GCE A- and AS-levels: CCD, Mature entry

Contact: As above

BA (Hons) Primary Education with History (7–11 years specialism) X1VC

4 years full-time

As above

BA (Hons) Primary Education with Mathematics (5–8 years specialism) X1G1

4 years full-time

Year 1: Algebra and calculus; discrete mathematics and statistics.

Year 2: Calculus and differential equations; mathematical methods and statistics.

Year 3: Transformation geometry and linear algebra; history of mathematics and introduction to analysis.

Entry requirements: BTEC NC/ND, CCCC: Irish Leaving Certificates: CCCC, SCE Higher: CCCCC, GCE A- and AS-levels: CDE, AVCEs: DD, Mature entry

Contact: As above

BA (Hons) Primary Education with Mathematics (7–11 years specialism) X1GC

4 years full-time

As above

BA (Hons) Primary Education with Physical Education (5–8 years specialism) X1C6

4 years full-time

Courses in primary games, athletics, dance, gymnastics, swimming, and outdoor and adventurous activities. Students will also study modules which examine the psychological and sociological context of children's participation in sport and exercise. In addition, the course offers an insight into the role of the PE curriculum leader and the ways in which young people's involvement in physical activity can be developed in community settings.

Year 1: Psychological and sociological perspectives of sport and leisure; children and physical activity: games, athletics, outdoor and adventurous activities.

Year 2: Research design/health and lifestyle; psychology of learning and teaching: gymnastics, dance and swimming in primary education.

Year 3: Curriculum leadership in PE; sport, exercise and health in special populations; young people in sport and leisure.

Entry requirements: BTEC NC/ND, AVCEs: CC, Irish Leaving Certificates: CCCC, SCE Higher: CCCCC, GCE A- and AS-levels: CCD, Mature entry

Contact: As above

BA (Hons) Primary Education with Physical Education (7–11 years specialism) X1CP

4 years full-time

Year 1: Psychological and sociological perspectives of sport and leisure; children and physical activity: Games, athletics, outdoor and adventurous activities.

Year 2: Research design/health and lifestyle; psychology of learning and teaching: Gymnastics, dance and swimming in primary education.

Year 3: Curriculum leadership in PE; sport, exercise and health in special populations; young people in sport and leisure.

Entry requirements: As above
Contact: As above

BA (Hons) Primary Education with Science (5–8 years specialism) X1F0

4 years full-time

Year 1: Science foundation: Energy.

Year 2: Biological sciences; introduction to chemistry and materials.

Year 3: Pollution and materials; energy, earth in space.

Entry requirements: BTEC NC/ND, Irish Leaving Certificates: CCCC, SCE Higher: CCCCC, GCE A- and AS-levels: CDE, AVCEs: DD, Mature entry
Contact: As above

BA (Hons) Primary Education with Science (7–11 years specialism) X1FA

4 years full-time

Students will spend the equivalent of 1 year in school based training and 2 years studying all aspects of primary education, focusing on the core subjects of: English; mathematics; science and ICT. Introduction to non-core subjects of the National Curriculum; 1 year of specialist subject study. All students train to teach the full 5–11 age range in addition to 3rd and 4th year work focused on their chosen age range.

Successful completion of this course leads to a recommendation for Qualified Teacher Status (QTS) after completion of skills tests.

Entry requirements: BTEC NC/ND, Irish Leaving Certificates: CCCC, SCE Higher: CCCCC, GCE A- and AS-levels: CDD, AVCEs: DD, Mature entry
Contact: As above

BA (Hons) Primary Education with Theology (5–8 years specialism) X1V6

4 years full-time

Year 1: Introduction to the Bible; the study of religion.

Year 2: Christology, 1–451 AD; ecclesiastical movements, 1789–1965.

Year 3: The origins of Christianity; Christian understanding of God.

Entry requirements: BTEC NC/ND, Irish Leaving Certificates: CCCC, SCE Higher: CCCCC, GCE A- and AS-levels: CCD, AVCEs: CC, Mature entry
Contact: As above

BA (Hons) Primary Education with Theology (7–11 years specialism) X1VP

4 years full-time

Year 1: Introduction to the Bible; the study of religion.

Year 2: Christology, 1–451 AD; ecclesiastical movements, 1789–1965.

Year 3: The origins of Christianity; Christian understanding of God.

Entry requirements: As above
Contact: As above

PGCE Secondary Education (Business Studies) N1X1

1 year full-time

Entry requirements: Candidates must be graduates of a British university or be holders of equivalent qualifications, and have passed GCSE minimum grade C (or equivalent) English language and mathematics. A first degree in business studies or a combined degree in which business studies is a significant component is required.
Contact: Ms Anne Welburn
         Admissions Assistant
         (Postgraduate)
         0113 283 7268
         a_welburn@tasc.ac.uk

PGCE Secondary Education (English) Q3X1

1 year full-time

Entry requirements: Candidates must be graduates of a British university or be holders of equivalent qualifications, and have passed GCSE minimum grade C (or equivalent) English language and mathematics. A first degree in English or a combined degree in which English is a significant component is required.
Contact: As above

PGCE Secondary Education (French) R1X1

1 year full-time
As above

Entry requirements: Candidates must be graduates of a British university or be holders of equivalent qualifications, and have passed GCSE minimum grade C (or equivalent) English language and mathematics. A first degree in modern languages with French or a combined degree in which

French is a significant component is required.

Contact: As above

PGCE Secondary Education (German) R2X1

1 year full-time

Entry requirements: Candidates must be graduates of a British university or be holders of equivalent qualifications, and have passed GCSE minimum grade C (or equivalent) English language and mathematics. A first degree in modern languages with German or a combined degree in which German is a significant component is required.

Contact: As above

PGCE Secondary Education (History) V1X1

1 year full-time

Entry requirements: Candidates must be graduates of a British university or be holders of equivalent qualifications, and have passed GCSE minimum grade C (or equivalent) English language and mathematics. A first degree in history or a combined degree in which history is a significant component is required.

Contact: As above

PGCE Secondary Education (Mathematics) G1X1

1 year full-time

Entry requirements: Candidates must be graduates of a British university or be holders of equivalent qualifications, and have passed GCSE minimum grade C (or equivalent) English language and mathematics. A first degree in mathematics or a combined degree in which mathematics is a significant component is required.

Contact: As above

PGCE Secondary Education (Mathematics, conversion) GXC1

2 years full-time

Entry requirements: An Honours degree in subject related to mathematics, including the successful completion of the equivalent of 1 year of mathematics studies; GCSE English and mathematics grade C.

Contact: As above

PGCE Secondary Education (Religious Education) V6X1

1 year full-time

Entry requirements: Candidates must be graduates of a British university or be holders of equivalent qualifications, and have passed GCSE minimum grade C (or equivalent) English language and mathematics. A first degree in theology or religious studies or a combined degree in which theology or religious studies is a significant component is required.

Contact: As above

PGCE Secondary Education (Spanish) R4X1

1 year full-time

Entry requirements: Candidates must be graduates of a British university or be holders of equivalent qualifications, and have passed GCSE minimum grade C (or equivalent) English language and mathematics. A first degree in modern languages with Spanish or a combined degree in which Spanish is a significant component is required.

Contact: As above

PgCert/PgDip in Media Education

PgDip: 2 to 5 years part-time

Entry requirements: Qualified Teacher Status.

Contact: Mr Graham Jarvis
0113 283 7290
a_bean@tasc.ac.uk

Trinity College, Carmarthen

College Road
Carmarthen
SA31 3EP
Tel: 01267 676767
Fax: 01267 676766
registry@trinity-cm.ac.uk
www.trinity-cm.ac.uk

Trinity College, Carmarthen is the second oldest institution of higher education in Wales. It was founded in 1848 to train teachers for Church schools. It is a campus-based college so all facilities are close to hand.

The Faculty of Education and Training is one of the main Teacher Training centres in Wales. The Faculty provides a range of undergraduate and postgraduate courses for prospective teachers and also programmes of Continuing Professional Development for teachers including a newly validated MA degree in Early Years Studies.

Trinity has a Teaching Resources Centre which provides books, resources and services for all the education courses. A library and IT suites provide extra academic resources and there are sports and leisure facilities including a new students' union on site. The accommodation at Trinity College is all located on the main campus. First-year students are usually accommodated in catered Halls of Residence. Second-, third-year and postgraduate students can opt for en-suite self-catering flats.

HOW TO APPLY

Degree courses: applications are made through UCAS.

PGCE: applications are made through GTTR.

Postgraduate: applications are made direct to the institution.

COURSES

BA (Hons) Addysg Gynradd (Primary Education) X123

3 years full-time

Course is taught through the medium of Welsh.

Contact: Registry
01267 676767
registry@trinity-cm.ac.uk

BA (Hons) Primary Education X120

3 years full-time

College-based studies cover: Professional teaching studies; core National Curriculum subjects (English; mathematics; science; information technology; Welsh 1st and 2nd language); foundation subjects and religious education (art; geography; history; music; physical education; technology; religious education); early years education; subject specialism. School-based studies: these form an integral part of the course. They take up a minimum of 24 weeks and students gain experience in both infant and junior phases of primary education in at least 3 primary schools in different geographical, linguistic and socio-educational settings.

Successful completion of this course leads to a recommendation for Qualified Teacher Status (QTS).

Entry requirements: Tariff: 140, IELTS: 5.5, BTEC NC/ND, Irish Leaving Certificates: CCCCC, Foundation / access qualification, Mature entry, SCE Higher
Contact: As above

PGCE Cynradd (Primary Education, 3–11, Welsh medium) X101

1 year full-time

Entry requirements: Gradd anrhydedd dda mewn pwnc sy'n addas ar gyfer y cwricwlwm cynradd ynghyd â chymhywster TAGE (Gradd A–C) mewn Iaith Saesneg, Mathemateg a phwnc Gwyddonol, ynghyd â Chymraeg i'r rhai sy'n dymuno astudio'r cwrs drwy gyfrwng y Gymraeg.
Contact: Shon Hughes
Director of College-based Studies
01267 676686
s.w.hughes@trinity-cm.ac.uk

PGCE Primary Education (3–11) X100

1 year full-time

Entry requirements: Applicants should be graduates whose previous education provides the foundation for work as a primary school teacher, and should have obtained GCSE grade C or above (or equivalent) in English language, science and mathematics.

Contact: As above

PGCE Secondary Education (Religious Education) V6X1

1 year full-time

Entry requirements: Applicants should be graduates in a related subject whose previous education provides the foundation for work as a primary school teacher, and should have obtained GCSE grade C or above (or equivalent) in English language and mathematics.

Contact: Vaughan Salisbury
Director of Studies
01242 225868
v.salisbury@trinity-cm.ac.uk

PGCE Secondary Education (Religious Education, Welsh medium) V6XC

1 year full-time

Entry requirements: Fe ddylech feddu ar radd mewn Astudiaethau Crefydd, Diwinyddiaeth, Astudiaethau Beiblaidd, Gradd Dyniaethau neu Astudiaethau Cyfunol gyda Chrefydd yn brif bwnc neu wedi astudio elfennau o Grefydd ar gyfer rhan sylweddol o'ch gradd. Ambell waith, fel amod cael mynediad ar y cwrs, byddwn yn gofyn ichi gwblhau'n llwyddiannus Fodylau Dysgu o Bell mewn rhai o'r crefyddau byd. Bydd hyn yn eich helpu i ychwanegu at eich gwybodaeth bynciol yn un neu ragor o'r crefyddau byd ac yn rhoi ichi'r hyder i addysgu'r pwnc yn effeithiol gyda disgyblion.

Gorau po gynted y byddwch yn gwneud cais gan fod y Cynulliad Cenedlaethol ond yn ariannu'r rhif targed ar gyfer y cwrs, sydd oddeutu 30 hyfforddai y flwyddyn.

Contact: As above

MA in Early Years Education

1 year full-time, 2 years part-time or variable

Entry requirements: Good Honours degree in suitable discipline.

Contact: Sian Wyn Siencyn
Head of the School of Early Years Education
01267 676798
s.w.siencyn@trinity-cm.ac.uk

MA in Education

Full-time or part-time

Entry requirements: Good Honours degree; applications may also be considered from candidates with alternative qualifications and experience in a teaching/training capacity.

Contact: Elaine Perry
Director, Continuing Professional Development
01267 676646
e.perry@trinity-cm.ac.uk

PgCert/PgDip/MA in Education (Children Under Five/Early Years)

MA: full-time or part-time

Entry requirements: Good Honours degree; applications may also be considered from candidates with alternative qualifications and experience in a teaching/training capacity.

Contact: As above

PgCert/PgDip/MA in Education (Education and Society)

MA: full-time or part-time
As above

PgCert/PgDip/MA in Education (Professional Education Studies)

PgCert: part-time, PgDip: part-time, MA: full-time or part-time
As above

MA (Ed) in Educational Drama and Theatre in Education

Part-time

Entry requirements: Good Honours degree in a relevant discipline or teaching qualification.

Contact: Kevin Matherick
Head of the Faculty of Creative,
Performing and Cultural Arts
01267 676606
k.matherick@trinity-cm.ac.uk

Msc in Management in Education and Training

Full-time or part-time

Entry requirements: Good Honours degree in a suitable discipline. Applications may be considered from candidates with another degree, subject to supportive references and interview. Non-graduates or mature students with relevant experience may also be considered.

Contact: Elaine Perry
Director, Continuing
Professional Development
01267 676646
e.perry@trinity-cm.ac.uk

University of Ulster

Cromore Road
Coleraine
County Londonderry
BT52 1SA
Tel: 08700 400 700
Fax: 028 7032 4908
online@ulster.ac.uk
www.ulst.ac.uk

The University of Ulster is the largest university in Ireland and currently caters for over 20,000 students. It is based over four campuses: Coleraine Campus, Jordanstown Campus, Belfast Campus and Magee Campus.

The School of Education provides postgraduate courses in Initial Teacher Education and programmes for Continuing Professional Development. Postgraduate opportunities are also available for individual research training or taught programmes.

Each campus offers a range of student services and leisure facilities. Academic resources and access to computers are available across the four campuses. University residences are available on all campuses except Belfast and there is also accommodation available in the local areas.

HOW TO APPLY

PGCE: applications are made direct to the institution.

Postgraduate: applications are made direct to the institution.

COURSES

PGCE in Primary Education (Key Stages 1–2)

1 year full-time

Entry requirements: Applicants should possess grade C or above in GCSE in English, mathematics and science or equivalent qualifications plus a good Honours degree from a recognised institution in a subject appropriately related to the National Curriculum. In addition, applicants should be able to demonstrate a knowledge of and an interest in the education of young children and must produce evidence of a satisfactory health record.

Contact: Miss I McComb
Head of Faculty Administration
028 9036 6184
ip.mccomb@ulst.ac.uk

PGCE in Secondary Education (Art and Design)

1 year full-time

Entry requirements: Honours degree in a cognate subject area plus grade C or above in GCSE (or equivalent) in English language and mathematics plus evidence of satisfactory health record.

Contact: As above

PGCE in Secondary Education (English/Drama and Media Studies)

1 year full-time

Entry requirements: Honours degree in a cognate subject area plus grade C or above in GCSE (or equivalent) in English language and mathematics plus evidence of satisfactory health record.

Contact: As above

PGCE in Secondary Education (Geography)

1 year full-time

As above

PGCE in Secondary Education (History)

1 year full-time

As above

PGCE in Secondary Education (Home Economics)

1 year full-time

As above

PGCE in Secondary Education (Music)

1 year full-time

As above

PGCE in Secondary Education (Physical Education)

1 year full-time

As above

PGCE in Secondary Education (Technology and Design)

1 year full-time

As above

PgCert/PgDip/MSc in Education

2–5 years part-time

Entry requirements: Degree or equivalent from recognised institution from UK, ROI or internationally recognised equivalent; recognised qualification in education (if not employed in a school or college, be in a role or profession with an education dimension); currently employed as a teacher or equivalent professional in compulsory education or related fields.

Contact: Miss I McComb
Head of Faculty Administration
028 9036 6184
ip.mccomb@ulst.ac.uk

EdD in Education

2 years full-time, 3 years part-time

Entry requirements: Master's degree in education or a related subject with an overall assessment mark of more than 60% and normally, more than 5 years' post-qualifying experience in education or a related profession.

Contact: As above

PgCert/PgDip in Further and Higher Education

1 year part-time

Entry requirements: For full-time or part-time teachers (normally graduates) in colleges of further and/or higher education or equivalent.

Contact: As above

PgCert/PgDip/MSc in Lifelong Learning

On-line study

Entry requirements: Degree or equivalent or equivalent standard in a PgCert or a recognised professional or other qualification.

Contact: As above

PgDip/MA in Teaching English to Speakers of Other Languages (TESOL)

1 year full-time, 2 years part-time

Entry requirements: Diploma in teaching English as a foreign language (TEFL) or in teaching English to speakers of other languages (TESOL) at an acceptable standard or equivalent required for MA, degree in English or in a modern foreign language or other relevant subject, or teaching qualification with at least 2 years' teaching experience required for Postgraduate Diploma. Experience of teaching will be considered an advantage.

Contact: As above

Urban Learning Foundation

Bede House
56 East India Dock Road
Westminster
London
E14 6JE
Tel: 020 7987 0033
Fax: 020 7536 0107
info@urbanlearning.org.uk
www.urbanlearning.org.uk

The Urban Learning Foundation is a registered charity and is focused on training teachers for schools in the inner city environment. It was initiated by the College of St Mark and St John in Plymouth and the Clouste Gulbenkian Foundation, and was originally launched in 1973. The Foundation began to develop in 1977 when the government proposed that part of the reorganised teacher training system could be used to benefit the inner city schools. Then in 1983, a commission established by the Archbishop of Canterbury produced a report that included a recommendation that the Church should sponsor training centres with an urban focus. Shortly afterwards Christ Church College in Canterbury, King Alfred's College, Winchester and St Martin's College, Lancaster joined, the Foundation was incorporated and was registered as a charity in 1984. The University of Gloucestershire is now also part of the consortium.

The Foundation now manages two School Centred Initial Teacher Training courses and aims to attract a significant number of Asian, African and African-Caribbean candidates. It offers the PGCE at early years and primary level or a degree course at primary level leading to qualified teacher status. There is accommodation available to students close to the location of training.

HOW TO APPLY

Degree: applications are made through UCAS, to St Martin's College.
PGCE: applications are made through the GTTR.

COURSES

BA (Hons) Advanced Study of Early Years Education (3–11 years) X104 T

Course is offered in partnership with St Martin's College. Please see entry under St Martin's.

PGCE in Primary Education (5–11 years) X171

1 year full-time

Entry requirements: Degree or equivalent in area relevant to chosen specialism; English language and mathematics GCSE grade C; experience of working with children and young people.
Contact: Enquiries
020 7987 0033
info@urbanlearning.org.uk

Wandsworth Primary School Consortium

Swaffield Primary School
St. Ann's Hill
Wandsworth
London
SW18 2SA
Tel: 020 8874 2825
swaffield@swaffield.wandsworth.sch.uk
www.scitt.co.uk

The Wandsworth Primary Schools' Consortium provides school-centred initial teacher training through a group of primary schools in Wandsworth, south west London, which have been accredited by the Teacher Training Agency. Swaffield Primary School is the lead school and the location for lectures.

Students are initially allocated one school as a base school in which the majority of their time will be spent during the first and third terms of the course. The second term is spent in one of the other schools. Assessed teaching practice takes place in the second term and the third term.

HOW TO APPLY

All applications are made through the GTTR.

COURSES

PGCE in Primary Education (Early Years, 3–5) X110

1 year full-time

Entry requirements: 2nd Class degree in an area relevant to primary curriculum with GCSE grade C or above in English language and mathematics, and science if born after 1st September 1979. Recent experience with children in primary school.

Contact: Enquiries
020 8874 2825
swaffield@swaffield.
wandsworth.sch.uk

PGCE in Primary Education (Lower Primary, 5–8) X121

1 year full-time
As above

PGCE in Primary Education (Upper Primary, 7–11) X171

1 year full-time
As above

University of Warwick

Coventry
CV4 7AL
Tel: 024 7652 3523
Fax: 024 7646 1606
Undergraduate:
ugadmissions@warwick.ac.uk
Postgraduate:
pgadmissions@warwick.ac.uk
www.warwick.ac.uk

The University of Warwick was founded in 1964 and is situated three miles from Coventry city centre. It has over 18,000 students and the green, landscaped campus is situated on three adjacent sites, Central Campus, Gibbet Hill Campus and Westwood Campus. Each campus is lively and modern with its own shops, banks, bars and restaurants.

The Institute of Education is located on Westwood campus. It is one of the largest centres for educational studies and research in the UK and is regarded as a leading centre for educational research. The University offers a wide range of teaching courses including initial teacher training at undergraduate and postgraduate level, taught Master's degrees, research opportunities and a range of Continuing Professional Development programmes. Flexible study is available when training to

teach some subjects.

Resources available at the University include a well-equipped library with a specialist education section and extensive computing facilities. Accommodation is available on and off campus.

HOW TO APPLY

Degree courses: applications are made through UCAS.

PGCE: applications are made through the GTTR.

Postgraduate: applications are made direct to the institution.

COURSES

BA (Hons) in Primary Education with a specialism in English X1Q3

4 years full-time

Course comprises 5 inter-related elements: Subject studies in specialist subject. Curriculum studies in the core areas of the National Curriculum. Whole curriculum studies: introduction to the National Curriculum requirements in other Foundation subjects (geography, history, physical education, art, music, design and technology) and in religious studies and information technology. Core professional studies (e.g. classroom management, special educational needs, assessment, reporting and recording). School experience.

Successful completion of this course leads to a recommendation for Qualified Teacher Status (QTS) subject to performance in skills tests.

Entry requirements: GCE A- and AS-levels: BCC to BBB, International Baccalaureate: 30, Irish Leaving Certificates: BBBBCC, SCE Higher: BCC to BBB
Contact: Mrs M Graham
Departmental Secretary
024 7652 3896
ba-qts@warwick.ac.uk

BA (Hons) in Primary Education with a specialism in Mathematics X1G1
4 years full-time
As above

BA (Hons) in Primary Education with a specialism in Science X1F0
4 years full-time
As above

PGCE in Primary Education (Lower Primary, 3/5–8) X121
38 weeks full-time

Entry requirements: Minimum 2nd Class degree or equivalent, normally in subject related to primary curriculum; GCSE grade C or above in English, mathematics and science normally required.
Contact: Admissions
024 7652 4208
pgce@warwick.ac.uk

PGCE in Primary Education (Upper Primary, 5–11) X100
38 weeks full-time
As above

PGCE in Secondary Education (Drama with English) W4XD
38 weeks full-time or part-time

Entry requirements: Degree in English language and/or literature preferred, or joint or combined degrees in English and other subjects, or in drama or theatre studies. GCSE grade C or above (or equivalent) in English language, mathematics and science.

Contact: Graduate Studies Secretary
Warwick Institute of Education
024 7652 4489
wie-grad@warwick.ac.uk

PGCE in Secondary Education (Economics and Business Studies) L1X1
38 weeks full-time or flexible

Entry requirements: 2nd Class Honours degree or graduate-equivalent status in related discipline plus GCSE grade C or above (or equivalent) in English language, mathematics and science.
Contact: As above

PGCE in Secondary Education (English and Drama) QX31
38 weeks full-time or flexible
As above

PGCE in Secondary Education (French with German) RX11
38 weeks full-time or flexible
As above

PGCE in Secondary Education (French with Spanish) RXD1
38 weeks full-time or flexible
As above

PGCE in Secondary Education (French) R1X1
38 weeks full-time or flexible
As above

PGCE in Secondary Education (German with French) RX21
38 weeks full-time or flexible
As above

PGCE in Secondary Education (German with Spanish) RX2C
38 weeks full-time or flexible
As above

PGCE in Secondary Education (German) R2X1
38 weeks full-time or flexible
As above

PGCE in Secondary Education (History) V1X1

38 weeks full-time

Entry requirements: 2nd Class Honours degree or graduate-equivalent status in related discipline plus GCSE grade C or above (or equivalent) in English language, mathematics and science.

Contact: As above

PGCE in Secondary Education (Information and Communications Technology) G5X1

38 weeks full-time

As above

PGCE in Secondary Education (Mathematics) G1X1

38 weeks full-time or flexible

As above

PGCE in Secondary Education (Religious Education) V6X1

38 weeks full-time or part-time

As above

PGCE in Secondary Education (Science, Biology) C1X1

38 weeks full-time or flexible

As above

PGCE in Secondary Education (Science, Chemistry) F1X1

38 weeks full-time or flexible

As above

PGCE in Secondary Education (Science, Physics) F3X1

38 weeks full-time or flexible

As above

PGCE in Secondary Education (Spanish with French) RX41

38 weeks full-time or flexible

As above

PGCE in Secondary Education (Spanish with German) RX4C

38 weeks full-time or flexible

As above

PGCE in Secondary Education (Spanish) R4X1

38 weeks full-time or flexible

As above

MA in Drama and Theatre Education

1 year full-time, 2–4 years part-time

Entry requirements: Degree (2nd Class Honours or above) in relevant discipline(s) normally required; other qualifications and experience may be considered in lieu of these.

Contact: Graduate Studies Secretary,
Warwick Institute of Education
024 7652 4489
wie-grad@warwick.ac.uk

PgCert in Drama Education

1 year part-time

As above

EdD in Education

3 years full-time, 4–5 years part-time

Entry requirements: Master's degree and at least 2 year's relevant professional experience normally required.

Contact: As above

MA in Educational Management

1 year full-time, 2–4 years part-time, distance learning

Entry requirements: Good Honours degree plus minimum 2 years' experience in educational organisation; candidates with relevant experience but without degree may be considered.

Contact: As above

MA in Educational Studies

1 year full-time, 2–4 years part-time

Entry requirements: Good Honours degree normally required but those with professional experience relevant to graduate study in their main field of interest are also welcome to apply.

Contact: As above

MA in Educational Studies (Further Education)

1 year full-time, 2–4 years part-time

As above

MSc in Mathematics Education

1 year full-time, 2–4 years part-time

As above

MA in Religious Education

1 year full-time, 2–4 years part-time

Entry requirements: Upper 2nd Class degree in relevant discipline normally required; other qualifications and experience may be considered; aimed at teachers but others with professional or personal interest in issues are welcome to apply.

Contact: As above

PgCert in Religious Education

1 year part-time, distance learning

As above

MSc in Science Education

1 year full-time, 2–4 years part-time

Entry requirements: Good Honours degree, but applications from those with professional experience relevant to graduate study in the main field of interest are also welcomed.

Contact: As above

West Midlands Consortium

Thomas Telford School
Old Park
Telford
TF3 4NW
Tel: 01952 200000
Fax: 01952 293294
pgce.ttsonline.net

The West Midlands Consortium has been running School Centred Initial Teacher Training courses since 1994 and offers subject routes in Design and Technology, Information Communication Technology and Physical Education through the secondary PGCE programme with Qualified Teacher Status. There are approximately 12 students on each subject route and the course is validated by the University of Surrey Roehampton.

There are nineteen secondary schools within the consortium and each student spends part of their time in two schools. Thomas Telford School is the main base and offers extensive teaching facilities with access to state-of-the-art equipment.

HOW TO APPLY

All applications are made through the GTTR.

COURSES

PGCE in Secondary Education (Design and Technology) W9X1

40 weeks full-time

Entry requirements: Degree in relevant subject; GCSE grade C or above in English language and mathematics, and science if born after 1st September 1979.

Contact: Enquiries
01952 200000

PGCE in Secondary Education (Information Technology) G5X1

40 weeks full-time

As above

PGCE in Secondary Education (Physical Education) X9C6

40 weeks full-time

As above

University of Wolverhampton

Wulfruna Street
Wolverhampton
WV1 1SB
Tel: 01902 321000
Fax: 01902 322686
enquiries@wlv.ac.uk
www.wlv.ac.uk

As one of the UK's largest universities, the University of Wolverhampton caters for over 22,000 students. It has four campuses in the West Midlands area: Compton Park on the outskirts of Wolverhampton, Telford Campus situated on a green field site on the outskirts of Telford, Walsall Campus a mile out of Walsall town and the largest, Wolverhampton Campus, in the city centre. Wolverhampton is one of the largest providers of teacher education and training in the public sector of British higher education.

The School of Education is based mainly at the Walsall Campus. It offers a wide range of courses including degrees, PGCEs and postgraduate programmes covering the primary and secondary age ranges through to post-compulsory education. It is supported by several specialist centres, including The Midland Leadership Centre, The Regional Primary Centre, The Centre for Design and Technology Education and The Centre for Rural Development and Training.

Each campus has excellent facilities including hi-tech learning centres, students' unions, sports facilities, shops and eating and drinking facilities. Accommodation is available either on or off campus.

HOW TO APPLY

Degree courses: applications are made through UCAS.

PGCE: applications are made through GTTR.

Postgraduate: applications are made direct to the institution.

COURSES

BEd (Hons) in Primary School Teaching X120

3 years full-time

Course provides students with practical experience of teaching in schools, alongside National Curriculum core subjects such as English, mathematics, science, information and communication technology, and foundation subjects including: art; music; physical education; design and technology, geography, history; religious education.

Entry requirements: Tariff: 200–260, Interview

Contact: Education Admissions
01902 321050
enquiries@wlv.ac.uk

BEd (Hons) in Secondary School Teaching (shortened) X101

2 years full-time

Specialist subjects: Design and technology; business studies; mathematics; the programme includes: school attachment; applied subject studies; further professional development; subject study and a period of practical teaching experience each year.

Successful completion of this course leads to a recommendation for Qualified Teacher Status (QTS) after completion of skills tests.

Entry requirements: Tariff: 200, BTEC NC/ND, HND, International Baccalaureate, Age restriction, Work experience

Contact: Education Admissions
01902 321050
enquiries@wlv.ac.uk

PGCE in Primary Education X100

1 year full-time

Entry requirements: UK degree or equivalent with GCSEs grade C or above in English, mathematics and science, or equivalent. All candidates are required to attend an interview. Work experiences in a primary school preferred.

Contact: Enquiries
01902 322222
enquiries@wlv.ac.uk

PGCE in Secondary Education (Business Studies) N1X1

1 year full-time

Entry requirements: Degree or equivalent, including substantial element of study of a subject appropriate to the secondary school curriculum; GCSE grade C or above, or equivalent, in English and mathematics; interview.

Contact: Enquiries
01902 322222
enquiries@wlv.ac.uk

PGCE in Secondary Education (Design and Technology) W9X1

1 year full-time
As above

PGCE in Secondary Education (English) Q3X1

1 year full-time
As above

PGCE in Secondary Education (Information Communication Technology) G5X1

1 year full-time
As above

PGCE in Secondary Education (Mathematics) G1X1

1 year full-time
As above

PGCE in Secondary Education (Modern Languages) R9X1

1 year full-time
As above

PGCE in Secondary Education (Physical Education) X9C6

1 year full-time
As above

PGCE in Secondary Education (Science) F0X1

1 year full-time
As above

PgCert in Basic Skills for Post-Compulsory Education

5 years full-time

Entry requirements: Degree or equivalent professional qualification

Contact: Dr Chris Rhodes
01902 322837
sed-enquiries@wlv.ac.uk

MA in Education

2 years full-time, 5 years part-time

Entry requirements: Degree, teaching qualification or relevant experience in subject area.

Contact: Central Dispatch Unit
01902 322222
enquiries@wlv.ac.uk

PgCert/PgDip/MA in Education (Professional and Postgraduate Development Programme)

2 years full-time, 5 years part-time

Entry requirements: Degree or equivalent qualification (substantial professional experience may substitute for graduate status).

Contact: Dr Chris Rhodes
01902 322837
sed-enquiries@wlv.ac.uk

PgCert in Information and Learning Technology for Post-Compulsory Education

5 years part-time

Entry requirements: Degree or equivalent qualification.

Contact: As above

MA in Management and Leadership in Education

2 years full-time, 5 years part-time

Entry requirements: Degree or Qualified Teacher Status or equivalent.

Contact: Central Dispatch Unit
01902 322222
enquiries@wlv.ac.uk

PgCert in Managing for Effective Learning

5 years part-time

Entry requirements: Degree or Qualified Teacher Status or equivalent.

Contact: As above

Pgcert in Mentoring

5 years part-time

Entry requirements: Applicants should have at least 2 years' successful teaching experience and be involved in mentoring, or managing mentoring within an institution.

Contact: Dr Chris Rhodes
01902 322837
sed-enquiries@wlv.ac.uk

University College Worcester

Henwick Grove
Worcester
WR2 6AJ
Tel: 01905 855000
Fax: 01905 855132
admissions@worc.ac.uk
www.worc.ac.uk

University College Worcester is based on a single site campus near to the centre of the City of Worcester. Worcester has many cultural attractions such as the Cathedral and the River Severn flows through the heart of the city. The shops, bars and restaurants of Worcester are all within walking distance of the university.

The Department of Education offers courses in initial teacher education and education and childhood studies as well as research opportunities and programmes for Continuing Professional Development.

The library and computer centre are based on the campus providing access to a multitude of academic resources and there are also sporting and recreational facilities. Accommodation is available through the university or in privately rented housing in the area.

HOW TO APPLY

Degree courses: applications are made through UCAS.
PGCE: applications are made through GTTR.
Postgraduate: applications are made direct to the institution.

COURSES

BA (Hons) in Primary Education (Early Years) X121

3 years full-time

Covers general teaching skills including classroom management and control, and teaching of language including reading, mathematics, expressive arts, humanities, science and physical education. Teaching practice. Students specialise in early years teaching.

Successful completion of this course leads to a recommendation for Qualified Teacher Status (QTS) after completion of skills tests.

Entry requirements: Tariff: 200 points, BTEC NC/ND, International Baccalaureate, Irish Leaving Certificates, Mature entry, SCE Higher
Contact: Julie Riley
Registry Admissions
01905 855111
j.riley@worc.ac.uk

BA (Hons) in Primary Education (Later Years) X122

3 years full-time

Covers general teaching skills including classroom management and control, and teaching of language including reading, mathematics, expressive arts, humanities, science and physical education. Teaching practice. Students specialise in later years teaching.

Successful completion of this course leads to a recommendation for Qualified Teacher Status (QTS) after completion of skills tests.
As above

PGCE in Primary Education (Early Years, 3–7) X121

1 year full-time

Entry requirements: Honours degree usually a Lower 2nd Class or above covering at least 1 of specialist subjects: mathematics; English; science; information communication technology; advanced early years; A-level and work experience in subject may suffice for those with different degree; GCSE or equivalent mathematics and English language grade C or above; science GCSE grade C or above (for those born after 1/9/79); evidence of recent experience in a primary school or nursery setting appropriate to the chosen age range option is required.

Contact: Jill Thompson
Registry Admissions
01905 855111
admissions@worc.ac.uk

PGCE in Primary Education (Later Years, 5–11) X171

1 year full-time
As above

PGCE in Secondary Education (Business Studies and Economics)

1 year full-time

Entry requirements: Degree or equivalent, with a substantial proportion of degree or professional qualification applicable to subject choice; GCSE (grade C or above), or equivalent, mathematics and English language. GCSE (grade C or above), or equivalent, in science is essential for those born on or after 1/9/79; some experience (at least 5 days) in a school before the course starts.

Contact: As above

PGCE in Secondary Education (Design and Technology: Food and Textiles) D6X1

1 year full-time
As above

PGCE in Secondary Education (Economics and Business) L1X1

1 year full-time
As above

PGCE in Secondary Education (English) Q3X1

1 year full-time
As above

PGCE in Secondary Education (Geography) F8X1

1 year full-time
As above

PGCE in Secondary Education (History) V1X1

1 year full-time
As above

PGCE in Secondary Education (Mathematics) G1X1

1 year full-time
As above

PGCE in Secondary Education (Modern Foreign Languages) R9X1

1 year full-time
As above

PGCE in Secondary Education (Music) W3X1

1 year full-time
As above

PGCE in Secondary Education (Physical Education) X9C6

1 year full-time
As above

PGCE in Secondary Education (Science: Biology) C1X1

1 year full-time
As above

PGCE in Secondary Education (Science: Chemistry) F1X1

1 year full-time
As above

PGCE in Secondary Education (Science: Physics) F3X1

1 year full-time
As above

Pgdip/MA/MSc in Education/Education Management

MA/MSc: 2–6 years part-time

Entry requirements: Qualified teacher status and minimum 2 years' professional experience required; plus degree in education or with education or cognate studies as major component; or degree plus DPSE or other appropriate advanced diploma; exceptionally, candidates with other qualifications admitted.

Contact: Susan Rennie
Pathway Administrator
01905 855056
s.rennie@worc.ac.uk

York St John, College of University of Leeds

Lord Mayor's Walk
York
YO31 7EX
Tel: 01904 624624
Fax: 01904 712512
admissions@yorksj.ac.uk
www.yorksj.ac.uk

York St. John was founded in 1841. It has been linked with the University of Leeds since 1920 and in 1990 became a full college of the University. It now has over 5,000 students. The main eight-acre site is on Lord Mayor's Walk, just a five-minute walk from city centre shops, restaurants, pubs, galleries and other attractions. The Heworth Croft site which currently houses the Sports Science and Psychology departments is just ten minutes away but these will transfer to the new facilities currently under construction at Lord Mayor's Walk. In addition to these developments a new Learning Centre, Health building and a new General Teaching block are also being built.

The college offers degree programmes, primary and secondary level PGCEs and other postgraduate and return to teaching options. The library, computer services and other facilities are all located on campus. University-owned accommodation is available although it cannot be guaranteed to all students so advice is also provided about privately rented accommodation.

HOW TO APPLY

Degree courses: applications are made through UCAS.

PGCE full-time: applications are made through the GTTR; PGCE part-time/flexible: applications are made direct to the institution.

Postgraduate: applications are made direct to the institution.

COURSES

BA (Hons) in Primary Education with English (nursery/lower primary) XQ13

4 years full-time

Scheme allows for specialisation in language or literature studies. All students must take 1 language module (introduction to the study of language) and 1 literature module (children's literature).

Language studies: Modules address important questions about the nature and study of language, with English as the main language under focus. Literature studies: Modules ask fundamental questions about the study of literature.

Teacher education includes: Core subjects of the National Curriculum (English, mathematics and science); curriculum studies: teaching National Curriculum foundation subjects (art, music, physical education, design and technology, geography, history, information technology) and religious education; general teaching issues, including planning, class management, assessing, recording and reporting children's attainment; practical school experience.

On completion students are recommended for Qualified Teacher Status (QTS) after completion of skills tests.

Entry requirements: Tariff: 220, International Baccalaureate: 28, Irish Leaving Certificates: BBBB, SCE Higher: BBB, BTEC NC/ND, Interview.

Contact: Admissions Department
01904 716598
admissions@yorksj.ac.uk

BA (Hons) in Primary Education with English (upper primary) XQC3

4 years full-time

As above

BSc (Hons) in Primary Education with Information Technology (nursery/lower primary) XG15

4 years full-time

Teacher education includes: Core subjects of the National Curriculum (English, mathematics and science); curriculum studies: teaching National Curriculum foundation subjects (art, music, physical education, design and technology, geography, history, information technology) and religious education; general teaching issues, including planning, class management, assessing, recording and reporting children's attainment; practical school experience.

Specialist subject study: Year 1 modules provide a sound basis for the development of all-round IT skills closely related to the role you will assume in schools; students develop understanding of the major software packages including word processing, spreadsheets, database, graphics, multimedia and web-based systems. In Years 3 and 4 students learn to design large database systems, develop educational computer programmes and develop understanding of the role of school co-ordinator for ICT.

On completion students are recommended for Qualified Teacher Status (QTS) after completion of skills tests.

Entry requirements: Tariff: 160, Inter-

national Baccalaureate: 24, Irish Leaving Certificates: CCCC, SCE Higher: CCC, BTEC NC/ND, Interview

Contact: Admissions Department
01904 716598
admissions@yorksj.ac.uk

BSc (Hons) in Primary Education with Information Technology (upper primary) XGC5

4 years full-time

As above

BSc (Hons) in Primary Education with Mathematics (nursery/lower primary) XG11

4 years full-time

Mathematics studies: In the first 2 years modules are taken which cover the basic concepts of the subject, putting students' previous knowledge of pure mathematics on a sound theoretical basis. Students also consider statistical ideas and the use of computers in mathematics and mathematical education. These modules are organised in such a way as to give insight into mathematical processes, applications and learning. The final-year module reflections on mathematics extends those ideas and provides the opportunity for extended projects in mathematics and mathematics teaching.

Teacher education includes: Core subjects of the National Curriculum (English, mathematics and science); curriculum studies: teaching National Curriculum foundation subjects (art, music, physical education, design and technology, geography, history, information technology) and religious education; general teaching issues, including planning, class management, assessing, recording and reporting children's attainment; practical school experience.

On completion students are recommended for Qualified Teacher Status (QTS) after completion of skills tests.

Entry requirements: Tariff: 160, International Baccalaureate: 24, Irish Leaving Certificates: CCCC, SCE Higher: CCC, BTEC NC/ND, Interview

Contact: Admissions Department
01904 716598
admissions@yorksj.ac.uk

BSc (Hons) in Primary Education with Mathematics (upper primary) XGC1

4 years full-time

As above

BA (Hons) in Primary Education with Music (nursey/lower primary) XW13

4 years full-time

Musical studies: Modular programme consisting of studies in performance; composition; listening and understanding; and music in education, with sufficient flexibility to allow students to develop personal interests.

Teacher education includes: Core subjects of the National Curriculum (English, mathematics and science); curriculum studies: teaching National Curriculum foundation subjects (art, music, physical education, design and technology, geography, history, information technology) and religious education; general teaching issues, including planning, class management, assessing, recording and reporting children's attainment; practical school experience.

On completion students are recommended for Qualified Teacher Status (QTS) after completion of skills tests.

Entry requirements: Tariff: 160, International Baccalaureate: 24, Irish Leaving Certificates: CCCC, SCE Higher: CCC, BTEC NC/ND, Interview

Contact: Admissions Department
01904 716598
admissions@yorksj.ac.uk

BA (Hons) in Primary Education with Music (upper primary) XWC3

4 years full-time

As above

BA (Hons) in Primary Education with Theology and Religious Studies (nursery/lower primary) XV16

4 years full-time

Theology and religious studies: Students study modules from 4 strands: world religions; theology and biblical studies; theology through story and the visual image; religion from a sociological and psychological perspective.

Teacher education includes: Core subjects of the National Curriculum (English, mathematics and science); curriculum studies: teaching National Curriculum foundation subjects (art, music, physical education, design and technology, geography, history, information technology) and religious education; general teaching issues, including planning, class management, assessing, recording and reporting children's attainment; practical school experience.

On completion students are recommended for Qualified Teacher Status (QTS) after completion of skills tests.

Entry requirements: Tariff: 160, International Baccalaureate: 24, Irish Leaving Certificates: CCCC, SCE Higher: CCC, BTEC NC/ND, Interview

Contact: Admissions Department
01904 716598
admissions@yorksj.ac.uk

BA (Hons) in Primary Education with Theology and Religious Studies (upper primary) XVC6

4 years full-time

As above

PGCE in Primary Education (Lower or Upper Primary)

18 months part-time

Entry requirements: Degree or equivalent acceptable to the University of Leeds, with passes at GCSE grade C (or equivalent) in English language and mathematics. Candidates born after 1 September 1979 also require GCSE minimum grade C in a science subject.

Contact: Admissions Department
01904 716598
admissions@yorksj.ac.uk

PGCE in Primary Education (Lower or Upper Primary, flexible route)
Flexible
As above

PGCE in Primary Education (Lower Primary, 3/5–8) X121
1 year full-time
As above

PGCE in Primary Education (Upper Primary, 7–12/13) X401
1 year full-time
As above

PGCE in Secondary Education (Religious Education) V8X7
1 year full-time
As above

PgDip/MA in Educational Studies
1–5 years part-time
Entry requirements: Qualified Teacher Status.
Contact: As above

University of York

Heslington
York YO10 5DD
Tel: 01904 430000
Fax: 01904 433538
admissions@york.ac.uk
www.york.ac.uk

The University of York was founded in 1963 and now has almost 10,000 students and over 30 academic departments and research centres. The University has a collegiate system consisting of eight colleges of which all students and staff are members. First-year or overseas students are guaranteed accommodation in one of the colleges or at nearby University residences.

The University consists of two campuses: Heslington and King's Manor. The main campus, Heslington, is a 200-acre landscaped park close to the City of York. The colleges and academic buildings are situated around a lake within close proximity of each other. King's Manor Campus is located in the City Centre.

Departments are based in specific colleges. The Department of Education is based at Langwith College, which is in a central position on the Heslington Campus and is convenient for the library, Central Hall and Heslington village. It offers a range of undergraduate and postgraduate courses. It supports and encourages work involving various research strategies and has an Educational Research Group (ERG) which was set up to cater for the needs of higher degree students. The purpose of the ERG is to promote research in schools and other educational institutions. Students on Master's programmes are encouraged to attend and weekend workshops are held once a term.

HOW TO APPLY
PGCE: applications are made through the GTTR.

Postgraduate: applications are made direct to the institution.

COURSES
PGCE in Secondary Education (English) Q3X1
1 year full-time
Entry requirements: Degree in English with GCSE grade C or above or equivalent in English language and mathematics.
Contact: Dr Judith Bennett
Director of Graduate Studies
01904 433455
educ15@york.ac.uk

PGCE in Secondary Education (History) V1X1
1 year full-time
As above

Entry requirements: Degree in history (or related) plus GCSE grade C or above or equivalent in English language and mathematics.
Contact: As above

PGCE in Secondary Education (History with Citizenship) VX1C
1 year full-time
As above

PGCE in Secondary Education (Mathematics) G1X1
1 year full-time

Entry requirements: Degree in mathematics plus GCSE grade C or above or equivalent in English language.
Contact: As above

PGCE in Secondary Education (Modern Languages: French with German) RX11
1 year full-time

Entry requirements: Degree in the relevant modern languages plus GCSE grade C or above or equivalent in English language and mathematics. Applications from graduate native speakers of the modern foreign languages are welcomed.
Contact: As above

PGCE in Secondary Education (Modern Languages: French with Spanish) RXD1
1 year full-time
As above

PGCE in Secondary Education (Modern Languages: French) R1X1
1 year full-time
As above

PGCE in Secondary Education (Modern Languages: German with French) RX21
1 year full-time
As above

PGCE in Secondary Education (Modern Languages: German) R2X1
1 year full-time
As above

PGCE in Secondary Education (Science: Biology) C1X1
1 year full-time

Entry requirements: Degree covering the relevant subject area(s) (science/biology) plus GCSE grade C or above or equivalent in English language and mathematics.
Contact: As above

PGCE in Secondary Education (Science: Physics) F3X1
1 year full-time

Entry requirements: Degree covering the relevant subject area(s) (science/chemistry) plus GCSE grade C or above or equivalent in English language and mathematics.
Contact: As above

PGCE in Secondary Teaching (Science: Chemistry) F1X1
1 year full-time

Entry requirements: Degree covering the relevant subject area(s) (science/physics) plus GCSE grade C or above or equivalent in English language and mathematics.
Contact: As above

Diploma in Applied Educational Studies
1 year full-time, 2 years part-time

Entry requirements: Applicants should be teachers or other education professionals
Contact: As above

MA in Early Childhood Studies
2 years part-time

Entry requirements: Candidates require a teaching certificate, first degree or equivalent qualification with 2 years' experience in an early years setting.
Contact: Dr C Kyriaco
Director of Graduate Studies
01904 433460
educ15@york.ac.uk

MA in Education
1 year full-time, 2 years part-time

Entry requirements: Applications welcome from those working in schools and also from those outside of schools, such as in nurse education, prison education and further education.

Contact: Dr Judith Bennett
　　　Director of Graduate Studies
　　　01904 433455
　　　educ15@york.ac.uk

MA in Educational Studies

1 year full-time

Entry requirements: Degree or advanced diploma in education or equivalent.
Contact: As above

MA in Primary Education

24 months part-time

Entry requirements: Degree or teaching qualification plus relevant primary school experience.
Contact: As above

MA in Science Education

2 years part-time weekend

Entry requirements: Teachers and others working in science education; and teachers at schools and colleges using curriculum development materials developed by University of York Science Education Group who wish to carry out research relating to implementation of materials.
Contact: As above

MA in Teaching English to Young Learners

2 years distance learning

Entry requirements: Designed for professionals including advisers, teacher-trainers, teachers, writers and publishers who are involved in various aspects of teaching English as a foreign language to young learners.
Contact: Secretary, EFL Unit
　　　01904 432483
　　　efl2@york.ac.uk

ADDITIONAL COURSES

The following are courses you can choose that lead to professional qualifications other than QTS, for example, for continuing professional development. This additional courses index will enable you to search for institutions offering post-A-level or post-graduate courses relevant to teaching, suitable for before or after you have gained QTS.

Institution	Qualification	Course	Level
Belfast Institute of Further and Higher Education	PgCert	Educational Technology	PG
Birkbeck, University of London	Certificate	Teaching in Lifelong Learning	PG
Blackpool and the Fylde College	Certificate	Information Technology for Educators	Post A-level
Bolton Community College	Certificate	Information Technology (Educational Use)	Post A-level
Bolton Institute	MA	Educational Management	PG
Bolton Institute	MA	Inclusive Education	PG
Bolton Institute	MEd	Professional Development	PG
Bolton Institute	MA/MEd	Technical and Vocational Education	PG
Bridgwater College	PgDip	Education (Early Years)	PG
British Institute in Paris, University of London	MA	Second and Foreign Language Teaching	PG
Buckinghamshire Chilterns University College	MA	Education	PG
Cardiff University	MA	Education	PG
Cardiff University	EdD	Education	PG
City of Bristol College	Certificate	Information Communication Technology for Teachers and Trainers	Post A-level
Coleg Gwent (Newport Campus)	Teacher's Certificate/ Teacher's Diploma	Information Technology	Post A-level
Coleg Gwent (Pontypool Campus)	Teacher's Certificate/ Teacher's Diploma	Information Technology	Post A-level
Crawford College of Art and Design	Diploma	Art and Design Education (Post-Primary)	PG
Crawford College of Art and Design	Diploma	Art and Design for Teachers	Post A-level
Croydon College	PgDip/MEd	Education	PG

Institution	Qualification	Course	Level
Dearne Valley College	Teacher's Certificate	Information Communication Technology	Post A-level
Doncaster College	PgCert/ PgDip/MA	Educational Studies	PG
East Berkshire College, Maidenhead, Windsor, Langley	Certificate	Teaching Pupils with Specific Learning Difficulties	Post A-level
East Down Institute of Further and Higher Education	Certificate/ Diploma	Teaching Pupils with Specific Learning Difficulties	Post A-level
Evesham College	Certificate/ Diploma	Teaching Students with Specific Learning Difficulties	Post A-level
Glasgow School of Art	MPhil	Art, Design and Architecture in Education	PG
Havering College of Further and Higher Education	MSc	Education Management	PG
Hornsby International Dyslexia Centre	Certificate	Dyslexia (fast-track)	Post A-level
Hornsby International Dyslexia Centre	Diploma	Dyslexia	Post A-level
Hornsby International Dyslexia Centre	Certificate	Specific Learning Difficulties	Post A-level
Hornsby International Dyslexia Centre	Diploma	Specific Learning Difficulties	Post A-level
Hull College	Certificate	Information and Communication Technology for Teachers	Post A-level
Kingston College	Diploma	Information Technology for Teachers and Trainers	Post A-level
Lancaster University	PgCert/ PgDip/MA	Education	PG
Lancaster University	PgDip	Educational Studies	PG
Leeds College of Technology	Professional Development Certificate	Information and Communication Technology for Teachers	Post A-level
Leo Baeck College, Centre for Jewish Education	Advanced Diploma	Professional Development (Jewish Education)	Post A-level
Leo Baeck College, Centre for Jewish Education	MA	Jewish Education	PG
London College, University College Kensington	PgDip/MA	Education	PG
Matthew Boulton College of Further and Higher Education	RSA Award	Teaching Learners with Specific Learning Difficulties	Post A-level
Napier University	PgDip/MSc	Careers Guidance (Special Needs)	PG
Napier University	PgDip/MSc	Computer-Enhanced Mathematics Education	PG
National College of Art and Design	Higher Diploma	Art and Design Teaching	PG
Newbury College	Award	Teaching Learners with Specific Learning Difficulties	Post A-level
North Hertfordshire College	Certificate/ Diploma	Teaching Learners with Specific Learning Difficulties	Post A-level

Institution	Qualification	Course	Level
Northumbria University, Longhirst Campus	PgCert/ PgDip/MA	Studies in Education	PG
Norwich City College	MSc	Education and Training	PG
Norwich City College	MSc	Educational Management	PG
Norwich School of Art and Design	MA	Art and Design Education	PG
St John's College Nottingham	MA	Religious Education	PG
St John's College Nottingham	Professional Certificate	Religious Education Policy	Post A-level
St John's College Nottingham	Professional Certificate	Religious Education Practice	Post A-level
Thames Valley University	PgCert	Teaching and Learning in Further and Higher Education	PG
Truro College	PgDip/MA	Education	PG
University of Cambridge	MPhil	Education	PG
University of Cambridge	MEd/Mphil/ PhD	Education	PG
University of Central Lancashire	MA	Education	PG
University of Central Lancashire	MA	Education (Leadership)	PG
University of Central Lancashire	PgDip	Education Administration and Management (Post-Compulsory)	PG
University of Central Lancashire	PgCert/PgDip	Educational Management	PG
University of Central Lancashire	MA	Strategic Leadership in Education	PG
University of Central Lancashire	Advanced Certificate	Teaching Local and Regional History in the Classroom	Post A-level
University of Essex	Diploma/MA	English Language Teaching	PG
University of Glamorgan	PgCert/PgDip/ MA	Educational Development	PG
University of Glamorgan	PgCert/PgDip/ MA	Educational Leadership and Management	PG
University of Lincoln	EdD	Education	PG
University of Lincoln	MBA (Inter- national)	Educational Leadership	PG
University of Liverpool	PgCert/ PgDip/MEd	Education	PG
University of London External Programme	PgDip/MA	Open, Distance and Flexible Learning	PG
University of Luton	MA	Professional Studies in Education	PG
University of Wales, Lampeter	MA	Teaching Philosophy at A-level	PG
Walford and North Shropshire College	Certificate/ Diploma	Teaching Learners with Specific Learning Difficulties	Post A-level
Walsall College of Arts and Technology	Teacher and Trainer Diploma	Information Technology	Post A-level
West Cheshire College	Certificate	Information and Communication Technology for Teachers/Trainers	Post A-level
West Hert College	Diploma	Teaching Learners with Specific Learning Difficulties	Post A-level

Institution	Qualification	Course	Level
Wiltshire College Chippenham	Certificate	Teaching Students with Specific Learning Difficulties	Post A-level
Wiltshire College Chippenham	Diploma	Teaching Students with Specific Learning Difficulties	Post A-level
Yeovil College	MEd	Education/Professional Studies in Education	PG

FE AND POST-COMPULSORY EDUCATION PGCE COURSES

Chapter 3 of the introduction to this Directory explored teaching in the Further Education and Higher Education sector. The following index lists all the institutions that provide Further Education PGCE/BEd courses and Post-Compulsory Education PGCE courses. Please contact the institutions for details.

Institutions running Further Education PGCE/BEd courses

Bexley College

Bishop Auckland College

Bolton Institute

Bristol College, City of

Cardiff University

Ceredigion, Coleg

Darlington College of Technology

Deeside College

Exeter College

Gloucestershire College of Arts and Technology

Gwent, Coleg (Ebbw Vale Campus)

Gwent, Coleg (Newport Campus)

Halton College

Hartlepool College of Further Education

Huddersfield Technical College

Hull College

Isle of Man College

Joseph Priestley College

Lincoln College

Llandrillo, Coleg

Meirion-Dwyfor, Coleg

Menai, Coleg

Merthyr Tydfil College

Mid-Cheshire College

Morgannwg, Coleg

New College Durham

New College Nottingham

Newcastle College

North East Worcestershire College

North Lindsey College

Northumbria University

Nottingham Trent University

Institutions running Further Education PGCE/BEd courses (*continued*)

Pembrokeshire College

Reading College and School of Art & Design

Redcar and Cleveland College

Ridge Danyers College

Rotherham College of Arts and Technology

Salford College

Sandwell College of Further and Higher Education

Sir Gar, Coleg

Solihull College

South Cheshire College

South Trafford College

South Tyneside

Stoke-on-Trent College

Sunderland College, City of

Sunderland, University of

Swansea College

Telford College of Arts and Technology

West Anglia, College of

West Cheshire College

West Kent College

Weymouth College

Institutions running Post-Compulsory Education PGCE courses

Accrington and Rossendale College

Amersham and Wycombe College

Anglia Polytechnic University, Chelmsford

Basingstoke College of Technology

Blackpool and the Fylde College

Boston College

Bracknell and Wokingham College

Bridgend College

Bristol, University of the West of England

Broxtowe College, Nottingham

Canterbury Christ Church University College

Cardiff, University of Wales Institute

Carlisle College

Central England in Birmingham, University of

Central Lancashire, University of

City Literary Institute

Cornwall College

Craven College

Darlington College of Technology

De Montfort University, Bedford

Doncaster College

Exeter, University of

Institutions running Post-Compulsory Education PGCE courses (*continued*)

Greenwich, University of

Grimsby College

Guildford College of Further and Higher Education

Gwent, Coleg (Abergavenny Campus)

Gwent, Coleg (Ebbw Vale Campus)

Gwent, Coleg (Newport Campus)

Havant College

Havering College of Further and Higher Education

Herefordshire College of Technology

Hertford Regional College

Hertfordshire, University of

Huddersfield, University of

Institute of Education, University of London

Keighley College

Kingston College

Lancaster and Morecambe College

Leeds Metropolitan University, Harrogate College Faculty

Leicester College

Llandrillo, Coleg

Middlesbrough College

Milton Keynes College

Nelson and Colne College

Newport, University of Wales College

North East Wales Institute of Higher Education

North Nottinghamshire College

Norwich City College

Oxford Brookes University

Penwith College

Peterborough Regional College

Preston College

Sheffield Hallam University

Skelmersdale and Ormskirk College

South East Essex College

Stockton Riverside College

Suffolk College

Swindon College

Thomas Danby College

Wakefield College

Walford and North Shropshire College

Weston College

Ystrad Mynach College

The subject index that follows will enable you to identify at a glance which institutio offer the subject areas of your choice at the relevant level. Once you have selected the ins tutions in the Directory that you are interested in applying to, you should consult th institution's prospectuses and/or websites before making your application.

	BA/BEd/BSc			PGCE		
	Primary	Middle Years	Second -ary	Primary	Middle Years	Second ary
ART/VISUAL ARTS						
Anglia Polytechnic University						*
Bangor, University of Wales	*					*W
Bath Spa University College						*
Bishop Grosseteste College						*
Bradford College	*					
Brighton, University of						*
Bristol, University of						*
Bristol, University of the West of England	*					*
Cambridge Faculty of Education, University of						*
Canterbury Christ Church University College	*					*
Cardiff, University of Wales Institute						*
Central England in Birmingham, University of						*
Chester College						*
Chiltern Training Group						*
De Montfort University, Leicester						*
East Anglia, University of				*		
Edge Hill College of Higher Education	*					*
Edinburgh, University of						*
Exeter, University of						*
Glasgow, University of						*
Gloucestershire, University of						*
Goldsmith's College, University of London						*
Greenwich, University of	*					*
Hertfordshire, University of	*					*
Institute of Education, University of London						*
King Alfred's Winchester	*					
Kingston University	*					
Leeds, University of						*
Liverpool Hope	*	*				
Liverpool John Moores University						*

KEY: C = Conversion course; W = Welsh medium; F/G = French or German medium; I = Irish Ga medium; S = Scottish Gaelic medium; M = includes French Maitrise; H = includes Austr Hauptschulqualifikation; O = aimed at overseas students; * = all other co

	BA/BEd/BSc			PGCE		
	Primary	Middle Years	Second -ary	Primary	Middle Years	Second- ary
anchester Metropolitan University						*
id Essex SCITT Consortium						*
iddlesex University						*
orth Bedfordshire Consortium						*
orthumbria University						*
xford Brookes University						*
ymouth, University of	*					*
ading, University of	*					*
Mark and St John, College of	*					*
Martin's College	*					*
Mary's University College, Belfast	*					
anmillis University College	*					
athclyde, University of						*
rrey Roehampton, University of	*			*		*
ansea Institute of Higher Education						*
ster, University of						*
NGALI						
st London, University of						*
athclyde, University of						*
JSINESS STUDIES						
erdeen, University of						*
ighton, University of				*		*
istol, University of the West of England						*
ge Hill College of Higher Education						*
asgow, University of						*
oucestershire Initial Teacher Education rtnership (SCITT)					*	
and Union Training Partnership						*
iddersfield, University of				*		*C
ill, University of						*
stitute of Education, University of London						*
nt and Medway Training						*
ngston University						*
anchester Metropolitan University				*		*
anchester, University of						*
iddlesex University						*
ottingham Trent University						*
isley, University of						*
rtsmouth, University of						*
effield Hallam University						*
Mary's University College, Belfast				*		
ffordshire University						*

	BA/BEd/BSc			PGCE		
	Primary	Middle Years	Second -ary	Primary	Middle Years	Second ary
Stirling, University of			*			
Stranmillis University College			*			
Strathclyde, University of						*
Sunderland, University of			*			*C
Surrey Roehampton, University of						*
Swansea Institute of Higher Education						*
Trinity and All Saints' College						*
Warwick, University of						*
Wolverhampton, University of			*			*
Worcester, University College						*
CITIZENSHIP						
Anglia Polytechnic University, Chelmsford						*
Birmingham, University of						*
Bristol, University of						*
Canterbury Christ Church University College						*
Edge Hill College of Higher Education						*
Exeter, University of						*
Goldsmith's College, University of London						*
Huddersfield, University of						*
Hull, University of						*
Institute of Education, University of London						*
Leicester, University of						*
Liverpool Hope						*
London Metropolitan University						*
Manchester Metropolitan University						*
Marches Consortium (SCITT)					*	*
Newman College of Higher Education						*
St Martin's College						*
Sussex, University of						*
York, University of						*
CLASSICS including Greek and Latin						
Cambridge Faculty of Education, University of						*
Centre for British Teachers						*
King's College London (University of London)						*
St Mary's, Strawberry Hill						*
Strathclyde, University of						*
DANCE						
Brighton, University of						*
De Montfort University, Bedford						*
Exeter, University of						*

	BA/BEd/BSc			PGCE		
	Primary	Middle Years	Second-ary	Primary	Middle Years	Secon-ary
Stranmillis University College			*			
Strathclyde, University of						*
Suffolk College						*
Sunderland, University of			*			*C
Surrey Roehampton, University of	*			*		*
Swansea, University of Wales						*
Titan Partnership Ltd						*
Ulster, University of						*
West Midlands Consortium						*
Wolverhampton, University of			*			*
Worcester, University College						*
DRAMA						
Aberdeen, University of						*
Aberystwyth, University of Wales						*W
Bishop Grosseteste College						*
Cambridge Faculty of Education, University of						*
Canterbury Christ Church University College						*
Cardiff, University of Wales Institute			*			
Central England in Birmingham, University of						*
Central School of Speech and Drama						*
Chester College						*
Devon Secondary Teacher Training Group						*
Durham, University of						*
Edinburgh, University of						*
Exeter, University of						*
Goldsmith's College, University of London						*
Institute of Education, University of London						*
King Alfred's Winchester	*					
Kingston University	*					
Leeds, University of						*
Liverpool Hope						*
London Metropolitan University						*
Manchester Metropolitan University						*
Middlesex University						*
Newcastle upon Tyne, University of						*
Plymouth, University of						*
Reading, University of						*
St Martin's College	*					*
Stranmillis University College	*					
Strathclyde, University of						*
Ulster, University of						*
Warwick, University of						*

	BA/BEd/BSc			PGCE		
	Primary	Middle Years	Second-ary	Primary	Middle Years	Second ary
Crawley College	*					
De Montfort University, Bedford					*	*
Derby, University of						*
Durham, University of						*
East Anglia, University of				*		*
East London, University of						*
Edge Hill College of Higher Education	*	*				*
Edinburgh, University of						*
Exeter, University of				*	*	*
Glasgow, University of						*
Gloucestershire, University of						*
Goldsmith's College, University of London						*
Grand Union Training Partnership						*
Greenwich, University of	*					
Hertfordshire, University of	*					*
Hull, University of	*					*
Institute of Education, University of London						*
Keele University						*
Kent and Medway Training						*
King Alfred's Winchester	*					
King's College London (University of London)						*
Kingston University	*					
Leeds, University of						*
Leicester, University of						*
Liverpool Hope	*					*
Liverpool John Moores University	*					
London Metropolitan University						*
Manchester Metropolitan University					*	*
Manchester, University of						*
Mid-Essex SCITT Consortium						*
Middlesex University						*
Newcastle upon Tyne, University of						*
Newman College of Higher Education		*	*			*
North Bedfordshire Consortium						*
North East Essex Coastal Confederation Initial Teacher Training				*		
Northampton Teacher Training Partnership						*
Nottingham Trent University						*
Nottingham, University of						*
Oxford Brookes University						*
Oxford, University of						*
Paisley, University of						*
Plymouth, University of	*					*
Portsmouth Primary SCITT				*		

	BA/BEd/BSc			PGCE		
	Primary	Middle Years	Second-ary	Primary	Middle Years	Second ary
Bath, University of						*
Birmingham, University of						*
Bradford College	*					
Brighton, University of		*				*
Bristol, University of						*
Bristol, University of the West of England	*					*
Bromley Schools' Collegiate						*
Cambridge Faculty of Education, University of						*
Canterbury Christ Church University College	*				*	*
Chichester, University College	*					
Chiltern Training Group						*
Durham, University of						*
East Anglia, University of				*		*
Edge Hill College of Higher Education						*
Edinburgh, University of						*
Exeter, University of				*		*
Glasgow, University of						*
Gloucestershire, University of						*
Goldsmith's College, University of London						*
Hertfordshire, University of						*
Hull, University of						*
Institute of Education, University of London						*
Keele University						*
King Alfred's Winchester	*					
Kingston University	*					
Leeds, University of						*
Leicester, University of						*
Liverpool Hope	*					*
Manchester Metropolitan University						*
Marches Consortium (SCITT)					*	*
Mid-Essex SCITT Consortium						*
Middlesex University						*
Newcastle upon Tyne, University of						*
North Bedfordshire Consortium						*
Nottingham, University of						*F/G
Open University						*
Oxford Brookes University						*
Oxford, University of						*
Plymouth, University of						*
Portsmouth, University of						*
Reading, University of						*
Sheffield Hallam University	*					
Sheffield, University of						*

	BA/BEd/BSc			PGCE		
	Primary	Middle Years	Second-ary	Primary	Middle Years	Second ary
Leeds, University of						*
Leicester, University of						*
Liverpool Hope	*					*
Manchester Metropolitan University						*
Marches Consortium (SCITT)					*	*
Newcastle upon Tyne, University of						*
North Bedfordshire Consortium						*
North East Essex Coastal Confederation Initial Teacher Training					*	
Nottingham, University of						*F/G
Oxford, University of						*
Plymouth, University of	*					
Reading, University of						*
Sheffield, University of						*
Southampton, University of						*
St Martin's College	*		*			*
St Mary's University College, Belfast	*					
Stirling, University of			*			
Stranmillis University College	*					
Strathclyde, University of						*
Surrey Roehampton, University of	*			*		*
Sussex, University of						*
Swansea, University of Wales						*
Trinity and All Saints' College	*					*
Ulster, University of						*
Warwick, University of						*
Worcester, University College						*
York, University of						*
HOME ECONOMICS						
Aberdeen, University of						*
Strathclyde, University of						*
Ulster, University of						*
HUMANITIES						
Canterbury Christ Church University College						*
Goldsmith's College, University of London						*
Institute of Education, University of London						*
INFORMATION TECHNOLOGY/ COMPUTING						
Aberdeen, University of						*
Anglia Polytechnic University, Chelmsford						*
Bangor, University of Wales						*W

	BA/BEd/BSc			PGCE		
	Primary	Middle Years	Second-ary	Primary	Middle Years	Second ary
St Mary's, Strawberry Hill	*					
Staffordshire University						*
Stirling, University of			*			
Stranmillis University College	*					
Strathclyde, University of						*
Sunderland, University of		*	*		*	*C
Surrey Roehampton, University of				*		
Swansea, University of Wales						*
Titan Partnership Ltd						*
Warwick, University of						*
West Midlands Consortium						*
Wolverhampton, University of						*
York St John, College of University of Leeds	*					
LEISURE, TRAVEL AND TOURISM						
Canterbury Christ Church University College						*
Edge Hill College of Higher Education						*
MANUFACTURING						
Edge Hill College of Higher Education						*
MATHEMATICS, including numeracy						
Aberdeen, University of						*
Bangor, University of Wales	*					*W
Bath Spa University College					C	
Bath, University of					*	*
Birmingham, University of						*C
Bishop Grosseteste College						*
Bradford College	*					*
Brighton, University of		*	*			*C
Bristol, University of						*
Bristol, University of the West of England						*
Bromley Schools' Collegiate						*
Brunel University						*
Cambridge Faculty of Education, University of					*	*C
Canterbury Christ Church University College	*				*	*
Cardiff, University of Wales Institute						*
Centre for British Teachers						*
Chester College						*
Chichester, University College	*	*				
Chiltern Training Group						*
Cornwall School Centred Initial Teacher Training						*
De Montfort University, Bedford					*	*
Derby, University of						*

	BA/BEd/BSc			PGCE		
	Primary	Middle Years	Second-ary	Primary	Middle Years	Second-ary
urham, University of						*
1st Anglia, University of				*		*
1st London, University of						*
dge Hill College of Higher Education	*	*	*			*
dinburgh, University of						*
xeter, University of	*				*	*
lasgow, University of						*
loucestershire, University of						*
oldsmith's College, University of London						*
reenwich, University of	*					*
ertfordshire, University of	*		*			*
uddersfield, University of			*			*C
ull, University of	*					*C
stitute of Education, University of London						*
eele University						*C
ent and Medway Training						*
ng Alfred's Winchester	*					
ng's College London (University of London)						*
eds, University of						*
icester, University of						*
verpool Hope	*					*
verpool John Moores University	*	*				
ondon Metropolitan University				*		*C
anchester Metropolitan University				*C	*	*C
anchester, University of						*
arches Consortium (SCITT)					*	*
id-Essex SCITT Consortium						*
iddlesex University						*
ewcastle upon Tyne, University of					*	*
ewport, University of Wales College				*		
orth East Essex Coastal Confederation tial Teacher Training					*	
orthampton Teacher Training Partnership						*
ottingham Trent University						*
ottingham, University of						*
pen University						*
xford Brookes University						*
xford, University of						*
isley, University of						*
ymouth, University of	*					*
rtsmouth Primary SCITT				*		
rtsmouth, University of						*
aeen's University of Belfast						*
ading, University of						*

	BA/BEd/BSc			PGCE		
	Primary	Middle Years	Second-ary	Primary	Middle Years	Second-ary
Sheffield Hallam University	*		*			*C
Sheffield, University of						*
Southampton, University of						*
St Mark and St John, College of			*			*
St Martin's College	*		*			*C
St Mary's University College, Belfast	*					
St Mary's, Strawberry Hill	*					*
Stirling, University of			*			
Stranmillis University College	*					
Strathclyde, University of			*			*
Sunderland, University of			*			*C
Surrey Roehampton, University of				*		*
Sussex, University of					*	
Swansea, University of Wales						*
Titan Partnership Ltd						*
Trinity and All Saints' College	*					*C
Warwick, University of	*					*
Wolverhampton, University of				*		*
Worcester, University College						*
York St John, College of University of Leeds	*					
York, University of						*
MEDIA						
Canterbury Christ Church University College						*
Central School of Speech and Drama						*
Keele University						*
Leicester, University of						*
London Metropolitan University						*
St Martin's College						*
Stirling, University of			*			
Ulster, University of						*
MODERN LANGUAGES						
Anglia Polytechnic University, Chelmsford						*
Bradford College					*	*
Brighton, University of		*	*			*
Bristol, University of						*
Bristol, University of the West of England						*
Bromley Schools' Collegiate						*
Cambridge Faculty of Education, University of					*	*
Cardiff, University of Wales Institute						*
Centre for British Teachers						*
Chiltern Training Group						*
Edinburgh, University of						*

	BA/BEd/BSc			PGCE		
	Primary	Middle Years	Second-ary	Primary	Middle Years	Second-ary
Institute of Education, University of London						*
Keele University						*
King's College London (University of London)						*
Kingston University						*
Leeds, University of						*
Leicester, University of						*
Liverpool Hope						*
Liverpool John Moores University						*
Manchester Metropolitan University						*
Manchester, University of						*
Newcastle upon Tyne, University of				*	*	*
Newman College of Higher Education				*		
Nottingham, University of						*
Open University						*
Oxford Brookes University						*M
Oxford, University of						*
Portsmouth, University of						*
Reading, University of						*C
Sheffield, University of						*
South West Teacher Training						*
Southampton, University of						*
St Martin's College						*M
Stirling, University of		*				
Strathclyde, University of						*
Swansea, University of Wales						*
Titan Partnership Ltd						*
Trinity and All Saints' College						*
Warwick, University of						*
York, University of						*
MODERN LANGUAGES (GERMAN)						
Aberdeen, University of						*
Aberystwyth, University of Wales						*W
Bangor, University of Wales						*W
Bath, University of						*
Birmingham, University of						*
Bristol, University of						*
Brunel University						*
Chester College						*
Cornwall School Centred Initial Teacher Training						*
Devon Secondary Teacher Training Group						*
Durham, University of						*

	BA/BEd/BSc			PGCE		
	Primary	Middle Years	Second-ary	Primary	Middle Years	Second-ary
East Anglia, University of						*
Edge Hill College of Higher Education						*
Exeter, University of						*
Glasgow, University of						*
Goldsmith's College, University of London						*
Grand Union Training Partnership						*
Hertfordshire, University of						*
Hull, University of						*
Keele University						*
King's College London (University of London)						*
Kingston University						*
Leeds, University of						*
Leicester, University of						*
Liverpool Hope						*
Liverpool John Moores University						*
Manchester Metropolitan University						*
Manchester, University of						*
Newcastle upon Tyne, University of						*
Nottingham, University of						*
Open University						*
Oxford, University of						*
Portsmouth, University of						*
Reading, University of						*
Sheffield, University of						*
South West Teacher Training						*
Southampton, University of						*
St Martin's College						*H
Stirling, University of			*			
Strathclyde, University of						*
Swansea, University of						*
Trinity and All Saints' College						*
Warwick, University of						*
York, University of						*
MODERN LANGUAGES (ITALIAN)						
Bristol, University of						*
Glasgow, University of						*
Leicester, University of						*
Oxford, University of						*
St Martin's College						*
Strathclyde, University of						*

	BA/BEd/BSc			PGCE		
	Primary	Middle Years	Second -ary	Primary	Middle Years	Second- ary
MODERN LANGUAGES (JAPANESE)						
Nottingham, University of						*
MODERN LANGUAGES (RUSSIAN)						
Nottingham, University of						*
Sheffield, University of						*
MODERN LANGUAGES (SPANISH)						
Bath, University of						*
Birmingham, University of						*
Bristol, University of						*
Chester College						*
Cornwall School Centred Initial Teacher Training						*
Durham, University of						*
Edge Hill College of Higher Education						*
Glasgow, University of						*
Hertfordshire, University of						*
Hull, University of						*
Keele University						*
King's College London (University of London)						*
Kingston University						*
Leeds, University of						*
Liverpool Hope						*
Liverpool John Moores University						*
Manchester Metropolitan University						*
Manchester, University of						*
Newcastle upon Tyne, University of						*
Nottingham, University of						*
Open University						*
Oxford, University of						*
Portsmouth, University of						*
Sheffield, University of						*
Southampton, University of						*
St Martin's College						*
Stirling, University of			*			
Strathclyde, University of						*
Swansea, University of Wales						*
Trinity and All Saints' College						*
Warwick, University of						*
York, University of						*
MODERN STUDIES						
Aberdeen, University of						*

	BA/BEd/BSc			PGCE		
	Primary	Middle Years	Second-ary	Primary	Middle Years	Second-ary
ınburgh, University of						*
ısgow, University of						*
athclyde, University of						*
JSIC						
erdeen, University of			*			
ıgor, University of Wales	*					*W
:h Spa University College					*	*
hop Grosseteste College						*
stol, University of						*
mbridge Faculty of Education, ıversity of						*
ınterbury Christ Church University College	*				*	*
rdiff, University of Wales Institute			*			*
ıtral England in Birmingham, University of						*
ıtre for British Teachers						*
von Secondary Teacher Training Group						*
rham, University of						*
ıt Anglia, University of				*		
ȝe Hill College of Higher Education						*
ınburgh, University of						*
ːter, University of				*		
ısgow, University of			*			
ɔucestershire Initial Teacher Education tnership (SCITT)					*	
ɔucestershire, University of						*
ɪdsmith's College, University of London						*
ɪddersfield, University of			*			*C
ɪitute of Education, University of London						*
gston University						*
ːds, University of						*
ːrpool Hope	*					*
ıdon Metropolitan University			*			*C
nchester Metropolitan University						*
rches Consortium (SCITT)					*	*
Jdlesex University						*
ːn University						*
ford Brookes University						*
mouth, University of	*					*
ıding, University of	*					*
ːal Northern College of Music						*
ːal Scottish Academy of Music and ıma			*			
thampton, University of						*

	BA/BEd/BSc			PGCE		
	Primary	Middle Years	Second -ary	Primary	Middle Years	Secondary
St Martin's College	*					
St Mary's University College, Belfast	*					
Stranmillis University College	*					
Strathclyde, University of						*
Sunderland, University of			*			*C
Surrey Roehampton, University of	*			*		*
Sussex, University of						*
Ulster, University of						*
Worcester, University College						*
York St John, College of University of Leeds	*					
OUTDOOR ACTIVITIES						
Bangor, University of Wales						*W
PERSONAL, SOCIAL AND MORAL EDUCATION						
St Martin's College						*
PHYSICAL EDUCATION/SPORTS STUDIES						
Bangor, University of Wales	*					*W
Bath, University of						*
Birmingham, University of						*
Brighton, University of		*	*			*
Brunel University			*			*
Canterbury Christ Church University College	*					*
Cardiff, University of Wales Institute						*
Chester College						*
Chichester, University College			*			
Chiltern Training Group						*
De Montfort University, Bedford			*			*
Durham, University of						*
East Anglia, University of						*
Edge Hill College of Higher Education	*					*
Edinburgh, University of	*		*			
Exeter, University of					*	*
Gloucestershire, University of	*					*
Greenwich, University of	*					*
King Alfred's Winchester	*					
Leeds Metropolitan University			*			*
Liverpool Hope	*					*
Liverpool John Moores University		*	*			*
London Metropolitan University						*
Loughborough University						*

	BA/BEd/BSc			PGCE		
	Primary	Middle Years	Second-ary	Primary	Middle Years	Secondary
Durham, University of	*					
Ealing, Hammersmith and West London College	*					
East Anglia, University of				*		
East London, University of				*		
Edge Hill College of Higher Education	*			*		
Edinburgh, University of	*			*		
Essex Primary Schools Training Group				*		
Forest Independent Primary Collegiate				*		
Glasgow, University of	*			*		
Gloucestershire, University of				*		
Greenwich, University of	*					
Hertfordshire, University of	*O			*		
High Force Education				*		
Hull, University of	*					
Institute of Education, University of London				*		
Isle of Man College				*		
Jewish Primary Schools Consortium				*		
Kingston, University of	*			*		
Leeds Metropolitan University	*			*		
Leeds, University of				*		
Liverpool John Moores University	*					
Manchester Metropolitan University	*			*		
Manchester, University of				*		
Middlesex University	*			*		
National SCITT in Outstanding Primary Schools				*		
Newman College of Higher Education	*			*		
Newport, University of Wales College	*			*		
North East Wales Institute of Higher Education	*					
Northampton, University College	*					
Northumbria University	*					
Nottingham Trent University	*			*		
Oxford Brookes University	*			*		
Paisley, University of	*			*		
Plymouth, University of	*			*		
Poole SCITT, Borough of				*		
Portsmouth Primary SCITT				*		
Primary Catholic Partnership				*		
Sheffield Hallam University	*			*		
Shire Foundation				*		
Somerset Teacher Education Programme				*		
South Bank University				*		

	BA/BEd/BSc			PGCE		
	Primary	Middle Years	Second-ary	Primary	Middle Years	Second-ary
）uthampton, University of				*		
Mark and St John, College of	*					
Martin's College	*			*		
Mary's University College, Belfast	*			I		
Mary's, Strawberry Hill	*			*		
ranmillis University College	*					
rathclyde, University of	*			*S		
ıffolk and Norfolk Primary SCITT				*		
ınderland, University of				*		
vansea Institute of Higher Education	*					
rinity College Carmarthen	*W			*W		
▌ster, University of				*		
ıban Learning Foundation				*		
⹃arwick, University of	*					
⹃olverhampton, University of	*			*		
RIMARY (LOWER/KEY STAGE 1), **ıcluding PRE-SCHOOL/EARLY YEARS**						
⹃berystwyth, University of Wales				*W		
▲ngor, University of Wales				*W		
ıth Spa University College				*		
⹃xley Primary Consortium for Teacher ⹃aining				*		
▐lericay Educational Consortium				*		
⹃rmingham, University of				*		
⹃shop Grosseteste College	*					
）urnemouth and East Dorset SCITT ⹃onsortium				*		
⹃adford College	*			*		
⹃ighton, University of	*			*		
⹃istol, University of the West of England	*			*		
⹃ımbridge Faculty of Education, ⹃ıiversity of				*		
⹃ınterbury Christ Church University College	*			*		
⹃ırdiff, University of Wales Institute	*					
⹃ntral England in Birmingham, ⹃ıiversity of				*		
⹃ıichester, University College	*					
⹃awley College	*					
⹃ Montfort University, Bedford				*		
⹃ırham, University of				*		
⹃st Anglia, University of				*		
⹃inburgh, University of	*					
⹃eter, University of				*		
⹃oucestershire, University of	*			*		

	BA/BEd/BSc			PGCE		
	Primary	Middle Years	Second -ary	Primary	Middle Years	Second-ary
Goldsmith's College, University of London	*			*		
Greenwich, University of	*			*		
Hertfordshire, University of				*		
Hull, University of				*		
Institute of Education, University of London				*		
King Alfred's Winchester	*			*		
Leeds Metropolitan University	*			*		
Leeds, University of				*		
Leicester, University of				*		
Lindisfarne Initial Teacher Training				*		
Liverpool Hope	*			*		
Liverpool John Moores University				*		
London Diocesan Board for Schools				*		
London Metropolitan University				*		
Manchester Metropolitan University	*			*		
Newcastle Upon Tyne, University of				*		
North East Wales Institute of Higher Education	*					
Northampton, University College	*			*		
Northumbria University	*			*		
Nottingham Trent University	*					
Oxford Brookes University				*		
Plymouth, University of	*					
Reading, University of	*			*		
Sheffield Hallam	*			*		
South Bank University				*		
St Mark and St John, College of				*		
St Martin's College	*			*		
Stranmillis University College				*		
Sunderland, University of	*					
Surrey Roehampton, University of	*			*		
Swansea, University of Wales				*		
Thames Primary Consortium				*		
Trinity and All Saints' College	*					
Wandsworth Primary School Consortium				*		
Warwick, University of				*		
Worcester, University College	*			*		
York St John, College of University of Leeds	*			*		
PRIMARY (UPPER/KEY STAGE 2)						
Aberystwyth, University of Wales				*W		
Bangor, University of Wales				*W		
Billericay Educational Consortium				*		
Bradford College				*		

	BA/BEd/BSc			PGCE		
	Primary	Middle Years	Second-ary	Primary	Middle Years	Second-ary
﹐ighton, University of				*		
﹐anterbury Christ Church University College	*			*		
﹐ardiff, University of Wales Institute	*					
﹐hichester, University College	*					
﹐rawley College	*					
﹐e Montfort University, Bedford				*		
﹐urham, University of				*		
﹐linburgh, University of	*					
﹐xeter, University of				*		
﹐loucestershire, University of	*			*		
﹐oldsmith's College, University of London	*			*		
﹐reenwich, University of				*		
﹐ertfordshire, University of				*		
﹐ull, University of				*		
﹐ing Alfred's Winchester	*			*		
﹐eeds, University of				*		
﹐eicester, University of				*		
﹐ndisfarne Initial Teacher Training				*		
﹐verpool Hope	*			*		
﹐ondon Metropolitan University				*		
﹐anchester Metropolitan University	*					
﹐ewcastle Upon Tyne, University of				*		
﹐orth East Wales Institute of Higher ﹐lucation	*					
﹐orthampton, University College				*		
﹐orthumbria University				*		
﹐eading, University of	*			*		
﹐ Mark and St John, College of				*		
﹐ Martin's College				*		
﹐nderland, University of	*					
﹐rrey Roehampton, University of	*			*		
﹐vansea, University of Wales				*		
﹐ames Primary Consortium				*		
﹐inity and All Saints' College	*					
﹐andsworth Primary School Consortium				*		
﹐arwick, University of				*		
﹐orcester, University College	*			*		
﹐ork St John, College of University of Leeds	*			*		
﹐IENCE (GENERAL)						
﹐nglia Polytechnic University						*
﹐angor, University of Wales	*					
﹐th Spa University College					C	*C
﹐th, University of					*	
﹐shop Grosseteste College						*

	BA/BEd/BSc			PGCE		
	Primary	Middle Years	Second-ary	Primary	Middle Years	Second ary
Bradford College	*				*	*
Brighton, University of		*	*			*C
Bromley Schools' Collegiate						*
Brunel University						*
Cambridge Faculty of Education, University of					*	
Canterbury Christ Church University College	*				*	
Cardiff, University of Wales Institute						*
Centre for British Teachers						*
Chiltern Training Group						*
Cornwall School Centred Initial Teacher Training						*
De Montfort University, Bedford					*	*
Durham, University of	*					
East Anglia, University of				*		
East London, University of						*
Edge Hill College of Higher Education	*	*	*			*
Exeter, University of				*	*	
Glasgow, University of						*
Gloucestershire, University of						*
Goldsmith's College, University of						*
Grand Union Training Partnership						*
Greenwich, University of	*					*
Hertfordshire, University of	*					*
Huddersfield, University of			*			C
Keele University						C
Kent and Medway Training						*
King Alfred's Winchester	*					
Kingston University	*					
Leicester, University of						*
Liverpool John Moores University	*	*	*			
Manchester Metropolitan University					*	*
Manchester, University of						*
Marches Consortium (SCITT)					*	*
Mid Essex SCITT Consortium						*
Middlesex University						*
Newcastle upon Tyne, University of				*		
Newman College of Higher Education		*				
Newport, University of Wales College			*			
North Bedfordshire Consortium						*
North East Essex Coastal Confederation Initial Teacher Training					*	
Northampton Teacher Training Partnership						*
Open University						*
Oxford Brookes University						*
Plymouth, University of	*					

	BA/BEd/BSc			PGCE		
	Primary	Middle Years	Second-ary	Primary	Middle Years	Second-ary
›rtsmouth, University of						*
›ueen's University of Belfast						*
›effield Hallam University	*		*			
›effield, University of						*
›uth London Teacher Training						*
›uth West Teacher Training						*
Mark and St John, College of			*			
Martin's College	*		*			*C
Mary's University College, Belfast	*					
Mary's, Strawberry Hill	*					*
›anmillis University College	*					
›nderland, University of			*		*	*C
›rrey Roehampton, University of	*			*		*
›ssex, University of					*	*
›vansea, University of Wales						*
›esside, University of					*	
›tan Partnership Ltd						*
›nity and All Saints' College	*					
›arwick, University of	*					
›olverhampton, University of						*
›IENCE (BIOLOGY)						
›erdeen, University of						*
›erystwyth, University of Wales						*W
›ngor, University of Wales						*W
›th, University of						*
›rmingham, University of						*
›istol, University of						*
›istol, University of the West of England	*					*
›unel University						*
›mbridge Faculty of Education, ›niversity of						*
›nterbury Christ Church University ›llege						*
›rham, University of						*
›st Anglia, University of						*
›inburgh, University of						*
›eter, University of						*
›asgow, University of						*
›ldsmith's College, University of London						*
›ddersfield, University of						*
›ll, University of	*					*
›titute of Education, University of London						*
›ele University						*

	BA/BEd/BSc			PGCE		
	Primary	Middle Years	Second-ary	Primary	Middle Years	Second ary
King's College London (University of London)						*
Kingston University						*
Leeds, University of						*
Leicester, University of						*
Liverpool John Moores University						*
Loughborough, University of						*
Manchester Metropolitan University						*
Manchester, University of						*
Newcastle upon Tyne, University of						*
Nottingham Trent University						*
Nottingham, University of						*F/G
Oxford, University of						*
Paisley, University of						*
Queen's University of Belfast						*
Reading, University of						*
Sheffield Hallam University						*C
Southampton, University of						*
St Mark and St John, College of						*
St Martin's College	*					*
Stirling, University of			*			
Strathclyde, University of			*			*
Surrey Roehampton, University of						*
Swansea, University of						*
Warwick, University of						*
Worcester, University College						*
York, University of						*
SCIENCE (CHEMISTRY)						
Aberdeen, University of						*
Aberystwyth, University of Wales						*W
Bangor, University of Wales						*W
Bath, University of						*
Birmingham, University of						*
Bristol, University of						*
Brunel University						*
Cambridge Faculty of Education, University of						*
Canterbury Christ Church University College						*
Durham, University of						*
East Anglia, University of						*
Edinburgh, University of						*
Exeter, University of						*
Glasgow, University of						*

	BA/BEd/BSc			PGCE		
	Primary	Middle Years	Second-ary	Primary	Middle Years	Second-ary
ɔldsmith's College, University of London						*
ɪddersfield, University of						*
ɪll, University of						*
ɪele University						*
ng's College London (University London)						*
ɪngston University						*
eds, University of						*
ɪcester, University of						*
verpool John Moores University						*
ɪughborough University						*
anchester Metropolitan University						*
anchester, University of						*
ɪwcastle upon Tyne, University of						*
ɔttingham Trent University						*
ɔttingham, University of						*F/G
ɪford, University of						*
ɪeen's University of Belfast						*
ɪading, University of						*
effield Hallam University						*C
uthampton, University of						*
Mark and St John, University of						*
Martin's College						*
ɪathclyde, University of			*			*
ɪansea, University of Wales						*
ɪrrey Roehampton, University of						*
ɪrrey, University of			*			
ɪrwick, University of						*
ɪrcester, University College						*
ɪrk, University of						*
IENCE (PHYSICS)						
ɪerdeen, University of						*
ɪerystwyth, University of Wales						*W
ɪngor, University of Wales						*W
ɪth, University of						*
mingham, University of						*
ɪstol, University of						*
ɪnel University						*
ɪmbridge Faculty of Education, ɪiversity of						*
ɪnterbury Christ Church University ɪllege						*
ɪrham, University of						*

	BA/BEd/BSc			PGCE		
	Primary	Middle Years	Second-ary	Primary	Middle Years	Second ary
East Anglia, University of						*
Edinburgh, University of						*
Exeter, University of						*
Glasgow, University of						*
Goldsmith's College, University of London						*
Huddersfield, University of						*
Hull, University of						*
Keele University						*
King's College London (University of London)						*
Kingston University						*
Leeds, University of						*
Leicester, University of						*
Liverpool John Moores University						*
Loughborough University						*
Manchester Metropolitan University						*
Manchester, University of						*
Newcastle upon Tyne, University of						*
Nottingham Trent University						*
Nottingham, University of						*F/G
Oxford, University of						*
Queen's University of Belfast						*
Reading, University of						*
Sheffield Hallam University						*C
Southampton, University of						*
St Mark and St John, University of						*
St Martin's College						*
Strathclyde, University of			*			*
Surrey Roehampton, University of						*
Swansea, University of Wales						*
Warwick, University of						*
Worcester, University College						*
York, University of						*
SOCIAL SCIENCES, including Politics, Psychology, Sociology						
Goldsmith's College, University of London						*
Institute of Education, University of London						*
Keele University						*
Leeds, University of						*
Leicester, University of						*
Manchester Metropolitan University						*
Queen's University of Belfast						*
Stirling, University of			*			

	BA/BEd/BSc			PGCE		
	Primary	Middle Years	Second-ary	Primary	Middle Years	Second ary
Paisley, University of						*
Queen's University of Belfast						*
Sheffield Hallam University						*
Southampton, University of						*
St Mark and St John, College of						*
St Martin's College	*		*			*
St Mary's University College, Belfast	*		*			
St Mary's, Strawberry Hill						*
Stirling, University of			*			
Stranmillis University College	*		*			
Strathclyde, University of						*
Surrey Roehampton, University of	*			*		*
Titan Partnership Ltd						*
Trinity and All Saints' College	*					*
Trinity College Carmarthen						*W
Warwick, University of						*
York St John, College of University of Leeds	*					*
URDU						
Edge Hill College of Higher Education						*
Strathclyde, University of						*
Titan Partnership Ltd						*
WELSH						
Aberystwyth, University of Wales						W
Bangor, University of Wales	*					W
Cardiff, University of Wales Institute			*			*
Swansea, University of Wales						*

KEY: C = Conversion course; W = Welsh medium; F/G = French or German medium; I = Irish Gae
medium; S = Scottish Gaelic medium; M = includes French Maitrise; H = includes Austri
Hauptschulqualifikation; O = aimed at overseas students; * = all other co